D1498891

DRUGS
IN SOCIETY

SIXTH EDITION

by michael d. lyman,

with additional materials by gary w. potter

DRUGS IN SOCIETY

SIXTH EDITION

CAUSES, CONCEPTS, AND CONTROL

AMSTERDAM • BOSTON • HEIDELBERG • LONDON
NEW YORK • OXFORD • PARIS • SAN DIEGO
SAN FRANCISCO • SINGAPORE • SYDNEY • TOKYO

Anderson Publishing is an imprint of Elsevier

Acquiring Editor: Ellen S. Boyne
Project Manager: André Cuello
Designer: Kelly Grondin

Anderson Publishing is an imprint of Elsevier
30 Corporate Drive, Suite 400, Burlington, MA 01803, USA

© 2011 Elsevier Inc. All rights reserved.

No part of this publication may be reproduced or transmitted in any form or by any means, electronic or mechanical, including photocopying, recording, or any information storage and retrieval system, without permission in writing from the publisher. Details on how to seek permission, further information about the Publisher's permissions policies and our arrangements with organizations such as the Copyright Clearance Center and the Copyright Licensing Agency, can be found at our website: www.elsevier.com/permissions.

This book and the individual contributions contained in it are protected under copyright by the Publisher (other than as may be noted herein).

Notices
Knowledge and best practice in this field are constantly changing. As new research and experience broaden our understanding, changes in research methods or professional practices, may become necessary. Practitioners and researchers must always rely on their own experience and knowledge in evaluating and using any information or methods described herein. In using such information or methods they should be mindful of their own safety and the safety of others, including parties for whom they have a professional responsibility.

To the fullest extent of the law, neither the Publisher nor the authors, contributors, or editors, assume any liability for any injury and/or damage to persons or property as a matter of products liability, negligence or otherwise, or from any use or operation of any methods, products, instructions, or ideas contained in the material herein.

Library of Congress Cataloging-in-Publication Data
Application submitted   2010935325

British Library Cataloguing-in-Publication Data
A catalogue record for this book is available from the British Library.

ISBN: 978-1-4377-4450-7

Printed in the United States of America

11 12 13 14 10 9 8 7 6 5 4 3 2

Working together to grow
libraries in developing countries

www.elsevier.com | www.bookaid.org | www.sabre.org

ELSEVIER   BOOK AID
International   Sabre Foundation

For information on all Anderson publications visit our website at www.andersonpublishing.com

Preface

Despite decades of widespread enforcement, interdiction, prevention efforts, and treatment initiatives, the problem of drug abuse and trafficking continues to flourish in communities and neighborhoods across the United States. The extent of the problem has accelerated to the point that most of us know of someone who has been affected in some way by substance abuse.

One of the many lessons to learn from studying the U.S. drug problem is that change is an inevitable part of the drug abuse crisis. We cannot develop a sound drug control policy unless we first become students of history. Things are different now in the twenty-first century than they were in the mid-1980s, when crack cocaine first appeared on the nation's drug scene. Drugs and those who produce and sell them are notably different than their counterparts of 20, 30, and even 50 years ago.

Not only do the drugs of abuse themselves change, but patterns and trends of drug abuse also shift from one decade to the next. For example, over the decades, the focus of the nation's drug abuse problem has shifted from opium to marijuana to LSD to PCP to cocaine; today many look at methamphetamine as one of the prevailing national threats to human health and public safety. Furthermore, people who traffic drugs are also keenly aware of the element of change in the drug business. When factors such as competition from rival criminal groups or effective law enforcement measures place pressures on criminal trafficking organizations, their methods of manufacturing, transportation, and marketing must also be modified. Many of today's drug-trafficking organizations have become extremely resourceful in adjusting to political, economic, and social changes in the drug trade.

Indeed, domestic political agendas greatly affect the manner in which our government and society deal with the drug problem, and clearly such changes vary from one presidential administration to the next. One of the ironies of the drug problem is that, for the most part, people want the same things: safe neighborhoods, safe highways, drug-free workplaces, drug-free schools, addiction-free babies, and so forth. However, individual politics and values often dictate different ways of achieving these goals. Political agendas affect the philosophies of dealing with both drug abuse and drug offenders, which in turn dictate which and how many resources will be made available to deal with the nation's drug problem. So, with all these variables at work, it is little wonder why finding a resolution to the U.S. drug problem is so difficult.

This brings us to the purpose of this book. *Drugs in Society: Causes, Concepts, and Control*, Sixth Edition, deals with the three most pivotal areas of today's drug problem: drug abuse, drug trafficking, and drug control policy. We should acknowledge that the preparation of any book is a considerable undertaking, and this one has been no exception. Furthermore, any text dealing with drug abuse necessitates periodic updating because it is a diverse subject that encompasses numerous disciplines such as sociology, politics, psychology, medicine, criminal justice, public policy, and law.

Many social, political, and private policy changes have set the stage for this text, and this is precisely the premise of this sixth addition—change. It is a book about drugs, addictions, dealers, corrupt officials, "narcs," the courts, personal and public values, public policy, the laws, and the rising numbers of ruined communities and families throughout the country. Put simply, it is designed to give the reader insight into formulating possible solutions to the U.S. drug dilemma.

Drug abuse is a sensitive public issue. Discussions typically generate the political volatility of other heated social issues such as abortion, gun control, and capital punishment. It is therefore one of our primary goals to address the subject in a realistic fashion with objective consideration given to both liberal and conservative social perspectives. This book, designed to offer a logical flow of information, is organized in three parts: "Understanding the Problem," "Gangs and Drugs," and "Fighting Back." Each part contains chapters that focus on the many critical areas of the U.S. drug problem and give the reader a foundation for critical thinking and rational decision making within this complex multidisciplinary field.

We would like to extend a sincere thank-you to the many individuals who assisted in the preparation of this project. Specifically, thanks is most offered to the many friends and associates in the drug enforcement profession, our colleagues in criminal justice and higher education, and the always helpful people at the National Institute of Justice, the National Center for Drugs and Crime Control, the Office of National Drug Control Policy, the Drug Enforcement Administration, the Federal Bureau of Investigation, and the Bureau of Justice Statistics. A special thanks is well deserved by the good people at Anderson Publishing (Elsevier) and their capable management, editorial, and production staff. Their belief in our work helped make this sixth edition of *Drugs in Society: Causes, Concepts, and Control* a reality.

In an effort to ensure accuracy and readability of the book's organization and content, we would like to encourage any and all comments about this text for use in future editions. Please feel free to contact us at any time in this regard. Again, we would like to thank you for adopting this textbook, and we hope that it provides you with a meaningful learning tool for understanding drugs in society.

Michael D. Lyman
Columbia College of Missouri

Introduction

For many Americans, the drug problem is an abstract one involving other people and occurring somewhere else: Heroin and crack are abused by the poor in outlying ghettos; cocaine and pharmaceuticals are used by the very rich; other drugs are consumed by fast-trackers in the entertainment industry. Even drug busts on local television feature characters from neighborhoods on the far side of town—certainly not where *we* live. However, as responsible citizens living in a modern society, we can no longer adopt an out-of-sight, out-of-mind mentality with regard to drug abuse. We must begin by being honest with ourselves about the realities of drug abuse and assume a more proactive attitude. For example, most of us are very well acquainted with the most abused drug in the country: alcohol. Statistics show that the fatal consequences of alcohol abuse outweigh those associated with any other drug. In addition, the scores of people involved with the illicit drug trade, from members of organized crime groups to casual dealers, have little respect for U.S. laws, legitimate forms of commerce, or a safe and prosperous society.

Perhaps accepting the problem—that is, not assuming that it is someone else's problem—is the first step in identifying workable solutions. This is the primary focus of Part I, "Understanding the Problem," which addresses the history of drug abuse and the development of drug control policy, drug pharmacology, theories of drug abuse, and the role of source countries in drug trafficking. Part I also focuses on drug-related crimes that support the illicit drug industry and are at the core of many senseless acts of violence in neighborhoods around the country.

Organized gangs bankrolled by the lucrative drug trade are not only rooted in major U.S. cities but have long since expanded to communities of all sizes. Not only are traditional organized crime groups such as the Mafia involved in drug trafficking, but also nontraditional gangs that include many inner-city youth groups as well as newly emerging Asian youth gangs. Such gangs have become reliant on the drug trade for fast money and local control of criminal enterprises in their communities.

In many American cities, Mexican cartels strive for control of neighborhoods sales of cocaine and methamphetamine by using violence to maintain that control. Outlaw motorcycle gangs such as the Hells Angels have added the drug trade to their many other criminal endeavors. These organizations and others are the focus of Part II of this book—"Gangs and Drugs"—which discusses the involvement of organized crime in the drug trade.

As Americans accept the reality of drug abuse, we are faced with many questions: How have things gotten so far out of hand? What do we do now? Do solutions to the problem lie in the area of public health, culture, sociology, education, or criminal justice? Each of these areas offers some explanation. Part III, "Fighting Back," considers what is being done and what can be done to best deal with the problem. In doing so, its chapters discuss the role of federal drug enforcement organizations, drug laws, and drug enforcement initiatives. Additionally, critical issues such as drug courier profiling, covert police initiatives, legalizing medical marijuana, needle exchange programs, drug testing in the workplace and at home, and drug abuse in sports are all examined.

As an aid to our readers, numerous critical thinking questions have been provided throughout each chapter. These are designed to promote thought and discussion about some of the more important dynamics of the U.S. drug abuse problem. We have also provided reading objectives at the beginning of each chapter, along with important terms at each chapter's conclusion. All these features are created to provide the student of drug abuse with a means not only to understand the problem but also to formulate realistic public policy responses.

Today, drugs in society present a myriad of social problems. Drugs threaten our standard of living and the quality of our neighborhoods. Drugs can ruin not only the lives of drug users but the lives of those who love them as well. They drain society of precious public resources that could be put to work elsewhere. Society has responded by passing criminal and civil laws as well as implementing myriad social programs, each designed to deal with some aspect of the nation's drug abuse problem. Some of these initiatives have proved more successful than others, but limited as any initiative is, we can only hope that we can rise as a nation to meet the challenge.

Part I

Understanding the Problem

One of the assumptions of this book is that an educated society is better prepared to respond to the problem of drug abuse than one that is ill-informed. To that end, the first six chapters are designed to give the reader the essentials regarding the nation's drug abuse crisis. To begin, we discuss the social and health consequences of drug use. Next is an in-depth review of the drugs most commonly abused in our schools and neighborhoods, followed by an overview describing how drugs of abuse emerged in modern society and what circumstances led to their gradual social control. We then offer an overview of the international and domestic drug-trafficking problem, providing an understanding of the origins of illicit drugs. Finally, drug-related crime is discussed in the context of predatory, political, and white-collar criminal behavior related to the drug trade. Each of these areas will prepare the reader for a discussion of organized criminal activity in the illicit drug trade, discussed in Part II.

Chapter 1

The Nature of the Drug Problem

This chapter will enable you to:

- Learn the social and individual consequences of drug abuse
- Understand the reasons that people use drugs
- Realize the extent of the drug abuse problem in the United States
- Consider the various theories and explanations of drug abuse

It all started innocently enough. In 1998, when Michelle Brown got pregnant, her doctor wrote her a prescription for Lortab, a potentially addictive painkiller similar to Vicodin, for relief of migraine headaches. Her migraines eventually got worse; the Lortab made her life bearable. However, it had a devastating effect: slowly she became addicted. She became a classic "doctor shopper," hopping from one physician to another to get multiple prescriptions. She discovered Percocet and soon she was mixing Lortab with OxyContin, a new super-strength painkiller she got through a street drug dealer. By early 2000, Brown, 25 years old and the mother of two small children, worked up the nerve to commit fraud. Pretending to phone from her doctor's office, she called her local pharmacy, read her physician's identification number off a prescription bottle, and won what she called "my key to the palace" (Kalb, 2001).

Nearly every citizen across the country is not only aware of the nation's drug problem but also most likely knows someone impacted by it. Family members, coworkers, friends, and neighbors all have the potential to become drug abusers or victims of drug abuse in one fashion or another.

DOI: 10.1016/B978-1-4377-4450-7.00001-1
© 2011 Elsevier Inc. All rights reserved.

In 2010, the U.S. government estimated the economic cost of the war on drugs to be roughly $215 billion (National Drug Intelligence Center, 2010). Additionally, the U.S. government reports that the cost of incarcerating drug law offenders was $30.1 billion—$9.1 billion for police protection, $4.5 billion for legal adjudication, and $11.0 billion for state and federal corrections. In total, in 2005 roughly $45.5 billion was spent on these efforts. The socioeconomic costs as well as the individual costs (i.e., the personal disadvantages in income and career) caused by the incarceration of millions of people are not included in this number.

In a 2010 report to Congress, President Barack Obama noted, "Drug abuse endangers the health and safety of every American, depletes financial and human resources, and deadens the spirit of many of our communities" (ONDCP, 2010). He continued, stating that drug overdose deaths surpass gunshot deaths in our country, and in 16 states, overdose deaths are a more common cause of accidental death than car crashes. "Drugged" driving has now been identified at higher levels than alcohol-impaired driving. Prescription drug abuse is at record levels (ONDCP, 2010).

Indeed, at the heart of the success in reducing drug use is a change in perceptions about not only the acceptability of using illicit substances but also the need to take responsibility for one's actions. These changes take place at the individual, family, and community levels.

Trends in cigarette, illicit drug, and alcohol use over time demonstrate that substance use is impressionable and that it follows public perceptions of the acceptability and harmful consequences of substances. These trends also show that government can play an important role in helping the public choose healthier lifestyles. From 1964 onward, the surgeon general issued multiple reports on the health consequences of smoking. A steady decline in cigarette smoking coincided with increased public awareness. Likewise, when President Nixon declared a war on drugs in 1971, use lowered before spiking again later that decade as popular culture embraced drug use. Subsequently, ballot initiatives to legalize marijuana for medical use in the late 1990s coincided with a rise in nonmedical use.

Additionally, trends in alcohol use show that the legal availability of alcohol, particularly to young people, has an impact on use rates. Although unpopular, Prohibition, established in 1919 and repealed in 1933, had a significant impact on the volume of consumption. Lowering the drinking age in the early 1970s was accompanied by increases in consumption, while alcohol consumption and alcohol-related fatalities showed marked declines after 1987, when most states had increased the drinking age to 21.

Over time, data show that baby boomers experienced some of the highest prevalence rates of illicit drug use during their youth. Rates of use among this group, now largely within the 50- to 60-year-old age category, remain unexpectedly high as its members continue to age. This trend underscores not only the importance of early identification and referral for treatment in order to break the cycle of addiction but, more important, the need for effective drug prevention to help young people avoid initiating drug use. For some, behaviors developed in youth can persist for decades. Furthermore, the adult population has proven to be more resistant to changes in use rates. Thus, baby boomers—the generation that was associated with high rates of drug use 30 to 40 years ago—continue to display elevated rates of use to this day.

Young people feel the greatest pressure to use drugs, primarily from their peers. This pressure is often reinforced through popular culture, creating the mistaken belief that "everyone is doing it" and that drug use is "cool" and free of consequences. This "social norm" effect creates the mistaken belief among some young people—and sometimes even their parents—that more kids use drugs than actually do. In the past year, the majority of 12- to 17-year-olds talked at least once with one or more parents about the dangers of substance abuse. These discussions were helpful: Rates of current substance use were lower for youths who did talk with parents than for those who did not.

Part of what might account for the decline in drug use among youths is an increased awareness of the dangers of drugs. Survey data show that drug use is inversely correlated with the perception of the harmful effects of drugs. The better young people understand the risks of drug use, the more likely they are to choose not to use drugs. Clearly, parental involvement, education, and community action are key to preventing drug use among youths.

Figure 1.1
Source: Monitoring the Future, 2009.

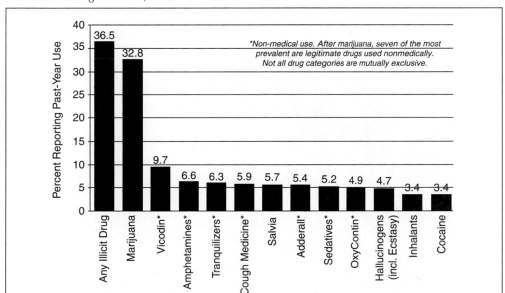

Drug Use Among 12th Graders, 2009

STATISTICAL EVIDENCE OF DRUG USE

According to national statistics released in 2010, each day in this country, almost 8,000 Americans illegally consume a drug for the first time. The risks posed by their drug use, like that of the other 20 million Americans who already use drugs illegally, will radiate to their families and to the communities in which they live. The scale of the problem and the suffering it causes are immense: More than 7.6 million Americans have a diagnosable drug abuse disorder; drug overdoses approach car crashes as a leading cause of accidental death; drug abuse contributes to more than one in eight new human immunodeficiency virus (HIV) infections; and substance abuse results in significant healthcare costs every year (ONDCP, 2010).

National data further show that in 2008, 14.2 percent of people 12 years of age and older had used illicit drugs during the past year. Marijuana is the most commonly used illicit drug, with 25.8 million individuals 12 years of age and older (10.3 percent) reporting past-year use. That rate remains stable from the previous year (10.1 percent). Psychotherapeutics ranked second, with 15.2 million individuals reporting past-year "nonmedical use" in 2008, a decrease from 16.3 million in 2007. In 2008, approximately 5.3 million individuals age 12 and older reported past-year cocaine use. A total of 850,000 reported past-year methamphetamine use, and 453,000 reported past-year heroin use. Rates of drug use vary by age. They are highest for young adults ages 18 to 25, with 33.5 percent reporting illicit drug use in the past year. Nineteen percent of youths ages 12 to 17 report past-year illicit drug use (National Drug Intelligence Center, National Drug Intelligence Center, 2010).

Figure 1.2
Source: SAMHSA. 2008. National Survey on Drug use and Health (2009).

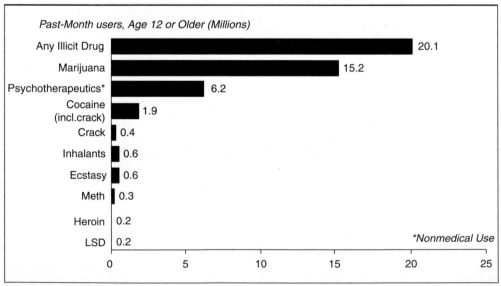

Past-Month Drug Use in 2008

THIS BOOK'S THEME

This text is designed to give the reader a realistic overview of the nation's drug problem, as well as to discuss what society is doing about it. Information is presented from medical, legal, public policy, and practical points of view that will help the reader formulate informed opinions.

OVERVIEW OF THE DRUG CRISIS

The social effects of drug trafficking are accentuated and reinforced by their direct and indirect economic impact. The sums spent on drugs represent resources lost to legitimate productive enterprises, and the money laundered by drug traffickers seems to corrupt all who come into contact with it. Consequently, drug traffickers who purchase legitimate businesses have learned that it is easy to integrate dealers into society. Drug traffickers who make use of existing legitimate businesses know that where such vast sums of money are involved, even "respectable citizens" can be induced to overlook the source of the money. In addition, the economic effect carries over into the workplace, where drug-using workers increase costs of production, raise levels of absenteeism, and raise the incidence of accidents on the job, all of which compel employers to implement expensive anti-drug abuse programs.

Severe health problems are also created when drug abuse prevails. These problems include drug overdoses and poisonings from "street" drugs as well as improperly consumed pharmaceutical drugs. Even marijuana can have devastating long-term effects. Not only is marijuana the drug with which many users begin, but marijuana cigarettes have many times the tar and carcinogens found in tobacco cigarettes. Additional problems include drug-addicted mothers who give birth to addicted babies, as well as the spread of diseases such as hepatitis and AIDS through drug users sharing contaminated needles. The proliferation of the crack house has given rise to the spread of the AIDS virus; in many crack houses, prostitution flourishes in the common sex-for-drugs transaction.

Drug abuse also has the ability to affect society on a much greater level—in terms of national security. Many larger drug organizations, particularly the South American and Southeast Asian cartels, have already become so powerful that they wield as much influence as many Latin and Central American governments. Drug money from these organizations has corrupted government officials, many of whom are themselves charged with the responsibility of drug control. In fact, the immense power and financial reserves of some of the largest drug-trafficking organizations have made them attractive partners in intelligence operations (such as those conducted during the Vietnam War and in Central America), thereby rendering U.S. policy confused and contradictory at times. Other drug-source countries that are hostile to the United States view drugs as a weapon to use against American society.

Figure 1.3

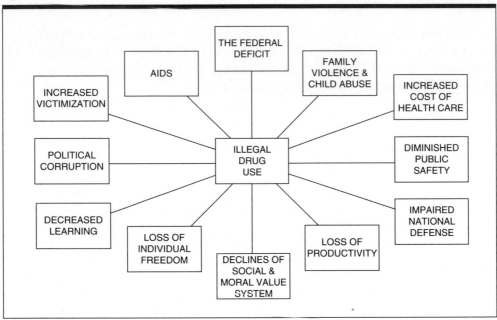

Overview of the Drug Crisis

Drugs and the Family

It is easy to see that the drug user can have a residual effect on the lives of family members. A portrait of the drug user is provided in Chapter 14, but experience has shown that the dependent drug abuser will lie and steal if necessary to support his or her habit. In many cases an occurrence called *backstabbing* takes place in families in which a member uses drugs. Here, young and middle-aged drug users who have depleted their own resources will turn to family members for drug money. In some cases, the family is unaware of the seriousness of the situation and provides money to the user, only to realize that more will be required soon. Many families cease to continue providing money, whereas others continue in an effort to "help" their dependent family member. This phenomenon gradually depletes the family's financial and emotional resources to the point at which family members lose faith in the drug user and begin to view him or her as troublesome, untrustworthy, or weak. In time, the person begins stealing items of value from the household to sell for drug money.

Sadly, in many cases, parents are part of the problem. Drug-dealing children who come home with hundreds of dollars are sometimes not disciplined by parents because that money, although obtained illegally, is needed to pay bills and buy food. The parents tend to rationalize their child's behavior by thinking that they will deal drugs anyway or that society has somehow failed to provide them with sufficient means to earn a legitimate income. When this occurs, the parents tend to take on a childlike role, leaving the major decisions up to the primary breadwinner—the drug-dealing child. In other cases, parents who are drug users themselves will often fail to provide adequate attention, care, and financial support for their family, resulting in many children being taken in by grandparents, other relatives, or the state social service system.

Studies have also shown that unemployment and frequent drug use have been major contributors to the demise of the two-parent household, whereas stable employment and low drug use are associated with high rates of forming a "traditional" two-parent family. Research has shown that although drug abuse adversely affects all ethnic groups, the hardest hit are poor and minority families and those with single female heads of households. Without help, many of these mothers experience great difficulty in controlling the actions of their young ones, who are charmed by drug dealing and other forms of street crime. Involvement in the drug culture also places youths in other types of jeopardy, including arrest, street violence, drug overdose, incarceration, and truancy.

Drugs and Schools

In recent years, more than one-third of Gallup poll respondents cited drug abuse as one of the biggest problems in schools. Several reasons are given for this phenomenon. For example, many students experience cognitive and behavioral difficulties that interfere not only with their studies but with their classmates' schoolwork as well. Even teachers and students who do not use drugs are hampered by the actions of those who choose to use drugs. Both categories of people are at risk of victimization by drug-related crimes and drug users. The availability of drugs in schools also has become a growing concern. Surveys have indicated that many students find that they can locate and purchase drugs without difficulty.

In 2010, the Office of National Drug Control Policy (ONDCP) made some instructive observations about teen drug use. They observed that in the late twentieth century, young Americans reached extraordinarily high levels of illicit drug use. By 1975, the majority of young people (55 percent) had used an illicit drug by the time they left high school. This figure rose to two-thirds (66 percent) by 1981 before a long and gradual decline to 41 percent by 1992—the low point. After 1992 the proportion rose considerably, reaching a recent high point of 55 percent in 1999; it was at 47 percent in 2008 (Monitoring the Future Study, 2009).

The most alarming trend is the increasing use of illegal drugs among school-age youths. In the 2010 annual report *The National Drug Control Strategy*,

Many states have implemented *drug-free school zones*—areas extending 1,000 feet away from a school within which penalties for drug crimes are enhanced.

the ONDCP referred to a study conducted by Columbia University's National Center on Addiction and Substance Abuse, which observed that children who smoke marijuana are 85 times more likely to use cocaine than peers who never tried marijuana. Furthermore, in 2009, 11 percent of youths ages 12 to 17 reported current use of illicit drugs. The use of ecstasy (MDMA) among tenth- and twelfth-graders has been increasing, according to a 2009 *Monitoring the Future* survey.

The Cost of Combating Drugs

The economic cost of drug abuse is immense, estimated at nearly $215 billion. The damage caused by drug abuse and addiction is reflected in an overburdened justice system, a strained healthcare system, lost productivity, and environmental destruction.

In 2010 the United States spent an estimated $215 billion on police, corrections, and courts (ONDCP, 2010). The drug war plays a significant role in these increased expenditures. At the federal level, in 1969, the Nixon administration spent $65 million on the war against drugs; by 1982, the Reagan administration had increased that figure to $1.65 billion; and by 2000, the Clinton administration had increased the price tag to $17.9 billion for the federal government (ONDCP, 2001:2). In 2007, the Bush administration called for $12.9 billion to fund the battle against the nation's drug crisis (ONDCP, 2007).

Spending at the state level, although more difficult to track, has similarly escalated dramatically due to draconian drug war policies. In 1998, for example, states spent $39.7 billion for adult and juvenile corrections and their court systems; 77 percent of those expenditures were directly related to the war on drugs (CASA, 2001:15). Of the $29.8 billion spent by the states on incarceration, probation, and parole, 81 percent is spent on drug war-related programs. It costs $8.6 billion a year to simply incarcerate convicted drug offenders (Criminal Justice Institute, 1997). State spending on law enforcement-related policies in the drug war amount to more than 10 times the spending on prevention, treatment, and education (CASA, 2001:15).

The Economics of Drug Control

Drug Prices

Our intense law enforcement campaign against drugs is supposed to make drugs more expensive for the consumer. After all, a law enforcement strategy built around interdiction, asset forfeiture, and arrest and seizure ought to make the drug business more costly. However, once again, the data clearly show that the drug war is an astounding failure. Consider the case of heroin.

The conversation about drug economics must be had in context with drug availability versus drug prices. This is because there is a direct correlation between drug availability and the price of drugs on the street (also see Chapter 4). A case in point is the way the price of cocaine has changed with its decreased availability. As of the writing of this text, based on numerous cocaine availability data indicators (seizures, price, purity, workplace drug tests, etc.), cocaine was considerably less prevalent in 2009 than in 2006. (Reasons for cocaine's decline in availability are discussed later in this book.) According to national statistics, federal cocaine seizures decreased 25 percent from 2006 (53,755 kg) to 2008 (40,449 kg) and remained low in 2009. Accordingly, the price per pure gram of cocaine increased from $94.73 in the third quarter of 2006 to $174.03 in the third quarter of 2009, whereas the purity of the drug decreased from 68.1 percent to 46.2 percent (National Drug Intelligence Center, 2010:27).

Drug Profits

Critics of the drug war argue that drug enforcement has failed to reduce use, has resulted in lower drug prices for both dealers and consumers, and has increased the quality and potency of drugs available for purchase in the United States. Despite the enormous expenditure of taxpayer dollars, the large number of arrests and subsequent incarcerations, and the proactive law enforcement strategy employed by law enforcement, the war on drugs has resulted in even greater profits for drug cartels. In fact, it can be argued that by the 1990s the drug war had failed so miserably that the drug trade had become a major component of international trade, commerce, and economics. The international drug trade generates about $400 billion in international trade and constitutes 8 percent of all international commerce (UNODCCP, 1998:3). Drug profits have been so inflated by the failed war on drugs that three-quarters of all drug shipments would have to be interdicted and seized in order to reduce the present profitability of the drug trade.

Some experts argue that it is the flawed logic of a law enforcement approach to drugs that directly results in this profitability. For example, a kilogram of coca base in Colombia costs about $950. The same kilogram, when it reaches wholesale distributors in the United States, sells for $25,000. A kilogram of heroin produced in Pakistan costs about $2,270 and sells for $129,380 in the United States. As political scientist Herbert Packer pointed out almost 40 years ago, efforts at prohibition lead directly to a "crime tariff" on prohibited substances, which is essentially a state-imposed tax that goes directly to organized crime (Packer, 1968). Colombian drug cartels bring $7 billion in drug profits back into the Colombian economy annually. Colombia's legal exports return profits of $7.6 billion annually (Trade and Environment Database, 1997:4). Almost all (98 percent) of Bolivia's foreign exchange earnings from international trade come directly from the coca market (Office of Technology Assessment, 1993). In essence, the drug war subsidizes drug production and distribution.

The Availability of Drugs

It is all but impossible to estimate with certainty the amount of drugs available in the United States. As such, the determination as to whether the availability of a particular drug is increasing or decreasing is based on the analysis of available data. Such data give us an indication of the price and purity of drugs as well as trends in transportation and distribution of drugs. For example, national data show that in 2009, cocaine availability was decreasing, whereas heroin, marijuana, methamphetamine, and MDMA were readily available (National Drug Intelligence Center, 2010).

Cocaine

Since 2006, cocaine availability decreased sharply in the United States. Evidence of this decrease can be seen in federal seizures, which decreased an estimated 25 percent from 2006. The price per pure gram of cocaine increased from $94.73 in 2006 to $174.03 in late 2009 (National Drug Intelligence Center, 2010). Accordingly, cocaine purity decreased from 68.1 percent to 46.2 percent in the same time period (National Drug Intelligence Center, 2010).

Heroin

As of the preparation of this book, heroin was widely available, and if anything, its availability was on the increase. This is evidenced by its high wholesale purity, low prices, increasing levels of abuse, and number of overdose deaths. For example, according to DEA Heroin Signature Program data, the wholesale purity of Mexican heroin in 2008 was 40 percent. Moreover, Mexican heroin represented 39 percent of all heroin seized in the United States. In comparison, the purity of South American heroin was reported at 57 percent in 2008 (National Drug Intelligence Center, 2010).

In spite of record heroin and opium production in Afghanistan, the United States remains a secondary market for Southwest Asian heroin. This is because most heroin from that region is consumed regionally in Southeast Asia. Organizations that traffic in Southwest Asian heroin are generally based in Afghanistan, Pakistan, and India (National Drug Intelligence Center, 2010).

Methamphetamine

The availability of methamphetamine is on the increase as of the preparation of this book. According to some government estimates, the increased availability of methamphetamine in the United States is based somewhat on increased production of the drug in Mexico—the primary source of methamphetamine consumed in the United States (National Drug Intelligence Center, 2010). The decreased availability of methamphetamine from Mexico in 2007–2008 was attributed to restrictions of precursor chemicals. In 2007, for example, prohibitions were placed on the importation of both pseudoephedrine and ephedrine into Mexico, and there was a ban on the use of both chemicals by 2008. By late 2008, however, Mexican traffickers adapted their trafficking process in a number of ways. These included using new smuggling routes for moving restricted chemicals, importing nonrestricted chemical derivatives instead of precursor chemicals, and establishing alternative production methods. For example, Mexican traffickers moved ephedrine and pseudoephedrine from sources in China and India using discrete smuggling routes through Central Africa, Europe, and South America (National Drug Intelligence Center, 2010). Furthermore, packages containing such chemicals are purposely mislabeled as other items during transit to avoid inspection by law enforcement in airports and seaports in Mexico.

> **A Closer Look: Restrictions on the Retail Sales of Pseudoephedrine**
>
> In September 2006, the federal Combat Methamphetamine Epidemic Act (CMEA) of 2005 became effective nationwide, setting restrictions on the retail sale of pseudoephedrine products. As of December 2009, 45 states had passed measures establishing or enhancing restrictions on over-the-counter sales or purchase of pseudoephedrine products in addition to those set forth by the CMEA. Of those states, 20 made pseudoephedrine a scheduled drug, 43 imposed point-of-sale restrictions, and 26 enacted pseudoephedrine tracking laws.

Source: National Drug Intelligence Center, 2010.

Marijuana

Marijuana has remained widely available in the United States, largely because of increasing production in Mexico. Statistics show that marijuana production in Mexico increased 59 percent between 2003 and 2009. Making things worse, there is an ongoing decrease of marijuana eradication in Mexico. This reduction is the result of the Mexican military's focus on anti-violence measures rather than crop cultivation. This differs from marijuana production in the United States, which has been hindered largely because of successful and increasing eradication efforts domestically. In fact, eradication of both indoor and outdoor plants more than doubled between 2004 and 2009. That said, more growers are establishing indoor sites to produce better marijuana and avoid the detection of outdoor growing operations (National Drug Intelligence Center, 2010).

Drug-Related Deaths

Illegal drug use is responsible for the deaths of thousands of Americans annually. SAMHSA's Drug Abuse Warning Network (DAWN) collects data on drug-related deaths for medical examiners in 41 major metropolitan areas. DAWN found that drug-related deaths steadily climbed throughout the 1990s (ONDCP, 2001).

According to the Centers for Disease Control and Prevention (CDC), in 2006, a total of 38,396 persons died of drug-induced causes in the United States. This category includes not only deaths from dependent and nondependent use of legal or illegal drugs but also poisoning from medically prescribed and other drugs (Heron et al., 2009). In addition, other causes of death, such as HIV/AIDS, are sometimes partially due to drug abuse.

Health Complications

Many health-related complications are associated with drug abuse. Users can die from overdose; medical reactions can result from taking certain types of drugs; users are exposed to HIV infection, hepatitis, tuberculosis, and other diseases; injuries can result from accidents caused by intoxication; injuries can result from violence in obtaining drugs or associating with persons with violent criminal backgrounds; dependence can form with certain drugs; and chronic physical problems can develop in some drug users. Some of these effects, such as overdose, are directly related to drug use; others, such as violence stemming from illegal drug transactions, are indirectly associated with drug-use behavior.

A brutal fact in the illicit drug industry is that some drugs sold on the streets are simply not what they are purported to be. This is sometimes due to increased purity of the drug over that to which the user has been accustomed, but another reason is that impurities are also commonly placed in drug solutions to either enhance or dilute the potency of the drug. Other times drugs are sold as being something completely different than what they actually are. For example, during the late 1970s, powdered PCP (phencyclidine), known as "angel dust," acquired such a bad reputation on the street that dealers chose to rename it THC, or cannabinol. In actuality, THC is one of the active ingredients in marijuana, giving it its intoxicating effects, but it has no connection whatsoever with the hallucinogen PCP. Dealers simply believed that THC sounded better than angel dust to potential drug buyers.

Use of certain drugs can result in specific physical reactions. For example, cocaine use can result in convulsions or even cardiovascular failure because it creates changes in heart rate and blood pressure. The reaction often occurs quickly and under circumstances in which medical treatment is not readily available. As we will see in the following chapter, the myth that cocaine is a harmless drug has been replaced with the realization that it may be more harmful than other so-called hard drugs, including heroin. In addition, the reinforcing properties of cocaine often lead to binge consumption, which in turn increases chances for dependence, overdose, withdrawal-like symptoms, or more serious cardiovascular complications, including death. Residual physical problems for cocaine abusers can include a ruptured aorta, central nervous system problems, and intestinal and obstetrical problems.

Specific reactions to other drugs can also be noted. Heroin, for instance, is a central nervous system depressant that can leave the user with acute toxic reactions resulting from overdose. More often than not, this occurs because users may not be aware that the purity of the heroin they inject is higher than their systems can tolerate. Other depressants and stimulants also can produce certain health complications, especially regarding drug-induced psychosis. Users lose contact with reality and experience a rapid pulse and elevated blood pressure.

Finally, health consequences are illustrated by the number of hospital emergency room admissions. In 2005, the Drug Abuse Warning Network (DAWN) provided a snapshot of the consequences of America's drug problem. It estimated that 1,449,154 emergency room visits were associated with drug use or misuse (DAWN, 2005).

Attitudes About Drugs

Perhaps the varying attitudes people harbor about drug abuse and control create confusion about the issue. Many positions about substance abuse or control are no longer clear-cut. Some drug users and former drug users have spoken out forcefully against drugs; others have urged a reconsideration of prohibition policies. Many parents, though strongly antidrug themselves, have ambivalent feelings about the drug laws when their sons or daughters are drug users. Drug use, which in the past has been more neatly confined to particular groups in society, has now taken root in all social strata. This means that virtually all of us either have friends, relatives, or associates who are or have been drug users.

Drug control policy is discussed in Chapter 13, but it might be helpful here to review the basis of some attitudes behind drug use and control. From earliest recorded time, society has exhibited social conflict over such heated issues as religion and politics, the latter of which is afforded greater attention in this book. One's willingness to criticize or accept public consensus frequently hinges on one's political attitudes. Such attitudes will most likely lean at least somewhat toward the conservative (right) or the liberal (left) view. Those of the former persuasion tend to be more traditional and resistant to change, whereas those holding liberal views tend to be more open-minded about change and willing to try the hitherto untried. Excesses in either of these convictions tend to foster unrealistic views and attitudes. The issues of drug use and control have blurred even these familiar political distinctions. Most conservatives, for example, favor tough laws, more police, and refined due process procedures for accused criminals, but some leading conservatives are actually arguing for repeal of the drug laws. They base their positions on two fundamental conservative tenets: first, the belief that the free market is self-regulating and will reduce drug abuse if allowed to operate, and second, the traditional conservative position put forward by John Stuart Mill that government should interfere with individual freedoms as little as possible. Liberals, on the other hand, have traditionally stressed due process rights, non-law enforcement approaches to crime and the belief that crime is rooted in a myriad of social problems. Yet leading liberal legislators, such as Representative Charles Rangel and the late Senator Edward Kennedy, have been among the strongest supporters of unyielding antidrug efforts.

WHY DO PEOPLE GET HIGH?

Whether it is caffeine, nicotine, alcohol, or another drug, abuse is an everyday part of our lives. So, several essential questions about drug abuse can be asked. For example, why do people willingly engage in behavior that might be dangerous, illegal, or unhealthy? Furthermore, many drugs fail to have obvious effects on the user, which makes us wonder why they are popular in the first place. For example, cigarette smokers generally don't appear to be in a state of euphoria when they smoke. The same is true for people when drinking a caffeine-based soft drink. How about harder drugs like heroin?

We think we know why a heroin user uses the drug: for its euphoric effect. However, the initial effects of many of today's popular drugs, like heroin, are in fact downright unpleasant. Stated differently, if 100 people were selected from the population and administered heroin, many would probably get sick and never want to see the drug again. So what's the point of taking the drug in the first place? The same could be said for alcohol or cocaine. One's first drink of whiskey or first experience with crack cocaine is not always pleasant. Given this premise, perhaps it is true that the more pleasant effects a drug has on a user, the more attractive that drug is to them. If this is so, why do people smoke without any noticeable effect from the nicotine? As you see, we have now come full circle in our quandary.

Although numerous explanations have been offered on the subject, another glaring question still remains unanswered: Is drug abuse representative of a universal human need? Some would argue that this is precisely the case and that one of today's great challenges is for society to develop a drug that is completely safe for recreational consumption. Although this is a controversial premise, it inspires thought. Some people are lifelong abstainers, whereas others use drugs on a regular basis. Whether it is our daily fortification of coffee, tea, or cigarettes or a reliance on prescription painkillers or antidotes for minor ailments, some form of drug use is an everyday part of living for most Americans.

Explanations for drug abuse are in constant debate. For example, some experts claim that there is a genetic basis for dependence and addiction, but others argue that it stems from a learned behavior. However, if a genetic propensity for drug abuse does exist, what created it? Alcohol abuse is a good example. Experts suggest that an insensitivity to the effects of this drug results in excessive drinking. Therefore, the insensitivity of some drinkers causes them to feel only slightly drunk when they are actually very intoxicated. As a result, they tend to drink more than others do. Some have suggested that this hypothesis extends to drug use in general.

> ### Critical Thinking Task
>
> Create the "perfect" recreational drug for American society. (Remember, your creation must be free of harmful physiological or psychological effects.) Describe its ingredients, methods of consumption, social applications, price, and method of distribution.

In opposition to the genetic theory of dependence, other experts, such as Benjamin Stein (1988), have argued that a syndrome known as the *addictive personality* exists. Under this theory, a drug user consumes drugs because the drugs help organize an otherwise disordered life. The theory suggests that drug abusers are lonely, sad, and frightened people who possess a character flaw for which drugs offer a crutch. In comparison, other experts have suggested that drug abuse is simply learned behavior whereby the abuser fails to act responsibly with the drugs he abuses.

Social explanations stress the influence of society, culture, and peers in a person's life. Some drugs are more likely to be abused by certain classes of people; other types of drugs are more available in specific areas of a city and, therefore, are more widely abused there. In addition, it has been argued that in many social circles it is more socially acceptable for men to drink more heavily than women. In some societies, drug consumption takes place in social, religious, or family settings. In any case, social explanations should be considered along with others when searching for answers to the question of why people use drugs.

The "Usefulness" of Drugs

As suggested earlier, to best deal with this perplexing issue, it is important to abandon our stereotypes of drug use for its pleasurable effects. For the sake of discussion, let's accept the proposition that people do not necessarily use a drug for its reputed pleasurable effects. Rather, let's assume that some drugs are used because people find them useful for less exotic reasons (Krogh, 1992). For example, hard-core heroin users generally do not use the drug for its euphoric effects but rather to help them get through the day—to survive. The same is also true for many smokers and coffee drinkers. So, for many, drug use allows people to function on a day-to-day level. After all, the ability to perform a job successfully and receive a regular paycheck is a powerful motivator for many people.

In an attempt to better understand reasons for drug use, let's take a closer look at the reasons for wanting to alter one's physical or mental state. Research has shown that, as a rule, people take illicit drugs for the effects they produce. These effects may include mood change, pleasure, stimulation, sedation, or enhanced physical or psychological performance. In fact, more so than for their physical results, illicit drugs are taken for their mind-altering effects. As we will discuss in this chapter, drugs such as heroin have limited accepted medical use but may be taken for the relief of pain. Others, such as stimulants and sedatives, have distinct medical applications but may be taken to produce excitement, alertness, or feelings of relaxation. Given the many different variables of human nature—personal values, morals, beliefs, habits, lifestyles—it is logical to assume that different people use drugs for different reasons. As we will see, some reasons are rational and others are more enigmatic.

Drug Abuse Forums

It is probably safe to generalize that millions of people abuse drugs for a number of reasons. Young people in junior high and high school, career people, and even the elderly from time to time use drugs unwisely or illegally. Therefore, many different reasons exist to explain drug abuse behavior; accordingly, there are many circumstances under which drug abusers engage in their activity. Next we will consider some of the most common social forums of drug abuse.

The Natural High

The term *natural high* refers to a desirable euphoric feeling naturally produced by the body. A multitude of studies by experts in social behavior suggest that people naturally want to alter their state of consciousness at certain times throughout their lives. For example, children may help illustrate the innate desire to alter consciousness by the very manner in which they play. For all their innocence, they sometimes spin themselves into dizziness or ride on the roller coaster at the local amusement park to achieve a thrill and the corresponding physical exhilaration. Many adults also enjoy adrenaline-inducing rides for the mere excitement of the experience. Such an indulgence in and of itself may raise or distort perceptions of reality while generating endocrine drug reactions, such as the production of adrenaline and noradrenaline. These "highs" are particularly appealing because they are produced naturally, without the interference of external chemical stimuli. However, the endocrine-producing glands in our bodies do not always produce "uppers" like adrenaline. In fact, the body also manufactures its own "downers," such as serotonin and gamma-amino butyric acid (GABA).

Chemicals such as these are called *endogenous*; that is, they are produced in the body. Endogenous chemicals produced by the brain and various glands change our moods and actions and even resemble some drugs taken by people for recreational purposes. For example, a group of endogenous chemicals called *endorphins*, discovered in 1975, closely resemble heroin or morphine in their chemical makeup, but they are naturally produced by the human body and act to relieve pain. The release of endorphins has been well documented in runners enjoying the so-called runner's high who seem to generate these chemicals to cope with pain and to provide energy while running.

Happy Hour

The term *happy hour* does not refer to a reason that people become intoxicated but rather to a social forum in which ritualistic recreational chemical use occurs in groups. Millions of people look forward to the traditional bar happy hour after a long day or week of work. The altering of one's mental state or "attitude adjustment" through alcohol consumption is lawful, socially acceptable, and even commonplace. Such indulgence, however, is regulated through each state's criminal code because of the potential for accidents or criminal behavior if drinkers become intoxicated.

Although it is legal, alcohol can drastically change one's psychological and physiological condition. For this reason, most states have established limits for alcohol consumption in ways such as (1) restricting where liquor can be purchased; (2) increasing penalties for driving while under the influence (of alcohol and illicit drugs alike); (3) establishing special criminal provisions for crimes committed while intoxicated; (4) criminalizing the transportation of liquor out of bars in groups; and (5) regulating open liquor containers in motor vehicles.

Medicinal Use

Ingesting "harder" and more dangerous drugs under certain circumstances is lawful if prescribed by a medical practitioner who has identified a physical or psychological requirement for such medication. Morphine, for example, is a dangerous and highly addictive narcotic drug, but when taken under a doctor's supervision, it can be an extremely effective painkiller during surgery and recovery. The lawful distribution of dangerous drugs mandates their legal manufacture by legitimate pharmaceutical companies. The highly controlled circumstances in the manufacturing, distribution, and storage of dangerous substances will be discussed in greater length later in this text.

Religious Use

Although some modern-day religions incorporate mind-altering substances such as wine in their ceremonies, few religions condone using enough of the substance for participants to become intoxicated. Exceptions to this rule, however, exist in certain cultures. For example, since the 1700s, North American Indian cultures have used peyote cactus, which produces a psychoactive drug, in religious ceremonies. Eating or smoking peyote was embraced in elaborate ancient ceremonies as a means to gain "oneness" with the spirits and with nature.

Today, in most states, members of the Church of the Native American Indian are authorized to use peyote in their religious ceremonics. Use of the drug outside a religious ceremony or by non-Indian participants is prohibited under law. Ironically, those Indian cultures that embrace the use of peyote in their religious practices also consider alcohol a curse. In a similar vein, followers of traditional Coptic Christianity, whose most recognizable U.S. denomination is the Rastafarians, use marijuana in their religious observations in much the same way other churches use wine.

To Alter Moods and Metabolism

When people are depressed, anxious, or bored, it is reasonable for them to desire a change in their mental state. Drugs are sometimes used both legally and illegally to create a shift in personalities, attitudes, and moods. Such measures might include the consumption of stimulants (uppers), depressants (downers), or even psychoactive drugs (hallucinogens that are either organic or clandestinely manufactured). In those cases in which the undesirable mood is due to a natural physiological chemical imbalance, physicians may lawfully prescribe certain drugs to help offset the body's chemical deficiencies. Excessive use of Valium and Librium, for example, was common in the 1950s to uplift a patient's depressed feelings.

These drugs were commonly prescribed because most doctors believed they were safe. In reality, not only can the drugs be dangerous by themselves, but they can be particularly dangerous if combined with other drugs. Polydrug use is common in situations in which drug users ingest amphetamines in the morning as a "pick-me-up" and then take barbiturates in the evening to help "wind down." This creates a classic abuse cycle in which one type of drug is required to counteract another. Another common example of polydrug use, particularly among people taking downers for medical purposes, is combining barbiturates and tranquilizers with alcohol, a combination that heightens inebriation and is potentially deadly.

To Inspire Creativity

Throughout the years, musicians, poets, and novelists have hailed the effects of certain drugs that supposedly promote creativity. Many artists have believed that drugs (often those belonging to the hallucinogen family) can release inhibitions and unleash a creative thought process. These individuals include American short-story writer and poet Edgar Allan Poe (1809–1849), who had a weakness for laudanum (tincture of opium); British writer Aldous Huxley (1894–1963), who experimented extensively with mescaline in the 1950s (and was quoted as stating that "pharmacology antedated agriculture"); the nineteenth-century author Oliver Wendell Holmes (1809–1894), who indulged in ether; and popular comedian Lenny Bruce (1926–1966), whose physical addiction to morphine ultimately cost him his life.

en.wikipedia.org

Edgar Allan Poe is a famous example of an artist who used drugs to inspire creativity. Poe regularly indulged in alcohol and laudanum (tincture of opium).

MEASURING DRUG ABUSE

The current state of affairs involving drug use clearly indicates that use of dangerous substances is widespread. In 2008, according to the finding of the *National Survey on Drug Use and Health*, an estimated 20.1 million Americans (about 8 percent of the household population age 12 and older) were current (past month) illicit drug users, meaning that they had used an illicit drug during the month prior to the survey interview. Considerable information exists regarding the extent of drug abuse throughout the country. However, most methods focus on households, high school seniors, and arrestees and offenders and do not give any indication about other groups that are more difficult to reach. For instance, many members of the homeless population may be involved in some form of drug abuse. These people are missed in the household surveys, just as high school dropouts are not surveyed in high school senior surveys. Surveys have also revealed other aspects of the drug abuse problem. For example, an alarmingly high number of young adults have used illicit drugs, and the most commonly abused drug is marijuana. In addition, one-third of the U.S. population knows someone who uses crack cocaine. Today, most of what we know about drug abuse is derived from the following surveys:

- *National Survey on Drug Use and Health (NSDUH)*. Formerly known as the *National Household Survey on Drug Abuse* (NHSDA), this survey has been conducted periodically since 1972 but is now an annual survey that randomly interviews people living in households and in specified group residences throughout the United States.
- *High School Survey*. Also referred to as *Monitoring the Future*, this survey was first developed in 1975. Results of the high school survey offer indications as to the frequency of drug abuse and drug abuse trends by high-school-age drug abusers.
- *Worldwide Survey of Substance Abuse and Health Behaviors among Military Personnel*. This survey is conducted annually and involves active-duty military personnel surveyed at military bases across the world.
- *Survey of Jail Inmates*. This survey comprises interviews of inmates who are awaiting trial or serving sentences in local jails. It was conducted annually.
- *Survey of State Prison Inmates*. This survey is conducted every five to seven years. On average, an estimated 14,000 inmates are interviewed in 275 facilities.

Who Are the Drug Users?

The surveys have also provided information regarding who the drug users are. For example, the 2005 *NIDA Household Survey on Drug Abuse* reports several interesting findings about drug users:

- Males are more likely than females to use drugs, but among youths aged 12 to 17, the rate of substance dependence or abuse was higher among females than males.
- People between the ages of 18 and 20 are more likely to have used illicit drugs in the past month.
- Current illicit drug use among people aged 12 or older varied by race/ethnicity in 2008, with the lowest rate among Asians (3.6 percent) and Hispanics (6.2 percent) and the highest rate (14.7 percent) for persons reporting two or more races (SAMHSA, 2009).

Of course, as drug patterns and trends change over time, these statistics will also change. As people get older, drug use rates shift. For instance, in 1995, lifetime rates of use became the highest among people age 31 through 39, reflecting the peak drug-using years of the late 1970s (NIDA, 1996d).

David Musto, professor of psychiatry at Yale University, has written that we have moved to a "two-tier system" of drug consumption, marked by declining use among middle-class whites and increasing use among poor minorities. In *The American Disease: Origins of Narcotic Control*, he states that the American society is repeating an earlier cycle of drug use. Musto points out that at the turn of the twentieth century, drugs were readily available and widely tolerated. As the incidences of abuse grew and people gained increased awareness, consumption dropped off and social attitudes became sterner. He further states that as the two-tier effect becomes more pronounced and minorities become more associated with drug abuse, public support for treatment might begin to wane. The result could be more public support for increased police, prisons, and harsher sentences, a reaction considered futile. "My concern is that as drug use declines among middle-class Americans, they will refuse to invest in the long-term needs of the inner city, like education and jobs. A primary task facing the [country's] Office of National Drug Control Policy is harnessing the current anti-drug energy and making it productive" (Musto, 1973).

Geographical Differences

Trends of drug use in 20 major U.S. cities have been monitored by the Community Epidemiology Workgroup. Findings reveal that the types of drugs used in different cities vary. Availability and price of drugs determine the extent of use in most areas, but in most cases, cocaine has remained the major drug of abuse. Heroin use has declined in some cities but has shown increased use in others. Stimulants, on the other hand, were most prevalent in Western cities. Furthermore, the *National Survey on Drug Use and Health* has shown that drug use varies across urban and rural areas, with higher instances of use in the larger metropolitan areas. In contrast, high school senior surveys have shown that use rates of stimulants, inhalants, and sedatives were similar in both rural and nonrural areas, with marijuana and cocaine being used more often in urban areas than in rural areas.

THE SOCIAL COSTS OF DRUG ABUSE

As we have indicated, law enforcement initiatives against drug abuse and trafficking are a financially exhausting proposition. Drug abuse also costs society billions of dollars in many other ways. These are seen in drug treatment and prevention programs, lost productivity on the job caused by impaired drug users, and the cost of other federal programs. The President's Fiscal Year (FY) 2011 National Drug Control Budget requests $15.5 billion to reduce drug use and its consequences in the United States. This represents an increase of 3.5 percent over the FY 2010 enacted level of $15 billion (Office of National Drug Control Policy, 2010a).

In addition to the financial burden imposed on Americans by drug abuse, there is yet a greater price to pay: the effects of drugs on our youths. Studies have revealed that most drug users began to use drugs as adolescents or even as preteens. Some reasons commonly offered are peer pressure, few legitimate means of income, and so-called broken homes. Adolescent drug abuse also impairs the learning capabilities of children and in some cases can cause severe emotional problems. Additionally, one should remember that most drug abuse is illegal activity, and when drugs are indiscriminately used around children, a message is sent to them that gives legitimacy to this activity, particularly when parents themselves are the drug users. Statistics vary, but studies have shown that many child maltreatment cases involve substance abuse.

Violence

The proliferation of drug-trafficking groups operating in the United States has increased substantially over the past 20 years. With the propagation of drug gangs interested in their share of the drug profit pie, drug-related crime has also spread to ancillary areas where the profit motive outweighs the motivation of the addict to stay "well." Drug-trafficking gangs wage turf wars and calculated acts of revenge over the control of neighborhoods. These gangs also recruit members as young as eight years old to deal drugs or act as spotters. Although drug markets seemed to stabilize in the 1990s, the potential for competitive violence still remains.

The pursuit of higher education and legitimate work is no longer considered by many of these individuals to be the best way to get ahead in life. The allure of gold chains, fast cars, status, and parties has affected the traditional maturation process for many gang members. Indeed, drugs represent a set of already stifling environmental factors that create a social gauntlet between children and their education and legitimate employment. The violence associated with drugs poses one of the greatest social concerns. In numerous recent polls, respondents consider drug trafficking to be one of the greatest national concerns and in many cases a serious threat to national security.

Addicted Babies

Another health concern is the problem of drug-addicted babies. Studies have shown that drug use can affect the development of a child, even before birth. Research has shown that marijuana and cocaine use during pregnancy are associated with substantial reductions in fetal growth. Moreover, infants exposed to drugs, especially heroin, are prone to exhibit withdrawal symptoms. Exposure to cocaine has been linked to various neurobehavioral and circulatory complications, including major congenital malformations. In 1996, a report by the National Institute on Drug Abuse showed that between 1992 and 1993, 5.5 percent of women (about 221,000) in the United States used an illicit drug at least once during their pregnancy. Infants born to mothers who use drugs often go through withdrawal or have other medical problems at birth (NIDA, 1996c). Health problems arising from drug abuse are a principal concern in drug control efforts. One particular issue is the problem of infants whose mothers have demonstrated a pattern of heavy cocaine use, especially in combination with alcohol.

Cocaine use by pregnant mothers can only be detected within 24 to 48 hours after use. Problems exist because the symptoms of a pregnant woman who suffers from cocaine addiction may not always be apparent to hospital officials. In many cases, pregnant addicts may not even visit hospitals until they are in labor.

Much attention was focused on the issue of cocaine-addicted babies during the late 1980s because of the serious health-related risks facing unborn children. Such hazards include strokes while babies are still in the uterus, physical malformations, and increased risk of death during infancy. In addition, because of the earlier-mentioned practice of "sex for drugs" by some pregnant woman, many babies are born with ancillary health problems, including sexually transmitted diseases.

Dr. Gordon B. Avery of Children's National Medical Center in Washington, D.C., stated that it is typical for cocaine babies to be born prematurely. He added, "In addition to the medical complications facing otherwise normal premature babies, cocaine babies face special hardships such as hydrocephaly (water on the brain), poor brain growth, kidney problems, and apnea (an unforeseen stoppage of breathing)" (Kantrowitz and Gonzalez, 1990). Confusion in this area of drug abuse partly exists because as recently as 1982 some medical textbooks on high-risk obstetrics still stated that cocaine had no harmful effects on the fetus. However, most sources agree that a fetus is particularly vulnerable to cocaine for several reasons:

- Although the placenta does shield the uterus from many large, complex molecules (particularly those that cannot defuse across fatty cell membranes), it is an open door to cocaine. This is true because cocaine is attracted to fatty compounds, and once the drug enters the blood and tissues of the fetus, it remains there longer than it does in an adult.
- The effects of cocaine on the mother-to-be also pose some threat to the fetus. That is, when a woman addicted to crack becomes pregnant, the well-being of the fetus and of her own body are not her primary concerns.
- An estimated 40 percent to 50 percent of cocaine-addicted pregnant woman have been exposed to the AIDS virus.
- Among cocaine-addicted babies, the average birth weight is approximately 21 ounces lower than normal, while the average head circumference is about three-quarters of an inch smaller than the average among normal babies. These differences may lead to future learning difficulties and an increased risk of infant mortality.

Demographically, the problem of cocaine-addicted babies extends beyond the inner city and across the national social spectrum. In many large cities such as New York, hospitals report that their obstetric and pediatric wards are overburdened and that drug-related costs contribute greatly to the overall cost of health care.

An emerging problem is children who were born to cocaine-using mothers but who survive for a few years: "They operate on an institutional level; they eat and sleep, and eat and sleep. Something has been left out" (Kantrowitz and Gonzalez, 1990). Social workers and hospital professionals claim that these cocaine children may have difficulty playing or relating with other children because they display symptoms of paranoia and distrust toward others. It has become a sobering reality that even if drug abuse were halted today, society would be forced to deal with its effects in one way or another during future decades (see Chapter 11).

Drugs and HIV

One of the most recent dangers of drug abuse is the threat of contracting deadly blood-borne viruses. Acquired immune deficiency syndrome (AIDS) and the human immunodeficiency virus (HIV) that causes AIDS are specific examples. In 2000, the CDC reported that more than 33 percent of new AIDS cases affected injecting drug users, their sexual partners, and their children (CDC, 2002). According to AVERT, a international AIDS charity, injection drug use was the transmission route in 10 percent of male and 16 percent of female diagnoses in 2007 (AVERT, 2010). Such viruses are real threats not just to the health of intravenous (IV) drug users but also to the health of others who associate with them. Statistics show that many heterosexual and pediatric AIDS cases in the nation can be traced directly to IV drug users. With the increase in the use of heroin in the 1990s, experts are predicting that there is even greater risk of HIV spreading throughout the drug-using community.

Lost Productivity

Drugs affect not only friends and families but logically the workplace as well. Employees who use drugs may miss more work and be late for work more often than those who do not use them. In addition, illness, injury, encounters with the justice system, and related family problems also may result. It is common for alcohol and other drugs to be used in combination, resulting in seriously affected coordination, concentration, risk taking, and other factors. Just how drugs affect the user depends largely on the user's dosage level, the rate of consumption, and the person's experience in using the drug. The extent of the drug use problem in the workplace was illustrated in a study of 2,500 postal workers (Zwerling, Ryan, and Endel, 1990) that found that postal workers who had used marijuana were:

- 1.6 times as likely as nonusers to have quit their jobs or have been fired
- 1.5 times as likely to have had an accident and nearly twice as likely to have been injured
- 1.5 times as likely to have been disciplined by a supervisor
- 1.8 times as likely to be absent from work

Concerns about safety mainly concentrate on high-precision or high-risk occupations such as transportation (e.g., airline pilots, air traffic controllers, railroad engineers, truck drivers, etc.). Other concerns focus on production of shoddily manufactured products, bad business decisions, slow-moving business services, drug-related absenteeism, sickness, and employee turnover. Furthermore, employee interaction can be negatively affected by drug-using employees' mood changes. Many people employed in the nation's public and private sectors are drug users. According to a Substance Abuse and Mental Health Services Administration report, of the 20.3 million adults classified with drug dependence or abuse in 2008, 12.5 million (61.5 percent) were employed full time (SAMHSA, 2009). Drug users tend to be less dependable than other workers and they decrease workplace productivity. An earlier SAMHSA report noted that they are more likely to have taken unexcused absences in the past month—12.1 percent do so, compared to 6.1 percent of drug-free workers. Furthermore, illegal drug users get fired more often (4.6 percent) than their non-drug-using counterparts (1.4 percent) (SAMHSA, 1997).

Drug Consumerism

The clandestine methamphetamine/crack market has created a new type of "consumerism" (for lack of a better term) that accompanies trafficking ventures. The new consumerism can be viewed from two angles: drug-user consumerism and drug-dealer consumerism. Because of drug-user consumerism, many supermarkets have noticed increased sales of items such as scouring pads, cough syrup, and over-the-counter bronchial inhalers. The sales of these and similar items illustrate their greater worth in a clandestine market than in a legitimate market. Scouring pads and steel wool are used for cleaning drug pipes and holding crack at the bottom of the pipe bowl. Grain alcohol is commonly used to ignite crack, and inhalers give drug users an added euphoric feeling, or *rush*, while under the influence of stimulants.

Stolen goods are a common means for drug users to get money for drugs. Studies have shown that "T-tops" from the roofs of sport cars are commonly bartered or sold for drugs. Other favorites include virtually anything electronic, such as videocassette recorders, microwave ovens (which are also used to make crack), stereos, and video games. At the opposite end of the consumerism spectrum is the drug-dealing side. Purchases of cellular phones, pagers, personalized license plates, jewelry, firearms, and automobiles for illegal purposes have actually boosted the legitimate market of these products. Cell phones and pagers are commonly used to arrange drug transactions, deliver supplies, and arrange for money pickups. Personalized license plates have emerged as a type of status symbol. Plates bearing variations of "boof" and "sling," for example, may refer to smoking and selling crack. Expensive rings and gold chains and watches are commonly used in bartering for drugs because such items are easily carried into crack houses and many dealers see them as status symbols.

Weapons such as the nine-millimeter semiautomatic gun have become popular with many drug dealers. The nine-millimeter, commonly referred to as a "muscle gun," is compact and has an intimidating appearance. Automobiles are also one of the most sought-after status symbols. Luxury vehicles have been seized by law enforcement agents after the vehicles have been purchased with cash earned from illicit sources. Expensive athletic shoes are also desired. In view of this connection, in 1998, the athletic shoe manufacturer Converse scrapped plans to launch a basketball shoe with the potentially controversial moniker "Young Guns," which was designed to attract urban teen males (Wells, 1998).

These buying trends pose serious ethical, moral, and legal dilemmas for retail merchants, who may be suspicious of some customers but may not have firm grounds for refusing business from those customers. Problems arise when customers present merchants with large sums of cash in exchange for goods. While merchants should not morally judge people because they possess large amounts of cash or because they are from a certain part of town, they should realize that the money they receive from any transaction may ultimately be subject to forfeiture under federal law if the customer turns out to be a drug dealer.

THEORIES OF DRUG ABUSE AND CRIME

The search for solutions for reducing drug abuse and crime has baffled law enforcement authorities, social scientists, and criminal justice academicians alike. Although many proposed solutions to the problem are discussed throughout this book, several widely accepted social theories explain why people use drugs and under what circumstances they become lured into criminal lifestyles. First, however, we will address the concepts of vice and victimless crime, terms commonly associated with drug crimes and drug abuse.

Vice and "Victimless" Crime

Although *vice* in normal parlance refers to any bad habit or evil conduct, in legal jargon it specifically refers to the supplying of any illicit good or service. For example, smoking cigarettes may be a vice in the ordinary sense, but only activities that have been specifically outlawed are considered *vice crimes*: drug trafficking, loan-sharking, gambling, and prostitution. Some vice crimes are actually legal under carefully regulated circumstances. Gambling, for instance, is legal in some states under some circumstances. Nonetheless, illegal gambling activity thrives on the skirts of controlled gambling institutions. Through uncontrolled illegal organizations, profits may exceed those that can be realized through legitimate channels.

Enforcement techniques, especially for vice crimes such as drug trafficking, can be controversial because a police officer's professional code of conduct and the letter of the law with regard to criminal investigations are sometimes compromised in order to obtain information. Enforcement is particularly difficult in these cases because there is usually no complainant or victim, as there is in other types of criminal violations. Therefore, law enforcement officers must rely on a high degree of surreptitiousness and ingenuity to make arrests. This can be illustrated, for example, by a drug investigator's tolerance of a certain amount of drug use on the part of his or her informant while other people are under investigation for drug use activity similar to that of the informant.

In a study of drug law enforcement, Peter K. Manning and Lawrence John Redlinger (2006) listed the questionable and corrupt practices that have been associated with narcotics agents. The list included taking bribes, using drugs, buying and selling drugs, arrogation of stolen property, illegal searches and seizures, protection of informants and their drug-trafficking activities, and violence. In contrast, drug enforcement professionals, though willing to admit that there is a certain degree of corruption in all law enforcement agencies, defend their profession by pointing to several factors. First, because of the accessibility of federal grant money in the early 1990s, professional training is more readily available to drug enforcement officials than ever before. Second, the adoption of a field training officer (FTO) program for drug enforcement personnel in larger departments has helped weed out individuals who are not considered competent for the job. Third, because of an increase in drug testing programs within law enforcement agencies, administrators have a new tool to check officers for drug abuse.

Regarding the term *victimless crime*, another distinction must be made. A crime is usually characterized by an act that hurts someone or something or by the potential for the act to hurt someone or something. The case of drug abuse is an exception because the primary victims (the drug abusers themselves) are willing participants in the activity. In addition, there are generally no complainants in vice crimes, for the reasons previously discussed. So when charges are filed in vice cases, the state (or government) is the complainant. However, though the term *victimless crime* came into use to describe these crimes, this does not change the fact that innocent people are also commonly victimized by drug abuse.

Why do people choose drug abuse as a social lifestyle? What fuels one's ambition to become involved in a criminal drug-trafficking organization or in a behavior that is considered criminal? These questions will be addressed in the context of sociological theories that attempt to explain the social nature of the drug problem.

Social Disorganization Theory

One popular explanation of drug abuse addresses the link with poverty, *social disorganization*, and a feeling of hopelessness. The correlation between drug abuse and young minority group members has often been tied to factors such as racial prejudice, low socioeconomic status, lack of positive self-esteem, and uncharitable urban surroundings. As a result, the link between drug use, poverty, and race has been associated with high levels of mistrust and defiance common to lower-class urban areas (Winick, 1965). In spite of a strong suggestion that drug abuse is linked with social disorganization, the relationship between class status and crime in general remains unclear.

Cultural Transmission

Today, social disorganization theory is most closely associated with the work of Chicago sociologists Clifford Shaw and Henry McKay. Their study, first published in the early 1940s, developed the theory of *cultural transmission* and focused on crime within the context of a changing urban environment. Shaw and McKay examined criminality, particularly among young people, in Chicago during the 1920s and 1930s. They concluded that the popular concepts of body build and IQ were no longer accurate predictors of criminality but that environmental factors in the cities were better predictors. Shaw and McKay saw criminality as a product of decaying "transitional neighborhoods" that were changing from affluence to deterioration. They examined certain areas that were consistently "high-crime" neighborhoods over several decades. Research revealed that although the ethnic composition of these neighborhoods changed over time, the level of criminality in these so-called *zones of transition* remained the same. As a result of this study, it has been suggested that the attitudes, values, and norms of these areas are not only conducive to crime but are transferred over time from one ethnic group to another. According to this theory, children become indoctrinated into a life of crime at an early age. This occurs particularly in males who associate regularly with criminals and drug dealers and look to them as role models.

Anomie

In 1938, Robert Merton introduced the concept of *anomie* to explain an individual's motive for involvement in deviant social behavior or crime. In his theory, Merton attempted to adapt the abstract concept of anomie to living conditions in U.S. society. Earlier, French criminologist Emile Durkheim had applied the term to explain a feeling of "normlessness" that results in a breakdown of social rules and order. Merton later adapted the concept to fit living conditions in U.S. society. In this theory, Merton argued, the ends become more important than the means, and an individual will resort to deviant means if no legitimate means (such as education, employment opportunities, etc.) are available. Merton went on to emphasize that modern American society is goal-oriented, with wealth and material goods being the most desired goals. The cultural goal of financial success is highly valued by the individual, but if that individual finds that (1) less value is attached by society to how that success is achieved, and (2) legitimate routes to financial success are blocked, he or she may opt for illegal means to achieve that particular end. For example, owning a home is generally considered one of the "great American dreams," but for many low-income families, this dream cannot be obtained through legitimate means. As a result, people from these families often "become estranged from a society that promises them in principle what they are deprived of in reality" (Merton, 1964:218).

To illustrate his theory, Merton cited a preoccupation with material success or *pathological materialism* endemic in American culture. A legitimate profit motive may be channeled through deviant means (drug dealing, for example) when social barriers preclude legitimate channels such as good schooling, quality jobs, and higher income. The result may be the creation of a criminal person willing to break the law to reach his or her goals. Merton further explained that there are five modes of individual adaptation to the contradiction between promised goals and available means: (1) conformity, (2) ritualism, (3) rebellion, (4) retreatism, and (5) innovation.

It is the first and third modes, conformity and rebellion, that may offer the most intelligible explanation of society's involvement in drug use. The fifth mode, innovation, creates one of the fundamental social infrastructures for involvement in organized crime. For example, the crime phenomenon of the California youth gangs that spread to many major cities in the mid-1980s suggests that Merton's philosophy has contemporary validity. Such gangs represent thousands of inner-city youths from the Los Angeles area who have become extremely organized, targeting large cities and realizing hundreds of thousands of dollars of drug money (see Chapter 8).

Opportunity Theory

Opportunity theory is another popular theory that parallels Merton's theory of anomie and one that attempts to explain that not only are legitimate social opportunities unequally distributed throughout society, but even some illegitimate criminal opportunities are blocked for some youths. Richard A. Cloward and Lloyd E. Ohlin (1960) wrote that many male adolescents experience extreme deprivation of opportunity. Therefore, many feel that their position within society is somewhat fixed and that there are few legitimate ladders to success. In fact, they argue that criminal opportunities are available only for youths who have grown up in areas where collusion exists between members of the underworld and the general society. In these areas, adult criminals have worked out arrangements (through corruption) among businesses, politicians, and the police that leave them all but immune from prosecution. Their criminal enterprises (drug trafficking, gambling, and so forth) offer a stable income and an alternative to legitimate economic success. Fostered by adult criminals, youths fit right into this model and create a criminal subculture, preparing to join adult crime organizations by first running with criminally active street gangs. Cloward and Ohlin identified three types of delinquent subcultures: (1) the retreatist subculture (in which drug use is the primary focus); (2) the conflict subculture (in which gang activities are dedicated to destruction and violence as ways of gaining status); and (3) the criminal rackets subculture (in which gang activity is devoted to utilitarian or profit-motivated criminal pursuits).

Essentially, Cloward and Ohlin view crime as a function of different opportunities provided to youths to attain both legitimate and illegitimate goals. When avenues for legitimate goals are blocked, illegitimate avenues are then pursued.

Differential Association

Some researchers embrace learning theories in which *differential association* attempts to explain a person's involvement in criminal activity. This theory, first formulated by Edwin Sutherland in 1939, suggests that a principal part of learning criminal behavior occurs within intimate groups. This occurs in two ways. First, individuals, particularly those living in economically depressed areas, identify with the financially successful role models in their communities (drug dealers, pimps, and gamblers). Second, individuals are exposed to the lifestyle and techniques of criminal behavior in their communities. The specifics of what is learned are based on the frequency of contacts and the intensity and duration of each association. According to Sutherland, the individual learns specialized techniques, attitudes, justifications, and rationalizations. Sutherland offered nine basics of differential association:

1. Criminal behavior is learned.
2. The fundamental basis of learning criminal behavior is formed in intimate personal groups (e.g., gangs).
3. Criminal behavior is acquired through interaction with other persons in the process of communication.
4. The learning process includes the techniques of committing the crime and specific rationalizations and attitudes for criminal activity.
5. General attitudes regarding respect (or lack of respect) for the law are reflected in attitudes toward criminal behavior.
6. A person becomes delinquent or criminal because of an excess of definitions favorable to violation of the law over definitions unfavorable to violation of the law.

7. Differential association may differ in duration, frequency, and intensity.
8. The processes for learning criminal behavior parallel those of any other type of learning.
9. Criminal behavior is an expression of general needs and values (as with noncriminal behavior), but it is not explained by those needs and values.

Sutherland believes that it is through the learning of these traits that a favorable predisposition to criminal lifestyles is developed.

SUMMARY

Today's drug situation is a result of complex social interactions affecting many different people, places, and things. It is referred to in a number of different ways by public speakers, politicians, the media, and private citizens. Terms used to describe the situation include the *drug crisis*, the *drug problem*, the *drug dilemma*, the *drug epidemic*, and the *war on drugs.* However people choose to refer to the issue, drugs have remolded the social fabric of communities, the work environment, the learning environment of schools, the criminal justice system, and the drug treatment industry, just to name a few. From all indications, drug abuse in one form or another is here to stay.

There is no single drug abuse problem. Drug problems are related to both health and public safety, and much controversy exists around the best solution for the problem. The existence of drugs in our communities poses a considerable financial burden for society. Costs include the financial expense of street crimes such as robbery and burglary, criminal justice system costs, medical costs for victims, and the loss of productivity in the workplace. Other hidden costs include the moral cost of corrupt public officials and family strife for drug users and their loved ones.

The very nature of the drug problem creates an element of criminality and comes with the violence associated with that element. Organized crime groups, such as the Jamaican posses and the California-based Crips and Bloods, have emerged since the "drug culture" materialized, and their presence has become well known in many communities throughout the nation. Long-established crime organizations have also flourished since the drug epidemic gained momentum.

The reasons that people take drugs are numerous. For example, some people desire a stimulation of the endocrine chemicals within the body. These internal chemicals tend to emulate the effects of morphine and give a feeling of euphoria. Other people use drugs to alter their moods in the traditional "happy hour" forum. Still others use certain drugs for treatment of physical or mental medical conditions. Drug trafficking and related drug activity is referred to by many as a "vice" crime. Additionally, many tend to refer to this type of behavior as "victimless" because all participants are willing to engage in the act. For that reason, many feel that the enforcement of such crimes is the equivalent of government attempting to police morals and personal values and that such crimes should not be considered crimes at all but should be regulated and taxed.

Several social theories have been posited to explain the criminal behavior that commonly accompanies drug abuse. Included are theories of social disorganization, anomie, cultural transmission, differential association, and differential opportunity. Each of these theories adds to our understanding of drug abuse and criminality and can be applied to the study of modern-day criminal behavior.

Do you recognize these terms?

- addictive personality
- anomie
- backstabbing
- cultural transmission
- differential association
- endogenous
- endorphins

- opportunity theory
- pathological materialism
- rush
- social disorganization
- vice crimes
- victimless crime
- zones of transition

DISCUSSION QUESTIONS

1. What is meant by the term "drug abuse"?

2. Other than drug users themselves, who are the victims of drug abuse in our society?

3. Discuss some of the reasons that the drug problem is considered such a major social problem in the United States.

4. Discuss some of the health-related problems inherent in drug abuse.

5. What are some social factors that contribute to a climate of drug abuse?

6. What are the distinctions between the terms *vice* and *victimless crime*?

7. List the ways that cocaine in addicted pregnant mothers affects their unborn.

8. What are endorphins, and how do they relate to drug abuse?

CLASS PROJECT

1. Discuss with fellow classmates or friends their perception of the country's drug problem and what can be done to solve it.

Chapter 2

The History of Drug Abuse

This chapter will enable you to:

- Understand the beginnings of the world's drug abuse problem
- Realize the many social implications of drug abuse
- Compare developments in drug control legislation during recent decades
- Appreciate the development of the United States' national drug control policy

Public perceptions of drugs and drug abuse have shifted dramatically over the past 200 years. Twice, Americans have accepted and then rejected drugs in our society. Understanding these striking historical swings helps us understand our current reactions to drug use. America's recurrent enthusiasm for recreational drugs and the resulting campaigns for abstinence present resounding problems for public policymakers as well as for the public they serve. Because the peaks of these episodes occurred about a generation apart, citizens rarely have an accurate picture (much less a recollection) of the latest wave of drug use. Criminologist David Musto (1991) suggests that fear and anger have been the primary causes of society's intolerance for drugs, and such emotions have distorted public memory so grotesquely that it becomes useless as a point of reference for policy formation. The lack of knowledge concerning our earlier encounters with drugs impedes the task of establishing a workable public policy toward dealing with the problem.

Due to the notoriety of drug use during the 1960s, many people assume that this decade was most responsible for our nation's current drug problem. Indeed, as we will see, the 1960s played a significant role in the development and propagation of certain drugs of abuse, but the roots of the problem go back much further in history.

DOI: 10.1016/B978-1-4377-4450-7.00002-3
© 2011 Elsevier Inc. All rights reserved.

History Repeats Itself

Humankind's drug abuse legacy began thousands of years ago in such diverse areas as China, Egypt, India, the Middle East, and the Americas, where cannabis, ephedra, and opium were used for medicinal purposes and as general health tonics. In many cases, the medicinal use of these plants turned to recreational use, creating a pattern of progression from use to abuse that has continued to the present. Seven thousand years ago the Sumerians left records of a "joy plant," presumably the highly addictive opium poppy (papaver somniferum). The euphoric effects of medicinal use of the plant led to recreational abuse of opium in Sumerian society.

The Chinese discovered alkaloid ephedrine *(Ephedra sinica),* an inhalant, as far back as 3000 B.C.E. and marijuana *(Cannabis sativa)* by 2000 B.C.E. Chinese emperors in the third millennium B.C.E. ate or brewed cannabis in tea. Later on, the custom of drying and smoking cannabis was imported from India. Within a few centuries, alcohol abuse in Babylonia was significant enough to inspire legal controls. In 1700 B.C.E., the Code of Hammurabi included censure of public intoxication. Likewise, opium abuse in ancient Egypt increased to such an extent that by 1500 B.C.E. Egyptian scriptures had censured the practice. Again, opium use, which had medicinal origins as a pain reliever in surgery, had become opium abuse.

In South America, the Incas chewed the coca leaf, the plant from which cocaine is derived. By 1000 B.C.E., the Incas believed that the coca leaf (Erthroxylon coca) aided in the digestion of food and the suppression of their appetites. So highly valued was the coca leaf that it was used instead of gold or silver to barter for food and clothing. Coca chewing is even reflected in the art of that period. For example, a ceramic statue now housed in a museum in Ecuador portrays an Indian with the characteristic chewer's bulge in the cheek.

Greek literature in the first millennium B.C.E. records an awareness of both opium and alcohol. The hero of Homer's epic tale *The Odyssey* forbids his sailors from eating the lotus flowers when visiting the African land of the Lotus Eaters. This imaginative tale about the lotus-eating dreamers suggests Homer's familiarity with opium use among North African cultures. Later, in 400 B.C.E., Hippocrates, the father of modern medicine (for whom the Hippocratic Oath is named), recommended drinking the juice of the white poppy mixed with the seed of nettle. Yet another myth deals with Dionysus, god of wine—and drunkenness. Under the influence of alcohol, the followers of Dionysus ran amok, killing people and destroying property. So, although wine festivals were an important part of Greek culture, they were surrounded by a legend that inspired laws restricting the excessive use of alcohol.

In still another early culture, hallucinogens were commonly used. Around 100 B.C.E., the Aztec Indians of North America used dried peyote cactus buttons in religious ceremonies. Tribe people believed they would get closer to the gods and nature if they consumed this magical plant. Magic mushrooms (psilocybin) and morning glory seeds (ololiuqui) were other organic hallucinogens commonly used by the Indians.

Ancient cultures all around the world established customs of drug use quite independently. However, with improved ships, more extensive sea travel, and political and military expansion, one culture began to influence another. For instance, the Roman conquest of the eastern Mediterranean in the first century C.E. contributed to the spread of opium use. Whether the drugs were imported or indigenous to a culture, drug use continued to flourish.

Drug use was so established in India, for both recreational and commercial purposes, that the Susruta treatise of C.E. 400 catalogued with unprecedented detail various types of cannabis preferred by the Indians. For example, bhang, a strain of cannabis generally considered weak in strength, was brewed into tea. Ganja, a more potent type of cannabis, was usually smoked. The high-grade charas, similar to hashish or sinsemilla, was commonly eaten by affluent Indians. In the ninth century, Arab traders introduced opium to China. Within a few more centuries, opium smoking in China ("chasing the dragon") would become a major public health threat.

Drugs even entered military rituals in several parts of the world. Some eleventh-century Persian warriors smoked hashish to prepare for battle and for their fate as martyrs. Al-Hassan-ibn-al Sabbah ("The Old Man of the Mountains") led such a band of Shiite Moslem warriors. (The word *assassin*, which later evolved through European use to mean the murderer of a political figure, comes from Hassan's name.) On the other side of the world, Incan warriors commonly chewed coca leaves. Some historians partially attribute Pizarro's defeat of the Incan empire in 1532 to the fact that many Incan warriors were so inebriated that they were mentally and physically unable to fight.

As we'll discuss in Chapter 3, in North America, Native American Indians have a long tradition of smoking tobacco, a custom that was eventually introduced to European sailors. Magellan took tobacco to parts of Africa, while the Portuguese carried it to Polynesia. In the 1600s, Sir Walter Raleigh introduced pipe smoking to England. Jean Nicot, who first took tobacco to France, claimed that it had great medicinal properties. In fact, the stimulant nicotine, the most dangerous chemical in tobacco, is named after him. The popularity of tobacco spread so rapidly in many Asian and European countries that some governments began to censure it. Japan, for example, prohibited smoking in the mid-1650s, and at about the same time, in parts of Europe, smoking tobacco was punished by disfigurement or death.

The age of exploration contributed greatly to the spread of culture, colonialism, commerce—and drugs. Whether mildly stimulating or dangerously addictive, drugs and the drug trade flourished. Explorers introduced some African cultures to tobacco and borrowed other drugs from them. In 1621, the Ethiopian coffee bean was introduced in England, and by the 1650s, coffee houses were well established in London and elsewhere.

THE OPIUM MENACE OF THE 1800S

Opium addiction established itself as a major health threat in China. During the 1800s, the Manchu dynasty tried to restrict opium use through legislation focusing on trade. The main target of such legislation was the East India Company of Great Britain, which supplied China with opium from India, which was then a colony of the British Empire. In fact, the British forced their colonial subjects into a widespread system of opium production that gave the British a virtual monopoly on the opium trade. Today's opium cultivators in Southeast and Southwest Asia are the descendants of farmers who were forced to participate in the British opium trade. Despite legal controls, the opium problem in China became so great that hostilities broke out between Great Britain and China.

In the early 1800s, the Manchu government passed a standing order for its army to detain and search any British vessel suspected of carrying opium. This led to the first of two great *opium wars* between China and Britain (1839–1842). The first war resulted in the defeat of China. The victorious British quickly claimed that opium consumption was harmless, encouraged its use, and reaped the profits from its trade. Chinese officials continued their objections, and a second war (1856–1860) broke out. In this second opium war (also called the *Anglo-French War*), a joint offensive by Britain and France resulted in the second defeat of China. Presumably, profit from the opium trade was more important than the welfare of the Chinese people to those warring countries (France, Britain, Russia, and the United States) that imposed the Tientsin Treaty (1858) on China. China at first refused to ratify the treaty, but by 1860 the defeated nation was forced to agree to key provisions: the legalization of opium and the opening of 11 more ports to Western ships.

Opium use had naturally spread to Britain and continental Europe, where decades earlier the Romantic poet Samuel Taylor Coleridge had fought addiction to the drug. Aiding in the perpetuation of the English addiction cycle was the manufacture of many opium-based over-the-counter preparations and tonics containing opium, morphine, and laudanum, each with harmless-sounding names such as Mother Bailey's Quieting Syrup and Munn's Elixir. Other over-the-counter cures had cocaine as their only active ingredient. Such "cures" were typically sold by street peddlers, mail order houses, retail grocers, and pharmacists. At the time, users could also gain unrestricted access to opium in opium dens and to morphine through retailers.

Throughout the eighteenth and nineteenth centuries, advances in chemistry led to derivatives from opium and new chemical preparations. German chemists developed anodyne, a liquid form of ether, in 1730. The British chemist Joseph Priestley, best known for his discovery of oxygen, held laughing gas parties in his home after he discovered nitrous oxide gas in 1776. During the early 1800s, chloroform gained popularity as an anesthetic.

Meanwhile, a German pharmacist named F. W. A. Serturner developed morphine, an opium derivative that he named after Morpheus, the Greek god of dreams and sleep. Codeine, another opium derivative, discovered in 1832, was used as a cough suppressant. Morphine use in surgery led to the invention of the hypodermic needle in 1853. Ironically, doctors at that time believed patient addiction to morphine could be avoided if the drug were injected rather than swallowed.

Figure 2.1

The History of Heroin

1874 Heroin is isolated from morphine.

1898 The Bayer Company of Germany commercially produces heroin, which is later found to be more potent than morphine.

1900 Heroin is determined to be highly addictive, even though it was originally believed to be a cure for opium addiction.

1914 In the United States, the Harrison Narcotics Act is passed, which restricts the manufacture, importation, and distribution of heroin.

1924 Heroin becomes readily available on the black market, as its manufacture is prohibited.

1930 The French Connection becomes the primary international supplier of heroin to the United States.

1964 The controversial methadone maintenance program is launched to treat opiate addicts.

1970 In the United States, heroin is classified as a Schedule I Narcotic by the Controlled Substances Act.

1985 The U.S. government estimates that there are 500,000 to 750,000 heroin addicts in the country.

2010 Heroin purity increases as the warring between powerful drug cartels in Mexico escalates.

The History of Heroin

During this time, because of a peculiarity of the U.S. Constitution, the powerful new forms of opium and cocaine were more readily available in the United States than in most nations (Musto, 1991). Under the Constitution, individual states assumed responsibility for health-related issues. This included the regulation of medical practice and the availability of pharmaceutical drugs. In actuality, the United States had as many laws regarding health professions as it had states. For much of the nineteenth century, many states chose to have no controls at all; instead, lawmakers reacted to the free-enterprise philosophy that gave physicians freedom to practice medicine virtually as they saw fit. In comparison, nations with a less restricted central government, such as Great Britain, had a single, all-encompassing pharmacy law controlling the availability of drugs that were considered dangerous. So, when we consider drug abuse in the nineteenth century, we are looking at an era of unbridled availability and limitless advertising of drugs.

LATE-NINETEENTH-CENTURY DEVELOPMENTS

In the 1860s, the American Civil War literally triggered a drug epidemic, resulting in hundreds of thousands of morphine addicts—400,000 in the Union Army alone (O'Brien and Cohen, 1984). The indiscriminate use of morphine and commercially available opium-based drugs prevailed on the battlefields, in prisons, and even on the home front. Self-medication for grief and pain often resulted in high dosages and, eventually, addiction. Meanwhile, opium use increased on the West Coast, and many Americans quickly associated opium smoking with Chinese immigrants, who were lured to California by the promise of work on the railroads. Chinese opium smoking was tolerated and even encouraged while the Chinese laborers worked for low wages, performing backbreaking tasks in jobs that few white Americans wanted. However, when a series of economic depressions in the late 1800s made jobs, even low-paying ones, a scarce commodity, nativist white anger was turned loose on the Chinese and their practice of opium smoking. This drug abuse cultural link was one of the earliest examples of a powerful theme in the American perception of drugs: an association of drugs with a feared or rejected group within society. Similarly, cocaine would be linked with blacks, and marijuana with Mexicans, during the first part of the twentieth century.

Opium dens were so commonplace in San Francisco that the city passed an ordinance in 1875 to ban opium smoking in opium dens. This was considered the first antidrug law in the United States, and it resulted in a series of state and local legislative actions. (By 1912, nearly every state and many municipalities had regulations controlling the distribution of certain drugs.) However, the absence of any federal control over interstate commerce in habit-forming and other drugs, the absence of uniformity among state laws, and a lack of effective drug enforcement had one important implication: The rising tide of legislation directed at opiates (and later cocaine) was more a reflection of changing public attitude toward these drugs than an effective strategy to reduce supplies to users (Musto, 1991). The reality is that the reduction of opiate use around 1900 was probably due more to a fear of addiction, particularly among physicians, than to any successful campaign to reduce drug abuse (Musto, 1991).

More newly discovered drugs contributed to the use-to-abuse pattern. Around 1870, Oscar Liebreich developed one of the first sedative hypnotics, chloral hydrate. In combination with alcohol, it was commonly abused as a recreational drug as well as for more nefarious purposes such as the famous "Mickey Finn," a knockout cocktail used by muggers and robbers. Meanwhile, in 1878, cocaine was first isolated in an alkaloid form in an attempt to cure many of the postwar morphine addicts in the United States. Early on, its retail price was exceedingly high (compared to industrial wages of the time)—$5 to $10 per gram—but it soon fell to 25 cents a gram and stayed there until price inflation after World War I (Musto, 1991). Although problems with cocaine were apparent almost from the beginning, by the 1880s this "cure" was used recreationally on a widespread basis. This was partly because popular opinion and leading medical "experts" touted cocaine as being both a beneficial and a benign stimulant. In fact, the crack cocaine epidemic that struck the United States during the mid-1980s was not the first cocaine epidemic. The nation's original cocaine epidemic occurred within roughly a 35-year period from the mid-1880s to 1920.

Contributing to the spread of cocaine use was the considerable support of its use by the European medical community and later by American medical professionals. In the absence of national legislation controlling the use of cocaine, its abuse spread. Initially, cocaine was offered as a cure for opiate addiction, an asthma remedy (the official remedy of the American Hay Fever Association), and an antidote for toothaches. In 1886, Atlanta-born John Styth Pemberton introduced the soft drink Coca-Cola, which, for the next 20 years, had a cocaine base. The soft drink was introduced as having the advantages of coca but lacking the dangers of alcohol.

Although cocaine failed as a cure for morphine addiction, it was still erroneously hailed as a cure for other problems. One report in 1883 explained how Bavarian soldiers given cocaine experienced renewed energy for combat. Sigmund Freud, inspired by American and German medical literature, first used cocaine as an aid in therapy in the 1880s. He used the "magical substance" in the treatment of depression and believed it to be helpful

An early Coca-Cola ad, featuring cocaine as an ingredient, is part of an exhibit at the Drug Enforcement Administration Museum and Visitors Center in Arlington, Virginia.

with asthma and certain stomach disorders. Freud's professional use led to his own secret habit that was known only to a few close friends and associates during the later years of his life.

As medicinal cocaine use spread throughout Europe, so did its commercial and recreational appeal. A popular European elixir called Vin Mariani (named after its inventor, Angelo Mariani) surfaced in Paris and consisted of red wine and Peruvian coca leaf extracts. Historians believe that in the 1880s Vin Mariani was probably the most widely used medical prescription in the world, used even by popes, kings, queens, and other rulers. At the same time, William A. Hammond, a prominent American neurologist, hailed cocaine as being no more habit-forming than coffee or tea. After all, how could any substance that makes the user feel so good be so bad? Within one year of the discovery of cocaine, the Parke-Davis Company was marketing coca and cocaine in 15 different forms, including coca cigarettes, cocaine for injection, and cocaine for sniffing. Cocaine kits were sold by Parke-Davis as well as by other companies. These kits even offered syringes for convenient injections. The company proudly announced that cocaine "can supply the place of food, make the coward brave, the silent eloquent and . . . render the sufferer insensitive to pain" (Musto, 1991). Musto further points out that several reports from the years before the *Harrison Narcotics Act* of 1914 suggest that both the profit margin and street price of cocaine were unaffected by the legal availability of cocaine from a physician. He suggests that "perhaps the formality of medical consultation and the growing antagonism among physicians and the public toward cocaine helped to sustain the illicit market."

As with other "cures" before it, cocaine had failed as a remedy for morphine addiction, so it was with great pride that the Bayer Company in Germany announced a "wonder drug" designed to cure morphine and cocaine addictions. The new drug, heroin, also a derivative of opium, was soon found to be at least three times as addictive as the morphine it was supposed to remedy. Cocaine abuse decreased considerably by the 1920s and then virtually disappeared from the American drug scene until the 1970s. Meanwhile, the Aztec custom of using peyote had spread northward in the Americas. The Comanche Indians first incorporated peyote into their religious ceremonies in the 1870s. This religious practice continues and is protected by U.S. law. Less than 20 years later, the drug mescaline was isolated as the hallucinogenic ingredient in peyote. (Many decades later, mescaline was thought by many to be a "risk-free" recreational drug.)

Figure 2.2

The History of Cocaine

1844 Cocaine, the principle alkaloid in coca leaves, is isolated.

1863 A preparation of coca leaves and wine called Vin Mariani gains popularity in Europe.

1878 Cocaine is used for morphine addiction.

1884 Sigmund Freud studies cocaine as a psychoactive drug to treat depression and fatigue.

1884 Karl Koller uses cocaine as a topical anesthetic in eye operations.

1886 Coca-Cola, a soft drink containing coca extract, comes on the market.

1906 The U.S. Pure Food and Drug Act prohibits interstate shipment of food and soda water containing cocaine.

1906 The Coca-Cola Company switches to "decocainized" coca leaves.

1914 The U.S. Harrison Narcotics Act lists cocaine as narcotic.

1922 Congress prohibits most importation of cocaine and coca leaves.

1970 The U.S. controlled Substances Act classifies cocaine as a Schedule II Stimulant.

1970s Cocaine use becomes popular as a glamour drug with affluent segments of society.

1985 Crack cocaine is introduced and replaces PCP as the inner-city drug of choice.

2010 The availability of cocaine in the U.S. is greatly reduced due to the demise of many cocaine cartels.

The History of Cocaine

Although peyote use was confined primarily to religious ceremonies, at the turn of the century alcohol abuse was spreading throughout society to all social classes and racial groups. Epidemic alcohol addiction in the United States finally led to the controversial Eighteenth Amendment and the era of Prohibition. Prohibition limited only the legal consumption of alcohol; illegal markets thrived. Alcohol—and even marijuana, which served as an inexpensive substitute for costly black-market alcohol—was easily available in (among other places) secret bars called *speakeasies*. Many famous jazz musicians performing in such speakeasies were thought to be drug abusers.

THE TWENTIETH CENTURY

As the twentieth century unfolded, so did the introduction of many new drugs. In 1903, barbiturates were discovered in Germany, and in 1912 amphetamines were mass-produced as an antidote for asthma. Benzedrine inhalers were introduced for the first time in 1932 for treatment of adverse respiratory conditions, and in 1938 the painkiller Demerol, which is today a highly prized substitute for heroin on the streets, was synthesized and placed on the market. Thus, drug abuse in the early twentieth century was nothing new or unusual. What was relatively new was the variety of drugs abused and the extent to which each decade since 1900 can be characterized by particular drug fads, especially in the United States.

As early as 1887 and in the absence of federal laws, some states had begun regulatory procedures. Finally, because of growing concern over opiate addiction and the nonmedical use of drugs at the turn of the twentieth century, several important federal legislative actions were taken. The first was a federal prohibition of the importation of opium by Chinese nationals in 1887 and a restriction of opium smoking in the Philippines in 1905. These actions were followed by the passing of the federal Pure Food and Drug Act in 1906, which required over-the-counter medicine manufacturers to correctly label the inclusion of certain drugs. However, the act failed to restrict the use of these drugs. In the following seven years, the U.S. government participated in several international conventions designed to motivate other nations to pass domestic laws dealing with drug control. In 1909, the Shanghai Opium Convention strongly supported such controls, but its recommendation generated little actual legislation among the nations involved, including the United States.

By 1910, President William Howard Taft presented Congress with a State Department report stating that cocaine was more appalling in its effects than any other habit-forming drug in the United States. A year earlier, President Theodore Roosevelt had led the effort to ban drugs in the nation's capital when he was informed by local police of their suspicions that the use of cocaine predisposes the user to commit criminal acts. Failure to pass the proposed Foster Anti-Narcotic Bill led to a debate at the famed 1911 International Conference at The Hague, which deliberated the issue of whether the United States would

Figure 2.3

The History of Marijuana	▐▐▐▐▐▐▐▐▐▐▐▐▐▐▐▐▐▐▐▐

c. 2000 B.C.E.	Reference to marijuana found in India.	**1937**	The Marijuana Tax Act is passed and outlaws untaxed possession or distribution of marijuana.
1545	Hemp is introduced to Chile.	**1950–60**	Recreational marijuana use spreads on college campuses and in high schools.
1611	Hemp is cultivated by early settlers in Virginia.		
1856	*Putnam's Magazine* publishes an account of Fitzhugh Ludlow's marijuana-consuming experiences.	**1970**	The Controlled Substances Act lists marijuana as a Schedule I hallucinogen.
1875	"Hashish houses" appear and are modeled after Chinese opium dens.	**1990**	Alaska "recriminalizes" marijuana after 15 years of relaxed marijuana laws.
1920	Marijuana use for recreational purposes increases during Prohibition.	**2010**	Medical marijuana laws have been passed in 14 states, but receive national criticism.

The History of Marijuana

actually enact such legislation. Resulting from The Hague conference, the Senate's ratification of the convention in 1913 committed the United States to enact laws to suppress the abuse of opium, morphine, and cocaine. The goal was a world in which narcotics were restricted to medicinal use. Both producing and consuming nations would have control over their own boundaries.

Returning from The Hague was the State Department's opium commissioner, Hamilton Wright, who began to structure a comprehensive federal anti-drug law. Blocking his efforts was the specter of states' rights. The major cause of addiction was thought to be indiscriminate prescription of dangerous drugs by health professionals, yet how could the federal government interfere with the prescribing practices of physicians or demand that pharmacists keep records? To Wright, the answer was obvious: the government power to tax. After extensive negotiations with pharmaceutical, export, import, and other medical interests, the Harrison Narcotics Act was passed in December 1914 and became the hallmark of federal drug control policy for the next 65 years. Many people viewed the Harrison Narcotics Act as a rational way to limit addiction and drug abuse through taxation and regulation. It was a regulatory device that, according to the American Opium Commission, "would bring the whole traffic and use of these drugs into the light of day and, therefore, create a public opinion against the use of them that would be more important, perhaps, than the act itself." The act was heralded as a method of drug abuse control and as a public awareness tool.

The success of the enforcement of the act was directly attributed to the chosen source of authority and constitutional power to collect taxes. Because it was basically a tax revenue measure, it required people who prescribed or distributed certain drugs to register with the government and buy tax stamps. In addition, the law stipulated that possession of drugs by an unregistered person was unlawful unless prescribed by a physician in good faith. The responsibility of enforcement rested with the Department of the Treasury.

Figure 2.4

Section 1—Any person who was in the business of dealing in the specified drugs was required to pay a special annual tax of one dollar. In 1918 the Revenue Act increased the special annual tax on importers, manufacturers, producers, and compounders to $24; on wholesalers to $12; on retailers to $6; and on practitioners to $3.

Section 2—The selling or giving away of any specified drugs was prohibited except pursuant to the written order of the person to whom the drug was being given or sold. The written order was required to be on a special form issued by the Commissioner of Internal Revenue.

Section 4—It was unlawful for anyone who had not previously registered to engage in interstate trafficking of the specified drugs.

Section 8—The possession of any of the specified drugs was illegal with the exception of employees of registrants and patients of physicians.

Section 9—The punishment for any violation of the act was to be not more than $2,000 or not more than five years in prison or both.

Section 10—The Commissioner of Internal Revenue was given responsibility for enforcing the act

Selected Provisions of the Harrison Narcotics Act

Because of so many ambiguities in the Harrison Act, conflict erupted between the medical community and law enforcement officials. From the beginning, the Treasury Department insisted that medical maintenance of opiate addicts (treatment through declining usage) was unlawful, but physicians opposed this belief. Lower courts of law initially upheld the practice of drug maintenance of addicts, but a series of Supreme Court decisions, including the 1919 ruling in *Webb et al. v. United States*, stated that maintaining addicts on narcotic drugs, even by prescription, was illegal.

Early enforcement of the Harrison Narcotics Act resulted in mass arrests of physicians, pharmacists, and unregistered users. In fact, some 30,000 physicians were arrested during this period for dispensing narcotics, and about 3,000 actually served prison sentences. Consequently, doctors all but abandoned the treatment of addicts for nearly half a century in the United States. Furthermore, although private sanitariums that claimed to cure addiction had existed since the mid-1800s, they were unable to serve all the remaining addicts when physicians became wary of prescribing opiates for maintenance. To respond to this need, between 1919 and 1921 44 cities opened municipal clinics to provide temporary maintenance for addicts. Such clinics soon found themselves aggressively targeted for investigation by agents of the Narcotics Division. By 1925, all these clinics had been closed. Despite popular criticism of the

Figure 2.5

1909	At the Shanghai Opium Convention, representatives of 13 nations met to discuss ways of controlling illicit drug traffic.
1912	At The International Opium Convention, the first binding international instrument governing the shipment of narcotic drugs was signed at The Hague, Netherlands.
1914	The Harrison Narcotics Act was passed and became the hallmark of U.S. federal drug control policy for the next 65 years.
1920	The First Assembly of the League of Nations established an Advisory Committee on Traffic in Opium and Other Dangerous Drugs. Under League auspices, three main drug conventions were developed over the next two decades.
1925	The Second International Opium Convention established a system of import certificates and export authorizations for licit international trade in narcotics.
1931	The Convention for Limiting the Manufacture and Regulating the Distribution of Narcotic Drugs introduced a compulsory estimation system aimed at limiting the amount of drugs manufactured to those needed for medical and scientific needs.
1936	The Convention for the Suppression of the Illicit Traffic in Dangerous Drugs was the first international instrument called for severe punishment for illegal traffickers.
1946	Drug control responsibilities formerly carried out by the League of Nations were transferred to the United Nations. The Division of Narcotic Drugs was also created to act as the secretariat for the commission and to serve as the central repository of United Nations expertise in drug control.
1961	The Single Convention on Narcotic Drugs codified all existing multilateral treaty laws. It placed under control the cultivation of plants grown as raw material for narcotic drugs. Controls were continued on opium and its derivatives, and coca bush and cannabis were placed under international control, obliging governments to limit production to amounts needed for scientific and medical use.
1971	Until 1971, only narcotic drugs were subject to international control. The Convention on Psychotropic Substances extended controls to include a broad range of man-made, mood-altering substances that could lead to harmful dependencies. These included hallucinogens such as LSD and mescaline, stimulants such as amphetamines, and sedative-hypnotics such as barbiturates.
1981	The International Drug Abuse Control Strategy was formed and implemented a five-year program. It included measures for wider adherence to existing treaties coordinating efforts to ensure a balance between supply and demand of drugs for a legitimate use and steps to eradicate the illicit drug supply and reduce traffic.
1984	In its Declaration on the Control of Drug Trafficking and Drug Abuse, the U.N. General Assembly characterized drug traffic and abuse as "an international criminal activity" that constituted "a grave threat to the security and development of many countries and peoples"
1987	The International Conference on Drug Abuse and Illicit Trafficking focused on developing long-term drug control strategies, policies, and activities to attack at the national, regional, and international levels of drug abuse and trafficking.

Milestones in U.S. Drug Control

prohibition of narcotic drugs during this period, the Harrison Narcotics Act proved to drastically reduce the consumption of narcotics in the United States. This conclusion is evident when we observe the reduction of the number of addicts during a 25-year period: In 1920, there were an estimated 500,000 addicts, and in 1945, the addict population was roughly 40,000 to 50,000.

The Prohibition Era

Although moderate drinking was generally accepted during the eighteenth century, by the early nineteenth century some people began to perceive an increase in the abuse of alcohol. The American Temperance Society, founded in 1826, began gathering pledges of abstinence. Within three years, more than 200 antiliquor organizations were active, and by 1830, temperance reform "constituted a burgeoning national movement" (Lender and Martin, 1987). In the 1840s, the Washington Temperance Societies conducted revival-style meetings to encourage similar pledges. These groups viewed the nation's growing cities, filled with the newly arriving Irish, Jewish, and Italian immigrants, as centers of deterioration and wickedness. The propensity of these immigrants to drink heavily was viewed as the driving force behind their supposedly deviant lifestyle. As early as 1846, the state of Maine was persuaded to outlaw alcohol; similar attempts followed elsewhere. However, these efforts were hampered by the Civil War, and despite the passage of many liquor laws, the sale and use of alcohol remained widespread.

The national *Prohibition movement*, also known as the Noble Experiment, was spearheaded by Prohibitionists, who felt alcohol was a dangerous drug that destroyed lives and disrupted families and communities. Consequently, they believed it was the responsibility of the government to prohibit its sale. Between 1880 and 1890, a new wave of prohibition sentiment swept the evangelical Protestant churches. Organized by the Women's Christian Temperance Union (WCTU), the Anti-Saloon League of America, and the National Prohibition Party, prohibitionists put pressure on their local politicians for an amendment to the Constitution.

In January 1919, the *Eighteenth Amendment* was passed, outlawing the manufacture and sale of alcohol except for industrial use. Prohibition marked a triumph of morality of middle- and upper-class Americans over the threat posed to their culture by the new Americans (Gusfield, 1963). Nine months after the Eighteenth Amendment was passed, it was followed by the passage of the Volstead Act, which provided an enforcement mechanism. The law was sporadically enforced and met with considerable public opposition. In fact, Erich Goode writes that most Prohibitionists were extremely naïve about both the feasibility of enforcing Prohibition and the impact the Volstead Act would have on drinking and related problems (1993). Soon bootlegging, speakeasies, and smuggling flourished under the direction and dominance of local gangsters. It was estimated that Chicago had approximately 10,000 speakeasies in operation at any given time during the Prohibition era. Opponents of the law claimed that it was ineffective and that it represented an unnecessary restriction of personal choice. As a result, a massive campaign was mounted to repeal the amendment, which became a reality in 1933 with the ratifying of the *Twenty-first Amendment*. Thereafter, the *temperance movement* faded. In Chapter 13, we discuss the policy lessons learned as a result of the Prohibition experience.

Prohibition created a virtual gold mine for crime that made millionaires out of criminals such as Meyer Lansky, Waxey Gordon, Owney Madden, Al Capone, Dutch Schultz, and many others. It affected the lives of many people throughout the country. It tainted politics and corrupted police officers. The stage was now set for one of the most lawless periods in the history of America: the *Roaring Twenties*. Despite the newly passed law, no one went thirsty during this period. Flappers, bobbed hair, the Charleston, coonskin coats, the hip flask, and other memorabilia combined to give this period its unique distinction.

It soon became clear to many entrepreneurial criminals that there was a need for an organized infrastructure to handle public demand for alcohol. Factories were needed to produce liquor; a transportation system was needed to deal with bulk shipments; and an importation system capable of dealing with large bulk shipments from England, Cuba, and Canada had to be constructed. This market demand for more complex organization combined with advances in electronic technology that would revolutionize communications to drastically revamp gambling and bring what we now know as organized crime into the modern age.

The Roaring Twenties set the stage for clandestine abuse of alcohol and marijuana in the shadow of Prohibition. Interestingly, the opiate problem—in particular, morphine and heroin—declined in the United States during the 1920s and 1930s until most of the problem was confined to individuals labeled by law enforcement and the powerful as social outcasts in urban areas. After World War I, America's international antidrug efforts continued as both the British and American governments proposed adding The Hague Convention to the Versailles Treaty. The result would mean the addition of domestic laws controlling narcotics. This incorporation resulted in passing the British Dangerous Drugs Act of 1920, a law often portrayed as a response to a bustling narcotics problem in Britain. During the 1940s, some Americans suggested that by adopting a medical model and supplying heroin to addicts (rather than relying on law enforcement efforts for drug control), the opiate problem in Britain had almost been eradicated. In fact, Britain had no such problem to begin with. This example illustrates how the desperate need to solve the drug problem in the United States creates misperceptions about a foreign drug predicament.

In the 1930s, partly due to the popularity of marijuana and amphetamines, the Federal Bureau of Narcotics (FBN) was created within the Department of the Treasury. Under the direction of Commissioner Harry Anslinger, the FBN separated the enforcement of alcohol laws from those dealing with other drugs. The FBN was charged with enforcing the Harrison Narcotics Act, among other drug laws, but the responsibility of interdiction remained with the Bureau of Customs. Although marijuana was not included in the Harrison Narcotics Act, the FBN did include an optional provision in the Uniform Narcotic Drug Act, which it extended to the states. During his tenure as bureau commissioner, Anslinger regularly issued reports and wrote books and articles for popular magazines, claiming that while under the influence, marijuana users rob, kill, rape, and chop up their families in a drug-induced frenzy (Goode, 1993). Consequently, concern about violent crime and the dangers of marijuana grew, and many states passed legislation prohibiting its use.

Post-Prohibition Drug Abuse

By the mid-1930s, national awareness about marijuana use resulted in its being placed on the FBN's enforcement agenda. Unlike opiates and cocaine, marijuana was introduced during a time of intolerance; consequently, it was not until the 1960s (40 years later) that it was widely used. Marijuana was not included in the 1914 Harrison legislation because at the time it was not considered a particularly dangerous drug.

In an effort to avoid assuming additional responsibilities at the federal level, the FBN had minimized the dangers of marijuana use and failed to support federal marijuana control measures. Instead, in its 1932 annual report, it urged the states to adopt a Uniform State Narcotics Law, which was adopted in 1932. By 1937, the FBN had changed its position. The desire to expand its power, budget, and personnel allocations led the FBN to engage in a scare campaign against marijuana and to support federal controls. Even scientific publications during the time fearfully described marijuana's alleged ominous side effects.

Due to public concern over its increasing popularity in recreational use during Prohibition, when marijuana was a cheap alternative to alcohol, states began passing legislation against its use or possession. Many of the early anti-marijuana laws were passed in the western states, where marijuana was linked with Mexican laborers and was seen as part of the "Mexican problem." Like the earlier Chinese immigrants, Mexicans had been brought into the United States to work the farms and ranches of the Southwest in difficult, low-paying jobs not wanted by the white majority. However, as the Great Depression of the 1930s settled over the United States, immigrants became an unwelcome minority linked with violence and the smoking of marijuana. By 1931, "all but two states west of the Mississippi and several more in the east had enacted prohibitory legislation against it" (PCOC, 1986a).

As a result of increasing public pressure, the FBN supported the federal *Marijuana Tax Act,* which was passed in 1937. This congressional measure was basically a nominal revenue measure patterned after the Harrison Narcotics Act. At the time, however, marijuana had some commercial use in the manufacture of rope, twine, veterinary medicines, and other products. In fact, at the time of the act's passage, it was estimated that there were more than 10,000 acres of marijuana being cultivated in the United States. The Marijuana Tax Act required a substantial transfer tax for all marijuana transactions. The act required that any person whose business was related to marijuana pay a special tax. Additionally, the transference of marijuana had to be pursuant to a written order on a special form issued by the Secretary of the Treasury. The person transferring the marijuana was then required to pay a tax of $1 per ounce if registered and $100 per ounce if not registered.

The Postwar Era

In addition to marijuana, amphetamines, which were originally prescribed to curb obesity and depression, became popular among students, professionals, and even homemakers who sought the euphoric effects of the drugs. The popularity of amphetamines continued through World War II, partly because they were so easily obtained with a doctor's prescription. As soon as the user market for amphetamines surpassed the legitimate sources of supply, an illicit market was created to meet the demand.

LSD (lysergic acid diethylamide) was popularized during the 1940s and 1950s in certain communities. It was initially discovered in 1938 by Albert Hoffman and W. A. Stoll, Swiss chemists who were experimenting with ergot fungus, a parasitic fungus that grows on rye. The use of LSD for mental disorders was widely researched in the 1940s and was praised by the psychiatric community in the 1950s. Soon, many members of the psychiatric community used LSD for both therapy and recreation. In 1962, Harvard professor Timothy Leary and Richard Alpert began treating inmates at the Massachusetts Correctional Institute with LSD. One year later, under a cloud of scandal, they were relieved of their positions at Harvard. LSD was also tested by the Central Intelligence Agency (CIA) as part of its efforts to find the ultimate "truth serum" and again later in an attempt to find a "mind control" drug. In fact, the CIA administered LSD to unsuspecting, nonconsenting victims, at least one of whom committed suicide.

Use of LSD through most of this time was restricted to a small part of the U.S. population. More common in the 1950s was the use of marijuana, tranquilizers, and various combinations of drugs. The coffee houses frequented by members of the 1950s' "Beat Generation" often served as clearinghouses for these drugs. Tranquilizers, ranging from the minor benzodiazepines to more dangerous barbiturates, can produce an intoxication similar to that produced by alcohol. Again, the easy availability of tranquilizers via prescription contributed to their abuse. Like many amphetamines, tranquilizers have been available through both legitimate and illicit markets. Mixed drug, or *polydrug*, use, such as taking "uppers" in the morning for energy and "downers" at night to induce sleep, also became more commonplace during the 1950s and 1960s.

In addition, some adolescents at this time began experimenting with such drug trends as sniffing glue or paint, occasionally with lethal consequences.

During the 1950s, two major laws were passed: the Boggs Act of 1951 and the Narcotics Control Act of 1956. Essentially, these laws severely increased the penalties for violations of the import/export and internal revenue laws relating to marijuana and narcotics. These penalties included mandatory minimum prison sentences along with expanded fines for drug violations.

The Turbulent 1960s

The 1960s are notorious for the celebration of drug abuse among youths. This proved to be a watershed decade. The use of most illegal drugs was greeted with increased tolerance, as were a wide range of unconventional behaviors, including the growth of movements opposing the war in Vietnam as well as challenging mainstream American culture; the popularization of rock music and its related lifestyle; the creation of psychedelic art; and enormous media publicity devoted to drugs, drug users, and drug proselytizers. A vigorous drug subculture came into existence. During this time, some social groups viewed drug use in positive terms, evaluated individuals on the basis of whether they used illegal drugs, and believed it a virtue to "turn on" someone who did not use drugs. This subculture proved to be a powerful force in recruiting young people into the use of illegal psychoactive drugs. Never before had drug abuse reached such a large, youthful audience.

In Vietnam, U.S. soldiers became addicts by the thousands, as had their counterparts in the Civil War. Heroin, marijuana, and hashish were widely available to the armed forces, many of whom, once becoming addicted, turned to drug trafficking. Since the Vietnam War, recreational use of heroin has escalated in the United States, especially in economically depressed inner cities. Controversial methadone clinics opened in 1964 to treat opiate addicts. Although methadone is effective, it is itself a highly addictive narcotic drug (see Chapter 14).

Soon there was a shifting of drugs of choice in the American drug scene. The use of psychedelic substances—such as LSD, MDA (methylenedioxyamphetamine), DMT (N-diethyltryptamine), heroin, and marijuana began in the 1960s and continued to be popular through the early 1970s. By the early 1970s, cocaine was gaining popularity as a recreational drug but was affordable only to affluent consumers. Despite the end of the Vietnam conflict in the early 1970s and the subsequent calming of the social and political waters, drug abuse failed to wane. The already popular use of PCP increased during this time, along with the newly developed depressant Quaalude (methaqualone). Cocaine was still growing in popularity to the point at which small gold cocaine spoons on necklaces were the rage in some social circles. In fact, during the 1970s, New York's exclusive disco, Studio 54, displayed a dance floor that was decorated with a huge coke spoon. It was rumored that preferred clientele were furnished free samples of the drug. By the end of the 1970s, use of cocaine and its close cousin, methamphetamine, was still gaining momentum. Methamphetamine and other domestic drugs—PCP (phencyclidine) and LSD—were illegally produced in the United States in an increasing number of clandestine laboratories.

Figure 2.6

The History of LSD

1938	LSD is first produced in Basel, Switzerland.	**1965**	New York is the first state to outlaw LSD.
1943	Dr. Albert Hoffman accidentally ingests a lysergic acid compound and experiences "fantastic visions." Hoffman later takes LSD purposely to study the effects.	**1967**	LSD is reported to damage white blood cells in laboratory studies.
		1968	Negative effects of LSD, such as "flashbacks" and "bad trips," are reported.
1949–1953	LSD is researched for treatment of mental disorders, alcoholism, and epilepsy.	**1968**	The popularity of LSD peaks and stabilizes in the late 1960s.
1962	Drs. Timothy Leary and Richard Alpert of the Harvard Center for Research in Human Personality use LSD on inmates at the Massachusetts Correctional Institute.	**1970–1995**	Different forms of LSD, such as blotter, microdot, and windowpane acid, appear on the illicit market.
		2002	LSD enjoys a relative stable user market with no notable increases or decreases in use.
1963	The illicit market for LSD begins, and different types of LSD appear.	**2010**	LSD remains a Schedule I Hallucinogen under U.S. federal law.

The History of LSD

Because of the growing epidemic of drug abuse across the nation, many drug laws were passed in an attempt to control the problem. In 1961, the United Nations adopted the Single Convention on Narcotics Drugs. The Single Convention established regulatory schedules for psychotropic substances and quotas to limit production and export of licit pharmaceuticals. In 1963, the President's Advisory Commission on Narcotics and Drug Abuse (also known as the Prettyman Commission) recommended a larger role by the federal government in the treatment of drug addicts. Accordingly, the 1963 Community Mental Health Centers Act became law and provided for federal assistance to nonfederal treatment centers. In 1965, the Drug Abuse Control Amendments were also passed. These brought the manufacture and distribution of amphetamines and barbiturates under federal control and imposed criminal penalties for illegally manufacturing these drugs. In addition, it created the Bureau of Alcohol and Drug Abuse Control within the Department of Health, Education, and Welfare (HEW), while enabling the HEW Secretary to add substances to the controlled list (LSD was added the following year). Toward the end of the

1960s, the 1966 Narcotic Addict Rehabilitation Act created a federal compulsory treatment program and gave financial support to community-based treatment programs. Finally, in 1968, the FBN was transferred to the Justice Department and merged with the Bureau of Drug Abuse Control to form the Bureau of Narcotics and Dangerous Drugs (BNDD).

Figure 2.7

The History of PCP			
1959	PCP is first developed as a disassociative anesthetic for use in surgery.	**1978**	President Jimmy Carter enacts special legislation against PCP.
1960	Medical use of PCP on human patients is discontinued because of violent side effects. Veterinary medicine adopts the use of PCP as an animal tranquilizer.	**1980**	Clandestine laboratory technology spreads in the manufacture of PCP.
		1985	The use of PCP drastically declines with the popularity of crack cocaine.
1965	Recreational use of PCP spreads because of illicit production of the drug.	**1990**	Criminal cases involving PCP all but dissappear from the criminal courts.
1970	PCP is sold as "THC" and "cannabinol" on the streets because people are beginning to associate the drug with negative experiences.	**2002**	PCP begins to emerge in larger U.S. cities.
		2010	PCP's popularity is moderate at best but it retains its Schedule II status under U.S. federal law.

The History of PCP

Late-Twentieth-Century Developments

Although media attention to drugs and drug use declined between the late 1960s and late 1970s, the actual use of drugs did not. Numerous surveys point to a strong increase during this period. The late 1970s and early 1980s probably represent another turning point in the recreational use of marijuana, hallucinogens, sedatives, and amphetamines. However, as seen in the previous chapter, studies have shown a considerable drop in the use of most drug types through the 1990s and beyond.

The shift in drug control policy was finalized in 1970 with the passing of the *Controlled Substances Act*, which created a common standard of dangerousness to rank all drugs rather than concentrating on specific substances. It also allowed the scheduling of substances to be done administratively. The year 1970 continued to be an eventful year for drug control legislation, with the passing of the federal Racketeer-Influenced and Corrupt Organizations (RICO) and the Continuing Criminal Enterprise (CCE) laws, which were designed to focus on the leaders of large criminal organizations. As discussed in greater detail in Chapter 11, this decade was the catalyst for many modern drug control policy issues and debates.

Finally, in 1972, the issue of decriminalization of marijuana as a policy option was debated by the Presidential Commission on Marijuana and Drug Abuse. This debate sprang from the rising number of persons arrested on marijuana charges during the 1960s and 1970s. This, in conjunction with a growing scientific debate about the dangers of marijuana, generated pressure to reduce penalties for marijuana violations. In fact, not only did the Comprehensive Drug Abuse Prevention and Control Act of 1970 reduce federal penalties for marijuana violations, but the Carter administration formally advocated legalizing marijuana in amounts up to one ounce. In addition, during the 1970s, 11 states decriminalized penalties for possession of marijuana, although some small penalties were retained. The Gallup poll on relaxation of laws against marijuana is instructive. In 1980, 53 percent of Americans favored legalization of small amounts of marijuana; by 1986, only 27 percent supported that view. At the same time, those favoring penalties for marijuana rose from 43 percent to 67 percent. As a result, many states revised or "recriminalized" their laws relating to marijuana violations, indicating a newfound concern about the potential hazards of the drug, a trend that began in the late 1970s and continues today.

Critical Thinking Task

Project yourself 35 years into the future. Predict the incidence of drug use, both legal and illegal, in the United States. Discuss the type and availability of drugs in the 2040s and 2050s, any interdiction efforts, internal efforts to deal with the drug problem, and the effects of drugs on future society. Base your prediction on past and current trends.

Hallmarks of the drug abuse story in the 1980s included the synthesis of drugs and the lifestyles of some music and sports celebrities. Designer drugs such as China White heroin and ecstasy (MDMA) are potentially deadly synthetic substances similar to opiates and hallucinogens. However, in some areas, they may be technically legal because they can be produced without certain illegal chemical analogs. Crack, a freebase form of cocaine, was developed about this time and provided a potent but cheap alternative to cocaine. The crack and methamphetamine markets of the 1980s spawned an upsurge in organized crime. Newcomers to the drug trade included such youth gangs as the Crips and Bloods as well as Jamaican gangs known as *posses*. Many cities across the United States are now terrorized by the drug-related violence of such gangs. This in turn provided a basis for much media and entertainment industry attention. One example is the 1988 film *Colors*, which portrays the violence of inner-city youth gangs involved in the drug trade.

Meanwhile, many top athletes were turning to anabolic steroids, a muscle builder, to maintain a competitive edge. Mass disqualification of athletes

Figure 2.8

The legal infrastructure to the federal drug control effort is the 1970 Comprehensive Drug Abuse Prevention and Control Act, Title II, which is also known as the Controlled Substances Act (CSA). This federal measure updated all previously existing drug laws and gave uniformity to federal drug control policy. Generally speaking, the CSA's four provisions consist of the following:

- mechanisms for reducing the availability of dangerous drugs;
- procedures for bringing a substance under control;
- criteria for determining control requirements; and
- obligations incurred by international treaty arrangements.

The CSA placed all substances that were in some manner regulated under existing federal law into one of five schedules. The criteria by which drugs are placed in these schedules are theoretically based on the medical use of the substance, its potential for abuse, and safety or addiction (dependence) liability. These five schedules are listed below:

Schedule I
- The drug or other substance has a high potential for abuse.
- The drug or other substance has no currently accepted medical use in treatment in the United States.
- There is a lack of accepted safety for use of the drug or other substance under medical supervision.

Schedule II
- The drug or other substance has a high potential for abuse.
- The drug or other substance has a currently accepted medical use in treatment in the United States or a currently accepted medical use with severe restrictions.
- Abuse of the drug or other substance may lead to severe psychological or physical dependence.

Schedule III
- The drug or other substance has a potential for abuse less than the drugs or other substances in Schedules I and II.
- The drug or other substance has a currently accepted medical use in treatment in the United States.
- Abuse of the drug or other substance may lead to moderate or low physical dependence or high psychological dependence.

Schedule IV
- The drug or other substance has a low potential for abuse relative to the drugs or other substances in Schedule III.

Figure 2.8—*continued*

- The drug or other substance has a currently accepted medical use in treatment in the United States.

- Abuse of the drug or other substance may lead to limited physical dependence or psychological dependence relative to the drugs or other substances in Schedule III.

Schedule V

- The drug or other substance has a low potential for abuse relative to the drugs or other substances in Schedule IV.

- The drug or other substance has a currently accepted medical use in treatment in the United States.

- Abuse of the drug or other substances may lead to limited physical dependence or psychological dependence relative to the drugs or other substances in Schedule IV.

In addition, the law imposes nine control mechanisms on the manufacturing, purchasing, and distribution of controlled substances.

The Comprehensive Drug Abuse Prevention and Control Act (1970)

thought to be using steroids dominated the coverage of the Pan Am games in Caracas, Venezuela, in 1983. In 1988, Ben Johnson gained notoriety but lost an Olympic gold medal due to his use of steroids. Other drugs ruined the lives of other celebrities. Comedian John Belushi died in 1983 as a result of respiratory complications from the use of cocaine mixed with heroin, a concoction called a *speedball*. The deaths of two athletes in June 1985 helped bring home the tragedy of cocaine. Len Bias had been drafted by the Boston Celtics; he celebrated his draft by using cocaine and died of cardiac arrest as a result of the drug and a preexisting heart ailment. Football star Don Rogers also died that month from cocaine poisoning.

As drug use increased among American youths, so did drug education programs aimed at curbing the problem. Former First Lady Nancy Reagan's Just Say No campaign was subjected to ridicule by those who accused it of being simplistic and unrealistic, while supporters defended it as a common-sense prevention strategy that focused on potential first-time users rather than hard-core street addicts. Despite lukewarm support for programs such as Just Say No, the public became more intolerant of drug-related tragedies. This public outrage finally resulted in the controversial drug testing of air traffic controllers, train engineers, bus drivers, and other employees whose jobs were associated with public safety.

The medical cover story of the 1990s—Acquired Immune Deficiency Syndrome (AIDS)—helped clarify the association between drug use and public safety. Among the high-risk groups for AIDS, a lethal, infectious disease for which there is no cure, are intravenous drug users such as heroin addicts. Because of the nature of heroin abuse and the illegality of heroin, activity commonly takes place in secluded settings, such as urban "shooting galleries" where the sharing of hypodermic syringes (also illegal in most jurisdictions) has become commonplace. American recreational drug use thrived in the 1980s, but not as a result of ignorance about the drugs themselves. Indeed, no society has been more aware of the tragic price paid for substance abuse.

As of 2000, the number of drug abusers had declined by almost 50 percent from the 1979 high of 25 million—a decrease that represents an extraordinary change of behavior (ONDCP, 2001). Despite that drop, statistics reveal that almost one-third of all Americans aged 12 and older have used an illicit drug. As of the preparation of this book, the primary drugs of abuse are marijuana, cocaine, heroin, and methamphetamine. However, club drugs such as MDMA (ecstasy) and OxyContin have seen considerable popularity, especially among youths.

Although drug abuse is still at an unacceptably high level, it does not approach the emergency situation of the 1970s and 1980s. As drug use declined during the 1990s, national attention also faded. Consequently, disapproval of drugs and the perception of risk by young people have also declined through the last two decades. As a result, since 1992, more youths have been using illicit drugs, alcohol, and tobacco. Maybe it could be said that adults have resigned themselves to teen drug use, since research suggests that nearly one-half of the "baby boomer" generation expects their children to use drugs (Luntz Research, 1996).

THE TWENTY-FIRST CENTURY AND BEYOND

It is difficult to speculate about the future of recreational drug use in our society because of the ever-changing social climate. As history has proven, the basis for social acceptance of some drugs and not others is neither rational nor consistent. Should certain drugs be authorized by law for recreational use? If lawfully sanctioned, under what circumstances should drug use be permitted? Given the high incidence of drug-related crime and drug-related health problems, can we responsibly consider the legalization of any dangerous substance? Or have the health problems associated with drug abuse and the ancillary crime associated with drug trafficking in the illicit market become so dangerous that a post-Prohibition approach is required?

It appears that the customary use of products containing legal drugs, such as coffee and tobacco, as well as certain over-the-counter drugs will continue indefinitely. Alcohol use will undoubtedly continue despite initiatives on community, state, and national levels for curbing many of the dysfunctional aspects of alcohol abuse. Illicit consumption of substances such as marijuana and cocaine will most likely continue, but to what extent is questionable. Perhaps public education and prevention programs in the future will meet the challenge of informing drug users and prospective drug users of the dangers of these substances. In addition, it is likely that continued research will provide insight into the psychological and physiological effects of these drugs. Based on the advancements in chemical technology, clandestine drug manufacturers will probably conceive of new ways to increase the potency of drugs and to reduce the retail price.

Responsibility for combating the drug problem in the future will rest with governmental functions such as law enforcement, treatment, and prevention programs as well as the court and correctional systems. Others who must share in this responsibility include parents, teachers, and community leaders. Only through this multidisciplinary approach can the incidence of drug abuse and drug-related crime be reduced and ultimately abolished.

SUMMARY

Of all the social phenomena affecting public health and safety, it is clear that drug abuse has superseded all other forms of widespread social deviance. There is much agreement that drugs can cause severe social problems and that some drugs are less harmful than others. However, there is little agreement as to which drugs are less harmful and to what extent they should be tolerated.

Cannabis and the opium poppy have been generally accepted as the oldest mind-altering drugs of abuse, since historic records of their use date back some 7,000 years. Further, these two drugs have been associated with both medical treatment and recreational uses. The regional origins for these drugs include South America for the coca plant; North America for alcohol, tobacco, and peyote; and Mexico, Southeast Asia, Southwest Asia, and China for opium and cannabis.

Before the late 1800s, drugs were, for the most part, legal and readily available. During and after the Civil War, morphine was widely used and abused as a painkiller. Toward the end of the nineteenth century, "cures" for morphine addiction were developed. For example, cocaine (1878) and heroin (1898), both thought to be nonaddicting antidotes for morphine addiction, were synthesized during the last quarter of the century. Other drugs, such as barbiturates and amphetamines, were also developed around the turn of the twentieth century and have proven to be some of the most widely abused drugs in history. Concern about the use of opiates led to the passing of several pieces of federal legislation, such as the 1914 Harrison Narcotics Act. This comprehensive act exemplified national concern over the abuse of coca- and opiate-based drugs. The Harrison Act marked one of the first laws to break away from the era of legalized drugs into a period of regulation. The public perception of drugs grew increasingly negative while drug abuse expanded during the early to mid-1900s, leading public policy into an attitude of prohibition.

Although Prohibition (1920–1933) was designed to reduce alcohol consumption, it inadvertently resulted in an increase of marijuana use. Along with this increase was an escalation in the clandestine abuse of other drugs, such as cocaine and heroin. Although alcohol prohibition failed to last, other drugs became controlled more often, as evidenced by the passing of the Marijuana Tax Act in 1937.

PCP was synthesized in the late 1950s. The drug ultimately proved to be harmful to human patients but was successful as a general anesthetic for animals. Shortly thereafter, LSD, originally developed in 1938, was studied by Harvard professor Timothy Leary and became one of the first widely used recreational "psychedelic" drugs. Much social and political unrest—civil rights protests, race riots, the women's liberation movement, and demonstrations against United States involvement in Vietnam—marked the era of the 1960s. Abuse of drugs, including cocaine, marijuana, amphetamines, LSD, and PCP, continued to flourish during this period, resulting in the passing of the 1970 Controlled Substances Act, which specified all drugs that were to be considered unlawful.

As the 1970s approached, however, the harmful effects of illicit drugs were downplayed by the media and entertainment industry as certain drugs such as cocaine achieved an elevated status among drug users. To supply the growing numbers of drug users, many entrepreneurial drug chemists began to cook their own batches of drugs, including methamphetamine and PCP. By the early 1980s, there was a significant increase in clandestine laboratory technology, which continues to spread across the United States. Designer drugs such as China White heroin and ecstasy are illicit drugs that were popularized during the 1980s. Each of these also represents innovative clandestine laboratory advances by domestic criminals entering the illicit drug market.

The drug-using population of the 1980s also witnessed the genesis of crack—a potent, freebase form of cocaine. The popularity of crack created a great profit margin, which lured many new organized crime groups into the drug trade. Competition over cities and neighborhoods as sales turf by street gangs and organized crime groups has thus become a primary concern of policymakers in the twenty-first century.

Do you recognize these terms?

- Controlled Substances Act
- Eighteenth Amendment
- Harrison Narcotics Act
- Marijuana Tax Act
- opium wars

- polydrug use
- Prohibition
- Roaring Twenties
- temperance movement
- Twenty-First Amendment

DISCUSSION QUESTIONS

1. Discuss China's role in global drug addiction and how that country attempted to deal with its own opium problem.

2. Discuss the early historical (both medical and recreational) use of cannabis.

3. How has the historical use of opium in China affected drug abuse in the United States today?

4. Discuss the American Civil War's unique association with the drug morphine.

5. Discuss the first antidrug law passed in the United States and the circumstances surrounding it.

6. Compare the drug abuse climate in the United States before and after the passing of Prohibition.

7. List the elements of the era that possibly accelerated drug use during the 1960s and early 1970s.

Chapter 3

Understanding Drugs of Abuse

This chapter will enable you to:

- Understand the meaning of the term *drug abuse*
- Discover reasons that people take drugs
- Realize the various social forums in which drugs are taken
- Learn the pharmacology of popular drugs of abuse
- Identify the effects of drugs on the drug user

The literature on drug identification and pharmacology is rich with varying opinions, but not much is really known about drugs' effects on the human physiology. For example, drugs such as alcohol and cocaine often affect different users in different ways. Not only do the user's moods differ from one drug to another, but the development of tolerance and addiction differs from one user to the next as well. In this chapter, we examine those drugs that are not only popular but potentially hazardous in society today. We also study legal distinctions and categories of drugs as well as the effects those drugs have on those who use them.

Defining Drugs

To some, attempting to define the word *drug* might seem absurd, since it is such a commonly used word in our everyday lives. Today, though, the word seems to serve as a catchall for just about any medicinal or chemical substance. In fact, it refers to both dangerous substances, such as heroin or

LSD, which are illegal to possess and have no medicinal use, as well as to more benign substances such as aspirin and nonprescription cold remedies. *Webster's Dictionary* attempts to define the word *drug* in a general sense as "a substance used by itself or a mixture in the treatment or diagnosis of disease." Although somewhat comprehensive, this definition still fails to recognize the use of drugs for applications other than the treatment of disease, such as recreational use. Therefore, at the risk of oversimplification, a more practical definition might be as follows: A drug is any substance that causes or creates significant psychological and/or physiological changes in the body.

It is here where we may first identify a primary misunderstanding about the word, because the traditional definition fails to recognize recreational or nonmedical use of certain substances. Certainly most drug use in accordance with a legitimate medical problem is not only lawful but appropriate, yet the word *drug* actually encompasses a much broader scope of definition. Webster's definition excludes consideration of the recreational category of drugs. Other "everyday" substances, such as sugar and caffeine, do not meet Webster's definition either, but they do alter the user's physical well-being and mental awareness and are, of course, perfectly lawful to possess. We could, therefore, recognize as a drug any substance that alters the user's physiological or psychological state, whether that substance is used for medicinal or nonmedical use.

Drug abuse is another term randomly discussed in substance abuse literature. Just exactly what does it mean? To some, drug abuse may refer to the taking of any illicit drug or the overuse of prescribed drugs. For others, drug abuse is illicit drug use that results in social, economic, psychological, or legal problems for the drug user. The Bureau of Justice Statistics (1991) describes drug abuse as the use of prescription-type psychotherapeutic drugs for nonmedical purposes or the use of illegal drugs.

DRUGS AND THE BRAIN

We know generally in what ways drugs affect the user. However, the pharmacological mechanisms through which some drugs exert their effects are only partially understood. Researchers have identified locations and substances in the brain that are closely associated with the effects of drugs and their reinforcement properties. Although the process is complex, the so-called neurotransmitter *dopamine* appears to play an important role in determining the effects of drugs such as cocaine and heroin. For example, cocaine acts on the pleasure center of the brain to the extent that in some people, particularly those with personality disorders already in place, cocaine becomes more important and pleasurable than some of the most basic human needs such as food, sex, or exercise. Normally, dopamine is released by nerve centers and is then withdrawn. In the case of cocaine, dopamine continues to be transmitted, significantly raising the blood pressure and increasing the heart rate.

How central is dopamine's role in the brain? Scientists are still trying to find an answer to that question, but what they do know is that it is no accident that people are attracted to drugs. The major drugs of abuse—for example, narcotics such as heroin or stimulants such as cocaine—mimic the structure of neurotransmitters, the most powerful mind-altering drugs the human body creates. Neurotransmitters underlie every thought, emotion, memory, and learning process. They carry the signals between all the nerve cells (or neurons) in the brain. Among some 50 neurotransmitters discovered to date, at least six, including dopamine, are known to play a role in addiction (Nash, 1997).

At a purely chemical level, every experience people find enjoyable—whether listening to music, embracing a lover, or savoring chocolate—amounts to little more than an explosion of dopamine. Dopamine, though, like most biologically important molecules, must be kept in strict bounds. Too little dopamine in certain areas of the brain triggers the tremors and paralysis of Parkinson's disease. Too much causes the hallucinations and bizarre thoughts of schizophrenia (Nash, 1997). Probably the most significant breakthrough in addiction came in 1975, when psychologists Roy Wise and Robert Yokel at Montreal's Concordia University reported on the behavior of drug-addicted rats. One day the rats were placidly dispensing cocaine and amphetamines to themselves by pressing a lever attached to their cages, and the next they were banging at the lever with frantic persistence. The reason was that the scientists had injected the rats with a drug that blocked the action of dopamine. In the years following, evidence has mounted regarding dopamine's role in drug addiction.

We also know that drug abuse may be a symptom of a larger problem. For example, people with certain psychiatric disorders may be prone to drug abuse. Alcohol and other drug problems often occur along with other psychiatric disorders. Those with drug problems frequently have affective, anxiety, or personality disorders. Sometimes, however, the reverse is also true. One example of this is the self-medication hypothesis. In this case, a person who is depressed may use drugs to elevate his or her mood, or a person who is suffering severe anxiety may seek relief through the relaxing effects of certain drugs. In other cases, people who are addicted to one drug may seek to counter that drug's effects by taking another drug with opposite effects. This polydrug use may result in an overdose or even the death of the user, depending on the mixture of drugs taken.

Side Effects

Adding to the dangers of substance abuse is the reality that drugs alter people's behavior. Psychoactive drugs alter people's moods, perceptions, attitudes, and emotions. As a result, concern is often expressed about the impact of drug use on work, family, and social relations. Another concern is that many drugs provide the user with unintended side effects. Although some of these side effects may be short term and relatively harmless in nature, some have just the opposite effects. Heroin users, for example, initially take the drug for its euphoric effects, but they soon discover that euphoria is also accompanied by nausea, constricted pupils, and respiratory depression. Cannabis products such as marijuana and hashish can result in memory loss and disorientation. Users of hallucinogens such as LSD often complain of bad hallucinations and imagined flashbacks. Just exactly what constitutes the effects of any particular drug depends on a number of factors, such as the mood of the user and how the drugs are taken. A good example is cocaine, a drug that usually elevates one's mood. In users who are depressed prior to drug consumption, however, a deeper depression may result. In addition, after the initial effects of the drug wear off, cocaine users experience anxiety, depression, fatigue, and an urge for more cocaine. Drug users will often look to drugs such as those in the stimulant family to enhance their intellectual or physical performance. Because these drugs increase one's alertness, there is a perception of improved performance, but in reality the user experiences severe fatigue and a reduced capacity for learning, which can offset any physical improvements caused by the drugs.

Outcomes of Drug Abuse

To best understand the many different drugs abused on our streets, we should first consider some clinical terms commonly associated with drug abuse. These terms define the predominant effects of drugs and are generally associated with the most dangerous drugs of abuse:

- *Physical dependence (or physiological dependence).* A growing tolerance of a drug's effects so that increased amounts of the drug necessitate the continued presence of the drug in order to prevent withdrawal symptoms.
- *Psychological dependence.* A controversial term that generally means the craving for or compulsive need to use drugs because they provide the user with a feeling of well-being and satisfaction. However, attempts to equate physical dependence or addiction with psychological dependence are highly questionable because psychological dependence may be developed for any activity, from listening to rock music to enjoying sex.
- *Tolerance.* A situation in which the user continues regular use of a drug and must administer progressively larger doses to attain the desired effect, thereby reinforcing the compulsive behavior known as drug dependence.
- *Withdrawal.* The physical reaction of bodily functions that, when a body is deprived of an addictive drug, causes increased excitability of the bodily functions that have been depressed by the drug's habitual use.

We should note that psychological dependence is subjective and difficult to define, but is characterized by a person's compulsive need to use drugs.

Furthermore, the extent to which drugs produce physical dependence will vary. Heroin, for instance, has an extremely high potential for physical dependence. In comparison, cocaine is not addictive in the same way as heroin, but its potential for psychological dependence is high in some people, particularly those with obsessive personality traits—especially when the cocaine used is in the form of crack, because of the intense initial dose in the vapor. This variation in the potential for physical dependence is one reason for the scheduling of drugs under federal and state laws (see Chapter 11).

DEPENDENCE VERSUS ABUSE

When addressing the task of understanding the many different drugs that have been popularized on the street, perhaps we should first consider certain clinical terms and definitions commonly associated with drugs and drug use. These terms define certain predominant effects of drugs and are generally associated with those drugs that are considered the most dangerous.

To begin, we should note that drug abuse can be described in many different ways. Generally, however, the pathological use of substances that affect the central nervous system falls into two main categories: substance dependence and substance abuse. Let's look closer at these two terms. The *Diagnostic and Statistical Manual of Mental Disorders* (DSM-IV, 1994), endorsed by the American Psychiatric Association, outlines the criteria for *substance dependence* as the presence of three or more of the following symptoms occurring at any time in the same 12-month period:

1. Tolerance, as defined by either of the following:
   (a) A need for markedly increased amounts of the substance to achieve intoxication or desired effect
   (b) Markedly diminished effect with continued use of the same amount of the substance
2. Withdrawal, as manifested by either of the following:
   (c) The characteristic withdrawal syndrome for the substance
   (d) The same, or closely related, substance is taken to relieve or avoid withdrawal symptoms
3. The substance is often taken in larger amounts or over a longer period than was intended.
4. There is a persistent desire or unsuccessful efforts to cut down or control substance use.
5. A great deal of time is spent in activities necessary to obtain the substance (e.g., visiting multiple doctors or driving long distances), use the substance (e.g., chain smoking), or recover from its effects.
6. Important social, occupational, or recreational activities are given up or reduced because of substance use.

7. The substance use is continued despite knowledge of having a persistent or recurrent physical or psychological problem that is likely to have been caused or exacerbated by the substance (e.g., current cocaine use despite recognition of cocaine-induced depression, or continued drinking despite recognition that an ulcer was made worse by alcohol consumption).

Substance abuse is another term commonly used in both conversation and in the literature of drug abuse. It has also been defined by the DSM-IV. Substance abuse differs from substance dependence in that it is a less severe version of dependence. In short, abuse is diagnosed when the person's use of a substance is maladaptive but not severe enough to meet the diagnostic criteria for dependence. Understanding these terms helps us not only categorize drugs but recognize abnormal behavior that often accompanies drug use.

DRUG CATEGORIES

To better understand the various types of drugs and their effects, a system of categories has been generally recognized. Each of these seven categories (stimulants, depressants, hallucinogens, narcotics, cannabis, steroids, and inhalants) may contain both legal and controlled substances. Each substance possesses unique characteristics. We discuss these categories next.

Stimulants

Stimulants, also known as *uppers*, reverse the effects of fatigue on both mental and physical tasks. Two commonly used stimulants are nicotine, which is found in tobacco products, and caffeine, an active ingredient in coffee, tea, some soft drinks, and many nonprescription medicines. Used in moderation, these substances tend to relieve malaise and increase alertness. Although the use of these products has been an accepted part of U.S. culture, the recognition of their adverse effects has resulted in a proliferation of caffeine-free products and efforts to discourage cigarette smoking.

A number of stimulants, however, are under the regulatory control of the Controlled Substances Act (CSA). Some of these controlled substances are available by prescription for legitimate medical use in the treatment of obesity, narcolepsy, and attention deficit disorders. As drugs of abuse, stimulants are frequently taken to produce a sense of exhilaration, enhance self-esteem, improve mental and physical performance, increase activity, reduce appetite, produce prolonged wakefulness, and "get high." They are among the most potent agents of reward and reinforcement that underlie the problem of dependence.

Stimulants are diverted from legitimate channels and clandestinely manufactured exclusively for the illicit market. They are taken orally, sniffed, smoked, and injected. Smoking, snorting, or injecting stimulants produces a sudden sensation known as a *rush* or a *flash*. Abuse is often associated with a pattern of binge use—sporadically consuming large doses of stimulants over a short period of time. Heavy users may inject themselves every few hours, continuing until they have depleted their drug supply or reached a point of delirium, psychosis, and physical exhaustion. During this period of heavy use, all other interests become secondary to recreating the initial euphoric rush. Tolerance can develop rapidly, and both physical and psychological dependence occur. Abrupt cessation, even after a brief two- or three-day binge, is commonly followed by depression, anxiety, drug craving, and extreme fatigue known as a *crash*.

Therapeutic levels of stimulants can produce exhilaration, extended wakefulness, and loss of appetite. These effects are greatly intensified when large doses of stimulants are taken. Physical side effects, including dizziness, tremor, headache, flushed skin, chest pain with palpitations, excessive sweating, vomiting, and abdominal cramps may occur as a result of taking too large a dose at one time or taking large doses over an extended period of time. Psychological effects include agitation, hostility, panic, aggression, and suicidal or homicidal tendencies. Paranoia, sometimes accompanied by both auditory and visual hallucinations, may also occur. Overdose is often associated with high fever, convulsions, and cardiovascular collapse. Because accidental death is partially due to the effects of stimulants on the body's cardiovascular and temperature-regulating systems, physical exertion increases the hazards of stimulant use.

Caffeine

Caffeine plays an important role in understanding drug abuse in many societies around the world. It is a bitter-tasting, odorless chemical that can be either manufactured synthetically or derived from coffee beans, tea leaves, or cola nuts. It was first extracted from coffee in 1820 and from tea leaves in 1827 and is currently found in cola drinks, cocoa, and some diet pills. As a rule, it acts as a mild stimulant and is generally harmless to people, except for its addicting nature. In larger doses, caffeine is known for causing insomnia, restlessness, and anxiety in users. Physical effects of caffeine include an increase in heart rate and possible irregularities in the heart. In fact, some researchers maintain that heavy coffee drinkers are more prone to develop coronary heart disease (Gilbert, 1984). Because caffeine is associated with insomnia, it has been used by many people to postpone fatigue. However, not all the effects of caffeine have proven to be negative. For example, because caffeine decreases blood flow to the brain, it has been used in treating migraine headaches, and physicians have used it to treat poisoning caused by depressants such as alcohol and morphine. Furthermore, studies suggest that it somewhat increases the effectiveness of common analgesics such as aspirin and helps relieve asthma attacks by widening bronchial airways (Gilbert, 1984). Caffeine has probably become the most popular drug in the world and has etched a niche in everyday American life.

Coffee

Of the caffeine drinks that have gained popularity over the centuries, coffee has become an American (and even a global) icon. The word *coffee* was derived from the Arabic word *gahweh* (pronounced *kehevh*). People drink it as a morning pick-me-up, as a midday break drink, and as a means to stay alert late at night. As a result of its popularity, the coffee industry is one of the most profitable in the world. In fact, the coffee bean is thought to be the world's most valuable agricultural commodity. Today, the United States remains the top global importer of coffee, although U.S. per-capita coffee consumption ranks only in the top 10, behind most countries in Western Europe and Scandinavia (Brooke, 1994).

Coffee, which is native to Ethiopia, has been cultivated and brewed in Arab countries for centuries. The drink was introduced into Europe in the mid-seventeenth century, and plantations in Indonesia, the West Indies, and Brazil soon made coffee cultivation an important element of colonial economies. Today, Latin America and Africa produce most of the world's coffee, with the United States the largest importer and consumer. Coffee's unique flavor is determined not only by the variety but also by the length of time the green beans are roasted. After roasting, the beans are usually ground and vacuum-packed in cans. Because the flavor of coffee deteriorates rapidly after it is ground or after a sealed can is opened, many coffee drinkers today buy whole roasted beans and grind them at home. Instant coffee, which makes up about one-fifth of all coffee sold, is prepared by forcing an atomized spray of very strong coffee extract through a jet of hot air, evaporating the water in the extract and leaving dried coffee particles that are packaged as instant coffee. Another method of producing instant coffee is freeze-drying. Decaffeinated coffee is another popular form of coffee. To make decaffeinated coffee, the green bean is processed in a steam or chemical bath to remove the caffeine, the substance that produces coffee's stimulating effect.

Nicotine

Nicotine is another stimulant found in most societies around the world. Since colonial times, nicotine has maintained a large and prosperous tobacco industry, and despite evidence of its ill effects on health, today it is consumed almost as fast as it is produced. In the early 1900s, cigarettes were the most common form of taking nicotine. This trend occurred after a series of public health warnings about the dangers of chewing tobacco and its link to tuberculosis. Unaware of the high risks to the lungs, heart, blood, and nervous system, people switched to smoking cigarettes instead of chewing tobacco. In addition, the cigarette industry utilized automatic rolling machines for cigarette production, making them more affordable, and relied on extensive advertising campaigns for mass sales. In 1964, the first surgeon general's report on smoking was issued, titled *Report of the Surgeon General's Advisory Committee on Smoking and Health*. It received mass media coverage and convinced many Americans of the dangers of smoking. In subsequent years, manufacturers produced low-tar and filtered cigarettes, which were touted as being "safer." Finally, during the 1990s, many antismoking campaigns emerged, rallying support for increased numbers of no-smoking areas in public places. In many cities today, smoking has been completely outlawed in stores, restaurants, and workplaces.

Critical Thinking Task

Assume that you are an attorney whose client, a non-smoker dying of lung cancer, is suing the tobacco industry for damages inflicted from secondhand smoke. Submit your summation speech to the jury.

In addition to the discomfort experienced by nonsmokers, nicotine has been proven to be an addictive substance creating a physical dependence on the part of the smoker. Those who have developed nicotine dependence often must seek specially designed programs to aid them in gradually cutting back on smoking. Nicotine, an extremely poisonous, colorless liquid alkaloid, turns brown on exposure to air. As the most potent ingredient of the tobacco plant, *nicotiana tabacum* is found mainly in the leaves. Nicotine, the addictive substance in the tobacco plant, was named for Jean Nicot, a French ambassador who sent tobacco from Portugal to Paris in 1560. Nicotine's effects on the human body after prolonged use can be devastating. It can affect the human nervous system, causing respiratory failure and general paralysis. It may also be absorbed through the skin. Interestingly, only two or three drops (less than 50 milligrams [mg]) of the pure alkaloid placed on the tongue are rapidly fatal to an adult (Hyman, 1986). A typical cigarette contains 15 to 20 mg of nicotine, but the actual amount that reaches the bloodstream—and hence the brain—through normal smoking is only about 1 mg. Nicotine is believed to be responsible for most of the short-term effects and many of the long-term effects of smoking as well as for tobacco smoking's addictive properties. Because of the popularity of filter-tipped cigarettes, nicotine yields have declined by about 70 percent since the 1950s. Nicotine is also produced in quantity from tobacco scraps and is used as a pesticide. Converted to nicotinic acid, a member of the vitamin B group, it is used as a food supplement.

Smoking

Smoking is a common practice in many societies and typically refers to the inhaling of tobacco smoke from a pipe, cigar, or cigarette. Despite a 1989 report issued by the U.S. Surgeon General concluding that cigarettes and other forms of tobacco are addictive and that nicotine is the drug that causes addiction, in 2009 the *National Survey on Drug Use and Health* reported that an estimated 70.9 million Americans aged 12 or older were current (past month) users of a tobacco product. More specifically, 59.8 million persons (23.9 percent of the population) were current cigarette smokers; 5.3 percent smoked cigars, 3.5 percent used smokeless tobacco, and 0.8 percent smoked tobacco in pipes (U.S. Department of Health; NSDUH, 2009).

The history of smoking is vast, and concerns about it have existed for years. Native Americans smoked pipes, and European explorers had introduced the practice into the Old World by the early sixteenth century. Controversy over the health effects of smoking have stemmed from that time. Much of this concern is with good cause; cigarette smoke consists of more than 4,700 compounds, 43 of which are carcinogens, such as tar (CDC, 1992). Nicotine is considered the addicting agent that makes quitting smoking so difficult.

By the early 1960s, numerous clinical and laboratory studies on smoking and disease had been conducted. In 1964, a committee appointed by the surgeon general of the U.S. Public Health Service issued a report based on the critical review of previous studies on the effects of smoking. The report concluded that nearly all lung cancer deaths are caused by cigarette smoking, which was also held responsible for many deaths and much disability from various illnesses such as chronic bronchitis, emphysema, and cardiovascular disease. The *Journal of the American Medical Association* has reported that more than 400,000 people die every year from smoking-related diseases—more than from alcohol, crack, heroin, murder, suicide, car accidents, and AIDS combined (McGinnis and Foege, 1993). A 1984 report by the U.S. Public Health Service also suggested that passive inhalation of smoke by nonsmokers (secondhand smoke) could be harmful. Although considered controversial at the time, studies have since confirmed many of these charges. Some experts estimate that passive smoke kills as many as 50,000 Americans a year, and it is the third leading preventable cause of death, behind smoking and drinking. Studies have shown that children are particularly sensitive to passive smoke and that smoking by pregnant women may harm the fetus.

Since 1964, tobacco advertising has been restricted, and health warnings have been mandated for advertisements. Most states in the United States have also passed laws to control smoking in public places such as restaurants and workplaces, where nonsmoking areas may be required. Most U.S. airlines have prohibited smoking on flights lasting six hours or less, whereas others have prohibited smoking on all flights. Among the military, the U.S. Army has been particularly strict in imposing smoking restrictions. The tobacco industry and many smokers regard antismoking measures as harassment, whereas many nonsmokers defend the measures on the grounds that the government has a duty to discourage unhealthful practices, that public funds in one form or another become involved in treating diseases caused by smoking, and that smokers pollute the air for nonsmokers.

Quitting smoking is thought to be extremely difficult, especially for chronic smokers. In fact, in 1993, the Centers for Disease Control and Prevention (CDC) reported that 70 percent of regular smokers try to quit, but only 8 percent succeed. In recent years, smoking-withdrawal clinics have become popular, although most people who quit smoking are thought to do it on their own. Nicotine gum and skin patches may be useful tools for quitting the habit. Nicotine gum, which has been around for years, tends to lessen early withdrawal symptoms. Nicotine patches, which are available by prescription, are yet another way to allow the smoker to deal with the behavioral aspects of quitting before confronting the physical effects of nicotine withdrawal.

Figure 3.1

Tobacco in the United States

1964 Surgeon general releases reports that conclude smoking causes lung cancer.

1965 Federal law requires the surgeon general's warnings on cigarette packs.

1980 Surgeon general reports smoking is a major threat to women's health.

1988 Surgeon general reports nicotine is an addictive drug.

1990 Smoking is banned on all domestic flights lasting six hours or less.

1994 Executives of the seven largest U.S. tobacco companies swear in congressional testimony that nicotine is not addictive.

1994 Tobacco company executives deny allegations that they manipulate nicotine levels in cigarettes.

1995 President Bill Clinton announces FDA plans to regulate tobacco for minors.

1997 Tobacco company Liggett concludes landmark settlement with states that insulates the company from tobacco litigation in return for admitting that cigarettes are addictive.

1997 A federal judge rules that the government can regulate tobacco.

1998 Attorney general and tobacco companies settle lawsuit for $246 billiion over a 25-year period.

2010 A smoking ban (either state, county, or local) has been enacted covering all bars and restaurants in each of the 60 most populated cities in the United States except these 16: Arlington, Atlanta, Fort Worth, Indianapolis, Jacksonville, Memphis, Miami, Las Vegas, Nashville, Oklahoma City, Philadelphia, Pittsburgh, San Antonio, Tampa, Tulsa, and Virginia Beach.

The History of Tobacco in the United States

Cocaine

Cocaine is the active alkaloid that is extracted from the leaves of the *Erythroxylon* coca plant, which contains between 0.5 percent and 1 percent cocaine. *Erythroxylon* coca grows in the high Andes region of South America.

Chewing the leaves of the plant as a remedy for fatigue, nausea, and altitude sickness has been a custom in the region for as long as written records of human practice exist (Van Dyke and Byck, 1986).

The actual word *coca* comes to us from the Aymara Indians, a local tribe living in the area now known as Bolivia, and translates as *plant*. The Aymara were conquered by the Inca in the tenth century. Coca received elevated religious status in the Incan Empire, being used prominently in religious ceremonies, marriages, rites of prophecy, and initiation rituals for *haruaca*, young Incan noblemen. Production and use of coca were tightly regulated in Incan society. Incan rulers restricted production to state-owned plantations and restricted its use to rituals and as a special gift bestowed on the favored only by Incan royalty. Use among the general population was heavily regulated and restricted (Grinspoon and Bakalar, 1985).

The use of coca was introduced to the general populace only after the Spanish conquest of the Incan empire. Under an edict issued by King Philip II, coca was made available as a labor-enhancing substance, a food substitute, and an ameliorative for hunger. Social norms that regulated its use among the Inca disappeared with the passage of time under Spanish rule (Grinspoon and Bakalar, 1985).

Coca use and production remained restricted because the plant does not grow in Europe and the harvested leaves lost their efficacy during the long voyage from South America. It was not until 1750 that botanist Joseph de Tussie was able to successfully transfer the first plants to Europe. Nonetheless, coca was highly praised in writings by visitors to South America for its stimulant attributes and its usefulness in easing breathing difficulties at high altitudes (Grinspoon and Bakalar, 1985).

Cocaine as a drug was not isolated from the plant until the mid-nineteenth century. Dr. Theodor Aschenbrant, a Bavarian army physician, initiated the first recorded use of cocaine as a medicine, treating asthenia and diarrhea with the drug. In 1859, the Italian physician Dr. Paolo Mantegazza published what is probably the earliest tract on cocaine, praising its widespread potential for medical use (Van Dyke and Byck, 1986).

It was at about the same time that cocaine began appearing in nonmedicinal substances as well. As discussed in Chapter 2, Angelo Mariani patented the formula for and produced Vin Mariani, a wine containing 6 mg of cocaine. Vin Mariani was used medicinally by some people but was also popular at social events and was the preferred drink served at social gatherings hosted by Pope Leo XIII and King William III. Another contemporary example of nonmedical use was the inclusion of cocaine in the original formula for Coca-Cola, patented in 1886 (Grinspoon and Bakalar, 1985).

Use of cocaine among the literati was common. Sir Arthur Conan Doyle used the drug and made his fictional hero Sherlock Holmes a user who found cocaine useful in sharpening his powers of deduction. Robert Louis Stevenson, it is believed, wrote his novel about Dr. Jekyll and Mr. Hyde under the influence of the drug. In addition, Alexander Dumas, Jules Verne, and Thomas Edison were acknowledged cocaine users who praised the drug's qualities (Grinspoon and Bakalar, 1985).

Dr. W. H. Bentley brought cocaine to the United States as a drug to cure opium, morphine, and alcohol addiction in 1878. Sigmund Freud was both a user and an advocate of cocaine, arguing it was effective in treating depression and morphine addiction. One of Freud's students, Dr. Koller, introduced the use of cocaine as a local anesthetic in 1884. The major pharmaceutical firm Parke-Davis was selling cocaine as an additive in cigarettes, as an ingredient in an alcohol-based drink called Coca Cordial, as a nose spray, as a tablet, and as an injectable fluid by 1890 (Van Dyke and Byck, 1986).

The first signs of medical resistance about cocaine use appeared between 1885 and 1890. Reports on the negative psychological and physical reactions associated with using cocaine as an antidote to morphine addiction surfaced in the medical literature. Because common medical practice at the time was to treat morphine addiction by combining cocaine and morphine, it is unclear whether these reports actually reflected problems with cocaine, the results of reducing morphine doses to addicts, or of combining two drugs with such antagonistic pharmacological properties. An unfortunate side effect of this confusion was the linking of cocaine and morphine in international attempts to control addictive or dangerous drugs, despite their almost opposite qualities and effects. This confusion is one of the reasons that early efforts to regulate cocaine were undertaken (Van Dyke and Byck, 1986).

By 1890 snorting cocaine was quite fashionable among the wealthy and among artists and writers in America. Several policies and practices implemented over the next several decades impacted use rates. For instance, in 1903, cocaine was removed as an active ingredient in Coca-Cola, and Novocain was developed and used as a local anesthetic, which led to a reduction in the medicinal use of cocaine. The passage of the Pure Food and Drug Act of 1904 and the Harrison Narcotics Act in 1914 instituted controls on over-the-counter medicines that limited availability. Around the same time, personal use of cocaine was criminalized in Europe, but medical use continued until the introduction of amphetamines in the 1930s (Grinspoon and Bakalar, 1985).

It was not until the 1970s that cocaine resurfaced in the United States, Canada, and Europe as a recreational drug. While very popular, increases in cocaine's use were slowed by its prohibitive price, selling in the United States for between $100 and $150 per gram. An acceleration in the growth of cocaine use began in the mid-1970s and extended into the early 1980s. The legal suppression of amphetamine use, failed U.S. drug control policies in South America, and the activities of CIA-backed paramilitary groups in Central and South America combined to increase availability and reduce the consumer price. By the end of the 1980s the supply of cocaine in the United States had increased by more than 400 percent, the purity of imported cocaine had more than doubled, and the wholesale price at a port of entry had declined by about 500 percent. Use, while relatively stable in terms of numbers, spread to all social strata of American society (Lyman and Potter, 1998).

In the 1980s, U.S. intelligence agents working with the Nicaraguan contras in an attempt to overthrow the government of Nicaragua (1) solicited funds for the operation from the Medellin Cartel; (2) provided logistical air support for cocaine flights to United States and allowed the cartels use of contra landing strips in Costa Rica; (3) arranged State Department payments to companies owned by drug traffickers, ostensibly as part of a humanitarian relief operation; and (4) allowed the contras to deal in large quantities of cocaine themselves. Recent investigations have revealed that a sizeable portion of the cocaine being sold to Los Angeles-based street gangs for the production of crack came from the contras (Scott and Marshall, 1991).

While snorting cocaine continued to be the most common modality of use (about 90 percent of users), increased availability led to new modalities, particularly smoking the drug, either freebasing it or smoking crack. In South America cocaine is smoked in the form of *basuko*, a coca paste created by the first steps in the extraction process, with a cocaine content as high as 90 (Van Dyke and Byck, 1986).

Cocaine works by extending and strengthening the activity of the neurotransmitters noradrenaline and dopamine, resembling the effects of amphetamines in a much milder fashion. Cocaine does not create tolerance, and its effects last for a maximum of one hour when snorted (less when smoked). Cocaine is not physically addictive. It is, however, a powerfully reinforcing drug that can lead to patterns of increased frequency of use (Fagan and Chin, 1991).

In the 1980s and 1990s, media and state portrayals of cocaine described it as a highly addicting drug. These accounts usually depicted cocaine addicts suffering the anguish of their cocaine "addiction" with horrifying consequences for their personal lives. This socially created view of cocaine addiction went uncontested for three basic reasons. First, there were very little data from which to evaluate the claims. Second, this view of cocaine as an addicting drug was promoted as part of the drug war and therefore was unlikely to be contested by the state itself. And finally, the only early data that were available came from alleged cocaine addicts in treatment or seeking treatment.

Over the years additional research has produced data that contradict this view. For example, the preponderance of the evidence shows that cocaine, no matter what the mode of administration, is not especially addictive for human beings (Fagan and Chin, 1991). For example, the 1990 NIDA household survey of drug use found that 11 percent of Americans reported they had used cocaine, but only 3 percent had used it in the past year and only 0.8 percent had used cocaine in the past month. This means that roughly 2.7 percent of cocaine users had patterns of use that might fall into a category of addictive behavior. A similar Canadian study found that only 5 percent of current cocaine users used the drug monthly or more frequently. Other studies demonstrate that only a very small proportion of cocaine users are persistent abusers, much less addicts (Lyman and Potter, 1998).

Among a small minority of long-term, persistent cocaine users, character-istics of dependence do develop. For example, of 50 regular, persistent cocaine users studied over a 10-year period, only five demonstrated the characteristics of compulsive users at any point in the 10 years. These persistent users, even during periods of heavily increased use, did not progress to habitual patterns of cocaine use. Similar studies of regular cocaine users in Canada, Scotland, Australia, and Holland all found controlled use to be the common pattern. These studies showed the level of use and problems associated with use came and went during the study period. The most frequent response to problems incurred in using cocaine was to quit or greatly cut back use, once again hardly the characteristics of addiction (Kappeler, Blumberg, and Potter, 2000).

Crack is a chemical form of cocaine sold on the streets. It is composed of water, cocaine, ammonia, and bicarbonate of soda. It has a melting point of 96 degrees Centigrade, which allows it to be smoked. Because cocaine's effects are increased when the concentration of the drug in the body rises quickly, smoking cocaine produces a more intense but shorter "high" than snorting the drug.

Studies have shown that in the United States, where street-level cocaine is highly adulterated with other substances, greater preference is shown for crack. In the Netherlands, where cocaine is less adulterated and less costly, consumer preference is strongly oriented toward sniffable forms of the drug. It is impor-tant to note that 92 percent of cocaine-related deaths result from smoking the drug, and only about 10 percent of all cocaine users smoke cocaine rather than snort cocaine (Kappeler, Blumberg, and Potter, 2000).

In the mid-1980s the media and the state's drug war bureaucracy worked in concert to create a "drug scare," a historical period in which all manner of social difficulties, such as crime, health problems, and the failure of the edu-cation system, were blamed on a chemical substance: crack. The crack scare linked the use of crack cocaine to inner-city blacks, Hispanics, and youths. In the 1970s, when the use of expensive cocaine hydrochloride was concentrated among affluent whites, both the media and the state focused their attention on heroin, seen as a drug of the inner-city poor. Only when cocaine became available in the form of inexpensive crack, and after its use spread to minor-ity groups and the poor, was it widely portrayed as a social problem (Beckett, 1994).

Media coverage of crack, beginning in 1986, was intense. *Time* and *Newsweek* ran five cover stories each on crack during 1986; NBC ran 400 eve-ning news stories on crack between June and December 1986; and all three networks ran 74 drug stories on their nightly news programs in July 1986. These stories repeated highly inflated and inaccurate estimates of crack use and warnings about the dangers of crack that were out of proportion to the available evidence (Reinarmann and Levine, 1989).

The fact is that by 1986 crack use was no longer growing. Research from the National Institute of Drug Abuse showed that the use of all forms of cocaine had reached its peak four years earlier and had been declining ever since. At the height of the drug scare, crack use was relatively rare. Surveys of high school seniors showed that experimentation with cocaine products had been decreasing steadily since 1980. The government's own drug use statistics showed that 96 percent of young people in the United States had never even tried crack. The media portrayal of crack use was not reflective of reality. The intense coverage of crack may have created new markets for the drug and slowed the decline in use that had already been under way for almost a decade (Beckett, 1994; Orcutt and Turner, 1993; Reinarmann and Levine, 1989).

As a result of the crack scare, new state and federal laws were passed that increased mandatory sentences for crack use and sales. Ironically, these laws resulted in a situation in which someone arrested for crack faced the prospect of a prison sentence three to eight times longer than a sentence for cocaine hydrochloride, the substance needed to produce crack. In addition, the crack scare resulted in the racialization of the drug war. Starting with the crack scare of the 1980s, both the state and the media have gone to extraordinary lengths to tie illicit drug use to African Americans while ignoring heavy drug use among affluent whites. Half of all television news stories about drugs feature blacks as users or sellers, while only 32 percent of the stories feature whites. This again is out of proportion to the known patterns of drug use. About 70 percent of all cocaine and crack users are white, and about 14 percent are black. The media's overemphasis on drug use by African Americans is matched by the police enforcement activity. Blacks represent 48 percent of all individuals arrested on drug charges, roughly three-and-a-half times their actual rate of use (Beckett, 1994; Kappeler, Blumberg, and Potter, 2000).

In the mid-1980s reports also began to surface about the negative effects of cocaine use by mothers on their developing fetuses. Though the use of any drug is unadvisable during pregnancy, the panic that resulted from early research claims about cocaine's damage to fetuses and the laws passed by the state and federal governments in response to that research clearly exaggerated the harm and created policies that did far more damage to the mother and fetus than the drug itself (Coffin, 1996).

The early research, particularly a 1985 case study, suggested that prenatal cocaine use could result in several health problems related to fetal development, the health of the newborn, and future child development. Quickly thereafter, several other studies linked prenatal cocaine use to maternal weight loss and nutritional deficits; premature detachment of the placenta; premature birth; low birth weight; reductions in infants' body length and head circumference; rare birth defects and bone defects; and neural tube abnormalities (Coffin, 1996).

The media widely repeated these research findings, creating the impression that an epidemic of "crack babies" was plaguing the medical community. The intense publicity and a proclivity for dealing with drug issues using harsh measures led to new laws in response to the "crack baby crisis." Laws were passed that required doctors and nurses to report pregnant drug users to child welfare authorities. Other laws required child welfare agencies to take children away from mothers who had used drugs while pregnant. And many states criminalized drug use during pregnancy. In July 1996 the South Carolina Supreme Court upheld a law that allowed women to be imprisoned for up to 10 years for prenatal drug use (Coffin, 1996).

In this flurry of activity, few took note of continuing research on the issue of prenatal cocaine use that seemed to call the whole "crack baby scare" into question. Subsequent reviews of the early studies on prenatal cocaine use found serious methodological difficulties, including the absence of any control groups, not distinguishing cocaine from other substances in the studies, and lack of follow-up studies noting the health and development of the newborn (Coffin, 1996).

One of the most serious problems with the early studies suggesting a "fetal cocaine withdrawal syndrome" was that they were "nonblind," meaning that the individuals making the observations were told in advance which infants had mothers who had used cocaine during pregnancy. This biased the research and contradicted other observations from doctors and nurses who reported cocaine-exposed children to be indistinguishable from other children. In subsequent blind studies, therefore, it came as no surprise that observers were unable to detect the presence of "fetal cocaine withdrawal syndrome" (Coffin, 1996).

In addition, research using control groups finds no increased risk of sudden infant death syndrome (SIDS) among cocaine-exposed infants. Earlier studies suggesting a possible relationship between SIDS and maternal cocaine use had failed to control for one of the most important variables in SIDS deaths: the socioeconomic status of the mother (Coffin, 1996).

In reviewing all the studies on both animals and humans, it is now clear that no study has been able to establish a causal link between maternal cocaine and poor fetal development, and epidemiological studies have not detected any increase in birth defects that could be associated with cocaine use during pregnancy. It is likely, though, that cocaine, like any other psychoactive substance that enters the bloodstream, has the potential to impact fetal and newborn development (Coffin, 1996).

Instead of maternal cocaine use, most of the scientific evidence points to the lack of quality prenatal care, the use of alcohol and tobacco, environmental agents, and heredity as primary factors in poor fetal development and birth defects. Inadequate prenatal medical services have been positively associated with prematurity and low birth weight. The provision of quality prenatal care to cocaine-using mothers and non-cocaine-using mothers significantly improves fetal development. Without question, it is the use of alcohol, resulting in fetal alcohol syndrome, that is responsible for the most severe birth defects. Tobacco use has also been strongly associated with low birth weight, prematurity, growth retardation, SIDS, low cognitive achievement, behavioral problems, and mental retardation. Additional factors far surpassing cocaine use in their impact on fetal and newborn development are poverty and lead exposure (Coffin, 1996).

The legal responses to the "crack baby scare" did much more harm than good to both the mothers and the children involved. Making substance abuse during pregnancy a crime kept mothers from prenatal medical care, thereby endangering the fetus far more than would be the case with drug use, and discouraged them from seeking drug treatment. When babies were removed from maternal care as a result of alleged drug use, social service agencies found it very difficult to find homes for infants labeled as "crack babies" because of the alleged behavioral problems that might occur during infancy and early childhood. In addition, enforcement of maternal drug abuse laws was also clearly and blatantly racist. More than 80 percent of the women subjected to prosecution under those laws were African American or Latina women (Coffin, 1996).

By the 1990s both cocaine use and the illegal cocaine markets had stabilized in the United States and Europe. As of 2001, 27.7 million adults in the United States had used cocaine, with at least 1.6 million using it on a monthly basis. Additionally, 6.2 million American adults had used crack, with 400,000 using it on a monthly basis (SAMHSA, 2002:109, 110, 129, 130). Although European use levels are not calculated for every country, the Netherlands, which measures use in a manner consistent with that used in the United States, reported much lower use levels, despite a much more lenient drug policy toward cocaine users. In 1999, the Netherlands reported that only 2.1 percent of their adult population had ever used cocaine, compared with 12.3 percent in the United States. So, in the Netherlands, with a no-arrest drug policy for possession and use, cocaine use was between 350 percent and 586 percent lower than in the United States (University of Amsterdam, 1999).

In addition, the economics of cocaine has demonstrated a clear stabilization in the cocaine market. Cocaine is available at a lower price, in greater quantity, and at a higher grade than ever before. In the United States the cost of cocaine at the retail level declined from $423.09 per gram in 1981 to $211.70 per gram in 2000. In addition, the purity level of that retail

---

Figure 3.2

1. Coca farmers, known as *campesinos,* cultivate plants throughout the Andean region of South America.
2. Depending on the method and variety of coca used, coca plants may take up to two years to mature fully.
3. Once harvested, coca leaves are sometimes allowed to dry in the sun to keep the leaves from rotting.
4. Cocaine base processors stomp the coca leaves to macerate the leaves and help extract desired alkaloids.
5. The solution is transferred by bucket to a second plastic lined pit, where lime or cement is added.

Cocaine: Cultivation to Product

gram has increased from 36 percent in 1982 to 61 percent in 2000. At the wholesale level, the cost of cocaine has declined even more markedly, from $125.43 a gram in 1981 to $26.03 a gram in 2000 (Abt Associates, 2001:43). Similarly, in Europe during the 1990s the price of cocaine fell by 45 percent (UNODCCP, 1999:86).

Cocaine and Addiction: A Scientific and Human Controversy

Addiction is a powerful and compelling word that carries with it medical, psychological, and social meanings. Until recently, addiction was a relatively easy concept to describe. It meant physical dependence associated with the use of a drug. Physical dependence was a product of a process that involved using a drug, developing a level of tolerance for the drug, increasing dosage or frequency of use, and the presence of withdrawal symptoms if the user attempted to break off his or her pattern of drug use. Defined in this precise medical and pharmacological manner, addiction was generally limited to heroin and other opiates. The advent of heavy cocaine use in the 1970s and the introduction of crack to the drug market in the late 1970s and 1980s led to claims that cocaine and its byproducts were addictive. The problem was that cocaine is usually thought of as a drug that does not produce physical dependence and therefore does not fit the traditional definition of addiction. Cocaine use and the laws passed to control it seemed to necessitate a revision in the concept of addiction, so focus was shifted from physical dependence to a psychological model of dependence.

It has been standard practice on tabloid television programs, television talk shows, and even the nightly news for the media to showcase alleged cocaine addicts discussing in graphic detail the anguish of their cocaine "addiction" and the horrifying consequences that have ensued from cocaine dependence. As mentioned earlier, this view of cocaine use and cocaine addiction went unchallenged for a number of reasons. First, there were very little, if any, data available from which to make a judgment. Second, this view of cocaine as an addicting and enslaving drug was consistent with the tone of the government's drug war and therefore was unlikely to be contested by the state itself. Finally, the data that were available came primarily from alleged cocaine addicts who were either in treatment or seeking treatment. The claim that cocaine is addictive went unchallenged for so long that it is now a "given" in the debate on drugs. Much like many other "givens," however, there are serious questions about its accuracy. Some research has suggested a startlingly different conclusion: that cocaine, no matter what the mode of administration (snorted, smoked, or injected), is not especially addictive for human beings (Erickson, 1993; Erickson and Alexander, 1989; Fagan and Chin, 1989).

A good place to begin assessing cocaine's addictiveness is with drug use surveys. For example, the 1995 *National Household Survey of Drug Use* found that 22 million Americans reported they had used cocaine, but only 2.6 percent had used it in the past year and only 1.2 percent had used it in the past month (NIDA, 1996b). Even more instructive is the fact that among current users only one in 10 used cocaine once a week or more. A similar Canadian study found that only 5 percent of current cocaine users used the drug monthly or more frequently (Adlaf, Smart, and Canale, 1991). So, the vast majority of current cocaine users use the drug only infrequently. In addition, it is fair to point out that monthly and weekly use, even when it occurs, is still a long way from addiction. Studies indicate that only a very small proportion of cocaine users are persistent abusers, much less addicts. It is true that a small minority of long-term, persistent cocaine users do exhibit the characteristics of addiction. However, it is a small number. For example, of 50 regular, persistent cocaine users studied over a 10-year period, only five demonstrated the characteristics of compulsive users at any point in the 10 years (Siegel, 1984). These persistent users, even during periods of heavily increased use, did not progress to habitual patterns of cocaine use. Similar studies of regular cocaine users in Canada, Scotland, Australia, and Holland all found controlled use to be the common pattern (Cohen, 1989; Ditton et al., 1991; Mugford and Cohen, 1989). All of these studies showed that the level of use and problems associated with use came and went during the study period.

Figure 3.3

The exact effects of cocaine on the human body are not quite clear. Research suggests, however, that the physical cyclical effects of cocaine are as follows:

- Upon ingestion, cocaine first enhances then later interferes with the transmission of the pleasure signals of the brain. A message is carried across the synapse between the axon of one nerve cell and the body of another by chemicals called *neurotransmitters.*

- Of the neurotransmitters released by cocaine, the most important is *dopamine.* Dopamine fills receptors on the body of the next cell and sparks a continuation of the message.

- Normally, pumps reclaim the dopamine, but according to a leading theory, cocaine blocks this process. Dopamine remains in the receptors, sending an enhanced message before breaking down. Prolonged cocaine use may also deplete dopamine, rendering the sensation of pleasure impossible for the user (White, 1989).

How Cocaine Works

Methamphetamine

As of the writing of this text, *methamphetamine* is second only to alcohol and marijuana as the drug used most frequently in many western and midwestern states. Seizures of dangerous laboratory materials have increased dramatically—in some states, fivefold. In response, many special task forces and local and federal initiatives have been developed to target methamphet-amine production and use. Legislation and negotiation with earlier source areas for precursor substances have also reduced the availability of the raw materials needed to make the drug.

Methamphetamine is a highly addictive drug with potent central nervous system stimulant properties. In the 1960s, methamphetamine pharmaceutical products were widely available and extensively diverted and abused. The 1971 placement of methamphetamine into Schedule II of the Controlled Substance Act (CSA) and the removal of methamphetamine injectable formulations from the United States market, combined with a better appreciation for the drug's high abuse potential, led to a drastic reduction in its abuse. However, a resurgence of methamphetamine abuse occurred in the 1980s and it is currently considered a major drug of abuse. The widespread availability of methamphet-amine today is largely fueled by illicit production in large and small clandestine laboratories throughout the United States and illegal production and importa-tion from Mexico. In some areas of the country (especially the West Coast), methamphetamine abuse has outpaced that of both heroin and cocaine.

The drug has limited medical uses for the treatment of narcolepsy, atten-tion deficit disorders, and obesity. Methamphetamine is included in Schedule II of the CSA. On the street, methamphetamine is called various names. These include speed, meth, ice, crystal, chalk, crank, tweak, uppers, black beauties, glass, biker's coffee, methlies quick, poor man's cocaine, chicken feed, shabu, crystal meth, stove top, trash, go-fast, yaba, and yellow bam.

Short–Term Effects

As a powerful stimulant, methamphetamine, even in small doses, can increase wakefulness and physical activity and decrease appetite. Methamphetamine can also cause a variety of cardiovascular problems, including rapid heart rate, irregular heartbeat, and increased blood pressure. Hyperthermia (elevated body temperature) and convulsions may occur with methamphetamine overdose and, if not treated immediately, can result in death.

Most of the pleasurable effects of methamphetamine are believed to result from the release of very high levels of the neurotransmitter dopamine. Dopamine is involved in motivation, the experience of pleasure, and motor function and is a common mechanism of action for most drugs of abuse. The elevated release of dopamine produced by methamphetamine is also thought to contribute to the drug's deleterious effects on nerve terminals in the brain.

Long–Term Effects

Long-term methamphetamine abuse has many negative consequences, including addiction. Addiction is a chronic, relapsing disease, characterized by compulsive drug seeking and use, accompanied by functional and molecular changes in the brain. In addition to being addicted to methamphetamine, chronic abusers exhibit symptoms that can include anxiety, confusion, insomnia, mood disturbances, and violent behavior. They also can display a number of psychotic features, including paranoia, visual and auditory hallucinations, and delusions (for example, the sensation of insects creeping under the skin). Psychotic symptoms can sometimes last for months or years after methamphetamine abuse has ceased, and stress has been shown to precipitate spontaneous recurrence of methamphetamine psychosis in formerly psychotic methamphetamine abusers. With chronic abuse, tolerance to methamphetamine's pleasurable effects can develop. In an effort to intensify the desired effects, abusers may take higher doses of the drug, take it more frequently, or change their method of drug intake.

Withdrawal from methamphetamine occurs when a chronic abuser stops taking the drug; symptoms of withdrawal include depression, anxiety, fatigue, and an intense craving for the drug. Chronic methamphetamine abuse also significantly changes the brain. Specifically, brain imaging studies have demonstrated alterations in the activity of the dopamine system that are associated with reduced motor speed and impaired verbal learning. Recent studies in chronic methamphetamine abusers have also revealed severe structural and functional changes in areas of the brain associated with emotion and memory, which may account for many of the emotional and cognitive problems observed in chronic methamphetamine abusers. Fortunately, some of the effects of chronic methamphetamine abuse appear to be at least partially reversible.

A recent neuroimaging study showed recovery in some brain regions following prolonged abstinence (two years, but not six months). This was associated with improved performance on motor and verbal memory tests. However, function in other brain regions did not display recovery even after two years of abstinence, indicating that some methamphetamine-induced changes are very long-lasting. Moreover, the increased risk of stroke from the abuse of methamphetamine can lead to irreversible damage to the brain.

Trafficking in Meth

Transportation of methamphetamine from Mexico appears to be increasing, as evidenced by increasing seizures along the U.S.-Mexico border. The amount of methamphetamine seized at or between U.S.-Mexico border ports of entry (POEs) increased more than 75 percent overall from 2002 (1,129.8 kilograms [kg]) to 2003 (1,733.1 kg) and 2004 (1,984.6 kg).

The sharp increase in methamphetamine seizures at or between U.S.-Mexico border POEs most likely reflects increased methamphetamine production in Mexico since 2002. Mexican drug-trafficking organizations (DTOs) and criminal groups are the primary transporters of Mexico-produced methamphetamine to the United States. They use POEs primarily in Arizona and southern Texas as entry points to smuggle methamphetamine into the country from Mexico. Previously, California POEs were the primary entry points used by these drug-trafficking organizations and criminal groups; however, increasing methamphetamine production in the interior of Mexico has resulted in Mexican DTOs and criminal groups shifting some smuggling routes eastward. Methamphetamine transportation from Mexico to the United States by these DTOs and criminal groups is likely to increase further in the near term as production in Mexico-based methamphetamine laboratories continues to increase in order to offset declines in domestic production.

The trafficking and abuse of methamphetamine—a leading drug threat in western states since the early 1990s—have gradually expanded eastward, reaching the point at which the drug now impacts every region of the country, although to a much lesser extent in the northeast region. In the early 1990s, methamphetamine trafficking was an evident threat to California drug markets such as Fresno, Los Angeles, Sacramento, San Diego, and San Francisco. By the mid-1990s that threat had expanded to other drug markets, including Denver, Las Vegas, Phoenix, Seattle, and Yakima, Washington. By the late 1990s and early 2000s—as methamphetamine production and distribution remained very high in western states—methamphetamine trafficking continued its eastward expansion (see 2006 National Drug Threat Assessment, Appendix A, Map 4), supported by distribution on the part of Mexican criminal groups and high levels of local production.

The eastward expansion of the drug took a particular toll on central states such as Arkansas, Illinois, Indiana, Iowa, Kansas, Missouri, and Nebraska. Increased methamphetamine trafficking in these states (see 2006 National Drug Threat Assessment, Appendix C, Chart 2), often in rural areas, is evidenced by a 126 percent increase (1,601 to 3,620) in reported methamphetamine laboratory seizures and an 87 percent increase (10,145 to 18,951) in methamphetamine-related treatment admissions from 1999 through 2003. Since 2003 methamphetamine trafficking has expanded farther east to areas such as southern Michigan, Ohio, and western Pennsylvania. The eastward expansion of methamphetamine trafficking and abuse has recently slowed because increasing regulation of the sale and use of chemicals used in methamphetamine production, particularly pseudoephedrine and ephedrine, has substantially decreased domestic production. However, Mexican DTOs and criminal groups have supplanted decreases in domestic production with methamphetamine that they are producing in Mexico. If they are successful, methamphetamine trafficking will spread farther eastward to encompass the entire United States.

Methamphetamine laboratories also contaminate surrounding property. It is estimated that one pound of methamphetamine produced in a clandestine lab yields five to six pounds of hazardous waste. The resultant environmental damage to property, water supplies, farmland, and vegetation where labs have operated costs local jurisdictions thousands of dollars in cleanup and makes some areas unusable for extended periods of time. Damage to some areas is extensive. For example, U.S. Forest Service officers have encountered tree "kills" in areas surrounding small toxic labs (STLs), and ranchers in Arizona have reported suspicious cattle deaths in areas downstream from labs.

Meth Users

According to the 2004 *National Survey on Drug Use and Health*, approximately 11.7 million Americans ages 12 and older reported trying methamphetamine at least once during their lifetimes, representing 4.9 percent of the population ages 12 and older. Approximately 1.4 million (0.6 percent) reported past-year methamphetamine use, and 583,000 (0.2 percent) reported past-month methamphetamine use.

Among students surveyed as part of the 2005 *Monitoring the Future* study, 3.1 percent of eighth graders, 4.1 percent of tenth graders, and 4.5 percent of twelfth graders reported lifetime use of methamphetamine. In 2004, these percentages were 2.5, 5.3, and 6.2, respectively.

The Youth Risk Behavior Surveillance (YRBS) study by the CDC surveys high school students on several risk factors, including alcohol and other drug use. Results of the 2005 survey indicate that 6.2 percent of high school students reported using methamphetamine at some point in their lifetimes. This is down from 7.6 percent in 2003 and 9.8 percent in 2001.

Available data on typical methamphetamine users reveal that most are white, are in their twenties or thirties, have a high school education or better, and are employed full- or part-time. Methamphetamine is used by housewives, students, club-goers, truckers, and a growing number of others. Almost as many women as men use methamphetamine (55 percent male, 45 percent female.)

Methcathinone

Methcathinone, known on the streets as "Cat," is a structural analogue of methamphetamine and cathinone. Clandestinely manufactured, methcathinone is almost exclusively sold in the stable and highly water-soluble hydrochloride salt form. It is most commonly snorted, although it can be taken orally by mixing it with a beverage or diluting it in water and injecting it intravenously. Methcathinone has an abuse potential equivalent to methamphetamine and produces amphetamine-like effects. It was placed in Schedule I of the CSA in 1993.

Methylphenidate

Methylphenidate, a Schedule II substance, has a high potential for abuse and produces many of the same effects as cocaine and amphetamines. Unlike other stimulants, methylphenidate has not been produced in clandestine labs, but the abuse of this substance has been documented among addicts who dissolve the tablets in water and inject the mixture. Complications arising from this practice are common due to the insoluble fillers used in the tablets. When injected, these materials block small blood vessels, causing serious damage to the lungs and retina of the eye. Binge use, psychotic episodes, cardiovascular complications, and severe psychological addiction have all been associated with methylphenidate abuse.

Methylphenidate is used legitimately in the treatment of excessive daytime sleepiness associated with narcolepsy, as is the newly marketed Schedule IV stimulant, modafinil (Provigil). However, the primary legitimate medical use of methylphenidate (Ritalin, Methylin, Concerta) is to treat attention deficit hyperactivity disorder (ADHD) in children. The increased use of this substance for the treatment of ADHD has paralleled an increase in its abuse among adolescents and young adults who either take the tablets orally or crush them and snort the powder to get high. Abusers have little difficulty obtaining methylphenidate from classmates or friends who have been prescribed it.

Anorectic Drugs

A number of drugs have been developed and marketed to replace amphetamines as appetite suppressants. These *anorectic drugs* include benzphetamine (Didrex), diethylproprion (Tenuate, Tepanil), mazindol (Sanorex, Mazanor), phendimetrazine (Bontril, Prelu-2), and phentermine (Lonamin, Fastin, Adipex). These substances are in Schedule III or IV of the CSA and produce some amphetamine-like effects. Of these diet pills, phentermine is the most widely prescribed and most frequently encountered on the illicit market. Two Schedule IV anorectics often used in combination with phentermine—fenfluramine and dexfenfluramine—were removed from the U.S. market because they were associated with heart valve problems.

Khat

For centuries *khat*, the fresh young leaves of the *Catha edulis* shrub, has been consumed where the plant is cultivated, primarily East Africa and the Arabian Peninsula. There, chewing khat predates the use of coffee and is used in a similar social context. Chewed in moderation, khat alleviates fatigue and reduces appetite. Compulsive use may result in manic behavior with grandiose delusions or in a paranoid type of illness, sometimes accompanied by hallucinations. Khat has been smuggled into the United States and other countries from the source countries for use by emigrants. It contains a number of chemicals, among which are two controlled substances, cathinone (Schedule I) and cathine (Schedule IV). As the leaves mature or dry, cathinone is converted to cathine, which significantly reduces its stimulatory properties.

Depressants

Historically, people of almost every culture have used chemical agents to induce sleep, relieve stress, and allay anxiety. Though alcohol is one of the oldest and most universal agents used for these purposes, hundreds of substances have been developed that produce central nervous system depression. These drugs have been referred to as downers, sedatives, hypnotics, minor tranquilizers, anxiolytics, and antianxiety medications. Unlike most other classes of drugs of abuse, depressants are rarely produced in clandestine laboratories. Generally, legitimate pharmaceutical products are diverted to the illicit market. A notable exception is a relatively recent drug of abuse, gamma hydroxybutyric acid (GHB).

Chloral hydrate and paraldehyde are two of the oldest pharmaceutical depressants still in use today. Other depressants, including gluthethimide, methaqualone, and meprobamate, have been important players in the milieu of depressant use and abuse. However, two major groups of depressants have dominated the licit and illicit market for nearly a century—first barbiturates and now benzodiazepines.

Barbiturates were very popular in the first half of the twentieth century. In moderate amounts, these drugs produce a state of intoxication that is remarkably similar to alcohol intoxication. Symptoms include slurred speech, loss of motor coordination, and impaired judgment. Depending on the dose, frequency, and duration of use, one can rapidly develop tolerance as well as physical and psychological dependence on barbiturates. With the development of tolerance, the margin of safety between the effective dose and the lethal dose becomes very narrow. That is, to obtain the same level of intoxication, the tolerant abuser may raise his or her dose to a level that could result in coma or death.

Although many individuals have taken barbiturates therapeutically without harm, concern about the addiction potential of barbiturates and the ever-increasing number of fatalities associated with them led to the development of alternative medications. Today, fewer than 10 percent of all depressant prescriptions in the United States are for barbiturates.

Benzodiazepines were first marketed in the 1960s. Touted as much safer depressants with far less addiction potential than barbiturates, today these drugs account for about one out of every five prescriptions for controlled substances. Although benzodiazepines produce significantly less respiratory depression than barbiturates, it is now recognized that benzodiazepines share many of the undesirable side effects of barbiturates. A number of toxic central nervous system effects are seen with chronic high-dose benzodiazepine therapy, including headaches, irritability, confusion, memory impairment, and depression. The risk of developing over-sedation, dizziness, and confusion increases substantially with higher doses of benzodiazepines. Prolonged use can lead to physical dependence, even at doses recommended for medical treatment.

Unlike barbiturates, large doses of benzodiazepines are rarely fatal unless combined with alcohol or other drugs. Although primary abuse of benzodiazepines is well documented, abuse of these drugs usually occurs as part of a pattern of multiple drug abuse. For example, heroin or cocaine abusers will use benzodiazepines and other depressants to augment their "high" or alter the side effects associated with overstimulation or narcotic withdrawal.

There are marked similarities among the withdrawal symptoms seen with most drugs classified as depressants. In the mildest form, the withdrawal syndrome may produce insomnia and anxiety, usually the same symptoms that initiated the drug use. With a greater level of dependence, tremors and weakness are also present, and in its most severe form the withdrawal syndrome can cause seizures and delirium. Unlike the withdrawal syndrome seen with most other drugs of abuse, withdrawal from depressants can be life-threatening.

Alcohol

Alcohol, one of the oldest drugs known, has been used as far back as records exist. In fact, legal codes limiting its consumption date as far back as 1700 B.C.E. As has been noted, growing concern about alcoholism and related social problems prompted Prohibition in the United States during the 1920s and early 1930s. As the moral approach to alcohol abuse was gradually abandoned, a more scientific approach was adopted, referring to it as a disease. However, some experts have suggested that alcoholism is not as much a disease as a learned social behavior (Bower, 1988).

Although various types of alcohol exist, ethyl alcohol is the type consumed in drinking. In its pure form, it is a colorless, odorless substance. As a rule, people drink alcohol in three categories of beverages: beers, which are made from grain through brewing and fermentation and generally contain from 3 percent to 8 percent alcohol; wines, which are fermented from fruits such as grapes and generally contain from 8 percent to 12 percent alcohol naturally and up to 21 percent when fortified by adding alcohol; and distilled beverages (spirits), such as whiskey, gin, and vodka, which typically contain from 40 percent to 50 percent alcohol. If not kept in check, drinkers may become physically addicted to any of these beverages.

The effects of alcohol vary considerably from one person to another. Mild sedation results from low doses; higher doses, insofar as they tend to reduce anxiety, may produce a temporary state of well-being leading to more serious effects such as depression and apathy. Intoxicating doses typically result in impaired judgment, slurred speech, and loss of motor skills. In addition to the safety dangers associated with drinking and driving and related accidents, chronic users incur risks of long-term involvement with depressants. Tolerance to the intoxicating effects of alcohol develops quickly, leading to a progressive narrowing of the margin of safety between a dose that is intoxicating and one that is lethal.

Alcohol's effects depend on the amount in the blood, known as *blood-alcohol concentration* (BAC), which varies with the rate of consumption and the rate at which the drinker's physical system absorbs and metabolizes alcohol. The higher the alcohol content of the beverage consumed, the more alcohol will enter the bloodstream. The amount and type of food in the stomach also tends to affect the absorption rate. Some studies have shown that drinking when the stomach is filled with food is less intoxicating than when it is empty; the foods in the stomach, which contain fat and protein, delay alcohol absorption. Body weight is also a factor: the heavier the person, the slower the absorption of alcohol. After alcohol passes through the stomach, it is rapidly absorbed through the walls of the intestines into the bloodstream and carried to the various organ systems of the body, where it is metabolized.

Although small amounts of alcohol are processed by the kidneys and secreted in the urine, and other small amounts are processed through the lungs and exhaled in the breath, most of the alcohol is metabolized by the liver. As the alcohol is metabolized, it gives off heat. The body metabolizes alcohol at about the rate of three-fourths of an ounce to one ounce of whiskey an hour. Technically, it is possible to drink at the same rate as the alcohol is being oxidized out of the body. Most people, however, drink faster than this, and so the concentration of alcohol in the bloodstream keeps rising. Alcohol begins to impair the brain's ability to function when the BAC reaches 0.05 percent, or 0.05 grams of alcohol per 100 cubic centimeters of blood. Most state traffic laws in the United States are based on the assumption that a driver with a BAC of 0.08 percent to 0.10 percent is intoxicated. With a concentration of 0.20 percent (a level obtained from drinking about 10 ounces of whiskey), a person has difficulty controlling the emotions and may cry or laugh excessively. The intoxicated person will experience a great deal of difficulty in attempting to walk and will want to lie down.

When the BAC reaches about 0.30 percent, which can be attained when a person rapidly drinks about a pint of whiskey, the drinker will have trouble comprehending and may become unconscious. At levels from 0.35 percent to 0.50 percent, the areas of the brain that control breathing and heart action are affected; concentrations above 0.50 percent may result in death, although a person generally becomes unconscious before absorbing a lethal dose. Moderate or temperate use of alcohol is not harmful, but excessive or heavy drinking is associated with alcoholism and numerous other health problems. The effects of excessive drinking on major organ systems of the human body are cumulative and become evident after heavy, continuous drinking or after intermittent drinking over a period of time that may range from 5 to 30 years.

Critical Thinking Task

Predict the effects on society if Americans, attempting to reduce body fat and strokes, greatly increase their consumption of wine. How would this activity affect social behavior, health, and the drug problem?

The parts of the body most affected by heavy drinking are the digestive and nervous systems. Digestive-system disorders that may be related to heavy drinking include cancer of the mouth, throat, and esophagus; gastritis; ulcers; cirrhosis of the liver; and inflammation of the pancreas. Disorders of the nervous system can include neuritis, lapse of memory (blackouts), hallucinations, and extreme tremors (as found in *delirium tremens*, or "the DTs," which may occur when a person stops drinking after a period of heavy, continuous imbibing). Permanent damage to the brain and central nervous system may also result from heaving drinking, including Korsakoff Psychosis and Wernicke's Disease. Evidence also indicates that pregnant women who drink heavily may give birth to infants suffering from *fetal alcohol syndrome*, which is characterized by face and body abnormalities and, in some cases, impaired intellectual facilities. Additionally, the combination of alcohol and other drugs (such as commonly used sleeping pills, tranquilizers, antibiotics, and aspirin) can be fatal, even when both are taken in nonlethal doses.

Drinking habits in different societies vary considerably. Virtually every culture has its own general beliefs or sense of etiquette about the use and role of alcoholic beverages within its social structure. In some cultures, drinking is either forbidden or frowned upon. The Koran contains prohibitions against drinking, and Muslims are forbidden to sell or serve alcoholic beverages. Hindus also take a negative view of the use of alcohol; this is reflected in the constitution of India, which requires every state to work toward the prohibition of alcohol except for medicinal purposes. Abstinence from alcohol has also been the goal of large temperance movements in Europe and the United States. Some Christian religious groups, including Christian Scientists, Mormons, Seventh-Day Adventists, Pentecostalists, and most Baptists and Methodists, strongly urge abstinence. In some ambivalent cultures, such as the United States and Ireland, the values of those who believe in abstinence clash with the values of mainstream society, which regards moderate drinking as a way of being hospitable and sociable. This accounts for an abundance of laws and regulations that restrict the buying of alcoholic beverages. Some psychologists say that this indecision in society makes it harder for some people to develop a consistent attitude toward drinking.

Some cultures, including those of Spain, Portugal, Italy, Japan, and Israel, have a permissive attitude toward drinking. The proportion of Israelis and Italians who use alcohol is high, but the rates of alcoholism among them are lower than in Irish and Scandinavian groups. Some cultures may be said to look too favorably upon drinking, as do the French. In France, the heavy consumption of alcohol has been related to the high number of people engaged in viticulture and in the production and distribution of alcoholic beverages. Various surveys indicate that subgroups within a society or culture do not all have the same attitudes toward alcoholic beverages or the same drinking patterns. Drinking behavior also differs significantly among groups of differing age, sex, social class, racial status, ethnic background, occupational status, religious affiliation, and regional location.

Teen Drinking

In spite of a nationwide campaign to overcome it, teen drinking remains a widespread problem in the United States. By 1988, the legal drinking age reached 21 in all 50 states, spurred by a 1984 federal law that tied federal highway funding to compliance by the states. After dropping significantly during the 1980s, when the legal drinking age was raised to 21, the amount of teen drinking leveled off but at alarmingly high rates; in 2005, there were 4,767 teens ages 16–19 who died of injuries caused by motor vehicle crashes (CDC, 2006).

The 2001 arrest of President George W. Bush's daughters Jenna and Barbara brought fake IDs and underage drinking to the forefront in the news. The sisters were cited by police after their May 2001 visit to a Mexican restaurant in Austin, Texas. Just two weeks earlier, Jenna Bush had pleaded "no contest" to underage drinking and was ordered to receive alcohol counseling and perform community service.

Research provided by the National Institute on Alcohol Abuse and Alcoholism suggests that the average age at which teens begin drinking dropped from about 18 in the mid-1960s to about 16 in the late 1990s. Furthermore, those who begin drinking younger are more likely to become alcohol-dependent. Teen drinking remains popular in high school, since many teens have access to liquor in their homes, through their friends, and through the use of fake IDs. According to a 1999 survey, about one-half of all students had consumed alcohol in the previous month.

Binge Drinking

On August 26, 1997, police were called to a fraternity house at Louisiana State University in Baton Rouge, where they found a pile of passed-out pledges on the floor. Three of them had to be hospitalized. A fourth one, 20-year-old Benjamin Wynne, was dead. Wynne had spent the night drinking at an off-campus bar and his blood-alcohol level was 0.588, nearly six times the legal limit of 0.10 for drunken driving. Less than one month after Wynne's death, Scott Krueger, an 18-year-old student at Boston's Massachusetts Institute of Technology, died after celebrating his official linking with his fraternity "big brother" that same night. The stories of Ben Wynne and Scott Krueger are not unusual; each year new stories emerge about alcohol abuse and its consequences.

Binge drinking, especially by college students, remains a serious concern. The term can be defined as consuming five or more drinks in one sitting for men and four for women. With each academic year comes a number of stories about young men and women who drank until they died or fell off a roof or out a window, or until they passed out and choked to death on their vomit. In 1995, Harvard University released a landmark study of more than

17,000 college students that suggested that going on frequent drinking sprees is a commonly accepted part of college life. Of that number, one-half the men and 39 percent of the women admitted binge drinking during the previous two weeks. The CDC reports that about 90 percent of alcohol consumed by youths under age 21 in the United States is in the form of binge drinking (CDC, 2007).

Barbiturates

Barbiturates were introduced for medical use in the early 1900s. More than 2,500 barbiturates have been synthesized, and at the height of their popularity, about 50 were marketed for human use. Today, about a dozen are in medical use. Barbiturates produce a wide spectrum of central nervous system depression, from mild sedation to coma, and have been used as sedatives, hypnotics, anesthetics, and anticonvulsants. The primary differences among many of these products are how fast they produce an effect and how long those effects last. Barbiturates are classified as ultrashort, short, intermediate, and long-acting.

The ultrashort-acting barbiturates produce anesthesia within about one minute after intravenous administration. Those in current medical use are the Schedule IV drug methohexital (Brevital) and the Schedule III drugs thiamylal (Surital) and thiopental (Pentothal). Barbiturate abusers generally prefer the Schedule II short-acting and intermediate-acting barbiturates that include amobarbital (Amytal), pentobarbital (Nembutal), secobarbital (Seconal), and Tuinal (an amobarbital/secobarbital combination product). Other short and intermediate-acting barbiturates are in Schedule III and include butalbital (Fiorinal), butabarbital (Butisol), talbutal (Lotusate), and aprobarbital (Alurate). After oral administration, the onset of action is from 15 to 40 minutes, and the effects last up to six hours. These drugs are primarily used for insomnia and preoperative sedation. Veterinarians use pentobarbital for anesthesia and euthanasia.

Long-acting barbiturates include phenobarbital (Luminal) and mephobarbital (Mebaral), both of which are in Schedule IV. Effects of these drugs are realized in about one hour and last for about 12 hours; they are used primarily for daytime sedation and the treatment of seizure disorders.

Benzodiazepines

The *benzodiazepine* family of depressants is used therapeutically to produce sedation, induce sleep, relieve anxiety and muscle spasms, and prevent seizures. In general, benzodiazepines act as hypnotics in high doses, anxiolytics in moderate doses, and sedatives in low doses. Of the drugs marketed in the United States that affect central nervous system function, benzodiazepines are among the most widely prescribed medications. Fifteen members of this group are currently marketed in the United States, and about 20 additional benzodi-azepines are marketed in other countries. Benzodiazepines are controlled in Schedule IV of the CSA.

Short-acting benzodiazepines are generally used for patients with sleep-onset insomnia (difficulty falling asleep) without daytime anxiety. Shorter-acting benzodiazepines used to manage insomnia include estazolam (ProSom), flurazepam (Dalmane), temazepam (Restoril), and triazolam (Halcion). Midazolam (Versed), a short-acting benzodiazepine, is utilized for sedation or treating anxiety and amnesia in critical-care settings and prior to anesthesia. It is available in the United States as an injectable preparation and as a syrup (primarily for pediatric patients).

Benzodiazepines with a longer duration of action are utilized to treat insomnia in patients with daytime anxiety. These benzodiazepines include alprazolam (Xanax), chlordiazepoxide (Librium), clorazepate (Tranxene), diazepam (Valium), halazepam (Paxipam), lorazepam (Ativan), oxazepam (Serax), prazepam (Centrax), and quazepam (Doral). Clonazepam (Klonopin), diazepam, and clorazepate are also used as anticonvulsants.

Benzodiazepines are classified in the CSA as depressants. Repeated use of large doses (or, in some cases, daily use of therapeutic doses) of benzodiaz-epines is associated with amnesia, hostility, irritability, and vivid or disturbing dreams as well as tolerance and physical dependence. The withdrawal syn-drome is similar to that for alcohol and may require hospitalization. Abrupt cessation of benzodiazepines is not recommended; tapering down the dose eliminates many of the unpleasant symptoms.

Given the millions of prescriptions written for benzodiazepines, relatively few individuals increase their dose on their own initiative or engage in drug-seeking behavior. Those individuals who do abuse benzodiazepines often main-tain their drug supply by getting prescriptions from several doctors, forging prescriptions, or buying diverted pharmaceutical products on the illicit market. Abuse is frequently associated with adolescents and young adults who take benzodiazepines to obtain a "high." This intoxicated state results in reduced inhibition and impaired judgment. Concurrent use of alcohol or other depres-sants with benzodiazepines can be life-threatening. Abuse of benzodiazepines is particularly prevalent among heroin and cocaine abusers. A large percentage of people entering treatment for narcotic or cocaine addiction also report abus-ing benzodiazepines. Alprazolam and diazepam are the two most frequently encountered benzodiazepines on the illicit market.

Flunitrazepam

Flunitrazepam (Rohypnol) is a benzodiazepine that is not manufactured or legally marketed in the United States but is smuggled in by traffickers. In the mid-1990s, flunitrazepam was extensively trafficked in Florida and Texas. Known as "rophies," "roofies," and "roach," flunitrazepam gained popularity among younger individuals as a party drug. It has also been utilized as a "date rape" drug. In this context, flunitrazepam is placed in the alcoholic drink of an unsuspecting victim to incapacitate him or her and prevent resistance from sexual assault. The victim is frequently unaware of what has happened to him or her and often does not report the incident to authorities. A number of actions by the manufacturer of this drug and by government agencies have resulted in reducing the availability and abuse of flunitrazepam in the United States.

Gamma Hydroxybutyric Acid (GHB)

In recent years, *gamma hydroxybutyric acid* (GHB) has emerged as a significant drug of abuse throughout the United States. Abusers of this drug fall into three major groups: (1) users who take GHB for its intoxicant or euphoriant effects; (2) bodybuilders who abuse GHB for its alleged utility as an anabolic agent or as a sleep aid; and (3) individuals who use GHB as a weapon for sexual assault. These categories are not mutually exclusive, and an abuser may use the drug illicitly to produce several effects. GHB is frequently taken with alcohol or other drugs that heighten its effects and is often found at bars, nightclubs, rave parties, and gyms. Teenagers and young adults who frequent these establishments are the primary users. Like flunitrazepam, GHB is often referred to as a "date rape" drug.

GHB involvement in rape cases is likely to be unreported or unsubstantiated because GHB is quickly eliminated from the body, making detection in body fluids unlikely. Its fast onset of depressant effects may render the victim with little memory of the details of the attack.

GHB produces a wide range of central nervous system effects, including dose-dependent drowsiness, dizziness, nausea, amnesia, visual hallucinations, hypotension, bradycardia, severe respiratory depression, and coma. The use of alcohol in combination with GHB greatly enhances its depressant effects. Overdose frequently requires emergency room care, and many GHB-related fatalities have been reported.

Gamma butyrolactone (GBL) and 1,4-butanediol are GHB analogues that can be used as substitutes for GHB. When ingested, these analogues are converted to GHB and produce identical effects. GBL is also used in the clandestine production of GHB as an immediate precursor. Both GBL and 1,4-butanediol have been sold at health food stores and on various Internet sites.

The abuse of GHB began to escalate seriously in the mid-1990s. For example, in 1994, there were 55 emergency department episodes involving GHB reported in the Drug Abuse Warning Network (DAWN) system. By 2002, there were 3,330 emergency room episodes. DAWN data also indicated that most users were male, less than 25 years of age, and taking the drug orally for recreational use.

GHB was placed in Schedule I of the CSA in March 2000. GBL was made a List I Chemical in February 2000. GHB has recently been approved as a medication (Xyrem) for the treatment of cataplexy, which is associated with some types of narcolepsy. This approved medication is in Schedule III of the CSA.

Paraldehyde

Paraldehyde (Paral) is a Schedule IV depressant used most frequently in hospital settings to treat delirium tremens associated with alcohol withdrawal. Many individuals who become addicted to paraldehyde are initially exposed during treatment for alcoholism and, despite the disagreeable odor and taste, come to prefer it to alcohol. This drug is not used by injection due to resulting tissue damage; in addition, taken orally, it can be irritating to the throat and stomach. One of the signs of paraldehyde use is a strong, characteristic smell to the breath.

Chloral Hydrate

The oldest of the hypnotic (sleep-inducing) depressants, *chloral hydrate* was first synthesized in 1832. Marketed as syrups or soft gelatin capsules, chloral hydrate takes effect in a relatively short time (30 minutes) and will induce sleep in about an hour. A solution of chloral hydrate and alcohol constituted the infamous "knockout drops" or "Mickey Finn." At therapeutic doses, chloral hydrate has little effect on respiration and blood pressure; however, a toxic dose produces severe respiratory depression and very low blood pressure. Chronic use is associated with liver damage and a severe withdrawal syndrome. Although some physicians consider chloral hydrate the drug of choice for sedation of children before diagnostic, dental, or medical procedures, its general use as a hypnotic has declined. Chloral hydrate, Noctec, and other compounds, preparations, or mixtures containing chloral hydrate are in Schedule IV of the CSA.

Glutethimide and Methaqualone

Glutethimide (Doriden) was introduced in 1954 and methaqualone (Quaalude, Sopor) in 1965 as safe barbiturate substitutes. Experience demonstrated, however, that their addiction liability and the severity of withdrawal symptoms were similar to those of barbiturates. By 1972, "luding out"—taking methaqualone with wine—was a popular college pastime. Excessive use leads to tolerance, dependence, and withdrawal symptoms similar to those of barbiturates. In the United States, the marketing of methaqualone pharmaceutical products stopped in 1984, and methaqualone was transferred to Schedule I of the CSA. In 1991, glutethimide was transferred into Schedule II in response to an upsurge in the prevalence of diversion, abuse, and overdose deaths. Today, there is little medical use of glutethimide in the United States.

Meprobamate

Meprobamate was introduced as an antianxiety agent in 1955 and is prescribed primarily to treat anxiety, tension, and associated muscle spasms. More than 50 tons are distributed annually in the United States under its generic name and brand names such as Miltown and Equanil. Its onset and duration of action are similar to the intermediate-acting barbiturates; however, therapeutic doses of meprobamate produce less sedation and toxicity than barbiturates. Excessive use can result in psychological and physical dependence. Carisoprodol (Soma), a skeletal muscle relaxant, is metabolized to meprobamate. This conversion may account for some of the properties associated with carisoprodol and likely contributes to its abuse.

More Recently Marketed Drugs

Zolpidem (Ambien) and *zaleplon* (Sonata) are two relatively new, benzodiazepine-like central nervous system depressants that have been approved for the short-term treatment of insomnia. Both of these drugs share many of the same properties as the benzodiazepines and are in Schedule IV of the CSA.

Figure 3.4
Source: National Coffee Association, 1997.

- *Heroin (200,000 users).* Triggers release of dopamine and acts on other neurotransmitters.
- *Amphetamine (800,000 users).* Stimulates excess release of dopamine.
- *Cocaine/Crack.* Blocks dopamine absorption.
- *Marijuana (10 million users).* Binds to areas of the brain involved in mood and memory. Also triggers release of dopamine.
- *Alcohol (11 million users).* Triggers dopamine release and acts on other neurotransmitters.
- *Nicotine (61 million users).* Triggers release of dopamine.
- *Caffeine (130 million coffee drinkers).* May trigger release of dopamine.

Getting High: How It Works

Hallucinogens

Hallucinogens are among the oldest known group of drugs used for their ability to alter human perception and mood. For centuries, many of the naturally occurring hallucinogens found in plants and fungi have been used for a variety of shamanistic practices. In more recent years, a number of synthetic hallucinogens have been produced, some of which are much more potent than their naturally occurring counterparts.

The biochemical, pharmacological, and physiological basis for hallucinogenic activity is not well understood. Even the name for this class of drugs is not ideal, since hallucinogens do not always produce hallucinations.

However, taken in nontoxic dosages, these substances produce changes in perception, thought, and mood. Physiological effects include elevated heart rate, increased blood pressure, and dilated pupils. Sensory effects include perceptual distortions that vary with dose, setting, and mood. Psychic effects include disorders of thought associated with time and space. Time may appear to stand still, and forms and colors seem to change and take on new significance. This experience may be either pleasurable or extremely frightening. It needs to be stressed that the effects of hallucinogens are unpredictable each time they are used.

Weeks or even months after some hallucinogens have been taken, the user may experience flashbacks—fragmentary recurrences of certain aspects of the drug experience in the absence of actually taking the drug. Flashbacks are unpredictable, but they are more likely to occur during times of stress and seem to occur more frequently in younger individuals. With time, these episodes diminish and become less intense.

The abuse of hallucinogens in the United States received much public attention in the 1960s and 1970s. A subsequent decline in their use in the 1980s may be attributed to real or perceived hazards associated with taking these drugs.

However, a recent resurgence of the use of hallucinogens is cause for concern. According to the 2003 *Monitoring the Future Study*, 10.6 percent of twelfth graders reported hallucinogenic use in their lifetime. According to the 2003 *National Survey on Drug Use and Health,* approximately 1 million Americans were current hallucinogen users. Hallucinogenic mushrooms, LSD, and MDMA are popular among junior and senior high school students who use hallucinogens.

A considerable body of literature links the use of some of the hallucinogenic substances to neuronal damage in animals, and recent data support that some hallucinogens are neurotoxic to humans. However, the most common danger of hallucinogen use is impaired judgment that often leads to rash decisions and accidents.

LSD

Lysergic acid diethylamide (LSD) is the most potent hallucinogen known to date. It was originally synthesized in 1938 by Dr. Albert Hoffman, but its hallucinogenic effects were unknown until 1943, when Hoffman accidentally consumed some LSD. Because of its structural similarity to a chemical present in the brain and the similarity of its effects to certain aspects of psychosis, LSD was used as a research tool to study mental illness decades ago.

After a decline in its illicit use after its initial popularity in the 1960s, LSD made a comeback in the 1990s. However, the current average oral dose consumed by users is 30 to 50 micrograms, a decrease of nearly 90 percent from the 1960 average dose of 250 to 300 micrograms. Lower potency doses probably account for the relatively few LSD-related emergency incidents during the past several years and its present popularity among young people.

LSD is produced in crystalline form and then mixed with excipients or diluted as a liquid for production in ingestible forms. Often, LSD is sold in tablet form (usually small tablets known as *microdots*), on sugar cubes, in thin squares of gelatin (commonly referred to as *windowpanes*), and, most commonly, as blotter paper (sheets of paper soaked in or impregnated with LSD, covered with colorful designs or artwork, and perforated into one-quarter-inch-square, individual dosage units). LSD is sold under more than 80 street names, including acid, blotter, cid, doses, and trips, as well as names that reflect the designs on the sheets of blotter paper.

Physical reactions to LSD may include dilated pupils, lowered body temperature, nausea, goose bumps, profuse perspiration, increased blood sugar, and rapid heart rate. During the first hour after ingestion, the user may experience visual changes with extreme variations in mood. The user may also suffer impaired depth and time perception, with distorted perception of the size and shape of objects, movements, color, sound, touch, and the user's own body image. Under the influence of LSD, the ability to make sensible judgments and see common dangers is impaired, making the user susceptible to personal injury. He or she may also injure others by attempting to drive a car or operate machinery. The effects of higher doses last 10 to 12 hours. After an LSD "trip," the user may suffer acute anxiety or depression for a variable period. Also, as mentioned previously, users may also experience "flashbacks."

Law enforcement officials show part of the 300 stamps soaked with LSD seized in February 2007. LSD is often sold soaked into sheets of paper covered with colorful designs or artwork.

AP Photo/Carabinieri Press Office

Much of the LSD manufactured in clandestine laboratories is believed to be located in northern California, and initial distribution sources for the drug are typically located in the San Francisco Bay area. A limited number of chemists, probably fewer than a dozen, are believed to be manufacturing nearly all the LSD available in the United States. LSD is available in at least retail quantities in virtually every state, with supply increasing in some states. Retail-level distribution often takes place during concerts and all-night raves. Users usually obtain LSD from friends and acquaintances.

Peyote and Mescaline

Peyote is a small, spineless cactus, *Lophophora williamsii*, whose principal active ingredient is the hallucinogen mescaline (3, 4, 5-trimethoxy-phenethylamine). From earliest recorded time, peyote has been used by natives in northern Mexico and the southwestern United States as a part of their religious rites.

The top of the cactus above ground—also referred to as the *crown*—consists of disc-shaped buttons that are cut from the roots and dried. These buttons are generally chewed or soaked in water to produce an intoxicating liquid. The hallucinogenic dose of mescaline is about 0.3 to 0.5 grams and lasts about 12 hours. Although peyote produced rich visual hallucinations that were important to the native American peyote users, the full spectrum of effects served as a chemically induced model of mental illness. Mescaline can be extracted from peyote or produced synthetically. Both peyote and mescaline are listed in the CSA as Schedule I hallucinogens.

Many chemical variations of mescaline and amphetamine have been synthesized for their "feel-good" effects. For example, *4-Methyl-2, 5-dimethoxyamphetamine* (DOM) was introduced into the San Francisco drug scene in the late 1960s and was nicknamed STP, an acronym for "Serenity, Tranquility, and Peace." Other illicitly produced analogues include *4-bromo-2, 5-dimethoxyamphetamine* (DOB) and *4-bromo-2,5-dimethoxyphenethylamine* (2C-B or Nexus). In 2000, *para-methoxyamphetamine* (PMA) and *para-methoxymethamphetamine* (PMMA) were identified in tablets sold as ecstasy. PMA, which first appeared on the illicit market briefly in the early 1970s, has been associated with a number of deaths in both the United States and Europe.

Newer Hallucinogens

A number of phenethylamine and tryptamine analogues have been encountered on the illicit market. Those recently placed under federal control include 2C-T-7 (dimethoxy-4-(n)-propylthiophenethylamine), permanently placed in Schedule I in March 2004, and 5-MeO-DIPT (5-methoxy-diisopropyltryptamine) and AMT (alpha-methyltryptamine), which were placed in Schedule I on an emergency basis in April 2003. In addition, a number of other analogues are being encountered. These include DIPT (N,N-diisopropyltryptamine), DPT

Figure 3.5

Source: National Institute of Drug Abuse. Found at http://www.nida.gov.

Substances: Category and Name	Examples of *Commercial* and Street Names	DEA Schedule/How Administered	*Intoxication Effects*/Potential Health Consequences
Cannabinoids			*Euphoria, slowed thinking and reaction time, confusion, impaired balance and coordination*/cough, frequent respiratory infections; impaired memory and learning; increased heart rate, anxiety; panic attacks; tolerance, addiction
hashish	boom, chronic, gangster, hash, hash oil, hemp	I/swallowed, smoked	
marijuana	blunt, dope, ganja, grass, herb, joints, Mary Jane, pot, reefer, sinsemilla, skunk, weed	I/swallowed, smoked	
Depressants			*Reduced anxiety; feeling of well-being; lowered inhibitions; slowed pulse and breathing; lowered blood pressure; poor concentration*/fatigue; confusion; impaired coordination, memory, judgment; addiction; respiratory depression and arrest; death
barbiturates	*Amytal, Nembutal, Seconal, Phenobarbital:* barbs, reds, red birds, phennies, tooies, yellows, yellow jackets	I, III, V/injected, swallowed	
benzodiazepines (other than flunitrazepam)	*Ativan, Halcion, Librium, Valium, Xanax:* candy, downers, sleeping pills, tranks	IV/swallowed, injected	*Also, for barbiturates—sedation, drowsiness*/depression, unusual excitement, fever, irritability, poor judgment, slurred speech, dizziness, life-threatening withdrawal
flunitrazepam	*Rohypnol:* forget-me pill, Mexican Valium, R2, Roche, roofies, roofinol, rope, rophies	IV/swallowed, snorted	*for benzodiazepines—sedation, drowsiness*/dizziness
GHB	*gammahydroxybutyrate:* G, Georgia home boy, grievous bodily harm, liquid ecstasy	I/swallowed	*for flunitrazepam—visual and gastrointestinal disturbances, urinary retention, memory loss for the time under the drug's effects*
methaqualone	*Quaalude, Sopor, Parest:* ludes, mandrex, quad, quay	I/injected, swallowed	*for GHB—drowsiness, nausea*/vomiting, headache, loss of consciousness, loss of reflexes, seizures, coma, death
			for methaqualone—euphoria/depression, poor reflexes, slurred speech, coma
Dissociative Anesthetics			*Increased heart rate and blood pressure, impaired motor function*/memory loss; numbness; nausea/vomiting
ketamine	*Ketalar SV:* cat Valiums, K, Special K, vitamin K	III/injected, snorted, smoked	*Also for ketamine—at high doses, delirium, depression, respiratory depression and arrest*
PCP and analogs	*phencyclidine:* angel dust, boat, hog, love boat, peace pill	I, II/injected, swallowed, smoked	*for PCP and analogs—possible decrease in blood pressure and heart rate, panic, aggression, violence*/loss of appetite, depression,
Hallucinogens			*Altered states of preception and feeling; nausea; persisting perception disorder (flashbacks)*
LSD	*lysergic acid diethylamide:* acid, blotter, boomers, cubes, microdot, yellow sunshines	I/swallowed, absorbed through mouth tissues	*Also for LSD and mescaline—increased body temperature, heart rate, blood pressure; loss of appetite, sleeplessness, numbness, weakness, tremors*
mescaline	buttons, cactus, mesc, peyote	I/swallowed, smoked	
psilocybin	magic mushroom, purple passion, shrooms	I/swallowed	*for LSD—persistent mental disorders*
			for psilocybin—nervousness, paranoia
Opioids and Morphine Derivatives			*Pain relief, euphoria, drowsiness*/nausea, constipation, confusion, sedation, respiratory depression and arrest, tolerance, addiction, unconsciousness, coma, death
codeine	*Empirin with Codeine, Fiorinal with Codeine, Robitussin A-C, Tylenol with Codeine:* Captain Cody, schoolboy; (with glutethimide) doors & fours, loads, pancakes and syrup	II, III, IV, V/injected, swallowed	*Also, for codeine—less analgesia, sedation, and respiratory depression than morphine*

Figure 3.5—*continued*

Substances: Category and Name	Examples of *Commercial* and Street Names	DEA Schedule/How Administered	*Intoxication Effects*/Potential Health Consequences
Opioids and Morphine Derivatives, continued			
fentanyl and fentanyl analogs	*Actiq, Duragesic, Sublimaze:* Apache, China girl, China white, dance fever, friend, goodfella, jackpot, murder 8, TNT, Tango and Cash	I, II/injected, smoked, snorted	
heroin	*diacetyl-morphine:* brown sugar, dope, H, horse, junk, skag, skunk, smack, white horse	I/injected, smoked, snorted	*for heroin—staggering gait*
morphine	*Roxanol, Duramorph:* M, Miss Emma, monkey, white stuff	II, III/injected, swallowed, smoked	
opium	*laudanum, paregoric:* big O, black stuff, block, gum, hop	II, III, V/swallowed, smoked	
oxycodone HCL	*Oxycontin:* Oxy, O.C., killer	II/swallowed, snorted, injected	
hydrocodone bitartrate, acetaminophen	*Vicodin:* vike, Watson-387	II/swallowed	
Stimulants			*Increased heart rate, blood pressure, metabolism; feelings of exhiliration, energy, increased mental alertness*/rapid or irregular heart beat; reduced appetite, weight loss, heart failure, nervousness, insomnia
amphetamine	*Biphetamine, Dexedrine:* bennies, black beauties, crosses, hearts, LA turnaround, speed, truck drivers, uppers	II/injected, swallowed, smoked, snorted	
cocaine	*Cocaine hydrochloride:* blow, bump, C, candy, Charlie, coke, crack, flake, rock, snow, toot	II/injected, smoked, snorted	*Also, for amphetamine—rapid breathing*—tremor, loss of coordination; irritability, anxiousness, restlessness, delirium, panic, paranoia, impulsive behavior, aggressiveness, tolerance, addiction, psychosis
MDMA (methylenedioxymethamphetamine	Adam, clarity, ecstasy, Eve, lover's speed, peace, STP, X, XTC	I/swallowed	*for cocaine—increased temperature*/chest pain, respiratory failure, nausea, abdominal pain, strokes, seizures, headaches, malnutrition, panic attacks
methamphetamine	*Desoxyn:* chalk, crank, crystal, fire, glass, go fast, ice, meth, speed	II/injected, swallowed, smoked, snorted	
methylphenidate (safe and effective for treatment of ADHD)	*Ritalin:* JIF, MPH, R-ball, Skippy, the smart drug, vitamin R	II/injected, swallowed, snorted	*for MDMA—mild hallucinogenic effects, increased tactile sensitivity, empathic feelings*/impaired memory and learning, hyperthermia, cardiac toxicity, renal failure, liver toxicity
nicotine	cigarettes, cigars, smokeless tobacco, snuff, spit tobacco, bidis, chew	not scheduled/smoked, snorted, taken in snuff and spit tobacco	*for methamphetamine—aggression, violence, psychotic behavior*/memory loss, cardiac and neurological damage; impaired memory and learning, tolerance, addiction
			for nicotine—additional effects attributable to tobacco exposure; adverse pregnancy outcomes; chronic lung disease, cardiovascular disease, stroke, cancer, tolerance, addiction
Other Compounds			
anabolic steroids	*Anadrol, Oxandrin, Durabolin, Depo-Testosterone, Equipoise:* roids, juice	III/injected, swallowed, applied to skin	*no intoxication effects*/hypertension, blood clotting and cholesterol changes, liver cysts and cancer, kidney cancer, hostility and aggression, acne; in adolescents, premature stoppage of growth; in males, prostate cancer, reduced sperm production, shrunken testicles, breast enlargement; in females, menstrual irregularities, development of beard and other masculine characteristics

Figure 3.5—*continued*

Substances: Category and Name	Examples of *Commercial* and Street Names	DEA Schedule/How Administered	*Intoxication Effects*/Potential Health Consequences
Dextromethorphan (DXM)	*Found in some cough and cold medications:* Robotripping, Robot, Triple C	not scheduled/swallowed	*Dissociative effects, distorted visual perceptions to complete dissociative effects*/for effects at higher doses, see "dissociative anesthetics"
inhalants	*Solvents (paint thinners, gasoline, glues), gases (butane, propane, aerosol propellants, nitrous oxide), nitrites (isoamyl, isobutyl, cyclohexyl):* laughing gas, poppers, snappers, whippets	not scheduled/inhaled through nose or mouth	*Stimulation, loss of inhibition; headache; nausea or vomiting; slurred speech, loss of motor coordination; wheezing*/unconsciousness, cramps, weight loss, muscle weakness, depression, memory impairment, damage to cardiovascular and nervous systems, sudden death

NIDA's List of Commonly Abused Drugs

(N,N-dipropyltryptamine), 5-MeO-AMT (5-methoxy-alpha-methyltryptamine), MIPT (N,N-methylisopropyltryptamine), and 5-MeO-MIPT (5-Methoxy, N,N-methylisopropyltryptamine), to name a few. Although these drugs are not specifically listed under the CSA, individuals trafficking in these substances can be prosecuted under the Analogue Statute of the CSA. The ever-increasing number of these types of hallucinogens being encountered by law enforcement is a testament to the efforts of individuals to engage in profitable drug enterprises while trying to avoid criminal prosecution.

MDMA ("Ecstasy")

As the twentieth century drew to a close, U.S. drug enforcement officials and policymakers began to focus on yet another illicit drug as a target for increased penalties and stepped-up enforcement. That drug, *MDMA,* usually referred to as *ecstasy* or XTC, had been around for two decades when fears began to surface about increases in use among middle-class youths. In particular, MDMA was associated with the "rave scene" and the music clubs and bars that are part of that cultural phenomenon, hence it's status as a so-called designer drug.

MDMA (3, 4-Methylenedioxymethamphetamine) is a Schedule I synthetic, psychoactive drug possessing stimulant and hallucinogenic properties. It was first synthesized in 1912 by a German pharmaceutical company researching the production of an appetite suppressant. In the 1970s, MDMA was used in psychotherapeutic treatment by many psychiatrists and therapists in the United States. Recreational use of MDMA appears to have increased in the late 1980s and continued into the 2000s. Most MDMA use occurs on an individual basis, but it is a popular drug at "raves," late-night music parties, rock concerts, and some nightclubs catering to the rave culture. Ironically, MDMA use often reduces alcohol use because alcohol is believed to suppress the invigorating effects of MDMA. In that alcohol is one of the most dangerous of the widely used psychoactive drugs, MDMA appears to suppress one dangerous type of drug use.

MDMA is generally ingested orally as a tablet or capsule but can be snorted, smoked, injected, or taken via suppository. Its maximum period of intoxication is about four hours. Users describe a wide range of pleasant effects from MDMA use, including anxiety reduction, increased empathy for others, and relaxation. Adverse symptoms sometimes attributed to MDMA include nausea, mild hallucinations, chills, teeth clenching, increases in body temperature, muscle cramping, and blurred vision. However, great care must be taken in attributing any of these effects to pure MDMA in that ingestion of the actual drug may be the exception rather than the rule due to adulteration and counterfeiting (discussed later in this section). The same cautions must be applied to alleged outcomes of MDMA overdoses, which are said to result in faintness, high blood pressure, panic attacks, and (in the most severe cases) loss of consciousness. But once again, these may be the symptoms of drugs that have been substituted for or added to MDMA.

Production and Distribution of MDMA

Most of the MDMA imported to the United States comes from clandestine laboratories operating in the Netherlands, Belgium, and other Western European nations. Most of the MDMA produced in these labs is consumed in Europe, where it is a very popular recreational drug, but some of the supply is diverted to the United States. Israeli and Russian organized crime groups appear to be the primary importers of the drug to the United States.

MDMA is most commonly smuggled into the United States through express mail delivery services or on commercial airline flights or concealed in air freight shipments of legal goods emanating from the major cities of Western Europe. The DEA asserts that the common quantity for a single importation batch is about 10,000 tablets.

MDMA sells for about $20 a dose on the streets and in clubs. Like other illicit drugs, MDMA traffickers make heavy use of brand names and logos to distinguish their product from those of their competitors. Common logo designs in the United States are butterflies and four-leaf clovers.

MDMA use appears to be increasing in the United States despite increased law enforcement attention and heavy penalties for the sale or use of the drug. The Drug Abuse Warning Network reported a 500 percent increase in use from 1993 to 1999, and the DEA reported a large increase in MDMA seizures through the 1990s. Law enforcement reporting indicates that federal seizures and arrests regarding MDMA have decreased each year since peaking in 2001 (National Drug Intelligence Center, 2005).

The MDMA Scare

Despite concerns voiced by law enforcement officials and politicians, the scientific evidence concerning MDMA is anything but alarming. In general, the evidence leads to some general conclusions: (1) there is considerable scientific evidence that MDMA is an effective therapeutic substance appropriate for a variety of medical uses; and (2) the evidence concerning potential harms from MDMA can be characterized as either mixed or leaning toward considerable doubt that MDMA is a compellingly dangerous substance when used illegally.

Prior to the outlawing of MDMA in 1987, psychiatrists and mental health therapists frequently engaged in MDMA-assisted psychotherapy for a variety of maladies, including the treatment of terminally ill patients, the treatment of serious trauma, the treatment of various phobias, therapy associated with marital problems, and, most interestingly, the treatment of drug addiction (Adamson, 1985; Adamson and Metzner, 1988; Downing, 1986; Greer and Tolbert, 1986; Grinspoon and Bakalar, 1986; Grob, 2000; Riedlinger and Riedlinger, 1994). In fact, not only is there a large body of scientific literature endorsing the therapeutic utility of MDMA, there is also much literature demonstrating positive outcomes for patients. In particular, these studies found significant improvements in patients' self-esteem, communication abilities, capacities for reaching empathic rapport, and capacities for establishing trust and intimacy relationships (Grinspoon and Bakalar, 1986; Grob and Poland, 1997). A study of MDMA use among psychiatrists who had utilized MDMA therapies found that in 85 percent of the cases MDMA had facilitated patients' abilities to be open and communicative with others, in 65 percent of the cases MDMA had decreased fear levels, and in 50 percent of the cases it had reduced aggression (Liester et al., 1992).

A five-year study of Swiss patients being treated with MDMA found that 90 percent had significantly improved their clinical status as a result of the therapy, whereas only 2.5 percent of those treated had suffered deterioration in their conditions (Liester et al., 1992). In addition, in the Swiss study, patients significantly reduced their use of nicotine, alcohol, and marijuana in the years following their MDMA therapy. Doctors also reported that patients undergoing MDMA therapy showed significant improvement with regard to their overall quality of life, their levels of self-acceptance, and their abilities to act autonomously.

A study in Spain of rape victims afflicted with post-traumatic stress disorder (PTSD) who underwent treatment with MDMA also yielded striking results. A similar study in the United States looking at MDMA to treat depression, anxiety, alienation, and pain in end-stage cancer patients also showed promising results (Grob, 2000).

The medical and scientific evidence on MDMA as a therapeutic drug is overwhelming and clearly indicates that the DEA's classification of MDMA as a Schedule I drug, subject to heavy and draconian control, is both in error and in contradiction to the evidence. In fact, DEA's own administrative law judge, in reviewing the scientific evidence, ruled that MDMA should be rescheduled as a Schedule III drug, subject to far looser controls. Unfortunately, in a socially constructed atmosphere of drug war hysteria, neither the DEA nor Congress could be persuaded to place scientific evidence over political expediency.

Although the evidence concerning the recreational use of MDMA is not as clear-cut, it is safe to say it is far removed from any justification for heavy criminal penalties or a new drug war directed at MDMA. A government-funded study conducted by George Ricaurte suggested that MDMA may pose some long-term risks to users, but even in that study the evidence was far from conclusive, and many scientists strongly disagree with the study's findings (Grob, 2000). The research indicating that MDMA has negative impacts on memory and cognitive skills is methodologically inadequate at best. It failed to control for multiple drug use, thereby confounding any findings; it failed to control for levels of drug use; and, most important, it failed to construct an adequate, scientifically valid control group as a point of comparison, which is a methodologically debilitating error (Grob, 2000).

All findings on MDMA use are invalidated by the legal status of MDMA. Simply put, because MDMA is illegal, there is very little actual MDMA on the market. As is the case with every other illegal drug, the market is polluted with adulterated and counterfeit substances. The impurities and imprecise pharmacology associated with these substances more than adequately explain any of the adverse scientific findings related to MDMA. The criminalization of MDMA by the DEA had the effect of turning production of much of the MDMA supply over to underground chemists who produce the drug in uncontrolled settings, with additives to expand the volume of their supplies. Unregulated, uncontrolled production is an inevitable consequence of prohibiting illicit substances, and MDMA is no exception. In the case of MDMA, this consequence has even greater compulsions. Drug traffickers and producers can be prosecuted under draconian criminal laws for producing and selling MDMA, a relatively safe psychoactive substance, but they can avoid those harsh penalties while producing counterfeit compounds that are not covered by the law but are far more dangerous than the outlawed substance. This inherent contradiction of drug prohibition occurs in other markets as well, but nowhere is its outcome more debilitating than in regard to MDMA. Virtually all the problems alleged to emanate from the ingestion of MDMA are actually problems associated with counterfeit and adulterated substances masquerading as MDMA.

A compelling example of this problem occurred at an Oakland, California, rave in the fall of 2000. More than 5,000 people participated in the rave, and nine ended up being sent to the hospital for treatment of problems that were alleged to be associated with MDMA. However, blood tests demonstrated that eight of the nine had not taken MDMA at all but rather had ingested counterfeit substances. DanceSafe, a national, youth-oriented drug control organization, has found in its research that 40 percent of the MDMA pills they tested were, in fact, substances other than MDMA, and an additional 20 percent of the pills they tested contain drugs in addition to MDMA ("Lure of Ecstasy," 2000). The most common adulterants added to MDMA are caffeine, cocaine, methamphetamines, and various over-the-counter medications. The most common counterfeits sold as MDMA are ketamine, PCP (phencyclidine), and

DXM (dextromethorphan), an inexpensive cough suppressant, which was the legal drug that actually incapacitated eight of the Oakland rave victims. DXM inhibits sweating, causes dehydration, and often leads to heatstroke. Of course, the ultimate irony of this situation is that a legal drug ingested because MDMA is illegal was the substance that caused eight of the nine drug-related problems at the Oakland rave. Probably no other example so clearly points out the absurdity of current drug prohibition policies.

The fact is that no one can say with certainty that MDMA does or does not have long-term effects related to its use. The fact is that we simply do not know. The drug laws make knowing that much more difficult by restricting research on MDMA and make the situation that much worse by encouraging counterfeiting and adulteration of the drug.

Phencyclidine and Related Drugs

In the 1950s, *phencyclidine* (PCP) was investigated as an anesthetic, but due to the side effects of confusion and delirium, its development for human use was discontinued. It became commercially available for use as a veterinary anesthetic in the 1960s under the trade name of Sernylan and was placed in Schedule III of the CSA. In 1978, due to considerable abuse, phencyclidine was transferred to Schedule II of the CSA and manufacturing of Sernylan was discontinued. Today, virtually all the phencyclidine encountered on the illicit market in the United States is produced in clandestine laboratories.

PCP is illicitly marketed under a number of other names, including angel dust, supergrass, killer weed, embalming fluid, and rocket fuel, reflecting the range of its bizarre and volatile effects. In its pure form, it is a white crystalline powder that readily dissolves in water. However, most PCP on the illicit market contains a number of contaminants resulting from makeshift manufacturing, causing the color to range from tan to brown and the consistency from powder to a gummy mass. Although sold in tablets and capsules as well as in powder and liquid form, it is commonly applied to a leafy material, such as parsley, mint, oregano, or marijuana, and smoked.

The drug's effects are as varied as its appearance. A moderate amount of PCP often causes the user to feel detached, distant, and estranged from his or her surroundings. Numbness, slurred speech, and loss of coordination may be accompanied by a sense of strength and invulnerability. A blank stare, rapid and involuntary eye movements, and an exaggerated gait are among the more observable effects. Auditory hallucinations, image distortion, severe mood disorders, and amnesia may also occur. In some users, PCP may cause acute anxiety and a feeling of impending doom; in others, paranoia and violent hostility; and in some it may produce a psychosis indistinguishable from schizophrenia. PCP use is associated with a number of risks, and many believe it to be one of the most dangerous drugs of abuse.

Modification of the manufacturing process may yield chemically related analogues capable of producing psychic effects similar to PCP. Four of these substances—N-ethyl-l-phenylcyclohexylamine, or PCE; l-(phenylcyclohexyl) pyrrolidine, or PCPy; l-[l-(2-thienyl)cyclohexyl]piperdine, or TCP; and l-[l-(2-thienyl)cyclohexyl]pyrrolidine, or TCPy—have been encountered on the illicit market and have been placed in Schedule I of the CSA. Telazol, a Schedule III veterinary anesthetic containing tiletamine (a PCP analogue), in combination with zolazepam (a benzodiazepine), is sporadically encountered as a drug of abuse.

Ketamine

Ketamine is a rapidly acting general anesthetic. Its pharmacological profile is essentially the same as that of phencyclidine. Like PCP, ketamine is referred to as a *dissociative* anesthetic because patients feel detached or disconnected from their pain and environment when anesthetized with this drug. Unlike most anesthetics, ketamine produces only mild respiratory depression and appears to stimulate, not depress, the cardiovascular system. In addition, ketamine has both analgesic and amnesic properties and is associated with less confusion, irrationality, and violent behavior than PCP. Use of ketamine as a general anesthetic for humans has been limited due to adverse effects, including delirium and hallucinations. Today it is primarily used in veterinary medicine, but it has some utility for emergency surgery in humans.

Although ketamine has been marketed in the United States for many years, it was only relatively recently associated with significant diversion and abuse and placed in Schedule III of the CSA in 1999. Known in the drug culture as Special K or Super K, ketamine has become a staple at dance parties or raves. Ketamine is supplied to the illicit market by the diversion of legitimate pharmaceuticals (Ketaset, Ketalar). It is usually distributed as a powder, which is obtained by removing the liquid from the pharmaceutical products. As a drug of abuse, ketamine can be administered orally, snorted, or injected. It is also sprinkled on marijuana or tobacco and smoked. After oral or intranasal administration, effects are evident in about 10 to 15 minutes and are over in about an hour.

After intravenous use, effects begin almost immediately and reach peak effects within minutes. Ketamine can act as a depressant or a psychedelic. Low doses produce vertigo, ataxia, slurred speech, slow reaction time, and euphoria. Intermediate doses produce disorganized thinking, altered body image, and a feeling of unreality, with vivid visual hallucinations. High doses produce analgesia, amnesia, and coma.

Narcotics

Narcotics constitute a category of drugs that includes opium and opium derivatives or their synthetic substitutes. Generally speaking, these drugs are painkillers that are indispensable in medical treatment but are also very potent and extremely addictive. The initial effects of the drugs may be unpleasant for the user and may include such side effects as nausea, vomiting, drowsiness, apathy, decreased physical activity, and constipation. Strong doses can lead to respiratory depression, loss of motor coordination, and slurred speech. Users who desire the brief euphoric effects of narcotic drugs may develop tolerance and increase their doses of the drug. Repeated use of narcotics will almost certainly manifest itself in both physical addiction and psychological dependence. Usually, narcotics are administered either orally or by injection. Intravenous drug users will commonly use one of two methods of injection:

- *Skin popping*. Injecting the drug just under the skin and into the muscle.
- *Mainlining*. Injecting the drug directly into the veins.

In the event that the physically addicted user is deprived of the drug, the first withdrawal signs are usually noticed shortly before the time of the next desired dose, which is anywhere from 36 to 72 hours after the last dose. Other symptoms (such as watery eyes, runny nose, yawning, and perspiration), however, will appear about 8 to 12 hours after the last dose. As the abstinence syndrome progresses, the user will experience loss of appetite, irritability, insomnia, goose bumps, and tremors, accompanied by severe sneezing. When the symptoms reach their peak, the user becomes weak and vomits while also experiencing stomach cramps, diarrhea, and an increase in heart rate. These symptoms linger for five to seven days and then disappear.

Narcotics are of both natural and synthetic origins. Of the natural-origin narcotics, the most common are opium, heroin, and morphine. All of these drugs are derived from the opium poppy plant. This plant only grows in certain parts of the world and is most commonly found today in South America, Southeast Asia, Southwest Asia, and Mexico.

The opium poppy produces a seed pod that when unripe was traditionally lanced with a knife by farmers to obtain a milky liquid that oozes out of the incision. A more modern method, however, is the industrial poppy-straw process of extracting alkaloids from the mature dried plant (see Chapter 4).

Narcotics of Natural Origin

The poppy plant, *Papaver somniferum*, is the source for nonsynthetic narcotics. It was grown in the Mediterranean region as early as 5000 B.C.E. and has since been cultivated in a number of countries throughout the world. The milky fluid that seeps from incisions in the unripe seed pod of this poppy has, since ancient times, been scraped by hand and air-dried to produce what is known as *opium*. A more modern method of harvesting is by the industrial poppy-straw process of extracting alkaloids from the mature dried plant. The extract may be in liquid, solid, or powder form, although most poppy straw concentrate available commercially is a fine brownish powder. More than 500 tons of opium or equivalents in poppy straw concentrate are legally imported into the United States annually for legitimate medical use.

Opium

There were no legal restrictions on the importation or use of opium until the early 1900s. In the United States, the unrestricted availability of opium, the influx of opium-smoking immigrants from East Asia, and the invention of the hypodermic needle contributed to the more severe variety of compulsive drug abuse seen at the turn of the twentieth century. In those days, medicines often contained opium without any warning label. Today state, federal, and international laws govern the production and distribution of narcotic substances.

Although opium is used in the form of paregoric to treat diarrhea, most opium imported into the United States is broken down into its alkaloid constituents. These alkaloids are divided into two distinct chemical classes: phenanthrenes and isoquinolines. The principal phenanthrenes are morphine, codeine, and thebaine; the isoquinolines have no significant central nervous system effects and are not regulated under the CSA.

Morphine

Morphine is the principal constituent of opium and ranges in concentration from 4 percent to 21 percent. Commercial opium is standardized to contain 10 percent morphine. In the United States, a small percentage of the morphine obtained from opium is used directly (about 20 tons); the remaining is converted to codeine and other derivatives (about 110 tons). Morphine is one of the most effective drugs known for the relief of severe pain and remains the standard against which new analgesics are measured. Like most narcotics, the use of morphine has increased significantly in recent years. Since 1998, there has been about a twofold increase in the use of morphine products in the United States.

Morphine is marketed under generic and brand name products including MS-Contin, Oramorph SR, MSIR, Roxanol, Kadian, and RMS. Morphine is used parenterally (by injection) for preoperative sedation, as a supplement to anesthesia, and for analgesia. It is the drug of choice for relieving the pain of myocardial infarction and for its cardiovascular effects in the treatment of acute pulmonary edema. Traditionally, morphine was almost exclusively used by injection. Today morphine is marketed in a variety of forms, including oral solutions, immediate and sustained-release tablets and capsules, suppositories, and injectable preparations. In addition, the availability of high-concentration morphine preparations (e.g., 20-mg/ml oral solutions, 25-mg/ml injectable solutions, and 200-mg sustained-release tablets) partially reflects the use of this substance for chronic pain management in opiate-tolerant patients.

Codeine

Codeine is the most widely used, naturally occurring narcotic in medical treatment in the world. This alkaloid is found in opium in concentrations ranging from 0.7 percent to 2.5 percent. However, most codeine used in the United States is produced from morphine. Codeine is also the starting material for the production of two other narcotics, dihydrocodeine and hydrocodone. Codeine is medically prescribed for the relief of moderate pain and cough suppression. Compared to morphine, codeine produces less analgesia, sedation, and respiratory depression and is usually taken orally. It is made into tablets either alone (Schedule II) or in combination with aspirin or acetaminophen (i.e., Tylenol with Codeine, Schedule III). As a cough suppressant, codeine is found in a number of liquid preparations (these products are in Schedule V). Codeine is also used to a lesser extent as an injectable solution for the treatment of pain. Codeine products are diverted from legitimate sources and are encountered on the illicit market.

Thebaine

Thebaine, a minor constituent of opium, is controlled in Schedule II of the CSA as well as under international law. Although chemically similar to both morphine and codeine, thebaine produces stimulatory rather than depressant effects. Thebaine is not used therapeutically but is converted into a variety of substances, including oxycodone, oxymorphone, nalbuphine, naloxone, naltrexone, and buprenorphine. The United States ranks first in the world in thebaine utilization.

Semisynthetic Narcotics

The following narcotics are among the more significant substances that have been derived from morphine, codeine, or thebaine contained in opium.

Heroin

First synthesized from morphine in 1874, *heroin* was not extensively used in medicine until the early 1900s. Commercial production of the new pain remedy was first started in 1898. It initially received widespread acceptance from the medical profession, but physicians remained unaware of its addiction potential for years. The first comprehensive control of heroin occurred with the Harrison Narcotics Act of 1914. Today heroin is an illicit substance having no medical utility in the United States. It is in Schedule I of the CSA.

Four foreign source areas produce the heroin available in the United States: South America (Colombia), Mexico, Southeast Asia (principally Burma), and Southwest Asia (principally Afghanistan). However, South America and Mexico supply most of the illicit heroin marketed in the United States. South American heroin is a high-purity powder primarily distributed to metropolitan areas on the East Coast. Heroin powder may vary in color from white to dark brown because of impurities left from the manufacturing process or the presence of additives. Mexican heroin, known as *black tar*, is primarily available in the western United States. The color and consistency of black tar heroin result from the crude processing methods used to illicitly manufacture heroin in Mexico. Black tar heroin may be sticky like roofing tar or hard like coal, and its color may vary from dark brown to black.

Pure heroin is rarely sold on the street. A "bag" (slang for a small unit of heroin sold on the street) currently contains about 30 to 50 milligrams of powder, only a portion of which is heroin. The remainder could be sugar, starch, acetaminophen, procaine, benzocaine, quinine, or any of numerous cutting agents for heroin. Traditionally, the purity of heroin in a bag ranged from 1 percent to 10 percent. More recently, heroin purity has ranged from about 10 percent to 70 percent. Black tar heroin is often sold in chunks weighing about an ounce. Its purity is generally less than South American heroin and it is most frequently smoked or dissolved, diluted, and injected.

In the past, heroin in the United States was almost always injected, because this is the most practical and efficient way to administer low-purity heroin. However, the recent availability of higher-purity heroin at relatively low cost has meant that a larger percentage of today's users are either snorting or smoking heroin instead of injecting it. This trend was first captured in the 1999 *National Household Survey on Drug Abuse*, which revealed that 60 percent to 70 percent of people who used heroin for the first time from 1996 to 1998 never injected it. This trend has continued. Snorting or smoking heroin is more appealing to new users because it eliminates both the fear of acquiring syringe-borne diseases, such as HIV and hepatitis, as well as eliminating the social stigma attached to intravenous heroin use. Many new users of heroin mistakenly believe that smoking or snorting heroin is a safe technique for avoiding addiction. However, both the smoking and the snorting of heroin are directly linked to high incidences of dependence and addiction.

According to the 2003 *National Survey on Drug Use and Health*, during the latter half of the 1990s heroin initiation rates rose to a level not reached since the 1970s. In 1974, there were an estimated 246,000 heroin initiates. Between 1988 and 1994, the annual number of new users ranged from 28,000 to 80,000. Between 1995 and 2001, the number of new heroin users was consistently greater than 100,000. Overall, approximately 3.7 million Americans reported using heroin at least once in their lifetimes.

Hydromorphone

Hydromorphone (Dilaudid) is marketed in tablets (2, 4, and 8 mg), suppositories, oral solutions, and injectable formulations. All products are in Schedule II of the CSA. The drug's analgesic potency is two to eight times that of morphine, but it is shorter-acting and produces more sedation than morphine. Much sought after by narcotic addicts, hydromorphone is usually obtained by the abuser through fraudulent prescriptions or theft. The tablets are often dissolved and injected as a substitute for heroin. In September 2004, the FDA approved the use of Palladone (hydromorphone hydrochloride) for the management of persistent pain. This extended-release formulation could have the same risk of abuse as OxyContin, which is discussed in more detail in the next section.

Oxycodone

Oxycodone is synthesized from thebaine. Like morphine and hydromorphone, oxycodone is used as an analgesic. It is effective orally and is marketed alone in 10, 20, 40, 80, and 160 mg controlled-release tablets (OxyContin), in 5 mg immediate-release capsules (OxyIR), or in combination products with aspirin (Percodan) or acetaminophen (Percocet) for the relief of pain. All oxycodone products are in Schedule II. Oxycodone is either abused orally or the tablets are crushed and sniffed or dissolved in water and injected. The use of oxycodone has increased significantly in recent years. In 1993, about 3.5 tons of oxycodone were manufactured for sale in the United States. In 2003, about 41 tons were manufactured.

Historically, oxycodone products have been popular drugs of abuse among the narcotic-abusing population. Recently, concern has grown among federal, state, and local officials regarding the dramatic increase in the illicit availability and abuse of OxyContin products. These products contain large amounts of oxycodone (10 to 160 mg) in a formulation intended for slow release over about a 12-hour period.

Abusers have learned that this slow-release mechanism can be easily circumvented by crushing the tablet and swallowing, snorting, or injecting the drug product for a more rapid and intense high. The criminal activity associated with illicitly obtaining and distributing this drug, as well as serious consequences of illicit use, including addiction and fatal overdose deaths, is of an epidemic proportion in some areas of the United States.

Hydrocodone

Hydrocodone is structurally related to codeine but more closely related to morphine in its pharmacological profile. As a drug of abuse, it is equivalent to morphine with respect to subjective effects, opiate signs and symptoms, and "liking" scores. Hydrocodone is an effective cough suppressant and analgesic. It is most frequently prescribed in combination with acetaminophen (i.e., Vicoden, Lortab) but is also marketed in products with aspirin (Lortab ASA), ibuprofen (Vicoprofen), and antihistamines (Hycomine). All products currently marketed in the United States are either Schedule III combination products primarily intended for pain management or Schedule V antitussive medications often marketed in liquid formulations. The Schedule III products are currently under review at the federal level to determine whether an increase in regulatory control is warranted.

Hydrocodone products are the most frequently prescribed pharmaceutical opiates in the United States, with more than 111 million prescriptions dispensed in 2003. Despite their obvious utility in medical practice, hydrocodone products are among the most popular pharmaceutical drugs associated with drug diversion, trafficking, abuse, and addiction. In every geographical area in the country, the DEA has listed this drug as one of the most commonly diverted. Hydrocodone is the most frequently encountered opiate pharmaceutical in submissions of drug evidence to federal, state, and local forensic laboratories. Law enforcement has documented the diversion of millions of dosage units of hydrocodone by theft, doctor shopping, fraudulent prescriptions, bogus "call-in" prescriptions, and diversion by registrants and Internet fraud.

Hydrocodone products are associated with significant drug abuse. Hydrocodone was ranked sixth among all controlled substances in the 2002 Drug Abuse Warning Network (DAWN) emergency department (ED) data. Poison control data, DAWN medical examiner (ME) data, and other ME data indicate that hydrocodone deaths are numerous, widespread, and increasing in number. In addition, the hydrocodone acetaminophen combinations (accounting for about 80 percent of all hydrocodone prescriptions) carry significant public health risk when taken in excess.

Synthetic Narcotics

In contrast to the pharmaceutical products derived from opium, synthetic narcotics are produced entirely within the laboratory. The continuing search for products that retain the analgesic properties of morphine without the consequent dangers of tolerance and dependence has yet to yield a product that is not susceptible to abuse. A number of clandestinely produced drugs as well as drugs that have accepted medical uses fall within this category.

Meperidine

Introduced as an analgesic in the 1930s, *meperidine* produces effects that are similar, but not identical, to morphine (shorter duration of action and reduced antitussive and antidiarrheal actions). Currently it is used for pre-anesthesia and the relief of moderate to severe pain, particularly in obstetrics and post-operative situations. Meperidine is available in tablets, syrups, and injectable forms under generic and brand name (Demerol, Mepergan, etc.) Schedule II preparations. Several analogues of meperidine have been clandestinely produced. During the clandestine synthesis of the analogue MPPP, a neurotoxic byproduct (MPTP) was produced. A number of individuals who consumed the MPPP-MPTP preparation developed an irreversible Parkinson's-like syndrome. It was later found that MPTP destroys the same neurons as those damaged in Parkinson's disease.

Dextropropoxyphene

A close relative of methadone, *dextropropoxyphene* was first marketed in 1957 under the trade name of Darvon. Its oral analgesic potency is one-half to one-third that of codeine, with 65 mg approximately equivalent to about 600 mg of aspirin. Dextropropoxyphene is prescribed for relief of mild to moderate pain. Bulk dextropropoxyphene is in Schedule II, whereas preparations containing it are in Schedule IV. More than 150 tons of dextropropoxyphene are produced in the United States annually, and more than 25 million prescriptions are written for the products. This narcotic is associated with a number of toxic side effects and is among the top 10 drugs reported by medical examiners in drug abuse deaths.

Fentanyl

First synthesized in Belgium in the late 1950s, *fentanyl*, with an analgesic potency about 80 times that of morphine, was introduced into medical practice in the 1960s as an intravenous anesthetic under the trade name of Sublimaze. Thereafter, two other fentanyl analogues were introduced: alfentanil (Alfenta), an ultrashort-acting (5 to 10 minutes) analgesic, and sufentanil (Sufenta), an exceptionally potent analgesic (5 to 10 times more potent than fentanyl) for use in heart surgery. Today, fentanyls are extensively used for anesthesia and analgesia. Duragesic, for example, is a fentanyl transdermal patch used in chronic pain management, and Actiq is a solid formulation of fentanyl citrate on a stick that dissolves slowly in the mouth for transmucosal absorption. Actiq is intended for opiate-tolerant individuals and is effective in treating breakthrough pain in cancer patients. Carfentanil (Wildnil) is an analogue of fentanyl with an analgesic potency 10,000 times that of morphine and is used in veterinary practice to immobilize certain large animals.

Illicit use of pharmaceutical fentanyls first appeared in the mid-1970s in the medical community and continues to be a problem in the United States. To date, more than 12 different analogues of fentanyl have been produced clandestinely and identified in the U.S. drug traffic. The biological effects of the fentanyls are indistinguishable from those of heroin, with the exception that the fentanyls may be hundreds of times more potent. Fentanyls are most commonly used by intravenous administration but, like heroin, they may also be smoked or snorted.

Pentazocine

The effort to find an effective analgesic with less dependence-producing consequences led to the development of pentazocine (Talwin). Introduced as an analgesic in 1967, it was frequently encountered in the illicit trade, usually in combination with tripelennamine and placed into Schedule IV of the CSA in 1979. An attempt at reducing the abuse of this drug was made with the introduction of Talwin Nx. This product contains a quantity of antagonist (naloxone) sufficient to counteract the morphine-like effects of pentazocine if the tablets are dissolved and injected.

Butorphanol

Although *butorphanol* can be made from thebaine, it is usually manufactured synthetically. It was initially available in injectable formulations for human (Stadol) and veterinary (Torbugesic and Torbutrol) use. More recently, a nasal spray (Stadol NS) became available, and significant diversion and abuse of this product led to the 1997 control of butorphanol in Schedule IV of the CSA. Butorphanol is a clear example of a drug gaining favor as a drug of abuse only after it became available in a form that facilitated greater ease of administration (nasal spray vs. injection).

Narcotics Treatment Drugs

Methadone

German scientists synthesized *methadone* during World War II because of a shortage of morphine. Although chemically unlike morphine or heroin, methadone produces many of the same effects. It was introduced into the United States in 1947 as an analgesic (Dolophine). Today methadone is primarily used for the treatment of narcotic addiction, although a growing number of prescriptions are being written for chronic pain management. It is available in oral solutions, tablets, and injectable Schedule II formulations.

Methadone's effects can last up to 24 hours, thereby permitting once-a-day oral administration in heroin detoxification and maintenance programs. High-dose methadone can block the effects of heroin, thereby discouraging the continued use of heroin by addicts in treatment. Chronic administration of meth-adone results in the development of tolerance and dependence. The withdrawal syndrome develops more slowly and is less severe but more prolonged than that associated with heroin withdrawal. Ironically, methadone used to control nar-cotic addiction is encountered on the illicit market. Recent increases in the use of methadone for pain management have been associated with increasing num-bers of overdose deaths.

LAAM

Closely related to methadone, the synthetic compound *levo alphacetyl-methadol*, or *LAAM* (ORLMM), has an even longer duration of action (from 48 to 72 hours) than methadone, permitting a reduction in frequency of use. In 1994, it was approved as a Schedule II treatment drug for narcotic addiction. Both methadone and LAAM have high abuse potential. Their acceptability as narcotic treatment drugs is predicated upon their ability to substitute for her-oin, the long duration of action, and their mode of oral administration. Recent data regarding the cardiovascular toxicity of LAAM have limited the use of this drug as a first-line therapy for addiction treatment.

Buprenorphine

Buprenorphine is a semisynthetic narcotic derived from thebaine. Buprenor-phine was initially marketed in the United States as an analgesic (Buprenex). In 2002, two new products (Suboxone and Subutex) were approved for the treatment of narcotic addiction. Like methadone and LAAM, buprenorphine is potent (30 to 50 times the analgesic potency of morphine), has a long duration of action, and does not need to be injected. Unlike the other treatment drugs, buprenorphine pro-duces far less respiratory depression and is thought to be safer in overdose. All buprenorphine products are currently in Schedule III of the CSA.

Cannabis

Cannabis sativa L., the cannabis plant, grows wild throughout most of the tropic and temperate regions of the world. Prior to the advent of syn-thetic fibers, the cannabis plant was cultivated for the tough fiber of its stem. Historically, in the United States, cannabis was legitimately grown only for scientific purposes. More recently, however, it has been grown for medicinal reasons in states authorizing its use.

Cannabis contains chemicals called *cannabinoids* that are unique to the cannabis plant. Among the cannabinoids synthesized by the plant are can-nabinol, cannabidiol, cannabinolidic acids, cannabigerol, cannabichromene, and several isomers of tetrahydrocannabinol. One of these, delta-9-tetrahydro-cannabinol (THC), is believed to be responsible for most of the characteristic psychoactive effects of cannabis. Research has resulted in development and marketing of the dronabinol (synthetic THC) product, Marinol, for the control of nausea and vomiting caused by chemotheraputic agents used in the treatment of cancer and to stimulate appetite in AIDS patients. Marinol was rescheduled in 1999 and placed in Schedule III of the CSA.

Cannabis products are usually smoked. Their effects are felt within minutes, reach their peak in 10 to 30 minutes, and may linger for two or three hours. The effects experienced often depend on the experience and expectations of the individual user as well as the activity of the drug itself. Low doses tend to induce a sense of well-being and a dreamy state of relaxation, which may be accompanied by a more vivid sense of sight, smell, taste, and hearing as well as by subtle alterations in thought formation and expression.

This state of intoxication may not be noticeable to an observer. However, driving, occupational, or household accidents may result from a distortion of time and space relationships and impaired motor coordination. Stronger doses intensify reactions. The individual may experience shifting sensory imagery, rapidly fluctuating emotions, fragmentary thoughts with disturbing associations, an altered sense of self-identity, impaired memory, and a dulling of attention despite an illusion of heightened insight. High doses may result in image distortion, a loss of personal identity, fantasies, and hallucinations.

Three drugs that come from cannabis—marijuana, hashish, and hash oil—are distributed on the U.S. illicit market. As mentioned, in a number of states, marijuana is authorized under state law to be sold as "medical marijuana". On the federal level, marijuana is listed as Schedule I—having no accepted medical use. Today cannabis is illicitly cultivated, both indoors and out, to maximize its THC content, thereby producing the greatest possible psychoactive effect.

Marijuana

Marijuana is the most frequently encountered illicit drug worldwide. In the United States, according to the 2003 *Monitoring the Future Study*, 57 percent of adults aged 19 to 28 reported having used marijuana in their lifetimes. Among younger Americans, 17.5 percent of eighth graders and 46.1 percent of twelfth graders had used marijuana in their lifetimes. The term *marijuana*, as commonly used, refers to the leaves and flowering tops of the cannabis plant that are dried to produce a tobacco-like substance. Marijuana varies significantly in its potency, depending on the source and selection of plant materials used.

The form of marijuana known as *sinsemilla* (Spanish, *sin semilla*: without seed), derived from the unpollinated female cannabis plant, is preferred for its high THC content. Marijuana is usually smoked in the form of loosely rolled cigarettes called *joints*, in bongs or pipes, or in hollowed-out commercial cigars called *blunts*. Joints and blunts may be laced with a number of adulterants, including phencyclidine (PCP), substantially altering the effects and toxicity of these products. Street names for marijuana include pot, grass, weed, Mary Jane, and reefer.

Figure 3.6
Source: Committee on Substance Abuse and Habitual Behavior, Commission on Behavioral and Social Sciences and Education. Copyright 1982 by the National Research Council, Academy of Sciences. Courtesy of the National Academy Press, Washington, DC. Reprinted with permission.

---

1. Marijuana is fat-soluble and is stored for months in the fatty tissues of the body. The lipid-soluble cannabinoid molecules (THC) become embedded in cell membranes and eventually saturate them. Once the cell membrane becomes saturated with THC, the vital nutrients can no longer be transported into and out of the cell, resulting in the loss of cell energy and ultimate cell death.

2. World renowned brain researcher Dr. Robert Heath of Tulane Medical School concluded from experiments on monkeys that the greatest damage occurs in the area of the brain that affects one's motivation.

3. Marijuana users claim that the drug is harmless because it is not physically addictive. The reason for this, however, is because it cannot be withdrawn rapidly. The body builds up its own supply. It takes one week for the stored marijuana to drop to one-half, two weeks to drop to one-fourth, three weeks to drop to one-eighth, etc.

4. More than 8,000 scientific research studies were published in the book *Marijuana: An Annotated Bibliography* (University of Mississippi Research Institute). These studies concluded that marijuana is harmful to the mind and body alike.

Summarizing Marijuana's Harmful Effects

Although marijuana grown in the United States was once considered inferior because of a low concentration of THC, advancements in plant selection and cultivation have resulted in North American marijuana containing higher levels of THC. In 1974, the average THC content of illicit marijuana was less than 1 percent. In 2007, the ONDCP reported that marijuana potency reached 8.5 percent, compared to an average 4 percent THC content in 1983 (ONDCP, 2007).

Marijuana contains known toxins and cancer-causing chemicals. Marijuana users experience the same health problems as tobacco smokers, such as bronchitis, emphysema, and bronchial asthma. Some of the effects of marijuana use also include increased heart rate, dryness of the mouth, reddening of the eyes, impaired motor skills and concentration, and hunger with an increased desire for sweets. Extended use increases risk to the lungs and reproductive system as well as suppression of the immune system. Occasionally, hallucinations, fantasies, and paranoia are reported. Long-term chronic marijuana use is associated with an *amotivational syndrome* characterized by apathy; impairment of judgment, memory, and concentration; and loss of interest in personal appearance and pursuit of goals.

Hashish

Hashish consists of the THC-rich resinous material of the cannabis plant, which is collected, dried, and then compressed into a variety of forms such as balls, cakes, or cookie-like sheets. Pieces are then broken off, placed in pipes or under glass, and smoked. The Middle East, North Africa, and Pakistan/Afghanistan are the main sources of hashish. The THC content of hashish that reached the United States, where demand is limited, averaged about 5 percent in the 1990s.

Hash Oil

The term *hash oil* is used by illicit drug users and dealers but is a misnomer in suggesting any resemblance to hashish. Hash oil is produced by extracting the cannabinoids from plant material with a solvent. The color and odor of the resulting extract will vary, depending on the type of solvent used. Current samples of hash oil, a viscous liquid ranging from amber to dark brown in color, average about 15 percent THC. In terms of its psychoactive effect, a drop or two of this liquid on a cigarette is equal to a single "joint" of marijuana.

Steroids

The issue of performance-enhancing drugs, especially *anabolic steroids*, has once again gained international attention. These drugs are used by high school, college, professional, and elite amateur athletes in a variety of sports (e.g., weightlifting, track and field, swimming, cycling, and others) to obtain a competitive advantage. Bodybuilders and fitness buffs take anabolic steroids to improve their physical appearance, and individuals in occupations requiring enhanced physical strength (e.g., bodyguards, night club bouncers, construction workers) are also known to use these drugs.

Concerns over a growing illicit market, abuse by teenagers, and the uncertainty of possible harmful long-term effects of steroid use led Congress in 1991 to place anabolic steroids as a class of drugs into Schedule III of the Controlled Substances Act (CSA). The CSA defines anabolic steroids as any drug or hormonal substance chemically and pharmacologically related to testosterone (other than estrogens, progestins, and corticosteroids) that promotes muscle growth.

Once viewed as a problem associated only with professional and elite amateur athletes, various reports indicate that anabolic steroid abuse has increased significantly among adolescents. According to the 2003 *Monitoring the Future Study*, 2.5 percent of eighth graders, 3 percent of tenth graders, and 3.5 percent of twelfth graders reported using steroids at least once in their lifetime.

Most illicit anabolic steroids are sold at gyms, at competitions, and through mail-order operations. For the most part, these substances are smuggled into the United States from many countries. The illicit market includes various preparations intended for human and veterinary use as well as bogus and counterfeit products. The most commonly encountered anabolic steroids on the illicit market include testosterone, nandrolone, methenolone, stanozolol, and methandrostenolone. Other steroids seen in the illicit market include boldenone, fluoxymesterone, methandriol, methyltestosterone, oxandrolone, oxymetholone, and trenbolone.

A limited number of anabolic steroids have been approved for medical and veterinary use. The primary legitimate use of these drugs in humans is for the replacement of inadequate levels of testosterone resulting from a reduction or absence of functioning testes. Other indications include anemia and breast cancer. Experimentally, anabolic steroids have been used to treat a number of disorders, including AIDS wasting (which is the involuntary loss of more than 10 percent of body weight, combined with more than 30 days of either diarrhea or weakness and fever), erectile dysfunction, and osteoporosis. In veterinary practice, anabolic steroids are used to promote feed efficiency and to improve weight gain, vigor, and hair coat. They are also used in veterinary practice to treat anemia and to counteract tissue breakdown during illness and trauma.

Used in combination with exercise training and a high-protein diet, anabolic steroids can promote increased size and strength of muscles, improved endurance, and decreased recovery time between workouts. They are taken orally or by intramuscular injection. Users concerned about drug tolerance often take steroids on a schedule called a *cycle*. A cycle is a period of between 6 and 14 weeks of steroid use, followed by a period of abstinence or reduction in use. Additionally, users tend to "stack" the drugs, using multiple drugs concurrently. Although the benefits of these practices are unsubstantiated, most users feel that cycling and stacking enhance the efficiency of the drugs and limit their side effects.

Another mode of steroid use is called *pyramiding*. With this method users slowly escalate steroid use (increasing the number of drugs used at one time and/or the dose and frequency of one or more steroids), reach a peak amount at midcycle, and gradually taper the dose toward the end of the cycle. The escalation of steroid use can vary with different types of training. Bodybuilders and weightlifters tend to escalate their doses to a much higher level than do long-distance runners or swimmers.

The long-term adverse health effects of anabolic steroid use are not definitely known. There is, however, increasing concern about possible serious health problems associated with the abuse of these agents, including cardiovascular damage, cerebrovascular toxicity, and liver damage. Physical side effects include elevated blood pressure and cholesterol levels, severe acne, premature balding, reduced sexual function, and testicular atrophy. In males, abnormal breast development (gynecomastia) can occur. In females, anabolic steroids have a masculinizing effect, resulting in more body hair, a deeper voice, smaller breasts, and fewer menstrual cycles. Several of these effects are irreversible. In adolescents, abuse of these agents may prematurely stop the lengthening of bones, resulting in stunted growth. For some individuals, the use of anabolic steroids may be associated with psychotic reactions, manic episodes, feelings of anger or hostility, aggression, and violent behavior.

A variety of nonsteroid drugs are commonly found in the illicit anabolic steroid market. These substances are primarily used for one or more of the following reasons: (1) to serve as an alternative to anabolic steroids; (2) to alleviate short-term adverse effects associated with anabolic steroid use; or (3) to mask anabolic steroid use. Examples of drugs serving as alternatives to anabolic steroids include clenbuterol, human growth hormone, insulin, insulin-like growth factor, and gamma hydroxybutyric acid (GHB). Drugs used to prevent or treat adverse effects of anabolic steroid use include tamoxifen, diuretics, and human chorionic gonadotropin (hCG). Diuretics, probenecid, and epitestosterone may be used to mask anabolic steroid use.

Over the last few years, a number of precursors to either testosterone or nandrolone have been marketed as dietary supplements in the United States. Some of these substances include androstenedione, androstenediol, norandrostenedione, norandrostenediol, and dehydroepiandrosterone (DHEA). New legislation has been introduced in Congress to add several steroids to the CSA and to alter the CSA requirements needed to place new steroids under control in the CSA.

Inhalants

Inhalants are a diverse group of substances that include volatile solvents, gases, and nitrites that are sniffed, snorted, huffed, or bagged to produce intoxicating effects similar to those of alcohol. These substances are found in common household products such as glues, lighter fluid, cleaning fluids, and paint products. *Inhalant abuse* is the deliberate inhaling or sniffing of these substances to get high, and it is estimated that about 1,000 substances are misused in this manner. The easy accessibility, low cost, legal status, and ease of transport and concealment make inhalants one of the first substances abused by children.

According to the *National Survey on Drug Use and Health,* there were more than 1 million new inhalant users in 2002. During 2003, almost 23 million (9.7 percent) of people age 12 and older reported using an inhalant at least once in their lifetimes. The 2003 *Monitoring the Future Study* from the University of Michigan reported that 8.7 percent of eighth graders, 5.4 percent of tenth graders, and 3.9 percent of twelfth graders used inhalants in the past year. The study also showed that 4.1 percent of eighth graders, 2.2 percent of tenth graders, and 1.6 percent of twelfth graders used inhalants in the past month.

The highest incidence of use is among 10- to 12-year-old children, with rates of use declining with age. Parents worry about alcohol, tobacco, and other illicit drug use but may be unaware of the hazards associated with products found throughout their homes. Knowing what these products are, understanding how they might be harmful, and recognizing the signs and symptoms of their use as inhalants can help a parent prevent inhalant abuse.

For example, volatile solvents are found in a number of everyday products. Some of these products include nail polish remover, lighter fluid, gasoline, paint and paint thinner, rubber glue, waxes, and varnishes. Chemicals found in these products include toluene, benzene, methanol, methylene chloride, acetone, methyl ethyl ketone, methyl butyl ketone, trichloroethylene, and trichlorethane. The gas used as a propellant in canned whipped cream and in small metallic containers called *whippets* (used to make whipped cream) is nitrous oxide or "laughing gas"—the same gas used by dentists for anesthesia. Tiny cloth-covered ampules, called *poppers* or *snappers* by abusers, contain amyl nitrite, a medication used to dilate blood vessels. Butyl nitrite, sold as tape head cleaner and referred to as rush, locker room, or climax, is often sniffed or huffed to get high.

Inhalants may be sniffed directly from an open container or huffed from a rag soaked in the substance and held to the face. Alternatively, the open container or soaked rag can be placed in a bag, where the vapors can concentrate before being inhaled. Some chemicals are painted on the hands or fingernails or placed on shirt sleeves or wristbands to enable an abuser to continually inhale the fumes without being detected by a teacher or other adult. Although inhalant abusers may prefer one particular substance because of its taste or odor, a variety of substances may be used because of similar effects, availability, and cost. Once the substance is inhaled, the extensive capillary surface of the lungs allows rapid absorption of the substance, and blood levels peak rapidly. Entry into the brain is fast, and the intoxicating effects are short-lived but intense.

Inhalants depress the central nervous system, producing decreased respiration and blood pressure. Users report distortion in perceptions of time and space. Many users experience headaches, nausea, slurred speech, and loss of motor coordination. Mental effects may include fear, anxiety, or depression. A rash around the nose and mouth may be seen, and the abuser may start wheezing. An odor of paint or organic solvents on clothes, skin, and breath is sometimes a sign of inhalant abuse. Other indicators of inhalant abuse include slurred speech or staggering gait; red, glassy, watery eyes; and excitability or unpredictable behavior.

The chronic use of inhalants has been associated with a number of serious health problems. Sniffing glue and paint thinner causes kidney abnormalities; sniffing the solvents toluene and trichloroethylene causes liver damage. Memory impairment, attention deficits, and diminished nonverbal intelligence have been related to the abuse of inhalants. Deaths resulting from heart failure, asphyxiation, or aspiration have occurred.

Diet Drugs

In 1990, an appetite-suppressant drug known as *fen-phen* (a combination of *fenfluramine* and *phentermine*) was hailed as the answer to many dieters' prayers. The drug was used widely and thought by many to be a valuable aid in weight control. But by the summer of 1997, a Mayo Clinic report surfaced on the potential dangers of fen-phen. The report identified 24 women who took a combination of fenfluramine and phentermine for an average of one year to lose weight and subsequently developed heart valve problems. Shortly after the release of the Mayo Clinic report, the Food and Drug Administration (FDA) reported nine more women who developed the same problems while taking these medications.

In an urgent step, the FDA sent thousands of letters to doctors asking them to examine their fen-phen patients for possible heart valve damage and report any cases to the agency. The urgency was legitimate, for during 1996 alone, physicians wrote more than 20 million prescriptions for fenfluramine and phentermine, which are designed to curb appetite by affecting the serotonin levels in the brain and making patients feel full.

Although obesity is associated with more than 300,000 deaths a year, the majority of those deaths are linked to heart problems (Hellmich, 1997). In September 1997, Florida was the first state to ban the sale of fen-phen and a similar drug, Redux, ordering physicians not to prescribe them. The drugs were later completely banned for medical use in the United States.

In the aftermath of the ban on fen-phen and Redux, new substitute products began to emerge. St. John's wort (hypericum), an herb used for years by German doctors, emerged in late 1997 as a weight-loss supplement. Also used for the treatment of clinical depression, it began appearing on the shelves of health-food stores almost immediately after the other two diet drugs were removed. The herbs are newly lined with herbal Phen Fuel, Diet Phen, and other St. John's wort blends designed to sound like the unavailable fen-phen. St. John's wort's negative effects are minimal and include dizziness, confusion, tiredness and sedation. St. John's wort, native to Europe, North Africa, Asia, and the western United States, has a 2,400-year history in folk medicine and is said to have been prescribed by Hippocrates.

SUMMARY

Perhaps one reason for drug abuse is a misunderstanding about the effects of drugs and their general pharmacology. Frequently, drug users listen to other drug users about the effects of a particular drug; such information is often incorrect. Drugs can be virtually anything that alters the user's physical or psychological makeup; they can be either legal or illegal to possess. Therefore, the word *drug* could rightfully refer to such compounds as heroin, LSD, and marijuana along with sugar, salt, and caffeine.

All drugs, whether or not they are controlled, fall into one of seven categories: stimulants, depressants, hallucinogens, narcotics, cannabis, steroids, and inhalants. Drugs in the stimulant category literally stimulate the central nervous system and make the user feel more alert. The most commonly abused illicit drugs in this category are cocaine (including crack), amphetamines, and methamphetamine. The depressant category represents drugs that have a different effect on the user. Although early stages of ingestion of depressants may create a feeling of exhilaration for the user, these drugs actually depress the central nervous system. Alcohol is a lawfully obtainable depressant, whereas depressants such as barbiturates and sedative hypnotics are usually physically addicting and pose great physical dangers to the drug abuser.

Hallucinogens are a unique category of drug; they are not physically addicting and their use is not as common as other categories of drugs. Hallucinogens such as LSD, PCP, and MDMA (ecstasy) are considered dangerous drugs for other reasons. For example, users of LSD encounter the possibility of "bad trips" or "flashbacks" resulting from the use of the drug. PCP users frequently become completely detached from reality while experiencing violent hallucinations. Those who use PCP can injure themselves (even breaking bones) unwittingly because PCP also acts as an anesthetic.

The narcotic category refers to drugs such as heroin, morphine, opium, and other derivatives and synthetic substitutes, which are physically addicting and emulate the effects of opium. All drugs within this category are controlled, and possession of lawfully manufactured narcotics is permitted only pursuant to a lawful prescription.

Cannabis is discussed as an individual category of drug, but the Drug Enforcement Administration considers it to be a mild hallucinogen. Although cannabis had a legitimate use during the early history of the United States, it is either outlawed or regulated to one extent or another in the United States. Its beneficial use in medicine is still under study, and 14 states have passed laws related to its medical use.

The use of inhalants has become popular for many (especially adolescents) because they are both readily available and legal to possess. Breathing the fumes of such household products as glue, paint, and gasoline, however, may pose more risk of physiological damage to the user's brain than other dangerous substances encountered on the street.

Do you recognize these terms?

- binge drinking
- blood-alcohol concentration
- delirium tremens
- dopamine
- drug abuse

- fetal alcohol syndrome
- physical dependence
- psychological dependence
- tolerance
- withdrawal

DISCUSSION QUESTIONS

1. Discuss the reasons that people use drugs.

2. Define the terms *psychological dependence* and *physiological dependence*.

3. Discuss the definition of the term *drug*.

4. List and discuss the different categories of drugs and give examples of each.

5. List and discuss some widely used synthetic narcotic drugs.

6. What are designer drugs, and how do they effect the drug user?

Chapter 4

The Illicit Drug Trade

This chapter will enable you to:

- Understand the various dynamics of the illegal drug business
- Comprehend the different facets of illicit drug marketing
- Understand the role of foreign drug source countries
- Discover the global magnitude of the world's drug problem

The criminal drug trade, by virtue of its illegal nature, is a covert enterprise in which people, business decisions, and transactions all occur outside the watchful eye of the public. Because of this secrecy, much misunderstanding exists about the inner workings of the illicit drug trade. For example, many questions exist regarding sellers, buyers, business decisions, business logistics, and organizational dynamics. Addressing these areas is the purpose of this chapter.

In 1927, bootlegger Al Capone told newspaper reporters that he was just a well-meaning businessman providing a public service that the government chose not to provide. Many of today's drug-trafficking entrepreneurs might also perceive themselves as businesspeople who are simply offering goods and services not legally available to the public. However, the realities of the drug trade are not as benevolent as this supposition suggests.

The truth is that the illicit drug business is a money-driven, calculated undertaking that gives little consideration to human anguish or social responsibility. Drug sellers and users alike demonstrate their disregard for law and order in their choice to participate and become involved with illegal drugs. In addition, compared to legitimate businesses espousing a "customer is always right" philosophy, the drug trade is anything but user-friendly. Allegiances are weak (or nonexistent) in virtually all levels of production, manufacturing,

125

DOI: 10.1016/B978-1-4377-4450-7.00004-7
© 2011 Elsevier Inc. All rights reserved.

transportation, and sales. Sellers typically lie about the quality and purity of drugs being sold; users distort information about the "benefits" of drugs to other potential users; arrested drug offenders regularly turn in long-time associates instead of going to prison; drug prices are inconsistent and unstable; and players in the drug trade are often suspicious about their associate's relationships with rival organizations or are paranoid about the presence of undercover agents in their operations. Indeed, trust—or the lack of it—is the hallmark of the illegal drug trade. To understand public policy approaches to the illicit drug problem, these premises must be understood.

Despite the many negative aspects of the drug business, the organizational dynamics of the illicit drug trade parallel those of legitimate industry in many ways, which helps to explain why this business has endured in the United States, in one form or another, for more than a century. Considerations such as personnel management, manufacturing costs, market acquisition, wholesale and retail sales, corporate security, and overhead are included in today's illicit cocaine, heroin, and marijuana businesses. Furthermore, these commercial aspects are found in both international and domestic trafficking organizations. An understanding of how these dynamics operate and interface is crucial in the formation of national drug policy as well as the development of criminal and constitutional law dealing with areas of drug control.

ILLICIT DRUG TRAFFICKING IN THE TWENTY-FIRST CENTURY

Most of the cocaine, heroin, and MDMA (ecstasy) and much of the methamphetamine consumed in the United States is smuggled into the United States by international criminal organizations from source countries in Latin America, Asia, and (for MDMA) Europe. Cocaine consumption in the United States, the world's most important and largest market, has declined somewhat since its peak in the late 1980s but has remained relatively stable for most of the past decade. Cocaine is produced in the South American Andean countries of Colombia, Peru, and Bolivia; Colombia is the source of an estimated 90 percent of the cocaine supply in the U.S. market (U.S. Department of State, 2000; United Nations, 2000).

Fueled by high-purity, low-cost heroin introduced into the U.S. market by Southeast Asian and Colombian traffickers, heroin use in the United States increased significantly in the early to mid-1990s and has leveled off in recent years. The purity of heroin currently available in the United States is higher than ever. Southwest Asia's "Golden Crescent" (Afghanistan, Iran, and Pakistan) and Southeast Asia's "Golden Triangle" (Myanmar, Laos, and Thailand) are the world's major sources of heroin for the international market, but Colombia is the largest source of supply for the U.S. heroin market (Mexico is the second largest). Colombia and Mexico account for about 75 percent of the U.S. heroin market, with heroin from Southeast Asia making up most of the remainder.

The use of synthetic drugs in the United States, many of which come from abroad, has increased over the past few decades. Beginning in the 1990s, there has been a dramatic surge in the worldwide production and consumption of synthetic drugs—particularly amphetamine-type stimulants, including meth-amphetamine and ecstasy. The majority of methamphetamine available in the U.S. market is produced by Mexican traffickers operating in the United States or in Mexico; the U.S. Drug Enforcement Administration (DEA) estimates that Mexican trafficking groups control 70 percent to 90 percent of the U.S. meth-amphetamine supply. There has been a significant increase in methamphet-amine production in Southeast Asia in recent years. Although little has found its way to the U.S. market from Southeast Asia, increasing quantities of "Thai tabs" have been seized in the western United States.

Most of the ecstasy in the U.S. market is produced in the Netherlands. Amsterdam, Brussels, Frankfurt, and Paris are major European hubs for trans-shipping ecstasy to foreign markets, including the United States. U.S. law enforcement reporting indicates that the Dominican Republic, Suriname, and Curaçao are used as transshipment points for U.S.-bound ecstasy from Europe and that Mexican and South American traffickers are becoming involved in the ecstasy trade.

Marijuana remains the most widely used and readily available illicit drug in the United States. Most of the marijuana consumed in the United States is from domestic sources, including both outdoor and indoor cannabis cultivation in every state, but a significant share of the U.S. market is met by marijuana grown in Mexico, with lesser amounts coming from Jamaica, Colombia, and Canada. Very little of the cannabis grown in other major producing countries—including Morocco, Lebanon, Afghanistan, Thailand, and Cambodia—comes to the United States.

International drug-trafficking organizations have extensive networks of suppliers as well as front companies and businesses to facilitate narcotics smug-gling and laundering of illicit proceeds. Colombian and Mexican trafficking organizations dominate the drug trade in the Western Hemisphere. Colombia supplies most of the cocaine and contributes the largest share of heroin to the U.S. market, and Mexico is the major avenue for cocaine trafficking into the United States as well as a major supplier of heroin, marijuana, and metham-phetamine. In the Asian source regions, heroin production is dominated by large trafficking organizations, but the trafficking networks smuggling heroin from Asia are more diffuse. Asian heroin shipments typically change hands among criminal organizations as the drug is smuggled to markets in the United States and elsewhere.

The evolution of the international drug trade in the past decade has included greater involvement by a growing number of players and more worldwide traf-ficking of synthetic drugs. Criminal organizations whose principal activities focus more on traditional contraband smuggling, racketeering enterprises, and fraud schemes have become increasingly involved in international drug trafficking. Although they generally are not narcotics producers themselves, many organized crime groups—including those from Russia, China, Italy, and Albania—have cultivated and expanded ties to drug-trafficking organizations to obtain cocaine, heroin, and synthetic drugs for their own distribution markets and trafficking networks. Traffickers from many countries are increasingly eschewing traditional preferences for criminal partnerships with single ethnic groups and collaborating in the purchase, transportation, and distribution of illegal drugs.

Taking advantage of more open borders and modern telecommunications technology, international drug-trafficking organizations are sophisticated and flexible in their operations. They adapt quickly to law enforcement pressures by finding new methods for smuggling drugs, new transshipment routes, and new mechanisms to launder money. In many of the major cocaine-and heroin-producing and transit countries, drug traffickers have acquired significant power and wealth through the use of violence, intimidation, and payoffs of corrupt officials.

The Economics of Drug Trafficking

With few exceptions, the drug trade attracts entrepreneurs who are motivated by profit. As with any business, illicit or not, certain principles apply to the successful operation of the trafficking system. For example, drug traffickers in retail markets typically use a "just in time" business strategy. That is, in many cases only small amounts of drugs are supplied to street vendors, which minimizes their losses should the vendor be arrested by police or robbed by competitors. In many cities, the "just in time" strategy makes it possible for sellers to provide just enough drug product for street vendors to sell in one day's time or for crack house operators to sell in about a week's time. Suppliers are aware that in addition to the type of drug seized, in some states the quantity of drugs seized plays a role in the severity of the criminal charge. So, if a vendor is in possession of small amounts when arrested, not only will he or she possibly be looking at a lesser charge, but the supplier's credit standing with their wholesaler will not be jeopardized for future sales. Any such losses can easily be compensated for with future sales. With the drug trade being profit-driven, both wholesale and retail pricing play an important role in realizing earnings.

Drug Prices

With profit being the mainstay of the drug business, a number of variables can be attributed to the establishment, rise, and decline of drug prices. In addition to other factors, the laws of supply and demand play a major role in determining whether a certain drug's price increases, falls, or remains stable. For example, drug dealers are keenly aware that police investigations result in the arrest and imprisonment of people associated with the drug trade. To insulate themselves from police detection, trafficking managers hire lower-level dealers to bear the risks of dealing on the street level. These sellers are often street-corner minions trading in small quantities of drugs, but they may also be couriers who have been entrusted with a greater amount of responsibility for transporting drug shipments. Occasionally, dealers are arrested and their stashes of drugs seized by police. In addition to seizure by police, some drug shipments are:

- Stolen by rival criminal organizations
- Thrown overboard vessels to avoid confiscation
- Not picked up because of a fear of police surveillance
- Flushed down toilets for fear of seizure by police
- Abandoned after dealers are arrested by police

All these circumstances result in the drug supply not arriving at the designated point of delivery. Consequently, subsequent shipments of the same drug might be affected by an increase in the street price. This brings up another important business variable that parallels legitimate commerce: Wholesale prices are much cheaper than retail prices. When cocaine, for example, is produced in South America, its wholesale price is often based on the amount that is purchased; the larger the purchase, the lower the price. After the drugs arrive in the United States for distribution, prices rise considerably. This occurs not only because of the cost of production and transportation of the drugs but also because of the risks undertaken by dealers and distributors. Here is a hypothetical example: Assume that 10 kilograms of opium from Mexico is valued at $40,000. Once this opium was transformed into heroin of 40 percent to 70 percent purity, it sold for anywhere from $150,000 to $260,000 per kilogram in the United States at the wholesale level. Once the drugs reached the midlevel stage of distribution, heroin at 20 percent to 70 percent purity could be sold for roughly $500,000 per kilogram. According to DEA Heroin Signature Program (HSP) data, the wholesale purity of Mexican heroin was 40 percent in 2008 (National Drug Intelligence Center, 2010).

Black tar heroin of 20 percent to 60 percent purity can sell for $850,000 per kilogram. In sum, the street price of this heroin is between 153 and 183 times the price it was at the time it was cultivated. Further complicating the price structure is the fact that the prices of drugs also depend on the country of origin or other geographical factors. This is evident when we consider that in 1990 the price of a gram of cocaine varied from $35 in Miami to $125 in Los Angeles.

It is common for different grades of drugs to dictate the street price of that drug. For example, in the marijuana business, wholesale and retail prices of both commercial and sinsemilla grades were lowest in Houston. This is because the drugs were transported through Mexico to Houston; thus the distribution chain was shorter than if the drugs were transported to Omaha or Boston.

The price of a drug may also affect how drug buyers conduct business. For example, higher prices for a drug may result in the potential buyer choosing not to purchase the drug until prices come down or until another dealer is located who is selling the drug for a cheaper price. Accordingly, the buyer may choose to cut back on the use of the drug because of the high price tag. Finally, buyers may opt to substitute a less expensive drug with similar effects for the expensive drug. In any case, it is clear that the more expensive a drug, the less likely it will sell as readily on the street. Knowledge of these business dynamics is the reason that drug control efforts by police often attempt to raise the prices of drugs, thus making them too expensive for users to afford. In addition, high drug prices are also thought to deter would-be users from beginning the use of that particular drug.

Figure 4.1

- Distances the drugs travel

- Number of rungs on the distribution ladder before reaching retail levels

- Shortages of drug supplies due to wholesale and retail losses

- Changes in pricing at the export/import and subsequent levels

- Buyer preferences for drugs from a particular nation and of certain varieties or grades of drugs

---

Why Prices of Illicit Drugs Vary

Demand Elasticity

Demand elasticity refers to the relationship between the change in the use of an item and the price of that item. In legitimate business, if the price of a commodity rises, the total purchases of that commodity decrease. So too in the illicit drug trade: The amount that the total use of a drug decreases (due to high prices) depends on how sensitive the demand is to that rise in price. A close examination of retail drug prices tells us that demand elasticity hinges on the type of drug in question. For example, price elasticity is greater for heroin than it is for marijuana because heroin is a physically addictive drug, whereas marijuana is not. Therefore, drug users are more willing to pay more for a drug they "need" than for a drug they may simply desire.

Financing Drug Deals

In the world of legitimate commerce, businesses are much less concerned with hiding profits than are their illegal business counterparts. For this reason, it is not uncommon for businesses to borrow millions of dollars of capital from legitimate banking institutions. Once profits are realized, regular deposits can be made into banks or other financial institutions for disbursement or reinvestment. As one might guess, the rules of the game are quite different for business transactions in the illicit drug trade. Instead of borrowing money from a bank or other lending institution, drug dealers will often have a "revolving credit" arrangement with their suppliers, whereby payment for the drugs is not required until they have been sold. In such cases, payments are not made until the dealers take delivery on a subsequent drug shipment. In time, as the dealer's financial base grows, shell or front corporations are sometimes established that help disguise or "launder" drug profits.

The hiding of drug revenues is an essential component of the illicit drug trade, since profits are earned without paying taxes on those earnings. In legitimate business operations, businesses pay taxes on their profits in proportion to the amount of money changing hands. As a result, a large part of the profit realized by drug dealers is money that would otherwise be paid to the government. Chapter 6 addresses the issue of money laundering.

MERCHANDISING AND DISTRIBUTION OF ILLEGAL DRUGS

The illicit drug-trafficking chain refers to large shipments of drugs that are transported from their point of origin to their destination, where they arc broken down into much smaller quantities for street-level distribution. With each stage in the distribution cycle, the price of the drug increases. Accordingly, as the shipment of drugs gets closer to the street, along with an increase in price of the drug, the purity of the drug decreases. The distribution chain refers to the players along the trafficking route. For example, in a cocaine-trafficking operation, the first level of players consists of the coca farmers, who cultivate the coca plant and sell by the bushel to traffickers, who then hire people to process the leaves into coca paste. Once the coca paste has been produced, it is sold to midlevel producers, who dry the paste on drying tables, where it becomes cocaine hydrochloride or powder. Next, smugglers are hired to transport the cocaine to the United States to be delivered to wholesalers, who in turn sell quantities to retail salespeople. Finally, the retail salesperson sells small quantities to low-level street dealers, who bear more of the risk of arrest than any other player in the distribution chain.

At the retail level, the buying and selling of drugs often entails a complex exchange of schemes and roles. For instance, some people who are not necessarily involved in the actual sale of drugs may be used as *steerers*, who locate potential customers for dealers. Others may act as guards or lookouts, charged with locating police vehicles spotted in the area of drug sales. In other cases, one player is assigned to sell the drugs while a different person takes the money from the sale. This structure represents the classic division of labor in the drug trade and illustrates how operatives can insulate themselves from detection because it may be more difficult for police investigators to observe transactions.

Marketing Illicit Drugs

It is common in the drug business for dealers to attempt to convince potential buyers of the purity or quality of their product. Typically, this is done by offering a specific drug with an identifiable label; for instance, Panama Red or Colombian Gold marijuana. In other cases, the seller asks the buyer to trust his or her reputation as an honest local drug dealer. In still other cases, drugs are sold based on the quantity offered. For instance, if a high price is being asked for a gram of cocaine, the seller may remind the buyer that there is actually a gram and a quarter available for the price of a single gram, giving the buyer the impression that he or she is getting more than his or her money's worth.

Marketing is also apparent in the packaging of certain drugs. In Columbia, Missouri, for example, blotter acid (LSD) appeared on the street in the form of Grateful Dead album covers. Virtually every album cover image ever produced by this rock group was available to buyers in blotter acid form. For the potential buyer to purchase the entire album cover image, however, he or she had to purchase 12 individual dosage units of the drug, since the picture of the album was spread out over all 12 squares of paper, each containing LSD. Heroin dealers also use marketing techniques to persuade buyers to purchase their heroin over that of another dealer. Techniques include marking bags with colored tape, symbols, or pictures or assigning a particular batch or dealer's heroin a brand name like Red Lion heroin. Brand names help users identify the heroin thought to be of a high quality. Interestingly, if an addict dies as a result of a drug overdose, other addicts will often seek out the specific drug used by the deceased, believing that the user failed to realize it was of such a high quality.

As drug enforcement efforts become more successful and effective and as different drugs become increasingly popular, drug dealers often shift their marketing strategies. These changes in drugs and drug use may result in the development of new drugs or analogues or the reemergence of older drugs that have not been popular for a while. In any event, it is always the drug dealer's desire to increase the potency of the drug he or she sells. Once this can be accomplished, word will spread among drug buyers, who will seek out the new, more potent drug.

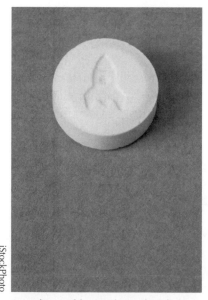

iStockPhoto

A rocket emblazoned on the designer drug ecstasy. Manufacturers and exporters of illegal drugs use identifiable labels and "brand names" to convince the buying public of the quality of their products.

Distributing Illegal Drugs

Drug sales networks differ somewhat from one case to the next. For example, trafficking not only differs from rural to urban areas but also depends on the type of drug and the techniques of the group distributing it. Most large urban areas have sections of town that are known as drug distribution areas. These areas, sometimes called *copping areas,* are typically well known to drug users. Often these areas are nothing more than street corners or public parks where small amounts of drugs are sold. Here it is common for many different drug sales to take place in a short period of time. Buyers go to the copping area, pay cash for the drugs, and leave—all in a matter of seconds. Investigations have shown that dealers operating in copping areas often sell to known customers and strangers alike. As a rule, dealers in copping areas will employ lookouts and steerers, who watch for both police and potential customers. Once dealers are tipped off about the presence of police in the area, they can dispose of their drugs before being caught in possession of them.

Neighborhood bars, truck stops, or homes in affluent areas of town are sometimes fixed locations for drug dealing. Studies into the habits of dealers and users have revealed that middle-class buyers will often make their purchases away from the typical urban copping area to avoid getting arrested. In some cases, drug deals are arranged by telephone and a drop-off location is chosen. Crack houses are yet another example of a fixed location for drug dealing. Such locations emerged during the mid-1980s and are often abandoned buildings or apartments in public housing projects located near copping areas. In the crack house are the necessary paraphernalia for taking cocaine. This equipment includes needles and syringes for injecting as well as pipes and heat sources for smoking crack. The Detroit Police Department identified two types of crack houses: (1) a "buy-and-get-high party" house, where drugs are consumed on the premises in conjunction with illicit sex acts, and (2) a "hole in the wall" house, where buyers would literally put cash into a hole in the wall at the front door of a house and receive crack cocaine from an unidentified seller on the other side.

Profit Margin

Although it is true that wholesale and midlevel drug dealers make hundreds of thousands of dollars and escape detection, people operating on the lower rung of the trafficking chain, especially those who are considered heavy drug users, accumulate few riches. The Bureau of Justice Statistics (1992) cited several reasons for this:

- Their profits often support their own drug use.
- The drug business is a fragile enterprise subject to considerable disruption by police efforts, frequent absence of a reliable supply of drugs, and a high potential for loss by predatory competitors and disloyal employees.
- Their involvement in drug sales is often sporadic.

Figure 4.2
Source: Bureau of Justice Statistics (1992). *Drugs, Crime, and the Justice System.* Washington, DC: U.S. Department of Justice.

Approximate role equivalents in legal markets	Roles by common names at various stages of the drug distribution business	Major functions accomplished at this level
Grower/producer	Coca farmer, opium farmer, marijuana grower	Grow cocoa, opium, marijuana; the raw materials
Manufacturer	Collector, transporter, elaborator, chemist, drug lord	All stages for preparation of heroin, cocaine, marijuana as commonly sold
Traffickers		
Importer	Multikilo importer, mule, airplane pilot, smuggler, trafficker, money launderer	Smuggling of large quantities of substances into the United States
Wholesale distributor	Major distributor, investor, "kilo connection"	Transportation and redistribution of multikilograms and single kilograms
Dealers		
Regional distributor	"Pound-and-ounce man," weight dealer	Adulteration and sale of moderately expensive products
Retail store owner	House connections, suppliers, crack-house supplier	Adulteration and production of retail level dosage units (bags, vials, grams) in very large numbers
Assistant manager, security chief, or accountant	"Lieutenant," "muscle man," transporter, crew boss, crack-house manager/proprietor	Supervises three or more sellers enforces informal contracts, collects money, distributes multiple dosage units to actual sellers
Sellers		
Store clerk, sales representative (door-to-door and phone)	Street drug seller, runner, juggler	Makes actual direct sales to consumer; private seller responsible for both money and drugs
Low-level distributors		
Advertiser, security guard, leaflet distributor	Steerer, tout, cop man, look-out holder, runner, help friend, guard, go-between	Assists in making sales, advertises, protects seller from police and criminals, solicits customers, handles drugs or money but not both
Servant, temporary employee	Runner of shooting gallery, injector (of drugs), freebaser, taster, apartment cleaner, drug bagger, fence, money launderer	Provides short-term services to drug users or sellers for money or drugs, not responsible for money or drugs

How Do the Roles and Functions at Various Levels of the Drug Distribution Business Compare with Those in Legitimate Industry?

- Earnings tend to be spent ostentatiously for expensive cars, gold jewelry, and other consumer goods.
- Many dealers spend a substantial amount of their time in jail or prison.

The mystique of drug dealing is shadowed by an illusion that all drug dealers make a lot of money. Unquestionably, this is not always the case.

Experts have also suggested that one reason for the small amount of money earned by low-level drug dealers is that they often deal drugs on a part-time basis. In fact, a study by the RAND Corporation concluded that the typical drug dealer netted between $25 and $2,500 per month from sales. Interviews during the study showed that 75 percent of these dealers held jobs in addition to drug dealing, and that drug dealing only supplemented their income. The study also revealed that most small-time drug dealers were heavy drug users as well as sellers and spent an average of 25 percent of their earnings on drugs. In the case of marijuana dealers, profits were shown to be considerably smaller than for other types of drugs, and dealings were much more casual and sporadic than transactions involving other, "harder" drugs (Reuter, MacCoun, and Murphy, 1990).

The enormous profits to be realized in the U.S. drug market have intrigued both domestic and foreign traffickers. Although many drugs, such as methamphetamine, LSD, and phencyclidine (PCP), are largely produced domestically and a rapidly increasing proportion of the marijuana consumed in the United States is grown domestically, foreign traffickers supply an estimated 75 percent of illicit substances consumed in the United States (DEA, 1996). Cocaine is a primary example of a drug imported by foreign drug networks. The United States' cocaine supply originates almost exclusively in South America; the coca plant is cultivated principally in Peru, Bolivia, Colombia, and Ecuador. Accordingly, processing laboratories have been seized in Colombia, Brazil, and Venezuela. Other South American and Caribbean countries have also served as transshipment centers for drugs.

Other drugs frequently smuggled into the United States from foreign countries are marijuana and hashish, both products of the hemp or cannabis plant. Mexico supplies an estimated 30 percent of cannabis to the United States; Colombia supplies an estimated 33 percent, although (as indicated previously) these percentages have been consistently declining due to increases in domestic production in the United States. Other foreign countries contributing to the U.S. marijuana market are Jamaica in the Caribbean and Belize in Central America.

THE INTERNATIONAL PERSPECTIVE

Drug trafficking is a generic term referring to the commercial exchange of illegal drugs, including the equipment and substances involved in producing, manufacturing, and using illicit drugs. Prohibition has been established by governments to enforce, deter, and eradicate the exchange of such illegal goods.

Despite vigorous enforcement efforts, the United Nations estimates that only 10–15 percent of heroin and 30 percent of cocaine is intercepted worldwide. It is estimated that at least 70 percent of international drug shipments need to be intercepted to substantially reduce the industry (Drug Policy Alliance,

2007). The drug market continues to produce the same, or even higher, quantities of illicit drugs in spite of record seizures by law enforcement. Developed efforts of drug control authorities in some countries have merely moved drug-trafficking operations to weaker jurisdictions and forced greater organizational sophistication. Economists call this the *balloon effect* because these efforts are like squeezing a filled balloon: When the air is squeezed out of one part, it is simply transferred to another.

This balloon effect is commonly seen in South and Central Asia and Latin America, where the majority of illicit drugs is produced and trafficked and where international interdiction efforts are focused. Drug trafficking continues to expand, with networks including cross-border cooperation and international connections. This growth and increased organization result not only from an expanding consumer market but from poverty. The war against drugs increases the cost of drugs, making drug production and sales more profitable and therefore more attractive—particularly to those living in poverty. Drug trafficking across the world exists as a $400 billion trade; drug traffickers earn gross profit margins of approximately 300 percent.

Mexico

Police in the United States have worked with Mexican authorities for decades to address the drug problem. In 2006, for example, Mexico extradited 63 criminals to the United States. Twenty-seven of these cases involved narcotics traffickers, including a member of the Tijuana-based Arellano-Félix organization. The eradication of illicit crops is still a priority for the Mexican Army, which eradicated nearly 30,000 hectares of marijuana in 2006. Mexican authorities also seize significant amounts of drugs as they flow into Mexico and toward the United States. Mexican President Felipe Calderón has vowed to pursue the strong counterdrug commitment he inherited from his predecessor, former President Vicente Fox.

Although Mexican criminal syndicates have been involved in drug trafficking for decades, primarily dealing in marijuana and heroin, only relatively recently have they made an important appearance in the cocaine market—first as surrogates for, and then as partners of, Colombian drug syndicates. Mexico's 2,000-mile border shared with the United States, much of which is in isolated rural areas with rugged terrain, makes it an obvious transshipment site for drugs. Moreover, its extensive coastal and inland mountain systems create perfect havens for growing marijuana and opium poppies (Eskridge, 1998; Macko, 1997; Schaffer, 1996).

Early Mexican drug-trafficking groups were primarily transshipment agents for larger drug organizations. In the 1980s, the Mexican drug organizations provided cross-border smuggling services, charging between $1,000 and $2,000 a kilogram for cocaine. Once the cocaine was safely inside the United States it would once again be turned over to Colombian traffickers for wholesale distribution.

By the end of the 1980s, Mexican drug traffickers were demanding increasingly greater remuneration for moving Colombian drugs. Now the Mexican drug syndicates wanted payment-in-kind, a share of the cocaine being transported (up to 50 percent of the load) for their smuggling services. This new arrangement offered Mexican drug syndicates an opportunity to get into the wholesale cocaine-trafficking business themselves, thereby vastly increasing their profits. Eventually this arrangement with the Colombians not only resulted in dividing the cocaine shipments down the middle but in dividing much of the U.S. market down the middle. As the arrangement evolved over time, the Colombians retained the wholesale market in the eastern United States as their own, and Mexican drug cartels took over the wholesale market in the midwestern and western states. By 1995 the Mexican syndicates had established themselves as major cocaine traffickers in their own right. Today that arrangement continues to evolve. Dominican traffickers have challenged Colombian hegemony in the east, particularly in New York and New Jersey, and Mexican syndicates have begun establishing cocaine trafficking operations in New York as well.

The structure and operations of Mexican drug syndicates are compartmentalized but exhibit a stronger chain of command from their Mexican bases than other drug syndicates. Mexican drug cartels have representatives or surrogates located throughout the United States who are responsible for managing the day-to-day activities of the syndicate. However, unlike many other drug syndicates that have insulated their home country operations by granting greater autonomy to cells operating in foreign countries, the Mexican syndicates still retain a system whereby Mexican-based syndicate leaders provide specific instructions to their foreign-based syndicates on such issues as warehousing drugs, whom to use for transportation services, and how to launder drug money. Despite the use of encrypted faxes, computers, pagers, and cellular telephones, this arrangement still leaves a longer trail of communications evidence for law enforcement to follow and is considerably more risky than allowing foreign-based cells to operate with autonomy.

About two-thirds of the cocaine sold in the United States is transshipped over the Mexican border. Typically, large loads of cocaine come into Mexico from Colombia by air or boat. The cocaine is transported across land, usually in trucks, to a number of repository cities such as Juárez or Guadalajara. From these warehousing sites cocaine loads are usually driven across the U.S. border to repository sites in the United States, most commonly in Los Angeles, Chicago, and Phoenix. Mexican trafficking syndicate representatives in those cities have contractual arrangements, usually with otherwise legitimate trucking companies, to move the cocaine across the country to smaller warehousing facilities closer to the point of sale. Individuals working in these "stash houses" guard the supplies and make arrangement for their distribution by cocaine wholesalers.

The size of Mexican cocaine operations is illustrated by a DEA investigation aimed at the U.S. operations of the Amado Carrillo-Fuentes organization, which resulted in the seizure of 11.5 metric tons of cocaine, more than $18 million in U.S. currency, almost 14,000 pounds of marijuana, and the arrest of 101 defendants. This particular investigation also illustrated the point made earlier that upper-echelon communications to local operatives in the drug market can be quite hazardous. It was through the interception and decoding of these communications that these arrests were made.

In addition to their expanded role in cocaine trafficking, Mexican drug syndicates continue to play a large role in the U.S. methamphetamine market. Mexican drug syndicates are now engaged in the large-scale production of methamphetamine. The meth market was revitalized as consumers shifted in the drug markets of the 1990s. The traditional control of the methamphetamine market by outlaw motorcycle gangs was broken by Mexican drug organizations operating in both Mexico and California.

Methamphetamine has a huge advantage over cocaine, heroin, and marijuana as a drug to be trafficked. Unlike the others, it is not dependent at all on agricultural production. Methamphetamine is manufactured directly from *precursor chemicals*, and those chemicals are easily available to Mexican syndicates from chemical companies in India, China, and the United States. Mexican drug syndicates operate clandestine laboratories in Mexico and California that are capable of producing hundreds of pounds of the drug. From the labs, the meth is moved to traffickers across the United States for sale.

From the 1930s onward—and certainly from the late 1940s and early 1950s when gangster Mickey Cohen struck a deal with the Los Angeles Police Department (LAPD) to allow him to traffic in Mexican heroin—the cultivation and refining of opium poppies has been an important source for the U.S. heroin market. Today about 29 percent of the heroin on the U.S. market comes from Mexico. Mexican drug syndicates produce about six metric tons of heroin a year for resale in the United States. Because of crude refining methods used in manufacturing the heroin, Mexican heroin is frequently dark in color ("black") and sticky or gummy (like "tar"), resulting in its name of "black tar" heroin. Black tar heroin is widely distributed through the southwestern, northwestern, and midwestern regions of the United States.

Mexico is the largest source of imported marijuana to the United States. At one time,

CON PESO APROX. DE 42.240 KGS. 2 VEHICULOS

AP Photo/Guillermo Arias

In this May 19, 2010, file photo, Mexican soldiers stand with Valentin Jaimes, center, in front of seized packs containing heroin during a presentation to the media in Tijuana, Mexico. According to the army, Jaimes was arrested with some 42 kg (more than 92 lbs) of heroin.

from 1930 through the 1960s, Mexico supplied as much as 95 percent of the marijuana consumed in the United States. Domestic U.S. production had cut that figure at least in half as of the 1990s, but Mexico retains its position as the largest foreign source for marijuana. That importing dominance was enhanced by the withdrawal of Colombian syndicates from the marijuana market in the 1970s. The Colombians simply decided that marijuana was too bulky a commodity to be safely transported. In addition, the profit margin for cocaine vastly exceeds that of marijuana. Mexican drug syndicates have begun to cultivate their marijuana in the United States. For example, in 1997, a group of people from Zacatecas, Mexico, were arrested in Idaho for cultivating 100,000 marijuana plants, weighing almost 20 tons.

Like most criminal organizations in the early stages of establishing their control of a market share in prohibited substances, Mexican syndicates cling to the excessive use of violence as a means of control. Like their centralized chain of command, this makes them particularly vulnerable, at least for the moment, to law enforcement intervention.

Mexican drug-trafficking organizations are still very much in the developmental stages. Their insistence on the heavy use of violence and centralized control from headquarters in Mexico makes them more vulnerable than other drug organizations. But as with the Colombian cartels, we can expect that these organizations will learn with time and restructure their operations accordingly. Today a variety of Mexican organizations, operating from many major cities in Mexico, dominate the Mexican drug trade.

The Arellano-Félix organization (AFO) was one of the most aggressive of the Mexican trafficking groups. They moved multiton quantities of cocaine and marijuana and smaller, but still significant, amounts of heroin and methamphetamine. Benjamin Arellano-Félix was the head of this syndicate, which operated in Tijuana, Baja California, and parts of the Mexican states of Sinaloa, Sonora, Jalisco, and Tamaulipas. Syndicate activities were coordinated through his brothers. Benjamin Arellano-Félix was captured in 2002, just weeks after his brother, Ramón Arellano-Félix, was killed in a gunfight. The other brothers were captured subsequently. It has been said that the cartel is still operational under the leadership of the Félix brothers' nephew, Luis Fernando Sánchez Arellano, dubbed El Alineado (The Aligner).

The Caro-Quintero syndicate is based in Sonora, Mexico, and specializes in trafficking cocaine and marijuana. The syndicate was founded by Rafael Caro-Quintero, who has been incarcerated in Mexico since 1985 for his involvement in the murder of DEA Special Agent Enrique Camarena.

The Juárez cartel was headed by Amado Carrillo-Fuentes until his July 4, 1997, death during surgery in Mexico City. The Juárez cartel is still heavily involved in the trafficking of cocaine, heroin, and marijuana. Following Amado's death, a power struggle broke out that resulted in 60 murders in the Juárez area between August 1997 and September 1998. Apparently, that outbreak of violence was resolved with Vicente Carrillo-Fuentes, Amado's brother, taking control of the organization. The Juárez cartel was featured battling a rival cartel in the 2000 motion picture *Traffic*. Since 2007, the Juárez cartel has been locked in a vicious battle with its former partner, the Sinaloa cartel, for control of Juárez. The fighting between them has left thousands dead in Chihuahua state.

The Amezcua-Contreras organization, also known as the Colima cartel, is based in Guadalajara and was directed by José de Jesús Amezcua Contreras and supported by his brothers, Adán and Luis. It is a massive methamphetamine-trafficking syndicate and a major supplier of precursor chemicals to other methamphetamine syndicates. This syndicate controls much of the legitimate trade in chemicals in Mexico as well. In October 2008, the U.S. Department of Treasury said that the organization has two leaders who are still at large: Patricia Amezcua (sister of Adán, Jesus, and Luis), who is responsible for the overall operations, and Telesforo Baltazar Tirado Escamilla (U.S. Department of the Treasury, 2008).

Mexican Drug Smuggling

For years, marijuana and heroin were the mainstay of exported drugs from Mexico. Beginning in the early 1990s, law enforcement officials observed that Mexican traffickers were active in aiding Colombian traffickers in the transshipping of cocaine through Mexico to the United States. In fact, since 1995, several large-scale Mexican cocaine-trafficking organizations have been identified. One such organization, the Gulf cartel, was headed by 52-year-old Juan Garcia Abrego, a one-time Texas laborer who controlled one-third of the cocaine sold in the United States. In 1996, he was arrested and convicted by a federal jury in Houston on 22 trafficking counts. He was also forced to forfeit $350 million in illegal proceeds.

For the most part, Mexican traffickers utilize overland smuggling methods as the most prevalent mode of moving illicit drugs from the Mexican interior to the United States. States most directly affected by Mexican traffickers are Texas, California, Arizona, and New Mexico, which share the Mexican border with seven ports of entry. Observing the Mexican border, it is immediately evident that there is no wall, fence, or barricade separating most of Mexico from the United States. Moreover, U.S. Customs and Border Protection officers assigned to watch for illegal aliens and drug smugglers find themselves understaffed and lacking much of the necessary equipment and resources to do an effective job. The remoteness of much of the border area and the great distances to be covered make patrol an almost insurmountable responsibility. In fact, drug smugglers literally walk over the Mexican border to meet fellow traffickers on the U.S. side, often free of detection by border patrol agents. Ground smuggling techniques for marijuana and heroin have proved to be quite ingenious over the years. Such methods include drugs concealed in false gas tanks as well as inside the backs of car seats, dashboards, and spare tires.

The movement of drugs through general aviation aircraft accounts for considerable drug-smuggling activity from Mexico. Illegal shipments of marijuana and heroin are flown from Mexico during the late hours of the night and are unloaded at predetermined locations by confederates in the United States. According to the DEA, more than 2,000 clandestine airstrips have been identified in Mexico; these are grouped into 10 different clusters. The number of these strips indicates the enormity of the air smuggling problem and illustrates Mexico's tenacious capacity for illicit drug production. It has been estimated that one-third of the airstrips are located around opium poppy-growing regions; the remainder are used for marijuana smuggling. Almost any type of plane can utilize these airstrips, ranging from small single-engine aircraft, such as the Cessna 172 and 182, to larger transports. The proximity of the Yucatán Peninsula to the United States also makes an ideal transit point for drug-smuggling flights, particularly those originating in the Guajira region of Colombia.

Figure 4.3
Source: Map Resources. Adapted by CRS. (K.Yancey 8/17/06).

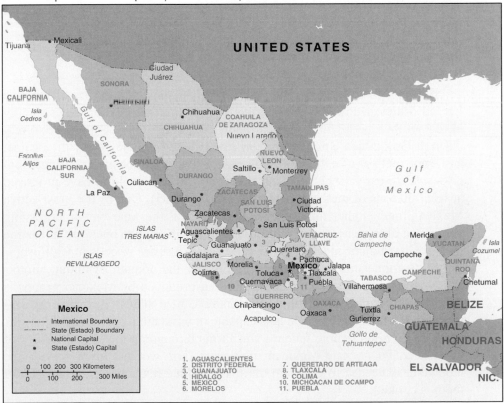

Because Mexico Shares a Border with the United States, the Criminal Cartels there are Able to Easily Deliver Illicit Goods to U.S. Markets

In a 1988 RAND Corporation study, project director Peter Reuter asserted that the Mexican government, unlike governments in Colombia, Bolivia, and Peru, does not incur any major political threats by cracking down on the drug trade. In fact, there is increasing willingness on the part of the Mexican government to do just that. This is due in part to the large numbers of Mexican police who have died in drug enforcement efforts. Indeed, it is likely that more Mexican than U.S. police have been killed while attempting to enforce U.S. drug policies.

Perhaps it is naïve to hope that Mexican officials could eliminate all transshipment efforts by Mexican traffickers, but a closer working relationship between the two countries is desirable. For example, as of the preparation of this text, there is no Mexican-U.S. provision for U.S. authorities to chase smugglers in "hot pursuit" across the border. Indeed, when U.S. chase planes approach the Mexican border, they are required under law to retreat.

Critical Thinking Task

Support or refute this statement: Interdiction officers of both nations should be allowed to cross the Mexican-U.S. border in pursuit of drug smugglers. Predict outcomes if the current policy is changed.

The Emergence of Mexican Meth

Because of the rising popularity of methamphetamine (meth) in the United States, many Mexican cartels have started trafficking it, especially in the southwestern United States. They realize that they do not have to rely on their Colombian counterparts for raw material, as they do with cocaine, and their meth is of extremely high purity. The statistics are sobering; from mid-1993 to early 1995, Mexican traffickers were thought to have produced at least 50 tons of methamphetamine (Eaton, 1995). One of the most active Mexican methamphetamine-trafficking groups is the Amezcua organization, composed of three brothers (Witkin, 1995). It is thought to operate clandestine labs in Guadalajara and Tijuana and to operate a series of cells in California.

Methamphetamine labs were traditionally the domain of outlaw motorcycle gangs, but the amount of meth being produced by Mexican groups is gaining considerable momentum. Within the United States, Mexican organizations are operating large-scale labs capable of producing 100 pounds at a time, many of them on remote ranches and farms throughout the inland valleys of California. Poorly paid Mexican immigrant farm workers often provide the labor that is needed to clean up the toxic residue remaining after a batch of meth is cooked.

One of the factors enabling the recent involvement of Mexican meth labs is the crucial ingredient *ephedrine*, a drug either extracted from the ephedra shrub or made synthetically for the treatment of asthma. In 1988, Congress imposed strict controls on ephedrine imports, which temporarily dried up the supply to U.S. labs, but by 1991 Mexican methamphetamine was appearing on U.S. streets. In one case in the mid-1990s, 3.4 metric tons of ephedrine traveling from Zurich to Mexico City was seized by customs agents at Dallas-Fort Worth Airport. It was then that the DEA learned that hundreds of tons of ephedrine were being shipped to Mexican front companies from India, China, and the Czech Republic. In the meantime, many traffickers have switched to *pseudoephedrine*, a similar drug that can be purchased as an over-the-counter decongestant.

Figure 4.4
Source: Drug Enforcement Administration, 1992.

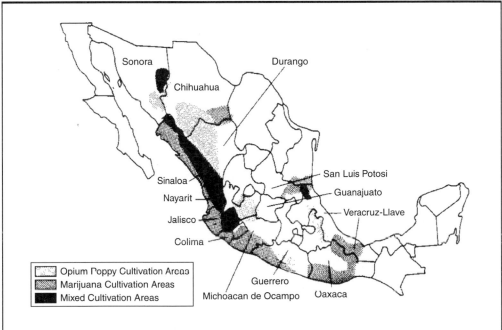

Mexico: Opium Poppy and Marijuana Cultivation Areas

The Mexican Heroin Trade

Mexico first emerged as a major heroin supplier during the early 1970s. This occurred just after the collapse of the *French Connection*, a massive heroin-trafficking operation between Marseilles, France, and New York. Mexico experiences an opium harvest season between September and April. This includes two harvests, which peak in November and March. After the opium harvest, raw opium gum is transported from the growing fields to nearby villages by pack mules, pedestrian couriers, or vehicles. Because of the vast number of back roads and footpaths in Mexico, interdiction at this stage is almost impossible. The opium reaches the heroin-processing laboratories by means of gatherers (called *acaparadors*). Their job is to purchase designated amounts of opium gum from the cultivators and deliver it, usually by general aviation aircraft, back to the processors who placed the order.

The process of converting raw opium to powdered heroin takes about three days and yields brown heroin with a wholesale purity of 65 percent to 85 percent. In contrast, white powdered heroin manufactured in the Middle East yields an average purity of 85 percent to 99 percent, which allows a much greater profit margin for traffickers. Most conversion laboratories are located in remote regions of the country, but some have been discovered in large cities such as Mexico City, Nuevo Laredo, and Tijuana.

Once the complicated laboratory processing is completed by experienced chemists, the traffickers transport the heroin to principal population areas and prepare it for clandestine shipment to the United States. Once in the United States, the principal market areas for Mexican heroin are in the western part of the country (DEA, 2005). Although areas such as Chicago still account for a significant percentage of the market, Mexican heroin is virtually unavailable in the northeastern and southeastern United States.

Drug Enforcement in Mexico

The primary authority for drug enforcement in Mexico is vested in the nation's chief law enforcement officer, the attorney general. It is the attorney general who dictates who will be prosecuted and for what drug offense. The responsibility for apprehension of drug offenders rests with the Mexican Federal Judicial Police (MFJP), which investigates all federal crimes, including drug offenses. Drug regulatory functions are the responsibility of the Department of Narcotics under the secretary of health and welfare and of the director of Food, Beverages, and Drugs. The Department of Narcotics is responsible for enforcing drug violations in Mexico City and surrounding areas.

The murder of a DEA agent in Mexico illustrates the extremes that Mexican traffickers will go to protect their trade. In her book *Desperados*, *Time* magazine correspondent Elaine Shannon exposed the circumstances surrounding the 1985 abduction and murder of DEA agent Enrique "Kiki" Camarena Salazar in Guadalajara (see Chapter 9). According to Shannon, certain Mexican officials not only helped plan the abduction and murder but also created an elaborate cover-up, one that continues as of this writing. According to Shannon's account, the Mexican government's involvement in narcotics is second only to that of the government in Panama (Shannon, 1988).

Colombia

Over the past several decades, Colombia has the dubious distinction of being the world's most active illicit drug-producing country. Although the United States has made numerous attempts over the years to work with the Colombian government to solve this problem, such efforts have been hampered by the ongoing problem of corruption among Colombia's public officials.

The Colombian involvement in U.S. cocaine trafficking can be traced back to the influx of Cuban refugees to South Florida in the 1960s, after the Castro revolution. In Florida, many immigrant Cubans formed ethnic communities that served as the economic base of continued operation for the so-called Cuban Mafia. The Cuban Mafia is a particularly pernicious organized crime group for two reasons. First, many of its leaders developed their illicit entrepreneurial skills under the tutelage of Meyer Lansky and Santo Trafficante when they ran massive gambling and drug-smuggling operations in prerevolutionary Cuba. Second, after the Cuban revolution, many of these future organized criminals were trained in the techniques of violence, smuggling, and other clandestine activities by the Central Intelligence Agency (CIA) as part of its efforts to raise and train an anti-Castro army. Once it was established in the United States, the Cuban Mafia became the major distribution organization for Colombian cocaine.

Figure 4.5

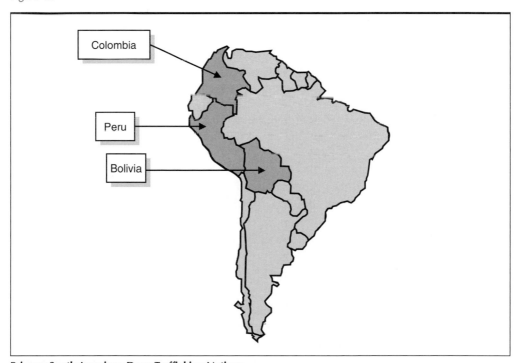

Primary South American Drug-Trafficking Nations

At first, the South Florida Cuban Mafia organizations, using their long-established Colombian cocaine connections, brought just enough cocaine to the United States for distribution in their own communities. Gradually, however, they began to import increasingly larger quantities of cocaine for expanding markets in the United States. By the mid-1960s, the Cuban networks expanded their distribution systems nationwide and relied on Colombian traffickers for nearly 100 percent of the cocaine distributed by the Cubans. The arrangement was simple: Colombians manufactured the drug, Cubans trafficked it in the United States.

Eventually, however, the Colombians came to want more control of the operation, and by the 1970s, they had expanded their own trafficking role in the United States. By 1978, the Colombians had severed most ties with the Cuban traffickers and assumed the dominant role that they now play in providing cocaine to the United States. It was also during the 1970s that the incidence of violence increased as a result of several localized cocaine-trafficking gang wars and gave rise to the Colombian trafficking cartel's notoriety.

When Colombia's extensive role as a source country is considered, one should also consider the reasons that have enabled Colombia to maintain consistent control of the cocaine market and much of the marijuana market for such a long period of time. Three reasons can be cited:

- Geographically, Colombia is well positioned both to receive coca from Peru and Bolivia and to export, by air or sea, processed cocaine to the United States.
- The country's vast central forests are effective in concealing hidden processing laboratories and air strips.
- Colombians have gained much experience over the years as early pioneers in the cocaine trade. Consequently, the drug organizations have progressed from small fragmented groups of criminals to sophisticated and professional criminal cartels that are quite proficient at their trade.

As noted, despite its many problems, Colombia is one of Latin America's richer countries, with an economy that has grown an average of about 3.5 percent a year. Investors are attracted to Colombia for its coal and oil. The cocaine business endures in Colombia largely due to its high profitability and the effective business practices initiated by the traffickers. Coca bushes grow best along the Andean mountain chain, mainly in Bolivia and Peru. Colombians import the semiprocessed coca paste, run the laboratories that convert the paste into cocaine powder, and skillfully control the trade northward to the United States through Caribbean and Atlantic Coast shipping routes.

The cocaine business incorporates more than one million people, from peasant growers in Peru and Bolivia to the chemists and processors in Colombia and the distributors on U.S. streets (Filippone, 1994). DEA officials estimate that Colombian traffickers over the past 10 years have increased tenfold the supply of cocaine to the United States. With the resultant market glut in the United States, traffickers are turning their attention to Europe by way of Spain, where cocaine brings about four times the retail price it does in Miami.

The major percentage of this traffic was controlled by large Colombian trafficking organizations. Marijuana is cultivated in several regions throughout Colombia; the largest of these is along the Guajira Peninsula. Members of large Colombian trafficking organizations purchase marijuana from growers and provide protection and financial incentives to them. Marijuana is harvested twice each year, with the largest harvest occurring in the fall. The predictable harvest pattern closely parallels the level of availability of Colombian ("Colombo" or "Bo") marijuana in the United States.

The U.S. government estimates that almost 90 percent of cultivated Colombian marijuana is shipped to the United States by sea, with the rest shipped by air through the use of general aviation aircraft. The ships used are commonly referred to as *mother ships* and are usually large fishing vessels or freighters (which can hold 50 tons for a 100-foot mother ship or 100 tons for a 400-foot mother ship).

Typically, these ships await their cargo while remaining at sea or stationed at selected Colombian ports. Once the shipment is ready for transportation to the United States, the ship travels to a beach site that is predetermined by the traffickers. An estimated 100 loading sites dot Colombia's north coast from Barranquilla to Portete, and all of these are linked by trails and airstrips to the major growing areas. When preparations are complete, the mother ship moves to a prearranged location about one-half to three miles off shore. Small boats then ferry loads of marijuana from the shore to the mother ship. This is usually done during the night to avoid detection.

Marijuana traffickers commonly use the same trafficking routes established by cocaine traffickers. These include the Windward Passage between Cuba and Haiti; the Yucatán Channel between Mexico and Cuba; and the Mona Passage, bordered by the Dominican Republic and Puerto Rico. It is from these routes that U.S. ports along the Gulf of Mexico and the East Coast are most accessible to smugglers.

Bolivia

Bolivia, a South American country that straddles the Central Andes mountain range, encompasses an area roughly equivalent to the combined size of Arizona, Colorado, Utah, and New Mexico. Bolivia consists of three primary topographical regions known as the Altiplano. Bolivia exhibits wide variations in geography and climate. For example, the climate ranges from the continuous humidity and heat of the Amazon basin to the extreme cold and heavy snowfall of the upper Andes. Bolivia has the lowest per capita income of all countries in South America (O'Brien and Cohen, 1984). Its notoriety as a drug source country is similar to Peru's as a coca-leaf-producing country for international traffickers. Although growing the coca leaf plant in Bolivia is perfectly legal, the processing of the plant into cocaine is against the law.

There are two principal areas of coca cultivation in Bolivia: the Chapare region in the department of Cochabamba and the Yungis in the department of La Paz. Bolivia's traditional role in international drug trafficking has revolved around the supplying of coca paste to traffickers in Colombia. Since the mid-1980s, however, Bolivia has been increasingly involved in the conversion of coca paste to cocaine hydrochloride. Cocaine laboratories have been discovered in the departments of the Beni and Santa Cruz. Ironically, the emergence of Santa Cruz as a cocaine-processing center was intimately connected to the pro-U.S. military dictatorship of Luis Garcia Meza Tejada.

It was under this regime that Roberto Suarez-Gomez Sr., the head of Bolivia's premier cocaine-trafficking family, consolidated his hold on the market with the assistance of Nazi war criminal Klaus Barbie, who helped reorganize both the security systems of the Suarez organization, one of the primary sources of cocaine paste in Bolivia, and Bolivia's internal security police. Under the leadership of Roberto Sr., also known as "little father," son Roberto Jr. and nephew Renato Roca Suarez produce an estimated 40,000 tons of coca paste per year and earn an estimated $600,000 per year. Roberto Sr. was forced to yield control of the organization in 1988 after his arrest.

A large portion of the Bolivian coca regions consist of flat, marshy lowlands that are virtually isolated from the outside world. Traffickers in Bolivia, therefore, primarily rely on general aviation aircraft for transporting drugs. Bolivia has averaged more than one government per year since 1825, so diplomatic efforts to establish eradication programs have been difficult (O'Brien and Cohen, 1984). Since the mid-1980s, however, the government of Bolivia has recognized the extent to which drug traffickers have used their tremendous financial resources to gain control over many political factions and financial institutions within the country. This has resulted in increased pressure from the government against traffickers.

The cocaine business in Bolivia is less institutionalized than in Colombia and Peru due to the organized crime influence of such historically well-known groups such as the Medellin cartel and the Sendero Luminoso (the Shining Path), a guerilla group closely affiliated with peasant and farming interests (see Chapter 4). Indeed, much of the farming in Bolivia is done by out-of-work miners who left the highlands when tin markets collapsed in the early 1980s.

In 1988, Bolivia outlawed the growing of coca for export, and the government has initiated a plan by which loans are offered to the estimated 37,000 farmers who are willing to switch crops. In other initiatives, Bolivia has torched more than 9,000 acres of coca since 1987 and has reduced its five-digit inflation rate to about 10 percent, the lowest in Latin America. Still, experts estimate that a farmer working a typical 2.5-acre coca plot can earn as much as $5,000 a year, 10 times the average annual income.

Peru

For more than 2,000 years, Peruvians have chewed the leaves of the coca plant, primarily to counteract the effects of high altitude and as an aid to digestion. A certain amount of coca is permitted under law for domestic use as well as pharmaceutical purposes. Although Peru is not considered a source country for cocaine, it is a primary contributor of coca leaves, which are cultivated and then sold to Colombian traffickers for processing. It has been estimated that Peru cultivates as much as 55 percent of the coca leaves used in world production of cocaine hydrochloride (Filippone, 1994).

Like its neighboring country, Bolivia, Peru suffers from a weak economy, and the cocaine trade provides hundreds of millions of dollars in income that otherwise would not be realized. The coca leaf is the principal source of income for thousands of Peruvian farmers, who find it far more profitable than coffee or other crops. In fact, a farmer who cultivates a little more than a hectare of coca leaf can earn the equivalent of several thousand dollars a year, at least 10 times more (and possibly 100 times more) than they could earn from any legal crop (Filippone, 1994). In Peru, it is estimated that as many as 60,000 families depend on the coca-growing business for their livelihood.

Critical Thinking Task

Considering the magnitude of the worldwide illicit drug trade and its impact on the United States, do you believe states should continue to criminalize drug use? Predict outcomes should current laws be either continued or abandoned.

Peru is the world's second leading producer of cocaine, and President Alan García has renewed Peru's commitment to counter illicit coca cultivation. Although the United Nations Office on Drugs and Crime estimates that Peruvian cocaine production dropped by 10 metric tons between 2004 and 2005, coca acreage in Peru increased from an estimated 27,500 hectares to some 38,000 hectares over the same period. To counter this increase, Peru employs a strong integrated counternarcotics strategy of eradication and alternative development. This nexus led to the eradication of more than 12,000 hectares of coca in 2006, the development of infrastructure projects, and millions of dollars in sales of licit products in coca-growing regions. Recently, Peru has implemented an aggressive container-screening program in its major ports, which resulted in the seizure of nearly 12 metric tons of cocaine in 2005—a threefold increase over seizures during the previous year (Braun, 2006).

Trafficking Trends in South America

It is evident that Colombia is maintaining its status as the largest producer of cocaine hydrochloride in South America (and the rest of the world). Although some coca leaf cultivation takes place there, the majority of coca leaves used in cocaine manufacturing come from the neighboring countries, Peru and Bolivia. The financial incentive for coca growers in these countries is augmented by the fact that the coca plant is far easier to grow and harvest than other conventional crops. This is evident for three reasons:

- Coca is a deep-rooted crop, with a lifespan of about 30 years.
- Income earned from growing the coca plant is many times the daily wage of growing a conventional crop.
- The coca plant can be harvested from three to six times a year and will grow in poor soil that is unable to support traditional crops.

The Colombian government's 1984 restrictions on the importation of ether and acetone, which are used in the cocaine conversion process, temporarily helped disrupt cocaine production, but these restrictions have not accounted for a major decrease in its production. This is because laboratory operators found chemical substitutes for these solvents and have also devised ways to smuggle essential chemicals into the country.

Bolivia's involvement in the cocaine trade remained somewhat consistent through the late 1980s. It is there that much of the required coca paste is manufactured for later production into cocaine. In addition, due to the tremendous profit margin, Bolivian traffickers have become increasingly involved with the conversion process of coca paste into cocaine hydrochloride.

Brazil's role in the South American drug trade is primarily that of a transshipment country, but it too may emerge as yet another source country for the finished cocaine hydrochloride product. This was evidenced by the 1987 seizures of six cocaine hydrochloride laboratories in various locations throughout the country. One of these laboratories, according to authorities, had been in operation for five months and was producing an estimated 2,000 kilograms per week.

One irony in the drug trade is that though many Americans claim drug abuse as the nation's number-one priority, U.S. chemical companies furnish an estimated 90 percent of the ethyl ether, acetone, and other processing agents required to make cocaine in South American jungle laboratories. Only in the late 1980s was there any type of governmental focus on this problem. For example, the Federal Chemical Diversion and Trafficking Act was implemented to require chemical firms to maintain strict records on sales and equipment. Although this law was designed to deter criminal diversion of chemicals to traffickers, the DEA reports that many phony "front" companies operating in the United States and Mexico have made it difficult to track chemicals. In addition, cocaine processors have successfully purchased precursor chemicals from German sources that either produced the chemicals themselves or purchased them from U.S. companies.

There has been some evidence of cocaine trafficking in some other South American countries. Some small cocaine labs have been seized in Ecuador; in Paraguay, where traffickers have easy access to Bolivia and where there is evidence that cocaine processing was encouraged by General Alfredo Stroessner's right-wing dictatorship; and in Uruguay, where some laboratory activity was detected in the late 1980s.

Figure 4.6

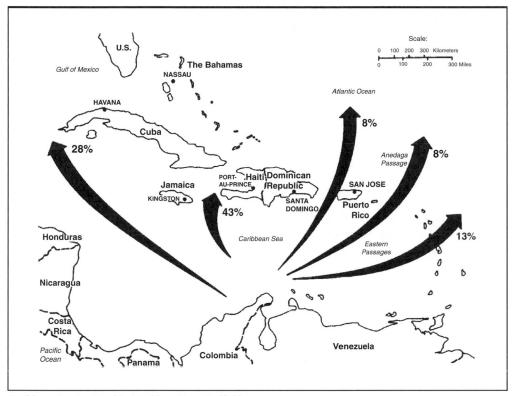

Caribbean Routes Used in Maritime Drug Trafficking

Trafficking Trends in the Caribbean

As of late 1996, most of the cocaine that reached the United States arrived from Colombia by way of Mexico. However, as pressure has been put on trafficking via that route, many cartels have turned to the eastern Caribbean to establish new routes. Since 1990, seizures have quadrupled to 18 tons of cocaine annually, and the DEA reports that more than 100 major traffickers are using the islands as storage and distribution points for both U.S. and European markets (Booth, 1996). Tourist guides make little mention of it, but drug cartels seem to permeate the region. They stash cocaine on the Virgin Islands and their boats lurk in the waters off St. Eustatius and Cuba. St. Lucia has a growing number of cocaine users, which coincides with the fact that it also has the world's second-highest murder rate (Booth, 1996). The DEA has reported drug gangs infiltrating Trinidad, and St. Martin has the reputation of being the world's meeting place for Italian, Colombian, and Russian drug cartels.

In the midst of all this activity is what is thought to be the new hub for the Caribbean drug trade: Puerto Rico. Since 1990, Puerto Rico has become the focal point for the exportation of cocaine to mainland United States from the Caribbean. The island's status as a U.S. commonwealth offers traffickers an extraordinary advantage because passengers and cargo undergo only perfunctory customs checks to enter the country. Once a shipment of cocaine has successfully been delivered to the island, it is easily relayed to U.S. cities. As in many other Caribbean countries, Puerto Rico's role in the international drug trade has coincided with a growing murder rate. Between 1993 and 1996, the country's murder rate exceeded that of the United States, and 90 percent of all violence is thought to be drug-related (Booth, 1996). Some say that San Juan has become what Miami used to be, with armed youngsters on the streets and people afraid to go out at night.

While Puerto Rico battles drug dealers and the accompanying violence, the consequences are even more devastating for the tiny island states that neighbor it, such as St. John, Antigua, and Trinidad. Because these are economies that rely on the tourist trade and perhaps small cash crops such as bananas or sugar, they are more susceptible to domination by drug cartels. After all, if large countries like Colombia can turn into "narco-democracies," what is to keep considerably smaller countries from a similar fate?

As smuggling through the Bahamas became more difficult, the Colombians switched their operations to Mexico for help, but as the United States focused on Mexico, drugs returned to the Caribbean—the point of least resistance.

The Bahamas is a major transit country for cocaine and marijuana bound for the United States from South America and the Caribbean. It is also a country of 700 islands and cays distributed over an area the size of California. There are both maritime and aerial routes between Colombia and the United States. Colombia is an attractive location for drug transshipments of cocaine, marijuana, and other illegal drugs (U.S. Department of State, 2010).

Southeast Asia

In the 1990s many of the countries of Southeast Asia benefited from a sizeable economic boom in the region. Lines of demarcation between legitimate business, law enforcement, politics, and organized crime have always been blurred at best in this region, but the economic surge of the 1990s created new bastions of wealth and political power that have benefited criminal organizations. In countries such as Thailand and Singapore, governmental programs designed to stimulate economic growth and improve the economic infrastructure strengthened the upper-world economy. However, those very same businessmen who accumulated wealth and power in response to these programs also used that new wealth and power to establish growing and highly profitable criminal enterprises ancillary to their legitimate holdings (Lintner, 1996; Renard, 1996; "Thai Democracy: Pass the Baht," 1996; Thayer, 1995).

Many of these new criminal enterprises centered around arms trafficking, prostitution, illegal gambling, and contraband smuggling, but the vast majority of them continued to specialize in the cornerstone of Southeast

Asia's illicit economy: drugs. In Myanmar, for example, major drug traffick-ers became heavy investors in infrastructure development, both as a means a profit-making enterprise in and of itself and as a means to facilitate drug smuggling and money laundering.

The opium-growing regions of Myanmar and Laos have made Southeast Asia the second-largest source region for the world's supply of heroin. Cultivating and harvesting the opium poppy is still the economic mainstay of the many hill tribes living in isolated, rural, impoverished areas of Southeast Asia. Poor weather patterns and climatic conditions negatively impacted opium cultivation from 1997 to 2000, but despite that fact, Myanmar alone accounted for 50 percent of the world's opium crop in 2003. Inefficiency in production and infrastructure problems, though, resulted in Myanmar producing only 21 percent of the world's supply of opium, despite its high rate of cultivation. Laos accounted for about 4 percent of the world's opium production in 2003.

Ready recruits for drug-trafficking organizations can be found in both urban ghettos and impoverished rural areas of Southeast Asia. Heroin is often smuggled on fishing boats down the Gulf of Thailand and then trans-ferred to the major international maritime shipping centers of Singapore and Hong Kong.

Massive criminal organizations, virtually immune from law enforcement interference because of widespread corruption in the governments and busi-ness communities of Southeast Asia, have been able to work in close collusion with police, the military, politicians, and otherwise legitimate businesspeople to spawn a massive drug-and-sex-trade empire in the region. The fact is that drug-trade profits are the source of most new commercial and business invest-ment in the region. Outside investors, including Russian criminal organiza-tions, have been enticed to invest in the prostitution and sex tourism industries, particularly in Thailand.

In addition to Thailand, Cambodia is now being increasingly utilized as a transshipment route for heroin. Cambodian government investments in eco-nomic development have greatly benefited the drug trade. For example, Teng Boonma, a major Cambodian shipping magnate and entrepreneur, is also a large-scale drug trafficker. He owns most of Kampong Saom, Cambodia's most important port city and the a key transit point for drugs.

Heroin and methamphetamine production in Southeast Asia is dominated by ethnic drug-trafficking armies operating mostly in Myanmar's remote opium-producing region. The drug-trafficking armies began as insurgent groups, often supported by the CIA, and still have an ethnically based political agenda. But over the years the biggest of these clandestine armies have become primarily engaged in the production and trafficking of heroin and methamphet-amine and in other illicit and lucrative economic activities—including gem smuggling and illegal logging and timber smuggling. As a result of its con-tinuing political repression directed at pro-democracy political groups, which began in 1988, the military regime in Myanmar has negotiated treaties with most of these ethnic armies in remote regions that have allowed the regime to fight any social or political changes in the country. In return, the government grants carte blanche to drug traffickers.

The arrest and subsequent retirement of heroin kingpin Khun Sa, for years a U.S.-funded client warlord in the region, resulted in his Mong Tai Army being broken up into smaller units. As a result, the United Wa State Army (UWSA) has become the largest drug producer in Southeast Asia. The UWSA is the largest regional producer of heroin and a major producer of methamphetamine, most of which is sold in Thailand.

Ethnic Chinese criminal organizations and some Thai criminal networks act as brokers, financial backers, and transporters in the Southeast Asian heroin trade. Operating out of major regional commercial centers such as Bangkok, Hong Kong, Singapore, and Taiwan and using a wide array of interchangeable front companies and legitimate businesses, Chinese and Thai criminal networks also arrange financing and transportation of drugs, routing drugs through many different ports—largely by commercial shipping—to their final destinations.

Southwest Asia

Following a decrease in illicit opium production in the 1970s in the Golden Triangle, three countries emerged as formidable producers of raw opium and heroin. These Southwest Asian countries—Iran, Pakistan, and Afghanistan—have been dubbed the Golden Crescent because of the rich opium poppy-growing regions in each country. Southwestern Asia is responsible for an estimated 60 percent of the world's heroin (ONDCP, 2007). Ironically, despite flagrant trafficking activities in this region, opium producers there have generally looked on the abuse of heroin as an "American problem." As of the preparation of this text, however, heroin addicts in Southwest Asia outnumber U.S. addicts almost two to one.

Opium use in the Middle East dates back thousands of years, but it was not until a few decades ago that the Middle Eastern countries making up the Golden Crescent became politically organized. While Iran was ruled by the Shah, the countries of Southwest Asia formed an opium system that had little impact on the West. This was because much of the opium produced in the border regions of Afghanistan and Pakistan was smuggled to Iran to serve that country's immense addict population, which consisted of one million addicts of a total population of 40 million. There the opium was usually eaten or smoked by older, rural dwellers, although Iranian modernization brought about an increasing number of heroin abusers among the urban middle classes.

In 1955, the Shah imposed a ban on domestic opium production in an attempt to suppress drug abuse. He did permit some legal production, however, to meet the requirements of registered addicts. As the Shah's dictatorship weakened and law and order in Iran became less prevalent, the farmers began to ignore the opium ban. Before the collapse of the Shah's regime in 1979, Iran served as a "sponge" for Afghan and Pakistani opium. After the fall of the royal family, Iran became a major producer of the drug for both its own domestic use and for exportation. The political chaos in Iran only aided traffickers in their operations. Soon there was more than enough heroin in the Golden Crescent to supply European and North American markets. The role of Turkey as a heroin transshipment country also increased. Turkish traffickers, using the large population of Turkish guest workers in Germany as a cover, first flooded Germany, then the rest of Europe, with inexpensive Southwest Asian heroin that frequently ranged into the 90-percent level in purity.

As evidence of Europe's heroin epidemic mounted, concerned U.S. officials suspected that it would spread to the United States. In 1979, the Department of State convened a meeting in Berlin to discuss the problem. Attending the meeting were State Department representatives and DEA narcotics coordinators from U.S. embassies in Europe and Southwest Asia. Other international efforts, such as exploring crop eradication operations in Iran, were also considered in 1979. With the untimely seizure of the U.S. embassy in Iran just one month after the Berlin meeting, all possibilities for a constructive dialogue ceased. Additionally, the Soviet invasion of Afghanistan foreclosed close cooperation with that country. Another of the many ironies of the international drug trade is the fact that the Soviet invasion seriously disrupted heroin supplies from Afghanistan. The heroin pipelines resumed the flow of drugs, in much larger volumes than before, after aid to fundamentalist Moslem guerrillas, the Mujahedeen, began to flow from Western nations. Only Pakistan remained as a possible area for diplomatic endeavors in the area of drug control.

Pakistan

Pakistan is one of the poorest countries in the world, and funds for narcotic suppression projects are extremely limited. Nevertheless, Pakistani leaders are aware of the enormous impact on other countries of the opium produced within Pakistan's borders, as well as domestic problems that the opium trade and addiction have produced. As an early response to the problem, the government of Pakistan issued an order banning cultivation and use of opium. This order was generally considered successful, and enforcement of it produced few problems despite the complicated tribal structure of the society in the growing regions. During the ban's first year, production fell from an estimated 650 metric tons in 1979 to less than 100 metric tons in 1980 (O'Brien and Cohen, 1984).

It soon became evident that U.S. assistance to Pakistan would be necessary to ensure that antidrug laws would be maintained. The initial phase, which involved a crop eradication program, was the easiest. What remained, however, was the toughest challenge: to control the illicit production of opium in extremely impoverished areas where the farmers had few, if any, acceptable economic alternatives. To help Pakistan with difficult enforcement initiatives, the United States provided vehicles and communications gear to antinarcotics units.

Since the mid-1970s, Pakistani traffickers have developed several unique but fairly unsophisticated networks for transporting drugs into the United States. Typically, the traffickers rely on family or friends in the United States to distribute drugs. They have also been known to make use of certain trusted black criminal organizations in cities such as Los Angeles, Detroit, and New York. In addition, Pakistani traffickers have aligned with their Italian criminal counterparts in New York City.

Afghanistan

Afghanistan produces nearly 90 percent of the world's opium poppy and is also the world's largest heroin-producing and -trafficking country. Trafficking activities include refining and traffic in all forms of unrefined (opium), refined (heroin), and semirefined (morphine-base) opiates. The International Monetary Fund (IMF) estimated licit gross domestic product (GDP) for the Afghan fiscal year ending on March 21, 2005, at $5.9 billion. UNODC estimated illicit opium GDP at $2.8 billion for the same period, which indicates that illicit opium GDP accounts for roughly one-third of total GDP. Criminal financiers and narcotics traffickers exploit the government's weakness and corruption. Reconstruction efforts, which began in 2002 in the aftermath of the September 11, 2001, attacks on the United States, are improving Afghanistan's infrastructure, laying the necessary groundwork to combat the cultivation and trafficking of drugs throughout the country (Drug Policy Alliance, 2007).

Afghanistan is landlocked, and drug traffickers must rely on land routes to move morphine base and heroin out of the country. Opiates are consumed regionally as well as smuggled to consumers in the West. The primary market for Afghan morphine base is traffickers based in Turkey. Morphine base is transported overland through Pakistan and Iran or directly to Iran from Afghanistan and then into Turkey. Shipments of Afghan-produced morphine base are also sent by sea from Pakistan's Makran Coast. Routes north through the Central Asia Republics, then across the Caspian Sea and south into Turkey, are also used.

Heroin is trafficked to worldwide destinations via many routes. Traffickers quickly make adjustments to heroin smuggling routes based on political and weather-related events. Reports of heroin shipments north from Afghanistan through the Central Asian States to Russia have increased. Tajikistan is a frequent destination for both opium and heroin shipments, although Tajikistan serves mostly as a transit point and storage location rather than a final destination. Some of the heroin is used in Russia, but some also transits Russia to other consumer markets. Heroin also transits India en route to international markets. Moreover, heroin continues to be trafficked from Afghanistan through Pakistan. Seizures are frequently reported at Pakistan's international airports. Heroin is also smuggled by sea on vessels leaving the port city of Karachi. Heroin produced in Afghanistan continues to be trafficked to the United States, although generally in small quantities.

Because of a changing political, social, and economic atmosphere, it is difficult to predict the future of Afghanistan's role in opium production. However, based on decades of survival in the illicit drug trade, it is likely that Afghanistan will remain a primary player in global illicit drug production for some time to come.

Figure 4.7

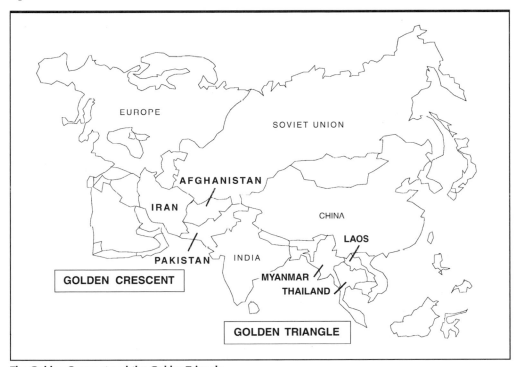

The Golden Crescent and the Golden Triangle

Turkey

As a key country bordering Iran and the Golden Crescent, Turkey remains a major contributor to opium and heroin production in that region of the world. Opium poppy farming has existed in Turkey for centuries and has represented a livelihood for thousands of Turkish farmers. For generations, opium was cultivated by private Turkish farmers, but in 1933 the Turkish government established an agency to buy the opium gum from the growers. The government then exported the opium gum to other countries, where opium alkaloids such as morphine and codeine were extracted for medicinal use. However, a considerable amount of gum was diverted and smuggled to the Middle East and France (the French Connection), where it was processed into heroin. Much of this heroin ultimately reached the United States. During the 1960s and early 1970s, an estimated 80 percent of the heroin on U.S. streets originated in Turkey.

In 1971, however, the Turkish government placed a ban on opium cultivation that became effective the following year. Because of trade losses after the 1971 ban, the Turkish government initiated the poppy-straw program in 1974, in which legal opiates were produced. The poppy-straw program operates under strict governmental control and allows for cultivation of the opium poppy on small licensed lots in seven provinces: Afyon (the Turkish word for opium), Isparta, Denizli, Usak, Burdur, Kutahya, and Konya. Harvesting is done by hand after the opium has passed the green stage and has completely dried. Only the poppy heads and parts of the stalks are removed, and the result is the poppy straw.

Figure 4.8

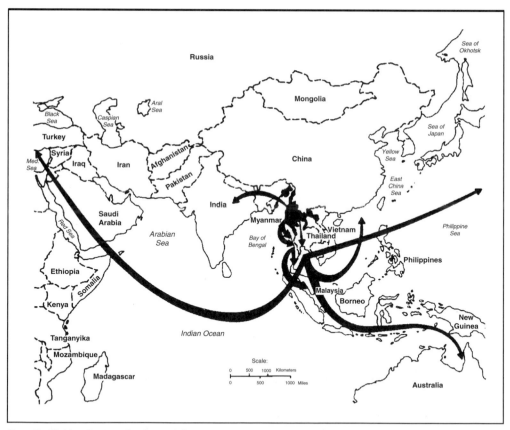

Drug-Trafficking Routes: Southeast Asia

Between 1976 and 1980, Turkey exported an average of 8,800 tons of poppy straw per year. Today much of the crop is purchased by the Dutch for processing in the Netherlands. India shares the market with the United States because of the "80–20 rule." This rule, supported by the United States, specifies that at least 80 percent of the raw narcotic material imported to the United States for legitimate use in medicine must originate either in Turkey or India. The remaining 20 percent can be imported from other countries.

One of the traditional opium producers in the region is the Pushtuns (also known as Pathans). This independent tribe, living on the border of Afghanistan and Pakistan, has produced great quantities of raw opium gum. The Kurds are another ethnic group in the Middle East who are heavily involved in traditional opium production.

The Kurds and Drug Trafficking

Because of the strict controls on opium cultivation, Turkey is not considered a primary source country. It does, however, remain a major transshipment country for opiates that are produced in Afghanistan, Pakistan, and Iran (the Golden Crescent). Most of the drug dealing and trafficking in Turkey is controlled by criminal groups in Istanbul.

One such group, which has a strong ethnic identity and contributes significantly to Turkish organized crime, is the Kurds. The Kurds speak Turkish and have a reputation for being family-oriented and independent. They are also known for being fierce fighters and devout Moslems. The Kurds have clans in both Turkey and Iran and do not recognize the border separating the two countries. Because the Kurds frequently travel across the border, they have a convenient network for smuggling drugs.

Although many Kurdish areas lie between eastern and southern Turkey, trafficking by Kurds is by no means restricted to those areas. Many of the main heroin wholesalers in Istanbul are Kurds who first migrated from remote villages as unskilled laborers and later became wealthy in the narcotics trade. In addition to the Kurds, many Iranians also traffic large amounts of heroin from Turkey to their Iranian contacts in the United States and Western Europe. Using Istanbul as a main distribution point, the Iranian traffickers smuggle both legitimate and illegitimate goods (drugs and weapons alike) to Western Europe and the United States.

Drug-smuggling routes in Turkey lie primarily along the eastern and southeastern areas of the country. Heroin is generally smuggled from Iran to Turkey by Turkish Kurds who travel through the mountainous border area, which is not heavily patrolled by either government. The DEA estimates that because of the harsh winters in this region, most drug smuggling into Turkey is somewhat seasonal and therefore is concentrated between May and December of each year. Authorities believe that most drug payloads arrive in the Turkish provinces of Van and Hakkiri, although some morphine base has been smuggled into Syria and Lebanon.

Although as a rule Turkey is not considered a source country for drugs, some refining of morphine base to heroin does occur there. In 1988, several

Turkish heroin refineries were seized but were found to be somewhat primitive. These labs were set up to convert a specific amount of morphine base to heroin and were designed to be easily dismantled and moved to a different location. As with heroin and morphine base, hashish (Turkey's biggest domestic consumer drug) is also commonly transported through Turkey from Lebanon. Other illicit commodities include firearms, which are often traded for drugs. In one specific case in 1987, Kintex, an import/export agency controlled by the Bulgarian government, was implicated in a guns- and drug-smuggling operation.

Iran

Iran, which also borders Afghanistan, has become a major bridge linking the drug-production zone to the lucrative consumer markets of the Persian Gulf, Turkey, Russia, and Europe. Afghanistan opium stocks have reached record highs; consequently, it is believed that large amounts of narcotics will continue to flow through Iran. The country's antinarcotic laws cover all aspects of offensive drug control. Punishments include fines plus lashings for smuggling opium or cannabis. Death penalty sentencing may be imposed for smuggling, selling, and distributing illicit drugs, but it is generally reserved for drug lords, organized criminals, and armed traffickers. Because Iran's prisons and hospitals are being filled with drug users, the government recently reformed drug laws to recognize addiction as a disease rather than a criminal offense. One treatment clinic is even experimenting with methadone treatment. The government hopes that this change in tactics may slow the flood of drugs into the country.

India

India is one of the world's top producers of licit opium, a business monitored by the Indian Central Bureau of Narcotics. However, reports reveal that tons of the licit opium are diverted to illegal markets, converted to heroin, and sold. Heroin use has effectively replaced opium and cannabis use in India. A growing number of people are also using licitly manufactured drugs, in particular codeine-based cough syrups and benzodiazepines, which are ingested, snorted, and injected, often in combination with illicit drugs like heroin. The main reason for this increase seems to be the lack of uniformity in monitoring compliance with prescription requirements. Drug laws have recently been altered to allow less severe prison sentences for those who prove possession for personal use only, and such offenders are also given the option of attending detoxification centers in place of imprisonment. Other drug-related offenders generally receive 10- to 20-year jail terms plus substantial fines. For those with previous convictions, the death penalty can be imposed.

Latin America

Latin America has been a major source of illicit drugs in the United States for decades. Over the past 15 years, the United States has spent more than $25 billion on source country eradication and interdiction. Despite these efforts, the prices of cocaine and heroin are at record lows while purity is at a record high—evidence that these drugs are more available than ever. In the Americas, opium poppy cultivation was reported from Colombia and Mexico; reports on eradication in Ecuador, Guatemala, Peru, and the Bolivarian Republic of Venezuela over the past years point to the existence of opium poppy cultivation in these countries as well (United Nations Office on Drugs and Crime, 2010).

Eradication refers to attempts to eliminate drug crops while they are being grown. One major reason that eradication programs have failed is the tendency for drug crops to be displaced rather than eliminated. For example, during the mid-1990s, eradication efforts in Bolivia and Peru created incentives to grow coca in Colombia. Although Peru experienced a 66 percent reduction in coca cultivation and Bolivia experienced a 53 percent reduction, coca cultivation in Colombia doubled. In addition, more potent strains of coca have been developed, leading to higher-yielding coca crops.

Interdiction refers to attempts to seize drugs while en route to the United States. Interdiction efforts have been unsuccessful in reducing drug use in the United States. Despite efforts by the Drug Enforcement Administration, U.S. Customs, U.S. Coast Guard, U.S. Army, and the Immigration and Naturalization Service, it is an impossible task to keep drugs from coming in through 19,924 kilometers of shoreline, 300 ports of entry, and more than 7,500 miles of border with Mexico and Canada. It is estimated that interdiction efforts only seize 10 percent to 15 percent of the heroin and 30 percent of the cocaine coming into the country.

Not only is U.S. antidrug intervention in Latin America ineffective, it also fuels violence and worsens human rights conditions. The Clinton and Bush administrations sent well over $1 billion in antidrug aid to Colombia in recent years as the instability and violence related to that country's 35-year-old civil war continued to worsen. Almost all the U.S. aid is going to Colombia's military and national police, despite their documented, ongoing ties to the violent right-wing paramilitary groups responsible for more than three-quarters of the political killings in the country. These groups, as well as guerilla groups such as the FARC and the ELN, depend on profits from the drug trade. Worsening economic conditions for the mostly poor farmers who grow coca make it even more unlikely that military intervention will reduce the amount of drug crops produced.

U.S. antidrug intervention in Latin America also has a devastating impact on the environment. For example, U.S.-sponsored and -backed eradication programs in Colombia have led to the clearing of more than 1.75 million acres of Amazon rainforest. Colombia is the second most biodiverse country in the world, but drug war deforestation has led experts to predict that Colombia could become another Somalia or Ethiopia within 50 years, meaning that the population would grow faster than its poor agricultural soils can produce food. In addition, aerial eradication efforts are responsible for the destruction of legal subsistence crops, and the pesticide glyphosate is suspected of causing a variety of health problems in Colombian children, including diarrhea, hair loss, and skin rashes.

Hong Kong

Like the Golden Triangle and the Golden Crescent, Hong Kong also plays a significant role in international drug trafficking, particularly in money laundering and transportation. In recent years, the Hong Kong Executive Council has considered legislative proposals giving the courts more power to confiscate the assets of major traffickers.

Legal proposals would allow the court to infer that all property acquired by the offender during the six-year period prior to his or her arrest for a drug-trafficking offense had been received as "payment or reward" for drug trafficking. The court would then levy a fine of an amount equivalent to the value of the property, with a provision for imposing a prison term on a sliding scale up to 10 years upon default on payment of the fine.

SUMMARY

The first part of this chapter illustrates the financial dynamics of the illicit drug trade in addition to describing the way the drug trade parallels legitimate industry. Factors such as supply and demand, manufacturing, transportation, marketing, and security are all considerations for every illicit drug dealer. Understanding these organizational dynamics aids policymakers in anticipating the needs and weaknesses of illicit trafficking organizations.

The extent of global involvement in the illicit drug trade illustrates the magnitude of the problem, since many countries play a major role in furnishing the United States with dangerous drugs. Ironically, the United States is frequently blamed by these countries for providing a drug user market and nurturing an incentive for drug production in their countries.

The closest neighbor to the United States on the south is Mexico, a major producer of heroin and marijuana. Mexico's widespread involvement in the drug trade gained considerable momentum just after the collapse of the French Connection in the early 1970s. Efforts to thwart drug trafficking in Mexico (and some other foreign countries) have been hampered by widespread corruption within the Mexican government. Allegations of corruption among Mexico's

Federal Judicial Police had been voiced for years but became more credible in 1985 with the abduction and murder of a federal DEA agent. Mexican police officers were ultimately charged with complicity in this crime.

In South America, the three Andean nations of Colombia, Peru, and Bolivia are the most active coca- and cocaine-producing countries in the world. Colombia primarily produces cocaine hydrochloride from dried coca leaves but also produces high-grade marijuana. Drug-trafficking cartels have expanded to the point at which they now threaten the democratically elected government in Colombia. A great deal of violence prevails as a result, but Colombian government officials, with aid furnished by the United States, are attempting to locate, arrest, and extradite members to the United States for prosecution. The leaves used in the production of cocaine are primarily grown in Peru and Bolivia; Peru is the primary supplier. As in Colombia, trafficking organizations also have attempted to exert control over the governments in Peru and Bolivia.

Do you recognize these terms?

- blotter acid
- copping areas
- demand elasticity
- drug cartels
- French Connection
- precursor chemicals
- steerers

DISCUSSION QUESTIONS

1. Explain the financial limitations of today's entrepreneurial drug trafficker.

2. Discuss to what extent the laws of supply and demand affect drug-trafficking organizations.

3. To what extent do marketing and distribution practices affect the drug trade?

4. Which areas of the world are most active in the production of raw opium and in heroin refinement?

5. What contributions do Peru and Bolivia make to the world's illicit drug situation?

6. Explain the roles of both the Golden Crescent and the Golden Triangle in global drug trafficking.

7. Discuss the volatile issue of extradition in Colombia.

CLASS PROJECTS

1. Locate three recent articles from a newspaper or magazine that address the international drug problem. Discuss any trends you observe in the drug policies of foreign governments.

2. Compare drug control initiatives in various foreign countries, and discuss similarities between them. Include in your discussion the strengths and weaknesses of the programs.

Chapter 5

Domestic Drug Production

This chapter will enable you to:

- Learn the role that the legitimate drug industry plays in the nation's drug abuse problem
- Understand the extent of the marijuana cultivation problem in the United States
- Realize the magnitude of the nation's clandestine laboratory problem
- Learn the consequences of pharmaceutical diversion in our country's drug problem

When we think of the nation's drug problem, we tend to think of drugs such as cocaine and heroin, which seem to dominate national media stories. We must, however, be cognizant of legal drug manufacturers' contribution to our nation's drug abuse problem. After all, more often than not, a visit to the doctor's office results in a prescription for some sort of drug to treat almost any ailment, mental or physical. As this chapter shows, the legal drug industry is more than just a benign wholesale and retail business. Rather, over the decades, it has grown into a massive marketing machine catering to doctors and lawmakers and often dictating to medical health professionals which—and how often—dangerous drugs should be prescribed.

As was discussed in the previous chapter, some illicit drugs, such as cocaine and heroin, are primarily produced in foreign countries. However, domestic drug producers and traffickers have also taken advantage of the opportunity to produce and cultivate illicit drugs. Marijuana, produced by both foreign and domestic traffickers, is used by an average of 10 million Americans each month (NIDA, 2006). Other drugs, such as methamphetamine, LSD, and PCP, are also produced in clandestine laboratories in

DOI: 10.1016/B978-1-4377-4450-7.00005-9
© 2011 Elsevier Inc. All rights reserved.

the United States and foster much criminal activity in the areas of drug manufacturing and trafficking. Yet another source of drugs exists in the United States: pharmaceutical drug diversion. Drugs that are legally manufactured for legitimate medical treatment are sometimes diverted from the legal source of distribution.

THE PHARMACEUTICAL DRUG INDUSTRY

We know that in addition to illicit drugs, there are legal drugs manufactured that are intended to serve a legitimate medical purpose. Painkillers are essential at the scenes of automobile accidents, in the operating room, and in treating people who suffer from diseases such as arthritis and cancer. For sufferers of toothaches or migraine headaches, painkillers can literally make the difference between being able to face the day and being miserable and dysfunctional at home or on the job. However, pain is not the only reason that people take pharmaceuticals. In recent years, pharmaceutical companies have made new claims to growing hair, controlling weight, reducing cholesterol, controlling impotence, and fighting breast cancer. Many of these claims have been at least partly proved in clinical trials.

The term *pharmaceuticals* is a general one referring to a category of drugs that includes capsules, pills, liquids, suppositories, lotions, and other preparations having a medical use. *Pharmacy Times*, a magazine reporting on drug sales for the United States, estimates that about 1.5 million prescriptions are written each year; one-half of these are new prescriptions and one-half are refills. The legal drug business (manufacturing and selling pharmaceuticals) is big business, comprising an estimated $30 billion or more per year (Goode, 1993).

In recent years the pharmaceutical drug industry has been criticized for its aggressive marketing methods. Critics complain that profit margin, not the elimination of human suffering, is the primary motivator for drug manufacturing. Quite literally, drugs are manufactured for treatment of most illnesses and levels of mental and physical discomfort.

Illegal Internet pharmacies are thwarting progress toward reducing pharmaceutical drug diversion. Pharmaceutical drugs appear to be increasingly diverted from legitimate and illegitimate sources of supply via the Internet, but the amount obtained through such sources is not quantifiable. Pharmaceutical drugs obtained through Internet pharmacies often are provided without proof of prescription, consultation, or doctor's examination. There are no conclusive estimates regarding the number or location of operational Internet pharmacies due to the vastness of the Internet and the ease with which such sites can be established, closed down, and reopened under different domain names. The number of such pharmacies could range from hundreds to thousands.

Figure 5.1

> • The availability of diverted pharmaceutical drugs is high and increasing, fueled by increases in both the number of illegal online pharmacies and commercial disbursements within the legitimate pharmaceutical distribution chain.
>
> • The implementation of pedigree systems such as Radio Frequency Identification (RFID) could help to eliminate the introduction of counterfeits as well as deter the diversion of commonly abused drugs from the legitimate pharmaceutical supply chain.
>
> • Demand for prescription narcotics may decline as some users switch to heroin, particularly in areas where law enforcement efforts curb the diversion and availability of prescription drugs.

Pharmaceutical Diversion at a Glance

Demand for diverted pharmaceuticals has fluctuated but remains relatively high: Data show that the estimated number of people age 12 or older reporting past-year use of prescription-type pain relievers, tranquilizers, stimulants, or sedatives remained relatively stable from 2002 (14,680,000) to 2005 (15,172,000). Moreover, the rate of past-year use among people age 12 or older reporting nonmedical use of prescription-type drugs in 2004 (6.2 percent) was second only to the rate of use for marijuana (10.6 percent)—and far surpassed rates of use for cocaine (2.4 percent) and heroin (0.2 percent).

There is currently no means of quantifying the actual amount of pharmaceutical drugs diverted and available in the United States, because illegal diversion occurs through several methods, including thefts from individuals, manufacturers, and dispensaries; prescription fraud; doctor shopping; and illegal Internet sales. As a result, it is difficult to measure progress against reducing pharmaceutical diversion.

The Business of Painkilling

For millions of Americans, painkillers make a notable difference in their quality of life. Cancer patients suffer the agony a little more easily; people with severe arthritis can now take walks and play with their grandchildren. Realizing that for years doctors neglected to include pain management in patient care, since 1990 the medical profession has taken a new, more aggressive approach to treating pain. In January 2001, a national accrediting board issued new standards requiring doctors in hospitals and other facilities to treat pain as a vital sign. This means they must treat pain as they treat blood pressure or heart rate. Even Congress, in the fall of 2000, passed legislation declaring the following decade the Decade of Pain Control and Research. In this environment, pharmaceutical companies are experimenting with new formulations of painkillers, and existing painkillers are being more widely used than ever before.

While the pharmaceutical market doubled to $145 billion between 1996 and 2000, the painkiller market tripled to $1.8 billion. Yet at the same time, the incidence of reported first-time abuse of painkillers also grew. Although there are no reliable statistics on how many people abuse prescription drugs, in 1999 an estimated 4 million Americans over the age of 12 used prescription pain relievers, sedatives, and stimulants for "nonmedical" purposes in the month prior to being surveyed (Kalb, 2001). According to the Drug Enforcement Administration, the most widely abused prescription drugs are oxycodone and hydrocodone, types of painkillers that contain addictive opioids.

Emergency room visits tell a similar tale of growing instances of painkiller abuse. For example, cases involving hydrocodone medications such as Vicodin and Lortab increased from an estimated 6,100 incidents in 1992 to more than 14,000 in 1999. Incidents involving oxycodone painkillers like Percodan and OxyContin rose from about 3,750 to 6,430, and those involving the antianxiety drug Xanax increased from 16,500 to more than 20,500. This compares to the abuse rate of illegal drugs, which also increased: cocaine from 120,000 to 169,000, and heroin and morphine from 48,000 to 84,000 (ONDCP, 2001).

OxyContin, which came on the market in 1996, is one of the most powerful painkillers available. It is a 12-hour time-release incarnation of the molecular compound of oxycodone, the active ingredient in drugs such as Percodan and Percocet. OxyContin allows patients to take fewer dosage units and offers pain relief that lasts three times longer than that of previous painkillers. However, when the drug is crushed and snorted, eliminating its time-release feature, it provides the user with an enormous "rush" to the brain. Abuse of OxyContin has become so chronic in some locations that users have resorted to armed robberies of pharmacies.

Painkillers are appealing in part because users think of them as safe; they are FDA-approved, easy to take without being noticed, and do not carry the same negative social stigma as illegal drugs. Once they are available on the street, painkillers are expensive. For example, Vicodin pills sell for about $6 each, Percocet and Percodan pills sell for up to $8 each, and an 80 mg OxyContin tablet will sell for as much as $80. Due to the increased abuse of OxyContin, during the summer of 2001 the DEA developed a national strategy to address illegal use of the drug by intensifying law enforcement at both state and federal levels.

So, who is to blame for the misuse of painkillers? Many people point fingers at doctors, saying they prescribe medication too quickly, without warning patients that some medications can be highly addictive. As this chapter shows, though, doctors are not deserving of all the blame, since many people take to deceiving doctors and pharmacists by phoning in false prescriptions or "doctor shopping" to get multiple prescriptions.

The Doctor's Dilemma

Physicians write millions of prescriptions each year for antibiotics, diet pills, tranquilizers, sleeping pills—almost anything their patients need or believe they need. However, with the continued high use of medications come unforeseen side effects and the rampant spread of bacteria, many of which have grown immune to antibiotics. Confronted with a patient who is sick and wants drugs, physicians are pressured to prescribe something. Their dilemma: Many patients today demand a "quick fix" and will search until they find a physician who will prescribe what they want. The demand for drugs has increased in recent years with advertising by drug companies. The statistics reflect the magnitude of the problem. In September 1997, the *Journal of the American Medical Association* reported that 21 percent of all antibiotic prescriptions written in 1992 were to treat colds, bronchitis, and unspecified upper-respiratory infections, even though 90 percent of such infections are caused by viruses that are impervious to antibiotics (Manning, 1997).

Figure 5.2
Source: National Prescription Drug Threat Assessment: 2009.

The recent increase in the extent of prescription drug abuse in this country is quite likely the result of a confluence of factors, such as significant increases in the number of prescriptions; significant increases in drug availability; aggressive marketing by the pharmaceutical industry; the proliferation of illegal Internet pharmacies that dispense these medications without proper prescriptions and surveillance; and a greater social acceptability for medicating a growing number of conditions. The fact that doctors are prescribing these drugs legitimately and with increasing frequency to treat a variety of ailments leads to the misguided and dangerous conclusion that the nonmedical use should be equally safe. This misconception of safety may contribute, for example, to the casual attitude of many college students toward abusing stimulants to improve cognitive function and academic performance.

A Closer Look: Factors That Contribute to Diversion and Abuse

The Cost Crisis

In addition to the crisis of illicit drugs in the United States, another crisis is ongoing: the rising cost of prescription medications. In the 1990s, the lion's share of the blame for Americans paying the highest medication prices in the industrialized world appeared to rest squarely on the shoulders of the drug manufacturers of this country (Pryor, 1994). In addition to being the beneficiary of considerable profits from drug sales, the drug industry also benefits from numerous tax breaks. These include receiving hundreds of millions of dollars in research-and-development tax credits, marketing and advertising deductions, and orphan drug tax credits. Moreover, the drug industry benefits from Internal Revenue Code 936, which permits pharmaceutical companies to move their operations to Puerto Rico, where millions of dollars in taxes and sales can be legally avoided.

Senior citizens use the most prescription drugs of any age group (an estimated 30 percent of all prescription drugs sold annually) and, as a result, a primary concern today is their ability to afford necessary medications. The American Association of Retired Persons (AARP) has reported that prescription medications are the highest out-of-pocket expense for three out of four older Americans. A follow-up survey by the AARP revealed that the crisis is still escalating. For example:

- An estimated 8 million Americans over age 45 claimed they were forced to cut back on necessary items such as food and fuel in order to pay for medications.
- More than 18 million elderly Americans reported they had trouble paying for their medications.
- An estimated 23 million men and women over age 55 have absolutely no prescription drug insurance coverage (Pryor, 1994).

The majority of older Americans do not have health insurance for prescription drugs; more than 65 percent of their medication costs are paid for out of pocket. In fact, Medicare, the government's healthcare program for the elderly and the disabled, fails to cover most outpatient prescription medications. For senior citizens living on fixed incomes, the problem is compounded considerably. Granted, Medicaid's prescription drug program can act as a safety net in helping the poor obtain their medications, but this number includes only about 1.9 million people who are eligible. This means that 84 percent of the poor (or near poor) do not qualify (Pryor, 1994). In August 1992, the General Accounting Office (GAO) released a report addressing the high cost of prescription drugs. The report addressed the responses of 29 manufacturers of widely used prescriptions. In explaining why costs were so high, the company gave the standard answer that price increases were necessary to fund research and development of new drugs. Pryor (1994) argues that the simple fact is that a manufacturer spending 15 percent of its sales on research and development would have to increase prices by only 1.5 percent each year to increase research and development by 10 percent. So it appears that all the excess profits are flowing into marketing and advertising and into the pockets of stockholders. It is yet to be seen whether the Patient Protection and Affordable Care Act, signed into law by President Barack Obama in 2010, will change the circumstances faced by seniors.

The drug price crisis can also be illustrated in the cost of combating AIDS. Initially, the drug AZT (zidovudine), used to treat HIV, was priced outrageously high, costing users up to $10,000 a year when it went on the market in 1987. AIDS activists protested, pointing out that the drug had actually been developed by government researchers at the National Institutes of Health, and asked that the manufacturer, Burroughs Wellcome Company, reduce the price. As a result, it was discovered that the drug works at one-half of the original dose, which brought down the price to about $3,000 per year (Rovner, 1992). Of course, because most Americans have insurance that fails to cover prescription drugs, even inexpensive medications can pose a considerable hardship.

Calls for reform of the pharmaceutical industry have become commonplace in newspapers, periodicals, and television commentaries. Although it is not likely that sweeping reforms will take place soon, some fine-tuning of the industry is still realistic. Suggestions have included placing caps on prescription prices, creating mechanisms for making physicians more aware of the prices of the drugs they prescribe, increasing the use of less expensive generic drugs, and reducing marketing costs for drug companies.

The Cost of Prescription Misuse

Prescription drug-related problems, often caused by patients failing to take their drugs properly, cost an estimated $75.6 billion in medical bills and cause 119,000 deaths a year (Friend, 1996a). Related morbidity and mortality represent a serious medical issue that is of some urgency. Problems include not following directions or forgetting to take a drug, taking doses that are too high or too low, being prescribed the wrong drug, not being prescribed a drug when one is needed, and side effects ranging from rashes to death. Of these, studies have shown that patient noncompliance is the most common problem.

Figure 5.3
Source: National Drug Intelligence Center/Drug Enforcement Administration.

On August 6, 2008, the Miami-Dade (Florida) Police Department and the Miami-Dade County State Attorney General's Office announced arrest warrants for 62 individuals, 52 of whom were public employees, charging them with crimes related to alleged health insurance fraud to obtain large quantities of OxyContin. According to the Florida state attorney's office, beginning in January 2003, six recruiters enlisted local government employees and others to participate in an illegal operation in which those recruited would provide their health insurance identification information to a recruiter. The government employees and others who were recruited allegedly obtained prescriptions for OxyContin (for which they had no medical need) from the complicit physician. They then presented the fraudulent prescriptions at a local pharmacy in Miami-Dade County to obtain the OxyContin tablets and sold the pills for cash to another individual involved in the scam. The government employees and others recruited also submitted health insurance claims to their employer-issued health insurance company, fraudulently claiming reimbursement for the cost of the prescriptions. Officials estimate that approximately 130 medically unnecessary prescriptions for OxyContin were presented to the pharmacies, accounting for more than 12,000 tablets with an estimated street value of almost $400,000.

Case in Point: Government Employees Arrested in Health Insurance/OxyContin scam

THE DRUG APPROVAL DILEMMA

Under federal law, no new drug can be marketed in this country until the Food and Drug Administration (FDA) approves it as safe and effective. This finding is made on the basis of the manufacturer's New Drug Application (NDA), which can contain thousands of pages of data from clinical tests and can take from 2 to 10 years to complete. During this period, the drug is not available for use except on a very limited basis as part of a clinical trial. Of course, the FDA is not the sole cause of clinical testing; such tests would be necessary even in the absence of FDA regulations. Clearly, though, these regulations have led to significant delays in the availability (not to mention considerable expense) of new pharmaceutical drugs for treatment of disease. Studies have revealed that over the past three decades, the FDA's requirements have more than doubled the development costs for new drugs as well as substantially reduced the rate at which new drugs are introduced, resulting in a considerable lag in the availability of new drugs. Those who defend the FDA's current procedures inevitably refer to the event that led to present-day practices: the thalidomide affair.

Thalidomide was introduced in Germany in 1957 as a nontoxic sedative. It was sold in 48 countries before it was associated with severe birth defects. The drug was never sold in the United States, although some Americans obtained it abroad or in research trials. Finally, in the United States, approval for thalidomide was requested in 1960 but withheld by FDA reviewer Frances Kelsey while she investigated reports that the drug caused peripheral nerve injury. Kelsey found that during the course of its widespread use, more than 12,000 babies were born with no limbs or tiny, flipper-like arms and legs. By 1961, news of the drug's fetal side effects was well known, and the drug was removed from the world market. Because of Kelsey's decision to withhold the drug pending investigation, it was never made available in this country; thus essentially thousands of children throughout the United States were spared birth defects. As a result, Kelsey was awarded the President's Gold Medal for Distinguished Service.

In 1997, a New Jersey company approached the FDA in an attempt to revive thalidomide as a treatment for a form of Hansen's disease (leprosy). The question was whether the drug's reemergence on the market would pose more of a benefit than a threat. After an intense debate of its approval, the FDA agreed to approve the sale of thalidomide in the United States for Hansen's disease patients suffering from inflammation, a condition called *erythema nodosum leprosum*. Once on the market, the drug was studied for use in a wider range of conditions, such as AIDS-related wasting and ulcers, cancer, lupus, rheumatoid arthritis, and autoimmune diseases. The FDA, though, has not forgotten the thalidomide horror stories of the 1960s and has recommended that it be sold under the tightest restrictions ever implemented for a drug in the United States—even demanding that a photo of a child thalidomide victim be shown to every doctor who prescribes it and every patient who takes it.

Resulting from the 1960s thalidomide decision, the powers of the FDA were expanded in 1962 under the Kefauver-Harris Amendments to the Food, Drug, and Cosmetic Act. The earlier statute, enacted in 1938, had prohibited the marketing of new drugs until they were found to be "safe" by the FDA. However, the 1962 amendments added a new criterion: that the drug be proven to be both safe and effective. Ironically, the thalidomide scare was one addressing safety and not efficacy. After the 1962 amendments, the FDA's role shifted from that of an evaluator of evidence to an active participant in the research process. Between 1962 and 1967, the average review time for new drugs more than quadrupled, rising from 7 to 30 months. Although in recent years the FDA has attempted to streamline this process, NDA review time has not improved. By the end of the 1980s, average NDA review time was 32 months (Kazman, 1991). In addition, the development time for new drugs, which averaged

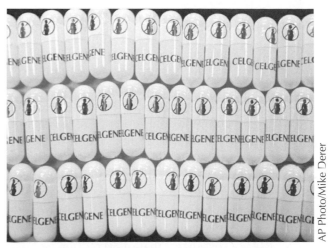

These capsules of thalidomide carry a symbol of a pregnant woman to warn women who are pregnant or plan to become pregnant against use of the drug that has caused thousands of infant deformities. In 1998, the Celgene Corporation was granted approval from the U.S. Food and Drug Administration to market thalidomide (with severe restrictions) to be used to treat leprosy.

AP Photo/Mike Derer

between four to six years in the 1960s, doubled to 10 years (Kazman, 1991).

The obvious policy question stemming from the thalidomide experience is: How many lives are lost or damaged during the lengthy development and review process for new drugs? Let's consider two examples. Misoprostol, approved in 1988, was the first medication used to prevent gastric ulcers that result from aspirin and other anti-inflammatory drugs. Such drugs are commonly taken by arthritis sufferers, who often develop ulcers, which are thought to cause 10,000 to 20,000 deaths each year through internal bleeding. Misoprostol is reported to produce a 15-fold reduction in such ulcers. By the time the drug was approved in the United States, it was already available in 43 foreign countries. Therefore, if the drug is 94 percent effective (as reported) and if the FDA's estimate that there are between 10,000 and 20,000 annual ulcer-related deaths is accurate, misoprostol could have saved between 8,000 and 15,000 lives during the FDA's nine-and-one-half-month review period.

Experts have debated the best way to deal with lengthy delays in the approval process for new drugs, but a consensus does not exist. Some have suggested that the FDA's veto power over new drugs be changed to a system of certification. Under this proposed system, new drugs that have not been approved could still be available by prescription but would be clearly labeled as unapproved. This system would enable critically ill persons to go beyond the circle of official approval but remain under the supervision of a physician. Regardless of what happens with the approval process, it is clear that the pharmaceutical drug business faces two critical issues in the upcoming years: the development time for new drugs and the built-in expense of developing those drugs. Both are problems of such enormity that quick-fix solutions are unlikely.

ADVERSE DRUG REACTIONS

Drugs can have wonderful benefits, but they also have risks. Consider the February 1997 case of four-year-old Harry Donnelly, who died while having his adenoids removed during routine surgery at a Peekskill, New York, hospital. It was not the operation that killed him but rather a deadly combination of two common drugs—nonprescription Neo-Synephrine, an allergy medicine that also controls bleeding, and a beta-blocking drug that lowers high blood pressure. Both drugs are widely used by doctors and hospitals, but Harry's death was no fluke. Investigators discovered 12 other cases in which combining these two drugs during surgery caused adverse reactions, including two additional deaths. Such tragedies occur with shocking frequency.

A 1998 study published by the *Journal of the American Medical Association* (*JAMA*) estimated that of 30 million people hospitalized each year, an average of 100,000 die from bad reactions to legal prescription drugs. Another 2.2 million suffer side effects so severe that they are permanently disabled or require long-term hospital stays. The *JAMA* study ranked adverse drug reactions as the fourth leading cause of death (Sternberg, 1998). Over the years, several observations have been made about drugs coming on the market:

- Heart medication can cause gum disease.
- Diet medication may result in heart problems.
- Hair-growth medication may cause liver problems and high blood pressure.
- New anti-breast cancer medicine may cause liver problems.

The problem begs the obvious question: Why are so many people being killed by our healthcare system? Some experts have argued that there is a systemwide breakdown in the manner in which powerful drugs are marketed, prescribed, and monitored, resulting in a lack of consumer protections. The protections that do exist depend on the voluntary efforts of the pharmaceutical companies interested in promoting their products and the doctors and hospitals, which may have a greater incentive to hide mishaps than to be proactive in preventing them.

- *Haphazard monitoring.* Although the Food and Drug Administration has sped up the approval process for newly developed drugs, it is approving the sale of drugs with more serious side effects, especially for treatment of fatal diseases such as cancer and AIDS. Drug companies are required to report toxic side effects found in prescription medicines, but there are no mandatory requirements for hospitals and doctors to report deadly problems. Instead, the FDA maintains only a database of problems reported voluntarily through its MedWatch system. Some pharmacist groups have complained that the voluntary system misses all but a fraction of the serious drug reactions and that it increases lag time to public notification about deadly side effects.

- *Hyping benefits over risks*. Drug companies spend more than $12 billion a year to promote the benefits of prescription drugs. It is safe to say that far fewer of their resources are directed at alerting hospitals and doctors to the dangers of drugs and educating them about the safest drug for any given medical condition. There is no legal requirement mandating that hospital patients receive information about the possible side effects of the medications they are given. Moreover, it was only after a 20-year fight that drug companies and pharmacists agreed in 1997 to begin providing warnings for prescriptions bought by consumers.

- *Medical ignorance*. Most medical schools provide doctors with little training in pharmacology. Moreover, the nurses who often administer drugs to patients frequently receive no formal education on drug therapy. In fact, both groups get most of their information from drug company representatives, who are interested in selling their particular product. As a result, health providers are often ill-informed about drug interactions and ways of spotting and counteracting deadly drug reactions.

- *Downplaying preventable mishaps*. Pharmacy associations estimate that only 40 percent of hospitals follow industry guidelines for monitoring and reporting adverse reactions. When mishaps occur, hospital officials admit that many hospitals discourage voluntarily alerting others to potential problems because of fear of malpractice suits. The *JAMA* report stated that 42 percent of the most serious drug reactions were preventable (Sternberg, 1998).

Speculation continues regarding what can be done to safeguard against adverse drug reactions, but one suggestion has been that diligent tracking of medical effects, along with increased communication among healthcare workers, is the key. It has been suggested that bedside computer terminals in hospitals could be one way to chart and track drugs. Another suggestion is federal regulations requiring hospitals to show that they regularly measure adverse drug events and medication error rates. Some feel that because hospitals, doctors, and pharmaceutical companies have little reason to move quickly, safeguarding requirements should be made law to protect unknowing and uninformed patients in future years.

DOMESTIC MARIJUANA CULTIVATION

Over the decades, marijuana has consistently remained one of the economic staples in the illegal drug business. So far in this book we have discussed several foreign cannabis sources that focus on smuggling their products into the United States. The majority of foreign marijuana operations consist of peasant farmers who grow the crop as their primary source of cash. Because marijuana grows in almost all 50 U.S. states, domestic cultivation also contributes greatly to the nation's overall drug production. Whether foreign or domestic enterprises are concerned, marijuana cultivation and trafficking have proven to be a relatively easy-entry illicit market. All that is required for a simple growing operation is seeds, a water source, land, and a willingness to enter into a criminal enterprise that in some states can result in a prison term as long as 25 years.

In spite of potentially long prison sentences, marijuana growing appears to be on the increase. For example, in 2010, the National Drug Intelligence Center reported that domestic marijuana cultivation was occurring at high levels, and eradication was increasing across the United States. Recent research shows that marijuana cultivation operations appear to be most prevalent in western states but have been increasing in many eastern states. The most active states for cultivation operations are California, Hawaii, Kentucky, Oregon, Tennessee, Washington, and West Virginia. The average potency of marijuana also steadily increased since the late 1980s to its highest recorded level in 2008 (National Drug Intelligence Center, 2010). This continuous yearly increase can be partially attributed to improvements in outdoor and indoor cultivation methods, discussed later in this chapter. No reliable estimates are available regarding the amount of domestically cultivated or processed marijuana.

Indoor marijuana cultivation has continued to be a preferred method for growers because this method helps them avoid heightened detection and potential eradication of outdoor grow sites. It also provides growers higher profits by trafficking higher-grade marijuana. Statistics show that more than 8 million plants were eradicated in 2008.

In spite of continuing increases in the amount of domestically grown marijuana, much of the cannabis consumed in the United States is foreign-produced. The two primary foreign source areas for marijuana distributed within the United States are Canada and Mexico. Mexican drug-trafficking organizations have relocated many of their outdoor cannabis cultivation operations in Mexico from traditional growing areas to more remote locations in central and northern Mexico, primarily to reduce the risk of eradication and gain easier access to U.S. drug markets. Asian criminal groups are the primary producers of high-potency marijuana in Canada.

The amount of marijuana available for distribution in the United States is unknown; an accurate estimate is not possible. Despite increasing eradication efforts in the United States, the availability of marijuana remains high, with stabilized prices.

Levels of marijuana use in the United States are higher than those for any other drug, particularly among adults; however, rates of marijuana use are decreasing among adolescents. Some law enforcement agencies identify marijuana as the greatest drug threat in their jurisdictions. Marijuana use can result in adverse health consequences to abusers, placing a burden on medical services.

No single criminal organization is thought to control domestic marijuana production and trafficking, probably due to the easy-entry nature of the business and the difficulty criminal organizations would experience in attempting to monopolize it. Consequently, the domestic marijuana market has spawned the development of a rural criminal who lives and operates in a scarcely populated agrarian area. Law enforcement in these areas is often diffused, resulting

Figure 5.4

> The National Guard Counterdrug Program has assisted local, state, and federal law enforcement agencies annually since 1989 with cannabis eradication. Soldiers and airmen provide aerial reconnaissance, ground reconnaissance, and criminal-analyst support in the 50 states and four territories. In 2008, 6,239,221 cannabis plants and 849,141 pounds of processed marijuana were seized by law enforcement officers with the assistance of the National Guard.

A Closer Look: National Guard Involvement in Cannabis Eradication

in growers who can operate with impunity while their operations are cloaked by thick forests, lush vegetation, and inaccessible mountain slopes. These factors also help conceal marijuana-growing operations from rival growers or "pot poachers" in the area.

To help hide their plants, outdoor growers frequently disburse them among corn and tomato plants or along riverbeds and creeks. Over the years, police agents have discovered deadly booby traps in and around marijuana patches that are difficult to detect. Other deterrents used

> **Critical Thinking Task**
>
> This section discusses the results of increased law enforcement efforts by rural police officers. In light of these results, do you agree or disagree that police should continue to vigorously enforce the law against marijuana cultivation in those areas?

by growers include hidden steel-jaw traps, guard dogs, and armed guards. These devices are designed not only to serve as a deterrent for police and poachers but as a signal to nearby growers, who may be heavily armed and potentially violent. As mentioned earlier, growers have resorted to indoor growing operations not only to conceal their operations but also to provide year-long harvesting opportunities.

Business Considerations

Marijuana growers are a somewhat fragmented group of traffickers who rely on kinship or local "good ole boy" networks. Operations are typically financed by either previous transactions or by "jobbers" furnishing special lighting, fertilizer, or other equipment in exchange for a percentage of the harvest. Police have documented cases, however, in which large-scale cultivation operations were financially backed by business executives looking for alternate ways to invest their money. The packaging of marijuana remains somewhat universal throughout the country. After harvest, it is usually placed in large trash bags for transportation to its destination. For smaller retail sales of one-quarter pound or less, smaller zipper-closing plastic bags are usually used.

Marijuana growers have learned that many police raids are a product of so-called search-and-destroy missions based on information from informants. Therefore, many growing operations are now automated, allowing the grower to be absent in case of a police raid. This explains why search-and-destroy operations are often unproductive and rarely are a top enforcement priority for police.

Types of Domestic Marijuana

As noted in Chapter 3, there are several types or grades of marijuana. It is becoming increasingly clear that the marijuana cultivation business is experiencing a horticultural revolution of sorts. That is, many growers, in search of higher profits, are continuously experimenting with techniques for producing more potent strains of marijuana. Each cultivated grade represents different types of growing technology and results in differing degrees of potency (and prices) for the manicured retail marijuana plant. Although state and federal drug laws do not differentiate among the grades of marijuana (they only require a showing that the drug evidence is cannabis), the grower is very interested in producing the most potent plant for greater profit margins. The DEA has identified three basic types of marijuana that grow domestically:

- *Indian hemp* (commonly referred to as *ditchweed*) is the most prevalent type of marijuana that grows in the United States. This is a wild-growing marijuana that has little market value and typically grows in uncultivated areas such as fields, ditch banks, and fence rows and along railroad tracks. Indian hemp grows in many types of soil and reproduces itself each year by its own seeds from the previous year's crop. These seeds can lie dormant for up to seven years. Because Indian hemp is not cultivated from potent seeds, its THC content is quite low, averaging around 0.14 percent. Because of its low potency, it will sometimes be mixed with other more potent marijuana as filler.
- *Commercial-grade marijuana* is the most common type of marijuana sold on the street. It is produced from cannabis plants that have been cultivated in a growing area where the male and female plants are permitted to grow in the same location and the female plants have been fertilized. As a rule, the entire marijuana plant (usually the female) is harvested, stripped of its leaves, and marketed. The growing season usually begins around mid-April, with harvest season beginning sometime during August. At maturity, plants may reach heights of 15 feet and can be harvested up until the first frost (usually some time in October). The THC content of the commercial marijuana plant ranges from 5 percent to 8 percent.
- *Sinsemilla*, a Spanish word meaning "without seeds," is a cannabis plant that represents the most potent type of marijuana on the illicit market and the type that will bring the highest profit return for the trafficker. Sinsemilla is produced from unfertilized female cannabis plants in a growing area where the male cannabis plants are removed before pollination. Marijuana plants allowed to grow in this fashion produce more flowers and resin in an

attempt to attract male pollen. It is the resin and flowers that contain the highest amounts of THC, usually averaging between 8 percent and 12 percent potency. Frequently, only the female flower tops (buds) are harvested and marketed.

One high-grade strain of sinsemilla grown in the United States is *cannabis indica*, imported from Afghanistan. This is popular because it grows into a short, squatty plant that produces one to two pounds of buds per plant. These buds are high in THC content and mature in four to five months.

Hashish is also produced from marijuana. This is accomplished by taking the drug-rich resinous secretions of the cannabis plant and drying and compressing them into a variety of forms such as balls or cookie-like sheets. Another form of cannabis, *hash oil*, is produced by repeated extraction of cannabis materials to yield a dark, tenacious liquid. The THC content of both hashish and hash oil is considerably higher than in the plant itself.

Figure 5.5
Source: University of Mississippi Potency Monitoring Project.

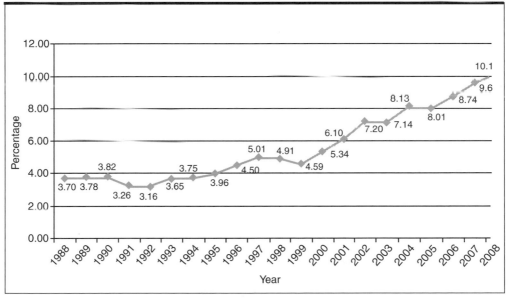

Average Percentage of THC in Samples Seized Marijuana, 1988–2008

Many marijuana growers have perfected indoor growing techniques that enable them to harvest plants year-round. According to the DEA, Oregon pot growers have developed a technique called *cloning*. In this technique, growers cultivate hybrid marijuana and select the most superior plants. A "cut" is then taken from the mother plant and soaked in a root stimulant. After the cutting develops roots, it is planted in pots and aided by a halide lighting system. Another technique, called *hydroponics*, is also used to grow marijuana in a greenhouse. Hydroponics is the science of growing plants in a soil-free, mineral-rich solution and is commonly used for indoor cultivation of tomatoes and cucumbers. Marijuana produced by the hydroponic method will typically produce a THC content at least twice that of marijuana produced by traditional methods. The DEA estimates that it takes only one square foot of space to grow a mature plant. Therefore, a facility with only 400 square feet of hydroponic growing area can, under optimal growing conditions, cultivate marijuana on a year-round basis and generate an estimated $5 million a year.

Figure 5.6
Source: Domestic Cannabis Cultivation Assessment, 2009.

	2004	2005	2006	2007	2008
Indoor	203,896	270,935	400,892	434,728	450,986
Outdoor	2,996,225	3,938,151	4,830,766	6,599,599	7,562,322
Total	**3,200,121**	**4,209,086**	**5,231,658**	**7,034,327**	**8,013,308**

Trends and Differences Between Outdoor and Indoor Marijuana Cultivation Production, 2004–2008

Marijuana cultivators and processors come from a wide range of backgrounds and operate in a variety of ways. For example, research by Ralph Weisheit (1992) found that many West Coast growers cultivate the plant for their own use and for sales to friends but are not necessarily large traffickers. In fact, he suggested that a considerable number of domestic cultivators were still operating within the context of a counterculture frame of reference. Weisheit's research in other areas, such as the Midwest, has generally shown marijuana cultivating and processing to be a disorganized, ancillary business often engaged in by otherwise law-abiding farmers. Some research on Kentucky, however, has indicated that cultivation there is becoming more highly organized, with law enforcement officials warning of a "cartelization" of the trade.

Law enforcement agents carry bundles of marijuana plants after clearing a patch of the plant from national forest land in Washington state. Illegal marijuana-growing operations are a problem in counties with huge tracts of open space and few resources to tackle them.

In eastern Kentucky, in particular, where high-grade marijuana with THC content as high as 18 percent is grown in small plots because of the rugged topography, there is increasing evidence of sophisticated organization in the marijuana market and of the creation of incipient organized crime groups. Ironically, one of the factors that appears to have stimulated the change from small, ad hoc, disorganized growing to the creation of highly organized criminal groups is Kentucky's federally funded law enforcement campaign against the marijuana industry. Stepped-up enforcement seems to have resulted in the creation of a more efficient and more dangerous marijuana industry.

CLANDESTINE LABORATORIES

As we have pointed out throughout this book, of the many different drugs that have become popular over the years, some are organic in nature and some are synthesized by chemists in illicit drug laboratories. It should be noted here that even though some drugs may be of an organic origin, a degree of chemical synthesis is necessary for the completion of the finished product. This is true, for example, with heroin and cocaine. Many popular drugs that have emerged over the years are synthetic in nature and originate in the clandestine laboratory. These include:

- Hallucinogens (LSD, PCP, MDMA)
- Stimulants (methamphetamine, amphetamines)
- Controlled substance analogues (designer drugs)

Drugs such as LSD seem to be available almost everywhere in the country, but their production appears to be regional. For example, for years LSD and PCP laboratories have been abundant in California, whereas much of the methamphetamine (meth) is produced in illegal laboratories in the West and Southwest. The size of most clandestine labs is relatively modest, since they generally produce one specific drug. Expertise to operate a lab is usually minimal, and much of the equipment and chemicals is readily available and inexpensive. This is true especially when the profits that can be realized are considered. One of the most commonly produced illicit drugs in the United States is methamphetamine. One of its immediate precursors, phenyl-2-propanone, is easily synthesized into methamphetamine. Like many other drugs, the production of methamphetamine is fairly cheap and effortless. The actual setting up of a lab can cost as little as $2,000 and can be enormously profitable, since one day's production can generate as much as $50,000 (DEA, 1996).

The spreading popularity of illicit labs is partly due to successes in federal drug interdiction efforts. Many traffickers feel safer making their own drugs domestically than they do risking detection and arrest as a result of dealing with foreign suppliers. As with the marijuana cultivator, the clandestine lab operator commonly seeks isolation in rural settings, where his or her activities will go unnoticed. For example, one of the largest illicit methamphetamine laboratories ever discovered in the United States was located in the mountains of rural McCreary County, Kentucky, and involved participants from Kentucky, Florida, Illinois, and Tennessee. Often this desire for rural isolation is due to the distinctive odors emitted by meth and PCP labs. In an urban setting, these odors can reveal the existence of a lab.

Figure 5.7
Source: Drug Enforcement Administration (2008), "Maps of Methamphetamine Lab Incidents," found at www.justice.gov/dea/concern/map_lab_seizures.html.

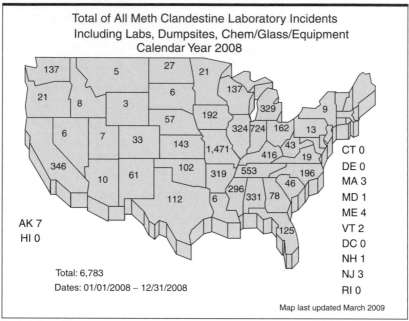

Meth Lab Incidents–2008

The Growing Meth Menace

In Salt Lake City, Utah, visitors are shown photographs of a woman in her late twenties who has been arrested several times for dealing in methamphetamine, a notoriously addictive and increasingly common street drug. She used the drug herself, and the photos show her appearance aging some 30 years over a five-year period: cheeks sinking, eyes turning glassy, teeth rotting. Utah, a predominantly Mormon state, largely denounces coffee, tobacco, and alcohol. However, by the middle of the decade, it ranked third nationally in the percentage of arrested men who tested positive for meth, and meth-related crimes were said to account for perhaps 80 percent of the criminal activity in the state (*The Economist*, 2005).

Meth—also known as ice, crank, crystal, or glass—is, in the eyes of many, America's leading drug problem. Limited to California and the Pacific Northwest in the 1990s, it has now spread across the country. In Missouri, 2,000 meth labs were discovered in 2004. Atlanta has become the gateway for meth distribution across much of the East Coast, with 174 pounds seized in one raid in 2005.

The growing presence of methamphetamine is supported by recent trafficking patterns and national statistics. For example, according to the National Drug Intelligence Center, in 2008 the flow of methamphetamine into the United States from Mexico was generally on the increase, but during 2007 its availability decreased in the United States, causing insta-bility in the methamphetamine supply chain. Before 2007, drug users in the United States relied on the strong flow of methamphetamine produced in Mexico, a supply system initially established in 2005 and strengthened in 2006. However, ephedrine and pseudoephedrine restrictions in Mexico resulted in a decrease in methamphetamine production there and reduced the flow of the drug from Mexico to the United States in 2007 and early 2008. By mid-2008, Mexican drug-trafficking organizations shifted their production operations from Mexico to the United States particularly to California (National Drug Intelligence Center, National Methamphetamine Threat Assessment, 2009). In addition, Mexican traffickers began adapt-ing their operating procedures in several other ways, including smuggling restricted chemicals through new routes, importing nonrestricted chemi-cal derivatives instead of precursor chemicals, using alternative production methods, and diverting precursor chemicals from sources in Southeast Asia and South America.

Methamphetamine can be made with a handful of ingredients—pseudoephedrine (a common ingredient in many cold remedies), red phos-phorus, muriatic acid, fertilizer, and iodine. Recipes can be found widely on the Internet. One day's work in a kitchen can yield a dozen doses. Injected or smoked, methamphetamine works almost instantly on the brain, releasing far more dopamines (the brain's primary pleasure transmitters) than cocaine or heroin. Users feel intense pleasure followed by an energetic high that can last for days.

Meth's physical consequences are shocking. The rotten teeth of a "meth mouth" are common in heavy users, a byproduct of the drug's effects on the metabolic system plus the large quantities of sugary soft drinks consumed to alleviate the dry mouth caused by the drug. Methamphetamine drastically alters the brain, shrinking it 1 percent a year with heavy use.

In May 2005, federal and local police in Salem, Massachusetts, raided a nearby meth "superlab" run by Mexican nationals, which was estimated to turn out 90 pounds of meth in two or three days, enough for 400,000 jolting doses. Big labs like this were common until recently, when restric-tions on the sale of medicines containing pseudoephedrine slashed their numbers. Oklahoma, Illinois, Missouri, California, Ohio, and several other states are limiting the sale of cold cures; Oregon is discussing a complete ban.

Another recent development with newly imposed restrictions on precursors is a technique adopted by some methamphetamine traffickers known as ephed-rine and pseudoephedrine smurfing. *Smurfing* is a method that enables traffick-ers to acquire large quantities of precursor chemicals. Meth producers purchase the chemicals at or below thresholds from multiple retail locations. Traffickers often employ friends or associates to increase the speed with which chemicals can be acquired (National Drug Intelligence Center, National Methamphetamine Threat Assessment, 2009).

Figure 5.8
Source: Organized Crime Drug Enforcement Task Force (1988). *Annual Report*. Washington, DC: U.S. Department of Justice.

The briefing from the California drug agent was to-the-point: "We have word that the cooker could be all screwed up from smelling this stuff, and he could be violent." The plan for the raid was simple: run into the suspected methamphetamine lab located just east of here in a wooded and hilly area, "grab the guy and come out." It was a scenario increasingly played out in the piney woods in this part of the country. Methamphetamine labs are sprouting like mushrooms, and the illegal stimulant, also known as crank, crystal, and speed, is rivaling the popularity of cocaine for a growing army of users.

Twenty minutes after the briefing, the investigators, armed to the hilt, turned off a gravel road and drove up a secluded drive. The movement of the men seemed at odds with the gentle spring country afternoon. The warm sun filtered through a thick stand of trees and danced off a small farm pond. The day would have otherwise seemed languid. Not today. A half-dozen drug agents dressed like Ninja warriors in black chemically resistant, flame retardant hoods, shirts, and pants charged breakneck from a van. Their target: a faded gray ranch-style house like any other a tourist might pass if roaming these hollows and hills.

State troopers took positions at the sides of the house. Two drug agents rigidly aimed automatic pistols and shotguns into a window and door. Other agents stormed the house.

It was over in seconds. "The house is clear," a sweating federal drug agent yelled hoarsely. His chest was heaving. The agents led out a groggy man of 55 that had moved into the house the previous year.

The air inside the house was tested for toxic fumes, but none were detected. The lab in the back would easily rival any high school chemistry laboratory. The walls were covered with plastic sheets, and a long hose ran from a condenser to a ceiling exhaust fan where gasses were released to the air. Thousands of dollars of flasks, beakers, glass tubing, and large glass pots lined the walls. Two 12-liter pots containing methamphetamine oil were still cooking on two stoves under the watchful eye of a closed-circuit camera.

In cluttered rooms and hallways and in a shed outside, agents found more evidence: 25 gallons of hydrochloric acid, 25 barrels of freon, and containers of red phosphorus, a chemical that when overcooked can produce deadly phosphine gas, used in World War I. Finally, in a back bedroom, the agents struck paydirt: 29 heat-sealed baggies of white methamphetamine powder.

Close-Up: The Meth Lab

Categories of Illicit Labs

Despite the numerous types of drugs produced by illicit laboratories, the manufacturing process can be broken down into three distinct categories:

- The *extraction lab* produces illicit substances by removing elements from one substance and creating another. Both hashish and methamphetamine are often manufactured using the benzedrine inhaler method of extraction.

- The *conversion lab* converts existing illicit drugs to a different form of the same drug. Crack is an example; it is cocaine that is converted into a freebase form for street sale.
- The *synthesis lab* transforms one substance to another, resulting in a different and more powerful drug. For example, the precursor phenyl-2-propanone is a dangerous drug used to manufacture methamphetamine powder. This process is different from the methamphetamine extraction method discussed earlier.

Investigating a clandestine lab is especially dangerous for police because of the explosive, corrosive, and hazardous materials usually associated with the drug-manufacturing process and because many labs are fortified with deadly booby traps. In many cases, even a slight spark can create a chain reaction resulting in a massive explosion of the laboratory. As noted earlier, in some instances agents have fainted from fumes emitted from the laboratories. For this reason, investigators who raid the labs now wear protective plastic jumpsuits, rubber gloves, respirators, and air tanks. Portable showers in vans are sometimes used to allow agents to wash off contaminants.

Figure 5.9
Source: National Drug Intelligence Center, National Methamphetamine Threat Assessment, 2009.

A one-pot methamphetamine laboratory actually uses a variation of the lithium ammonia method of production; however, in the one-pot method, a combination of commonly available chemicals is used to synthesize the anhydrous ammonia essential for methamphetamine production. Cooks using this method are able to produce the drug in approximately 30 minutes at nearly any location by mixing, or "shaking," ingredients in easily found containers such as a 2-liter plastic soda bottle, as opposed to using other methods that require hours to heat ingredients. Producers often use the one-pot cook while traveling in vehicles and dispose of waste components along roadsides. Discarded plastic bottles may carry residual chemicals that can be toxic, explosive, or flammable.

A Closer Look: "One-Pot" or "Shake-and-Bake" Methamphetamine Production

Criminal drug lab operators have not only been documented mixing deadly toxic chemicals, but they also have been found to dump toxic waste down bathroom drains or in holes dug outside in the ground. These actions make some lab locations akin to hazardous waste sites.

Clandestine laboratories are often operated by nonprofessional individuals with a limited knowledge of chemistry. Some labs are run by people that have learned various processing techniques through their peers in the criminal underworld. The methamphetamine market, for example, was dominated for many years by the Pagans motorcycle club. The skills utilized in drug processing and the safety procedures initiated by a group like the Pagans are highly suspect.

Controlling Precursor Chemicals

Legally obtained substances that are typically used by illicit lab operators to make their final product are known as *precursors*. Essential chemicals
called *solvents* are also needed to produce the final drug product, but they do
not actually become part of the drug itself. In 1988, the Chemical Diversion
and Trafficking Act was passed, requiring detailed record keeping and reporting of transactions of all purchases over a designated quantity of each chemical
and reporting of all "suspicious" purchases to the DEA. In turn, the DEA has
power to deny the sale of chemicals to any person or company they deem likely
to use them for the making of an illegal drug.

By 2005, 42 state governments had passed their own legislation regulating the sale of precursor chemicals (ONDCP, 2005). Several states require
companies that manufacture these chemicals to obtain a license with a state
agency and to maintain records that are regularly supplied to that agency.
Essentially, the controlling of precursors is yet another way in which manufacturers of illicit drugs can be identified for arrest or possibly deterred from
drug trafficking activity.

PHARMACEUTICAL DIVERSION

In August 2001, FBI agents arrested Kansas City pharmacist Robert
Courtney for diluting expensive drugs used for chemotherapy cancer treatment. They charged that Courtney diluted the drugs Gemzar and Taxol to
39 percent of the prescribed dose, enabling him to skim hundreds of dollars per
prescription. More alarming is that the diluted drugs were lifesaving prescriptions for cancer patients who were under the impression they were taking full-
strength medications for their ailments. Though this case represents only one
act of malfeasance on the part of pharmaceutical professionals, it illustrates
the growing problem of drug diversion.

The DEA estimates that because of growing popularity on the street, more
than 200 million dosage units of legally made drugs find their way from legitimate sources, such as hospitals and pharmacies, to the street drug abuser every
year. Some are lost through drugstore thefts and others through forged prescriptions. It is estimated that the greatest amount of these drugs are diverted
by a handful of corrupt physicians, pharmacists, osteopaths, veterinarians,
dentists, nurses, and other medical professionals. As discussed in earlier chapters, society foots the bill for drug abuse in terms of shoplifting, street crime,
and predatory criminal acts relating to drug abuse. Society also pays the bill
for drugs diverted through Medicaid and prepaid prescription plans offered by
some companies and unions.

The 1970 Controlled Substances Act authorized the DEA to regulate all
aspects of the drug-manufacturing and distribution process in the United States.
For the more potent drugs, the DEA can even dictate the thickness of warehouse

walls where they are stored (i.e., eight inches of concrete with steel rods). The DEA also controls the order form needed to purchase drugs (three copies, with one forwarded to DEA headquarters). Through these mechanisms, the DEA claims that much of the diversion from warehouses and factories has been controlled. The result has been increased diversion at the retail level, marked by a sharp rise in drugstore robberies and burglaries, along with increased pressure on some doctors and druggists to cross the line from "professional" to "pusher." Problems in drug diversion involve both medical professionals and people who attempt to acquire drugs through deceit and trickery. Persons in the latter category are often called *scammers*.

The Scammer

To aid in understanding the problem of drug diversion, investigators should look at the various scams used by street criminals to obtain pharmaceutical drugs. The word *scam* is defined by *Webster's Dictionary* as "to cheat or swindle, as in a confidence game." This is precisely what is happening within the medical care community. This criminal, known as the *scammer* or *professional patient*, acquires drugs through deceit and sells them on the street for profit.

Of all the scammer's targets, the most likely is the physician, because once a prescription has been successfully conned out of a physician, the scammer will experience little trouble having it filled by the pharmacist, since it appears to be legitimate. Pharmacists are the second most likely target of the scammer, especially in trying to pass forged or altered prescriptions. In addition to forgery and alterations of prescriptions, a pharmacist can be an unwitting partner to a scammer. Three methods are the most common: (1) filling prescriptions for the same drugs for the same patient from different physicians; (2) filling prescriptions for the same patient too frequently; and (3) accepting refills for prescriptions when the scammer calls in the prescription pretending to be the physician. Literally hundreds of diversion schemes have been uncovered throughout the years. The following examples, however, will give some insight into the practices of "professional patients."

The Fat Lady Scam

The "fat lady" scam is a common deception that is usually perpetrated by several women who are severely overweight. The plan involves the women moving into a new community and developing a schedule requiring each member to visit a maximum number of physicians each day for a week or so. The scam unfolds as each woman tells the physician that she is chronically unhappy with her life because of being overweight. Details may be added, such as that her husband is going to leave her and fight for custody of the children, she is considering having her stomach stapled, and so forth. At this point, the patient begins hinting about a particular drug, such as preludin, amphetamines, or another Schedule II drug. The physician will usually refuse to prescribe Schedule II drugs for this purpose but might be willing to prescribe Didrex. After the patient is issued a prescription for this drug, the woman might request a prescription for Valium to keep her from getting too edgy. Instead of taking the prescribed drugs themselves, the women sell them for profit on the street.

The Breast Cancer Scam

This scam is a fairly common one in many states and involves individuals who are actually experiencing a legitimate medical problem. For example, the scam was first documented in the St. Louis area and involved a woman who truly suffered from breast cancer. The woman would simply appear at a physician's office and present her case for treatment. In the St. Louis case, Dilaudid was the only drug determined to give her relief, and physicians would usually agree to give her a prescription. The patient saw seven doctors on a regular basis in different surrounding towns. As with the previous scam, the prescription drugs she obtained were sold on the street for a substantial profit.

The Toothache Scam

The toothache scam is popular among narcotics addicts who are also experiencing a tooth-decay problem. These scammers will try to obtain Schedule II narcotics from dentists and physicians at the same time. Sometimes scammers have attempted to obtain telephone prescriptions for the desired drug without even seeing the dentist. If the scammers choose to see the dentist, they will appear with a concocted legitimate reason for having to be somewhere else, so the dentist will be pressured to issue a prescription for painkillers such as Demerol or Dilaudid. Once obtained, the drugs are sold on the illicit market.

The Altered "Scrip" Scam

Those prescribers who shortcut the proper prescription-writing practice, especially by using Arabic numerals for dose amounts (not reinforced by a written number), are easy targets for professional patients. By simply matching the ink color of the prescriber's pen, a prescription for "10" can be altered to "40," "5" can become "25," and so forth. A prudent prescription becomes excessive and proportionally more profitable to the professional patient.

Many other scams are facilitated by confidence artists who are elderly, handicapped, or simply clever or brazen enough to attempt such a fraud. All professionals within the medical community are obligated, however, to report any such attempts by criminals when they are first detected.

Doctors as Offenders

What is it that makes a professional registrant choose to become a law violator and a "white-collar" drug dealer? The following are some motivating factors.

- *Greed*. Pharmacists and physicians have easy access to drugs that command top dollar on the street. For example, they pay only about $50 for 500 tablets of Knoll Pharmaceutical Company's Dilaudid, a synthetic narcotic similar to morphine (see Chapter 2). On the street, Dilaudid will easily bring between $50 and $60 per tablet. Some corrupt professionals barter drugs or prescriptions for merchandise. Others make their living by operating "diet clinics," in which they freely dispense or prescribe amphetamine tablets, even though the use of the drug for weight control is questionable.
- *Sexual favors*. Some investigations have revealed instances in which physicians and pharmacists give drugs or prescriptions in return for sexual favors. There have been cases of amphetamines being given to prostitutes to help them stay awake.
- *Salvaging a failing medical practice*. Drug diversion is a particular problem in cases of failing medical practices, caused by such circumstances as incompetence, impending retirement, or location problems. Illicit activity on the part of these physicians often results from being deep in debt or having been accustomed to high incomes that have been reduced. An unethical solution to the problem is to write illegal prescriptions or dispense pills for the easy income.
- *Self-addiction*. The addiction to drugs is an occupational disease for some members of the healthcare community. Long hours and the easy availability of drugs make the medical professional susceptible to drug abuse. Physicians who have become addicted may turn to diversion to finance their addiction.
- *Senility*. Some senile doctors and pharmacists have unwittingly yielded to the demands of drug abusers. In other cases, a nurse, medical receptionist, or family member has "taken over" the practice of a senile professional and allowed dangerous drugs to be diverted.
- *Rationalization*. Some professionals justify selling to abusers by rationalizing that they will get drugs anyway, perhaps through street crime or prostitution.

Some of the specific methods that physicians have commonly used to divert prescription drugs include:

- Physicians writing prescriptions in a patient's or family member's name, picking up the drugs themselves, and then telling the pharmacist they will deliver them to the patient.
- Physicians sending patients to pharmacies to have prescriptions filled but requiring the patient to bring the drugs back to the doctor's office, where only part of the drug is administered; the physician keeps the rest.

- Physicians writing prescriptions in their own name at various pharmacies at the same time.
- Physicians (and nurses) self-administering injectable drugs taken from nurses' stations, hospital emergency rooms, or hospital pharmacies.
- Physicians ordering drugs from a number of pharmacies at the same time using DEA official order forms, while ordering the same drugs from one of the many mail-order drug companies.
- Physicians obtaining drug samples and self-administering them.

Although medical institutions have both a legal and a moral obligation to their employees, many shun the responsibility of reporting a suspected diversion problem, or they simply look the other way rather than address the situation. Responsible hospitals, through their boards of directors, regulate their personnel and establish formal policies regarding impairment with strict enforcement (or treatment) provisions. In the case of addicted registrants, many state hospital boards have adopted a policy whereby a physician or nurse can voluntarily submit to treatment under an employee assistance program and remedy the problem before it results in the prosecution of the physician and embarrassment to the hospital. Similar problems are observed with nurses working within the medical field. A distinction should be made here between diversion of drugs for resale and diversion because of personal addiction. Studies have shown that many of those nurses who are diverting drugs do so because of personal physical addictions to those drugs rather than a desire to profit from their sale.

Theft of Drugs

Most healthcare institutions experience some degree of diversion, and generally it is the employees who are the culprits. As indicated, employees who steal drugs are those who have access to drugs—for example, physicians, nurses, pharmacists, and others—and they will most commonly divert drugs such as Valium, morphine, Demerol, Tylenol III with Codeine, Percodan, Percocet, and Ritalin. The type of drug user and available opportunities will have a bearing on whether tablets, capsules, or injectable substances are preferred. Diversion may occur in many different areas of the healthcare facility but are most commonly at one of the following locations: (1) the hospital pharmacy, (2) the nursing area, or (3) the recovery floor.

Substituting Drugs

In the event that the outright theft of drugs is not considered safe by the diversion criminal, the substitution of a controlled drug for a noncontrolled substance might be considered. Substituting drugs may be accomplished, for instance, by appearing to inject a patient with the prescribed medication while, in fact, a worthless substance may be used in its place. This may cause the patient to suffer and could result in additional medical setbacks for the patient. Techniques for substitution vary but commonly include (1) theft through charting (a technique for backdating) and (2) forging the names of other nurses.

Addressing the Problem

Drug diversion persists, in part, because many facilities fail to discipline the people involved. Compounding the problem is the fact that in many cases violators themselves have ways of avoiding punishment. For example, suspected users might quit their positions and join other hospitals. This might happen if drug users on the job are suspected by one or more employees; in an effort to avoid being confronted, the users simply change jobs. In such cases, when the diverter's new employer calls for an employee reference, incriminating information is frequently not shared, thereby allowing the user to carry on with unlawful activities.

Critical Thinking Task

Assume that you are a member of the board of directors for a major hospital. Suggest a policy for the control of prescription drugs within your hospital. Include procedures for the prevention of diversion and for enforcement of the policy.

In other cases, employees who are caught diverting drugs are transferred rather than disciplined. Medical care professionals, like many other types of professionals, are somewhat clannish and reluctant to "snitch" on fellow workers. So, by transferring suspect employees, embarrassing publicity for the institution is avoided. Of course, these reactions offer no incentive for violators to discontinue their involvement in drug diversion activity.

Problems in Diversion Investigations

Even though pharmacists are required by law to account for every dose of dangerous drugs they order, suspicious fires, robberies, and break-ins can destroy prescription files and cover shortages of pills. For these and many other reasons, evidence of diversion is difficult to acquire. For example, undercover agents investigating this type of criminal behavior may find that the suspect doctors claim that they were just "practicing medicine" and attempting to cure a patient by prescribing drugs for an illness. Other violations are more blatant, such as when physicians literally sell drugs to friends and associates or barter prescriptions for merchandise.

Other problems arise in the prosecution of diversion cases. For example, prosecutors are usually eager to file charges against drug dealers from the street, but when the drug dealer happens to be a physician in the community, charges are sometimes difficult to bring. Moreover, prosecutors are often reluctant to try "respectable" citizens who have the resources to mount an active defense against the charges. In addition, there are other pressures on prosecutors. They may have a social or political relationship with the registrant. If they are in a rural county where doctors' offices are few and far between, they know that any doctor forced out of business could leave some families without easy access to medical care. Furthermore, inconvenienced voters often have good memories when the prosecutor has to stand for reelection, creating a situation in which the prosecutor may actually be punished by the very public he or she serves for attempting to apply diversion laws to physicians. Even when charges are brought against physicians, prosecutors may have a difficult time convincing juries of the seriousness of the violation, or it may be difficult to explain the complexities of the diversion case to the jury. Because of these considerations, a conviction may not be forthcoming in the case.

The Drug Audit

One of the nine control mechanisms contained within the 1970 Controlled Substances Act is a record-keeping requirement for all registrants. This provision requires that full records of quantities of all controlled substances, regardless of which schedule they are under, be kept by registrants. This requirement applies to drugs manufactured, purchased, sold, or inventoried. Limited exceptions to this requirement are available only to researchers and physicians. It is from these records that audits can be performed to trace the flow of any drug from the time it is first manufactured, through the wholesale level, through its final destination at a pharmacy, hospital, or physician's office, and on to the patient. The mere existence of this requirement is often enough to discourage many types of diversion. Under the record-keeping requirement, one distinction is made: The records for Schedule I and II drugs must be maintained separately from all other records of the registrant. The purpose of this requirement is to allow investigators the ability to audit the most abusable drugs more expeditiously.

SUMMARY

Although foreign traffickers make significant contributions to the drug problem in the United States, many domestic criminals also play a significant role. Domestic drug production primarily centers on three types of illicit activities: marijuana cultivation; clandestine laboratories, which primarily manufacture methamphetamine and PCP; and pharmaceutical diversion.

Figure 5.10
Source: Organized Crime Drug Enforcement Task Force, 1988.

The Five Star Health Club in Fairmont, West Virginia, was in reality a gambling casino. Just three days prior to a police raid that closed it forever, the club was locked up by its owners. This was not the owners' only line of work. Three of the "five stars," the Spadafore brothers, Donnie, John, and Ralph, were drug dealers. The others were their attorney and an ex-cop that was a convicted gambler.

Over a period of years beginning in 1979, the Spadafore organization smuggled multi-kilo quantities of cocaine into Fairmont, then broke it into smaller consignments for distribution in central West Virginia and in Erie, Pennsylvania. Among many other local endeavors, they owned a grocery where, on inquiry, the grocer would pour grams of cocaine from the middle Bisquick box on the shelf.

The gang originally made their wholesale purchases in Miami but soon tired of paying stateside prices and branched out into their own version of international drug smuggling. Donnie, the leader, brought in an Erie, Pennsylvania, organized crime figure, Joseph Scutelli. The organization began to specialize in complicated logistical planning in order to avoid leaving trails. A Peruvian connection was established, improving certainty of supply and reducing price.

In a typical instance, three different private planes were used by the smuggling team. A ring member pilot flew his own aircraft from Lima to Stella Maris in the Bahamas where "the vacationers" were about to leave for Pittsburgh on a charter. "The vacationers" were a retired Erie Police Department detective and his wife, who were used repeatedly because of their ability to blend in with Caribbean tourists. Arriving in Fort Lauderdale at midnight, the couple (and the "dope") boarded another of the organization's planes, which dropped them in Pittsburgh and delivered the cocaine to an unused, unlighted runway of the Morgantown, West Virginia, airport.

At the South American end, drugs were usually packed in a pillow stuffed with llama hair. When transported by car in the United States, the drugs were wrapped in a shoe box and addressed for mailing. If challenged, the driver would report having found the box at a rest stop and say that he planned to mail it.

The Five Star attorney was versatile. At times he stored drugs or money at his home for the group. When an insurance arson was planned by the gang, this "corporate counsel" gave such advice as "put a dog and cat in the house, and you'll get paid easier." According to other defendants, it was he who arranged for and delivered monthly payments to "the Charlies" to give the gang protection from law enforcement. "The Charlies," Anderson and Dodd, were the county prosecutor and the sheriff, both convicted at later dates. The lawyer also was accused of acting as a lookout while the brothers broke into the police garage seeking to recover cash and cocaine that they thought was hidden in an impounded car. (Somebody else got there first.)

A fellow barrister (actually a city judge) was hired to keep police occupied inside the station next door during the break-in. The young judge was seduced into drug dealing by Donnie's offer of a trip to South America to "run some errands." He was halfway to Peru when he learned that the only errand was to pick up drugs and that he would be paid $65,000 for doing so. The temptation was too great.

The information and evidence necessary to bring down the "stars" was developed over a period of four years by agents of the FBI, IRS, West Virginia State Police, and Fairmont Police Department under auspices of the Organized Crime Drug Enforcement Task Force. Faced with a possible life sentence in prison, the Spadafores all entered plea agreements. The mastermind, Donnie, pleaded guilty in the Northern District of West Virginia to

Figure 5.10—*continued*

charges of operating a continuing criminal enterprise, unlawful possession of an unregistered firearm, and filing a false income tax return. He was sentenced to 20 years without parole. John Spadafore's primary role in the organization had been providing the muscle; he pleaded guilty to RICO charges in connection with drugs and also received 20 years. Ralph's role was to provide financial services and present a legitimate front for the organization. He was the overseer of the gambling operation and was responsible for all hiring. Ralph pleaded guilty to violating the RICO statute in connection with gambling and was sentenced to six years. All but one of the 21 persons indicted have been convicted or have pleaded guilty. The last is a fugitive believed to be somewhere in South America.

One of those convicted was Carol Rae Olson, a key supplier to the Spadafore organization and a vice president of an oil company whose jet aircrafts were used to move drugs. Her conviction was especially important because it severed a direct cocaine pipeline from Peru to the United States. Olson was apprehended in Hawaii with Donnie Spadafore's help and found guilty of six counts of racketeering, conspiracy, and cocaine importation. Others found guilty included Scutelli, the ring's lawyer, the city judge, two pilots, and "the vacationers."

Case Study: The Five Star Health Club

The marijuana cultivator will produce one of two types of marijuana: commercial or sinsemilla. The commercial grade is the most common type of marijuana and is generally the easiest to grow. Sinsemilla, on the other hand, is a more potent type of marijuana and will bring twice the street price of the commercial strain. Explaining why fewer marijuana growers are involved with sinsemilla farming than with growing commercial marijuana is the fact that sinsemilla is much more difficult to grow and requires more personal attention and time on the part of the cultivator.

The clandestine lab problem is one of growing proportions in the United States. Lab operators are the most active in the manufacturing of methamphetamine and PCP, both of which have achieved a growing popularity throughout the nation.

Finally, we examined the problem of pharmaceutical diversion by both scammers (also known as *professional patients*) and registrants. The diversion of addictive and dangerous drugs happens for many reasons. Some reasons involve a profit motive; others are related to personal addictions developed by the registrants themselves. In either case, the problem results in the diversion of a significant amount of dangerous drugs that are eventually marketed on the street for exorbitant prices.

Do you recognize these terms?

- cloning
- commercial grade
- conversion lab
- extraction lab
- hash oil
- hashish
- hydroponics

- Indian hemp
- precursors
- professional patient
- scammer
- sinsemilla
- smurfing
- synthesis lab

DISCUSSION QUESTIONS

1. List the three most common types of marijuana grown in the United States.

2. How is sinsemilla grown, and why is its potency so much higher than that of commercial marijuana?

3. What are the two most common methods of indoor growing of marijuana?

4. List the primary drugs manufactured by domestic clandestine laboratories, and explain why these labs are considered dangerous for police investigators.

5. Who are the most likely candidates for the diversion of pharmaceutical drugs?

6. What factors explain why a registrant might become involved in the diversion of pharmaceutical drugs?

7. Discuss some ways in which controlled drugs can be diverted from legal channels of distribution.

8. Explain why the pharmaceutical drug case is usually so difficult to prosecute.

Chapter 6

Drugs and Crime

This chapter will enable you to:

- Understand the relationship between various types of crime and drug abuse
- Comprehend the extent of the police corruption problem as it pertains to drug trafficking
- Understand the domestic and international problem of money laundering
- Realize who the money launderers are and how they operate
- Understand what legal tools are available to prosecutors to combat money laundering

In addition to the physiological effects and medical complications associated with drug abuse, one of the greatest public concerns is the rising spectrum of crime as it relates to the use of drugs. Clearly, a definitive but complex correlation exists between drug crimes and other types of crime, but the nature and extent of the link between drugs and crime are far from being understood. Therefore, the catch phrase *drug-related crime* remains somewhat general. Criminal justice researchers hope to clarify this category of crime in coming years, to predict both drug-trafficking patterns and nondrug-related criminal behavior.

The drugs and crime issue causes one to consider one fundamental question: To what extent does one perpetuate the other? For example, it is clear that abuse and trafficking and use of some substances are by their very nature illegal—users of heroin must possess the drug to use it, but possession of it is forbidden under law. Accordingly, stricter penalties exist on both the state and federal level for heroin's transportation and sale. Moreover, some forms

DOI: 10.1016/B978-1-4377-4450-7.00006-0
© 2011 Elsevier Inc. All rights reserved.

of drug abuse are more likely than not to spur particular types of antisocial behavior. For instance, amphetamine use has been linked to an increase in level of aggression, which has been shown to lead to assaultive behavior in some cases. Frequency of drug use is another factor. One who uses drugs several times a day is at a greater risk of involvement in crime than one who is an occasional user. Finally, many crimes not normally associated with drug use or drug dealing result from drug-related behavior. For example, a user might steal to support his or her habit, or prostitution might finance one's drug use. In fact, studies have shown that criminal activity is almost two to three times higher among frequent users of heroin or cocaine than among irregular users or nonusers of drugs. This does not imply that if drugs were to be eliminated, so would crime, but it does suggest that a causal link may exist.

This chapter identifies and discusses three critical forms of drug-related crime: drug use and predatory crime, police corruption, and money laundering. Each of these plays a significant role in the overall drug problem and should be considered in seeking solutions to the nation's drug dilemma.

Drug Use and Predatory Crime

Some law enforcement officials and researchers have long suspected that a link exists between addictive drugs and the propensity of drug users to commit crime. The available empirical research indicates that drug addicts, particularly heroin addicts, commit crimes more frequently than other population groups. Drug addiction appears to escalate the rate of criminal participation, but that does not mean that drug use causes crime. The need for financial resources to ensure a steady supply of the drug appears to escalate the already manifest criminal involvement of drug users. Several important sources of information about drugs and crime are currently available for helping to determine the extent of drug use (for example, urine testing of arrested persons; surveys of offender populations; criminal justice system records of arrests, convictions, and incarcerations; and surveys of drug users who have entered drug treatment programs).

One tool for measuring drug use and crime was the *Arrestee Drug Abuse Monitoring*, or ADAM, a survey conducted by the U.S. Department of Justice to gauge the prevalence of alcohol and illegal drug use among prior arrestees. ADAM was a reformulation of the prior Drug Use Forecasting (DUF) program. In 2004, the ADAM program was halted due to funding concerns. Other federal measures of drug use focus on self-reporting or on broad national trends. In the majority of cities, more than one-half of arrestees tested were found to have used drugs recently (Zhang, 2003). Of course, one of the problems with this measure is the absence of a nonarrested control group with whom to compare arrestees.

Jail inmate surveys also provide data regarding the link between drugs and crime. Twenty-nine percent of convicted offenders surveyed in 2002 reported that they had used illegal drugs at the time of their offense (Bureau of Justice Statistics, 2005). Prison inmate surveys tell a similar story. In the 2004 *Survey of Inmates in State and Federal Correctional Facilities*, 32 percent of state prisoners and 26 percent of federal prisoners said they had committed their offense under the influence of drugs (Bureau of Justice Statistics, 2006).

Finally, two national studies have shown that most people in treatment for drugs had been arrested or had admitted committing crimes for economic gain prior to entering treatment. The *Drug Abuse Reporting Program* (DARP) concluded that 71 percent had been in jail before entering treatment; the *Treatment Outcome Prospective Study* (TOPS) discovered that about 60 percent of people entering residential treatment programs reported they had committed one or more crimes for economic gain during the year before treatment.

It is also logical to assume that people who buy or sell drugs or who are under the influence of drugs may make likely targets for predatory attacks because they are likely to possess some cash or drugs on their person. Because these people are involved in criminality themselves, other offenders may assume that they will be less likely to report robberies, assaults, or thefts to the police. In addition, a drug buyer or seller who chooses not to report being victimized to the police may choose to take the law into his or her own hands. This can lead to violent encounters such as murder, assault, drive-by shootings, and so forth.

DRUGS AND VIOLENT CRIME

Legal drugs such as alcohol, as well as illicit drugs such as cocaine, amphetamine, and PCP, affect one's physiological functions, cognitive abilities, and moods. However, there is no existing evidence that shows a pharmacologically based drugs–violence relationship. It is the general impression of most experts in the field that the effects of alcohol and other drugs do not directly precipitate violence, but a combination of factors such as the type of drug, the user's personality, and other situational factors may influence one's propensity for aggressive behavior.

A study showing the relationship between certain drugs and violent criminality was conducted by Jeffery Roth for the National Institute of Justice (1994). In the study, several general observations were made. First, it was noted that violence is diverse, with acts as different as drive-by shootings and thoroughly planned serial killings. Second, the report noted that causes of violence are complex, involving a wide variety of factors that were broken down into four levels for study:

- *Macrosocial*. Broad and economic forces that include cultural practices related to alcohol use as well as the economic and social processes surrounding the sale of illicit drugs.
- *Microsocial*. Encounters between people in particular settings that include group drinking in locations where violence is expected and even socially acceptable.
- *Psychosocial*. Individual behavior development from childhood through adulthood. Examples include patterns of heavy drinking and aggression that develop during adolescence and continue into adulthood.
- *Neuro-behavioral*. Processes that underlie all human behavior, which can include the effects of substance abuse on fetal development during pregnancy and the effects of chronic drug abuse on brain functioning.

These factors may operate long before the occurrence of violent events, but it is evident that the causal events for violence are often linked to alcohol or other drugs (Roth, 1994). Specific findings include:

- For the past several decades, alcohol drinking by either the perpetrator of a crime, the victim, or both has immediately preceded at least one-half of all violent crimes.
- Chronic drinkers are more likely than others to have histories of violent behavior.
- Criminals who use illegal drugs commit robberies and assaults more frequently than do nonuser criminals, and they commit them especially frequently during periods of heavy drug usage.
- About 60 percent of arrestees booked for violent crimes were confirmed by laboratory tests to have used at least one illegal drug in the hours before arrest.

Interestingly, alcohol and other drugs modify encounters between people in ways that make such substances a particular risk for violence. Specifically in the case of alcohol, the risk of violence tends to be associated with the substance's effects on the user, compared to illegal drugs, for which most violence is associated with the business of drug purchases and sales. This is illustrated by the fact that many therapists who treat violent sex offenders have reported that their patients have both histories of alcohol abuse and high levels of testosterone. This is further validated by animal studies showing that although alcohol tends to reduce levels of testosterone in some animals, in those with high testosterone levels it promotes aggression at greater levels (Roth, 1994).

As indicated in prior chapters, the business of drug trafficking is also linked to violent crime. Drug markets, which operate outside the world of contract law as a means for arbitrating disputes, substitute illegal mechanisms developed for handling "business-related" problems. Violence is often used to protect or expand markets, intimidate competitors, and retaliate against sellers and buyers who are thought to be cheating. In addition, violence is focused against the police, witnesses, and informers who threaten to identify and convict the trafficker. It has even been suggested that the illicit drug trade attracts people who are prone to violence (Haller, 1989).

Problematic situations abound in the drug trade and can include:

- Protection of drug-producing crops during harvest season
- Territorial disputes between rival drug organizations
- Robberies of drug dealers and their subsequent retaliation
- Interpersonal violence between buyers and sellers of drugs
- Elimination of drug informers and witnesses
- Punishment for selling poor-quality or adulterated drugs
- Failure to pay debts
- Violence involving people other than buyers and sellers, such as victims of robberies

Finally, it is important to mention that a great deal of violence is related indirectly to the illicit drug trade. Examples include the robbery of a business by a person who has spent his rent money on drugs, or spousal assaults arising out of disputes over money.

Other Factors

Cities both large and small across the United States are now targeted by an array of drug gangs claiming turf for drug sales. According to a report by the Department of Justice, an estimated 80 percent of these individuals have already been in jail or prison, with one of every five having six or more convictions on his or her record (Brantley and DiRosa, 1994). Based on these figures, it seems apparent that a more specifically defined public policy is needed in the many areas of drug abuse, and a closer interaction between antidrug programs and the criminal justice system is necessary.

POLICE CORRUPTION

Corruption, regardless of who perpetuates it, erodes communities and the governments that oversee them. Where official corruption exists, an overall lack of public trust and credibility can result. The tentacles of the drug trade sometimes extend to those sworn to protect us from it.

Similar to the alcohol prohibition of the 1920s, current drug prohibition legislation breeds police corruption and abuse. A report by the General Accounting Office noted that on-duty police officers involved in drug-related corruption engage in serious criminal activities such as: (1) conducting unconstitutional searches and seizures, (2) stealing money and/or drugs from drug dealers, (3) selling stolen drugs, (4) protecting drug operations, (5) providing false testimony, and (6) submitting false crime reports. Approximately half of all police officers convicted as a result of FBI-led corruption cases between 1993 and 1997 were convicted for drug-related offenses, and nationwide more than 100 cases of drug-related corruption are prosecuted each year. Every one of the federal law enforcement agencies with significant drug enforcement responsibilities has seen an agent implicated in a corruption case (Drug Policy Alliance, 2007).

Explaining the growth of corruption is not a difficult task. Relative to other opportunities, legitimate or illegitimate, the financial temptations are enormous. Many police officers are demoralized by the scope of drug trafficking. No matter how diligent an officer may be, eradication programs and millions of arrests have done little to stop the illicit supply of drugs, which are now cheaper, purer, and more available than ever. Given the dangers of the law enforcement job, the indifference of many citizens and the frequent lack of appreciation are no doubt disheartening. Some police also recognize that their real function is not so much to protect victims from predators but to regulate an illicit market that cannot be suppressed and that much of society prefers to keep underground.

One of the United States' worst cases of drug-related police corruption occurred in 2001 in California after an officer caught stealing eight pounds of cocaine from a police department's evidence locker turned on his fellow officers to get a reduced sentence. In what was known as the *Rampart scandal*, more than 100 convictions were overturned as police misconduct—ranging from the planting of evidence to "confessions" obtained through beatings—was uncovered. Officers were indicted on corruption charges, including torture, murder, drug dealing, and framing innocent people. The unit's criminal behavior became known as the "Rampart way." *Rampart* refers to a predominately poor, immigrant neighborhood in East Los Angeles that was patrolled—and during that time controlled—by the police officers (Drug Policy Alliance, 2007). Some other examples of police corruption include:

- In Detroit, federal agents arrested three city police officers who were planning a home invasion in the suburb of Southfield, Michigan, with the intent to steal $1 million in cash.
- Starr County (Texas) Sheriff Eugenio Falcon resigned from office after pleading guilty to conspiracy to commit burglary. The investigation revealed that Falcon and other officers referred prisoners to a local bail bond business in exchange for kickback payments. On some occasions, payments were made directly at the sheriff's department.
- In a 69-count federal indictment in New Jersey, nine current or former west New York police officers were charged with taking part in a $600,000 bribery and kickback scheme.

Cases such as these differ somewhat from those of earlier generations of police officers, when officers were simply paid to look the other way while prostitution or gambling rings prospered. It is becoming increasingly clear that

many police officers are choosing
to cross the line and become active
participants in crime.

It is impossible to gauge exactly
how much corruption there is in U.S.
policing today. However, despite the
fact that many police officers are
reluctant to openly discuss the problem of corruption, a substantial body
of literature is available to help provide a general understanding of the
magnitude of the problem.

As far back as 1930, the *Wickersham Commission* declared that in
nearly all large cities there existed an
alliance between criminals and politicians. Since then, it has generally
been the case that efforts to control

Former Los Angeles police officer Rafael Perez reacts
after a judge orders his release from prison in Los Angeles
Superior Court. The former antigang officer, a key informant in the probe of corruption within the LAPD's Rampart
Division, served nearly three years of his five-year jail sentence for stealing cocaine from a police evidence room.

corruption have proved ineffective at best. Even in cases in which corruption
was identified and successfully dealt with by police administrators, it was not
uncommon to see its return.

James Inciardi (1992) wrote that one of the more pervasive problems in the
political arena is the wholesale corruption of both individuals and institutions.
With regard to institutional corruption, money laundering has long tainted the
banking industry. Official corruption also affects law enforcement and public
safety. For example, it permits criminals to continue in their activities, erodes
the reputation of the department and the morale of officers, and hampers the
general effectiveness of community crime control efforts.

Corruption on the official level may take many forms. Specifically, one who
has been compromised by criminal elements may take either a passive or an
active role in corruption. A good example of this situation occurred in 1988,
when more than 75 Miami police officers were under investigation at one time
for possible involvement in criminal activities. Allegations included drug dealing, robbery, theft, and even murder. One investigation in particular revealed
several officers who had ambushed drug dealers bringing cocaine into Miami.
This investigation revealed that officers stole $13 million in cocaine from a boat
anchored in the Miami River and loaded it into marked police vehicles. Duffel
bags full of cocaine were reportedly stacked to the ceilings of the patrol cars.
Three of the suspects, in an effort to escape, jumped into the river and drowned.

Preconditions for Corruption

The problem of corruption has been exacerbated by the problem of drugs and drug abuse. Millions of dollars in seized currency create temptations for officers predisposed toward wrongdoing. Some argue that police officers involved in proactive investigative enforcement efforts regarding drugs, gambling, and prostitution are more vulnerable to corruption than uniformed officers. This is primarily because crimes discovered by the undercover officer have not yet come to the official attention of the department. Therefore, the vice officer can "easily agree to overlook offenses known only to him or to even participate in illegal transactions (e.g., buying and selling drugs) for his own gain rather than the organization's advantage" (Abadinsky, 1990:401).

A management dilemma relating to the drug abuse problem is the number of police officer applicants who have drug abuse in their past. Many police departments are now receiving applications from individuals who are former or even current drug users. In fact, a study by Peter Kraska and Victor Kappeler (1988) found that more than 20 percent of the police officers in a local police department used marijuana and nonprescription drugs while on duty. Corruption opportunities are not limited to vice or narcotics officers, however; they are also readily available to officers working in the patrol capacity. Money and drug seizures made by patrol officers may actually take place with much less supervision than those made by the drug enforcement division; this creates a greater opportunity for corruption.

The *police socialization* process also contributes to the corruption problem in that rookie officers are often advised to forget all they have learned in the police academy and learn the "rules of the street" in order to survive. The implication is that some rules need to be bent or even broken in order to survive on the streets and to climb the career ladder in police work. Sherman suggests that the socialization process also creates a situation in which officers learn to "map out the environment." This means that as officers gain experience on the job and encounter various circumstances, they develop attitudes that rationalize their own deviant behavior. Sherman (1982:10-19) identified some common rationalizations:

- The public is the enemy and doesn't want the law enforced.
- Politicians are crooked and shouldn't be trusted.
- Minorities are amoral, a drain on society's resources, and cop haters who are not to be believed or shown respect.
- Everybody's on a hustle.
- Judges are too lenient.
- Police administrators are the enemy.

When such attitudes become a part of a police officer's view of police work, it is likely they become part of that officer's attitude toward society as well.

Types of Police Corruption

As definitions of the term suggest, corruption is not limited to its most conspicuous form—the acceptance of cash in exchange for an official favor. Several experts have identified different varieties of police corruption. For example, Michael Johnston (1982:75) cited four major corruption categories:

1. *Internal corruption.* This includes acts among police officers themselves and involves behaviors ranging from bending rules to outright commission of illegal acts.
2. *Selective enforcement.* Police officers exploit their discretion. For example, a detective who arrests and releases a drug trafficker in exchange for valuable information about the trafficker's organizations is not abusing his or her authority, but one who releases the same trafficker for money is in clear abuse of his or her discretion and authority.
3. *Active criminality.* Police officers participate in serious criminal activity using their positions of power and influence to commit the criminal acts they are entrusted to enforce.
4. *Bribery/extortion.* This occurs when police officers use their vested authority to generate a personal source of money. Bribery is initiated by the citizen, whereas extortion is initiated by the officer.

Another researcher, Ellwin Stoddard (1968), constructed a list of several specific forms of behavior that he considers corrupt in nature:

- *Bribery.* The receipt of cash or a "gift" in exchange for past or future assistance in avoidance of prosecution, as by a claim that the officer is unable to make a positive identification of a criminal, by being in the wrong place at a time when a crime is to occur, or by any other action that may be excused as carelessness but not offered as proof of deliberate miscarriage of justice. It is distinguished from "mooching" (see below) by the higher value of the gift and by the mutual understanding in regard to services to be performed upon the acceptance of the gift.
- *Chiseling.* The demand for price discounts or free admission to places of entertainment regardless of any connection with official police work. This differs from "mooching" (see below), because it is initiated by the officer, not the business proprietor. In this case, business owners and workers comply out of fear that the police officer will be less than responsive when and if a crime is ever committed on the premises or from fear that the officer will look closer for some kind of violations committed by the business or its employees if the favor is not granted.
- *Shakedown.* The common practice of holding "street court" by which minor traffic tickets can be avoided with a cash payment to the officer and no receipt given. Using the shakedown, police have also been known to extort money from tavern owners and other businesses by threatening to enforce city health and zoning codes.

- *Favoritism.* The practice of issuing license tabs, window stickers, or courtesy cards that exempt users from arrest or citation from traffic offenses (frequently extended to family members of officers).

- *Mooching.* The acceptance of free coffee, cigarettes, meals, liquor, groceries, and the like, justified by the police being in an underpaid profession or for future acts of favoritism performed for the donor. Many restaurant chains as well as doughnut and coffee shops have adopted policies of providing discount meals on a regular basis. This ensures that there will be a continued police presence at the establishment at virtually all times and is justified as being cheaper than hiring a full-time security guard for protection.

- *Perjury.* A willingness to lie under oath to provide an alibi for fellow officers apprehended in unlawful activity.

- *Prejudice.* Treatment of minority groups in a manner less than impartial, neutral, or objective, especially members of such groups who are unlikely to have "influence" in city hall that might cause trouble for the arresting officer.

- *Premeditated theft.* Predatory criminal activity that includes planned burglary involving the use of tools, keys, or other devices to gain entry, or any prearranged plan to acquire property unlawfully. This form of corruption, unlike some others, is rarely tolerated by police departments.

- *Shopping.* Opportunistic theft, such as picking up small items such as cigarettes, candy bars, jewelry, money, and so on, at a store that has accidentally been left unlocked at the close of business hours or at the scene of a fire or burglary.

Even seemingly benign actions such as accepting a free cup of coffee or free admittance to the local movie theater may constitute corruption or at least a predisposition for such behavior. More (1998:273) suggested that although on the surface the acceptance of a free meal or cup of coffee may seem insignificant, there is every reason to believe it creates an atmosphere conducive to corruption. So, to ensure a police force that can function within the community while being free of compromises, all such behavior should be closely scrutinized. This will protect the citizenry from a police force that gives preferential treatment to businesses that offer gratuities.

Police corruption is nothing new in the United States. A good deal of official corruption in the areas of liquor and gambling was documented during the early part of the century, when Prohibition was in effect. In many such cases, a link was established between police and politicians in which favored clients would be protected while competitors would be harassed.

Corruption in New York City

Of the many examples of police corruption in America, perhaps the most highly publicized investigation in twentieth-century history stemmed from charges made in the 1970s by two New York Police Department (NYPD) police officers: Frank Serpico and David Durk. The corruption problem surfaced when the officers began to protest to fellow officers about corrupt practices in their precinct. They were told to shut up and mind their own business or go along with the others and their corrupt practices. Out of frustration, Serpico and Durk then complained about corruption to top brass high up in the police department. Although they were assured that their charges were being fully investigated, nothing was ever done. Finally, Serpico and Durk took their story to *The New York Times*, and the paper ran a series of stories about the corruption problem in the NYPD. As a result of widespread public concern, the *Knapp Commission* was appointed to investigate the allegations.

Serpico's testimony before the Knapp Commission provided revealing information about corruption within the New York Police Department. Although the commission's findings revealed that minor offenses were much more commonplace than serious ones, it still concluded that overall corruption was widespread in the department. The majority of officers who received outright bribes usually did not vigorously seek cash payments but rather took advantage of offers that came their way from contractors, trucking operators, and criminals. Specific findings of the commission included that: (1) plainclothes officers received regular payoffs on a semiweekly or weekly basis; (2) detectives in some divisions were involved in shakedowns; (3) undercover officers in the narcotics division were receiving payoffs; (4) midlevel managers such as sergeants and lieutenants had been taking bribes; and (5) uniformed officers were receiving payoffs from local business owners and gamblers.

In addition, the commission found that in 5 of the 17 plainclothes divisions, corruption followed the same basic pattern. That is, officers assigned to the vice divisions were receiving payoffs from criminals. Detectives collected payoffs ranging up to $3,500 per month from each gambling location. This amount represented a "nut" (the officer's share) that ranged anywhere from $300 to $1,500 of the "pad" (list of payoff money). As might be expected, those officers who were higher in rank would receive a higher payoff. Specifically, supervisors would receive a share-and-a-half, which ranged from $450 to $2,250. Plainclothes officers who were newly assigned were required to wait two months before they were eligible for payoff "benefits" (Knapp, 1972).

Critical Thinking Task

Suppose that large-scale corruption is discovered within the police department in your community. You are a member of a citizens' group who has been asked by the city council to study the corruption problem and suggest means of correcting it and preventing future incidents. What suggestions will you make to the city council?

The commission also reported that uniformed officers were receiving much smaller payoffs than their plainclothes counterparts—typically less than $20. Such payoffs included shakedowns from small-time gamblers, payoffs for "fixing" traffic tickets, and bribes and payoffs from bars, grocery stores, and other places of business. Although these payoffs were small, they were plentiful enough to significantly enhance an officer's income.

Another form of corruption identified by the commission was the incidence of payoffs between officers on the force. These consisted of bribes to receive more desirable assignments or to speed up certain police procedures. Other types of corruption included special "pads" for sergeants only, excluding participation by subordinate officers. However, the Knapp Commission was unable to identify evidence of corruption on the part of officers above the rank of lieutenant, although much circumstantial evidence supported this assertion. The lack of evidence was partly due to the fact that superiors would commonly use lower-ranking officers to collect payoffs or serve as "bagmen" (participants who collect payoffs), and as a result it was extremely difficult to implicate supervisory personnel.

Arising out of the Knapp Commission's findings were two unique descriptive terms used to characterize corrupt officers: *grass eaters* and *meat eaters*. The grass eater is an officer who accepts payoffs as they are presented to him or her while performing normal police duties. In comparison, the meat eater is considerably more aggressive and contentious in his or her pursuit of illegal abuses of police power for personal gain. However, the commission reported that, "Although meat eaters get huge payoffs, getting all of the headlines, they represent a small percentage of corrupt officers. The truth is the vast majority on the take don't deal in large amounts of graft" (Knapp, 1972). In fact, the commission felt that grass eaters were at the center of the problem and that other officers looked at those who were involved as respectable.

The specter of police corruption in New York City came into the public spotlight once again in September 1993, when a special commission was appointed by Mayor David Dinkins to investigate police corruption in the 30,000-member police force. The *Mollen Commission*, headed by former appeals judge Milton Mollen, made new inquiries into the problem. The Mollen Commission's star witness was 32-year-old police officer Michael Dowd, who described his indoctrination by superiors into petty crime and brutality and an evolution of behavior that resulted in his own drug dealing. Ultimately, more than 25 police officers were implicated in organized corruption activities.

Dowd shocked listeners in describing how he would do lines of cocaine off the dashboard of his patrol car while his partner watched. His testimony revealed that his weekly "take" rose from $200 per week to an $8,000 payoff from a drug dealer. In his statement he said that he became a "hero" to rookie cops who wanted to know how he acquired his red Corvette, expensive wardrobe, and many vacations. Probably the most troubling testimony Dowd provided was regarding his education into corruption, which began at the police academy. He claimed that officers at the academy promoted an "us-against-them" mentality—"Us is the police officers and them is the public." Dowd's testimony also revealed how drinking on the job sealed a social pact of illegal activity by officers. In doing so, officers comprising literally the entire patrol force in Brooklyn's 75th Precinct would "regularly rendezvous at a hidden location for drinks, laughs, shooting off guns and other 'immature stuff'" (Frankel, 1993). In addition to Dowd's testimony, the commission focused on issues of brutality by officers. One such officer was Bernie Cawley. Also known as "the Mechanic," Cawley gave statements about how he would "tune [beat] people up with night sticks and lead-lined gloves." According to his testimony, "it was nothing to kick 'johns' out of bed and force prostitutes to have sex with him … and nothing to lie before grand juries as well as steal drugs and money from drug dealers" (Frankel, 1993).

Perhaps one of the more disturbing aspects of the Mollen Commission's findings was the involvement of upper-echelon police managers and administrators in corrupt activities. In fact, one of the common denominators in the inquiry was the specter of widespread corruption coupled with a total disregard for the police department's system of internal scrutiny. During the inquiry, internal affairs detective Sergeant Joseph Trimboli testified about how the five-year investigation was systematically stymied by top police supervisors working within the internal affairs division itself. In fact, after presenting a Brooklyn police commander with the identities of corrupt officers in the 75th precinct, the commander advised his officers to cover it up.

Corruption in Other Cities

The quality of law enforcement was studied in Philadelphia in the mid-1970s by the *Pennsylvania Crime Commission*, which found that corruption was continuing, prevalent, and organized at all levels of the police department. In fact, the corruption problem was almost identical to that found in New York City. During the course of the investigation, virtually all districts within the department had some degree of corruption involving officers holding ranks up to the position of inspector. As in New York City, Philadelphia corruption included the use of "bagmen" who made periodic rounds to illegal gambling operations, nightclubs, prostitutes, and business owners to collect payoff money that was later distributed to participating officers. More than 400 officers were identified by name or badge number as recipients of cash monies, merchandise, sexual favors, meals, or services. As with the New York investigation, the commission reported that officers viewed drug money to be the dirtiest kind of graft. However, that attitude failed to deter some officers from "scoring" suspected drug dealers for sizable payoffs. The commission also heard reports that in an estimated 65 to 75 percent of all drug arrests, at least part of the drugs were not turned in as evidence. Instead, officers used these drugs as "plants" to frame suspected drug dealers or sold them on the black market for cash profits.

More writes that the police department in Philadelphia had endured corruption since its inception (1992:260). During the twentieth century alone, three grand jury investigations revealed the existence of widespread corruption in the Pennsylvania Police Department. "Numerous interacting factors" were cited by the Pennsylvania Crime Commission during the mid-1970s as reasons for corruption. One factor was the department's general attitude toward the problem of corruption. Other reasons included perceived pressures on law enforcement officers and the reaction to corruption by other parts of the criminal justice system. The specific types of corruption identified by the Pennsylvania Crime Commission (1974:677-801) included the following:

- Payments to overlook liquor law violations
- Payments from after-hours clubs that operate beyond the legal closing time
- Payoffs from illegal nightclubs
- Payments for allowing illegal gambling, including numbers, horse-racing bets, and sports wagering
- Payoffs for allowing gamblers to use illegal gambling machines
- Cash payments for allowing prostitution
- Promises to prostitutes that charges would be dropped in exchange for sexual favors
- Extortion of money and drugs from drug offenders
- Illegal cash payments from businesses, in exchange for services such as providing escorts to banks and guarding business premises
- Cash payments from motorists for traffic violations
- Theft of unprotected valuables from premises
- The stripping of impounded cars
- The filing of false reports and committing perjury in court

Problems of police corruption in both New York and Philadelphia touched off calls by the public for reform. These cases were underscored in the 1980s and 1990s by accounts of corruption in other cities such as Miami, Boston, and San Francisco.

In 1999, a drug sting operation in the small town of Tulia, Texas, resulted in the arrest of 46 people, 40 of whom were black. The remaining six individuals were either Latinos or whites who were dating blacks. The drug bust incarcerated almost 15 percent of the black population and has been denounced as a form of *racial profiling* by the National Association for the Advancement of Colored People (NAACP) and the America Civil Liberties Union (ACLU). Those organizations filed a complaint with the Civil Rights Division of the Department of Justice; four years later, in 2003, the testimony of the key witness was deemed not credible and prosecutors agreed not to go to retrial.

All the evidence presented against those arrested came from the uncorroborated testimony of Tom Coleman, a private informant hired by the Sheriff of Tulia to conduct the sting operation. Coleman supposedly sought to buy powder cocaine and other drugs from area residents. In choosing his sting targets, he used a list of 60 "known drug dealers" that the Sheriff had previously compiled during a racially motivated local drug scare. Agent

Coleman worked alone and did not wear a wire during any of the alleged transactions.

Seven of those arrested were convicted and sentenced to prison terms, one for 99 years. Fourteen defendants took pleas and were sentenced to prison. Others were sentenced to probation. Most of the prison sentences were increased because the drugs were allegedly sold within 1,000 feet of a school, yet most of the defendants lived in trailer parks miles away from the nearest school. Coleman claimed to neither remember nor have records of any of the exact locations of the individual drug transactions.

Slowly, as suspicions rose around the credibility of Coleman's evidence, cracks in his story began to show. For a lucky few, cases were dismissed—one defendant was cleared when his employer showed time cards proving he was at work at the time of the alleged buy; another defendant had bank records proving that she was out of state.

A trial was ordered to determine whether the defendants were convicted solely on Coleman's word and to investigate whether prosecutors had failed to turn over information from Coleman's background that may have cast doubt on his testimony. It was stipulated by all parties and approved by the court that Coleman was not a credible witness under oath. As a result, all criminal cases Coleman investigated were dismissed.

It should be noted that although there appear to be areas of widespread corruption within some police departments, other forms of corruption exist in other parts of the criminal justice system as well. For example, prosecutors enjoy considerable discretion in filing cases, dismissing cases, and plea bargaining, and judges are vested with powers that can mold the trial process and make determinations regarding sentencing of offenders.

Institutional Corruption

Lawrence Sherman (1974) suggests that *institutional corruption* can also exist in police departments themselves. Such organizations can be categorized on the basis of the level and type of corruption existing within them. He identifies three types:

- *Type I—Rotten pockets and rotten apples*. A Type I police department consists of a few scattered corrupt police officers using their position for personal gain ("rotten apples"). When these officers get together, they form a "rotten pocket." Rotten pockets help institutionalize corruption because they expect newcomers to conform to their corrupt practices and to a code of secrecy.

- *Type II—Pervasive unorganized corruption*. A Type II police department employs a majority of officers who are corrupt but who have little relationship to one another. Although each officer may be involved in a variety of styles of corruption, most are not working in collusion with others on the police force for personal gain.

- *Type III—Pervasive organized corruption.* A Type III police department represents a police force in which almost all the officers are involved in organized and systematic corruption for personal gain. Such a situation was identified in New York by the Knapp Commission when a group of corrupt officers working out of the vice division would regularly extort money from local criminals and businesses. Such behavior was accepted by the officers as part of the job.

In addition to the blatant acceptance of currency for official services rendered, corruption may also include subtle arrangements in which an agreement is implied. Sometimes referred to as conflicts of interest, such agreements (as with those discussed previously) often encompass situations in which the officer becomes the beneficiary of favors or gifts from people with whom the officer conducts his or her duties.

Fighting Police Corruption

It is difficult to offer a simple and comprehensive explanation for some of the abuses of police power and authority. Clearly, however, better formal training and socialization may be the key to reducing deviant behavior among police officers. Policy changes are necessary to address those officers who are borderline or who have already become tainted by corruption.

Why, then, do some police officers become corrupt while others do not? Several explanations can be considered. For example, some argue that the type of individual who becomes a police officer is at the root of the problem. Studies show that most police personnel have been recruited from lower-class neighborhoods, and many lack the financial wherewithal to adopt a middle-class lifestyle. As the cynical, authoritarian police personality develops, the acceptance of graft seems to be a logical method of attaining financial security (Johnston, 1982:82).

Corruption can also be viewed as a function of police institutions and practices (Sherman, 1974:40-41)—for example, in terms of the degree of discretion police officers enjoy. The police officer's ability to intervene or not, coupled with low visibility and lack of supervision in communities and within agencies, may create an atmosphere conducive to corruption. Institutionalization of corruption is also evident when corrupt officers are protected by the code of secrecy within their ranks as well as by their own supervisors, who have risen up through the ranks and may be less than willing to report any wrongdoing.

A third explanation holds that corruption is a product of society's reservations toward the enforcement of many types of vice-related crimes. Because vice crime is so difficult to control and because a large segment of society wants it to persist, officers who are charged with enforcing vice laws might feel they are justified in accepting money from criminals involved in these types of crimes.

CORRUPTION IN FOREIGN COUNTRIES

When we consider the problem of official corruption in the drug trade, it is often difficult to determine whether complicity in criminal actions is on an individual basis by officials seeking their own financial enhancement or whether it is systematic and under the sanction of an entire government or official unit of that government. The corrupt official is the *sine qua non* (essential element) of drug trafficking, and it is his or her participation through the corruption of an official office that protects and aids sophisticated criminals in manufacturing, smuggling, and distributing illicit drugs. We have briefly discussed how corruption affects law enforcement domestically; let's now examine how corruption affects drug control in illicit drug source countries.

Cuba

The U.S. government first suspected the Cuban government's complicity in the drug trade during the early 1960s, but many of the allegations were unsubstantiated. Finally, in the early 1980s, many of these accusations were verified. In particular, in November 1982 the United States District Court indicted four major Cuban officials on charges of conspiring to traffic drugs. Among those four were the vice admiral of the Cuban navy and the former Cuban ambassador to Colombia. According to the indictment, the officials were allowing Cuba to be used as a transshipment center for drug shipments destined for the United States. On one occasion, in exchange for its participation in this scheme, the Cuban government was to receive $800,000 for the sale of 10 million methaqualone tablets (Quaaludes) and 23,000 pounds of marijuana.

Other reports of official corruption have surfaced, alleging Cuban cooperation with drug smugglers who flew smuggling aircraft through Cuban airspace. According to the President's Commission on Organized Crime (PCOC, 1986a), this was accomplished by assigning the smuggling pilots a corridor or "window" through which they could pass without any interference from the Cuban government. Cuban government officials have previously tried and convicted several high-ranking military and government officials for participating in drug trafficking.

Mexico

In January 1995, Mexico's newly elected President Ernesto Zedillo took over a nation in crisis. The reason was drugs. His advisors tried to paint a clear picture for the incoming president: The increasing number of the nation's drug cartels endangered Mexico's stability and threatened to make the country ungovernable. This was being accomplished through a number of high-level assassinations as well as the arrest of a multitude of high-ranking officials within the Mexican government.

U.S. government officials have been hesitant to make public accusations of Mexican involvement in criminal activity, particularly in the drug trade. One of the reasons for this hesitation is that Mexico is not only one of the United States' closest neighbors but is a staunch ally and trading partner as well (see Chapter 9).

Since the early 1980s, however, evidence has surfaced to support the assertion of official corruption in both the Mexican Directorate of Security and the Mexican Judicial Police. Probably one of the most widely publicized and tragic events that illustrated the complicity of several governmental officials in the Mexican drug trade was the 1985 abduction and murder of U.S. Drug Enforcement Agent Enrique Camarena Salazar and his pilot, Alfredo Zavala Avelar, in the city of Guadalajara. As a result of the subsequent investigation into this incident, six Mexican police officials were indicted on related charges, including protection of personnel and goods, custody of drugs while in transit, and providing information. The officers cited in this investigation were reportedly receiving payoffs for official protection that ranged from $200 to $6,250 a month. One of these six officials, the First Commandante Jorge Armando Pavon Reyes of the Mexican Judicial Police (who also headed the Camarena investigation in Mexico), accepted a bribe from drug suspect Rafael Caro Quintero in exchange for Caro's freedom.

Subsequent to the Camarena incident, then-President Miguel de la Madrid announced a major reorganization and consolidation of police forces. Under the reorganization, one governor dismissed an entire judicial system, including the state attorney general and more than 100 security agents.

Another incident in the mid-1990s also typifies Mexican corruption. Mexican officials were alerted by U.S. authorities that a Caravelle cargo jet packed with 8.5 tons of cocaine was headed from Colombia into Zacatecas, located in north central Mexico. By the time police were finished inventorying the aircraft, there were only 2.5 tons left. Days later, packages of cocaine with the same markings were intercepted at the U.S. border.

For decades, corruption in the police and judiciary has been common in Mexico, but the drug trade is now affecting the country's economy as well. The lucrative Mexican tourist trade has afforded traffickers a natural opportunity to launder millions of dollars of drug money. Traffickers and politicians who protect them invest millions in beach resorts, financial markets, shopping centers, and other enterprises. In August 1996, Mexico's Attorney General Antonio Lozano Garcia made an unprecedented gesture by dismissing more than 700 members of the judicial police in an attempt to reform its largest antinarcotics force. The action came in the aftermath of criticism that the police had become ineffective because of widespread corruption within their ranks. Lozano had fired 513 other police just two years earlier, putting the total number of dismissed officers at almost one-fourth of the 4,400-member force.

Figure 6.1
Source: U.S. Money Laundering Threat Assessment: 2007.

Illicit proceeds destined for Mexico often are transported through Texas on U.S. Interstate 59, which extends from the U.S.-Mexico border at Laredo to Houston and then north to other markets throughout the Midwest. Currently, a portion of U.S. Interstate 59 is slated to become part of U.S. Interstate 69. The proposed new highway will create a direct corridor between the U.S.-Mexico border and the U.S.-Canada border. On February 8, 2005, Texas Department of Public Safety (DPS) troopers seized $2.3 million as a result of a vehicle stop along U.S. Interstate 59 north of Nacogdoches. The Texas DPS trooper stopped the driver of a southbound tractor-trailer for a speeding violation. The driver, who was hauling boxes of frozen chicken, appeared to be nervous; his driver's log indicated that this was his first trip for the company. A search of the vehicle revealed a hidden compartment in the refrigerated trailer, and an inspection of the compartment uncovered the currency. DPS officers confiscated the currency, and the driver was arrested on state money-laundering charges. This was the fourth-largest traffic stop seizure of currency in Texas DPS history.

Case in Point: Smugglers Route—U.S. Interstate 59

Corruption among Mexico's police has been a critical and increasing concern of U.S. antinarcotic agents. Colombian traffickers ship an estimated 70 percent of their U.S.-bound cocaine through Mexico. The judicial police are in many ways the counterparts of the FBI in the United States, but Mexican federal police are political appointees who are often linked to the long-ruling Institutional Revolutionary Party, which has a history of unsavory conduct. Its officers have often been accused of crimes from torturing suspects to working as bodyguards for drug lords (Sheridan, 1996). Of course, the role of some judicial police officers in the murder of Kiki Camarena cast considerable doubt on their international credibility. In an article in *The Los Angeles Times*, Lozano commented that "things have gotten so bad that young people are seeking to enter the force principally because of its bad reputation—they want to be police to gain power" (Sheridan, 1996).

In 1997, Mexico was again shaken by the specter of high-level corruption when its top antinarcotics official General José de Jesús Gutiérrez Rebollo was indicted on charges that he cooperated with drug cartels. Shortly after Rebollo's arrest and dismissal, 36 officers in his employ were also dismissed for fear that they too were involved in unsavory practices with drug traffickers. In the United States, the Clinton administration was sufficiently concerned to place Mexico on notice that its certification as a "fully cooperative" nation might be withdrawn, costing Mexico millions of dollars in financial aid. According to federal law, the President of the United States must annually evaluate the cooperation of 32 countries that are sources or traffic routes for illegal drugs. With the arrest of Rebollo, Clinton was under considerable pressure from U.S.

politicians to decertify Mexico, whereas Mexican officials warned that doing so would only sour relations between the two countries.

In 1997, the United States made the following demands of Mexico for the country's certification to be continued:

- To allow more U.S. narcotics agents into the country
- To allow U.S. law enforcement officers to carry weapons in Mexico
- To allow extradition of Mexicans sought by the United States
- To improve air security over the border
- To allow drug traffickers to be chased into Mexican waters by the U.S. Coast Guard

Finally, in May of that year, in a meeting between President Clinton and Mexican President Ernesto Zedillo, both sides pledged close cooperation on drug-fighting efforts. Both leaders recognized the importance of international cooperation, for in Mexico alone more than 200 police had been murdered and 25 major assassinations had occurred in connection with drug trafficking (Hunt, 1997).

Despite current President Felipe Calderón's war on Mexican drug cartels, which has been a centerpiece of his administration, corruption in Mexican government continues to be a problem. In 2009, former "drug czar" Mariano Francisco Herran Salvatti was arrested on corruption charges of embezzlement and criminal association, among other things. Herran served as drug czar for President Ernesto Zedillo from 1997 to 2000. In that post, he was involved in the prosecution of more than 60 members of the Juárez drug cartel and the investigation that led to the 2001 arrest of former Quintana Roo Governor Mario Villanueva Madrid for his connections to drug traffickers. As mentioned earlier, Herran's predecessor, General Gutiérrez Rebollo, was fired in 1997 after an investigation revealed he had received payments from the Juárez drug cartel (CNN, 2009).

In 2008, Noe Ramirez Mandujano, who was the nation's top antidrug official from 2006 until August 2008, was arrested on charges that he accepted $450,000 a month in bribes from drug traffickers. Ramirez was accused of meeting with members of a drug cartel while he was in office and providing information on investigations in exchange for the bribes (Ellingwood, 2008).

The Bahamas

The Bahamas and other countries in the Caribbean basin are ideally located for transshipment and refueling for drug smugglers from Mexican and South American countries. In fact, many allegations about the role of smugglers transshipping drugs in this region have surfaced since the early 1980s. In 1986, U.S. government intelligence reports alleged that widespread corruption had reached high government offices in the Caicos Islands, where in March 1985 the Bahamas' Chief Minister Norman Saunders was convicted of conspiracy in a drug-trafficking scheme. Witnesses in the Saunders trial testified that he received a total of $50,000 for allowing drugs from Colombia to pass freely through his country.

In yet another case, in 1984, Bahamian Prime Minister Lynden Pindling was suspected of complicity with drug traffickers when an investigation revealed that his personal bank accounts reflected deposits of $3.5 million in excess of his salary during a six-year period. Convicted drug trafficker Carlos Lehder also commonly used Norman's Cay as a refueling and transshipment point for cocaine runs between 1978 and 1982. Subsequent to Lehder's arrest in 1987, it was learned that he paid "substantial bribes" to police and customs officials to aid him in trafficking cocaine to the United States (PCOC, 1986a).

Panama

In the late 1980s, Panama and its leader at the time, General Manuel Antonio Noriega, a longtime U.S. ally, became engaged in a complicated web of corruption and drug trafficking. In 1988, Noriega was indicted by U.S. federal grand juries in Miami and Tampa (Florida) on charges of drug trafficking, racketeering, and money laundering. Drug enforcement officials had been aware of Noriega's involvement in the drug trade since the early 1970s, but until December 1989, concern for maintaining stability in Panama and the Canal Zone outweighed U.S. concern about illicit drug activity there.

Noriega had previously worked as an informer for the Central Intelligence Agency (CIA) and allowed the agency to operate a listening post in Panama, monitoring Central and South America. U.S. Lieutenant Colonel Oliver North, then a junior member of the National Security Council, and General Richard Secord also used Panama as a base for training soldiers and a place for setting up "dummy" corporations to help fund Nicaraguan contras (rebels fighting Nicaragua's Sandanista government).

In 1988, DEA reports disclosed that Noriega did provide information to the United States regarding certain drug-smuggling operations. During that same time, he was accepting large bribes from Colombia's Medellín cartel for his assistance in drug-trafficking operations and for offering cartel members a safe haven in Panama to avoid prosecution. In 1985, Senator Jesse Helms of North Carolina proposed legislation cutting off aid to Panama, only to be persuaded to withdraw it later because of Noriega's assistance to the contras.

In the summer of 1987, the second-in-command of Panama's defense forces, Colonel Roberto Díaz Herrera, went public with several charges aimed at Noriega. Diaz first accused Noriega of fraud in the 1984 presidential election.

He also implicated Noriega in the 1981 death of Panama's President General Omar Torrijos, which at the time it occurred was thought to be accidental. In the late 1980s, it became increasingly clear that Noriega had no intention of restoring democracy to Panama, in particular in the aftermath of national elections in 1989, in which Noriega dispatched "goon squads" to intimidate his opposition and the voters of Panama. Political corruption of the caliber seen in Panama, Mexico, and the Bahamas is slow in development but, once entrenched, is difficult to purge (see the following section on cocaine money and Panama).

Noriega's reign as leader of Panama ended on December 20, 1989, as President George H. W. Bush authorized Operation Just Cause, a surprise overnight invasion in which 2,000 U.S. troops invaded Panama. Although the initiative resulted in 23 U.S. soldiers being killed and more than 200 being injured, it was successful in restoring the democratically elected government to power. The target of the invasion, Noriega, escaped during the attack and remained on the run for about 48 hours. The deposed dictator then turned himself over to the Vatican Embassy on Christmas Eve, seeking political sanctuary and asylum. This sparked international diplomatic concern over the legality and appropri-

ateness of using embassies to shelter suspected international drug traffickers who are wanted by the governments of other countries. On January 3, 1990, Noriega turned himself into authorities of the DEA outside the Vatican Embassy. He was then transported to Miami to face federal drug-trafficking charges. He was convicted and sentenced to 40 years' imprisonment. In 2007 Noriega's prison sentence ended but in 2010 he was extradited to France where in July of that year he was sentenced to seven additional years in prison.

On left, General Manuel Antonio Noriega raises his fists to acknowledge the crowd's cheers during a Dignity Battalion rally in Panama City on May 20, 1988. Less than two years later, Noriega, seen in the January 1990 photo at right, was in the custody of U.S. marshals after his seizure during the U.S. invasion of Panama.

MONEY LAUNDERING

Money laundering is the process drug traffickers use to introduce the monetary proceeds gained through the sale or distribution of controlled substances into the legitimate financial market. The International Monetary Fund (IMF) estimated in 2000 that money laundering amounts to between 2 percent and 5 percent of the world's gross domestic product (GDP), about $600 billion annually (UNODCCP, 2000). Money laundering allows concealment of the true source of the funds gained through the sale and distribution of drugs and converts the funds into assets that appear to have a legitimate legal source. The need to launder conspicuously large amounts of small-denomination bills renders the traffickers vulnerable to law enforcement interdiction. Tracking and intercepting this illegal flow of drug money is an important tool used to identify and dismantle international drug-trafficking organizations.

Current Money-Laundering Trends

Drug traffickers use various methods to launder their profits both inside and outside the United States. Currently, some of the more common laundering methods include the Black Market Peso Exchange, cash smuggling (couriers or bulk cash shipments), gold purchases, structured deposits to or withdrawals from bank accounts, purchase of monetary instruments (cashier's checks, money orders, travelers checks, and the like), wire transfers, and forms of underground banking, particularly the Hawala system (a system whereby money is transferred via brokers).

Today's organized crime leaders are strong, sophisticated, and destructive, and they have the capability to operate on a global scale. Organizational leaders have at their disposal airplanes, boats, vehicles, radar, communications equipment, and weapons in quantities that rival the capabilities of some legitimate governments.

Whereas previous organized crime leaders were millionaires, the Colombian drug traffickers and their counterparts from Mexico are billionaires. They have learned to exploit a variety of weaknesses to protect their drug profits, which are the lifeblood of these organizations. Their ultimate purpose is to amass large sums of money to maintain their lavish lifestyles, free from the boundaries or confines of the law.

Today, money laundering remains an ongoing problem in the fight against drugs and drug trafficking. Recent statistics bear this out. For example, in 2007, the National Money Laundering Strategy identified some significant trends. These include:

- Banks and other depository institutions remain the primary gateway to the U.S. financial system.
- Internet and remote banking present ongoing challenges in identifying people involved in electronic financial transactions.
- Money service businesses offer an alternative to banks for money laundering.
- Smuggling cash out of the country is a well-established money-laundering method and is on the rise.
- The most complex money-laundering methods involve international business transactions to disguise cash transfers.
- Casinos are cash-intensive businesses that provide money-laundering opportunities.

Figure 6.2
Source: U.S. Money Laundering Threat Assessment: 2007.

Bank records seized pursuant to search warrants revealed that the subject, using a personal account and his business (a convenience store) account, sent checks totaling approximately $300,000 to various individuals in Yemen during the years 1998–2002. Cash deposits were made simultaneous to the writing of the checks and slightly exceeded the amounts of the checks (indicative of a fee being charged). The checks were subsequently negotiated at various banks in Yemen. The tracking of the flow of funds stopped there.

The subject, during his interview, stated that he knew what a hawala was and the types of fees associated with its operation. [*Note:* The *hawala system* refers to an informal channel for transferring funds from one location to another through service providers—known as *hawaladars*—regardless of the nature of the transaction and the countries involved.] However, he insisted that he was not operating one and that he was simply sending money to support family members in his native Yemen. No lists or records of clients were ever uncovered; investigators were unable to corroborate any testimony, because the primary witnesses were in Yemen; and no one in the local Yemeni community was able to state that the subject and/or others were operating hawalas. Because of the lack of cooperation, the 18 USC 1960 part of the case was discontinued and the subject was indicted on other charges.

A Closer Look: Law Enforcement Challenges

Overview

Illegal narcotic sales in the United States generate billions of dollars annually, most in cash. Efforts to legitimize or "launder" this cash by the Colombian drug cartels are subject to detection because of intense scrutiny U.S. banks place on large financial transactions. To avoid detection, the cartels have developed a number of money-laundering systems in an attempt to avoid financial transaction reporting requirements and manipulate facets of the economy unrelated to the traditional financial services industry.

The various money-laundering methods utilized in today's financial world can be reduced to four categories: bulk movement, the use of financial institutions, the use of commercial businesses, and movement through the underground banking system. However, an organization may use several of these methods in a chain to arrive at its goal: the integration of drug money into the economy as licit profits.

Colombia

Despite the rise to power by the Mexican crime syndicates and their increasing influence on the drug trade in the United States, Colombian traffickers still control the manufacture of the vast majority of cocaine in South

America and a majority of the wholesale cocaine market in the eastern United States. They move cocaine from their clandestine laboratories in the jungles of southeast Colombia to Mexico and through the Caribbean, using commercial maritime vessels, go-fast boats, containerized cargo, and private aircraft. The methods are varied, and to thwart interdiction efforts traffickers frequently alter both their routes and their modus operandi.

The Colombian trafficking organizations' influence in the Caribbean remains overwhelming. Several major organizations based on the North Coast of Colombia have established command and control functions in Puerto Rico and the Dominican Republic. These drug traffickers use the Caribbean Basin to funnel tons of cocaine to the United States each year, and they direct networks of transporters that oversee the importation, storage, exportation, and wholesale distribution of cocaine destined for the continental United States. Seizures of 500 to 2,000 kilos of cocaine are common in and around Puerto Rico, the Dominican Republic, and the Bahamian island chain (Guillen, 2000).

The Dominican trafficking groups, already firmly entrenched as low-level cocaine and heroin wholesalers in the larger northeastern cities, were uniquely placed to assume a far more significant role in the multibillion-dollar cocaine and heroin trade. From Boston to Charlotte, North Carolina, well-organized Dominican trafficking groups are controlling and directing the sale of multi-hundred-kilogram shipments of cocaine and multikilogram quantities of heroin. This change in operations somewhat reduces profits for the syndicate leaders; however, it succeeds in reducing their exposure to U.S. law enforcement.

Due to geographical considerations, Colombian traffickers face many difficulties during the initial placement phase of the money-laundering process that Mexican syndicates do not encounter. Colombian drug organizations have in the past relied on a multifaceted collection process. They have amassed currency in strategic locations, used a variety of methods—including smuggling and bribery—to introduce the cash into the U.S. banking system, and subsequently transferred the cash to Colombia. In an effort to avoid the high risks associated with direct deposits in U.S. or European banks, many Colombian drug traffickers have returned to the simplest of money-laundering methods, the bulk movement of cash. Currently, the vast majority of U.S. currency bound for the bank accounts of the Colombian drug lords leaves the United States either through air cargo or commercial cargo freighters. Due to the enormous amount of commercial trade the United States has with Colombia, this method makes the traffickers' operations not only less complicated but also less vulnerable to discovery by law enforcement.

In addition, Colombian drug trafficking will exploit any means possible to safely launder their drug proceeds. One such form of money laundering is known as the Black Market Peso Exchange (BMPE). The BMPE is a complex system used by drug-trafficking organizations to launder billions of dollars of drug money each year utilizing the advantages of Panama's Colon Free Zone (CFZ), which serves as an integral link in the Colombian money-laundering chain.

Mexico

Mexico is not only a major drug transshipment and producer nation, it is also a conduit and repository for the laundering of drug proceeds generated in the United States. The 2,000-mile U.S.-Mexico border, close working relationships between Colombian and Mexican drug-trafficking organizations, widespread corruption, and the relative ease with which large amounts of U.S. currency can be absorbed into the Mexican financial systems make Mexico an ideal target for money-laundering organizations.

Laundering drug proceeds for Mexican crime syndicates is commonly accomplished by relatively simple and direct means: the bulk shipment of currency back to Mexico. Tractor trailers and cars with hidden compartments are frequently used to smuggle drugs out of Mexico into the United States, and then these same vehicles are packed with the proceeds from the street sale of the drugs and returned to Mexico. Drug traffickers based in Colombia also move the proceeds from their operations in the United States to Los Angeles, New York, and Miami for bulk shipment out of the United States. Both the Colombians and the Mexicans frequently use vehicles with hidden compartments to carry large quantities of U.S. currency. The bulk movement of U.S. cash to Mexico has resulted in significant increases of financial seizures along U.S. roadways. It is estimated that most of the seized currency was destined for drug-trafficking organizations operating out of Mexico.

Once the U.S. currency arrives in Mexico, a variety of alternatives for laundering it are available. The U.S. currency transported to Mexico is generally in small-denomination bills, such as tens and twenties. Money service businesses

Figure 6.3
Source: U.S. Money Laundering Threat Assessment: 2007.

In 2002, an individual defendant laundered more than $700,000 worth of drug proceeds for a money-laundering group associated with Colombian narcotics traffickers. The defendant wired funds to bank accounts in Panama and Honduras. As part of the defendant's money-laundering scheme, between November 1998 and June 2000 he made structured cash purchases of money orders totaling more than $600,000, without ever causing a currency transaction report (CTR) to be filed. On more than 50 occasions, the defendant made multiple small purchases of postal money orders at various post office locations, as many as 11 on a single day, keeping them below the $3,000 record-keeping threshold. The defendant completed the money orders in his name, the name of his company, and names of relatives and friends, then deposited the money orders into his company's businesses bank account. The defendant also exchanged more than $500,000 worth of what he understood was drug money for checks from various business accomplices, including numerous carpet dealers. This activity was determined to have been an intentional circumvention of the federal reporting requirements.

Case in Point: Layering Through MSBs

(MSBs), which include wire remittance services, cashier check companies, and *casas de cambio* (money exchange house) systems, are readily available for the transfer and exchange of dollars, in these small denominations, to pesos. The MSBs function as a parallel banking system in Mexico. In addition to the ability to exchange currency, they have the capability of transferring funds into any banking system worldwide. They provide currency conversion, exchanges, and money movement services for a fee. Legitimate businesses as well as drug-trafficking organizations seek the services MSBs provide. For example, Mexican immigrants have traditionally used wire remittance services to send dollars they've earned in the United States back to Mexico to support their families.

The Laundering Specialists

Technology and modern conveniences of the twenty-first century make it possible for modern-day money launderers to ply their craft. However, because most criminals fear detection by police agents, many have chosen to employ specialists to aid them. For a fee, laundering specialists sell their services to criminals, often in the form of multiservice packages but sometimes in a simple one- or two-step laundering process. Three types of laundering specialists can be identified for this purpose.

- *Couriers* arrange for the movement of currency to a site designated for laundering, where the cash is converted to another method of payment, such as money orders. In the event the courier is employed by a foreign trafficker, cash may be smuggled out of the country to a safe foreign jurisdiction with strict bank secrecy laws. The value of the courier rests in apparent legitimacy and lack of any obvious connection with the criminal who actually owns the money. In many cases, couriers do not even know the identity of the true owner of the currency.
- *Currency exchange specialists* operate both formal and informal businesses that can either be a front for laundering operations or dedicated to illegal clientele. Of the most common formal exchanges is the *casa de cambio*, which exchanges dollars for pesos. As a rule, the exchanges are legitimate foreign currency exchange houses used by criminals seeking quasi-banking services.
- *Business professionals* include attorneys, accountants, and even bankers, who provide investment counseling, create nominee trust accounts, handle international funds transfers, and take advantage of tax avoidance schemes in foreign countries. The goal is to conceal the true origin of the assets under their control.

Specialists who launder cash for large criminal organizations may create informal organizations to facilitate their services. Many laundering organizations are loose confederations united by a common criminal objective: profit. On only the rarest occasion does a laundering organization operate as part of a larger organization. Instead, specialists operate as part of a loose-knit network of entrepreneurs who sell their services on a piecemeal basis. Such organizations might work for more than one criminal organization at a time in addition to working for individuals who manage large criminal organizations at high levels.

Concealment

The first and foremost objective of the money-laundering process is to conceal cash, the source of its ownership, and the future destination of the illegal funds. If money launderers are not successful in hiding their cash and the ownership of it, they run the risk of exposure to police, subsequent forfeiture of those assets, and possible imprisonment. To this end, launderers must consider a second objective—anonymity. This option becomes more practical with the threat of detection by police. So, the backup strategy becomes obvious: Even if the illegal cash is discovered, its connection to the owner becomes obscure. One of the most typical ways of deterring investigation is through layers of false ownership and sales documents.

Money-Laundering Techniques

Illegal drug transactions are usually cash transactions that use large amounts of currency to pay off the different actors in each drug deal and to purchase sophisticated equipment. It is important for the trafficker to legitimize cash proceeds in a fashion that permits the trafficker to spend it wherever and whenever he or she desires, without attracting suspicion. Obviously, the trafficker could choose to store the cash in a strongbox or wall safe, but such methods would not be plausible for one who generates hundreds of thousands or even millions of dollars in illegal cash each year.

The techniques for laundering illicit proceeds are limited only by a trafficker's imagination and cunning. An entire "wash cycle" to transform small denominations of currency to legitimate business accounts, money market deposits, or real estate may take as little as 48 hours. The chosen method used by any given trafficker will reflect his or her own situation and any unique circumstances involved.

Money laundering consists of a three-stage process (Schroeder, 2001). The first stage involves the *placement* of proceeds derived from the illegal activities—the movement of proceeds, frequently currency, from the scene of the crime to a place or into a form that is less suspicious and more convenient for the criminal. For example, a government official may take a bribe in the form of cash and place it in a safe-deposit box or bank account opened under the name of another person, to hide its existence or conceal ownership.

Figure 6.4
Source: Office of National Drug Control Policy, 1994.

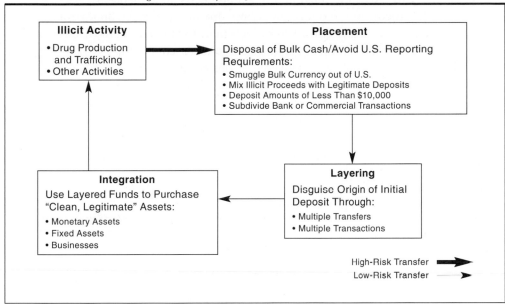

Money Laundering

Layering constitutes the second stage of the laundering process. It involves the separation of proceeds from the illegal source through the use of complex transactions designed to obscure the audit trail and hide the proceeds. This phase of the laundering process can include the transfer of money from one bank account to another, from one bank to another, from one country to another, or any combination thereof. Criminals layer transactions to increase the difficulty of tracing the proceeds back to their illegal source. They frequently use shell corporations and offshore banks at this stage because of the difficulty in obtaining information to identify ownership interests and acquiring necessary account information from them.

Integration, the third stage of money laundering, represents the conversion of illegal proceeds into apparently legitimate business earnings through normal financial or commercial operations. Integration creates the illusion of a legitimate source for criminally derived funds and involves techniques as numerous and creative as those used by legitimate businesses to increase profit and reduce tax liability. Common techniques include producing false invoices for goods purportedly sold by a firm in one country to a firm in another country, using funds held in a foreign bank as security for a domestic loan, commingling money

Critical Thinking Task

Write a letter to one of your U.S. senators or representatives asking that stricter laws be enacted to combat money laundering by drug traffickers. Be specific in your suggestions.

in the bank accounts of companies earning legitimate income, and purchasing property to create the illusion of legal proceeds upon disposal.

The successful money-laundering operation closely approximates legal transactions routinely employed by legitimate businesses. In the hands of a skillful launderer, the following strategies may be used: (1) the payment for goods that appeared to have been delivered by one company based on an invoice of sale prepared by another company covers the laundering of the purchase price when the goods never existed and the companies are owned by the same party; (2) the sale of real estate for an amount far below market value, with an exchange of one-half the difference in an under-the-table cash transaction, launders what on the surface appears to be capital gain when the property is sold again; and (3)

Figure 6.5
Typical Cycle of Money Laundering Using Money Orders

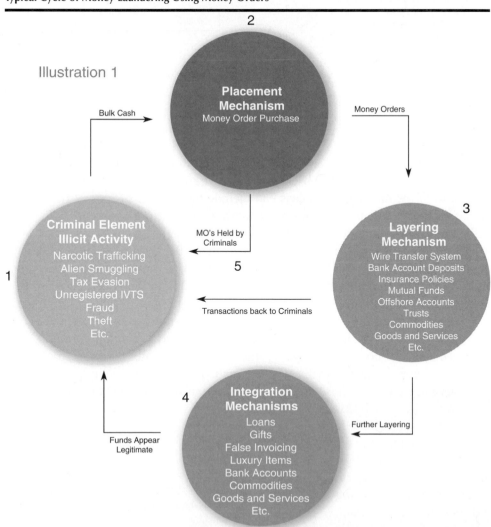

a variety of lateral transfer schemes among three or more parties or companies covers the trail of monetary transactions between any two of them.

Fighting Money Laundering

One principal tool utilized to detect, measure, and punish money laundering is the Bank Secrecy Act (BSA), originally passed into law in 1970. The BSA can help authorities flag the movement of illegally acquired cash moving through banking institutions and across international borders. However, the very inclusion of a minimum dollar amount has given traffickers a way to skirt around the law. Criminals can simply deposit less than the $10,000 amount that triggers banking records of a deposit. In any case, the current regulations under this act, issued by the Secretary of the Treasury, provide law enforcement with several basic tools to investigate money laundering:

- A paper trail of bank records must be maintained for up to five years.
- A *Currency Transaction Report* (CTR) must be filed with the Internal Revenue Service within 15 days when a currency transaction is more than $10,000. Notably omitted from the reporting requirements, however, are wire transfers, bank checks, bank drafts, or other written orders of transfer. In 1989, the U.S. government processed an estimated 7 million CTRs, compared to an estimated 100,000 just 10 years earlier. Traffickers quickly circumvented this requirement by bribing bank employees.
- A *Currency* or *Monetary Instrument Report* (CMIR) must be filed whenever currency or monetary instruments of more than $10,000 are taken into or out of the United States. CMIRs are filed with the U.S. Customs Service. Cashier's checks and bearer bonds made out to cash (rather than to an individual) are not covered by the reporting requirements.

Another powerful tool to combat money laundering is the Currency and Foreign Transactions Reporting Act, which empowers the U.S. government to compel other countries to maintain certain records similar to those used under the BSA. Finally, one of the greatest prosecutorial and investigative aids in years was the enactment of the Money Laundering Control Act. Prior to its passage by Congress in 1986, money laundering per se was not a crime, although various federal statutes were used to prosecute different stages of the money-laundering process. Under the new act, money laundering was made a separate violation of federal law punishable by a fine of $500,000 or twice the value of the property involved, whichever is greater, and 20 years' imprisonment. Powerful forfeiture clauses were also added to federal law in 1988, which provide for the seizure of any property associated with a money-laundering scheme.

The Money Laundering Prosecution Improvement Act of 1988 included a provision authorizing the U.S. Department of Treasury to require financial institutions to verify the identity of people who purchase bank checks or money orders in amounts of $3,000 or more. The law also authorized the Secretary of the Treasury to target certain types of institutions or geographic areas for special reporting requirements. More recently, the Money Laundering and Financial Crime Strategy Act of 1998 called for the development of a national strategy to combat money laundering and related financial crimes. In response, the Department of Justice and the Treasury Department developed a strategy designating high-risk money-laundering zones to direct coordinated efforts by police, providing for greater scrutiny of suspicious transactions, creating new legislation, and intensifying pressure on nations that lack adequate money-laundering controls.

These techniques represent only a few of the ways traffickers hide their illicit revenues from drug sales. It is generally thought that traffickers, regardless of their national origin, make regular use of these techniques. The fact that so many different mechanisms exist for money laundering makes investigation of these crimes difficult and presents many unique challenges to the investigator.

Figure 6.6

During the 1990s, the Cali Cartel of Colombia was one of the world's most powerful criminal organizations, estimated to be responsible for up to 80 percent of the cocaine smuggled into the United States. Today the cartel is in ruins, with its leaders imprisoned and their assets seized. In September 2006, Miguel and Gilberto Rodriguez-Orejuela, the brothers who ran the infamous Cali Cartel, pleaded guilty to a charge of conspiracy to import cocaine into the United States and agreed to plead guilty to conspiracy to commit money laundering. The Rodriguez-Orejuela brothers also agreed to the entry of a final forfeiture judgment in the amount of $2.1 billion. The Rodriguez-Orejuela family members, whose names were used as "fronts" on the brothers' businesses and other assets, agreed to relinquish these businesses and assist in their forfeiture by Colombia and the United States. After several years of investigation, Miguel and Gilberto Rodriguez-Orejuela (62 and 67 years old, respectively) were finally sentenced to 30 years in an American prison.

The convictions of the Rodriguez-Orejuela brothers resulted from Operation Cornerstone, an OCDETF investigation led by ICE, with the cooperation of the Drug Enforcement Administration, the Department of Justice, and Colombian law enforcement agencies. Since its inception in August 1991, Operation Cornerstone has led to the conviction of more than 140 members of the Cali Cartel and the seizure of 47.5 metric tons of cocaine. Through records seizures and witness testimony, Operation Cornerstone produced documentation of the smuggling of 200 metric tons of cocaine into the United States, representing $2.1 billion in drug proceeds. Thanks to the dedicated efforts of U.S. and Colombian law enforcement authorities, the Cali Cartel will no longer be able to benefit from these ill-gotten gains.

Figure 6.6—*continued*

> In the end, the Cali Cartel was incapacitated through the relentless investigation and immobilization of its hidden finances and assets. The four leaders of the Cali Cartel—Helmer Herrera Buitrago, Jose Santacruz Londono, and the two Rodriguez-Orejuela brothers—were initially identified as Specially Designated Narcotics Traffickers in 1995, pursuant to Executive Order 12978 under the International Emergency Economic Powers Act (IEEPA). The Treasury Department's Office of Foreign Assets Control (OFAC) then used IEEPA economic sanction authorities to attack the financial empire built by the Cali Cartel. Subsequent sanctions investigations by OFAC led to the addition of hundreds of front companies and individuals in Colombia and 10 other countries to the list of Specially Designated Narcotics Traffickers. OFAC's continued aggressive actions severely impacted the Cali Cartel's ability to reap the benefits of its drug trafficking activities, and ultimately pressured the conspirators into a plea agreement, signaling the end of this once-powerful drug-trafficking organization.

Following the Money to the Fall of the Cali Cartel

SUMMARY

When the so-called drug problem is discussed, the subject of drug-related crime is also deliberated. The very term *drug-related crime* means different things to different people because it represents many types of criminal activity. Although many people consider drug crimes to be street crimes (e.g., robbery, assault, burglary, and murder), other crimes also accompany drug abuse.

Studies of the behavior of drug users have revealed that the crime rate (street-type crimes) for users may be anywhere from four to six times as high as for people who do not use drugs. In addition to street crimes associated with drug use, ancillary crimes such as corruption and money laundering accompany drug use. Official corruption in the United States poses a major problem for drug-control strategists and enforcement officials. Corruption is pervasive and may take any of several forms, from bribery, extortion, favoritism, and mooching to more serious types of corruption such as perjury, premeditated theft, and shakedowns of suspects. Both the Knapp and the Mollen Commissions' inquiries into police corruption in New York shed light on corruption within police departments. In addition, many cases of police and official corruption have surfaced around the country, making it clear that the drug trade can penetrate even the most reputable of professions.

The problem of foreign corruption parallels that experienced in the United States with even greater repercussions. Many drug source countries, such as Colombia, Peru, and Myanmar, are experiencing criminal forces that threaten to rival the legitimate government because of political influence gained through payoffs. Unscrupulous links have been documented between Panama's former dictator Manuel Noriega and Fidel Castro, between Colombian traffickers and Honduran officials, and between high-ranking Mexican Federal Judicial Police officials and known heroin traffickers in Mexico. For decades, the laundering of illegally obtained currency has been a logistical problem for many organized crime operations. The trafficker's basic concern is how to transform illegally obtained money to currency that appears to be legitimate.

The 1970 Bank Secrecy Act has provided investigators with much-needed legal tools with which to combat this type of crime. These tools consist of specific reporting requirements for banking institutions and individuals alike. These reporting requirements enable investigators to follow the path of illicitly gained currency to its source.

Do you recognize these terms?

- Currency Transaction Report (CTR)
- Drug Abuse Reporting Program
- grass eaters
- institutional corruption
- integration
- Knapp Commission
- layering
- meat eaters
- Mollen Commission
- money laundering
- Pennsylvania Crime Commission
- placement
- police socialization
- Treatment Outcome Prospective Study
- Wickersham Commission

DISCUSSION QUESTIONS

1. List three reasons that corruption is considered a threat to public safety.

2. Discuss the different types of corruption commonly practiced by corrupt police officers.

3. Discuss the use of currency exchanges in money-laundering operations.

4. Discuss the Bank Secrecy Act (1970) and the use of the CTR and the CMIR as each pertains to money-laundering investigations.

5. What is the difference between corrupt officials who are termed *grass eaters* and those called *meat eaters*?

6. List and explain the four basic legal tools used to investigate money laundering as provided for under the Bank Secrecy Act.

7. List and discuss the most common techniques traffickers use to launder illicitly gained currency.

Part II

Gangs and Drugs

Organized crime has historically played an important role in U.S. society. The drug problem specifically has afforded many organized criminals increased sources of revenue with which to expand their operations and influence throughout the nation's communities. Accordingly, conflicts between these organizations have also escalated, resulting in gangs warring with each other over territory as well as recruiting new members from schools. Furthermore, larger crime organizations have developed the resources and capabilities to insulate themselves from detection by infiltrating legitimate businesses and corrupting public officials. This section examines the concept of organized crime, its origins and growth, and its increasing alliance with the illicit drug trade.

Part II

Gangs and Drugs

Chapter 7

Organized Crime and the Drug Trade

This chapter will enable you to:

- Understand the term *organized crime*
- Differentiate between traditional and non-traditional organized crime
- Understand the alien conspiracy theory
- Understand the factors that contribute to the growth of nontraditional organized crime

THE NATURE OF DRUG TRAFFICKING

As noted in Chapter 1, there is no single drug problem in the United States but rather myriad separate drug problems that interact with one another. Likewise, there is no single, predictable pattern for drug-trafficking organizations. They vary widely in size, sophistication, area of operation, clientele, and product. They also have varying degrees of vertical and horizontal integration, different proclivities for the use of violence, and distinct patterns of interaction with one another.

Drug-trafficking organizations share the distinct characteristic of being engaged in the same illegal business. For that reason, however, they do not have access to and are not subject to the normal channels of production, distribution, sales, finance, taxation, regulation, and contract enforcement that shape the legitimate business arena. Ironically, a dichotomy presents itself, since this illicit business is still subject to many of the same dynamics as the laws of supply and demand, the need for efficiency in operation, and the necessity for a set of rules by which to operate. Traffickers must operate outside the normal financial and legal structures of commerce while at the same time

DOI: 10.1016/B978-1-4377-4450-7.00007-2
© 2011 Elsevier Inc. All rights reserved.

remaining subject to all the market pressures normally accommodated by that structure. Recognizing this dichotomy is one of the keys to understanding the nature of drug-trafficking organizations.

To best understand this nature, we must realize that such organizations recreate the structures of legitimate commerce. Experience shows us that many of these organizations do so with astonishing precision, yet they are skewed by the limitations of the illicit nature of their activities. Some of the more well-established organizations may have a board of directors, a chief executive officer (CEO), and a bureaucracy that is disciplined and whose functions and benefits mirror those of the management in modern corporations. To that extent, many participants enjoy amenities such as expense accounts, bonuses, and even company cars. On the other hand, the normal commercial concept of contracts (in which disputes are adjudicated by an impartial judiciary) and restitution (which is almost always of a financial nature) is skewed in the world of drug trafficking. Here a system exists in which the rule of law has been replaced by the threat of violence and retribution.

Although there is no single type of organizational structure that describes major drug-trafficking organizations, a few well-defined patterns have been identified. First, there are major international, vertically integrated trafficking organizations that are best exemplified by the Mexican cartels (see Chapter 6). In addition, other groups (e.g., outlaw motorcycle gangs) operate domestically and tend to have smaller, less sophisticated operations. For example, their lines of supply are shorter, bank accounts are fewer, and the quantities of drugs transported are not as great. Next, there are city-based groups (e.g., youth gangs) that operate in many large inner-city areas. These groups tend to have minimal organization at the management end of their operations but still have extensive distribution networks run by low-level operatives, many of whom work directly on the street and concentrate primarily on local distribution and retail aspects of drug distribution (see Chapter 4).

Two features common to many of the larger trafficking organizations are their abilities to tap into alternate sources of supply and to adapt to readily changing conditions. For example, the Cali cartel can buy its coca leaves or paste in Peru, Bolivia, Ecuador, or Colombia itself. This flexibility enables the major traffickers to regroup and redirect a segment of their operations without disrupting the entire organization. In many respects, Colombian trafficking organizations are on the cutting edge of international technology. They operate across international borders, and the flexibility of their organizational structure enables them to form partnerships with other groups.

Like large legitimate corporations, major traffickers are immense because they are good at what they do. Careless errors are few, as are unnecessary risks. Leaders of these organizations are keenly aware of the importance of being insulated from street-level drug sales. One of the characteristics that prevails in the world of drug trafficking is the predilection for dealing in cash and the incentive to transfer that cash into the legitimate economy so that it can be converted into goods and services from the legitimate business community. This alone represents one of the biggest problems for trafficking organizations. In fact, so much cash is involved in the drug trade that it is often more advantageous for police to track cash proceeds than the drugs themselves. Indeed, it is money from which even the most cautious drug manager cannot be totally isolated. Accordingly, tracking this money remains one of the most challenging investigative endeavors for drug control agents.

Reminiscent of Prohibition-era gangs, today's drug-trafficking organizations are varied and have become increasingly organized and powerful. With an array of ethnically and geographically based groups, today's illicit drug-trafficking organizations have surpassed the sophistication and influence of many of their early twentieth-century counterparts.

Crime in the United States has undergone many significant changes since the 1920s. It has become more pernicious due to two interrelated developments: drug abuse and organized crime. For decades, the Mafia was thought to have monopolized the drug trade, but today many different criminal groups compete for territory and the tax-free profits offered by illicit drugs. For many years, the term *organized crime* was synonymous with La Cosa Nostra, or the Mafia. This term generally refers to the popular public view of Italian and Sicilian criminal groups. Although both Sicilian and Italian-American criminal organizations are involved in the lucrative drug trade, so are many other criminal groups. All these groups have their sights set on the immense profits to be earned in drugs. Today, groups whose criminal enterprises focus on the illegal drug trade include outlaw motorcycle gangs, Jamaican posses, African American organized crime groups, and California-based youth gangs, to name a few.

Organized crime has demonstrated not only an alarming degree of violence but also an ability to corrupt public officials at the highest levels. The pervasiveness of such activity threatens legitimate businesses and neighborhoods. To operate both efficiently and effectively, large-scale drug-trafficking operations require superb organization. This is essential to avoid police detection while maintaining the ability to compete with other criminal groups. To this end, these organizations can be characterized by a number of common activities. These include:

- Obtaining the illicit substances (or the raw materials with which to manufacture them)
- Making "connections" to acquire the illicit substances
- Arranging for the processing of drugs (either through overseas or domestic sources)
- Developing smuggling networks with which to transport illicit materials
- Arranging for protection of the operation through corrupting public officials or hiring enforcers
- Locating distributors on both the wholesale and retail levels
- Developing a process whereby illegal money can be laundered or otherwise concealed from detection by law enforcement authorities
- Utilizing the Internet to recruit new members

The coming chapters examine some of the significant actors on the criminal side of the "war on drugs." The following segment, however, is intended to acquaint the reader with various gang characteristics so that rational conclusions can be drawn regarding the role of organized crime in the U.S. drug scene.

Figure 7.1
Source: National Drug Assessment, 2010.

Drug cartels are large, highly sophisticated organizations composed of multiple drug-trafficking organizations and cells with specific assignments such drug transportation, security/enforcement, or money laundering. Drug cartel command-and-control structures are based outside the United States; however, they produce, transport, and distribute illicit drugs domestically with the assistance of organizations that are either a part of or in an alliance with the cartel.

Drug trafficking organizations (DTOs) are complex organizations with highly defined command-and-control structures that produce, transport, and distribute large quantities of one or more illicit drugs.

Criminal groups operating in the United States are numerous and range from small to moderately sized, loosely knit groups that distribute one or more drugs at the retail level and midlevel.

Street gangs are defined by the National Alliance of Gang Investigators as groups or associations of three or more persons with a common identifying sign, symbol, or name, the members of which individually or collectively engage in criminal activity that creates an atmosphere of fear and intimidation.

Prison gangs are highly structured criminal networks that operate within the federal and state prison system and in local communities through members who have been released from prison.

Outlaw motorcycle gangs (OMGs) are highly structured criminal organizations whose members engage in criminal activities such as violent crimes and weapons and drug trafficking. OMGs maintain strong centralized leadership that implements rules regulating membership, conduct, and criminal activity.

Drug Cartels, Drug Trafficking Organizations, Criminal Groups, and Gangs

GANGS

Gangs represent a serious public threat in many communities throughout the United States. Recent investigations show that gang members are increasingly migrating from urban to suburban areas and are responsible for a growing percentage of crime and violence. To a great extent, gang-related criminal activity involves drug trafficking, but recently gang members are increasingly engaging in alien and weapons trafficking (National Gang Intelligence Center, 2009). Additionally, a rising number of U.S.-based gangs are seemingly intent on developing working relationships with U.S.- and foreign-based drug-trafficking organizations and other criminal organizations to gain direct access to foreign sources of illicit drugs.

Recent statistics show the prevalence of gangs in the United States and the extent they are involved in criminal activity. For example, the National Gang Intelligence Center reported that in the United States in 2008 there were approximately 20,000 gangs with an estimated one million members. These gangs have been reported as operating in 58 percent of state and local law enforcement agency jurisdictions. Furthermore, law enforcement groups report that criminal gangs are thought to commit as much as 80 percent of the crime in many communities. These crimes include alien smuggling, armed robbery, assault, auto theft, drug trafficking, extortion, fraud, home invasions, identity theft, murder, and weapons trafficking. Gang members are also the primary retail-level distributors of most illicit drugs (National Gang Intelligence Center, 2009).

The gang migration from urban areas to suburban and rural locations, which began more than two decades ago, is a significant and growing problem in most areas of the country. Gangs are now fully well established in many communities across the nation. Most gangs were formed in major cities and then expanded into neighboring communities in the 1970s. By the 1990s, full-scale migration was taking place. Many notable gangs (e.g., Gangster Disciples, Latin Kings) were originally formed as organizations of political and social reform during the 1960s, but soon thereafter the focus of many of these gangs changed from reform to criminal activity in the pursuit of profit.

The movement of gang members to suburban areas often resulted in territorial conflicts between rival gang members competing for the new territory, in addition to conflicts with the few existing suburban gang members. Gang members who migrated from urban areas often formed new, neighborhood-based local gangs, and generally these gangs controlled their territories through violence and intimidation. Moreover, they sought to increase their size by recruiting new members who were typically from single-parent, low-income households and who possessed limited education. Local gangs engaged in a wide range of criminal activity, including retail-level drug distribution.

During the 1980s, some gangs began to expand their drug distribution networks into suburban communities influenced by local gangs. The larger gangs, who already controlled drug distribution in city drug markets, were motivated to move into adjoining communities to generate additional income by capitalizing on the growing cocaine (both powder and crack) markets. Billions of dollars were generated from trafficking illegal drugs, and this money enabled the gangs to recruit new members and forced smaller local gangs to either disband or join forces with the larger groups. As large urban gangs increasingly dominated and expanded into drug markets in suburban and rural communities, they often were met with initial resistance by local gangs. This resistance resulted in an increased number of homicides and drive-by shootings.

Gang-related violence and drug trafficking became fully ingrained in suburban areas throughout the 1990s. Because of violent gang activity, law enforcement devoted significant resources to fighting gun crime and disrupting the most violent gangs. The crackdown on violent gang activity targeted key gang leaders in an effort to dismantle highly structured gangs. In conjunction with this practice, federal law enforcement officers began to target violent gang members from Mexico and Central America, most of whom were in the United States illegally. Moreover, a large number of gang members in prison formed associations along ethnic lines in an attempt to protect their organizations and operations, giving rise to large, influential prison gangs.

Gang migration has led to the recruitment of new, younger gang members in many suburban and rural communities. According to recent statistics, the percentage of suburban students age 12–18 who reported that gangs were present at school during the previous six months increased by 17 percent from 2003 to 2005 after remaining stable from 2001 to 2003 (Bureau of Justice Statistics, 2009). Gang activity at schools is rising, in part because gangs are using middle schools and high schools as venues for drug distribution. Law enforcement agencies in numerous jurisdictions report that gangs are directing teenage members who had dropped out of school to reenroll, primarily to recruit new members and sell drugs.

Gang Membership

Gang membership in the United States was conservatively estimated at one million members as of September 2008. However, current estimates include approximately 900,000 gang members residing within local communities across the country and more than 147,000 documented gang members incarcerated in federal, state, and local correctional facilities. Increased gang membership is most likely the result of gang recruitment efforts and the release of incarcerated gang members (National Gang Intelligence Center, 2009).

Gang Types

Gangs vary extensively regarding membership, structure, age, and ethnicity. However, three basic types of gangs have been identified over the years: street gangs, prison gangs, and outlaw motorcycle gangs (OMGs).

Street Gangs

Street gangs operating throughout most of the United States control a large geographical area, and therefore, criminal activities such as violence and drug trafficking perpetrated by street gangs pose a great threat. The threat becomes magnified as national- and regional-level street gangs migrate from urban areas to suburban and rural communities, expanding their influence in most regions and broadening their presence outside the United States to develop associations with drug-trafficking organizations (DTOs) and other criminal organizations in Mexico, Central America, and Canada.

Currently, 11 national-level street gangs have been identified in the United States, and associates or members have been identified in foreign countries, according to analysis of federal, state, and local law enforcement (National Drug Intelligence Center, 2008b). National gangs typically have several hundred to several thousand members nationwide who operate in multiple regions. Established cells in foreign countries assist gangs operating in the United States for further developing associations and drug-trafficking organizations as well as other organizations in those countries.

Regional-level street gangs increasingly distribute drugs at the wholesale level. According to recent statistics, at least five street gangs, specifically Florencia 13, Fresno Bulldogs, Latin Disciples, Tango Blast, and United Blood Nation, have been identified as operating at a regional level. Regional-level gangs are usually organized with several hundred to several thousand members. They may have some members in foreign countries and maintain contacts with drug-trafficking organizations operating in the United States (National Drug Intelligence Center, 2009a).

Local street gangs, which are sometimes referred to as *neighborhood-based gangs* or *drug crews*, also present an ongoing problem for local law enforcement agencies. As of the preparation of this text, most street gangs are local-level gangs that operate in single locations. Membership generally ranges from three to several hundred members. Most of these gangs engage in violence in conjunction with a variety of crimes, including retail-level drug distribution; however, they usually have no direct ties to larger criminal organizations. But recent reports by police agencies claim that a few local gangs have established ties to wholesale-level drug trafficking organizations operating along the U.S.-Mexico border (National Drug Intelligence Center, 2009a).

Prison Gangs

Over the past three decades *prison gangs* have gained prominence in society. This is especially so with national-level prison gangs that affiliate with Mexican drug-trafficking organizations and maintain a considerable amount of influence over street gangs in the communities in which they operate. Prison gangs are highly structured criminal networks that operate within the federal and state prison systems. They operate in local communities through members who have been released from prison as well. Released members typically return to their home communities and resume their former street gang affiliations, acting as representatives of their prison gang to recruit street gang members who perform criminal acts on behalf of the prison gang.

Prison gangs often control drug distribution within correctional facilities and heavily influence street-level distribution in some communities. These

A few months prior to his resignation in August 2009, Los Angeles Police Chief William Bratton speaks at a news conference to announce the indictment naming 24 leaders, members, and associates of MS-13, part of the Mara Salvatrucha gang affiliated with the Mexican Mafia prison gang.

gangs exert considerable control over mid- and retail-level drug distribution in the southwestern United States and southern California. Their trafficking activities are facilitated through their connections with Mexican drug-trafficking organizations, which ensure access to a continuous supply of illicit drugs that are distributed through their networks in prison or are supplied to affiliated street gangs. Three different levels of prison gangs have been identified:

- *National-level prison gangs.* Prison gangs at this level maintain ongoing relationships with drug-trafficking organizations. Of the five identified national-level prison gangs, two have members or associates in at least two foreign countries. Prison gangs at this level are well organized and governed by established sets of rules and codes of conduct that are rigorously enforced by gang leaders. For example, the California-based Mexican Mafia (*La Eme*) uses fear and intimidation to control Hispanic street gangs whose members are in prison and on the street in California, giving them command over an estimated 50,000 to 75,000 gang members and associates (National Gang Intelligence Center, 2009a).
- *Regional-level prison gangs.* Gangs at the regional level are increasingly developing associations with known drug-trafficking organizations. Regional-level prison gangs have organizational structures similar to those of national-level gangs but typically are limited to operating in one or two state prison systems. The most significant regional-level prison gangs operate in Texas, and most have ties to at least one Mexican drug-trafficking organization (National Gang Intelligence Center, 2009a).
- *Local or state-level prison gangs.* Gangs at the local or state level, particularly those operating along the U.S.-Mexico border, are an ongoing concern for law enforcement. Local prison gangs typically operate within the Department of Corrections in a single state. As members are released from prison, they settle in local communities, where they recruit and associate with local street gang members and conduct criminal activities on behalf of the prison gang (National Gang Intelligence Center, 2009a).

Outlaw Motorcycle Gangs

Outlaw motorcycle gangs (OMGs) pose a threat to communities because of their wide-ranging criminal activity, propensity to use violence, and ability to counter law enforcement efforts. OMGs are highly structured criminal organizations, and their members engage in violent crime, weapons trafficking, and drug trafficking. These groups maintain a strong centralized leadership that implements rules regulating membership, conduct, and criminal activity.

Membership in outlaw motorcycle gangs is considerable. As of June 2008, state and local law enforcement agencies estimated that between 280 and 520 law motorcycle gangs were operating in United States. These organizations range in size from a single chapter to hundreds of chapters worldwide. Current law enforcement intelligence estimates indicate that more than 20,000 validated OMG members, divided among the hundreds of OMGs, reside in the United States (National Gang Intelligence Center, 2009a). As with other organized crime groups, OMGs can be identified on three different levels:

- *National-level OMGs.* With memberships ranging into the thousands, these groups maintain strong associations with transnational drug-trafficking organizations and other criminal organizations. In addition, national-level OMGs maintain criminal networks of regional and local motorcycle clubs, commonly referred to as *support, puppet,* or *duck* clubs, whose members conduct criminal activities in support of the larger group and which serve as a source for new members. Moreover, some members of support clubs have acquired employment with private businesses or government agencies, which enables them to provide national-level OMGs with business, government, and financial information that can be used to protect their criminal enterprises.

- *Regional-level OMGs.* OMGs on the regional level range in size from 50 to several hundred members. In the United States, 109 regional-level OMGs have been identified by law enforcement; most support one of the national-level groups. A number of regional-level OMGs maintain independent contact with transnational drug-trafficking organizations (National Gang Intelligence Center, 2009a).

- *Local-level OMGs.* The local-level OMG typically operates in a single state or in a few neighboring states and has fewer than 50 members. They are often support clubs for regional- and national-level OMGs. In general, OMGs on this level have no ties to international drug-trafficking organizations.

Criminal Activities

Gangs are responsible for much of the crime in many urban and suburban communities across the United States, and much of it is associated with drug-trafficking activities. Recent statistics show that gang members are responsible for as much as 80 percent of the crime in some locations. Violence resulting from disputes over control of drug territory and enforcement of drug debts frequently occurs among street gangs. Gang members also engage in a host of other criminal activities such as auto theft, assault, alien smuggling, burglary, drive-by shootings, extortion, firearms offenses, home invasion robberies, homicide, identity theft, insurance fraud, mortgage fraud, operation of prostitution rings, and weapons trafficking (National Gang Intelligence Center, 2009a).

Drug distribution by gang members on the retail level is on the increase, as is their participation in wholesale-level drug distribution in urban and suburban communities. For example, in 2004 it was estimated that 45 percent of gangs were involved in drug distribution; in 2008, that figure rose to 58 percent. The primary drug distributed by gangs is marijuana, followed by powder and crack cocaine and MDMA (ecstasy), methamphetamine, diverted pharmaceuticals, and heroin (National Gang Intelligence Center, 2009a).

Gang-related violent crime is also increasing in many areas around the country. In San Diego, for example, fatal gang-related homicides increased 56 percent, from 18 in 2006 to 28 in 2007 (National Gang Intelligence Center, 2009a). Accordingly, recent research shows that gang members are increasingly using firearms in conjunction with their criminal activities. Gang members typically buy, sell, and trade firearms among their associates. Gang members often obtain these firearms through thefts and straw purchases. These firearms are for personal use or for use by fellow gang members in committing homicides and armed robberies. For example, members and associates of the Los Angeles-based Black P. Stone Bloods and Rolling 20s Crips were arrested in July 2008 for illegally selling more than 119 firearms. Furthermore, members of California-based Mara Salvatrucha obtain weapons for their personal use and sell weapons and ammunition to members of other gangs in California for profit (National Gang Intelligence Center, 2009a).

Financing Illicit Operations

Gangs earn the profits essential to maintaining their criminal operations and the lifestyles of their members primarily through drug distribution. Most gang members are retail-level dealers who use drug proceeds to make typical consumer purchases, pay their living costs, or purchase luxury goods such as vehicles and jewelry.

Recent statistics show that gang members typically launder profits from criminal activities through front companies and real estate investments. Gang members use front companies such as clothing stores, hair salons, and music recording and production companies to co-mingle in illicit proceeds earned from drug sales with licit income from these businesses. Some gang members also use mortgage fraud schemes or purchase real estate as investments or as a means to co-mingle in illicit funds with rental payments. For example, members of the Chicago-based Latin Kings, Black Disciples, Vice Lords, and Gangster Disciples use mortgage fraud schemes that employ straw purchases and unscrupulous mortgage brokers and appraisers to purchase property at a minimal cost and sell it at a higher value to a third party. The gang members receiving the profits from the sales seemingly legitimatize the income, whereas their associates typically default on loans, often defrauding banks or mortgage companies (National Gang Intelligence Center, 2009a).

Gang Communications

Gang members use cell phones and the Internet to communicate and promote their illegal activities. Street gangs often use voicemail and text messaging to conduct drug transactions and prearranged meetings with customers. Members of street gangs use multiple cell phones that frequently are discarded while conducting their traffic operations. For example, the leader of an African American street gang operating in Milwaukee was found to use more than 20 cell phones to coordinate drug-related activities. Most were prepaid telephones that the leader routinely discarded and replaced. Internet-based methods such as social networking sites, encrypted e-mail, Internet telephones, and instant messaging are also used by gang members to communicate with one another and with drug customers (National Gang Intelligence Center, 2009a).

For example, members of the Crips gang in Hampton, Virginia, used the Internet to intimidate rival gang members and maintain websites to recruit new members. On October 23, 2007, a 15-year-old Crips gang member was arrested for shooting a rival gang member in the leg. Additionally, he was charged with the recruitment of persons for a criminal street gang through the use of the gang social network site (National Gang Intelligence Center, 2009a).

DEFINING ORGANIZED CRIME

Organized crime is a complex criminal phenomenon that conjures up the image of gangsters with broad-brimmed hats, dark pinstriped suits, and Thompson submachine guns. Over the years, this popular image has been perpetuated by movies, television, and novels and tends to leave the average person with a limited concept of the term. Contributing to the enigma of organized crime is the absence of a codified, legal definition of the term. Ironically, despite the lack of an official definition, many federal statutes address types of criminal activity typically involving organized crime. For example, statutes exist dealing with criminal conspiracies, continuing criminal enterprises (CCE), and racketeer-influenced and corrupt organizations (RICO), but all these are separate from and more specific than the general term *organized crime*.

The very words *organized crime* imply criminal involvement by a group of individuals operating in an organized fashion. However, it is not clear whether this broad definition includes a group of three youths involved in a shoplifting scheme or whether it should be applied only to larger, more sophisticated criminal organizations. The general term itself fails to give adequate guidelines to criminal justice professionals, who are in need of a more precise distinction between the high-level organized drug-trafficking organization and a group of two or three low-level "street-corner" drug dealers. In 1968, Congress passed into law the first major organized crime bill, the Omnibus Crime Control and Safe Streets Act, which is the only federal statute that uses the term *organized crime*. In the act, the term is loosely described as:

> [Organized crime includes] the unlawful activities of members of a highly organized, disciplined association engaged in supplying illegal goods or services, including but not limited to gambling, prostitution, loansharking, narcotics, labor racketeering, and other unlawful activities....

Clarity was given to the term when the President's Commission on Organized Crime concluded in 1986 that several variables that make up an organized crime unit can be identified (PCOC, 1986c). These include (1) the criminal group, which is made up of core people who share certain bonds, (2) the protectors, who protect the group's interests, and (3) specialized support, which consists of people who knowingly render services on an ad hoc basis.

The Criminal Group

The *criminal group* is composed of individuals who are usually bound by ethnic, racial, geographic, or lingual ties. The individuals display a willingness to engage in criminal activity for profit while using violence and intimidation to protect their criminal interests and to avoid detection. Organized crime (hereinafter referred to as *OC*) groups are characterized by the longevity of the groups themselves, which outlasts the lives of individual members. Such a group maintains rules and a code of conduct while its management is structured in a hierarchical or pyramid-style chain of command. Membership in the OC group is restricted and is usually based on a common trait, talent, or need of the group. Acceptance into the criminal group is closely scrutinized by the existing members, and typically an initiation is required for all recruits. Motivation for individual membership is based on the premise that the successful recruit will enjoy economic gain, protection by the group, and a certain prestige within the organization.

The Protectors

The *protectors* are usually associates of the criminal group who appear (at least on the surface) to be law-abiding members of the community. In fact, this group may include prominent members of the community such as corrupt politicians, bankers, attorneys, or accountants. They work to insulate the criminal group from government interference and to protect the assets of the organization.

Specialized Support

The larger the criminal group, the more it is in need of *specialized support*. Those individuals offering specialized support for the OC unit possess talent that enables the group to attain its goals and objectives. Unlike the seemingly lawful existence of the protectors, specialists include laboratory chemists, smuggling pilots, and enforcers (professional killers) for the OC unit. Most OC specialists are overtly involved in illicit aspects of criminality.

In addition to these specialists, the OC group relies on outside individuals (members of the general public) for financial and other support:

- *User support* includes those individuals who purchase the OC group's illegal goods and services. These individuals include drug users, patrons of prostitutes, bookmakers, and those who willfully purchase stolen goods.
- *Social support* includes individuals and organizations who grant power and an air of legitimacy to organized crime generally and to certain groups and their members specifically. Social support includes public officials who solicit the support of organized crime figures, business leaders who do business with organized crime figures, and others who portray the criminal group or organized crime in a favorable or glamorous light.

In considering organized crime organizations in both the United States and in foreign countries, several operative characteristics can be recognized. One such characteristic is the group's attempt to compete with the functions of legitimate government. Examples include the following:

- *In Colombia.* Cocaine cartels such as the Medellín and Cali cartels were competing with the legitimate government in attempting to control segments of the society, offering to pay off the country's national debt and generally acting like an alternative government.
- *In Italy.* The Sicilian Mafia has been responsible for the assassinations of many investigators and federal police who were assigned to anti-Mafia investigations. In addition, judges, mayors, union leaders, and government representatives have been killed by organized crime members because those individuals opposed the political or criminal activities of the Mafia.

In the United States, such displays of violence against the government are not quite as blatant, but many of the same principles are still at work. In one case, for example, organized crime members in Chicago attempted to levy a "street tax" on bookmakers and pornographers. Although these activities are illicit, the function of taxing can be viewed as one rightfully belonging to legitimate government. Additionally, many cities that have experienced the influx of youth gangs recognize that these groups have attempted to take control of neighborhoods for crack distribution. In many cases, witnesses who have offered to testify against criminal organizations have been intimidated because of the organization's reputation and have been encouraged (through threat of violence) not to cooperate with the government. Clearly, this characteristic of the OC unit threatens many of the fundamentals of a free, civilized society.

According to the U.S. Department of Justice, for a criminal group to be considered an OC group, several variables must be present. It must have an organizational structure, it has to engage in a continuing criminal conspiracy, its underlying goal must be the generation of profits, and it must have sufficient continuity to carry out its purpose over a long period of time (PCOC, 1986a). Groups that fit into this category include both foreign and domestic organizations.

> ### Critical Thinking Task
>
> Hollywood occasionally produces films and programs about organized crime (e.g., *Bugsy, Casino, Donnie Brasco, The Godfather, Goodfellas, Scarface*, HBO's *The Sopranos*). Evaluate the role the entertainment industry plays in supporting organized crime.

Numerous similarities are evident between the groups discussed in the forthcoming chapters. They all have taken advantage of the burgeoning market for illegal drugs and the numerous international sources for those drugs. Other similarities include a common disrespect for the law, a willingness to use violence to further their individual group goals, and the use of corruption to aid them in achieving their criminal intentions. Individually, each organized crime group poses an individual threat to society and public order, but collectively they make up what is generally considered the true scope of organized crime in the 1990s.

THE ALIEN CONSPIRACY THEORY

The term *organized crime* tends to invoke images of men of foreign descent, steeped in feudal traditions and sharing a blind allegiance to the organization to which they belong. These images are what some criminologists have dubbed the *alien conspiracy theory* of organized crime. This theory holds that OC is a direct spin-off of a secret society: the Mafia, a criminal organization dating back to Sicily during the mid-1800s. The basic premise of the theory is that the Mafia is a single organization that is centrally coordinated through a national commission that arbitrates disputes and mandates policy (Cressey, 1969).

There is considerable debate among scholars as to whether such a multinational organization actually exists, although some local, state, and federal law enforcement agencies are convinced of its existence and base the formation of public organized crime policy on that premise. Disbelievers in the alien conspiracy theory argue that the Mafia is a figment of both the media's and law enforcement's imagination. They insist that organized crime consists of numerous ethnically diverse groups who compete for profits in the provision of illegal goods and services. Furthermore, they claim that these groups are not bound by a single, national organizational leadership but act independently, on their own.

Supporters of the alien conspiracy theory conceive two OC contingencies: traditional organized crime (the Mafia) and nontraditional organized crime. The latter represents OC groups that

Critical Thinking Task

Do you believe the Mafia exists, or is it merely a myth or an exaggerated stereotype? Support or refute your belief in the alien conspiracy theory.

have emerged during the past two decades and have focused on the illegal drug trade as their major source of illegal revenue. They are largely made up of ethnic groups, including blacks, Hispanics, and Asians. The next section briefly discusses the alleged role of the Mafia as traditional organized crime participants in the drug trade, followed by a discussion of some emerging nontraditional drug-trafficking groups.

The Mafia

At the core of the alien conspiracy theory is the traditional crime group known as the *La Cosa Nostra* (which means "this thing of ours") or, more commonly, the *Mafia*. Operating in different factions in both Sicily and the United States, the Mafia is thought to be composed of "crime families" in 24 or so major United States cities. It is estimated that although total membership is around 1,700 "made men" or "wise guys," the influence of the organization is much greater due to a vast network of associates who are not actual members. In 1986 the President's Commission on Organized Crime estimated that as many as 17,000 associates are criminally involved in the businesses of the "mob" (PCOC, 1986c).

Mafia crime families are believed to operate in geographically assigned areas around the United States. In New York City, for example, five families—Gambino, Colombo, Lucchese, Bonnano, and Genovese—operate, each named after their founding godfathers and heavily involved in both illicit and legitimate businesses.

Most traditional crime families got their start during Prohibition (1920–1933) in the illegal liquor business. This time period created a multimillion-dollar bootlegging business following violent wars over territory and the control of illegal rackets. Today, believers of the alien conspiracy theory argue that the Mafia represents a highly sophisticated criminal network with a complex structure and chain of command emulated by many other new and emerging crime groups. Although not every Mafia family participates in the illicit drug trade, many do. For decades, the primary illicit drug sold by alleged Mafia members was heroin. Today, heroin is still worth an estimated $40 million per year to the organization, but trafficking in cocaine and marijuana has also been

AP Photo/Richard Drew

Reputed mob boss John Gotti sits smugly in New York Supreme Court in Manhattan in January 1990. Gotti was later convicted of murder and racketeering and sentenced to life in prison in 1992. He died in prison in June 2002 of complications from head and neck cancer.

documented. In addition to drugs, Mafia families deal in loan sharking, illegal gambling operations, public corruption, money-laundering operations, and an array of legal business enterprises designed to cloak their criminal rackets.

In many cities, the nontraditional crime organizations, such as the Colombian cartels and the youth gangs, have rivaled the Mafia for territory. In some cases, drug territory has even been surrendered to the newer gangs, with drugs being viewed as too risky or competitive. In recent years, advocates of the alien conspiracy theory argue that the Mafia is still a strong criminal organization with criminal interests all over the world. However, they assert that a new breed of Mafioso is beginning to emerge. The new Mafiosi are more willing to inform on fellow Mafiosi and seem to be more oriented toward individual gain than family organization. For example, in 1992, New York mob boss John Gotti was convicted after his underboss became a federal witness and offered damaging testimony regarding Gotti's role in the murder of former mob boss Paul Castellano.

DRUG GANGS AS ORGANIZED CRIME

Criminal organizations concerned solely with drug trafficking share many of the same characteristics as more established organized crime. In the decade of the 1970s, a new kind of drug-trafficking organization began to emerge. Four fundamental factors can be seen as contributing to the genesis of this new configuration of organized crime:

- Profound social, political, and economic changes in the drug-producing and drug-consuming nations combined to accelerate and intensify the spread of drugs.
- There was vastly increased mobility within and among consuming and producing nations, aided by cheap, readily available, international transportation. Immigration also greatly increased from South America and the Far East to the United States.
- In the opium-producing countries, many peasants and urban workers had surplus time for the kinds of work needed to sustain the drug traffic.
- In the consuming nations, old restrictions against many types of behavior, including the taking of drugs, declined sharply.

All these factors made possible a new kind of trafficking.

In attempting to understand these organizations as a whole, one should first recognize that no one drug-trafficking organization is "typical." Rather, a multiplicity of trafficking organizations follow a few well-defined patterns. Thus, as mentioned, several conditions exist that seem to lend cohesiveness to the modern-day drug-trafficking organization:

- *Vertical integration*. Vertical integration is illustrated by the major international trafficking groups, such as the Colombian cartels, and some domestic criminal groups, such as outlaw motorcycle gangs, that control both the manufacturing and wholesale distribution of drugs. Also, city-based operations such as the California street gangs, which concentrate on domestic distribution and retail sales, represent organizations with operations that are more directly linked to the end user than are the Colombian cartels or the motorcycle gangs.

- *Alternate sources of supply*. Among the various types of organizational structures and operational types, most have common distribution channels and operating methods. Many cocaine- and heroin-trafficking groups acquire illicit drugs outside the United States and from any of a number of sources. This principle was illustrated when the Turkish government clamped down on the illicit cultivation of opium poppies; drug organizations shifted their production to regions in the Golden Triangle in Southeast Asia and the Golden Crescent in Southwest Asia. Exceptions are marijuana and certain drugs made in domestic clandestine labs. Consequently, distribution channels are long and complicated. For instance, there are numerous links between the coca leaves grown and harvested in the Huallaga Valley of Peru and the destination of the finished product—a U.S. city.

- *Exploitation of social and political conditions*. Drug-trafficking organizations today demonstrate a willingness to capitalize on vulnerable social and national milieus. This occurs, for instance, in inner-city areas and even countries where labor markets are willing to take risks to partake of the huge profit potential offered in drug-trafficking operations. Generally, most players drawn into drug trafficking are expendable, provided that the leaders remain untouched. The leaders can then choose individuals from a large pool of unskilled labor. These individuals must be willing to take personal risks and be able to learn one or two menial duties in the trafficking system. Traffickers have demonstrated that they can manipulate market conditions to make trafficking more profitable. In particular, the introduction of black tar heroin in the mid-1980s was a response to heroin shortages, whereas the change from cocaine hydrochloride to crack in the mid-1980s was also an effort to offer the nonaffluent drug user affordable cocaine.

- *Insulation of leaders*. The organizational structure of a drug-trafficking group can be described as a solar system, with the leaders at the center. It is only these leaders (or *kingpins*) who see the organization as a whole. Trafficking leaders minimize any contact with drug buyers or the drugs themselves as a strategic effort to insulate themselves from governmental detection.

Although the four preceding operational variables help explain how drug-trafficking organizations function, they fail to explain adequately the tremendous growth of such groups. The growth of a particular organization can be partially attributed to highly addictive qualities of some drugs such as heroin. This accounts, at least in part, for a certain degree of return business for many trafficking organizations. Here the drug users themselves effectively become sales representatives, or *ambassadors*, who work on behalf of the drug-trafficking organization by introducing drugs to new users. Additionally, drugs in powder form, such as heroin, can be much more easily transported (smuggled) than a bulkier commodity such as marijuana.

Critical Thinking Task

Applying your personal code of ethics, do you believe that the benefits of participating in organized crime outweigh the risks, or is the reverse true? Do you think you would ever be tempted to participate in organized crime?

The political climate in foreign source countries also contributes to the growth of trafficking organizations. In many countries, the cultivation of raw materials for drugs is actually encouraged. Five of the most significant source countries—Mexico, Colombia, Ecuador, Peru, and Myanmar—are currently experiencing serious economic and political problems reflective of their move from conventional crops to coca, opium poppies, and marijuana; legitimate crops simply fail to provide incomes parallel to those realized by the illicit harvest.

Figure 7.2

Source: Organized Crime Drug Enforcement Task Force, 1988.

During the course of the Droznek/Rosa case, two dozen defendants pleaded guilty, individually and in small groups, leaving only two to be tried in this four-year-long OCDETF investigation by the FBI, DEA, IRS, ATF, and the Pennsylvania Bureau of Narcotics. Among those entering agreements with the government were Marvin "Babe" Droznek and Joseph Rosa, both are self-proclaimed members in the LaRocca/Genovese LCN [La Cosa Nostra] family of western Pennsylvania.

Having confessed to participating in a continuing criminal enterprise, Droznek made consensually recorded phone calls and "wore a wire" while pursuing business as usual—dealing cocaine. This risky activity made Droznek a devastating witness in a case noteworthy for the lack of physical evidence. There were plenty of guns but no cocaine. Droznek eventually testified against Rosa and most of the other defendants.

The prime target of Droznek's testimony was a friend that he never quite trusted, Joe Rosa. When Rosa invited him to bring $200,000 along and join him on a buying trip to Florida, Droznek set up a unique "death insurance" policy. A third party was to hold $20,000 to pay for Rosa's murder if anything happened to Droznek. Fortunately for both, the trip was canceled. When Droznek later told Rosa of his "insurance," Rosa admitted that he had indeed considered a rip-off. Droznek lived his adult life in a violent world. He admitted using threats and violence as an enforcer. He owned many guns, including submachine guns, and on occasion would fire one into the ground as a "demonstration."

Figure 7.2—*continued*

Close associates of Droznek that met untimely deaths included Robert George and Mark Puzas. George was a hotel operator, drug addict, and cocaine dealer. On a Tuesday, he told Droznek that he was suspicious that a man with whom he had been dealing might be "a dirty cop." The man was, in fact, an undercover county detective. The next day, George confronted the detective with a loaded shotgun. The brave officer slapped the gun away and killed George with one shot from his .357 Magnum. Mark Puzas became a confidential informant who was used by county narcotics detectives when they searched Droznek's home for marked cash after Puzas had purchased a kilogram of cocaine from him. A county grand jury recommended prosecution of Puzas during its separate investigation of Droznek. Two days after a visit from Droznek, Puzas hanged himself in jail.

Droznek worked his way up through the gambling ranks: first, as a numbers writer, then as a bookie, then as a collector and loan shark, and then as a "beard," a lay-off man paid a commission to keep big bookmakers from recognizing the real source of a bet. In 1984, having lost a Las Vegas sports informer that had enabled him to make some sure-thing bets, Droznek made his first "coke" deal. In the next three years, he and his associates distributed more than 200 kilos of cocaine in the Pittsburgh area.

During early 1985, Droznek was introduced, by a mutual customer, to a drug dealer and vending machine entrepreneur, William Kostrick. This customer had been a part of Kostrick's prior operation, in which Kostrick and Rosa had obtained cocaine in south Florida and utilized couriers to transport the drug to Pennsylvania. The cocaine was cut, stashed, and redistributed to various dealers. In a process that continued throughout the conspiracy, Kostrick and/or Rosa would travel to Florida to purchase quantities of cocaine. Couriers would fly to Miami or Fort Lauderdale and rent cars for transportation back to Pittsburgh and redelivery to Kostrick, Rosa, or Droznek. Throughout 1985 and 1986, each of the three principals developed separate sources and systems of delivery, and each would supply the others according to their needs. Kostrick, for example, developed contacts with a family from western Pennsylvania that had relocated to the west coast of Florida. This family had developed its own contacts with various Colombian and Cuban suppliers. The family members would transport cocaine in multi-kilogram lots to Kostrick in Pittsburgh. Rosa had developed contacts through his LCN connections. The three partners each maintained various stash houses that concealed both the cocaine and the money generated from the sale thereof. As a sideline, Droznek and Rosa, together with various other members of the conspiracy, also trafficked extensively in automatic and silenced weapons.

Each of the principals generated large amounts of cash during the operation of the enterprise. Droznek purchased a restaurant in Pittsburgh and a comfortable home in the suburbs. He also invested in certificates of deposit and utilized a number of safe deposit boxes to store his cash. Through his gambling and cocaine operations, Droznek established associations with a number of racketeers that owned and operated semi-legitimate businesses. Droznek used these associates to purchase fictitious W-2 wage statements to shelter him from income tax evasion charges. One such business operated as a pollution spill cleanup business. Droznek purchased his W-2 by paying the owner, a compulsive gambler and fraud artist, a 10 percent commission for each check.

Kostrick lived relatively modestly, investing his money in the vending business, possibly stashing some of his profits with family members. Most of the locations where Kostrick's machines were placed were owned by cocaine customers or loan shark victims. Rosa spent large amounts of income for automobiles, jewelry, and entertainment. He made a number of expensive real estate purchases, which he attempted to conceal

Figure 7.2—*continued*

> through the use of nominees. Rosa also formulated a construction and landscaping business in an attempt to generate a legitimate income in response to an extensive IRS investigation. Much of Rosa's ill-gotten gains, including $175,000 worth of jewelry Rosa had stolen from his own store in an insurance scam, were passed on to the LCN underboss.
>
> The membership of this criminal organization included a number of past and present law enforcement officers. Robert George, a hotel owner and a major dealer for all three of the principals, had been the chief of police for a small township in the northern suburbs of Pittsburgh. George had been fired from that position in the early 1980s as a result of various acts of administrative misconduct. Kostrick and two of his convicted associates had been former North Versailles Borough police officers. Michael Monaco, who provided Droznek with gun permits, had been an Allegheny County Deputy Sheriff prior to his arrest for cocaine trafficking in 1985. Perry Perrino, convicted and sentenced to 10 years incarceration, had been an Allegheny County Assistant District Attorney during the course of the conspiracy. At Perrino's sentencing, it was alleged that he had accepted both money and cocaine from Droznek while employed as a District Attorney and that Perrino had discussed with Droznek the status of an informant in an investigation then pending against Droznek. According to Charles Sheehy, the Acting U.S. Attorney, many of the persons contacted during this investigation have abandoned their jobs, careers, or professions as a result of cocaine addiction. Almost without exception, each individual that became involved in heavy cocaine use turned to criminal activity in order to support the habit. The lure of cocaine and the wealth that can be generated from its sale were shown to have corrupted numerous public officials entrusted with the responsibility of law enforcement.

Case Study: The Droznek/Rosa Case

The structure of today's drug-trafficking organizations poses serious tactical and investigative challenges to law enforcement officials. Additionally, significant public policy issues with regard to the law, personal freedoms, and priorities addressing the social order arise from investigations of drug-trafficking organizations. The volume of drugs entering the United States, the great number of trafficking organizations in existence, and the fact that methods of operation used by these groups can change so quickly dictate that unconventional approaches to detecting and prosecuting drug-related organized crime be considered by public officials.

SUMMARY

To understand the many problems associated with the illicit drug trade, one must first comprehend what constitutes organized crime. Defining organized crime is no easy task, and there is no official definition of the term. According to researchers, certain characteristics are unique to the "criminal group" or members of the organized crime unit. Such characteristics include the provision of illicit goods or services; the arbitrary use of violence; the establishment of a code of conduct for members; the ability to corrupt public officials; and a recruitment strategy based on ethnic, racial, geographical, or kinship factors.

Those who belong to the criminal group are usually supported by individuals belonging to two other categories of criminals: the protectors and specialized support. The protectors are not full-fledged members of the group but still work on behalf of the organization while appearing to be legitimate members of society. Protectors include accountants, attorneys, and government officials. The specialized support groups also consist of individuals who are not official members of the organization but who possess certain talents necessary for the success of the organization. Professionals with such traits are pilots, enforcers, and chemists.

Modern-day gangs are in part distinguished from traditional organized crime organizations by their recent vintage. For instance, the genesis of groups such as the Jamaican posses, the California youth gangs, and the Colombian cocaine cartels occurred around 1970, when drug abuse began to flourish in the United States. Four characteristics unique to the emerging groups are vertical integration, the use of alternate sources of supply, a propensity to exploit social conditions to further the organization, and the insulation of leaders from street-level dealers.

Do you recognize these terms?

- alien conspiracy theory
- criminal group
- La Cosa Nostra
- Mafia
- organized crime
- outlaw motorcycle gangs

- prison gangs
- protectors
- specialized support
- support clubs
- street gangs
- vertical integration

DISCUSSION QUESTIONS

1. Define the term *traditional organized crime* and discuss how it pertains to the illicit drug trade.

2. Compare and contrast the differences and similarities between legitimate and illegal business enterprises.

3. Discuss the three kinds of gangs active in the United States and differentiate their influence on the drug market.

4. Having examined the organized crime criminal and protector groups, discuss and compare them to the players in an organized crime support group.

5. What factors created the spawning of the new drug-trafficking groups during the early 1970s?

6.   Discuss some of the more successful drug-trafficking organizations and how they have been able to manipulate the drug-user market to improve profits.

7.   List and discuss the four conditions that lend a cohesiveness to the modern-day drug-trafficking organization.

8.   Give examples of criminal drug-trafficking groups that may be considered vertically integrated.

CLASS PROJECT

1.   Research the historical roots of traditional organized crime groups in the United States. Compare their emergence to the emergence of today's drug-trafficking organizations.

Chapter 8

Domestic Drug-Trafficking Organizations

This chapter will enable you to:

- Distinguish between traditional and nontraditional organized crime
- Learn about the origins of the criminal group known as the Mafia
- Understand the role of outlaw motorcycle gangs in the illegal drug trade
- Understand the role of youth gangs in the drug trade
- Learn the origins of prison gangs and their involvement in the illicit drug trade

The problem of organized crime in the United States is nothing new. In fact, it has been an American phenomenon for close to 100 years. The drug trade, however, has reshaped organized crime by creating new, violent, and more sophisticated criminal groups. Although these groups frequently clash with one another, increasingly more of them are learning to work together, as they did during Prohibition, to maximize profits and minimize their risk of detection. This chapter examines some of the largest and most active organized crime groups in the domestic illicit drug trade.

TRADITIONAL ORGANIZED CRIME: THE MAFIA

As discussed in the previous chapter, the Mafia, or La Cosa Nostra, has been a source of controversy in criminology and law enforcement in the United States for more than 80 years. Because its roots are in Italy and Sicily during

255

DOI: 10.1016/B978-1-4377-4450-7.00008-4
© 2011 Elsevier Inc. All rights reserved.

the mid-1800s, this group could very well be discussed in the following chapter dealing with foreign trafficking organizations; however, because some argue it plays such a significant role in criminality in the United States and because a great number of its alleged members are United States citizens, the Mafia is commonly referred to as a *domestic* criminal organization. Today, two factions of traditional organized crime operate in the United States: the alleged American Mafia (also called the Italian Mafia or Italian-American Syndicate) and the Sicilian Mafia.

The Mafia's History

The Sicilian Mafia has established itself as Italy's premier criminal group through corruption, assassination, extortion, and manipulation. Its criminal influence reaches around the globe, with particular strength in Western Europe, North America, and South America. Sicily is an island located off the southwestern coast of Italy and is the main region of influence of the Sicilian Mafia. This area, known as the *mezzogiorno*, is a territory claimed by another powerful Italian organized crime group, the Camorra.

The Camorra has a lengthy history as a prison gang originating in Italy. Spanish kings ruled Naples and Sicily between the years 1504 and 1707 and again between 1738 and 1860. The Camorra was organized during the first Spanish reign. The Sicilian Mafia, which was considered the most powerful criminal organization during the eighteenth and nineteenth centuries, was formed during the second reign. The Camorra and the Sicilian Mafia shared similar traits:

- Each existed by selling criminal services to either individuals or corrupt members of the government.
- Each had a formal organizational structure: the Camorra was organized into brigades, or *brigata*, while the Sicilian Mafia was organized into *families*.
- Each had a strict code of silence, or *omerta*, that (1) dictated that family members never cooperate with government officials, and (2) instituted the *vendetta*, the code of retribution against anyone that in any way attacked or insulted a member of the family.

The word *Mafia* appeared for the first time in a newspaper in November 1860, when it was acknowledged that a Camorra group had established itself in the general area of Palermo, Sicily. In 1878, Giuseppe Esposito, a Sicilian Mafioso, was credited as being the first Sicilian Mafia member to relocate, along with six others, to the United States. Upon arrival in New York, Esposito and his men not only found America hostile to non-English-speaking immigrants—they also witnessed a criminal underworld dominated by Irish and Jewish groups. Consequently, Esposito moved to New Orleans with his Sicilian entourage, where he organized and headed the flourishing Sicilian

Mafia. After being arrested in 1881 by Police Chief David Hennessey on an outstanding Italian fugitive warrant, Esposito was transported to New York and then extradited back to Italy.

Joseph Macheca, an American-born member of the organization, succeeded Esposito as crime boss of New Orleans. He soon began reinforcing the numbers of the New Orleans Mafia with new immigrants from Sicily, a practice commonly used by the American Mafia over the years. In 1890, Police Chief David Hennessey was assassinated; 10 members of the Macheca crime family were charged with the murder. After a lengthy trial, all were acquitted amidst claims of jury tampering. The acquittals created public outrage, and an angry crowd stormed Parish Prison, where 19 Sicilian prisoners were housed. The ensuing carnage resulted in the largest lynching in history—16 prisoners were murdered. Some were shot and many were hanged from the city's lampposts. However, this violence failed to prevent the rise of the Mafia in New Orleans. Indeed, as the turn of the century approached, other Sicilian Mafia families formed around the United States in cities such as San Francisco, St. Louis, Chicago, New York, and Boston.

Figure 8.1
Source: President's Commission on Organized Crime, 1987.

During January 1986, the President's Commission on Organized Crime solicited testimony from Martin Light, an attorney with close ties to La Cosa Nostra. Light, formerly a government witness, was sentenced to 15 years in prison for a drug conviction. He testified that prospective members are watched closely from childhood on, judged on their toughness and ability, and on their respect for superiors. Their willingness to "do the right thing" may be to share criminal profits with family leaders, to risk jail terms for refusal to cooperate with a grand jury, or to plead guilty to a crime actually committed by more important members in the family. It is to follow unquestioningly the self-perpetuating practices of a most secret exclusive criminal society.

The World of the "Made Man"

Lasting from 1920 to 1933, the Prohibition era was probably the single most influential factor in providing up-and-coming Mafia families with what they needed most: enough money to infiltrate legitimate business. Such capital would make their illicit enterprises more difficult to detect and would give the Mafiosi an aura of public respectability. During this time, some of the more notorious Mafiosi were arriving in the United States. Carlo Gambino, Joe Profaci, Joe Magliocco, Mike Coppola, and Salvatore Maranzano joined the likes of Joe (Joe Bananas) Bonanno and Charles (Lucky) Luciano. During the 1930s, Luciano and other Italian organized crime bosses solidified their base of operation, which some believe grew into a national organization that now occupies 24 U.S. cities with close to 2,000 made members. One of the most important developments during the 1930s was the formation of a national Mafia alliance, or *commission*, whereby heads of some of the most influential

Mafia families would meet to divide territory, choose rackets, approve new members, and arbitrate disputes between families.

Figure 8.2
Source: President's Commission on Organized Crime, 1986.

Boss. The head of the family. He does not participate in the day-to-day activities of the organization but is supposed to receive a cut from every income source. He usually has his own legitimate and illegitimate businesses.

Underboss. Assistant to the boss. Usually he is being groomed to succeed the boss, but succession is not automatic. There is only one underboss per family.

Consigliere. Literally, "counselor." He assists the boss but has no leadership authority. He is generally an older, experienced member that can advise family members. There is usually only one consigliere per family.

Capo. Caporegima, or captain; supervisors of the family's day-to-day criminal operations; represents the family among the soldiers, whom the capos oversee. A capo gains his position by proving his ability as an "earner"—one that earns a great deal of profit for the family. Capos may have their own legitimate and illegitimate ventures and retain a part of the income paid by their soldiers before passing it on to the leadership. The number of capos in a family depends on the size of the family.

Soldier. The basic rank in the family. Sometimes known as a "wise guy," "buttonman," or "made man"; the last term refers to any formal member of the LCN, one that has undergone the initiation ritual. To be "made," a man must be of Italian ancestry.

Associates. An informal position, yet one that is crucial to the family. An associate need not be of Italian descent; he is someone whose skills or position make him of value to the organization. Some are used as soldiers while others are more distantly connected. The FBI has estimated that for every formal member of La Cosa Nostra there are 10 criminal associates that cooperate with members and share their enterprises.

Protectors. Among any family's associates is a support network of "protectors." These are corrupt public officials, bankers, lawyers, accountants, and other professionals that protect the criminal group from governmental intervention, both civil and criminal.

La Cosa Nostra Organizational Structure

The Mafia and the Drug Trade

During the late 1960s and early 1970s, France became well known as a distribution point for an estimated 80 percent of the world's heroin. Marseilles became the center of heroin laboratories that processed raw opium brought in from Turkey. Heroin was then smuggled into the United States by French Corsicans as well as Sicilian Mafia members (the "French Connection"). In the early 1970s, the French Connection was broken up as a result of a joint investigative effort by U.S. and French authorities. Today, France is no longer considered a major producer of heroin sold on the U.S. market.

In 1986, the President's Commission on Organized Crime stated that "heroin is the biggest moneymaker for the Mafia." It is thought that since the collapse of the French Connection, Italy and Sicily became distribution points for heroin. Intelligence sources also indicated that French chemists assumed their traditional role of converting raw opium into heroin. The opium is transported from sources in the eastern Mediterranean countries of Syria, Lebanon, Pakistan, and Jordan. The Sicilian Mafia controls the transshipment of heroin through Italy to the United States from both Southwest Asia (SWA) and Southeast Asia (SEA) (see Chapter 4). Methods of smuggling by the Sicilian Mafia have included the following: members or associates traveling by air and wearing body packs of two to three kilograms of heroin, as well as heroin secreted in toys, statues, wheels of provolone cheese, film canisters, coffee machines, dry cell batteries, cans of baby powder, electronic appliances, mail, and clothing.

The Pizza Connection

The investigation that revealed the extent to which the Sicilian Mafia operated in the United States is popularly known as the *Pizza Connection*. The Pizza Connection was a massive operation involving heroin smuggling and money laundering by Sicilian Mafia members operating in the United States, an operation headed by Sicilian crime boss Gaetano Badalamente. Through the aid of crime-boss-turned-witness Tommaso Buscetta, arrests stemming from the Pizza Connection were made possible.

The operation ultimately led to the 1984 indictments in New York of 35 alleged members of the Sicilian Mafia. The investigation revealed that between 1982 and 1983, the Sicilian Mafia had scheduled 1.5 tons of heroin with an estimated wholesale value of $333 million for importation to New York. In addition, between 1980 and 1983, the New York Sicilian Mafia was reported to have shipped in excess of $40 million in cash from New York to Sicily via Switzerland.

The breadth of the investigation expanded worldwide, with Mafia members identified in such countries as Brazil, Canada, Spain, Switzerland, Italy, and the United States. So vast was the investigation that it took federal prosecutors one full year to try the case. Ultimately, the trial turned out to be the most costly and lengthy criminal proceeding in U.S. history but proved rewarding by securing convictions of all but two of the defendants. Those convicted received lengthy sentences. As a result of the information produced at this trial, some argue that not enough is being done to fight drug trafficking. Columnist Shana Alexander (1988:B11) stated, "[The case] did not make the slightest dent in the nation's desperate drug problem. More heroin and cocaine are on the streets today than before 'Pizza' began. The trial severely overtaxed every branch of our legal system law enforcement, bench, and bar and taxed unfortunate jurors worst of all."

Testimony revealed that one member of the Sicilian Mafia operating in the United States, Salvatore Salamone, was entrusted with the job of changing small-denomination bills to large-denomination bills and transporting the money in suitcases overseas. Once the money arrived in Switzerland, several other individuals converted the bills into Swiss francs and then to Italian lira for delivery to Sicily. The Pizza Connection illustrates a working relationship between the Sicilian and U.S.-based Mafia operatives and their "common interests" in drug trafficking and money laundering. Each organization needed the other, and the relationship was established on a basis of mutual trust and respect. In 1987, the FBI observed the following:

- The Sicilian Mafia operates in the United States as a separate criminal organization specializing in heroin smuggling. The first allegiance of its members is to the "family" in Sicily.
- Before initiating a major heroin-smuggling operation, the Sicilian Mafia obtains the sanction of certain American Mafia families.
- As payment for the American Mafia family granting its sanction for the operation, the Sicilian Mafia pays the American Mafia family up to $5,000 per kilogram of heroin brought into the United States.

The number of Sicilian Mafiosi operating in the United States is hard to predict. They are, however, thought to concentrate in the northeastern United States, principally in New York City and New Jersey, and are thought to operate without geographical jurisdictions.

The Mafia Wars

Over the decades, Italy's Mafia has undergone several periods of severe repression by police authorities. For example, in the 1920s, Mussolini attempted to purge La Cosa Nostra from the island of Sicily, which resulted in many members migrating to the United States seeking safe havens in U.S.-based families. Many of these refugees later became formidable bosses of the most influential crime families in the nation.

During the early 1980s, Italy experienced an increase in violence among members of the estimated 20 Mafia families operating in and around Palermo. The violence resulted in the murders of mobsters, police officers, judges, and politicians in what was dubbed the "heroin wars." The central government of Italy has since taken initiatives toward controlling Mafia-related criminal activity. These initiatives include anti-Mafia legislation enacted on September 11, 1982, which features these measures:

- "Association" with known Mafia types is illegal, whether a crime is committed or not.
- "Association" also applies to the Camorra and other "Mafia-type" groups.

- "Exile" locations for convicted Mafiosi have been established in towns with populations of fewer than 10,000, and an unauthorized exit of the location shall result in imprisonment.
- Property and other assets are subject to confiscation.
- Telephone wiretaps are authorized on persons suspected of belonging to "Mafia-type" organizations.
- The term *omerta* is defined in its most negative connotation as a "conduct of noncooperation with public safety officials due to fear."

The implementation of this law resulted in the 1984 arrests of more than 450 suspected Mafiosi and the subsequent trial that has become known as the Maxi-Processo (maxi-trial). The arrests, which are considered the greatest Mafia crackdown since Mussolini's 1920s Mafia purge, resulted from a 40-volume, 8,632-page indictment that outlined more than 90 murders, countless kidnappings, and even the use of torture chambers. Additionally, the indictment included charges of heroin smuggling and money laundering for Mafia members. In spite of all the media fanfare over the Mafia trials, it now appears they were little more than just show trials, for the Mafia continues to operate with virtual impunity in Italy and Sicily.

Figure 8.3

- Buffalo, New York (The Arm)
- Chicago, Illinois (Chicago Outfit)
- Cleveland, Ohio (Cleveland crime family)
- Dallas, Texas (Dallas crime family)
- Detroit, Michigan (Detroit Partnership)
- Kansas City, Missouri (Kansas City crime family)
- Los Angeles, California (Los Angeles crime family)
- New England (Patriarca family)
- New Jersey (DeCavalcante family)
- New Orleans, Louisiana (Marcello family)
- New York, New York (The Five Families)
- Bonanno family
- Colombo family
- Gambino family
- Genovese family
- Lucchese family
- Northeastern Pennsylvania (Bufalino Family)
- Philadelphia, Pennsylvania (Scarfo family)
- Pittsburgh, Pennsylvania (Pittsburgh crime family)
- St. Louis, Missouri (St. Louis crime family)
- Tampa, Florida (Trafficante family)

A Selected List of Mafia Families in the United States

The Mafia Controversy

While there is a substantial body of opinion arguing that La Cosa Nostra (LCN), or the Mafia, is the dominant organized crime group in the United States and plays a major role in drug trafficking, considerable controversy surrounds what this organization actually is and what it actually does. Many scholars and law enforcement officials have come to doubt the view presented by the FBI and other federal agencies that it is a hegemonic Italian organized crime syndicate. They argue that the evidence to support the existence of such a group is weak and open to other interpretations and that empirical research has failed to confirm the existence of such a dominant, complex, hierarchically organized criminal group.

Criticisms of the Mafia model fall into two distinct categories: (1) the historical evidence is sometimes weak and contradictory, and (2) empirical research conducted on organized crime fails to demonstrate the existence of the Mafia as a single criminal conspiracy, and there are alternative models of organized crime that explain the reality of criminal entrepreneurship. To this list we will add a third criticism: The evidence of LCN or Mafia "domination" of the drug trade is fragmentary and debatable.

Historical Controversies

Anthropological, historical, and social studies of the Sicilian Mafia, such as those conducted by Henner Hess and Anton Blok, have failed to turn up evidence of a single criminal organization (Hess, 1973; Blok, 1974). Rather, the studies point strongly to a series of localized village-based organizations, which were primarily created to protect the interests of absentee landlords and foreign invaders. These organizations formed a kind of "shadow government" in Sicily, meting out justice, controlling jobs, and providing for social control in an unstable society. Though the Mafia may have had its origins in such a rural ruling class, it is not the same Mafia proposed by conspiracy theorists.

In addition, evidence relating to Italians' importation of organized crime to the United States is open to similar questions. For example, proponents of the Mafia theory cannot tell us how it is that Italian immigration brought this criminal organization to the United States while similar waves of Italian immigration did not bring the same organization to England, Australia, and other nations.

Supporters of the Mafia model have failed to account for organized crime's existence in the United States long before the inception of Italian immigration. Further, proponents of the Mafia model must engage in considerable factual acrobatics to account for non-Italian figures who appear to have been dominant forces in the history of American organized crime—men like Arnold Rothstein, Meyer Lansky, Abner "Longie" Zwillman, Benjamin "Bugsy" Siegel, George "Bugs" Moran, Dutch Schultz (Arthur Flegenheimer), Owen "Owney" Madden, and dozens of others. Finally, specific historical "facts" presented by proponents of the Mafia model appear weak under close scrutiny. The Mafia's 1890 assassination of New Orleans Police Chief David Hennessey is a prime example. Was Hennessey killed by the Mafia? Or was the Mafia concept created, as Dwight Smith Jr. suggested (Smith, 1975), to justify the "lynching" of innocent immigrants? The fact is that the New Orleans grand jury failed to turn up any evidence of an Italian conspiracy, and the courts failed to convict any of the defendants. Similarly, questions have been raised about other proofs offered for the Mafia model.

Research on Organized Crime

Far more significant to this discussion, however, is the failure of empirical research on alleged LCN families to substantiate the model proposed by the federal government. For example, Francis A. J. Ianni's study of an LCN family in New York suggested that the only organizational arrangement was one of an extended family (Ianni, 1972). For Ianni, kinship became the prime variable in explaining how and why Italian-Americans worked together in both legal and illegal businesses. He found no evidence of an interconnected, national Italian-American crime syndicate. Joseph Albini's study of organized crime in Detroit also failed to confirm the existence of a monolithic crime structure (Albini, 1972). Albini reviewed historical documents and journalistic accounts, interviewed both law enforcement officials and participants in organized crime operations, and concluded that organized crime was based on a series of loosely constructed "patron-client relations," not on a massive criminal conspiracy.

Other studies, such as the one conducted by William Chambliss (1971), focused on organized crime in Seattle and found a syndicate composed of local political and business leaders, leading Chambliss to argue that "organized crime" was a misnomer and that the study of official corruption would be more revealing in describing criminal syndicates. In addition, Mark Haller's study (1989) of organized crime operations in Chicago, New York, and Florida concluded that rather than being dominated by a tightly organized criminal conspiracy, organized crime was a series of complex and often overlapping business partnerships in illicit enterprise. ·

Peter Reuter's exhaustive study (1983) of the gambling and loan-sharking industries in New York City failed to turn up either LCN domination or even widespread participation in those industries. Reuter argued that if the Mafia existed at all, it was a "paper tiger" living off its popular reputation, which was fueled by journalistic and law enforcement speculation. Finally, a study of organized crime in Philadelphia revealed that not only did the Mafia not dominate organized crime in the past (at best, its alleged members were functionaries of other, very large criminal syndicates) but that the alleged Cosa Nostra family of Angelo Bruno was only one of several dozen major organized crime syndicates operating in that city. Additional studies by Alan Block, John Gardiner, Virgil Peterson, Jay Albanese, and many others have served to dispute the theory of any dominant role of La Cosa Nostra (Albanese, 1996; Block, 1983; Gardiner, 1970; Peterson, 1983).

Although the views of some law enforcement officials tenaciously cling to the view of LCN as a single, massive criminal conspiracy, others have moved away from that position. The Pennsylvania Crime Commission, for example, has been quite active in exploring the role of other organized crime groups, particularly black crime groups and motorcycle gangs, in drug trafficking and other illicit business ventures. Potter and Jenkins (1985), in their study of organized crime in Philadelphia, identified black gangs, Greek-American gangs, the Irish K & A gang, and motorcycle gangs as more important in drug trafficking than traditional Italian-American groups.

There is little doubt that some individuals linked with Italian-dominated criminal organizations in both the United States and Sicily have been involved in large-scale drug trafficking, as we have seen in the case of the Pizza Connection. However, one should be cautious in attributing any degree of hegemony to these groups in the drug market. Drug trafficking is conducted by thousands of different criminal organizations, many of which are complex and quite large compared to LCN groups. Despite many successful Mafia-related drug investigations, the focus on the Mafia or La Cosa Nostra has tended to distort the perception of organized crime's role in drugs. For example, it ignores the vital role played by organizations headed by Frank Matthews, Nicky Barnes, Jeff Fort, and other crime figures. It also ignores the role of non-Italians, such as Meyer Lansky and Nig Rosen, who played the major coordinating role in the infamous French Connection. Finally, it ignores the major role in the organization of drug trafficking played by some truly pioneering organized crime figures, such as Arnold Rothstein, Happy Meltzer, "Dopey" Bennie Fein, and others. The role of the Mafia must be kept in perspective, and the roles of other major drug-trafficking groups must be given attention.

OUTLAW MOTORCYCLE GANGS

OMGs have etched a historic role in organized crime and the drug trade. According to the U.S. Treasury's Bureau of Alcohol, Tobacco, Firearms and Explosives (ATF), outlaw motorcycle gangs have evolved into one of the most "reprehensible" types of criminal organizations, consisting of "killers, psychotics, panderers, and social misfits" (ATF, 1988). Hunter S. Thompson, an authority on the Hells Angels (there is no apostrophe in the official club name), traced the origin of OMGs back to 1947, when the POBOB, or the "Pissed Off Bastards of Bloomington" (later known as the Hells Angels), transformed an American Motorcycle Association (AMA)-sponsored hill climb in Hollister, California, to a week-long brawl. Later that same year, in Riverside, California, thousands attended a motorcycle run that resulted in riot, destruction, and two deaths. The following year, a similar motorcycle event in Riverside ended up as a riot. The police chief then blamed the outcome of the event on the visiting "outlaws," which is a term now commonly associated with members of some motorcycle gangs.

The outlaw motorcycle phenomenon continued during the 1950s and 1960s and soon became a symbol of lawlessness and rebellion. That is to

Figure 8.4

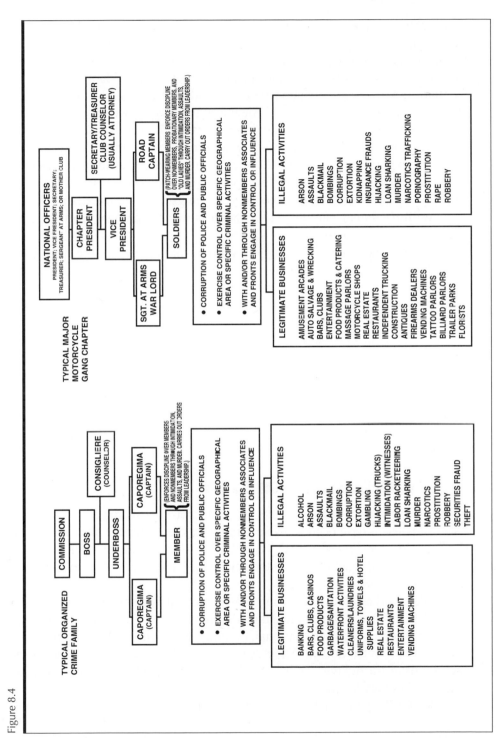

Similarities of Organizational Structure

say, for the most part, the bikers were more concerned with uninhibited good times than with organized criminal endeavors. The entertainment industry portrayed these outlaw gangs in popular films such as *The Wild Ones* and *Angels on Wheels*. In the late 1960s, the former president of the AMA, William Berry, became irritated about the bad publicity outlaw bikers gave to law-abiding motorcycle riders. He declared that only 1 percent of the motorcyclists in the United States functioned outside the spirit and intent of the law. The statement, of course, was a public relations effort on the part of the AMA to explain that only a small number of motorcycle riders represented a criminal element. The term "one percenter," however, was immediately adopted by the larger outlaw motorcycle gangs as a public affirmation of their criminal intent, and the "1%" patch is now commonly worn by gang members.

The years between 1947 and 1967 were formative ones for the early gangs such as the POBOBs, and imitators soon began to appear. In addition, larger gangs absorbed smaller ones or just muscled them out of existence. Roaming members calling themselves *nomads* traveled throughout the United States and formed alliances with other gangs. Formal organizational structures were formed, and leaders were placed in charge of the various gangs, or *chapters*. Still, gangs in this period lacked focus and were rarely considered to be more than troublemakers by local law enforcement.

Critical Thinking Task

Suggest creative methods by which society can protect itself from organized crime, both traditional and nontraditional.

By 1970, however, outlaw motorcycle gangs were viewed differently. The gangs contributed to a monumental social change that was under way in the United States. This change was characterized to some degree by an explosion of drug use. First as drug users and then as dealers, motorcycle gangs were drawn into the phenomenon. As the Treasury Department proclaimed in 1988, "whatever else the 1960s changed in America, it changed outlaw motorcycle gangs" (Bureau of Alcohol, Tobacco, and Firearms, 1988).

Today, outlaw motorcycle gangs have emerged into sophisticated criminal groups. In 2008, it was estimated that between 280 and 520 outlaw motorcycle gangs were operating at the national, regional, and local levels (National Gang Intelligence Center, 2009a). Their criminal activities are many and varied but include drug trafficking, contract killings, extortion, arson, fraud, embezzlement, and money laundering.

The OMG philosophy is of particular significance to law enforcement because it illustrates the sociopathic nature of the organization. "Fuck the World" (FTW) is the motto and attitude of outlaw motorcycle members, and the phrase is frequently embroidered on patches or even tattooed on the members themselves. Members generally choose renegade lifestyles and sport their own dress code. Acts typically considered outrageous and shocking only serve to enhance the biker's image within his or her own environment.

With the obvious exception of minority or ethnically dominated gangs, most OMGs embrace racist beliefs that closely parallel those of the Ku Klux Klan and the neo-Nazis. This white-supremacist philosophy is evidenced by the wearing of Nazi swastikas, white-power fists, and other symbols of white supremacy.

In addition to generally racist values, OMGs also tend to practice a chauvinistic attitude toward female associates of the organization. In fact, in most clubs, females fall into one of two categories: "mamas/sheep" or "old ladies." Because females are not permitted to be members of the gang, their roles in the organization are limited. For example, the mamas are considered property of the gang at large and must consent to the sexual desires of anyone at any time. In addition, they also perform menial tasks around the clubhouse. Old ladies, on the other hand, are wives or steady girlfriends of members and therefore "belong" to only one member of the club. Old ladies proudly wear colors similar to those of male members, with the difference being the words "property of . . . ," which are displayed on the bottom "rocker" of the club patch.

As indicated, OMG members place a great deal of importance on respect for the club's *colors*, which are basically the uniform of the gang. A gang's colors are typically a sleeveless denim or leather jacket with the club name and claimed territory affixed to the back. The colors consist of a top rocker with the name of the gang and a bottom rocker that usually claims territory, states, or cities occupied by the gang. The gang colors are a valued possession of a gang member, and members are expected to protect their colors at all costs.

The gang member's motorcycle also plays a major role. So esteemed is the motorcycle that its destruction or loss to a rival gang member not only results in loss of face but also could be grounds for expulsion from the club. The motorcycle is not just a means of transportation for the gang member but a requirement for club membership and a status symbol in its own right. The motorcycle, along with the dress of the gang members, perpetuates the image of a disciplined and paramilitary organization and has a certain "shock" value in dealing with members of the general public or other gangs.

There are two prerequisites for motorcycles frequently enforced by OMGs: They must be a certain size (usually a 900 cubic centimeter engine minimum), and they must be American-made. Bikers will commonly spend more time with their motorcycles than with anything else, and it is not uncommon for a biker gang member to park his motorcycle inside his home.

Outlaw motorcycle gangs tend to place great emphasis on the club's colors, which basically serve as the uniform of the gang. Many bars frequented by bikers prohibit the wearing of colors in an attempt to maintain peace in the establishment.

Finally, the club's bylaws or charter, which most clubs enforce, are of particular importance in the role that bikers play. The charter outlines accepted standards of conduct for gang members and administrative procedures for the gang's operations. Charter rules might include the following:

- No member will strike another member.
- All members must attend funerals of fellow bikers in the same chapter.
- Chapters must have one organized meeting per week.
- Chapter meetings may be attended by chapter members only.
- Members must respect their colors.
- A club prospect must be sponsored by one member who has known the prospect for at least a year.

Although hundreds of outlaw motorcycle gangs operate in the United States today, four have emerged as the largest and most criminally sophisticated. These are the Hells Angels, the Outlaws, the Pagans, and the Bandidos.

The Hells Angels

In 1950, POBOB leader Otto Friedli formed a new gang, the Hells Angels, named after a World War II bomber. The Angels' "mother chapter" was originally established in San Bernardino, California, where it remained until the mid-1960s. During that time, Ralph Hubert (Sonny) Barger, then president of the Oakland chapter, became national president and moved the mother chapter to Oakland, where it currently remains.

The Hells Angels (HA) are distinctive because they are considered the most professional and the wealthiest of the outlaw motorcycle gangs. They are also an international organization that, according to the U.S. Drug Enforcement Administration, has 33 U.S. chapters, 18 foreign chapters, and an estimated 900 members (450 to 600 are active members). Because of its lengthy and colorful history, the Hells Angels have evolved into a model gang that is emulated by other gangs, both large and small.

The FBI reports that during the mid-1960s, the Hells Angels began drug trafficking in the San Francisco area, with LSD as the main commodity. Later, their inventory expanded to cocaine, PCP, marijuana, and methamphetamine. Today they are still active in methamphetamine manufacturing and trafficking, and it is estimated that most of the methamphetamine trafficked in California is directly or indirectly tied to the Hells Angels organization.

Figure 8.5

National President. The national president is often the founder of the club. He will usually be located at or near the national headquarters. In many cases, he will be surrounded by a select group of individuals who answer only to him and who serve as bodyguards and organizational enforcers. Quite often, the national president will possess the authority to make final decisions.

Territorial or Regional Representative. The individual in this position is also called the vice president and is in charge of whatever region or district to which he is assigned. His duties usually include decision making on all problems that local chapters are unable to solve. Any problems that involve the club as a whole will usually be dealt with through the national headquarters.

National Secretary-Treasurer. The responsibility for handling the club's money, including collecting dues from local chapters, is that of the national secretary-treasurer. He makes changes in existing club bylaws and drafts new ones. He records the minutes and maintains the records of all headquarters or regional office meetings.

National Enforcer. The national enforcer answers directly to the national president. He ensures that the president's orders are carried out. He may act as the president's bodyguard, and he may also handle all special situations, such as retrieving the colors from a member that has left the club. He has also been known to locate ex-members and remove club tattoos from them.

Chapter President. Usually the chapter president, through a combination of personal strength, leadership, personality, and skills, has either claimed the position or has been voted in. He has final authority over all chapter business and members. Usually his word is law within that chapter.

Vice President. Second in command and "right hand" of the chapter president is the vice president. He presides over club affairs in the absence of the president. Normally, he is hand-picked by the president and is heir apparent to the club's leadership.

Secretary-Treasurer. Usually the chapter member possessing the best writing skills serves as secretary-treasurer. He will keep the chapter roster and maintain a crude accounting system. He records the minutes at all chapter meetings and collects the dues and/or fines. He is responsible for paying the chapter's bills.

Sergeant at Arms. Due to the unruly and violent nature of outlaw motorcycle gangs, each chapter has an individual whose principal duty is to maintain order at club meetings and functions. The sergeant at arms is normally the strongest member physically and is completely loyal to the president. He may administer beatings to fellow members for violation of club rules and is the club enforcer for that chapter.

Figure 8.5—*continued*

Road Captain. The road captain fulfills the role of gang logistician and security chief for the club-sponsored "runs." The road captain maps out routes to be taken during runs and arranges for refueling, food, and maintenance stops. He will also carry the club's funds and use them for bail if necessary.

Members. The rank-and-file, dues-paying members of the gang are the individuals that carry out the decisions of the club's leadership. Limiting membership affords the president greater control over the affairs of the gang. At the same time, it helps to ensure that the gang's criminal efforts are not compromised to law enforcement. When a gang becomes too large, it tends to divide the membership into various chapters, based on geographic location.

Probate or Prospective Members. These are the club hopefuls that spend from one month to one year in probationary status and must prove during that time that they are worthy of becoming members. Many clubs require the probate to commit a felony with fellow members observing, so as to weed out weak individuals and infiltration by law enforcement. Probates must be nominated by a regular member and receive a unanimous vote for acceptance. They carry out all menial jobs at the clubhouse and for other members. They are known to carry weapons for other club members and stand guard during club parties. The probates will not wear the club's colors; instead, they wear jackets with the bottom rocker of the club patch showing the location from which they come. Until he is voted in, completes his initiation, and is awarded his colors, a probate has no voting rights.

Associate or Honorary Members. An individual that has proved his value to the gang is known as an associate or honorary member. The associate may be a professional that has in a manner commensurate to his profession been supportive of the gang, or he may be a proven criminal with whom the gang has had a profitable, illicit relationship (see Chapter 8). Some of the more noted associates are attorneys, bail bondsmen, motorcycle shop owners, and auto wrecking yard owners. These individuals are allowed to party with the gang, either in town or on runs; they do not, however, have voting status, attend club meetings, or wear club colors.

Outlaw Motorcycle Gang Organizational Structure

The Outlaws

The Outlaws motorcycle gang was founded in 1959 by John Davis in Chicago. The Outlaws quickly expanded across the country and, with the absorption of the Canadian Satan's Choice gang, became an international organization. Under the leadership of Harry Joseph Bowman, the Outlaws are considered the largest motorcycle gang in the United States, with an estimated membership between 1,200 and 1,500, located in 25 U.S. cities and with six Canadian chapters. The Outlaws are engaged in trafficking of cocaine as well as Valium tablets manufactured by Canadian laboratories and distributed from Chicago to locations throughout the United States.

Figure 8.6

Source: Bureau of Alcohol, Tobacco, and Firearms, 1992.

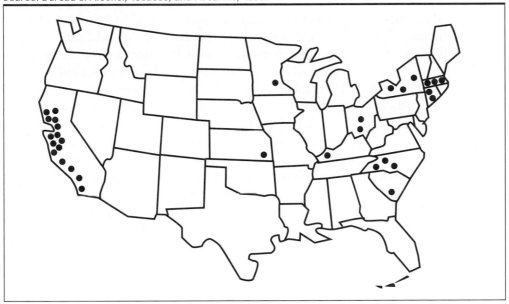

Location of Hells Angels Chapters in the Continental United States

Figure 8.7

Source: Bureau of Alcohol, Tobacco, and Firearms, 1992.

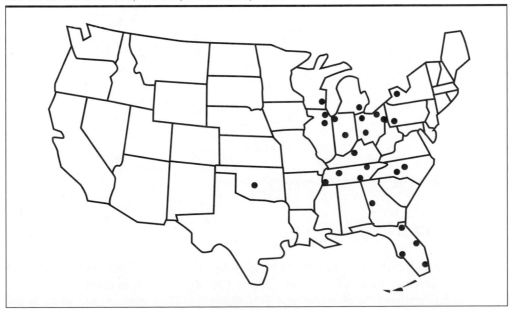

Location of Outlaws Chapters in the Continental United States

The Pagans

The Pagans originated in Prince George's County, Maryland, under the presidency of Lou Dolkin. The Pagans are concentrated on the East Coast and differ from the other four major gangs because they do not have a geographically fixed "mother chapter." It is therefore directed by a "mother club," which is made up of 13 to 18 members who are in charge of other chapters.

The Pagans have a particular presence in the Philadelphia area. Between New York and Florida, there are 44 chapters, with an estimated 700 to 900 members. The Pagans have earned the reputation of being one of the most ruthless motorcycle gangs. The Pagans have also become commonly associated with other, more traditional organized crime groups, frequently acting as killers and enforcers. In addition, the Pagans play a major role in the illicit sex industry, since they have considerable business interests in massage parlors and other prostitution outlets and often work closely with local pornography syndicates to provide protection, models, and the like.

Figure 8.8
Source: Bureau of Alcohol, Tobacco, and Firearms, 1992.

Location of Pagans Chapters in the Continental United States

The Bandidos

The Bandidos were formed in 1966 by Donald Chambers in Houston and are currently headquartered in Corpus Christi, Texas. It is estimated that the Bandidos have 26 chapters and 500 members. They concentrate in both the southern and northern regions of the country and are generally considered less sophisticated than the three OMGs previously discussed. The Bandidos are heavily involved in the manufacture and distribution of methamphetamine.

Figure 8.9
Source: Bureau of Alcohol, Tobacco, and Firearms, 1992.

Location of Bandidos Chapters in the Continental United States

Street Gangs and Youth Gangs

Reports of violent youth gang activity are not merely media hype but are an actual social phenomenon in many U.S. communities. The gang violence inspired by the drug trade poses real problems for certain neighborhoods. In many cases, residents are either fearful of leaving their homes or afraid to let their children play in the public parks taken over by gangs. Neighborhood businesses suffer economically because residents are hesitant to leave their homes to shop. The cost of dealing with gangs via community efforts, law enforcement efforts, and the court system is escalating.

A powerful mystique has evolved around gang activity over the years, partially as a result of movie and television programs focusing on gang-related themes. It is difficult to estimate exactly how many gangs exist today, but according to the National Youth Violence Prevention Resource Center (2007), there are more than 24,500 youth gangs around the United States, with more than 772,500 members. Although many other cities experience such problems, Los Angeles has become well known for its exceedingly sizeable gang problem. The major difficulty in predicting gang numbers is the secrecy and ever-changing nature of most juvenile gangs, making it burdensome for authorities to determine identities of both members and associates.

The origin of youth gangs dates back to the early 1900s. As late as 1990, they were generally localized into an estimated 10 cities that were thought to have a "gang problem." However, in 1994, that number had grown to 125 United States cities, with the most serious problems in the Midwest and in western states (Klein, 1991). One of the most compelling reasons for gang expansion is the expansion of the drug trade, particularly with regard to crack cocaine. The crack trade is a relatively easy-entry business, generating thousands, if not millions, of dollars each year. Because cocaine can be easily cooked by makeshift chemists and because it is easy to conceal, crack provides a considerable financial incentive for gang members in poverty-stricken, jobless neighborhoods. Furthermore, because crack is powerfully reinforcing, the entrepreneurial crack dealer can look forward to a substantial return business.

In addition to profits generated from drug sales, illegal firearms sales, which include AK-47s and Uzi machine guns, are also escalating. Accordingly, not only are youth gangs of today more heavily armed, they are increasingly violent as well. Disputes over gang turf and drug deals often result in murder. As a result, the widespread notoriety of gang violence spreads throughout neighborhoods, serving to intimidate law-abiding citizens who live in gang-infested communities. Sadly, police reports reveal that most gang-related murders are not a result of soured drug deals but rather spontaneous shootings (e.g., drive-by shootings) in which innocent people not associated with the gangs are killed.

Special Youth Gang Problems

Police experience great difficulty in monitoring and controlling youth gangs. Undercover agents are more effective in targeting adult gangs than youth gangs because most youth gang recruiters know their recruit from the neighborhood. Additionally, a youthful gang member is dealt with in a considerably more lenient fashion by the juvenile justice system than is his or her adult counterpart in the adult justice system. One factor making it hard for police to estimate the number of gang members is difficulty determining the status of a possible member. For example, a hard-core leader is commonly called an *original gangster*, while the part-timer and would-be member is called a *wannabe*. Confusing the matter is the varied ethnic composition of youth gangs. In 1989, a U.S. Justice Department survey estimated that about 50 percent of the nation's youth gang members are black, 35 percent are Hispanic, and the rest white or Asian (National Institute of Justice, 1989). Another problem with most youth gangs is difficulty in determining whether a particular assault, robbery, or murder was committed by an individual who happened to belong to a gang or by a gang member furthering the gang's objectives.

Asian gangs, one of the fastest-growing segments of ethnic gangs, are posing special problems for authorities. Language and cultural barriers in particular make investigation of these gangs difficult. In addition, Chinese, Vietnamese, Laotian, and Cambodian gangs have a fluid membership and are highly mobile. A new trend of the Asian gangs in the 1990s is the *home invasion*. Home invasions against Asian nationals have resulted in many rapes, robberies, beatings, and shootings of innocent people. Most of the violence occurs when valuables are not readily surrendered. Victims of home invasions are often distrustful of the criminal justice system and many times are reluctant to report the crimes for fear of retaliation.

Police departments respond in different ways to the gang problem and have adopted various approaches. In Chicago, special gang units exist with as many as 400 officers, compared to other large cities such as

> ### Critical Thinking Task
> Place yourself in the position of a youth gang member. Describe what would have to happen to induce you to leave the gang.

New York and Philadelphia that designate fewer than 10 officers as gang specialists. The creation of such units can cause controversy within the community. For example, some critics argue that a police department that recognizes a gang problem in the community may do so to justify a greater operational budget. Accordingly, members of the community may become unrealistically fearful of the gang problem. On the other hand, police departments that fail to recognize a gang problem in light of mounting evidence may not be adequately serving the needs and best interests of the community.

In the 1950s and 1960s, the typical police approach to gangs was intervention. That is, officers encouraged youths not to join gangs or employed social service agencies to work with gang members themselves. During the 1970s and 1980s, most police departments used a suppression policy that focused on identifying gangs and arresting their members. It is unclear which, if either, method worked. Today, debate still exists about which approach is more effective.

Defining the Youth Gang

A major problem in the study of youth gangs is the lack of consensus as to what defines a youth gang. Is it correct to refer to any congregation of youths as a gang? Many law enforcement agencies use the term narrowly to refer to a group of delinquents who hold and defend self-claimed territory, or *turf*. Frederick Thrasher (1927), a sociologist in a pioneering study, attempted to define the term *youth gang*:

> A gang is an interstitial group originally formed spontaneously and then integrated through conflict. It is characterized by the following types of behavior: meeting face-to-face, milling, movement through

Figure 8.10

Source: Office of National Drug Control Policy (2005). *National Drug Control Strategy*. Washington, DC: U.S. Department of Justice, p. 31.

In Chicago, street gangs, narcotics, and violent crime are intertwined. In 2006, the Chicago Police Department (CPD) tracked 68 active street gangs comprised of more than 500 factions with a total membership estimated at 68,000 members. The four Major Chicago street gangs—Gangster Disciples, Latin Kings, Black Disciples, and Vice Lords—are present in more than half of the states in the country. Street gangs control almost all local distribution of narcotics because of their sophisticated organizational structures, propensity for violence, and large membership. In 2003, almost 50% of all homicides in Chicago were street gang– or narcotics-related.

A number of strategies have been developed by local and federal authorities to combat street gangs. For example, local and federal officers meet monthly to share information to target Main 21 gang members. The Main 21 consists of gang leaders and members who exert significant influence over their membership and the community in the areas of gang activity, drug distribution, and violence. The meetings determine which participating agency has the best opportunity to successfully pursue a criminal case against a list member.

Most of the drugs distributed in Chicago are sold in open-air drug markets, which are operated by street gangs throughout the city. Targeted operations have been developed to clamp down on street gangs and open-air drug markets via physical and audio surveillance, undercover buys, court-approved eavesdropping devices, and other investigative tools. Known as *street corner conspiracies*, the number of operations has increased from 20 in 2003 to more than 50 in 2005. One example is operation Day Trader, targeted against a group called the Mafia Insane Vice Lords. The operation used 15 wires over a two-year period, which resulted in identification of the sources of supply for heroin and cocaine sold by the group. The operation led to 49 federal and 53 state indictments.

Street-corner conspiracies use the full range of law enforcement techniques to address open-air drug markets. Reverse sting missions, where undercover officers pretend to be drug dealers at open-air drug markets, have led to significant arrests and vehicle seizures. Pole-mounted cameras have been installed to monitor strategic street corners and properties owned by the Chicago Housing Authority. The cameras have dramatically reduced drug dealing and violence at those locations. Also, members of the CPD Deployment Operations Center analyze information generated from street-corner conspiracies to strategically deploy manpower and resources. The resulting presence of police manpower often reduces or eliminates potential gangs/drug activity and/or violence in targeted areas in the city. Agents from the Internal Revenue Service have joined the CPD and other agencies in identifying and seizing the assets of gang members, including a radio station used to advertise locations to buy narcotics, several buildings, numerous luxury vehicles, jewelry, and substantial amounts of cash. The CPD has concentrated its efforts on seizing weapons, which has resulted in Chicago leading other major cities in the seizure of guns.

These operations have resulted in a 39 percent reduction in aggravated batteries with firearms and a 25 percent reduction in homicides in Chicago between 2003 and 2005. Furthermore, there have been a substantial number of arrests for narcotic violations and numerous disruptions of drug trafficking organizations. The gang strategy in Chicago can be used as a model for other cities seeking ways to cope with street gangs, drugs, and violence.

A Closer Look: Disrupting Chicago's Violent Gangs

space as a unit, conflict, and planning. The result of this collective behavior is the development of tradition, unreflective internal structure, esprit de corps, solidarity, morale, group awareness, and attachment to local territory.

This definition, first appearing in 1927, still seems to capture the essence of group cohesiveness that remains the prevailing characteristic of many gangs.

Yet another behavioral scientist, Malcolm Klein, offered a more recent description of a youth gang, which includes the element of danger:

> Any denotable group of youngsters who (1) are generally perceived as a distinct aggregation by others in their neighborhood; (2) recognize themselves as a denotable group (almost invariably with a group name); and (3) have been involved in a sufficient number of delinquent incidents to call forth a consistent negative response from neighborhood residents and/or law enforcement agencies (1971:13).

Sociologist Lewis Yablonsky (1966) made an important contribution to the understanding of the youth gang with his definition of a *near group*. According to Yablonsky, human collectives tend to range from highly cohesive, tight-knit organizations to mobs with anonymous members who are motivated by their emotions and led by disturbed membership (1966:109). Teenage gangs fall somewhere in between and are therefore categorized as near groups. Near groups have the following traits:

- Diffuse role definition
- Limited cohesion
- Impermanence
- Minimal consensus norms
- Shifting membership
- Disturbed leadership
- Limited definition of membership expectations

Gang Formation

Unlike legitimate businesses, organized crime groups such as youth gangs do not have employment recruiting drives. In many inner-city areas, programs such as Little League baseball are nonexistent, leaving gangs as the only membership option for many. Typically, social scientists have suggested that gangs appeal to kids in areas marked by poverty, racial strife, broken families, and limited job and educational opportunities. In fact, that premise is widely supported by media accounts and scholars alike. Experts have suggested that when minority youths do not have jobs or an education, they attempt to demonstrate their power in other ways. The gang represents a means whereby members can feel they are a part of something. This is not to suggest, however, that gangs do not exist in middle-class America—they do.

Historically, gang formation has been closely linked with surges in immigration. With many such groups, especially those with strong language and cultural barriers, well-paying jobs were nonexistent. In other cases, social prejudice made it difficult for immigrants to secure jobs and earn a respectable living. Essentially, however, ethnic groups who found themselves at the bottom of the social ladder were more likely to end up involved in gang activity.

Youth gangs of many ethnic origins have been a nuisance throughout U.S. history. In fact, Benjamin Franklin lamented the trouble caused by youth gangs in pre-Revolutionary War Philadelphia. However, only since the early to mid-1980s have youth gangs become violent and well established in most major U.S. cities.

Mark C. Ide

Youth gang formation is often closely linked with surges in immigration. Gangs frequently provide youths with a feeling that they are a part of something bigger than themselves. Gang members may use symbols and signs to convey a sense of solidarity with one another.

PRISON GANGS

In studying the evolution of many major organized crime groups, it becomes clear that inmate associations in both state and federal prisons often help sow the seeds of criminal activity. The existence of prison gangs is nothing new. Recall that the Italian Camorra had its beginnings in the Spanish prisons of Naples in the 1860s. Indeed, a similar criminal phenomenon has taken place in the United States and has produced many violence-prone criminal organizations. It is difficult to estimate the exact number of prison gangs in the United States today, but the National Gang Intelligence Center (2009a) notes the following as major players: Mexican Mafia, Aryan Brotherhood, Black Guerrilla Family, Barrio Azteca, Hermanos de Pistoleros Latinos, Mexikanemi, and Ñeta.

The more sophisticated prison gangs share similar traits with regard to their dedication to the organization and members. Other traits are also prevalent:

- Prison gangs commonly have a *blood in—blood out" policy*, which requires prospective members to injure or kill a designated target individual in the prison system.
- Prison gangs operate both inside and outside prison walls.
- Prison gangs commonly form alliances within prisons to build presence, strength, and clout within the prison walls.

Most gangs are typically formed as protection organizations for members. Once accepted, the recruit enjoys the power, prestige, influence, and protection that the organization offers. Prison gangs in the United States became widely known in 1957 when the Mexican Mafia (EME) first organized at the Deuel Vocational Institute in Tracy, California. The gang originally formed as a protection organization for gang members, but membership grew rapidly. After gaining considerable size and influence in the prison system, gang members acquired control over such activities as homosexual prostitution, drug trafficking, debt collection (extortion), and gambling. The group focuses most of its aggression against white and black inmates while leaving Mexican inmates alone.

Five major prison gangs to note are the Mexican Mafia, the Nuestra Familia, the Aryan Brotherhood, the Texas Syndicate, and the Black Guerilla Family. The Mexican Mafia (EME)

> **Critical Thinking Task**
>
> If prison gangs in fact operate within the walls of prisons, do they pose a threat to public safety? Defend your answer.

established a goal for itself to control drug trafficking in all areas in which the group had become established. The gang gained a reputation for violence after the 1967 stabbing death of a suspected police informer operating within the ranks of the gang. As violence grew, even some members of the gang felt uneasy. It was the same year that a group of EME members formed its own gang, called Nuestra Familia (NF), meaning "our family." The NF waged war with the EME; over the years this war has resulted in numerous deaths. Because of the ongoing war with the EME, the NF formed an alliance with the Black Guerrilla Family as well as with other ethnic prison gangs. The NF eventually surpassed the EME in organizational capabilities and became one of the largest prison gangs in the United States.

Another prison gang that has achieved considerable notoriety is the Nazi-oriented Aryan Brotherhood. A characteristic of particular significance is the association between outlaw motorcycle gang members and the Aryan Brotherhood. Frequently, when members of outlaw motorcycle gangs are convicted and sent to prison, they no longer have the protection of their gang. The Aryan Brotherhood, being a white supremacist organization, has commonly accepted outlaw bikers, who share a racist philosophy, into the gang. The hierarchy of the Aryan Brotherhood consists of a commission and a governing council. Members are promoted through the ranks based on individual acts of violence committed on behalf of the gang's organizational goals.

The Black Guerrilla Family (BGF) was founded in 1966 by the late George Jackson in San Quentin Prison. The BGF is a politically motivated organization following a Maoist philosophy. It operates on a command structure that incorporates a supreme commander, central committee, field generals, and captains of security. As with the adoption of bikers by the Aryan Brotherhood, the BGF recruits members of black street gangs in prison. Members of the Crips and Bloods have been known to become instant members of the BGF once they are in the prison system.

The Texas Syndicate (E Ts E) is another prison gang; it organized in Folsom Prison in 1974. Although considered relatively small in membership, the Texas Syndicate is very violent. The gang consists of Mexican-American inmates who originally hailed from the areas of El Paso and San Antonio, Texas. One characteristic common in Mexican-oriented prison gangs is an intense loyalty between members, which contributes to their reputation for violence. The gang is active in assaults and extortion and has targeted drug trafficking as its primary criminal enterprise both inside and outside the prison.

ANCILLARY TRAFFICKING ORGANIZATIONS

In addition to those organizations already discussed, many other smaller organizations operate throughout the United States. These organizations do business in both urban and rural settings and account for a significant segment of the domestic drug-trafficking picture.

The urban trafficking organizations make up a significant category of drug dealers. These organizations are frequently well organized and highly structured and are usually composed of extremely violent career criminals. In many cases, the groups consist of younger criminals who assume a leadership role as they age. Many are later convicted and sent to prison or they are killed. This places the urban trafficking organizations in a constant state of metamorphosis.

Urban drug gangs exist throughout the country but have been particularly active in such cities as Chicago, Detroit, St. Louis, and East St. Louis, Illinois. It is common for members to be heavily armed with fully automatic weapons and to be especially violence-prone. Violence by these organizations frequently occurs because of rivalries between trafficking groups over "turf," but the violence may also manifest itself as aggression toward police, prosecutors, and witnesses in drug prosecutions.

As discussed earlier in this text, most drug sources are either Mexican or Latin American nationals. Women are commonly used as couriers from the source city to the ultimate destination. Profits acquired for drugs are usually considerably high. For example, a kilogram of cocaine purchased in a source city may cost $12,000 to $15,000 but can be resold for much more. Because of this enormous profit margin, control of the industry is a primary goal of the urban trafficking organization.

There are also other small-time trafficking organizations operating in rural America. In some cases, drug trafficking may be a variation of another type of criminal activity that has been going on for some time. For example, in some parts of the southeast, rural dwellers whose families once produced

Figure 8.11
Source: Organized Crime Drug Enforcement Task Force, 1988.

The Black Guerrilla Family [BGF] is a close-knit gang that originated in the 1970s in California prisons. BGF members and affiliates are engaged in many types of crime and are best characterized as "simply prone to violence."

This OCDETF [Organized Crime Drug Enforcement Task Force] case involved an investigation by a Task Force team consisting of the DEA, IRS, ATF, Los Angeles County Sheriff's Office, California Department of Justice, and local police officers from four jurisdictions. Their goal was to uncover and prosecute the narcotics, strong-arming, and homicide activities of the Elrader "Ray Ray" Browning organization. After two years of investigation, working undercover and using informants; six months of intensive surveillance; and three months of wiretaps on residences, automobiles, and portable phones, 28 defendants were indicted on a variety of cocaine, heroin, and firearms charges. Browning's drug couriers, whose consignment of cocaine was seized by the DEA in Detroit, were also indicted.

Browning was released from prison in 1979 after serving part of a state term for a murder that he committed as a juvenile. In August of that year, a man identified as Browning walked into a cafe and shot two men to death. The attack was to avenge a drug robbery of James "Doc" Holiday, Ray Ray Browning's associate. Ray Ray's conviction was overturned when a California Supreme Court decision rendered inadmissible the testimony of a witness that had been hypnotized in an attempt to refresh her memory.

In 1983, Browning was found guilty of firebombing and shooting into a Pasadena home in an incident related to drug territories. Again, his conviction was overturned, and he was released in September 1985. Browning then began organizing his major drug ring.

Like a corporation's chief executive officer, Ray Ray headed a broad narcotics empire with senior executives in at least four cities. Gross sales were estimated at $1 million to $3 million per month! Profits were funneled into a pricey lifestyle for Browning, his girlfriend and second-in-command, Nei Marie Wells, and a very small group of top confederates such as "Doc" Holiday. The rest were mainly small-time drug dealers ordered by Ray Ray to work for him or close up shop.

At home in Pasadena, everyone knew Ray Ray. Seeing him being driven in his white limousine or smiling behind the wheel of his Rolls-Royce, young boys watched in reverence and adults spoke in hushed tones. To those that knew him, Browning always seemed to beat the system. Folklore produced a man larger than life. Tales of drug rivalries, intimidation, and murder abounded.

The turning point was an incident in Detroit. Big John Milan, a Browning operative, arrived by bus with 18 kilos of cocaine in two suitcases. Observing two men and a dog examining his luggage, Big John refused to claim it. The agents had been alerted to his arrival by their Los Angeles counterparts, who were tapping Ray Ray's phone. They later testified that they did not detain Milan in order to protect the integrity of the wiretap.

Milan called Nei Marie Wells to ask permission to abandon the bags but was told that he might as well get arrested because Ray Ray wouldn't believe his story. He then approached the baggage clerk, who gratuitously told Milan not to claim the bags because the police had discovered the "bricks" inside. At that, John departed without the bags and checked into a Detroit hotel that the gang customarily used. Within a few hours, he changed hotels at Ray Ray's direction. The next evening, two men

Figure 8.11—*continued*

---

fired several .45 caliber slugs into Big John's room, wounding him seriously. At that point, Big John decided to cooperate with authorities in order to save his life. Nei's to-the-point comment registered on tape was: "We never heard of dogs sniffing buses before."

John Milan would make a zealous witness but not a particularly well-informed or reputable one. Nei Marie Wells, however, was all of these things. Nei functioned at the center of the web and knew more of the details than anyone but Ray Ray himself. Facing CCE charges and sentencing possibilities of up to 80 years, Nei decided to cooperate, provided she and her children could be protected from Ray Ray's wrath. Nei Marie Wells became "the most diligent, conscientious, cooperating witness" that the prosecutor had ever seen. She is presently out on bond awaiting sentencing, and she and her family are secure in the U.S. Marshal's Witness Security Program.

The raid that closed down the Ray Ray Browning operation involved several hundred officers and agents, who went to 17 locations simultaneously and seized 15 pounds of cocaine, $300,000 in cash, four homes, an apartment building, and 10 cars. They arrested 21 persons, and seven more were later detained on additional federal warrants. The Browning case and several immediate spin-offs resulted in seizures totaling almost a million dollars in cash and several million dollars worth of real estate, jewelry, and vehicles.

Twenty of the 28 charged defendants were prosecuted in federal court. Of those 20, 18 pled guilty and received sentences of up to 20 years in prison without parole; the only defendants to go on trial in federal court were Browning and Holiday. After a three-week trial in which they chose to handle their own defense, both were convicted. While awaiting sentencing, Browning tried to escape from Terminal Island Federal Prison by posing as an attorney, complete with wig, mustache, briefcase, and law book, but was foiled by an alert guard that recognized Ray Ray's "swagger."

Ray Ray is presently serving two life sentences plus 120 years in Leavenworth. He was among the nation's first defendants to be prosecuted under the 1986 statute mandating a life term for a conviction as the chief of a continuing criminal enterprise involving drugs. He was ordered to pay $2 million in fines (just in case anything should be left after forfeitures and the collection of unpaid taxes on the drug income). "Doc" Holiday was sentenced to life without possibility of parole.

The judge remarked at sentencing on August 29, 1988, "When Congress passed the [statute] it had a certain individual in mind. Well, Mr. Browning, you are it." Under the newest drug law, which took effect November 21, 1988, a defendant in Browning's position that is proven to have committed or ordered a drug-related murder faces the death penalty. Perhaps Ray Ray lucked out once again.

Case Study: Ray Ray and the BGF

moonshine have discovered that marijuana is more profitable. The isolation of many rural areas enables traffickers to conduct operations such as marijuana farming and clandestine laboratories. In doing so, traffickers remain relatively free of detection from law enforcement authorities. In many cases, such locations are also good areas for use as "drop zones" or secluded landing strips for smuggling pilots.

SUMMARY

Because of the profit potential for drug trafficking, criminal organizations with both foreign and domestic origins compete for market share. This chapter deals with domestic drug-trafficking organizations; many of these have their roots in foreign countries or are relatively new to the illegal drug trade.

The term *traditional organized crime* is most commonly associated with Italian criminal groups or La Cosa Nostra (LCN, also known as the Mafia). The LCN originated in Italy and Sicily during the 1800s and is now considered the premier criminal group in Italy and a major criminal phenomenon in the United States. The origin of Italian organized crime in prisons parallels that of many domestic prison gangs in the United States.

The first Mafioso arrived in the United States in the late 1800s and gained a foothold in New York and New Orleans. Prohibition (1920–1933) was conducive to Mafiosi criminal activities, which spread to other large cities throughout the United States. The FBI website estimates that the LCN has approximately 25,000 members total, with 250,000 affiliates worldwide. There are more than 3,000 members and affiliates in the United States, scattered mostly throughout the major cities in the Northeast, the Midwest, California, and the South. Their largest presence centers around New York, southern New Jersey, and Philadelphia (Federal Bureau of Investigation, n.d.).

Outlaw motorcycle gangs represent yet another type of domestic criminal group actively involved in the drug trade. Originating in the late 1940s, gangs such as the Hells Angels, the Pagans, the Bandidos, and the Outlaws have now cornered much of the methamphetamine market and frequently dwell in cities outside the continental United States. These gangs have also gained a reputation for violence and on many occasions have worked in collusion with other criminal groups such as LCN. The DEA has estimated that there are several hundred outlaw motorcycle gangs currently operating in the United States. Some of these organizations have demonstrated considerable sophistication and pose a very real threat to many major United States cities.

Do you recognize these terms?

- blood in–blood out policy
- gang colors
- home invasion
- near group
- original gangster
- Pizza Connection
- wannabe

DISCUSSION QUESTIONS

1. Discuss the hierarchical structure of La Cosa Nostra.

2. Review some of the reasons that some researchers perceive La Cosa Nostra as a fragmented group of semiorganized criminals.

3. List the domestic criminal organizations most actively involved in cocaine trafficking.

4. What is the relationship between the American Mafia and the Sicilian Mafia in the illicit drug trade?

5. Name and discuss the structure and other similarities of the four major outlaw motorcycle gangs that operate in the United States.

6. To what extent does the Mexican Mafia (EME) play a role in drug trafficking?

Chapter 9

Foreign Drug-Trafficking Organizations

This chapter will enable you to:

- Understand the role of Colombian drug criminals in global drug trafficking
- Understand the development of Mexican domination of the illicit drug market
- Understand the link between drug trafficking and terrorism
- Differentiate between various organizations of Asian drug traffickers
- Learn about the role of foreign drug-trafficking organizations as it relates to the United States market

In Chapter 4, some general dynamics of foreign drug source countries were discussed. This chapter takes a closer look at the criminal trafficking groups originating in those countries. Today, it is clear that drug abuse in the United States has created a growing incentive for escalating foreign involvement in the drug trade; the allure of profits for traffickers is considerable. The degree to which various criminal organizations are involved depends greatly on factors such as the type of drug trafficked, the source country's proximity to the United States and established trafficking routes, and the ability to move money and personnel in and out of the country.

In 2010, the operational landscape of drug trafficking has changed dramatically since the last publication of this book. No longer are the Colombian cartels the most significant manufacturers and importers of illicit drugs to the United States. Rather, Mexican trafficking organizations have gained international prominence and have become considerably more able than ever in

285

DOI: 10.1016/B978-1-4377-4450-7.00009-6
© 2011 Elsevier Inc. All rights reserved.

controlling all aspects of the trafficking of many drugs from their production to transportation to both wholesale and retail distribution. Thus, the focus of this chapter is on the rise in prominence of Mexican criminal organizations in the trafficking of marijuana, heroin, methamphetamine, and MDMA. Although cocaine is still a problem, its availability and use have decreased dramatically in recent years. We also examine other drug-trafficking groups that still fill a niche in the overall transnational drug-trafficking scheme.

DRUG TRAFFICKING ON THE SOUTHWEST BORDER

The Southwest border (SWB) of the United States is the main delivery zone for most of the illegal drugs smuggled into the country. Specifically, most of the cocaine, marijuana, methamphetamine, and Mexican heroin available in the United States is smuggled into the country across the southwestern border. This area of the United States is particularly vulnerable to drug smuggling because of the enormous volume of people and goods legitimately crossing the border between the two countries every day. Furthermore, large sections of the nearly 2,000-mile land border between Mexico and the United States are both expansive and remote, providing considerable drug-smuggling opportunities for Mexican traffickers. Once at the border, Mexican traffickers use every method imaginable to smuggle drugs into this country, including aircraft, backpackers, couriers, horses and mules, maritime vessels, rail, tunnels, and vehicles.

As of the preparation of this text, no other country in the world has a greater impact on the drug situation in the United States than does Mexico. Because of the shared border, the influence of Mexico on the U.S. drug trade is unmatched. Moreover, Mexico's success in the illicit drug trade is complemented by (1) its strategic location between drug-producing and drug-consuming countries; (2) a long history of cross-border smuggling; and (3) the existence of diversified, polydrug, profit-minded drug-trafficking organizations.

Each of the four major drugs of abuse—marijuana, cocaine, heroin, and methamphetamine—are either produced in or transshipped through Mexico before reaching the United States. The great majority of bulk currency intercepted within the United States originates from drug-trafficking activities. It is estimated that approximately $18–$39 billion annually is moved from the interior of the United States to the southwest border on behalf of Mexican and Colombian drug-trafficking organizations. As such, billions of dollars in U.S. currency are sent back to Mexico annually. From the Mexican perspective, the flow of large sums of money creates corruption that hinders drug enforcement. As discussed earlier in this book, it is instructive to briefly consider Mexico's illicit drug products:

- *Heroin.* Mexico is an opium poppy-cultivating and heroin-producing country. Though the country accounts for only about 6 percent of the world's opium poppy cultivation and heroin production, it is a major supplier of heroin to abusers in the United States (Perkins and Placido, 2010). Mexican black tar and brown heroin have appeared increasingly in the eastern

United States. Mexico was identified as the source country for 39 percent of the samples classified under the DEA's Heroin Signature Program (HSP) during 2008, the largest representation of Mexican-source heroin in the United States in the past 20 years (Perkins and Placido, 2010).

- *Marijuana.* Mexico is also the number-one foreign supplier of marijuana abused in the United States. In fact, according to 2008 statistics, marijuana is the top revenue generator for Mexican drug-trafficking groups. The profits derived from marijuana trafficking—an industry with minimal overhead costs, controlled entirely by the traffickers—are used not only to finance other drug enterprises by Mexico's multidrug-producing cartels but also to pay ongoing "business" expenses, purchase weapons, and bribe corrupt officials.

- *Methamphetamine.* In addition to Mexico's involvement in heroin and marijuana production, it is also the number-one foreign supplier of methamphetamine to the United States. Although the Mexican government has seen some success in controlling—even banning—the importation of methamphetamine precursor chemicals such as ephedrine, pseudoephedrine, and phenyl acetic acid, Mexican trafficking organizations have proven to be extremely resourceful in circumventing regulatory measures put in place by Mexico's Calderón administration. As with heroin, there is considerable financial incentive for the Mexican traffickers to maintain a trade they control from manufacture to distribution. In fact, Mexican authorities seized more methamphetamine labs in 2009–2010 than in the five previous years combined (Perkins and Placido, 2010).

- *Cocaine.* Mexican traffickers also maintain an important role in the cocaine trade. Since the 1980s, Mexico has served as a primary transportation corridor—transshipment point—for cocaine destined for the United States. Though Mexico is not a coca-producing country and therefore cannot control the trade from beginning to end, traffickers in Mexico have managed nonetheless to exert increasing control over the trade in exchange for shouldering the greater risk inherent in transporting the cocaine and ensuring its distribution in the United States.

Since 2007, Mexican trafficking organizations have established cooperation with Colombian sources of supply and developed relationships with alternate sources of supply in other cocaine-producing countries—particularly Peru. Consequently, Mexican drug traffickers have developed into intermediate sources of supply for cocaine in Europe, Australia, Asia, and the Middle East. Moreover, Mexican traffickers control the wholesale distribution of cocaine and other drugs of abuse throughout the United States. As of the preparation of this book, estimates suggest that approximately 93 percent of the cocaine leaving South America for the United States moves through Mexico.

During 2009, however, the majority of cocaine stopped first in a Central American country before moving onward to shipment into Mexico (Perkins and Placido, 2010). This suggests that drug control efforts by the Calderón administration are having a positive impact on how the cartels do business—requiring them to take the extra (and more costly and risky) step of arranging multistage transportation systems (Perkins and Placido, 2010).

Changes in cocaine movement patterns are not the only measurable trend. Beginning in January 2007—immediately after the Calderón government was installed—the price per gram of cocaine in the United States began to rise, with a correlative drop in cocaine purity. During this period, prices increased by almost 72 percent and purity fell by nearly 33 percent (Perkins and Placido, 2010).

MEXICAN DOMINATION OF THE ILLICIT DRUG MARKET

Much activity has occurred in the realm of Mexican drug trafficking since the last edition of this text. Many trafficking groups have expanded operations and spread their influence in intimidating and corrupting Mexican authorities, rival traffickers, and innocent citizens both in Mexico and the United States. In 2009, the National Drug Threat Assessment stated, "Mexican drug trafficking organizations represent the greatest organized crime threat to the United States and control most of the U.S. drug market" (National Drug Intelligence Center, 2008). They have proven to pose even a greater U.S. threat than Asian, Colombian, or Dominican organized crime groups. Between 2008 and 2009, more than 7,000 people have been murdered in connection with Mexico's drug cartel wars (Johnson, 2010).

Mexican cartels allegedly have used their vast financial resources to corrupt Mexican public officials, who either turn a blind eye to cartel activities or work directly for them. Beginning in 2005, the Mexican government began to make continued efforts to purge corrupt police. In December 2006, President Felipe Calderón launched operations against the cartels in nine of Mexico's 32 states. He has pledged to use extradition as a tool against drug traffickers and sent 64 criminals to the United States as of August 2007, including the alleged head of the Gulf Cartel (Congressional Research Service, 2007).

Calderón's efforts have had some notable results. For example, from January 2000 through September 2006, the Mexican government arrested more than 79,000 people on charges related to drug trafficking. Of these arrests, some 78,831 are low-level drug dealers. Mexico also arrested 15 cartel leaders, 74 lieutenants, 53 financial officers, and 428 hitmen (*sicarios*). Mexican authorities arrested nearly 10,000 people on drug-related charges from December 2006 through August 2007. On August 16, 2006, the U.S. Drug Enforcement Administration (DEA) and Coast Guard arrested Tijuana cartel leader Francisco Javier Arellano Félix, along with other Tijuana cartel leaders, on a boat off the Mexican coast. His brother, Francisco Rafael Arellano Félix, was extradited to the United States in September 2006. In January 2007, Mexico extradited 15 people wanted for prosecution in the United States, including four senior drug traffickers (Congressional Research Service, 2007).

Police agencies in the United States have reported Mexican drug-trafficking operations in an estimated 230 U.S. cities. These operations have been found to employ maritime, air, and overland transportation methods. Furthermore, Mexican traffickers have taken advantage of high-technology communication methods to avoid detection. For example, "cross-communication" centers have been discovered on both sides of the U.S.-Mexico border, using methods such as voice-over-Internet protocol (VoIP), satellite technology (broadband satellite instant messaging), encrypted messaging with rolling codes, cell phone technology, two-way radios, scanner devices, and text messaging to communicate with members (National Drug Intelligence Center, 2008).

Figure 9.1

Source: National Drug Intelligence Center, *National Drug Threat Assessment 2007*, adapted by CRS (P. McGrath, 3/1/2007).

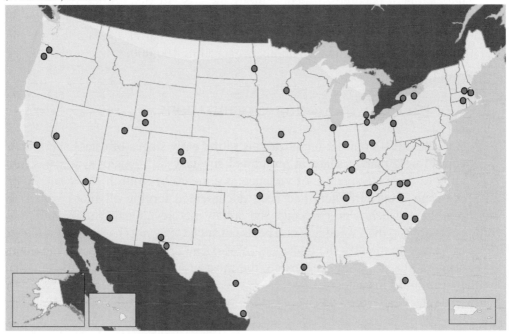

Mexican Cartel Presence in the United States

The Mexican Takeover of the Cocaine Trade

As of 2010, Mexican drug traffickers are slowly assuming control of Colombia's multibillion-dollar cocaine industry, which was previously controlled by well-known cartels from cities such as Medellín and Cali. With the dismantlement of the former Colombia cartels and the retraction of these cartels from key geographic locations outside Colombia, the Mexican cartels have filled the void, first by assuming supremacy of the cocaine distribution market in the United States and in recent years in a much broader global context.

That was illustrated in a case that unfolded in 2009 in which a conglomerate of Mexican drug cartels were arrested while attempting to smuggle 1,200 tons of cocaine into the United States from Colombia. That case demonstrated how Mexicans, including the Beltran-Leyva and Sinaloa cartels, were in charge in major drug shipments from Colombia to the United States, with Colombians assuming a diminished role.

The Mexican cartels have representatives in Colombia who coordinate with Colombian drug-trafficking organizations on the acquisition of cocaine and transportation to Central America and Mexico. As recently as 2000, the exact opposite could be said, in that the Colombian cartels were embedded in Mexico and coordinating with the Mexican drug-trafficking organizations.

Despite current efforts by Mexican President Felipe Calderón to quash the cartels, the drug organizations have become more aggressive in expanding their global operations. In doing so, law enforcement officials say they have strangled the communities in the regions they control. The situation has led to the deaths of hundreds of people along the U.S.-Mexico border. By not stopping the cartels when they were first organizing more than 10 years ago, narco-traffickers like Chapo "Shorty" Guzman's Sinaloa cartel, the Gulf cartel, and others have grown in size to numbers exceeding 100,000.

Key Mexican Trafficking Organizations

Like most criminal organizations in the early stages of establishing their control of a market share in prohibited substances, Mexican syndicates still cling to the excessive use of violence as a means of control. As of late 2009, Mexican drug traffickers had been documented forging alliances with U.S. drug gangs such as prison gangs and outlaw motorcycle gangs to expand their operations in the United States. The use of such U.S. gangs has made it difficult for police to identify the managers of Mexican drug operations. Of the many drug cartels operating in Mexico, the most prominent are the Gulf, Sinaloa, Juárez, and Tijuana cartels.

The Gulf Cartel

The *Gulf cartel* is a Mexican drug cartel based in Matamoros. The Zetas, a criminal group in Mexico, have created their own niche among drug enforcer gangs in that they operate "as a private army under the orders of Cárdenas' Gulf cartel, the first time a drug lord has had his own paramilitary." Most reports indicate that the Zetas were created by a group of 30 lieutenants and sublieutenants who deserted from the Mexican military's Special Air Mobile Force Group (Grupo Aeromovil de Fuerzas Especiales, GAFES) to the Gulf cartel in the late 1990s. As such, the Zetas were able to carry out more complex operations and use more sophisticated weaponry (Congressional Research Service, 2007).

The Zetas were instrumental in the Gulf cartel's domination of the drug trade in Nuevo Laredo and have fought to maintain the cartel's influence in that city following the 2003 arrest of its leader, Osiel Cárdenas. Press reports have charged that these soldiers-turned-cartel-enforcers were trained in the United States; however, the Washington Office on Latin America was unable to confirm this claim. Estimates on the number of Zetas range from 31 up to 200. Reports indicate that although the Zetas initially comprised members of special forces, they now include federal, state, and local law enforcement personnel as well as civilians. In September 2005, testimony to the Mexican

Congress by then Defense Secretary Clemente Vega indicated that the Zetas had also hired at least 30 former Guatemalan special forces (*Kaibiles*) to train new recruits because "the number of former Mexican special forces men in their ranks had shrunk from 50 to no more than a dozen, and they were finding it hard to entice more members of the Mexican military to join" (Congressional Research Service, 2007).

The Zetas act as assassins for the Gulf cartel. They also traffic arms, kidnap, and collect payments for the cartel on its drug routes. Mexican law enforcement officials report that the Zetas have become an increasingly sophisticated, three-tiered organization with leaders and middlemen who coordinate contracts with petty criminals to carry out street work. The Zetas have maintained the territory of the Gulf cartel in the northern cities of Matamoros and Nuevo Laredo, and in addition they are believed to control trafficking routes along the eastern half of the U.S.-Mexico border. Thus, the Zetas now have a presence in southern Mexico, where the Gulf cartel is disputing territory previously controlled by the Juárez and Sinaloa cartels. A recent federal investigation found that the Zetas also engage in kidnapping, drug dealing, and money laundering. In July 2006, local police in the southern state of Tabasco unknowingly arrested Mateo Díaz López, believed to be a leader of the Zetas. The arrest prompted an assault on the police station, killing four people, including two police officers. However, the assault did not succeed in liberating Díaz López, who was subsequently transferred to a prison in Guadalajara (Congressional Research Service, 2007). The Zetas also trained the Michoacán-based La Familia enforcer gang, which has carried out numerous executions in that state. The Familia maintains close ties to the Zetas but are a smaller entity.

Figure 9.2
Source: U.S. Customs and Border Protection; National Southwest Border Counternarcotics Strategy, 2009.

A Closer Look: Traffickers Use Subterranean Tunnels Along the Southwest Border

The number of tunnels extending from Mexico into the United States has increased, suggesting that drug traffickers consider these tunnels useful investments to smuggle drugs into the United States. For example, in 2008, U.S. Border Protection officials discovered 16 subterranean tunnels, the majority of which were in the Tucson Sector, which encompasses a border area of 262 miles from the New Mexico state line to Yuma County, Arizona. In 2009, 26 subterranean tunnels were discovered; 20 of those were in the Tucson area, primarily in the area of Nogales. During this same period, five tunnels were discovered in California. In February 2009, U.S. Customs and Border Protection initiated a program designed to hamper the construction of tunnels in Nogales's extensive drainage system. The initiative involved the construction of a 12-foot-deep steel and concrete underground wall that extends 100 yards along the border near the DeConcini point of entry in Nogales.

A Closer Look: Traffickers Use Subterranean Tunnels Along the Southwest Border

The Sinaloa Cartel

The *Sinaloa cartel* is another powerful cartel in Mexican drug trafficking. It claims the territory of Baja California, Sinaloa, Durango, Sonora, and Chihuahua. The cartel also goes by the names of the Guzmán-Loera Organization and the Pacific cartel, the latter due to the coast of Mexico from which it originated.

The Sinaloa cartel is known to have smuggled many tons of cocaine and large amounts of heroin into the United States between 1990 and 2008 (Drug Enforcement Administration, 2009d).

Pedro Avilés Pérez was a pioneer drug lord in the Mexican state of Sinaloa in the late 1960s. He is considered the first generation of major Mexican drug smugglers of marijuana who marked the birth of large-scale Mexican drug trafficking. He also pioneered the use of aircraft to smuggle drugs to the United States (Congressional Research Service, 2007). Second-generation Sinaloan traffickers such as Rafael Caro Quintero, Ernesto Fonseca Carrillo, Miguel Ángel Félix Gallardo, and Avilés Pérez's nephew Joaquín "El Chapo" Guzmán would claim they learned all they knew about narcotrafficking while serving in the Avilés organization. Miguel Ángel Félix Gallardo, who eventually founded the Guadalajara cartel, was arrested in 1989. While incarcerated, he remained one of Mexico's major traffickers, maintaining his organization via mobile phone until he was transferred to a maximum-security prison in the 1990s. At that point, his old organization broke up into two factions: the Tijuana cartel, led by his nephews, the Arellano Félix brothers; and the Sinaloa cartel, run by former lieutenants Héctor Luis Palma Salazar, Adrián Gómez González, and Joaquín Guzmán Locra El Chapo (Congressional Research Service, 2007).

The Sinaloa cartel used to be known as *La Alianza de Sangre* (Blood Partnership). When Héctor Luis Palma Salazar (a.k.a. El Güero) was arrested by elements of the Mexican Army, his partner Joaquín Guzmán Loera took leadership of the cartel. Guzmán was captured in Guatemala in 1993 and extradited to Mexico, where he was jailed in a maximum-security prison, but in January 2001 he escaped and resumed his command of the cartel. Guzmán has two top lieutenants, Ismael Zambada García and Ignacio Coronel Villareal. Guzmán and Zambada became Mexico's top drug kingpins in 2003, after the arrest of their rival Osiel Cardenas of the Gulf cartel. Another close associate, Javier Torres Félix, was arrested and extradited to the United States in December 2006. According to the Mexican embassy, as of mid-2007, Guzmán and Zambada have evaded operations to capture them (Embassy of the United States, Mexico, 2007).

The Sinaloa cartel has a presence in 17 states, with important centers in Mexico City, Tepic, Toluca, Cuautitlán, and most of the state of Sinaloa. The cartel is primarily involved in the smuggling and distribution of Colombian cocaine, Mexican marijuana, methamphetamine, and Mexican and Southeast Asian heroin into the United States (Drug Enforcement Administration, 2009c). It is believed that a group known as the Herrera Organization would transport multiton quantities of cocaine from South America to Guatemala on behalf of the Sinaloa cartel. From there it is smuggled north to Mexico and later into the United States. Other shipments of cocaine are believed to originate in Colombia from Cali and Medellín drug-trafficking groups. The Sinaloa cartel handles transportation across the U.S. border to distribution cells in Arizona, California, Texas, Chicago, and New York.

By the mid-1990s, according to one court opinion, the Sinaloa cartel was believed to be the size of the Medellín cartel during its prime. The Sinaloa cartel was believed to be linked to the Juárez cartel in a strategic alliance following the partnership of their rivals, the Gulf cartel and Tijuana cartel. Following the discovery of a tunnel system used to smuggle drugs across the U.S.-Mexico border, the group has been associated with such means of trafficking (Congressional Research Service, 2007).

By 2005, the Beltrán-Leyva brothers, who were formerly aligned with the Sinaloa cartel, had come to dominate drug trafficking across the border with Arizona. By 2006, the cartel had eliminated all competition across the 330 miles of Arizona border; it was suspected they had accomplished this by bribing state government officials. The Beltrán-Leyva cartel are now allies of the Zetas of the Gulf cartel (Congressional Research Service, 2007).

In January 2008, the cartel allegedly split into a number of warring factions, and this is a major contributor to Mexico's current drug violence epidemic. On February 25, 2009, the U.S. government announced the arrest of 750 members of the Sinaloa cartel across the United States in *Operation Xcellerator*. They also announced the seizure of more than $59 million in cash and numerous vehicles, planes, and boats (Drug Enforcement Administration, 2009c, 2009d).

In March 2009, the Mexican government announced the deployment of 1,000 federal police officers and 5,000 Mexican Army soldiers to restore order in Ciudad Juárez, where the Sinaloa cartel has been battling the Zetas of the Gulf cartel. The city has suffered more than 1,600 deaths related to drug trafficking, the highest in the country (Drug Enforcement Administration, 2009b).

The Sinaloa cartel's loss of partners in Mexico does not appear to have affected its ability to smuggle drugs from South America to the United States. On the contrary, based on seizure reports, the cartel appears to be the most active smuggler of cocaine. It has also demonstrated the ability to establish operations in previously unknown areas, such as Central America and South America, even as far south as Peru, Paraguay, and Argentina. It also appears to be active in diversifying its export markets; rather than relying solely on U.S. consumers, it has made an effort to supply distributors of drugs in Latin American and European countries (Congressional Research Service, 2007).

The Sinaloa cartel has been waging a war against the Tijuana cartel (the Arellano-Félix Organization) over the Tijuana smuggling route to the border city of San Diego, California. The rivalry between the two cartels dates back to the Miguel Ángel Félix Gallardo setup of Palma's family. Félix Gallardo, following his imprisonment, bestowed the Guadalajara cartel to his nephews in the Tijuana cartel (Drug Enforcement Administration, 2007b). In 1992, Palma struck out against the Tijuana cartel at a disco in Puerto Vallarta, Jalisco, where eight Tijuana cartel members were killed in the shootout, the Arellano-Félix brothers having successfully escaped from the location.

In retaliation, the Tijuana cartel attempted to set up Guzmán at Guadalajara airport on May 24, 1993. In the shootout that followed, six civilians were killed by the hired gunmen from the Logan Heights, San Diego-based 30th Street gang. The deaths included that of Roman Catholic Cardinal Juan Jesús Posadas Ocampo (National Drug Intelligence Center, 2008a).

The Juárez Cartel

The *Juárez cartel* is another influential drug-trafficking organization. It is based in Ciudad Juárez, Chihuahua, Mexico, across the border from El Paso, Texas. The Juárez cartel is an important player in modern-day drug trafficking because it controls one of the main transportation arteries for illegal drug shipments entering the United States from Mexico. The Juárez cartel has a reputation for being a brutal and dangerous drug-trafficking organization. For example, its members have been known to decapitate their rivals, mutilate their corpses, and dump them in public to intimidate the public, the police, and their rivals (Trahan et al., 2005).

Rafael Aguilar Guajardo founded the cartel in the 1970s and in 1993 handed it down to Amado Carrillo Fuentes. Amado's brothers and his son were later brought into the business. In 1997, after Amado died following complications from plastic surgery, a brief turf war began over the control of the cartel, where Amado's brother Vicente Carrillo Fuentes surfaced as leader (Trahan et al., 2005).

As recently as 2005, the Juárez cartel was the leading player in the center of the country, controlling a large percentage of the cocaine traffic from Mexico into the United States (Burton, 2007). The death of Amado Carrillo Fuentes in 1997, however, was the beginning of the decline in the cartel's prominence. This has resulted in some elements of the group being absorbed by the Sinaloa cartel, a relatively new but aggressive organization that has taken over much of the Juárez cartel's former territory (Drug Enforcement Administration, 2009c, 2009d; National Drug Intelligence Center, 2008a). Since 2007, the Juárez cartel has been at war with its former partner, the Sinaloa cartel, for control of Juárez. The fighting between them has left thousands dead in Chihuahua state.

The Juárez cartel relies on two enforcement gangs to exercise control over both sides of the border: La Linea, a group of current and former Chihuahua police officers, is prevalent on the Mexican side; the large street gang Barrio Azteca operates on the U.S. side of the border in Texas cities such as El Paso, Dallas, and Austin as well as in New Mexico and Arizona (National Drug Intelligence Center, 2008a).

The Tijuana Cartel

The *Tijuana cartel*, based in Tijuana, Baja California, is another powerful Mexican trafficking organization. Covering the northwestern part of Mexico, the Tijuana cartel competes with the Juárez cartel (central), the Gulf cartel (east), and the Sinaloa cartel. The Tijuana cartel has been called "one of the biggest and most violent criminal groups in Mexico" (Steller, 1998).

For the most part, the majority of Mexico's smuggling routes are controlled by three key cartels: Gulf, Sinaloa, and Tijuana—the latter being the least powerful. The Tijuana cartel was weakened in August 2006 when its leader, Javier Arellano Félix, was arrested by the U.S. Coast Guard on a boat off the coast of southern California. In January 2007, Mexican army troops were sent to Tijuana in an operation to restore order to the border city and expel corrupt police officers who were cooperating with the Tijuana cartel. As a result, the Tijuana cartel has been unable to project much power outside its base in Tijuana.

The Arellano-Félix family was initially composed of seven brothers and four sisters, who inherited the organization from Miguel Ángel Félix Gallardo upon his incarceration in Mexico in 1989 for his complicity in the murder of DEA Special Agent Enrique Camarena. Although the brothers' arrest was a blow to the Arellano-Félix cartel, it did not dismantle the organization, which currently is led by Eduardo's nephew, Luis Fernando Sánchez Arellano (Burton, 2007).

The Tijuana cartel has infiltrated the Mexican law enforcement and judicial systems and is directly involved in street-level trafficking within the United States. This criminal organization is responsible for the transportation, importation, and distribution of multiton quantities of cocaine and marijuana as well as large quantities of heroin and methamphetamine. The organization has a reputation for extreme violence. Ramón Arellano Félix ordered a hit that resulted in the mass murder of 18 people in Ensenada, Baja California, on September 17, 1998. Ramón was eventually killed in a gun battle with police at Mazatlán, Sinaloa, in 2002 (Burton, 2007).

The Tijuana cartel is present in at least 15 Mexican states, with important areas of operation in Tijuana, Mexicali, Tecate, and Ensenada in Baja California and in parts of Sinaloa. Fourteen Mexican drug gang members were killed and eight others were injured in a gun battle in Tijuana near the U.S. border on April 26, 2008, one of the bloodiest shootouts in the narco-war between the Tijuana cartel and the Sinaloa cartel.

Figure 9.3

Source: U.S. Drug Enforcement Administration, adapted by CRS (P. McGrath 3/2/2007).

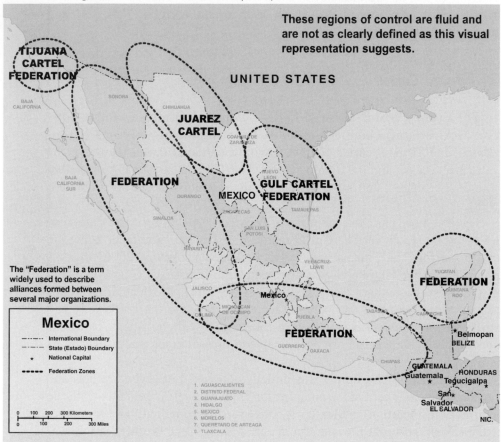

Mexican Cartel Areas of Influence

The Sonora Cartel

The *Sonora cartel* was formerly a Mexico-based criminal cartel. When the cartel collapsed, its leaders were brought into the Tijuana and Sinaloa cartels. The DEA considered the Sonora cartel one of the oldest and best-established cartels. Its roots were in the Guadalajara cartel, which dissolved after the 1989 arrest of its co-founder, Miguel Ángel Félix Gallardo (Congressional Research Service, 2007). The Sonora cartel had direct links to Colombian drug cartels and operated routes into California, Arizona, Texas, and Nevada.

The Sonora cartel is believed to be one of the earliest cartels to begin shipping cocaine from Colombia, particularly from the Cali cartel. The cartel was involved in the cultivation and distribution of marijuana primarily; however, secondary functions included the transportation and distribution of methamphetamine. Operating out of northern central Mexico, the cartel was believed to smuggle drugs into Arizona, Texas, and California from a network of ranches along the northern border region, where the drugs were stored prior to shipment. The Sonora cartel has been specifically linked to Hermosillo, Agua Prieta, Guadalajara, Culiacán, San Luis Potosi, Durango, Sinaloa, and Sonora (Congressional Research Service, 2007).

The La Familia (the Family) Michoacana Cartel

La Familia Michoacana is yet another powerful drug-trafficking cartel based in the Mexican state of Michoacán. Formerly allied to the Gulf cartel—as part of the Zetas— in 2006, La Familia Michoacana split off as its own organization. Its leader, Nazario Moreno González, known as El Más Loco (The Craziest One), advocates the cartel's right to eliminate enemies. He carries a "bible" of his own sayings and insists that his army of traffickers and enforcers avoid using the drugs they sell. Nazario Moreno's partners are José de Jesús Méndez Vargas, Servando Gómez Martínez, and Dionicio Loya Plancarte, each of whom has a bounty of $2 million for his capture (Congressional Research Service, 2007).

La Familia was first established in the 1980s with the stated purpose of bringing order to Michoacán and helping to protect the poor. Initially, La Familia formed as a group of vigilantes, spurred to power to counter interloping kidnappers and drug dealers, who were their stated enemies. Since then, it has capitalized on its reputation, building its myth, power, and reach to transition into a criminal gang itself (Drug Enforcement Administration, 2009e).

La Familia emerged to the foreground in the 1990s as the Gulf cartel's paramilitary group, designed to seize control of the illegal drug trade in Michoacán state from rival drug cartels. Trained with Los Zetas, in 2006 the group splintered off into an independent drug-trafficking operation. La Familia has a strong rivalry with both Los Zetas and the Beltrán-Leyva cartel but strong ties with the Sinaloa cartel and the Tijuana Arellano Félix cartel, making them one of the strongest cartels in Mexico (Grayson, 2009).

The La Familia cartel is sometimes described as quasi-religious because its current leaders, Moreno González and Méndez Vargas, refer to their assassinations and beheadings as "divine justice." They may have direct or indirect ties with devotees of the New Jerusalem religious movement, which is noted for its concern for justice issues.

The "bible" of La Familia's boss Nazario Moreno González was seized by Mexican federal agents and was shown to reveal an ideology that mixes evangelical-style self-help practices with insurgent peasant slogans. Moreno González seems to have based much of his doctrine on the work of Christian writer John Eldredge. The Mexican justice department stated in a report that Gonzalez Moreno has made Eldredge's book, *Salvaje de Corazón* (*Wild at Heart*), required reading for La Familia gang members and has paid rural teachers and the National Council of Educational Development (CONAFE) to circulate Eldredge's writings throughout the Michoacán countryside. An idea central to Eldredge's message is that every man must have "a battle to fight, a beauty to rescue and an adventure to live." Eldredge quotes from Isaiah 63, which describes God wearing blood-stained clothes, spattered as though he had been treading a wine press.

The La Familia cartel emphasizes religion and family values during recruitment and has placed banners in areas of operations, claiming that it does not tolerate substance abuse or exploitation of women and children. According to Mexico Public Safety Secretary Genaro Garcia Luna, it recruits members from drug rehabilitation clinics by helping addicts recover and then forces them into service for the drug cartel (those who refuse are killed). Advancement within the organization depends as much on regular attendance at prayer meetings as on target practice. The cartel gives loans to farmers, businesses, schools, and churches, and it advertises its benevolence in local newspapers to gain social support (Grayson, 2009; Drug Enforcement Administration, 2009e).

In April 2009, about 400 federal police agents raided a christening party for a baby born to a cartel member. Among the 44 detained was Rafael Cedeño Hernández (El Cede), the gang's second in command and in charge of indoctrinating the new recruits in the cartel's religious values, morals, and ethics (Associated Press, 2010; Drug Enforcement Administration, 2009e). In July of the same year, Servando Gómez Martínez (La Tuta) identified himself as the "chief of operations" of the cartel. In his televised message, Gómez stated, "La Familia was created to look after the interests of our people and our family. We are a necessary evil." And when asked what La Familia really wanted, Gómez replied, "The only thing we want is peace and tranquility." President Felipe Calderón's government refuses to strike a deal with the cartel and has rejected their calls for dialogue.

Even by Mexican standards, La Familia has been known to be unusually violent. Its members use murder and torture to quash rivals while building a social base in the Mexican state of Michoacán. It is the fastest-growing cartel in the country's drug war. In one incident in Uruapan in 2006, the cartel members tossed five decapitated heads onto the dance floor of the Sol y Sombra night club along with a message that read "The Family doesn't kill for money. It doesn't kill women. It doesn't kill innocent people, only those who deserve to die. Know that this is divine justice" (Drug Enforcement Administration, 2009e).

The cartel has moved from smuggling and selling drugs and turned itself into a much more ambitious criminal organization that acts as a parallel state in much of Michoacán. It extorts "taxes" from businesses, pays for community projects, controls petty crime, and settles some local disputes. Despite its short history, it has emerged as Mexico's largest supplier of methamphetamines to the United States, with supply channels running deep into middle America, and has increasingly become involved in the distribution of cocaine, marijuana, and other narcotics (Richey, 2009).

Michael Braun, former DEA chief of operations, states that the cartel operates *superlabs* in Mexico that are capable of producing up to 100 pounds of meth in eight hours. However, according to DEA officials, the cartel claims to oppose the sale of drugs to Mexicans. It also sells pirated DVDs, smuggles people to the United States, and runs a debt-collecting service by kidnapping defaulters. Because cartel members often use fake (and sometimes original) uniforms of several police agencies, most of their kidnap victims are stopped under false pretenses of routine inspections or report of stolen vehicles and then taken hostage (Drug Enforcement Administration, 2009e).

Twenty municipal officials have been murdered by La Familia in Michoacán, including two mayors. Having established its authority, the cartel then names local police chiefs. In May 2009, the Mexican Federal Police detained 10 mayors of Michoacán and 20 other local officials suspected of being associated with the cartel. On July 11, 2009, a cartel lieutenant—Arnoldo Rueda Medina—was arrested; La Familia members attacked the federal police station in Morelia to try to free Rueda shortly after his arrest. During the attacks, two soldiers and three federal policemen were killed. When that failed, cartel members attacked federal police installations in at least a half-dozen Michoacán cities in retribution (Richey, 2009). Three days later, on July 14, 2009, the cartel tortured and murdered 12 Mexican federal police agents who were investigating crime in Michoacán state and dumped their bodies along the side of a mountain highway, along with a written message: "So that you come for another. We will be waiting for you here." President Calderón responded to the violence by dispatching an additional 1,000 federal police officers to the area.

The infusion of police, which more than tripled the number of officers patrolling the area, angered Michoacán Governor Leonel Godoy Rangel, who called it "an occupation" and said he had not been consulted. The governor's half-brother, Julio César Godoy Toscano, who was elected in July 2009 to the lower house of Congress, was discovered to be a top-ranking member of the La Familia Michoacana drug cartel and accused of being in charge of protection for the cartel. Days later, 10 municipal police officers were arrested in connection with the slayings of the 12 federal agents (Drug Enforcement Administration, 2009e; Richey, 2009).

President Calderón stated that the country's drug cartels had grown so powerful that they now posed a threat to the future of Mexican democracy. His strategy of direct confrontation and law enforcement is not popular with some segments of Mexican society, where battling violent drug gangs has brought out several human rights charges against the Mexican military.

Official Corruption in Mexico

The role of corruption in organized crime was discussed in Chapter 1. Corruption's influence has profoundly impacted the Mexican drug-trafficking industry and hampered enforcement efforts in that country. Like many organized crime groups, Mexican cartels advance their operations, in part, by corrupting or intimidating law enforcement officials. One example is the Nuevo Laredo Police. Nuevo Laredo municipal police have reportedly been involved in the kidnapping of Gulf cartel competitors to hand them over to the Zetas. The Zetas then hold them for ransom or torture them for information about their drug operations (Congressional Research Service, 2007).

Research has shown that some agents of Mexico's Federal Investigative Agency (AFI) work as enforcers for the Sinaloa cartel. The Attorney General's Office (PGR) reported in December 2005 that one-fifth of its officers were under investigation for criminal activity. Specifically, nearly 1,500 of AFI's 7,000 agents were under investigation for suspected criminal activity and 457 were facing charges (Congressional Research Service, 2007). In November 2005, a video depicting the interrogation of four Zetas who revealed their methods of torture, ties to Mexican law enforcement agencies, and recruitment techniques was given to *The Dallas Morning News*. The video ends with the murder of one of the Zetas. The Mexican government sent "mixed signals" about the involvement of AFI agents in the kidnapping of the Zetas, first announcing that eight agents were under investigation and then announcing that AFI agents had no connection to the kidnapping and murder of the four Zetas. However, a report from a nongovernmental organization concluded that AFI agents probably kidnapped the Zetas in the resort city of Acapulco, then handed them over to members of the Sinaloa cartel to be interrogated and executed (Congressional Research Service, 2007).

Since 2005, the Mexican federal government has conducted purges and prosecution of police forces in Nuevo Laredo; Apatzingan, Michoacán; and Tijuana, Baja California. The presidential administration of Vicente Fox (2000–2006) launched *Operation Secure Mexico* in 2005 to combat drug violence and police corruption in cities with high incidences of drug violence. Federal officers arriving in Nuevo Laredo were fired on by municipal police, leading to the arrest of 41 municipal police and the suspension of the entire 700-member police force in order to investigate corruption. Less than one-half were later cleared to return to duty (Congressional Research Service, 2007). Later in that same year, federal police rescued 44 people, most of whom claimed they had been kidnapped by municipal police before being transferred to Gulf cartel safe houses. In spite of these efforts, reports indicate that the Zetas continue to have influence over Nuevo Laredo's municipal police and that warring cartels are gaining influence in all law enforcement present in the city (Congressional Research Service, 2007).

In 2006 Mexico launched the Northern Border (*Frontera Norte*) initiative, which included the deployment of 800 Federal Protective Police (PFP) officers to Nuevo Laredo. These officers are in addition to the 300 federal officers already deployed in Nuevo Laredo under Operation Secure Mexico. In March 2006, four PFP officers were killed after locating a cartel safe house. Federal officials announced that initial evidence indicated that municipal police officers were responsible for the killings (Pinkerton, 2005).

The anticartel operations begun by President Calderón in 2006 included ballistic checks of police weapons in places such as Tijuana, where there is concern that police are also working for the cartels. In 2007 more than 100 state police officers in the northern state of Nuevo León were suspended due to corruption concerns, and 284 federal police commanders were ousted, including federal commanders of all 31 states and the federal district. These commanders were suspended and subjected to drug and polygraph tests. The Mexican government immediately named replacements for the dismissed commanders, who were able to pass an array of examinations designed to weed out corrupt officers, including financial checks, drug testing, and psychological and medical screening.

Drug Violence in Mexico

Since 2008, Mexico has experienced an extraordinarily high incidence of violence. To some extent, the high levels of violence are an indicator of the successful crime crackdown campaigns by military and law enforcement officials there. Three types of violence have been identified in Mexico:

- Intra-cartel violence that occurs among and between members of the same criminal syndicate
- Inter-cartel violence that occurs between rival groups
- Cartel-versus-government violence

Intra- and inter-cartel violence has long been associated with the Mexican drug trade, but the current levels of violence are unprecedented. It is instructive to consider the background of the "culture of violence" associated with Mexican drug-trafficking organizations, along with the cyclical nature of the "violence epidemics" seen in Mexico. A recent historical example is the cross-border killing spree engaged in by Zetas operatives in the Laredo–Nuevo Laredo area during 2004–2005 (Congressional Research Service, 2007). Since 2007, there have been more than 22,000 drug-related murders in Mexico, as reported by the Mexican Attorney General's Office. Stories abound about the arrest of a "pozolero" (stew-maker), a killer who disposes of his victims' body parts in barrels of acid, or the discovery of a mass grave containing the remains of countless victims decomposing under layers of lime. These and other grisly tactics are not new, however; what is new are the sustained efforts of Mexican trafficking organizations to use violence as a tool to weaken public support for the government's antidrug efforts.

Traffickers have made a determined effort to send a public message through their reign of violence. Particularly worrisome are tactics intended to intimidate police, public officials, and law-abiding citizens. The cartels are known today to resort to leaving the beheaded and mutilated bodies of their tortured victims out for public display with the intent of intimidating government officials and the public alike. Moreover, the intimidation of public and police officials through violence or the threat of violence has a more insidious side. Not all corruption is a clear-cut, money-for-cooperation negotiation.

Rather, the intimidation of officials, which includes threats against their lives or their families' lives, is a much more widespread and effective tactic and probably accounts for the extent to which law enforcement officials have been corrupted in Mexico.

Pressure on the Traffickers

To a great extent, successes by the military and law enforcement have provided the basis for much of the violence. Tens of thousands of military troops have been deployed specifically to confront traffickers in "hot spots" throughout the country. Moreover, specialized law enforcement operations targeting specific cartel members or import/export locations have interrupted supply routes both in and out of Mexico. Additionally, since 2008, entry ports for large maritime shipments of cocaine from South America, previously controlled by the cartels, are patrolled and inspected by members of Mexico's armed forces. The lucrative transportation corridors within Mexico and into the United States, which were once completely controlled by cartel "gatekeepers" and "plaza bosses," are now populated with military checkpoints and monitored by Mexican law enforcement. As a result, closed supply routes translate to extreme competition between the drug-trafficking organizations that control routes that are still viable. Making things worse are drifting alliances, longstanding feuds, and record-breaking seizures by the Mexican national government.

The Problem of Spillover Violence

Extreme violence by Mexican traffickers presents problems for both Mexico and the United States. For example, in 2009, U.S. intelligence and law enforcement agencies worked to reach a consensus view on what has been termed "spillover" violence and the violent tactics used by Mexican trafficking groups. *Spillover violence* involves deliberate, planned attacks by drug cartels on U.S. assets, including civilian, military, or law enforcement officials, innocent U.S. citizens, or physical institutions such as government buildings, consulates, or businesses. This definition does not include trafficker-on-trafficker violence.

AP Photo/Str

Police forensic experts examine the scene where three men were found dead along a highway on the edge of Nuevo Laredo, Mexico, on May 11, 2007. The men were tortured and shot in the head and were found near a sign bearing a threat to the Sinaloa drug cartel from a rival gang. Another body was later found nearby.

Spillover violence presents a complicated issue. It is important to understand the difference between the intentional targeting of innocent civilians in the United States (or official U.S. government interests in Mexico or the United States) and actions that are characteristic of violent drug culture, such as the killing of someone who owes a drug debt to the organization. Certain isolated incidents in the United States, such as the torture by a Mexican trafficker of a Dominican drug customer in Atlanta, are frightening but do not represent a dramatic departure from the violence that has always been associated with the drug trade.

Younger-generation traffickers pose much of the risk of spillover violence, since their approach to the drug trade is less rational and profit-minded than that of their "elders," or multinational street and prison gangs working in concert with Mexican cartels as enforcers and street-level drug distributors. As the Mexican government has successfully disrupted the trafficker's organizational structure, less experienced "junior" cartel members have been assuming roles formerly held by traffickers of long standing who, though violent, tended to be more thoughtful and cautious in their actions.

One of the most significant ramifications of the unrest along the border has been a string of kidnappings involving U.S. citizens. Between May 2004 and May 2005, there were 35 reported abductions of U.S. citizens in this region. Thirty-four of these abductions occurred in Nuevo Laredo and involved people who had crossed the border.

It is reported that these numbers probably represent only a fraction of the actual occurrences because many kidnappings of U.S. citizens go unreported. There are two reasons for the underreporting of abductions along the border: First, victims and their families fear reprisal from kidnappers. Second, because many victims are alleged to be involved in drug trafficking, they and their families are reluctant to cooperate with law enforcement.

Nuevo Laredo

The city of Nuevo Laredo, directly across the border from Laredo, Texas, has been particularly hard hit by drug violence since the Sinaloa cartel began to contest the Gulf cartel's domination of Nuevo Laredo following the arrest of Osiel Cárdenas. The warring cartels are thought to compete for influence over law enforcement and the media, and they use intimidation and murder to further their cause. This is the most publicized of Mexico's turf wars due to the intensity of the violence and its proximity to the United States. More than 60 U.S. citizens have been kidnapped in Nuevo Laredo since the beginning of the turf war, and as of 2007, at least 20 were still missing (Congressional Research Service, 2007). Reports indicate that hundreds of Mexicans have been kidnapped in Nuevo Laredo, and murders continue to increase. Nuevo Laredo has not had a police chief in nearly a year due to the violence. The most recent chief resigned, and his predecessor was murdered.

U.S. Ambassador Tony Garza closed the U.S. consulate in Nuevo Laredo from July 29 to August 8, 2005, due to safety concerns and submitted a diplomatic note to the Mexican government in January 2006 expressing concern over violence in this border city. Journalistic enterprises have been affected as well. In 2006, gunmen suspected of ties with drug traffickers critically injured a reporter in an attack on offices of the daily *El Mañana* after it published a picture of a federal police officer, linking him to the Sinaloa cartel. The paper subsequently announced that it would scale back coverage of drug violence. In July 2007, drug cartels reportedly threatened to kill an unnamed U.S. journalist in Laredo for writing reports on the cartels. Around this time, the Committee to Protect Journalists noted a high level of self-censorship among media in Nuevo Laredo and other parts of northern Mexico, and both the *Dallas Morning News* and *San Antonio Express-News* took measures to protect their journalists working in the area (Congressional Research Service, 2007).

On February 19, 2007, the day after President Calderón announced the expansion of his counternarcotics operation into Nuevo Laredo, gunmen believed to be working for the Gulf cartel wounded Mexican Congressman Horacio Garza and killed his driver in Nuevo Laredo. In April 2007, the State Department began advising Americans to use caution when traveling in Mexico due to drug violence.

NARCOTERRORISM

A distinction exists between the motives of organized crime groups and the motives of terrorist groups. Organized crime is generally associated with a profit motive, as opposed to terrorist groups, who share more political motives. On the other hand, *narcoterrorism* is characterized as "a subset of terrorism in which terrorist groups or associated individuals, participate directly or indirectly in the cultivation, manufacture, transportation, or distribution of controlled substances and the monies derived from these activities" (Hutchinson, 2002).

The term *narcoterrorism* originated in 1983 with former President Fernando Belaúnde Terry of Peru, when he described terrorist-type attacks against his nation's antinarcotics police. Narcoterrorism is generally understood to mean the attempts of narcotics traffickers to influence the policies of a government or a society through violence and intimidation and to hamper the enforcement of the law by the threat or use of such violence. As a case in point, Colombian Pablo Escobar's ruthless violence in his dealings with the Colombian and Peruvian governments is probably one of the best-known examples of narcoterrorism.

The term has become a subject of controversy, largely due to its use in discussing violent opposition to the U.S. government's "war on drugs." The term has also been used increasingly for known terrorist organizations that engage in drug-trafficking activity to fund their operations and gain recruits and expertise. These organizations include FARC (Revolutionary Armed Forced of

Colombia), ELN (National Liberation Army), and AUC (United Self Defense Forces of Colombia) in Colombia and Peru's PCP-SL (the Communist Party of Peru).

The links between narcoterrorism groups and drug trafficking include these:

- Some groups raise funds through extortion or by protecting laboratory operations. In return for cash payments or possibly in exchange for weapons, the groups protect cocaine laboratories in southern Colombia. They also encourage coca planting and discourage licit alternative development.
- In 2001, three members of the Irish Republican Army (IRA) were arrested in Colombia for collaborating with the FARC. The three men were charged with traveling on false passports and providing the FARC with weapons instruction.
- Some terrorist groups apparently have assisted drug-trafficking groups in transporting and storing cocaine and marijuana within Colombia. In particular, some groups protect clandestine airstrips in southern Colombia.
- Elements of some FARC units in southern Colombia are directly involved in drug-trafficking activities, such as controlling local cocaine-base markets. At least one FARC front has served as a cocaine source of supply for one international drug-trafficking organization.
- Although there is no evidence that the FARC or ELN have elements established in the United States, their drug-trafficking activity impacts the United States and Europe.
- Several self-defense groups also raise funds through extortion or by protecting laboratory operations in northern and central Colombia (Office of National Drug Control Policy, 2010b).

The FARC has been characterized as the most dangerous international terrorist group based in the Western hemisphere. It occupies large swaths of territory in Colombia and is a hierarchical organization, which in 2010 comprised 12,000 to 18,000 members (DEA, 2010). At the lowest level, the FARC is made up of 77 distinct military units, called *fronts*, organized by geographical location. These in turn are grouped into seven *blocs*. The FARC is led by a seven-member Secretariat and a 27-member Central General Staff, or Estado Mayor, responsible for setting the cocaine policies of the FARC. The FARC is responsible for the production of more than half the world's supply of cocaine and nearly two-thirds of the cocaine imported into the United States, and it is the world's leading cocaine manufacturer (DEA, 2010). The FARC initially involved itself in the cocaine and cocaine paste trade by imposing a "tax" on individuals involved in every stage of cocaine production.

Later, FARC leadership ordered that the FARC become the exclusive buyer of the raw cocaine paste used to make cocaine in all areas under FARC occupation. In the late 1990s, the FARC leadership met and voted unanimously in favor of a number of resolutions, including resolutions to expand coca production in areas of Colombia under FARC control; expand the FARC's international distribution routes; increase the number of crystallization labs in which cocaine paste would be converted into cocaine; appoint members within each Front to be in charge of coca production; raise prices that the FARC would pay to *campesinos* (peasant farmers) from whom they purchased cocaine paste; and mandate that better chemicals be used to increase the quality of cocaine paste (DEA, 2010).

In April 2010, the U.S. Department of Justice indicted two top members of the 16th Front of the FARC, including Juan Jose Martinez-Vega, known as Chiguiro, and Erminso Cuevas Cabrera, known as Mincho. Martinez-Vega worked as the FARC's chief associate in its 16th Front, exchanging large quantities of cocaine for tons of weapons, explosives, ammunition, and other logistical supplies. In that capacity, Martinez-Vega coordinated a network of arms suppliers and cocaine traffickers throughout Colombia and neighboring countries. Cuevas Cabrera, the brother of FARC Southern Bloc commander Fabian Ramirez, worked as the chief of cocaine manufacturing for the FARC's 14th Front. In that capacity, Cuevas Cabrera directed the weekly production of thousands of pounds of cocaine at hidden jungle laboratories controlled by the FARC and coordinated the sale and transportation of this cocaine (DEA, 2010).

The 16th Front has been known for operating out of a remote village in eastern Colombia, where they operate an airstrip, engage in trafficking activities, and control all the operations in that particular arena. The cocaine that the 16th Front transports out of that area is paid for with currency, weapons, and equipment (Office of National Drug Policy, 2010b).

In March 2002, the Colombian Army and the Colombian National Police reclaimed the demilitarized zone from the FARC and uncovered significant evidence of the FARC's involvement in drug trafficking. The police went in, and in the demilitarized zone they found two major cocaine laboratories. In all the police seized five tons of processed cocaine from that particular site, demonstrating the enormity of this one processing site alone. Also present at the site was a 200-foot communications tower that the FARC operated. This seizure was significant in that it was the first time evidence was uncovered that the FARC was involved in the cocaine trade from start to finish, from cultivation to processing and distribution.

The violent activities of the FARC and other groups have not been limited to the country of Colombia. They have also become a destabilizing force along the northern border of Ecuador, where violence and coca-processing activities have increased. Similarly, the FARC's violence and coca-processing activities have also spread to Panama. Venezuela, too, is experiencing increased violence.

In response to insurgent violence, right-wing "self-defense groups" emerged in Colombia during the 1980s. Hundreds of illegal self-defense groups—financed by wealthy cattle ranchers, emerald miners, coffee plantation owners, drug traffickers, and so on—conduct paramilitary operations throughout Colombia. The loose coalition known as the AUC (*Autodefensas Unidas de Colombia*) is the best known of these self-defense groups. Carlos Castano is the most well-recognized leader of the AUC.

In 2000, the United States began funding Plan Colombia, intending to eradicate drug crops and to take action against drug lords accused of engaging in narcoterrorism (e.g., the leaders of the FARC and the AUC). The U.S. government is funding large-scale drug eradication campaigns and supporting Colombian military operations seeking the extradition of notorious commanders such as Manuel Marulanda Velez, among others.

Manuel Marulanda Velez, left, the leader of Colombia's Revolutionary Armed Forces (FARC), listens to the government's chief negotiator, Victor G. Ricardo, center, accompanied by rebel negotiator Raul Reyes, right, during peace talks in 2000.

AP Photo/ANCOL, German Enciso

Although al-Qa'ida is often said to finance its activities through drug trafficking, the *9/11 Commission Report* notes that "while the drug trade was a source of income for the Taliban, it did not serve the same purpose for al-Qa'ida, and

Critical Thinking Task

Terrorists sometimes use drug trafficking as a means of raising funds. How can law enforcement differentiate between terrorists and drug runners when these crimes overlap? Should penalties differ depending on the motive behind the trafficking operation?

there is no reliable evidence that bin Laden was involved in or made his money through drug trafficking." The organization gains most of its finances through donations, particularly those from "wealthy Saudi individuals."

CUBAN DRUG TRAFFICKERS

A discussion of Latino drug-trafficking organizations should also include the historic role of Cuban criminals. Since 1959, more than one million Cuban refugees have arrived in the United States. Although many have come seeking political freedom, a significant number of Cuban immigrants have been documented as having close involvement in drug-trafficking operations. Three periods of mass Cuban immigration to the United States occurred as follows:

1. Before and after the fall of the Batista regime until Fidel Castro halted emigration in 1959

2. Between 1965 and 1972, during the Camarioca boatlift "freedom flotilla," prompting the family reunification program under which more than 250,000 Cubans migrated to the United States
3. Between April 21 and November 10, 1980, during a boat lift from Mariel Harbor, bringing nearly 125,000 new Cuban refugees to the United States

Unquestionably, the greatest concentration of criminals came in the Mariel Harbor exodus, with nearly 2 percent of those arriving in the United States having been classified as prostitutes, criminals, drug users, or vagrants. The criminal element of these Cuban immigrants was soon given the name *marielito*, meaning criminal or undesirable.

The sophistication and organizational structure of the criminals who immigrated during the first two boatlifts was greater than that of the Cubans who came over on the Mariel boatlift. In particular, many of the earlier Cuban immigrants had ties with more traditional and well-established criminal organizations in the United States, particularly gambling and drug operations associated with Meyer Lansky and Santo Trafficante Jr. In addition, many of the early Cuban refugees participated in U.S. government-supported paramilitary and intelligence operations directed against the Castro government. As a result, they were given considerable training in intelligence techniques (including smuggling) by the CIA and were provided with financial and logistical support. When U.S. support for these activities ended in the 1960s, many of these immigrants had no lawful trade to fall back on, so they initiated organized crime activities to support themselves. The marielitos, on the other hand, demonstrated a great propensity for violence from the beginning.

During the 1960s, two major Cuban groups became well established in the United States: La Compana, a well-known drug-trafficking organization that concentrates primarily on cocaine trafficking, and The Corporation, headed by Jose Miguel Battle, which concentrates primarily on gambling operations.

The marielitos have been documented as joining established crime organizations such as La Compana, working as collectors and enforcers. They have also been associated with Colombian cartels in the same capacity. Although some debate continues over the exact number of marielitos that were part of the Mariel boat lift, there have been widespread reports of violent marielito activity in such cities as Miami, New York, Las Vegas, and Los Angeles.

As of the preparation of this book, the influence of Cuban trafficking organizations is expanding, albeit at a slower rate than other groups. The extent of their expansion relates largely to their establishment of indoor marijuana sites in the Southeast United States—in particular Georgia, Alabama, and North Carolina (National Drug Threat Assessment, 2010). Due to their expanding working relationships with Mexican drug-trafficking organizations, Cuban traffickers are becoming more and more involved with methamphetamine, cocaine, and heroin trafficking.

Figure 9.4
Source: President's Commission on Organized Crime, 1986.

> The Mariel boatlift had its genesis on April 1, 1980, when a small band of Cubans on a city bus attempted to gain political asylum by crashing the gates of the Peruvian Embassy. One Cuban guard at the gate accidently killed another guard while trying to stop the bus. Fidel Castro was enraged and publicly announced the removal of all guards from the gates. Within days over 10,000 people had crowded into the embassy grounds, requesting political asylum. Eventually Castro allowed them to be flown out of the country. This group and those that followed later included primarily decent and working-class people that genuinely sought liberty. Castro, however, proclaimed the refugees to be the scum of Cuban society. When the exodus continued, he tried to prove his description by forcibly including convicts, hard-core criminals, prostitutes, and the mentally ill among those that left by boat from Mariel.

The Mariel Boatlift

SOUTHWEST ASIA

Afghanistan, the Taliban, and Osama bin Laden

The Islamic State of Afghanistan has been a major source country for the cultivation, processing, and trafficking of opiate and cannabis products. In 2000, Afghanistan produced more than 70 percent of the world's supply of illicit opium. Morphine base, heroin, and hashish produced in Afghanistan are trafficked worldwide. Due to the warfare-induced decimation of the country's economic infrastructure, narcotics are a major source of income in Afghanistan.

U.S. intelligence confirmed a connection between Afghanistan's former ruling Taliban and international terrorist Osama bin Laden and the al-Qa'ida organization. Al-Qa'ida leader Osama bin Laden has been documented as being involved in the financing and facilitation of heroin-trafficking activities (Hutchinson, 2002). For decades, Afghanistan has been a formidable producer of opium. According to the official U.S. government estimates for 2001, Afghanistan produced an estimated 74 metric tons of opium from 1,685 hectares of land under opium poppy cultivation. This is a significant decrease from the 3,656 metric tons of opium produced from 64,510 hectares of land under opium poppy cultivation in 2000 (Hutchinson, 2002).

In 2002, opium prices in Afghanistan ranged from 9 to 11 times higher than in 2000 (February 2000: $30–43/kilogram, March 2002: $333/kilogram). The war on terrorism during 2001 markedly affected the production of opium in Afghanistan. During that year, the U.S. government estimated that 74 tons of opium were produced, down from more than 3,600 metric tons (75% of world production) one year earlier (Hutchinson, 2002). By October 2009, the Taliban were back in the opium production business and supporting the opium trade and deriving funding from it (Schmitt, 2009).

The United Wa State Army

Methamphetamine and heroin trafficking finances the efforts of the United Wa State Army (UWSA), which, at 20,000 members, is said to be the largest ethnic army in Myanmar (formerly known as Burma) (Johnston, 2009). The UWSA exists primarily as a separatist organization, seeking autonomy from Myanmar's central government. There is no recognized Wa State in Myanmar, which is divided into divisions, states, and special regions. UWSA funds its separatist activities by being the major international drug-trafficking organization in the region.

ASIAN ORGANIZED CRIME

Asian gangs compose yet another type of organized crime group involved in the drug trade. Chinese gangs in particular have demonstrated considerable growth in drug-trafficking activities. From 1970 to 1980, for example, the number of Chinese immigrants in the United States escalated from approximately 435,000 to about 806,000. This increase in population might partially reflect the fact that Chinese traffickers are becoming more proficient in their smuggling of Southeast Asian heroin to the United States.

In 2010, the National Drug Threat Assessment concluded that Asian trafficking organizations have filled a niche by trafficking high-potency marijuana and MDMA—a drug not typically trafficked by Mexican, Colombian, or Dominican trafficking organizations (National Drug Threat Assessment, 2010).

Chinese Organized Crime

Chinese organized crime groups have always posed a particular difficulty for U.S. law enforcement. Culturally and ethnically organized groups are among the most difficult to infiltrate and accumulate intelligence about. Chinese syndicates, operating primarily in ethnically defined, tightly organized Chinese communities of many major cities, have been virtually impossible to penetrate. The triads, tongs, and Chinese street gangs operating in the United States have traditionally been able to deflect most law enforcement efforts to control their activities. That problem has become even more difficult at the turn of the twenty-first century because a fourth Chinese organized crime entity—syndicates from mainland China—has now also established a presence in the United States (Chin, 1996; Robinson, 1999).

The large, traditionally organized *triads*, headquartered in Hong Kong, Macau, and Taiwan, continue to be the largest Chinese organized crime groups operating worldwide. Triads, most of which trace their origins to seventeenth-century China, continue to control traditional illicit enterprises such as extortion, illegal gambling, gun running, and drug trafficking. However, these newer mainland criminal organizations may be more aggressive and more difficult to control. First, they are not encumbered by the traditional organizational structure of the triads, which is more ceremonial than functional in the world of organized crime. The newer groups tend to be more loosely organized and more flexible. They are therefore much more responsive to law enforcement pressure and to economic fluctuations and opportunities. Second, they have moved more aggressively than the triads into newer enterprises such as software piracy, product counterfeiting, credit card fraud, and computer chip theft, allowing them to quickly build vast reserves to finance their forays into drug trafficking.

Traditionally, the triads established close working relationships with ethnic Chinese groups in major cities on the Pacific Rim of the United States and in Europe. Working with *tongs* and street gangs, they easily established local criminal structures to facilitate their enterprises and to purchase their drugs. The newer criminal syndicates from the mainland have apparently broken this monopoly and now deal directly with the tongs and the street gangs themselves. This means that, like the more traditional triads, they now have a broad range of criminal contacts in many countries that can broker deals and provide logistical support.

Chinese organized crime groups have for decades had a strong presence in the many ethnic Chinese neighborhoods and urban enclaves around the world. Gambling operations, prostitution, loan sharking, and narcotics trafficking were the mainstay of these criminal organizations operating through the triads, tongs, and street gangs. What has changed is that another, newer type of criminal syndicate has been added to the milieu.

Chinese criminal organizations, no matter their origin, have always derived great strength from their ability to overlook ethnic differences and cooperate freely and openly with other groups around the world. In the United States and Europe, for example, Chinese organized crime groups have worked closely with Italian, Dominican, and even, on occasion, Mexican and Colombian drug traffickers in trafficking heroin.

The well-established ethnic Chinese communities of Europe and North America have created established and relatively safe footholds for Chinese organized crime, thus making the United States and Europe major markets for illegal goods and services. In addition to the United States, Chinese organized crime activity is particularly prominent in the Netherlands, the United Kingdom, and Germany. Since the late 1980s and early 1990s, Chinese criminal organizations have also established strong footholds in central Europe, a major conduit for moving illegal Chinese immigrants to Western Europe.

Triads and Tongs

Although traditional triad societies are based in Hong Kong, Macau, or Taiwan, they have also exercised great power in every country that has a sizeable émigré Chinese community. Estimates are that the triads, collectively, have a worldwide membership that exceeds 100,000. The triads are traditionally organized associations of Chinese businessmen and Chinese organized criminals who are involved in a panoply of criminal enterprises. Most Hong Kong-based triads have evolved over the years from traditional cultural groups into loose-knit associations of both illicit and licit businessmen, cooperating with other and sharing mutual business interests. Contrary to some perceptions, triad leaders neither dictate what criminal enterprises their members should pursue nor receive any direct monetary remuneration from those enterprises. They simply provide introductions and facilitate mutual association.

There are 60 different triad societies operating in Hong Kong alone. Hong Kong's largest triad is the Sun Yee On, which is also the only remaining triad with the traditional hierarchical structure. The 14K triad, probably the second most influential in Hong Kong, has abandoned traditional hierarchies and is now a loose confederation of more that 15 separate groups. In addition to their drug-trafficking activities, the Hong Kong triads have been expanding their criminal enterprises into new ventures, including high-tech computer crimes and the manipulation of the stock and futures markets. By the 1990s the Hong Kong triads were engaged in an expansion that would have been unthinkable just a few years earlier, extending their criminal activities from Hong Kong into the Guangdong region of south China.

The largest triads, such as Hong Kong's 14K and Sun Yee On and Taiwan's United Bamboo, have autonomous branches extending worldwide. It is important to understand that these are affiliated organizations—not extensions of one massive criminal organization into other countries. In addition, in response to the booming economy of the United States during the Clinton administration, the triads began investing heavily in legitimate businesses in the United States and Europe.

Triad groups frequently share resources and cooperate on specific projects, but it is important to understand that there is no international triad organization and no centralized control of triad groups. Enterprises such as alien smuggling tend to center on small-scale triad-affiliated organizations, whereas drug trafficking seems to involve more ad hoc collusion. The key distinction, though, is that it is ad hoc collusion based on mutual interests in a specific project or at a particular point in time, not an overarching criminal conspiracy.

The Chinese Tongs

Chinese criminal enterprises are those ethnic Chinese organized crime groups engaged in racketeering activities. Chinese criminal enterprises can be categorized into two types: traditional criminal enterprises (e.g., Wo Hop To Triad, 14K Triad) and nontraditional Chinese criminal enterprises (e.g., Fuk Ching Gang and Tai Huen Chai, a.k.a. Big Circle Boys). Traditional Chinese criminal enterprises are based in Hong Kong, Macau, and Taiwan. Many nontraditional Chinese criminal enterprises are based in various countries that have sizeable Asian communities.

Traditional Chinese criminal enterprises are triad groups that share the following similarities: (1) a historical origin that can be traced back several hundred years, and (2) a rigid hierarchical organizational structure and a ritual that binds their members together.

For example, San Yee On of the Chiu Chow group was formed exclusively by the Chiu Chow minority people in Hong Kong, has a rigid hierarchical organizational structure, and uses the triad rituals, such as an initiation ceremony for the new members and a promotion ceremony for members promoted to the Office Bearer rank. Leaders of triad societies do not direct the activities of their members in other countries, but their influence is international due to their financial strength and global business and personal connections.

Most of the senior members of these well-established triad societies are quasi-legitimate businessmen. Many of them have obtained foreign passports for themselves and their family members and have diversified their businesses and invested their criminal proceeds in other countries. They cooperate with overseas triad members to undertake international crimes, such as drug trafficking, alien smuggling, credit card fraud, theft of computer equipment and automobiles, piracy of intellectual property, and money laundering.

With some exceptions, the organizational structure of modern-day Chinese triads is flatter and simpler. Most triad societies have been decentralized to the extent that there is no ultimate central committee to unify different factions of the society that fight against one another for turf control. Modern triad members who only look out for their personal benefits are individualistic entrepreneurs. They switch triad societies almost at will and are rarely loyal to the organization to which they belong. They weigh the benefits they can get out of their Dai Lo (Big Brother). If they are not satisfied with the relationship, they can approach a new Dai Lo from another triad group and request to come "under his wings." They use their triad organization as a power base that provides them a network through which they can assemble resources to organize criminal activities for fast money.

Nontraditional Chinese criminal enterprises are organized crime groups operating outside of Hong Kong, Macau, Taiwan, and the People's Republic of China (PRC) that may or may not share the name of a Hong Kong or Taiwan triad but are not otherwise related. Although many nontraditional Chinese criminal enterprises in the United States have ties to Chinese criminal groups in other countries, they are independent entities. For example, Tung On Gang was a major criminal organization in New York City and had expanded its activities in the northeastern and mid-Atlantic states of the United States. The former leader of this gang was a Red Pole (high-level Office Bearer) of San Yee On Triad in Hong Kong. In addition to its usual street gang activities, such as debt collection, protection, and enforcement, Tung On Gang also conducted organized crime activities such as extortion, murder, illegal gambling, alien smuggling, drug trafficking, and money laundering. Tung On Gang's activities were directed locally. San Yee On Triad in Hong Kong was its connection only for importing and distributing Southeast Asian heroin at the wholesale and retail level.

After the 1989 Tiananmen Square incident, the United States adopted a liberal policy in granting People's Republic of China citizens "political asylum," which attracted a large number of Chinese immigrants to this country. Fueled by the dramatic increase of Chinese immigrants and the large amount of money that has continuously flowed into North America from Hong Kong, Taiwan, and recently China, the Chinese communities in North America have grown rapidly and prosperously. This has provided a huge market for local gang members to expand their influence.

To maintain their competitiveness, some strong gang leaders have attempted to solidify their power bases in various Asian communities by forming alliances with gangs in other regions. The dominant position of members of old triad societies from Hong Kong, Taiwan, and Macau and criminally influenced Tongs2 is challenged by newer criminal groups, such as Big Circle Boys and Fuk Ching Gang, which originated in mainland China. It is reported that the freedom with which these newer Chinese organized crime groups can operate in China is unmatched by any other crime groups. They also have contacts worldwide that enable them to carry out various sophisticated crimes that require extensive coordinated efforts of members in other regions or countries. Chinese criminals represent the entire spectrum of Asian criminal enterprises in their criminal activities and their levels of criminality (from the simple street gang members to the quasi-legitimate businessmen with international connections).

Chinese Syndicates from the Mainland

Criminal syndicates based in mainland China (the People's Republic of China, or PRC) are typified by the Big Circle Gang and the Fuk Ching. Both of these gangs have smaller cells operating in Chinese communities around the world. These cells cooperate with each other and with the mainland organizations on an ad hoc basis, but the cells themselves operate autonomously, without centralized authority or direction. Local cell leaders use their connections in Chinese ethnic communities and with the mainland groups to mount what appear to be some very complex criminal operations that are well planned and highly organized. Once again, though, that planning and organization are integral to the cell—not to the overall criminal organization. Because cells have contact with other cells worldwide, they are able to carry out large-scale drug-trafficking, arms-trafficking, and human-trafficking enterprises with surprising ease and success.

Canadian and U.S. law enforcement intelligence analysts report that the Big Circle Gang, the largest of the mainland groups, has become the most active Asian criminal organization in the world and has achieved that status in less than a decade. By the end of the 1990s, the Big Circle Gang had established cells in Canada, the United States, and Europe and was extensively engaged in drug trafficking, human trafficking, vehicle theft and trafficking, financial fraud, product counterfeiting, and high-tech crimes. Big Circle Gang cells are also highly sophisticated in their use of technology, which has made them virtually immune from electronic eavesdropping and surveillance. The Big Circle Gang first surfaced in the United States in the early 1990s and by the end of the decade had major criminal organizations operating in New York, Boston, Seattle, San Francisco, and Los Angeles. The Fuk Ching is best known for its human-trafficking activities but is also heavily involved in drug trafficking, particularly heroin and methamphetamines.

Yakuza

When all the many criminal organizations composing the *yakuza* are considered, the yakuza would have to be among the most powerful and largest of the world's organized crime confederations. Yakuza organizations are extremely diverse in their criminal enterprises. They also tend to be highly structured and well organized. Yakuza organizations not only dominate the Japanese underworld; they are also powerful actors in the legitimate economy. In fact, using their extortionate practice of "sokaiya," they have successfully penetrated all aspects of social, economic, and political life in Japan (Huang and Vaughn, 1992; Shibata 1996; Song and Dombrink, 1994).

There are at least 3,000 separate yakuza-affiliated criminal organizations in Japan, with about 90,000 members. Approximately 60 percent of them are housed under the aegis of three large yakuza organizations: the Yamaguchi-Gumi, the Sumiyoshi-Kai, and the Inagawa-Kai. These three associations of yakuza groups control most gun trafficking, drug trafficking, human trafficking, prostitution, illegal gambling, extortion, and white-collar criminal activity in Japan. Scholars estimate the scope of yakuza activity in Japan amounts to an annual revenue of about $13 billion.

Most yakuza criminal enterprises are based in Japan, although yakuza groups have a well-established presence (often in legitimate business activities) in Australia, the United States, and most of Asia. Transnational criminal activity engaged in by yakuza groups primarily involves drugs, guns, and trafficking in women for prostitution in the Japanese market.

Most yakuza organizations purchase their heroin and methamphetamine supplies from Chinese organized crime groups based in Taiwan and Hong Kong. In recent years, yakuza organizations have also established working relationships with South American drug traffickers as a means of obtaining cocaine to be sold in Japan. Chinese and Russian organized crime groups are primary yakuza sources for firearms. The arms-trafficking business is one of the most profitable for yakuza groups because of extremely restrictive Japanese laws regulating firearms. About 90 percent of the firearms in Japan originate from international sources.

Yakuza organizations also are heavily involved in the international trafficking of human beings, particular foreign workers for the Japanese construction industry and foreign women for yakuza-owned entertainment and prostitution businesses. Yamaguchi-Gumi-affiliated groups are particularly active in the prostitution business and rely heavily on women imported from Russia, Southeast Asia, and Latin America. There is little or no evidence that yakuza groups traffic women to the United States.

Most yakuza transnational crime activities are used to supply or support criminal enterprises internal to Japan. In the 1990s, yakuza organizations apparently began developing more permanent working relationships with Russian organized crime groups. In 1992 the Yamaguchi-Gumi established a more permanent working relationship with Russian organized groups as suppliers of firearms and prostitutes. The establishment of more open trade arrangements between Japan and Russia and the scheduling of regular flights between major cities in Russia and Japan have facilitated this relationship.

Yakuza groups traffic drugs in Japan, but there is little evidence that they are involved in drug trafficking in the United States. The real threat posed by yakuza in the United States is in the area of legitimate business investment and money laundering. Yakuza groups are heavy investors in U.S. and Canadian real estate, with particularly heavy investments in golf courses and hotels. Yakuza groups also launder their criminal profits in the United States by playing the U.S. stock market and making substantial and potentially destabilizing investments. The Inagawa-Kai yakuza confederation, which is involved in drug and arms trafficking, extortion, investment frauds, and money laundering, has invested heavily in Hawaii and the states on the West Coast of the United States.

Vietnamese Gangs

A growing threat to Vietnamese communities throughout the United States is the expansion of Vietnamese youth gangs. Preying mostly on members of their own communities, their crimes include extortion, rape, assault, auto theft, murder, and a relatively new brand of robbery: the home invasion. The ages of the members typically range from 14 to 23. Gambling houses are often operated in the homes of Vietnamese gang members and their associates, making it difficult for police to conduct surprise raids.

NIGERIAN DRUG TRAFFICKERS

Nigerian-based organized crime groups have been heavily involved in the smuggling of large quantities of Southeast Asian heroin to the United States since the mid-1980s. Early Nigerian drug trafficking revolved around groups of Nigerian naval officers who were being trained in India and gained access to Southwest Asian heroin, which they subsequently moved on to the United States. Subsequently, Nigerian criminal organizations shifted their sourcing from Southwest to Southeast Asian heroin, primarily from Thailand. Nigerian traffickers obtain their heroin in Thailand and then pay couriers (usually fellow Nigerians) to smuggle small amounts of heroin to the United States on commercial aircraft. The fee paid to drug couriers is far in excess of what a Nigerian citizen could legitimately earn in a year (Rake, 1995; Smith, Holmes, and Kaufmann, 1999).

Nigerian drug couriers tend to use rudimentary and rather crude techniques to move drugs. Devices such as hollowed-out shoes and false-bottom suitcases are common modalities of smuggling. In addition, some couriers engage in a practice known as *swallowing*, which involves the ingestion of up to 150 condoms full of heroin that will be expelled upon the couriers' arrival in the United States. This is a dangerous practice because the breakage of just one condom will result in a fatal overdose of high-purity heroin.

Because of law enforcement targeting of Nigerian citizens, Nigerian drug traffickers are increasingly turning to couriers of other nationalities, in particular young women of European or U.S. citizenry who they believe are less likely to be selected for search. Members of the U.S. military traveling in uniform are also frequently recruited by Nigerian traffickers. Some Nigerian criminal organizations have actually set up courier training schools to instruct couriers in methods to avoid or divert the attention of customs officials and to instruct them in how to avoid drug courier profiling.

The usual pattern followed by Nigerian-employed couriers begins with the acquisition of the heroin in Bangkok. The courier then flies to a transit country (often Indonesia or Egypt), where the drugs are handed off to a second courier, who flies to another transit country where they are less likely to raise suspicions of U.S. customs officials. There the drugs are transferred to a third and last courier. The point of these complicated arrangements is to conceal the point of origin for the drug (Bangkok) from U.S. officials.

Nigerian traffickers also frequently employ an additional smuggling technique known as *shotgunning*, which is the practice of placing many couriers on the same flight to the United States. The hope is to overwhelm customs officials upon arrival. If some couriers on the flight are detained, the others will inevitably get through. The profit margin for heroin is so high that the loss of even a significant portion of a shipment still leaves the traffickers with immense profits. In addition to human couriers, some Nigerian trafficking syndicates have begun to use express mail as means of getting the drugs to the United States.

Once in the United States, the heroin is sold by Nigerian wholesalers. Nigerian syndicates are especially active in cities with large Nigerian émigré populations, such as Chicago, which is home to 200,000 Nigerian nationals. In the city, the Nigerian wholesalers sell the heroin to street-level retailing organizations, particularly street gangs such as the Blackstone Rangers and the Vice Lords.

By the end of the twentieth century, Nigerian traffickers controlled 57 to 90 percent of the market for Southeast Asian heroin in the United States. During the 1980s, high-purity Southeast Asian heroin was the most common substance on the U.S. market. However, the entry of Colombian drug syndicates into the heroin market in the late 1990s seriously undercut the Nigerian share of the market. Importing heroin from Southeast Asia is very expensive; importing from Colombia is far cheaper. High-grade Colombian heroin is now available at a much lower price than Nigerian-imported Southeast Asian heroin. This competition from the Colombians has caused the Nigerians to begin to seek markets for their heroin in Europe.

DOMINICAN DRUG-TRAFFICKING ORGANIZATIONS

The Dominican Republic is one of the poorest countries in the world. Dominican drug-trafficking organizations started out as retail cocaine dealers in emigrant communities in the United States. Perhaps the most famous of these communities was the Washington Heights area of Manhattan, in New York City. Starting in the mid-1970s, Dominican immigrants moved into this community and began handling Colombian-supplied cocaine. Soon thereafter their trafficking activities had spread into New Jersey, Connecticut, and some of the affluent suburbs of New York (Jackall, 1997; Pellerano and Jorge, 1997).

Dominican drug traffickers were for the most part retail operators until the 1990s. It was at that point that many Colombian drug syndicates began to divest themselves of wholesale operations, passing them on to Mexican drug syndicates. The Mexicans were charging a transport fee of 50 percent of the drug shipment. Traffickers from the Dominican Republic saw this as an opportunity to get into the wholesale cocaine business. The Dominican Republic is closer to New York City than is Mexico; emigrant Dominican communities had already been established in New York; and drug distribution systems had already been established in those communities. The Dominican trafficking syndicates made the Colombians an offer they couldn't refuse. For transportation of wholesale cocaine shipments to the New York City area, they would charge only 25 percent of the shipment as a fee, thereby undercutting the Mexican syndicates.

As a result of this business arrangement with Colombian cocaine traffickers, two major Dominican drug syndicates emerged. One syndicate, operating out of the Dominican Republic itself, provides stash sites for cocaine shipments from Colombia. This cocaine is transported into the Dominican Republic in small boats or by air drops. Traffickers from the Dominican Republic take it from there, smuggling the drugs into Puerto Rico in boats, repackaging the drugs, and shipping them to the continental United States by way of containerized maritime cargo ships or routine commercial air flights.

Once in New York City, the drugs are distributed by ethnic Colombian wholesalers or, increasingly, by a second syndicate of ethnic Dominicans, which now operates up and down the East Coast. Dominican drug syndicates also operate in smaller cities on the East Coast, including Fall River, Massachusetts, and Lewiston, Maine. Many of these smaller cities have brought in Dominican immigrants to work in low-wage, labor-intensive industries, such as garment manufacturing. Operations in these smaller cities have several advantages for Dominican syndicates. First, they expand their customer base. Second, they face virtually no competition from other established drug-trafficking organizations.

Dominican syndicates rotate members in the United States. Typically, they move operatives in for a two-year stay and then retire them to the island. Once back on Dominican soil, drug traffickers are protected by restrictive extradition laws to the United States.

Like many newer trafficking syndicates, the Dominicans still make heavy use of violence as a means of establishing their reputation and protecting their turf. One Dominican syndicate in New York City was directly linked to seven murders, including the shooting of a police officer who had been ambushed after responding to a false 911 call. In the early 1990s, incidents in Massachusetts indicated the violent nature of these traffickers. In Lowell, six people were found hogtied and choked to death as a result of a dispute with Dominican traffickers; in Lawrence, 146 houses were subjected to arsons in a turf battle between several emerging Dominican gangs.

ALBANIAN DRUG-SMUGGLING NETWORKS

The break-up of Yugoslavia in the early 1990s and the subsequent local conflicts between ethnic Serbs, Croats, Bosnians, and Albanians have focused attention on small, highly localized, but increasingly important organized crime groups of Albanian decent, operating primarily from Kosovo or from Albania itself. Albanian organized crime groups tend to be tightly organized groups of individuals related to one another in an ethnic clan system. Though these groups are primarily located in the Balkans and are frequently associated with Kosovo Liberation Front, their drug-trafficking activities have resulted in a proliferation of small criminal organizations throughout Europe and now in the United States (DeStefano, 1985; Galeotti, 2000).

Albanian organized crime groups typically started out in partnership with larger Italian or Russian organized crime syndicates. Their criminal enterprises are varied but usually include smuggling drugs, arms, and cigarettes; alien smuggling; and trafficking women for the purpose of prostitution. Partly as a result of regional conflicts in the Balkans, Albanian émigré and refugee communities have sprung up in many large Western European cities. Using these communities as an organizing base, Albanian organized crime groups have followed.

Initially drug smuggling was just an activity ancillary to arms trafficking, but in the mid-1990s Albanian organized crime groups began purchasing large amounts of heroin from Turkish wholesalers. In the years that followed, Albanian drug syndicates developed their own sources for Southwest Asian (Golden Crescent) heroin, moving the drug to central and northern Europe and becoming major competitors to their former Turkish partners. In addition, by 1999, Albanian crime syndicates were challenging the hegemony of Italian syndicates in heroin trafficking and alien smuggling in Italy. Indeed, Italian law enforcement sources believe the Albanians had taken over most of the prostitution enterprises in Italy by 1999 and were trafficking heroin, hashish, weapons, and cigarettes through Italy for shipment to other European destinations. According to Italian law enforcement, by 2000 the Albanians had literally taken the illicit trade in women and children away from traditional Italian syndicates in Italy itself.

Although Albanian prostitution and heroin operations in the United States are still small scale, it is clear that Albanian syndicates have been moving into the cities of the northeastern United States for the last several years.

SUMMARY

Illicit drugs in the United States finance drug-trafficking organizations with both domestic and foreign origin. The Mexican cartels, which dominate the news in recent years, were preceded by Colombian cartels, which at one time were one of the more visible types of modern-day drug-trafficking organizations.

Drugs have also attracted the participation of terrorist and insurgent groups in the cocaine trade, such as Colombia's FARC (Revolutionary Armed Forced of Colombia), ELN (National Liberation Army), and AUC (United Self Defense Forces of Colombia), and Peru's PCP-SL (The Communist Party of Peru). Such groups have been documented as operating in Latin American countries and exerting influence over significant portions of the drug trade. The existence of these groups is fueled by the unstable governments and economies of many source countries. The influence of these types of terrorist organizations reaches other Latin American countries as well.

Asian criminal organizations, such as the Chinese triads and tongs and the Japanese yakuza, operate in both the United States and Hong Kong. They also are active in the illicit drug trade. With the increase in Asian nationals in the United States, the ranks of the Chinese tongs are growing in Los Angeles, New York, and other cities.

Do you recognize these terms?

- cartels
- marielito
- narcoterrorism
- Operation Secure Mexico
- Operation Xcellerator

- spillover violence
- superlabs
- tong
- triad
- yakuza

DISCUSSION QUESTIONS

1. List the various foreign organized crime groups that are considered the greatest contributors to the United States' drug abuse problem. Specify the drugs with which each organization is most likely to be involved.

2. What role do the Mexican cartels play in the illicit global drug trade?

3. Identify and discuss the link between FARC (and other insurgent groups in Colombia and Peru) and drug traffickers.

4. Discuss the interplay between drug trafficking and insurgent terrorists.

5. Historically, what events have played the most significant roles in Cuban immigration into the United States?

6. Explain the role of Asian organized crime groups in the illicit drug trade.

Part III

Fighting Back

Because drug abuse is so diverse and because it touches so many different lives, many concerned people throughout our communities have strong commitments to combating the problem. These people include police officers, social workers, educators, church officials, and concerned parents, to name only a few. Each of these people seeks new and innovative ways to control drug abuse and crime in their neighborhoods. To this end, some important questions can be asked: In addition to relying on the police, what other community resources can be used to confront drug abuse? Should drug control policy focus on controlling the supply side or the demand side of the drug abuse problem? What role should churches and schools play in ensuring a drug-free community? To what extent can the average person make a difference in society's fight against drugs? The remaining five chapters of this book deal with these questions and more by addressing both the government's and the public's responses to the nation's drug abuse dilemma.

Chapter 10

The Drug Control Initiative

This chapter will enable you to:

- Understand the various goals of drug control
- Learn the different categories of drug laws
- Learn the strategies of drug enforcement agencies
- Understand the role of federal interdiction efforts
- Gain insight regarding the assorted efforts involved in drug control

Many controversial and vital issues must be considered in designing drug control strategies. A paradox of sorts becomes evident when we see, for instance, one interest group demand that law enforcement officers be given more police authority with which to perform their drug control duties, while others protest that expanding the roles of government authority decreases the constitutional and personal freedoms of individuals.

Controlling dangerous drugs involves a profusion of tasks that are sometimes contradictory; these include reducing the overall demand for drugs, reducing both the international and the domestic supplies of drugs, controlling organized crime, minimizing the spreading of dangerous diseases (such as AIDS) through intravenous drug use, using nontraditional drug enforcement tactics such as reverse stings and criminal profiling, and minimizing the use of dangerous drugs in professional and amateur sports.

The government's response to the nation's drug problem on both state and federal levels has been shaped by a number of important variables. For example, both levels of government must consider their statutory and constitutional authority to intervene. In addition, the jurisdiction of each law

DOI: 10.1016/B978-1-4377-4450-7.00010-2
© 2011 Elsevier Inc. All rights reserved.

enforcement agency must be considered along with the realization that the extent of drug use across the country varies according to cities and communities. For instance, crack cocaine and heroin are predominantly big-city problems, with marijuana and methamphetamine primarily plaguing rural areas.

Strategies to combat the drug problem also vary widely depending on community public opinion, the resources and jurisdiction of the law enforcement agencies in those communities, and the type of drugs most commonly abused and sold on the streets. Common community strategies include drug education, drug testing of workers, and police intervention on both the supply and demand sides of abuse and trafficking.

THE GOALS OF DRUG CONTROL

In addition to controlling drug use and crime associated with drug use, it is the goal of law enforcement agencies to disrupt criminal organizations that infiltrate neighborhoods and communities. As discussed in Chapter 4, many business-related facets exist in the drug trade, including the production, manufacturing, transportation, and sale of drugs. It is these various components of the drug trade that drug law enforcement attempts to upset. Therefore, each level of the drug business remains a viable enforcement target. These levels are (1) the source of the drugs, which concerns cultivation and production of opium poppies, coca leaves, and marijuana; (2) smuggling operations, which transport drugs into the country and across state lines; (3) wholesale distribution of drugs; and (4) retail sales.

It could be argued that the enforcement of drug laws makes selling drugs all that much more enticing and exciting for criminals. In addition, it increases the cost of the drugs while making the drug business more dangerous for those involved in it. Risks incurred by law enforcement officials at each stage of the drug trade increase from one level to another. The philosophy behind enforcement efforts is that if police seize drugs and other assets belonging to traffickers, and then they arrest and imprison the traffickers and their associates, it will deter others who are considering entering the trade. For those not deterred, incarceration prevents their continued participation in the drug trade.

Figure 10.1

- • To control drug use
- • To control drug-related crime and violence
- • To disrupt the development and growth of criminal organizations
- • To protect neighborhoods

Drug Enforcement Goals

DRUG LAWS

An illegal sale of drugs violates both state and federal laws. Depending on which law enforcement agency is able to document the violation, either state or federal charges are brought against the offender. In any case, those laws provide the essence of reducing the supply and demand of drugs. Drug laws are specific about what constitutes a criminal violation, and although specific features of those laws vary across jurisdictions and levels of government, three categories of law can be identified:

- *Possession or use*. This category of law prohibits people from possessing controlled drugs on their person, in their car, or in their home. The only notable exception is possession of drugs pursuant to a lawful prescription. Some states even go so far as to prohibit persons from being under the influence of drugs or using them. The specific levels of proof, such as the amount of the drug that differentiates simple possession from possession with intent to sell, vary from one state to another.
- *Manufacturing*. These laws generally include any activity related to the production of controlled drugs. The term *manufacturing* is broadly used in some legal language and can include cultivation, conversion of certain chemicals to other forms, and preparation and packaging of drugs for retail sale.
- *Distribution*. This category of laws generally refers to the sale and delivery of drugs on both the wholesale and retail levels. Also included are provisions for transportation, importation, and storage of drugs. Generally, the type of drug involved will dictate the specific charge to be filed against the offender.
- *Other prohibited activity*. In addition to the three categories of laws discussed here, many other types of laws are available for the prosecution of drug offenses. These include:
  - Drug paraphernalia laws
  - Drug precursor laws
  - Money-laundering laws
  - Conspiracy laws
  - Forfeiture laws
  - Racketeering laws (RICO)
  - Drug-diversion laws

A virtual alphabet soup of federal law enforcement agencies are charged in one fashion or another with the task of domestic and/or international drug enforcement. These agencies include the Drug Enforcement Administration (DEA), the Federal Bureau of Investigation (FBI), the United States Customs and Border Protection, the Coast Guard, and United States Immigration and Customs Enforcement (ICE). In addition, a wide variety of other federal agencies have been organized to coordinate certain aspects of drug enforcement activities. Because of the bureaucratic fragmentation of federal law enforcement agencies charged with drug enforcement, the exchange of information as well as coordination and cooperation between agencies is often problematic and difficult to achieve.

THE HISTORY OF FEDERAL DRUG ENFORCEMENT

Alcohol prohibition marked the first legal recognition of problems emanating from substance abuse. The enforcement mechanism for the National Prohibition Act was placed under the Commissioner of Internal Revenue. In addition, a narcotics unit was created, originally employing 170 agents and with an appropriation of $250,000. The narcotics unit operated between 1919 and 1927. By 1927, all powers of drug enforcement were transferred to the Secretary of the Treasury.

During the years of the narcotics unit's operation, the general public associated narcotics enforcement with the unpopular liquor enforcement efforts of the era. Additionally, scandals tarnished the image of narcotics agents when some agents were found to be falsifying arrest records and accepting payoffs from drug dealers. In response, Congress moved the responsibility of narcotics enforcement to the newly created Federal Bureau of Narcotics (FBN) in 1930. It was after the creation of the FBN that the term *narcotics agent* was generally adopted to refer to FBN drug enforcement personnel.

For the next 35 years, the mission of federal drug enforcement remained somewhat consistent. Through the mid-1960s, the federal government's drug suppression efforts were primarily directed toward the illegal importation of drugs into the country. The authority of the FBN was expanded in 1956 with the passing of the Narcotics Control Act, which, among other things, authorized narcotics agents to carry firearms and granted them authority to serve both search and arrest warrants.

In 1965, the Drug Abuse Control Amendments (to the 1956 Narcotics Control Act) were passed. These amendments addressed the problem of drugs in the depressant and stimulant category being diverted from legal channels. In 1966, another agency was created to enforce the amendments: the Bureau of Drug Abuse Control (BDAC), within the Department of Health, Education, and Welfare's Food and Drug Administration (FDA). Another advance in drug enforcement occurred in the late 1960s as a result of a study conducted by the Katzenbach Commission. The study concluded with the following recommendations to reduce both the supply and demand of drugs:

1. Substantially increase the enforcement staffs of the FBN and the Bureau of Customs.
2. Permit courts and correctional authorities to deal flexibly with violators of the drug laws.

3. Undertake research to develop a sound and effective framework of regulatory and criminal laws relating to dangerous drugs.
4. Develop within the National Institute of Mental Health a core of educational and informational materials relating to drugs.

In 1968, for the first time in history, the U.S. Department of Justice was given authority for the enforcement of federal drug laws. With this authority, the FBN and the BDAC were abolished and enforcement responsibility was passed to the newly created Bureau of Narcotics and Dangerous Drugs (BNDD). This was done to eliminate friction between enforcement agencies and to minimize bureaucratic fragmentation within the federal government's drug enforcement effort.

To assist state and local drug enforcement agencies, the Office for Drug Abuse and Law Enforcement (ODALE) was established in 1972. Several months after the creation of ODALE, the Office of National Narcotic Intelligence (ONNI) was created to serve as a clearinghouse for any information considered useful in the administration's antidrug initiative. ONNI was also charged with disseminating information to state and local law enforcement agencies for which there was a demonstrated "legitimate official need."

In 1973, President Richard Nixon implemented a drug enforcement reorganization plan that addressed the supply side of drug abuse as well as the demand component of the problem. One of the most important directives of the plan was the creation of the Drug Enforcement Administration (DEA) within the Department of Justice. Under the plan, the administrator of the DEA would report directly to the attorney general and would assume all personnel and budgets of the BNDD, ODALE, and ONNI. As of the writing of this text, the drug enforcement agencies discussed here are the agencies responsible for drug control on the national level.

The Drug Enforcement Administration (DEA)

As previously mentioned, the DEA, established in 1973, was declared the lead agency in the federal government's efforts to suppress the illicit drug trade. Acting under the U.S. Department of Justice, the DEA is the only federal law enforcement agency for which drug enforcement is the only responsibility. The DEA has primary responsibility for investigating drug-related events as well as collecting and disseminating drug-related intelligence information. In addition, the agency tries to coordinate efforts among federal, state, and local law enforcement agencies also involved in drug suppression.

The dominant philosophy of the DEA is to eliminate drugs as close to their sources as possible and to disrupt the drug-trafficking system by identifying, arresting, and prosecuting traffickers. In furtherance of this philosophy, drug shipments are sometimes permitted to enter the United States while under close surveillance by agents. Once a shipment is delivered, agents can arrest traffickers and, hopefully, leaders of the drug-smuggling organizations. The DEA philosophy, focusing on investigation and conviction, conflicts with the mission of other agencies, such as the U.S. Customs and Border Protection, which are charged with interdiction of drugs as soon as they enter the United States. Interagency rivalries are therefore created that tend to hamper the overall effectiveness of the federal drug enforcement initiative.

The DEA's mission is both domestic and foreign, with a total of more than 5,000 special agents and intelligence analysts located throughout the United States and in 42 other countries (DEA, 2006). Agents stationed in foreign countries possess no arrest powers and act primarily as liaisons with the host law enforcement agencies. DEA agents and analysts provide information about general trends in drug trafficking as well as specific information regarding the actions of drug criminals. The information collection process begins in drug source countries and includes analysis of drug production (illicit farming operations and laboratories) and transportation methods (smuggling) used by traffickers.

Intelligence collected by the DEA is a major source of information about drugs in transit, and it is shared with other law enforcement agencies. Through the DEA's El Paso Intelligence Center (EPIC), intelligence is collected, analyzed, and disseminated from all enforcement agencies. During recent decades, the DEA's budget and workforce have burgeoned. For example, in 1980, the DEA employed a total of 4,149 employees, with 1,941 special agents; by 2006, the DEA workforce included 10,891 employees, including 5,320 special agents. Although supporters of the federal drug enforcement initiative claim that the greater numbers of agent personnel account for the rising number of arrests and seizures, detractors of federal drug policy claim that hiring more enforcement agents is not the best way to approach the drug problem. In 1990, John Lawn expressed his frustration with drug enforcement initiatives by resigning his post as DEA administrator and conceding that the DEA is unable to keep pace with many of today's drug-trafficking organizations. Many analysts agree and suggest that the best way to confront the drug problem is to make a systematic analysis of every aspect of the way that major drug-trafficking organizations operate and then attack the *choke points* of distribution, as opposed to mounting an all-out effort on "every front." In short, the suggestion is to make better use of raw intelligence information by drug enforcement personnel who are already in place.

The Federal Bureau of Investigation (FBI)

The FBI is the chief law enforcement arm of the federal government and is a division of the Justice Department. In 1982, Attorney General William French Smith delegated to the FBI concurrent jurisdiction with the DEA for the overall drug law enforcement effort. This was a major change in the FBI's

Figure 10.2

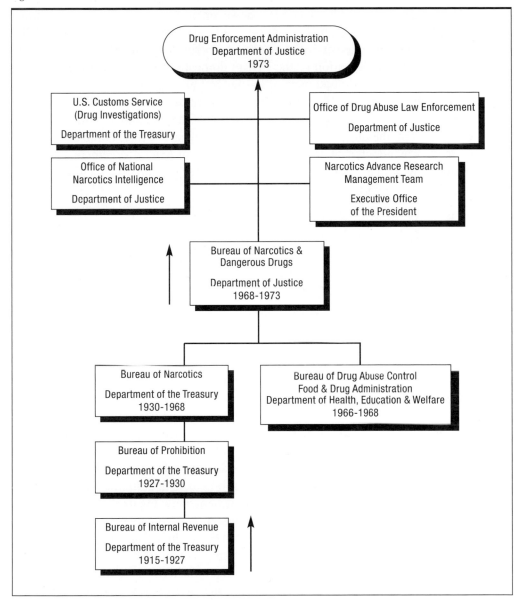

DEA Genealogy

normal jurisdiction, which had traditionally included all federal laws not specifically assigned to other enforcement agencies.

Since assuming these new drug enforcement responsibilities, the FBI has assigned more than 1,000 special agents to drug investigations. The primary impetus of the FBI's role in drug enforcement is the investigation of organized crime activity in the drug trade. These activities include probing into specific trafficking organizations as well as scrutinizing illegal financial transactions pertaining to drug trafficking.

Both the DEA and FBI are responsible for enforcement of the Controlled Substances Act of 1970. The FBI, however, is more concerned with drug-related violations of such laws as the Continuing Criminal Enterprise (CCE) statute and the Racketeer-Influenced and Corrupt Organizations (RICO) law. Although the participation of the FBI in domestic drug enforcement benefits the overall goals and objectives of the federal effort, some degree of conflict, overlapping responsibilities, and confusion about jurisdiction between the DEA and the FBI still exists. As an offshoot of the FBI's involvement in drug enforcement, the Organized Crime Drug Enforcement Task Force (OCDETF) concept was adopted in 1983. Through this joint law enforcement initiative, many high-level cases have been culminated (see section on OCDETF).

DRUG INTERDICTION

In September 2004, the U.S. Navy and Coast Guard intercepted a fishing vessel, the *Lina Maria*, 300 miles off the coast of the Galapagos Islands. Agents discovered more than 15 tons of cocaine secreted in compartments. As a result, 10 suspects were arrested (Kakesako, 2004).

The *Lina Maria* seizure was one of the largest single seizures in an ongoing investigation to stop the pipeline of drugs from the eastern Pacific to the shoreline of the United States. But it also demonstrates the success of combined efforts by the U.S. Navy, the U.S. Coast Guard, and federal law enforcement.

The process of interdicting drug smugglers is one of the primary focuses of U.S. drug control policy. Through intercepting and seizing contraband, *interdiction* prevents the entry into the United States of illegal drugs from foreign sources. As we have learned, drugs enter the country in a variety of ways, and drug smugglers regularly vary their methods to counter enforcement actions. Basically, interdiction consists of five rather broad categories of activity: (1) intelligence, (2) command and control, (3) surveillance, (4) pursuit, and (5) capture. The interdiction process addresses areas off shore and within the 12-mile "customs search" radius surrounding the United States as well as all ports of entry.

In 1990, the U.S. Air Force introduced a new long-range radar system that was originally designed to provide early warning of a Soviet attack. Its newer application is to detect airborne drug smugglers. The system, located in Maine, consists of two gigantic antennas, each spreading more than two-thirds of a mile and forming the first "over-the-horizon" radar capable of seeing 10 times farther than conventional systems—up to 1,800 miles.

The system is operated by bouncing signals off the ionosphere, and a series of computer screens maps every plane flying over a four-million-square-mile area of the Atlantic, from Iceland to South America. In theory, the system will match the aircraft against known flight plans and air traffic control information, identifying suspected drug flights and scrambling U.S. Customs and Border Protection or Coast Guard pursuit planes.

Figure 10.3

Source: Drug Enforcement Administration, 2007.

Beginning in the early 1980s, New Mexico state troopers grew suspicious following a sharp increase in the number of motor vehicle violations, particularly along Interstate 40, that resulted in drug seizures and arrests. Simultaneously, troopers in New Jersey began making similar seizures during highway stops along the Interstate 95 "drug corridor" from Florida to the Northeast. Independently, troopers in New Mexico and New Jersey established their own highway drug interdiction programs. Their drug and money seizures grew immediately. Seizure and arrest increases signaled to law enforcement officers that the nation's highways had become major arteries for drug transportation. In addition, they found that tons of illicit drugs were flowing north and east from Florida and the nation's southwestern border while millions of dollars of drug profits returned south and west—as though traveling through a pipeline.

Over time, as seizures mounted, highway officers found that highway drug couriers shared many characteristics, tendencies, and methods. Highway law enforcement officers began to ask key questions to help determine whether motorists they had stopped for traffic violations were also carrying drugs. These interview techniques proved extremely effective. The road patrol officers also found it beneficial to share their observations and experiences in highway interdiction at conferences and other multiagency gatherings. The success of the highway interdiction programs in New Mexico and New Jersey eventually led to the creation of Operation Pipeline in 1984.

Pipeline, a nationwide highway interdiction program that focuses on private motor vehicles, is one of the DEA's most effective operations and continues to provide essential cooperation between the DEA and state and local law enforcement agencies. The operation is composed of three elements: training, real-time communication, and analytic support. Each year, the El Paso Intelligence Center (EPIC), with the assistance of state and local highway officers, conducts dozens of training schools across the country, attended by other state and local highway officers. These classes are intended to inform officers of interdiction laws and policies, to increase their knowledge of drug trafficking, and to sharpen their detection of highway couriers.

Training classes focus on (1) the law, policy, and ethics governing highway stops and drug prosecution; and (2) drug-trafficking trends and key characteristics, or indicators, that are shared by drug traffickers. In addition, through EPIC, state and local agencies continue to share real-time information with other agencies and can immediately obtain the results of their record checks and receive detailed analysis of drug seizures to support their investigations.

Although Operation Pipeline relies in part on training officers to use characteristics to determine potential drug traffickers, it is important to understand that the program does not advocate such profiling by race or ethnic background. The

Figure 10.3—*continued*

issue of suspect profiling has been reviewed extensively over the course of the past decade in an effort to assure government officials that all the necessary precautions have been and will continue to be taken to ensure the fair, ethical, and impartial treatment of criminal suspects. Officers are trained to recognize a number of exceptional indicators that would lead law enforcement personnel to suspect criminal activity. During training, they are exposed to both the visual and audio indicators of deception and their potential link to criminal activity. Participants in this training learn concealment methods used by criminals based on prior interdiction efforts and how particular indicators of deception have led officers to extend their roadside interviews during traffic stops.

In 1990, Operation Convoy, Pipeline's sister operation, was created to target drug transportation organizations that use commercial vehicles to traffic drugs. Operation Convoy conducts long-term surveillance undercover operations and other enforcement activities aimed at transportation organizations. Much of the investigative work conducted through Operation Convoy occurs at truck stops, cargo transshipment areas, and motels. In addition, Operation Convoy began training DEA special agents to drive large commercial motor vehicles during undercover investigations. The DEA also assists state agencies with investigations following seizures of commercial vehicles on the nation's highways.

Operations Pipeline and Convoy

The U.S. Coast Guard

The Coast Guard focuses on identification and interdiction of maritime smuggling, principally by private, seagoing vessels. The Coast Guard concentrates on larger cases in the open ocean, although it also conducts patrols and makes seizures in near-shore areas, where it has concurrent jurisdiction with the U.S. Customs and Border Protection. Primarily, the Coast Guard concentrates on the areas in and around the Gulf of Mexico, the Caribbean, and South Florida. U.S. Coast Guard seizures are of three distinct types:

- *Incidental seizures.* These occur while officers are carrying out other, more standard missions. Many incidental seizures occur during search-and-rescue missions in which the vessel in trouble turns out to be involved in smuggling activity.
- *Intelligence-based seizures.* The second most common type of Coast Guard seizure is one that results from hard criminal intelligence. Such intelligence pinpoints the specific location and time of the smuggling operation. This type accounts for a large percentage of Coast Guard seizures.
- *Interdiction patrol operations.* The third and predominant type of seizure results from drug interdiction patrol operations. U.S. Coast Guard cutters, usually accompanied by Coast Guard interdiction aircraft, search for, identify, visually inspect, and board suspect target vessels.

Designated "choke points" are heavily patrolled by Coast Guard cutters in four Caribbean and Gulf of Mexico areas. The primary goal of this operation is to identify, through a system of profiling, "mother ships," which meet contact boats near the coast that deliver drugs into the United States. The Coast Guard's ability to intercept illicit drug shipments is restricted in several ways. Although the Coast Guard will focus on choke points, these areas frequently are expanses of ocean that are up to 100 miles wide and patrolled by a single cutter. The number of vessels traveling through the choke points is large, and only a small number of the vessels can be searched. The Coast Guard can conduct choke point coverage only part of the time. Not only does it have limited equipment and personnel resources, but its cutters must escort seized vessels to a port, which could tie a cutter up for several days at a time and leave the choke point unpatrolled. Finally, the mission of the Coast Guard interdiction and search and rescue will always take precedence over investigating a suspected smuggling operation.

U.S. Customs and Border Protection

U.S. Customs and Border Protection, under the auspices of the Department of Homeland Security, has primary interdiction responsibilities for border smuggling through official ports of entry on land as well as concurrent jurisdiction with Coast Guard vessels in coastal waters of the United States up to 12 miles offshore, also known as the *Customs zone*.

Prior to 2003, the Border Patrol was part of the Immigration and Naturalization Service (INS), an agency within the U.S. Department of Justice. The INS was disbanded as of March 2003. With the establishment of the Department of Homeland Security, the functions and jurisdictions of several border and revenue enforcement agencies were combined and reconstituted into Immigration and Customs Enforcement (ICE). The agencies that were either moved entirely or merged in part, based on their law enforcement functions, included the investigative and intelligence resources of the United States Customs Service, the law enforcement resources of the Immigration and Naturalization Service, and the United States Federal Protective Service.

The priority mission of the Border Patrol, as a result of the 9/11 attacks and the organization's merging into the Department of Homeland Security, is to prevent terrorists and terrorist weapons from entering the United States. However, the Patrol's traditional mission remains the deterrence, detection, and apprehension of illegal immigrants and individuals involved in the illegal drug trade who generally enter the United States other than through designated ports of entry.

Currently, the U.S. Border Patrol employs more than 11,000 agents, and is responsible for patrolling 19,000 miles of land and sea borders. Border Patrol personnel are deployed primarily at the U.S.-Mexico border, where they are assigned to control drug smuggling.

Figure 10.4

Coastal interdiction is difficult because smugglers:

- Easily conceal drugs
- Use small, fast boats to travel short distances, requiring fast response time
- Blend in easily with ordinary marine traffic
- Are unlikely to be inspected on arrival to the United States if they declare what cargo they are bringing into the country

---

Coastal Interdiction

Cargo, vessels, and passengers from foreign locations are regularly inspected by customs officials to ensure the payment of required duty as well as to stop the flow of contraband. Each of these is a formidable task.

Dogs trained to smell illicit drugs are used at ports of entry and are an important tool in interdiction. In 2005, U.S. Customs and Border Protection Canine Enforcement Program teams at ports of entry seized more than 407,447 pounds of narcotics and more than 20 million illegal drug units (including various pills, capsules, or vials). At checkpoints and between the official ports of entry, canine teams made 3,809 seizures totaling more than 504,290 pounds of narcotics (U.S. Customs and Border Protection, 2006).

It is also the responsibility of the customs inspectors to inspect all international cargo; all vessels entering seaports from foreign countries; all aircraft entering the United States from foreign countries (including general and commercial aircraft); all land vehicles such as trucks, automobiles, trains, and buses; and all international mail. The service's interdiction strategy at ports of entry has several components:

- It operates most effectively when it has prior reliable intelligence. Intelligence sources include informants, private citizens, transportation companies, and intelligence agencies.
- Profiles of people, vehicles, and cargo are used to initiate searches. Profiles include data such as the origin of the individual or cargo and the sex, age, or citizenship of the individual (see Chapter 11).
- Inspectors conduct periodic blitz-type inspections of passengers and cargo.
- Officials use dogs, along with metal detection devices and a variety of support and detection technologies to track suspect aircraft, to sniff out hidden drugs.

One responsibility of U.S. Customs and Border Protection is to interdict drugs in the nation's near-shore waters. This initiative utilizes the marine branch of the service, which uses a system of stopping and searching incoming vessels that behave suspiciously (especially small boats referred to as "go-fast" boats).

The best-developed marine interdiction capabilities appear to be in the Miami area, where the Blue Lightning Operations Center (BLOC) operates. This initiative was implemented in February 1986 and is a joint operation between Customs and the Coast Guard that is designed to collect and coordinate information from air and marine centers. The BLOC tracks suspicious vessels, plots the course and speed of the suspect target, and directs interceptors toward it.

The customs air branch is responsible for interdicting airborne drug smuggling. Drug smugglers prefer light, twin-engine, general aviation aircraft and will usually fly at a low altitude, placing them under the line-of-sight coverage of coastal scanners. These smugglers will typically operate at night to minimize their chance of detection by law enforcement. Once suspicious aircraft have been sighted, they are normally tracked both by cutters and/or by high-speed chase planes. The interdiction process usually involves customs strike teams that are transported to the landing site by helicopters.

As will be discussed further in Chapter 13, a 1988 study by the RAND Corporation revealed some disturbing conclusions regarding the military's ability to affect drug demand successfully through interdiction. The study, commissioned by the U.S. Department of Defense and directed by Peter Reuter, concluded that it was more costly for the government to attempt to interdict drugs than it was for traffickers to replace seized shipments. In the study, Reuter found that the drug traffickers' assets are so vast that the losses caused by interdiction go unnoticed. Dealers have to spend more on transporting shipments than police can on stopping them. He claims this is because raw materials and highly skilled labor are surprisingly cheap in the markets utilized by drug traffickers.

To facilitate the study, Reuter developed a computer model called SOAR to estimate more exactly how smugglers would adapt if interdiction efforts were increased. In an all-out drug war, assuming that the interdiction rate on 10 of 11 routes could be more than doubled, SOAR estimated that the cost of smuggling would increase 70 percent, but the retail price of drugs would increase only 10 percent. The increase would therefore affect the street crack user by $2 per purchase.

Interdiction Support Agencies

In addition to the interdiction efforts by the U.S. Coast Guard and the U.S. Customs and Border Protection, other support agencies share certain responsibilities. Such support services share intelligence, equipment, and other resources. The primary support groups used in the interdiction effort are the Department of Defense, the Federal Aviation Administration (FAA), and various state and local law enforcement agencies.

- *The Department of Defense (DOD).* The historical separation of powers between the police and the military is defined under a law known as the Posse Comitatus Act. It was refined in 1981, resulting in a relaxation of the provisions for using military equipment and personnel for domestic law enforcement. Though DOD personnel cannot make arrests, the new provisions of the law allow sharing of intelligence equipment and assisting in certain operations that lead to arrests.

- *The Federal Aviation Administration (FAA)*. The FAA supports the drug interdiction effort with its flight information systems. The FAA requires all pilots of private aircraft flights originating in foreign countries to file flight plans 24 hours in advance and to land at the airport nearest to their point of entry that has a customs officer. Those aircraft crossing the border without having filed a flight plan are automatically considered suspicious and are subsequently investigated.

Other agencies sharing certain drug enforcement responsibilities include the Internal Revenue Service (IRS), the United States Marshals Service, and the Bureau of Alcohol, Tobacco, Firearms and Explosives. Most of this cooperation is carried out on a case-by-case basis.

Coordination Organizations

Drug traffickers are mobile and respect neither political boundaries nor the division of jurisdictions between law enforcement agencies. Therefore, police have responded to the drug problem by joining their efforts. Coordination efforts can be either horizontal, involving efforts between agencies operating in a particular region, or vertical, involving agencies at various levels of government. Several agencies offer services to the primary drug enforcement agencies in the federal and state governments.

Operation Alliance

Operation Alliance was developed as a multiagency effort to prevent drug smuggling across the Mexican border. Essentially serving as a task force under the direction of the INS's Border Patrol, the alliance includes officers from DEA and INS, people from the U.S. Attorney's Office, and officers from state and local law enforcement agencies. The philosophy of Operation Alliance is to share resources while seeking to interdict the flow of drugs coming from Mexico.

The National Drug Enforcement Policy Board

The National Drug Enforcement Policy Board (NDEPB) was created by the 1984 National Narcotics Act. The board originated as a cabinet-level agency consisting of the Attorney General as chair and the secretaries of State, Treasury, Defense, Transportation, and Health and Human Services, as well

Figure 10.5

During a six-month period beginning in late 2005, the *U.S.S. Gettysburg*, with a U.S. Navy helicopter detachment and a U.S. Coast Guard Law Enforcement Detachment (LEDET), severely impacted trafficker operations in the deep eastern Pacific Ocean and the Caribbean Sea. Patrolling an area exceeding the entire width of the United States, this formidable mix of counterdrug assets, with U.S. interagency and partner nation support, disrupted the movement of more than 28 metric tons of cocaine and arrested 42 drug traffickers.

The hunt began in early October 2005. After receiving intelligence from Joint Interagency Task Force South (JIATF-South) and EPIC, a *USS Gettysburg* helicopter disrupted a drug-trafficking speedboat operation near Honduran waters, where the traffickers rushed the boat ashore and fled into the countryside.

When a U.S. Customs and Border Protection P-3 maritime patrol aircraft located three suspect fishing vessels 1,100 miles from the nearest shoreline, JIATF-South directed the *Gettysburg* to move in. Once on scene, the U.S. Coast Guard LEDET boarded one of the vessels and seized 244 bales of contraband, resulting in the seizure of more than 9 metric tons (20,470 lbs.) of cocaine and the arrest of seven drug traffickers.

Less than a week later and more than 1,300 miles from the previous interdiction, the *Gettysburg* detected a go-fast operating well off the coast of Panama and U.S. maritime patrol aircraft were diverted to assist in tracking it down. A maritime patrol aircraft caught the suspect dumping contraband overboard and quickly guided the *Gettysburg* into position for the intercept. The *Gettysburg* recovered 48 bales (1.5 metric tons) of illicit drugs and detained another four suspects.

In late February 2006, maritime patrol aircraft cued by fused intelligence detected a suspect fishing vessel and a go-fast operating almost 1,000 miles west of the Galapagos Islands. The now-seasoned *Gettysburg* team intercepted the fishing vessel and the go-fast, adding to their seizure tally another 211 bales (5 metric tons) of contraband and detaining eight drug traffickers.

The highly successful *Gettysburg* deployment highlights the importance of synchronized interagency action and the rapid fusion and dissemination of actionable intelligence in effectively detecting, interdicting, and apprehending drug smugglers on the high seas. Throughout the duration of her six-month deployment, the *U.S.S. Gettysburg* repeatedly proved that with the right combination of end game capability, intelligence, and maritime patrol aircraft support, impressive interdiction successes can be achieved in the transit zone.

Success in the Transit Zone: The *U.S.S. Gettysburg* Makes Her Mark

as the directors of Central Intelligence and the Office of Management and Budget, as members. Despite the diversity of federal agencies involved, it was the board's objective to coordinate and focus strategies in the fight against drug abuse. Specifically, the statutory language outlining the mission of the National Drug Enforcement Policy Board was as follows:

1. Maintain a national and international effort against illegal drugs.
2. Coordinate fully the activities of the federal agencies involved.

3. Charge a single, competent, and responsible high-level board of the U.S. government, chaired by the attorney general, with responsibility for coordinating U.S. policy with respect to national and international drug law enforcement.

In 1988, the NDEPB was dissolved to make way for the Office of National Drug Control Policy.

Office of National Drug Control Policy (ONDCP)

In 1988, the Office of National Drug Control Policy (ONDCP) was created to assume control of the federal drug policy effort and was to be directed by a high-level *drug czar.* Director William Bennett, the former U.S. Secretary of Education, was the first person to assume this office (in 1989) and was charged with formulating a workable plan for drug control on a nationwide basis. Each year, the ONDCP releases a number of reports detailing the national drug control strategy. Each of these reports specifies goals and objectives of both domestic and foreign drug control initiatives.

In 1990, ONDCP designated five areas as *high-intensity drug-trafficking areas:* New York, Miami, Los Angeles, Houston, and along the southwestern U.S. border. The program's goals are to identify and disrupt drug-trafficking organizations operating in these areas that are thought to be major contributors to the drug problem in the nation. Funding for this program is provided to federal and state local law enforcement projects that cannot be funded on individual agency budgets.

The Regional Information Sharing System (RISS)

The Regional Information Sharing System program is an innovative, federally funded program that was created to support law enforcement efforts and to combat organized crime activity, drug trafficking, and white-collar crime. The RISS project began with funding by the Law Enforcement Assistance Administration (LEAA) discretionary grant program. Since 1980, the U.S. Congress has made a yearly appropriation of funds to the RISS project as a line item in the Department of Justice budget.

The primary impetus of the project is to augment existing law enforcement agencies with intelligence information on criminal activities in their jurisdictions. Additionally, the RISS project provides services to member agencies regarding assistance in asset seizures, funds for covert operations, analysis of investigative data on organized criminals, loans of investigative equipment, and training in the use of such equipment in criminal investigations. The RISS program operates within seven Regional Information Sharing Projects:

- *Mid-State Organized Crime Information Center (MOCIC).* Missouri, Kansas, Illinois, Iowa, Nebraska, South Dakota, North Dakota, Minnesota, and Wisconsin.

Figure 10.6

Source: President's Commission on Organized Crime, 1986c.

Adler Barriman Seal, a former TWA 747 captain, flew cocaine from Colombia to the United States for more than seven years during the late 1970s and early 1980s. Seal was recruited as a trafficking pilot by a personal friend who worked for the Colombian cocaine-trafficking organization headed by Jorge Ochoa. Seal eventually worked directly with that organization's leadership.

Initially, Seal flew direct trafficking flights between Louisiana and Colombia. He piloted a number of different smuggling aircraft, the largest of which was a Vietnam-vintage C-123 capable of holding tons of packaged cocaine. Seal always departed and returned to his Louisiana base late at night, to reduce chances of interdiction. His typical route took him over the Yucatán Peninsula (not over the more heavily patrolled Yucatán Channel) and directly over Central America to the eastern tip of Honduras, then south to any one of a number of airstrips and airports in north Colombia.

According to Seal, the Ochoa organization paid Colombian officials bribes of $10,000 to $25,000 per flight for a "window," that is a specific time, position, and altitude designated for the smuggling flight's penetration of Colombian airspace. If this payment was not made, the aircraft was susceptible to interception by Colombian authorities. Seal generally arrived in Colombia at dawn. His aircraft was loaded with cocaine and refueled within an hour, sometimes within 15 minutes, and he returned immediately to the United States.

Seal used two fairly simple techniques to avoid interdiction on his return trip to the United States; both were effective because of the heavy helicopter traffic running between the Gulf Coast states and the hundreds of oil rigs located offshore. First, when he reached the middle of the Gulf on his return trip, Seal slowed his aircraft to 110 to 120 knots, which caused monitoring to mistake it for a helicopter. Second, at a distance of about 50 miles off the U.S. coast, he dropped the aircraft to an altitude of 500 to 1,000 feet in order to commingle with helicopter traffic and thereby arouse even less suspicion.

Once in U.S. airspace, Seal proceeded to prearranged points 40 to 50 miles inland. The points were mapped out in advance with Loran C, a long-range navigational instrument. Further inland, he was generally joined by a helicopter. The two aircraft continued to a drop zone, where the helicopter hovered close to the ground. Seal then dropped the load of cocaine from the airplane on a parachute; the helicopter picked up the load from the drop zone and delivered it to waiting automobiles, which eventually moved the cocaine to Miami. Seal then landed his drug-free aircraft at any nearby airport.

Seal was paid well for his services. He claims his top fee for smuggling a kilogram of cocaine was $5,000; an average load was 300 kilograms. His most profitable single load netted him $1.5 million. He was never apprehended in connection with this operation.

Author's note: Subsequent to testifying before the President's Commission on Organized Crime, Seal was killed in Louisiana by gunmen believed to be contracted by the Medellín Cartel.

Case Study: Barry Seal

- *Western States Information Network (WSIN).* California, Oregon, Washington, Hawaii, and Alaska.
- *Rocky Mountain Information Network (RMIN).* Colorado, New Mexico, Arizona, Nevada, Wyoming, Idaho, and Montana.
- *Regional Organized Crime Information Center (ROCIC).* Texas, Oklahoma, Arkansas, Louisiana, Tennessee, Mississippi, Alabama, Georgia, Florida, Kentucky, South Carolina, North Carolina, Virginia, and West Virginia.
- *Middle Atlantic Great Lakes Organized Crime Law Enforcement Network (MAGLOCLEN).* Indiana, Ohio, Pennsylvania, New York, Michigan, Rhode Island, New Jersey, Maryland, and Delaware.
- *New England State Police Information Network (NESPIN).* Massachusetts, Maine, Vermont, Connecticut, New Hampshire, and Rhode Island.
- *LEVITICUS.* Alabama, Georgia, Indiana, Kentucky, New York, Pennsylvania, and Virginia. The LEVITICUS Project also provides coordination to agencies investigating crimes related to the coal, oil, and natural gas industries.

The National Narcotics Border Interdiction System (NNBIS)

The National Narcotics Border Interdiction System (NNBIS) was created to provide guidance for interdiction systems and is under the direction of the vice president. Regional NNBIS units are established at six locations throughout the country. These regional components are chaired by the heads of various regional enforcement agencies who have responsibility for that particular geographical area. For example, three of these regional directors are admirals in the U.S. Coast Guard.

The Organized Crime Drug Enforcement Task Force (OCDETF)

In 1981, the effects of drug trafficking and drug abuse in South Florida had so greatly affected the quality of life there that several particularly vocal public groups demanded immediate attention be given to the problem. In 1982, President Ronald Reagan established a cabinet-level South Florida task force known as Operation Florida to address the problem. The primary focus of Operation Florida was interdiction, arrest, and prosecution of drug smugglers. The task force was staffed with officers from federal agencies such as the DEA, FBI, Customs, ATF, the marshals service, the Department of Defense, and the Coast Guard.

The establishment of the Operation Florida task force led to the creation of the Organized Crime Drug Enforcement Task Force (OCDETF) in 1983. The primary focus of the South Florida program was interdiction; the focus of the OCDETF program is the detection and prosecution of leaders of large criminal organizations that control illicit drug importation and distribution. As of the preparation of this text, the OCDETF has proved to be one of the most effective enforcement initiatives in the nation's drug control effort.

Figure 10.7
Source: Office of Technology Assessment, 1987.

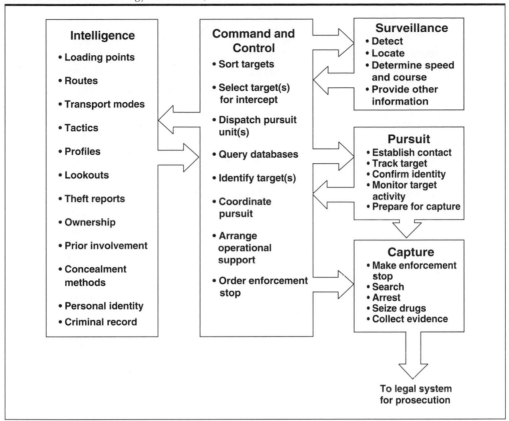

Interdiction Functions

Particularly supportive of the OCDETF program is the sustained use of the investigative grand jury (see Chapter 11). Prosecutors have employed the grand jury as an investigative technique in more than 60 percent of all task force cases. Additionally, investigators have made extensive use of undercover techniques in the development of cases that result in indictments. This technique is particularly suited to the OCDETF mission, in which there is a need for a long-term, complicated investigation that requires agents to follow all leads in pursuit of major dealers, whether manufacturers, suppliers, or money launderers. Today, the OCDETF concept remains the principal federal weapon in investigation and prosecution of drug traffickers and their organizations.

Other Task Forces

In addition to OCDETF, 44 formal and 12 provisional DEA-funded state and local task forces operate throughout the country. Augmenting this effort, another 700 multijurisdictional drug enforcement task forces operate with funding provided by the Anti-Drug Abuse Acts of 1986 and 1988.

The Task of Agency Coordination

A formidable task in the nation's drug war is the coordination of enforcement efforts between agencies located within both the state and federal governments. As mentioned, both NNBIS and OCDETF were designed to pool resources in the enforcement effort, but many organizational problems still prevail. On the federal level, "turf wars" and inter-agency bickering often result in a reluctance to share information or coordinate enforcement efforts. Confusion often results when many different departments play some role in the drug suppression effort. For example, U.S. Customs and Border Protection is responsible for interdiction, yet the armed services also monitor the military's role in interdiction. The FBI and DEA have similar roles in investigating federal violations of the Controlled Substances Act.

Critical Thinking Task

Refute or defend a need for additional drug enforcement agencies in the United States. What, if any, changes would you support in the jurisdiction of existing agencies?

The primary responsibility for coordination on the federal level rests with the director of the Office of National Drug Control Policy. Former Director William Bennett, appointed by President George H. W. Bush in 1989, assumed an uncomprising attitude on this problem and stated: "If they're not in line, we'll get them in line." These examples partially illustrate the problem:

- The DEA, the FBI, the U.S. Customs and Border Protection, the State Department, the CIA, and the Department of Defense all gather intelligence information separately.
- Customs and Border Protection and DEA have been involved in feuds about who keeps assets and money seized during drug investigations.
- An FBI-DEA National Intelligence Center, proposed in William Bennett's 1989 National Drug Strategy, was rejected after officials at the Justice Department claimed that it would infringe on Attorney General William Thornburgh's power.

Cannabis Eradication

Each year during the summer months, marijuana cultivation becomes big business. To counter the growers who cultivate marijuana, an alliance between DEA and state and local law enforcement agencies has been formed. Initiated in 1979 by the DEA, the Domestic Cannabis Eradication/Suppression Program (DCE/SP) gives state and local police such resources as technical assistance, training, and special equipment for this task. By 1985, all 50 states were participating in the program, which operates in conjunction with other federal agencies. Included are the U.S. Forest Service, the Bureau of Land Management, the Bureau of Indian Affairs, and the Department of Defense. In many states, the National Guard has also provided a workforce and equipment for this undertaking. According to the Drug Enforcement Administration, in 2009 the DCE/SP was responsible for the eradication of almost 10 million cultivated outdoor cannabis plants and more than 400,000 indoor plants. In addition, the DCE/SP has documented 10,073 arrests and the seizure in excess of $37.3 million of cultivator assets. The program also removed 5,569 weapons from cannabis cultivators (DEA, n.d.).

As discussed in Chapter 5, indoor growing operations pose special problems to police. By the late 1980s, these operations had emerged in great numbers throughout the nation, and government statistics indicate that the number of indoor operations is increasing. One initiative designed to identify such operations was the DEA's Operation Green Merchant, organized in the late 1980s to target suppliers of cannabis seeds, growing equipment, and cultivation information as well as the growers themselves (Bureau of Justice Statistics, 1992).

Investigating Illicit Laboratories

As with marijuana cultivation, illegal drug laboratories also pose serious problems for drug control officials. During the 1980s, the number of such labs soared, and in addition to their being illegal in nature, they pose specific dangers for investigators. The federal government estimated that one in five discovered illicit laboratories are uncovered as a result of fire or explosion. As discussed in

A ranger is shown supervising a marijuana eradication operation in Crystal Cave, Sequoia National Park, California, in August 2009. Authorities said the proximity of the pot plants to such a heavily trafficked tourist site reflects a newfound boldness among growers.

Chapter 5, drug labs are volatile and unstable, posing dangers to both lab operators and police alike. Adding to the dangers of investigating drug labs are countersurveillance measures such as cameras, automatic weapons, and booby traps, all commonly associated with these operations.

Because of the nature of illicit drug laboratories, many pose an environmental hazard when dangerous chemicals are indiscriminately disposed of by lab operators. In one case, a California drug lab operator dumped chemicals into the sewer system in a remote rural area. Consequently, the lab's chemicals killed the bacteria that was used to treat sewage, resulting in the raw sewage being returned to the environment.

Another problem associated with investigating the drug lab is disposal of the chemicals used in the drug-making process once they are seized. Most chemicals used in LSD, methamphetamine, and PCP labs are corrosive, explosive, and unstable, and when they are seized by police, they must be disposed of properly. One of the challenges police face is the identification and tracking of precursor chemicals used in the laboratory process. Aiding police was the passing of the 1988 Chemical Diversion and Trafficking Act, which is designed to prevent the use of legal chemicals to process illicit drugs. According to the provisions of the law, domestic distributors of precursor and essential chemicals must meet specific reporting and records requirements. The law requires distributors to:

- Identify their regular customers
- Maintain records of sales for a specified period of time
- Declare the import of such chemicals
- Report questionable orders to the DEA

Under the law, it is the seller who makes the decision as to whether a specific purchase is shady. A classic example is an order for a large quantity of chemicals that is under the minimum amount of chemicals required for reporting purposes from a buyer who is not involved in the type of business in which that chemical is normally used.

STRATEGIES FOR STREET-LEVEL ENFORCEMENT

Although the problem of foreign drug traffickers smuggling dangerous drugs into the country is one of the federal government's highest priorities, the coexisting problem of controlling local street-level dealers prevails. Adopting a policy that effectively deals with the street-level dealer is a major priority.

Discreet and Nondiscreet Markets

Primary responsibility for this task has typically rested with the local law enforcement agency and has been associated with two distinct illegal street markets: *discreet markets* and *nondiscreet markets*. Discreet drug markets are those in which the drug seller and the drug buyer are well acquainted. Drug transactions taking place under these circumstances typically involve exchanges of drugs for money in the workplace or within a social environment such as a bar or nightclub. It is often difficult for police to discover these operations because of the private nature of the transactions, and therefore, they may go undetected for long periods of time.

In comparison, nondiscreet drug markets differ from the discreet drug trade in that the drug seller is rarely acquainted with the drug buyer. The nondiscreet market accounts for the so-called open-air trade that flourishes in public places. This type of drug market is attractive for the drug dealer because it will generate more profits due to the greater number of available customers. The nondiscreet market is also an easy target for police intervention and control, since its whereabouts are easily learned through police surveillance operations and informants.

The Kingpin Strategy

Enforcement strategies differ from one jurisdiction to another. Some are aimed at the heads, or *kingpins*, of the organizations. Under this strategy, police believe that once the top manager of a drug-trafficking organization has been eliminated from the organization, the rest of the organization will shut down. Thus, the quantity of drugs on the streets will be reduced and the price of drugs available to buyers will rise, making them less attractive to consumers. Some research, however, has shown no documented cases in which these drug-reduction strategies had actually resulted in a reduction in drug consumption (Kleiman and Smith, 1990). Some experts also disagreed with the assumption that no new management figures would assume control of the organization once the "kingpin" was removed.

However, one expert in the field, Mark Moore (1990), suggested that strategies such as undercover operations targeting drug kingpins tend to make the organization more cautious, which results in some transactions being restricted out of fear of discovery by police. In addition, Moore argues that enforcement successes against organizations result in a loss of inventory and the future capacity to supply drugs.

Marijuana Citations

One original approach by many municipalities in dealing with offenders caught with small amounts of marijuana is the issuing of citations by uniformed patrol officers. For example, when a small amount of marijuana is seized as a result of a vehicle stop, instead of the officer taking the violator into custody, a citation is written and signed by the violator. This process basically works like a traffic citation, since it requires the offender to appear in court on a later date.

This procedure has generally been considered a successful street-level enforcement tactic because it reduces the commitments of time and money by the police, the prosecutor, and the courts through streamlining the adjudicatory process. At the same time, the practice enables law enforcement agents to identify and convict drug users in the community who might otherwise escape detection by the criminal justice system.

Undercover Operations

Due to the secret nature of drug-trafficking organizations, information on their activities is difficult to obtain. In Chapter 4 we discussed the fact that the number of people involved in drug-trafficking organizations is limited to ensure control by managers. So one method of learning the inner workings of such operations is through the use of *undercover* operatives. The typical undercover operation involves an undercover officer buying drugs and then arresting the seller; this is called a *buy-and-bust*.

Both police officers and informants are used in the undercover capacity, which typically focuses on street-level dealers who are easily persuaded to exchange information for leniency. Undercover operations also depend heavily on surveillance, which sometimes includes wiretaps, examination of financial records, and the use of other electronic monitoring devices.

Other Concerns

It is clear that law enforcement initiatives alone are not successful in adequately containing the existing problem of street drug trafficking. Modern-day strategies must include tactics such as the enlistment of the support of community groups, seizing assets of both sellers and users, and cracking down on all street-sales operations.

Drug dealing, a fragmented and broadly generalized term, addresses all levels of illicit drug distribution and many different types of drugs. Although different types of drugs, such as marijuana, methamphetamine, heroin, and so forth, are prevalent in different geographical areas of the country, many law enforcement departments have identified the problem of crack cocaine sales as an enforcement priority. The popularity of crack cocaine among dealers is closely related to its popularity among the drug-using public; that is, crack is a highly addictive drug that consequently creates much repeat business for the seller and generates a correspondingly high profit margin. Street sales of crack cocaine and powdered cocaine seem to follow two distinct patterns: the use of the crack house and the nondiscreet market.

The crack house is the most common means of dealers' street distribution of crack cocaine. Frequently, the crack house is an abandoned residence that has been commandeered by street dealers for use as a base of operation. These houses are often structurally fortified with steel bars on windows and metal doorjambs to prevent easy access by police. The crack house sometimes operates in an "open" fashion, which enables the drug buyer or user to enter the house, purchase the crack, and ingest it on the premises.

Street-corner sales have also contributed greatly to the proliferation of the crack cocaine problem. Although primarily an inner-city phenomenon, this

Figure 10.8

Source: Marx, G. (1988), *Undercover Police Surveillance in America*. Berkeley: University of California Press.

Of the many drug control initiatives employed over the years, the traditional hallmark has been the use of undercover agents in covert operations. Because criminal organizations depend on concealing information about their dealings, getting information about those operations is difficult. One successful way to learn important information about members of such criminal operations is to get them to reveal how they operate through undercover operations. While undercover work is considered one of the most dangerous components to any drug enforcement operation, it provides police with a special advantage that would otherwise be unobtainable. Operatives, once in place, are empowered to witness first-hand the discussions and decisions made by drug dealers. Often, these discussions result in crimes carried out with the undercover agent poised for surreptitious observation—a proactive advantage not enjoyed by police in most conventional investigations.

Critics of undercover work argue that it borders on the infringement of a suspect's constitutional right to privacy—especially when an undercover officer is invited into the home of a suspect with the suspect believing the officer is a true friend. However, the Supreme Court has considered such circumstances and has refused to see deception as a violation of a suspect's rights. In *United States v. Baldwin* (1963) the Court found that police do not require prior judicial approval in the form of a warrant or court order before utilizing an undercover agent. In a related case, *Hoffa v. United States* (1996), the Court held that the Fourth Amendment does not protect a wrongdoer's misplaced belief that a person to whom he voluntarily confides his wrongdoing will not reveal it.

While the benefits of using undercover agents are clear, drawbacks exist. For example:

- Undercover police agents work under minimum supervision and little immediate protection.
- Suspects may expect agents to use drugs or alcohol; a contingency plan must be adopted to ensure the officers integrity and the integrity of the investigation.
- Undercover operations are expensive (drug buy money, investigative expense, training).
- For safety purposes, each undercover contact requires numerous surveillance agents, posing a drain on a department's resources.
- Equipment for covert operations is expensive.

In addition to the dangers associated with undercover work, many experts have questioned the ability of agents to infiltrate the higher levels of crime organizations successfully. Larger criminal organizations are not receptive to newcomers who might be undercover police, and in some cases new members are required to commit violent crime to prove they are not working for the government.

One of the most comprehensive and compelling research analyses of undercover police operations was conducted by Gary Marx (1988), who points to a number of paradoxes, ironies, and trade-offs associated with undercover work.

Figure 10.8—*continued*

Marx argues that undercover police operations are based on deceit, trickery, and lies. He points out that many undercover operations, particularly those involving drugs, revolve around the police actually facilitating or unintentionally increasing crime in an effort to reduce crime.

Marx concluded that undercover operations frequently lead to role reversals, with police involved in criminal activity and criminals acting as police. Marx's ultimate evaluation of undercover tactics is that they are probably a necessary evil but should be utilized only as a last resort and should be subject to stringent controls and oversight. Initiating these controls becomes even more important as powerful new surveillance technologies become available to police agencies.

Problems with Undercover Work

Critical Thinking Task

Suggest guidelines by which law enforcement agencies may better monitor the activities of undercover drug agents and thus reduce police corruption.

nondiscreet method for retail crack sales has, in some cases, created vehicular traffic congestion because of dealers who literally approach any passing automobile and ask the driver if he or she is interested in purchasing crack. This system of illicit drug trafficking illustrates the arrogance and lackadaisical attitude that many street dealers share with regard to the criminal justice system.

Specific tactics used to reduce street sales largely depend on the scope of the problem in each community. The task force concept (previously discussed) is one such tactic and has proven to be one of the more effective enforcement tools in the fight against street trafficking and for use in interdiction.

Newer nontraditional strategies of street enforcement are being considered by many law enforcement agencies. One such tactic is the use of the reverse sting. This innovative approach to controlling street drug sales involves undercover police officers posing as drug dealers rather than buyers (as in the "buy-and-bust" technique mentioned earlier). The focus of this strategy is to arrest people who purchase crack or attempt to engage in an illicit drug transaction. The reverse sting concept has three primary advantages: (1) the ability to identify and seize personal assets of the drug dealer (discussed later in this chapter), (2) the ability to arrest large numbers of street dealers and thus deter criminal activity, and (3) the ability to generate positive media coverage of police department activities.

A common problem for police crackdowns on street-level drug operations is displacement. For decades, traditional vice units have dealt with the problem of the displacement of offenders in attempting to control operations such as prostitution. Typically, once a strong police presence is detected by potential violators, alternative markets for the criminal activity are identified and pursued. If law enforcement efforts are not as concentrated in outlying areas as in the area of the crackdown, drug dealers will almost assuredly set up their operations in these outlying areas (also see Chapter 10).

Figure 10.9

The U.S. Drug Enforcement Administration lists current drug trafficking penalties at its website: www.justice.gov/dea/agency/penalties.htm.

Drug Trafficking Penalties

POLICE-COMMUNITY DRUG CONTROL EFFORTS

In neighborhoods infested with drugs and drug traffickers, law-abiding people are sometimes aware of who the drug dealers and users are. Granted, the specific names and addresses of those involved with illicit drugs may not be known, but drug transactions are routinely witnessed as dealers come and go from crack houses and as acts of violence are committed. As discussed in Chapter 10, the practice of community and problem-oriented policing is designed to tap into this crucial source of information by cultivating community-police partnerships. The premise of this philosophy rests on two realities: First, the police need public assistance in pinpointing locations of drug production and sales as well as learning the identities of those responsible. Second, the community relies on the police to eradicate drugs and drug dealers from neighborhoods within the community. Many studies have been conducted in areas where such partnerships have been tried, and it is clear that closer ties between the police and the community result in safer neighborhoods. For example, experience has shown that the implementation of foot patrol programs in some cities has raised citizen satisfaction with the police as well as the quality of life for residents.

Community Policing

Apprehending and incarcerating retail drug dealers is not the only way to intercept street-level drug sales. Maintaining a high police profile in the community often can deter street dealers from initially entering a neighborhood. The *community policing* concept integrates the police into the community so that its citizens will be more receptive and willing to exchange information with the police. Patrols on foot are thought to be one of the most important aspects of community policing because citizens in that setting are apt to feel that the police are greater contributors to the overall safety of the community.

Some communities have even found that the presence of police officers who stand in the vicinity of open-air drug markets (blatant street drug dealing) or conspicuously take pictures of dealers and prospective drug buyers tended to deter potential customers and forced drug dealers to leave the area. In one case, patrol officers in Charleston, South Carolina, kept drug dealers moving from block to block, preventing them from establishing a foothold in a neighborhood. Officers also knock on the doors of suspected crack houses, which often frightens the dealers into flushing their illegal drug inventory down the drain. In other cases, officers in both Yakama, Washington, and Fort Lauderdale, Florida, deterred drug dealers by sending owners of cars seen cruising near drug markets notice that their vehicles were observed in an area known to be filled with drug dealers.

Summary

When we study the extensive history of U.S. federal drug control policy, we can observe many interesting occurrences in drug abuse trends and in the formation of public policy relating to drug abuse. Prohibition created the need for enforcement of the federal antiliquor laws. From the first narcotics unit operating under the Commissioner of Internal Revenue in 1919 to the current Drug Enforcement Administration, formed in 1973, many policies and agencies have been implemented. Some of these have been more successful than others.

To date, the primary thrust of drug enforcement is carried out by the Drug Enforcement Administration, the Federal Bureau of Investigation, and U.S. Customs and Border Protection. Many other federal agencies share different degrees of enforcement responsibility with regard to drug control. A priority of the federal drug enforcement initiative is interdiction, which is the interception of drugs coming into the country. U.S. Customs and Border Protection and the U.S. Coast Guard play major roles in this effort.

Other organizations exist that act as task forces for drug trafficking in the United States. The Office of National Drug Control Policy serves as the coordinating agency for the federal drug control effort. The ONDCP is charged with coordinating efforts with all federal agencies to reduce drug abuse and trafficking. The federal Organized Crime Drug Enforcement Task Force (OCDETF) also plays a major role in detecting and prosecuting domestic drug traffickers. The OCDETF is made up of agents representing the Drug Enforcement Administration (DEA), the Federal Bureau of Investigation (FBI), U.S. Immigration and Customs Enforcement (ICE), the Bureau of Alcohol, Tobacco, Firearms, and Explosives (ATF), the U.S. Marshals Service, the Internal Revenue Service (IRS), and the U.S. Coast Guard, in cooperation with the Department of Justice Criminal Division, the Tax Division, and the 93 U.S. Attorney's Offices and state and local law enforcement.

On the local level, many different drug enforcement/suppression organizations and strategies exist. Strategies include ways to reduce or eliminate both discreet and nondiscreet drug markets operating in communities. This is accomplished by the use of community policing and problem-oriented policing by the patrol function of local police departments. These initiatives are designed to unite the police more closely with the general public as well as to empower police to make certain managerial enforcement decisions within their own jurisdictions.

Do you recognize these terms?

- choke points
- community policing
- Customs zone
- discreet markets
- drug czar
- high-intensity
- drug-trafficking areas
- interdiction
- nondiscreet markets
- undercover

DISCUSSION QUESTIONS

1. Explain the evolution of the Drug Enforcement Administration (DEA) and its current role in federal drug control policy.

2. Under what circumstances was OCDETF developed, and what purpose does it serve in the overall federal drug suppression effort?

3. Explain why there was so much bureaucracy in the development of the various drug enforcement agencies during and after Prohibition.

4. Explain the role of the RISS project in drug enforcement.

5. Describe the concepts of community policing and how they relate to drug control in communities.

6. Discuss some drug enforcement strategies that deal with reducing the supply of illicit drugs.

7. Characterize and discuss the differences between discreet and nondiscreet illicit drug markets.

Chapter 11

Critical Issues in Drug Control

This chapter will enable you to:

- Discover contemporary policy options in drug control
- Understand how the reverse sting tactic is used by police
- Understand the utility of electronic surveillance and its legal implications
- Learn the issues surrounding drug-testing policies
- See how officials attempt to control drug use in sports

Accepting responsibility is often a first step in problem solving on any scale. Just as an alcoholic must first acknowledge his or her condition to be able to overcome it, the United States must acknowledge the extent to which it provides a market for drugs in order to combat the drug menace. This leads to several critical issues facing actors in the war on drugs: Are U.S. strategies properly balanced? Are U.S. strategies aimed at both domestic and international criminals? Are U.S. strategies tackling both ends of the supply/demand cycle? Are U.S. strategies sufficiently flexible to protect civil liberties for the general public while giving adequate authority to drug enforcement officials? These are just a few of the issues facing drug enforcement policymakers.

Many strategies for drug control are controversial. Conventional methods often seem to offer little hope for controlling the problem. Unconventional methods frequently create controversy because they tend to rely on expanded police powers, leading some citizens to fear an erosion of personal freedom. On the other hand, many unconventional methods of drug enforcement have proven more effective and innovative than the traditional approaches.

DOI: 10.1016/B978-1-4377-4450-7.00011-4
© 2011 Elsevier Inc. All rights reserved.

DRUG LORD ABDUCTIONS

One example of an unconventional drug control tactic is the controversial police practice of kidnapping or abducting drug lords in foreign countries. Such a practice is favored by some, partly due to the degree of official corruption observed in many foreign countries that commonly protect drug lords from prosecution or extradition. One such case was the abduction of multimillionaire drug baron Juan Ramon Matta Ballesteros, who was taken from his home in Honduras by U.S. marshals in 1988 to face trial in Los Angeles. He was convicted of drug trafficking and conspiracy in the kidnapping-murder of DEA agent Enrique "Kiki" Camarena in 1985. Though the 50-year-old Matta argued that he was illegally kidnapped by U.S. authorities, judges found no gross misconduct by the federal agents that would warrant overturning of the verdicts. Matta was given a life term in prison.

In a related case, Humberto Alvarez-Machain, a Mexican citizen, was abducted in April 1990 from his medical office in Guadalajara, Mexico, by a group of Mexican mercenaries working for the DEA. Alvarez was one of 19 people also wanted by the federal government in connection with the 1985 kidnapping-murder of Camarena (see Chapter 6).

Although this practice usually occurs on foreign soil, many detractors claim it is an erosion of police authority. The issue was resolved in 1992 when the U.S. Supreme Court reviewed the Alvarez-Machain abduction case (*United States v. Alvarez-Machain*, 1992). In court, Alvarez-Machain moved to dismiss the indictment against him, claiming that the federal court system had no jurisdiction to try him because he had been abducted in violation of an extradition treaty between the United States and Mexico. After reviewing the case, the Court decided that Alvarez-Machain's abduction was not in violation of the extradition treaty; therefore, such abductions did not deprive the U.S. District Court of jurisdiction in a criminal trial.

The practice of abducting criminal suspects in foreign countries and bringing them to U.S. soil for trial is nothing new. In fact, it is more than a century old, and in numerous cases, the U.S. courts have found it perfectly legal. Other official abductions include:

- Mexican trafficker Rene Verdugo-Urquidez, accused of involvement in the Camarena murder along with Juan Ramon Matta Ballesteros, was shoved through a border fence by Mexican authorities in 1986. He was ultimately convicted in U.S. courts.
- Roberto Suarez Levy, the son of Bolivian trafficker Roberto Suarez Gomez, was arrested in Switzerland in 1980 on drug charges. After nine months of waiting, federal agents arranged with local police to have Suarez smuggled out of the country to Miami to face charges.

The precedents addressing abductions clearly show that judges need not consider how a defendant got into their courtroom. Such morality judgments have generally been left to law enforcement agencies. In deciding the

Alvarez-Machain case, the courts cited the case of Frederick Ker, recognizing that the practice of abducting criminals from foreign countries began more than a century ago. Ker was an embezzler who absconded to Peru (*Ker v. Illinois*, 1886) but was hunted down and brought within the court's jurisdiction by reason of a "forcible abduction." Although Ker's lawyer argued that he was kidnapped, the Supreme Court ruled in 1886 that Ker had no right to due process while abroad and that how he was brought to the courtroom in Chicago had nothing to do with the charges he was facing there.

In another abduction case, however, an exception was delineated by the courts. In 1974, Francisco Toscanino was abducted in Uruguay and transported to the United States. Toscanino's attorney claimed his client had been tortured en route to the United States. In that case, the court held that it is appropriate for judges to consider the apprehension of defendants if there is a suggestion that the behavior of apprehending officers might "shock the conscience of the court." The Toscanino case also recognized that a U.S. judge may throw out an arrest if another country objects to the manner in which an arrest was made within its borders.

We will now examine several enforcement alternatives currently in effect or under consideration by drug enforcement authorities in the United States.

Drug Courier Profiling

The practice of law enforcement officers profiling suspected drug couriers is another innovative method of apprehending drug traffickers. The technique, originally developed in the 1970s by the DEA for use in detecting drug smugglers in airports, has been extended to the highways for identifying automobiles driven by drug couriers.

Drug courier profiling involves trained officers watching vehicles on highways and looking for certain characteristics common to drug traffickers. The practice gained national attention in 1987 after a segment on *60 Minutes*. The CBS news-magazine television show featured an interview with a Florida state trooper who had achieved a certain reputation for his ability to spot or profile such vehicles. To make the stop, the officer must watch cars on those traveled routes most likely to be used by smugglers. If the officer identifies any traffic violation, such as speeding, the car can be stopped. The officer then looks for other telltale signs of a typical "drug runner." These include "inappropriate dress," a large roll of cash, nervousness around police, the use of a rental car with no car rental papers available for inspection, and the lack of any travel gear such as luggage. Finally, the officer asks the driver for consent to search the vehicle.

Although drug courier profiling has resulted in numerous drug seizures and arrests, it has been criticized by the American Civil Liberties Union (ACLU), which views it as a violation of one's personal freedoms and an unfair infringement of one's Fourth Amendment rights regarding search and seizure.

Critics of the technique argue that a vague profile is not enough to create "reasonable suspicion" in the officers' minds.

The decision in *United States v. Sokolow* (1989) addressed the issue of whether the use of drug courier profiles is valid under the Fourth Amendment. The Supreme Court said there is nothing wrong with such use in this case because the facts, taken in totality, amounted to a reasonable suspicion that criminal conduct was taking place. The Court suggested that whether the facts in the case fit a "profile" was less significant than the fact that, taken together, they establish a reasonable suspicion. So, in essence, the Court was saying that though a drug courier profile might be helpful, the totality of the circumstances is more important in establishing the legality of the stop and the subsequent search (del Carmen and Walker, 2006).

Lawyers for the DEA's criminal law division claimed in 1989 that agents did not make stops on the basis of profiles. Defense attorneys, on the other hand, maintain that suspicion triggered by a profile will often lead to an arrest on the pretext of a traffic violation. They also assert that "voluntary" questioning and searches by police can in fact be highly coercive. Yet another unanswered question is by what standard should one's behavior be analyzed to determine whether it is suspicious? For example, to some officers, the first person getting off a plane may be suspicious, whereas to other officers, the last person getting off a plane may seem suspicious.

Some previous high-court decisions have upheld informal questioning of suspects fitting a suspect profile but have prohibited coercive searches and formal arrests unless the police have additional evidence on which to base a decision. Until terms such as *coercive, profile,* and *voluntary* have been further defined, the U.S. Supreme Court may have to continue to fine-tune its conclusion regarding the constitutionality of this drug enforcement technique.

Drug Evictions

In the early 1990s, President Bill Clinton vowed to drive drug dealers from public housing, but the policy has resulted in innocent citizens being evicted from their homes along with criminals; that is, elderly tenants have been evicted because household members or visitors have been arrested on drug charges. Under an executive order issued by President Clinton in 1996, that is all the justification a public housing agency needs to evict. The executive order, dubbed "one strike and you're out," created rules that sped up evictions, bypassing the usual requirement of a pre-eviction hearing. Congress laid the groundwork for the new system by making noncriminal but offensive conduct grounds for eviction, even if it occurs away from housing projects. The White House then ordered local housing authorities nationwide to apply the expulsion standards or face a reduction in federal funding or even a takeover. During the first six months of the policy, evictions rose 84 percent over the previous six months, to 3,847 people evicted nationwide (Katel, 1998). It is unclear, however, how many of those evicted were elderly.

For years, drug dealers have terrorized law-abiding tenants by carrying weapons in plain sight. Drug-dealing tenants tend not to fight eviction; challenges to the law are mostly being levied by the elderly.

Enforcement of such orders varies from city to city because housing authorities have considerable flexibility to make decisions on a case-by-case basis. A class action suit was filed in Chicago in 1996 by the Legal Assistance Foundation, limiting evictions of tenants who "knew or reasonably should have known" about the behavior of a household member or visitor. Attorneys argue that the Chicago standard should be the rule rather than the exception and that it was never the intent of Congress to make a tenant automatically responsible for the acts of a relative or visitor.

A unanimous 2002 Supreme Court decision overturned a ruling by a federal appeals court in San Francisco that had interpreted the provision of the Anti-Drug Abuse Act of 1988 to bar the eviction of "innocent" tenants who had neither knowledge of nor control over their family members' drug use. The plaintiffs who challenged the evictions in Oakland included two whose grandchildren, who lived with the plaintiffs, were caught smoking marijuana in a housing project parking lot; one whose daughter was found with cocaine three blocks from the apartment; and a disabled 75-year-old man whose caretaker was found with cocaine in his apartment. The Court said that there was nothing unconstitutional about "no-fault evictions" of tenants who failed to meet a condition of their lease (Greenhouse, 2002).

THE REVERSE DRUG STING

The *reverse sting* is an undercover operation in which the officer poses as a drug dealer and places buyers under arrest after certain necessary conversations and actions have been documented. Controversy about the appropriateness of the reverse sting as a police tactic centers on the legal question of *entrapment*, which takes place when government agents or police officers induce a person to commit a crime that was not originally contemplated by that person. Since the initiation of this covert police tactic, some courts have excluded all but the most compelling evidence obtained in such operations. Other courts, however, have accepted this practice as lawful and appropriate.

Other dangers are also inherent in this type of operation. For example, an undercover officer working in this capacity must maintain constant contact with street dealers, who will

> ### Critical Thinking Task
> Profile the "typical" drug dealer in your community; that is, how would you recognize this individual?

soon become familiar with the physical description of the officer and spread the description to other drug dealers. On the other hand, an advantage of the reverse sting operation is that it requires little funding for "buy money," which is often needed in greater amounts in long-term drug investigations. In many instances, law enforcement agencies may actually generate revenue to help compensate for future drug investigations. In Washington, D.C., for example, undercover officers sold inert substances to would-be drug buyers, who were penalized by the loss of their cash (through forfeiture) rather than by arrest.

Entrapment and Reverse Stings

In a related case, *Jacobson v. United States* (1992), the U.S. Supreme Court limited the authority of police in reverse sting-type operations. The *Jacobson* case involved a 1984 reverse sting operation conducted by the U.S. Postal Service. In February of that year, Jacobson ordered two magazines from an adult bookstore, *Bare Boys I* and *Bare Boys II*, each containing photographs of nude preteen and teenage boys. Although Jacobson's purchase was not illegal at that time, the Child Protection Act of 1984 criminalized the receipt through the mail of a "visual depiction that involves the use of a minor engaging in sexually explicit conduct...." After finding Jacobson's name on a mailing list, postal inspectors sent him a letter and application for membership from a fictitious organization associated with pornographic material. Over the following 26 months, Jacobson was contacted by five different organizations. In one contact, Jacobson was sent a brochure advertising photographs of young boys engaging in sex. Finally, Jacobson ordered the magazine *Boys Who Love Boys* from a brochure. The magazine was delivered and Jacobson was arrested.

The question in *Jacobson* was: Did the government's operation, which lasted more than two years, offer enough inducement to cause the "unwary innocent" to commit a crime, constituting entrapment? The U.S. Supreme Court said yes. The Court stated that "in their zeal to enforce the law … government agents may not originate a criminal design, implant in an innocent person's mind the disposition to commit a criminal act, and then induce commission of the crime so that the government may prosecute." This case is important because the Court reversed Jacobson's conviction on the basis that the government agents used entrapment to make their case by implanting in the defendant's mind the desire to commit a criminal act.

In drug cases in which reverse stings are employed, similar principles apply. As a rule, these operations target the novice drug user rather than one who has spent more time on the street. Experienced users usually patronize a specific dealer, thereby reducing their need to purchase drugs from a stranger on the street corner who might be a police officer or informant.

ZERO TOLERANCE

The *zero tolerance* enforcement initiative was implemented in 1988 under the Reagan administration, with the support of Customs Commissioner William Von Raab. Essentially, the policy directed the U.S. Coast Guard, Customs, and other arms of the federal government to enforce existing law to the utmost degree, thereby addressing the demand side of the drug abuse problem. The plan focused on the seizing of vehicles, boats, and planes if even a tiny amount of any controlled substance was found on board.

Zero tolerance has its roots in the seizure sanctions of federal law in which "administrative seizures" are possible without the owner necessarily being convicted of any crime. Police in cities such as New York and Miami have used this method to impound the automobiles of drug buyers whose drug purchases themselves would only result in a misdemeanor charge. Commissioner Von Raab said in 1988 that the purpose of the zero tolerance program was to "put pressure on drug users who ordinarily are not reached by criminal penalties."

Jamaican musician Buju Banton, right, poses with singer Wyclef Jean, left, at the Source Hip-Hop Music Awards in 2003. In court in early 2010, facing felony charges of possession of cocaine with intent to distribute, Banton claimed to be the victim of a government-run scheme in which an informant was paid to convince him to buy cocaine.

In May 1988, Customs seized the *Atlantis II*, an $80 million research vessel once used to explore the wreck of the *Titanic*, after a routine search netted traces of marijuana and two marijuana pipes in a crew member's shaving kit. The ship was returned, but only after its owner, the Woods Hole Oceanographic Institution, agreed to send Customs a letter supporting the antidrug campaign and promising to tighten security.

Controversy about this policy arose over the argument that many owners of such vessels and vehicles may risk the loss of their property without personal knowledge of any controlled substance being aboard. Members of the ACLU have stated that this is an unconstitutional practice because of the traditional premise in U.S. jurisprudence that the punishment must fit the crime.

THE WAR ON DRUGS AS A WAR ON WOMEN

One of the most devastating aspects of America's drug war has been its impact on women in general and minority women in particular. According to the 2008 *National Survey on Drug Use and Health* (NSDUH), approximately 42.9 percent of female respondents age 12 or older reported using an illicit drug at some point in their lives. Approximately 12.2 percent of females age 12 and older reported past-year use of an illicit drug, and 6.3 percent reported past-month use of an illicit drug (U.S. Department of Health and Human Services, 2009).

A study by the Correctional Association of New York, focusing on the arrests and prosecutions of "drug mules" in Queens, illustrates the impact of the drug war on women. The study found a drastic increase in the number of women arrested and subsequently charged with felony narcotics offenses. Many of these women were first-time offenders arrested for attempting to smuggle drugs through JFK International Airport, a major entry point for international travelers. As a result of the combined effect of New York's "Rockefeller Drug Laws" and the accessorial liability statute, women suspected of being drug couriers in the employ of smuggling syndicates faced mandatory prison sentences of 15 years to life on their first felony arrests. If they were also charged under federal laws, they faced the additional risk of a 50-years-to-life federal sentence (Correctional Association of New York, 1992).

Investigations determined that many of these women were either unwitting agents of drug smugglers or were women only marginally involved in drug-smuggling operations. Because of the severe sentences they faced, most of these women did not go to trial. Instead they accepted plea bargains carrying sentences of three years to life, a sentence that is out of proportion to other first-time felony sentences. Many of these women were mothers who were either unable or unwilling to be separated from their children for potentially very long periods if they were convicted of the original charges. In fact, it has been found that 80 percent of all women prisoners in the United States are the sole caretakers of children under the age of 18 (Greenfield and Harper, 1991). Moreover, according to the study, many female drug couriers who were charged pled guilty even if they had valid defenses or were innocent of the charges being proffered (Correctional Association of New York, 1992).

In many drug courier cases, women are disproportionately impacted by restrictions on judicial discretion in mandatory sentencing drug statutes. The defendant's inability to present evidence of mitigating circumstances in such cases is particularly crippling (Letwin, 1994:2). As a result, the rate of incarceration for women grew dramatically in the 1980s, increasing by 275 percent from 1980 to 1992 in the United States as a whole and increasing by 433 percent (from 2,370 to 12,633) between 1986 and 1991 for drug defendants incarcerated in state prison. By 1991, one out of every three women incarcerated in a state prison was there as the result of a drug conviction, up from one in eight in 1986 (Mauer and Huling, 1995).

The impact of the drug war on women does not end with women as drug defendants. With drug policy emphasizing enforcement and punishment rather than education and rehabilitation, the impact on families is profound. When fathers are incarcerated on drug trafficking or, more likely, drug possession charges, it is usually women who are left as single heads of households to raise the children. When male children are arrested for drug sales, it is their mothers who bear the brunt of the civil forfeiture laws, losing possessions as well as what meager funds they may have accumulated in bank accounts and facing almost certain eviction from their domiciles. When male addicts share needles because of a policy that makes the provision of clean needles a criminal offense, the women with whom they have sex also face the risk of HIV infection.

For women who are not drug couriers or traffickers but merely users with addictions, legal discrimination is the most intense. These women face not only the threat of arrests for possession but also mandatory reporting requirements and child abuse and neglect laws that can deprive them of access to medical care, prenatal care, and even drug counseling and treatment. Pregnant and new mothers face the danger of criminal prosecution on charges ranging from drug distribution to assault and murder. This discourages any effort to seek drug treatment, prenatal care, or even postnatal care for their babies. These kinds of criminal charges are the most discriminatory of all, excluding men from any participation and possibly endangering the health of mothers and children far more egregiously than any pattern of drug use ever could.

The "Crack Babies" Scare

Increases in cocaine use as well as the introduction of cocaine in smokable form ("crack") in the early 1980s raised concerns about the potential impact of cocaine use on pregnant women and their fetuses. Although it is clear that use of any drug, whether alcohol, tobacco, or crack, is unadvisable during pregnancy, the panic that resulted from early research claims about cocaine's damage to fetuses and the laws passed by state and federal governments in response to that research clearly exaggerated the potential harm and created policies that did more damage to the mother and fetus than the drug itself.

Early research, particularly a 1985 case study, suggested that prenatal cocaine use could result in several health problems related to fetal development, the health of the newborn, and future child development. Shortly thereafter, several other studies linked prenatal cocaine use to maternal weight loss and nutritional deficits; premature detachment of the placenta; premature birth; low birth weight; reductions in infants' body length and head circumference; and rare birth defects, bone defects, and neural tube abnormalities (Coffin, 1996).

The media widely repeated these research findings, creating the impression that an epidemic of "crack babies" was plaguing the medical community. The "crack baby crisis" resulted in the passing of laws that required doctors and nurses to report pregnant drug users to child welfare authorities. Other laws were quickly passed that required child welfare agencies to take children away from mothers who had used drugs while pregnant. Consequently, many states criminalized drug use during pregnancy.

However, in this flurry of media activity and legislative frenzy to pass harsh laws, few took note of continuing research on the issue of prenatal cocaine use that seemed to call the whole "crack baby scare" into question. For example, subsequent reviews of the early studies on prenatal cocaine use found serious methodological difficulties, including the absence of any control groups, a failure to distinguish cocaine from other substances in the studies, and lack of follow-up studies on the health and development of the newborn (Coffin, 1996).

One of the most serious problems with early studies suggesting a "fetal cocaine withdrawal syndrome" was that they were "nonblind," meaning that the individuals making the observations were told in advance which infants had mothers who had used cocaine during pregnancy. It has been argued then that the resulting research was biased and that it contradicted other observations from doctors and nurses who reported cocaine-exposed children to be indistinguishable from other children. In subsequent blind studies, therefore, it came as no surprise that observers were unable to detect the presence of "fetal cocaine withdrawal syndrome" (Coffin, 1996).

In addition, research using control groups finds no increased risk of sudden infant death syndrome (SIDS) among cocaine-exposed infants. Earlier studies suggesting a possible relationship between SIDS and maternal cocaine use had failed to control for one of the most important variables in SIDS deaths: the socioeconomic status of the mother (Coffin, 1996).

In reviewing all the studies on both animals and humans, it is now clear that most found no direct effects on newborns from social cocaine use, or they arrived at inconsistent results suggesting the presence of factors other than cocaine use. No study has been able to establish a causal link between maternal cocaine and poor fetal development, and epidemiological studies have not detected any increase in birth defects that could be associated with cocaine use during pregnancy. However, it is likely that cocaine, like any other psychoactive substance that enters the bloodstream, has the potential to impact fetal and newborn development (Coffin, 1996).

Rather than maternal cocaine use, most of the scientific evidence points to the lack of quality prenatal care, the use of alcohol and tobacco, environmental agents, and heredity as primary factors in poor fetal development and birth defects. Inadequate prenatal medical services have been positively associated with prematurity and low birth weight. The provision of quality prenatal care to both cocaine-using and noncocaine-using mothers significantly improves fetal development. There is little question that it is the use of alcohol, resulting in fetal alcohol syndrome, that is responsible for the most severe birth defects. Tobacco use has also been strongly associated with low birth weight, prematurity, growth retardation, SIDS, low cognitive achievement, behavioral problems, and mental retardation. Other factors that surpass cocaine use in their impact on fetal and newborn development include poverty and exposure to lead (Coffin, 1996).

If Lindesmith Center is correct in their observations, the legal responses to the "crack babies scare" clearly did more harm than good to both mothers and the children. Making substance abuse during pregnancy a crime kept mothers from prenatal medical care, thereby endangering their fetuses more than would be the case with drug use, and discouraged them from seeking drug treatment. When babies were removed from maternal care as a result of alleged drug use, social service agencies found it difficult and often impossible to find homes for infants labeled "crack babies" because of the alleged behavioral problems that might occur during infancy and early childhood. In addition, enforcement of maternal drug abuse laws also appeared to be blatantly racist. More than 80 percent of the women subjected to prosecution under those laws were African Americans or Latinos (Coffin, 1996).

Cocaine use during pregnancy is certainly not a good idea, but the fact remains that at least one recent study on cocaine use by pregnant women suggests that the pharmacological impact of cocaine has been greatly exaggerated, that many other factors impact fetal and newborn development, and that legal responses to maternal cocaine use have in some cases made the problem worse. As a responsible society we must ask ourselves one important question: When a new drug, or a new form of a drug, appears on the street, as with crack in the mid-1980s, what stance should we take? Should we consider the drug harmless until we discover that it is not, or should we first outlaw it as a precaution until such time that it is found to be harmless? In spite of the Lindesmith Center findings, we still know that crack is cocaine, and evidence abounds that cocaine is dangerous. We also realize, now more than ever, that virtually anything a pregnant mother ingests (cigarettes, alcohol, etc.) may present a risk to the unborn child. While some might consider "crack baby legislation" to be draconian and overbearing, to many it is a form of responsible, preventive safety for children who cannot yet speak for themselves.

Rachael Lowe and her husband await the start of her court hearing. After attempting to obtain counseling for an addiction to OxyContin, Lowe was confined for drug treatment under Wisconsin's "cocaine mom" law. Although the law is purportedly designed to protect the fetus of a pregnant woman from her abuse of alcohol or other drugs, her husband contended that the facility allowed only access to psychiatric care and not to prenatal care for her fetus.

MANDATORY MINIMUM SENTENCING

As suggested in the previous section, one of the more controversial issues in drug control today is the mandatory minimum sentencing policy of the federal court system. At the core of the issue is the realization by police and prosecutors that drug dealers are innovative and cunning and will employ many measures to avoid detection. Because one of the drug dealer's greatest fears is a prison sentence, experts have suggested that the best deterrent to drug crime is the threat of mandatory incarceration. So, under mandatory minimum sentencing laws, an arrested offender has two choices: to go to prison if convicted or to become a government witness against his or her supplier. This is the basis and hallmark of mandatory minimum sentencing, one that police argue is an effective tool for legal leverage against drug dealers. It gives prosecutors the option to not file a drug charge provided that the offender agrees to work with police in collecting evidence against others in the drug-trafficking operation. As experience has shown, the informant who is cooperating with authorities in exchange for prosecutorial leniency ("working a beef") has proved to be one of the most powerfully motivated players in the criminal investigation process, and clearly it is the codefendant who is most knowledgeable about a drug-trafficking enterprise.

In 1986 Congress enacted mandatory minimum sentencing laws, which force judges to deliver fixed sentences to individuals convicted of a crime, regardless of culpability or other mitigating factors. Federal mandatory drug sentences are determined based on three factors: (1) the type of drug, (2) the weight of the drug mixture (or alleged weight, in conspiracy cases), and (3) the number of prior convictions. Judges are unable to consider other important factors such as the offender's role and motivation and the likelihood of recidivism. Only by providing the prosecutor with "substantial assistance" (information that aids the government in prosecuting other offenders) may defendants reduce their mandatory sentences. This creates huge incentives for people charged with drug offenses to provide false information in order to receive a shorter sentence.

Although Congress intended mandatory sentences to target "kingpins" and managers in drug distribution networks, the U.S. Sentencing Commission reports that only 5.5 percent of all federal crack cocaine defendants and 11 percent of federal drug defendants are high-level drug dealers. This is because the most culpable defendants are also the defendants who are in the best position to provide prosecutors with enough information to obtain sentence reductions—the only way to reduce a mandatory sentence. Low-level offenders, such as drug mules or street dealers, often end up serving longer sentences because they have little or no information to provide the government.

Critical Thinking Task

Support or refute the federal court system's policy of mandatory minimum sentencing for the possession of crack cocaine.

The U.S. Sentencing Commission and the Department of Justice have both concluded that mandatory sentencing fails to deter crime. Furthermore, mandatory minimums have worsened racial and gender disparities and have contributed greatly toward prison overcrowding. Mandatory minimum sentencing is costly and unjust. Mandatory sentencing does not eliminate sentencing disparities; instead it shifts decision-making authority from judges to prosecutors, who operate without accountability. Mandatory minimums fail to punish high-level dealers. Finally, mandatory sentences are responsible for sending record numbers of women and people of color to prison. For example:

- *Prison overcrowding.* More than 80 percent of the increase in the federal prison population from 1985 to 1995 is due to drug convictions.
- *Racial injustice.* In 1986, the year Congress enacted federal mandatory drug sentences, the average federal drug sentence for African Americans was 11 percent higher than for whites. Four years later, the average federal drug sentence for African Americans was 49 percent higher.
- *Women.* Between 1986 and 1996, the number of women in prison for drug law violations increased by 421 percent. This led U.S. Bureau of Prisons Director Kathleen Hawk-Sawyer to testify before Congress, "The reality is, some 70-some percent of our female population are low-level, nonviolent offenders. The fact that they have to come into prison is a question mark for me. I think it has been an unintended consequence of the sentencing guidelines and the mandatory minimums" (Drug Policy Alliance, 2007).

ELECTRONIC SURVEILLANCE

The past 40 years have seen a virtual revolution in technology relevant to electronic surveillance. Advances in electronics, semiconductors, computers, imaging, databases, and related technologies have greatly increased technological options for police surveillance activities. Although the use of electronic surveillance in drug control is nothing new, techniques such as the wiretap have raised renewed concerns over the protection of privacy.

Title III of the Omnibus Crime Control and Safe Streets Act of 1968, the major law addressing electronic surveillance, was designed to protect the privacy of wire and oral communications. At the time this act was passed, electronic surveillance was primarily limited to telephone taps and hidden microphones (bugs). Since then, however, basic communications have undergone rapid technological changes with the advent of such technologies as personal pagers, personal computers, cellular telephones, e-mail, electronic bulletin boards, social networking sites, and more. Many of these devices are now commonly used by drug traffickers to assist them in communicating with drug suppliers and customers.

Figure 11.1
Source: Office of Technology Assessment, 1985.

1. *Movements.* Where someone is. Individuals can be tracked electronically via beepers as well as by monitoring computerized transactional accounts.

2. *Actions.* What someone is doing or has done. Electronic devices to monitor action include keystrokes on computer terminals, telephone numbers called with pen registers, cable TV monitoring, financial and computerized accounts, and computerized law enforcement or investigatory systems.

3. *Communications.* What someone is saying, writing, hearing, or receiving. Two-way electronic communications can be intercepted (whether the means be analog or digital communication) via wired telephones, cordless or cellular telephones, or digital electronic mail. Two-way nonelectronic communication can be intercepted via a variety of microphone devices and other transmitters.

4. *Actions and communications.* The details of what someone is doing or saying. Electronic visual surveillance, generally accompanied by audio surveillance, can monitor the actions and communications of individuals in both public and private places and in daylight or darkness.

5. *Emotions.* The psychological and physiological reactions to circumstances. Polygraph testing, voice stress analyzers, and brain wave analyzers attempt to determine an individual's reactions.

Categories of Behavior Subject to Electronic Surveillance

Because new and increasingly mobile drug gangs are evident throughout the country, law enforcement agencies at both the state and federal level are making more frequent use of electronic surveillance technology to combat drug trafficking. Public concerns arise with regard to the circumstances under which these technologies are applied and how they might infringe on First, Fourth, and Fifth Amendment rights. At the same time, however, the public is also concerned about crime (especially violent crime) and generally supports the use of electronic technology in criminal investigations. As a result, balancing these concerns remains a critical issue in drug control.

The primary purpose of electronic surveillance is to monitor the behavior of individuals, including individual movements, actions, communications, emotions, and/or various combinations of these. From a law enforcement and investigative standpoint, the potential benefits offered through new technologies may be substantial—for example, the development of more accurate and complete information on suspects, the possible reduction in time and human resources required for case investigation, and the expansion of options for preventing and deterring crimes. From a societal perspective, the possible benefits are also important, including the potential for increasing one's physical security in the home and on the streets, strengthening efforts to prevent drug trafficking, and enhancing the protection of citizens and government officials from terrorist actions.

Electronic surveillance is used primarily in gambling and narcotics cases. For years, gambling was the most common object of electronic surveillance, and narcotics was second most common; more recently, the order was reversed. The difficulty in using intrusion as a principle by which to evaluate a "reasonable expectation of privacy" and the appropriateness of using a particular surveillance device is that no criteria have yet been explicitly formulated to determine intrusiveness. Instead, the facts of individual cases seem to determine individual courses of action.

Still, based on court rulings, congressional statutes, and executive orders, it is possible to isolate five important dimensions in determining whether the situation warrants violation or protection of ordinary civil liberties. The five dimensions are: (1) the nature of the information, (2) the nature of the area or communication to be placed under surveillance, (3) the scope of the surveillance, (4) the surreptitiousness of the surveillance, and (5) preelectronic analysis. In evaluating the legitimacy of the government's use of surveillance devices, three dimensions are considered: (1) the purpose of the investigation, (2) the degree of individualized suspicion, and (3) the relative effectiveness of the surveillance.

Figure 11.2
Source: Office of Technology Assessment, 1985.

Civil liberty interest:
1. *Nature of information.* The more personal or intimate the information that is to be gathered about a target, the more intrusive is the surveillance technique and the greater the intrusion to civil liberties.
2. *Nature of the place or communication.* The more "private" the area or type of communication to be placed under surveillance, the more intrusive is the surveillance and the greater the threat to civil liberties.
3. *Scope of the surveillance.* The more people and activities that are subject to surveillance, the more intrusive is the surveillance and the greater the threat to civil liberties.
4. *Surreptitiousness of surveillance.* The less likely it is for the individual to be aware of the surveillance and the harder it is for the individual to detect it, the greater the threat to civil liberties.

Government's investigative interest:
1. *Purpose of investigation.* Importance is ranked as follows: national security, domestic security, law enforcement, and the proper administration of government programs.
2. *Degree of individualized suspicion.* The lower the level of suspicion is, the harder it is to justify the use of surveillance devices.
3. *Relative effectiveness.* More traditional investigative techniques should be used and proven ineffective before using technologically sophisticated techniques.

Dimensions for Balancing Civil Liberty Interest Against Government Investigative Interest

It appears that the use of higher technology in surveillance activities by law enforcement agencies will prevail. With the more frequent use of detection devices and electronic equipment by drug traffickers, surveillance equipment will become more sophisticated. Implementing such technology will no doubt continue to fall under close scrutiny by courts and public groups in the coming years. Its use, however, is clearly an important factor in the detection and documentation of covert criminal activity in the drug trade.

DRUG TESTING

Hardly a day goes by without more news detailing the extent of drug abuse in our society. The statistics are clear evidence that something must be done to curtail the problem. Naturally, because most drug abuse is done in private, it is difficult to detect. Studies in recent years have shown that drug testing may play an important role in deterring drug use. For example, experts have discovered that drug testing by the government during the Vietnam War played a significant role in deterring soldiers from using drugs, especially when testing was linked to punishment. In the early 1970s, when the Department of Defense began testing troops returning from Vietnam, about 5 percent tested positive for drugs, even though the troops were aware that they would be tested and that their departure for home would be delayed. After the first six months of testing, the number dropped to 2 percent. Today, the criminal justice system regularly tests criminal defendants during different stages of the criminal process, including arrest, incarceration, and supervised release. The idea is to deter continued drug use by defendants by detecting use through drug tests.

Testing employees in the workplace has also been suggested by some as an effective way to identify, treat, and control drug abuse. The goal of workplace testing is to enhance on-the-job performance and safety by identifying people who are impaired on the job. Armed security guards and transportation workers, for example, may pose a public threat if impaired while on the job. Testing also helps employers identify drug users so they can be referred to treatment and may serve to promote public trust in companies that have established drug-testing policies.

Despite critics' claims that it is an invasion of privacy and an unreasonable search in violation of federal and state constitutions, drug testing in various forms is either legal or in the process of becoming legal. For example, in 1988, Congress passed the Drug-Free Workplace Act. A Gallup poll taken that year found that 11 states had passed laws regulating the confidentiality and accuracy of drug-testing programs, 7 states regulated who can be tested and under what circumstances, and 14 states had introduced legislation for drug testing, most of it regulating testing procedures but not the circumstances under which testing can be performed. Additionally, federal and state executive departments and agencies have promulgated drug-testing rules. For example, a 1990 survey of state and local police agencies found that 23 percent of local police agencies had adopted policies authorizing testing of applicants, and 14 percent of those authorized drug testing of officers working in drug-related positions.

Because the workplace offers a captive pool of subjects, proponents of the drug-testing control strategy have advocated that drug testing be accomplished in that forum. The U.S. Supreme Court has legitimized some kinds of drug testing. Accordingly, testing in the workplace is generally concerned with the following five areas: (1) whom to test, (2) when to test, (3) what procedure to follow, (4) what to test for, and (5) what sanctions to impose on employees with positive test results.

Federal and state courts have generally held that an employer may test an applicant for drugs if the applicant is told of the testing beforehand. An employer may, therefore, withhold an employment offer based on a confirmed test result. The issue of testing employees raises other concerns. Arguments in favor of drug testing for employees generally focus on concerns for employee safety and employer liability. Other arguments in favor of testing address issues such as decreased job performance and productivity, rising absenteeism, and rising healthcare costs.

Most of the controversy over drug testing stems from the arbitrary, random, or unannounced testing of the worker on the job, as mentioned. Civil libertarians argue that this is an invasion of one's privacy and that drug testing in the workplace is a violation of one's Fourth and Fifth Amendment rights.

Despite these assertions, most courts have held that employees may indeed be tested under certain circumstances. Specifically, if the employee is put on notice of being tested for drugs, an employer may test upon reasonable suspicion of drug use after a reportable injury or a chargeable accident. In addition, legal trends indicate that employee testing as part of a physical examination, or random testing if the employee is in a safety-sensitive position, will become more customary.

The Department of Transportation's extensive drug-testing program delineates many specific procedures for administrators to follow. In particular, the program addresses the confidentiality of records and employee identity, specimen tampering, control over the transfer of collected specimens (the chain of custody), certification of laboratories, testing methods (including confirmation of an initial positive test result by mass spectrometry and gas-liquid chromatography technology, as discussed later in this section), medical evaluation of test results, and sanctions for confirmed test results of employees. At the time of this writing, current law does not uniformly identify the drugs for which an employee may be tested. Many companies and agencies have chosen to follow the lead of the Department of Transportation and test only for the NIDA-5 (NIDA is the National Institute on Drug Abuse): marijuana, cocaine, opiates, phencyclidine, and amphetamine. Most drug-testing programs have adopted one of three ways of screening for drugs. These are as follows:

- *Preemployment screening.* This method tests all or selected applicants for employment, usually in conjunction with a preemployment physical. A positive result is usually followed up by a second or confirmatory test. In some cases, the applicants are informed of the drug test ahead of time and are questioned about any medication they are on, including reasons for the medication. This is because both prescription and nonprescription drugs can be abused, and the presence of these drugs should be investigated.
- *For cause.* Supervisors or employers can request this test if they suspect that an employee is unfit for work or is impaired by alcohol or other drugs. A specimen may be requested to determine whether the employee has indeed been under the influence of alcohol or other drugs. Typically, this method occurs after an accident or an observable change in behavior of the employee.
- *Random urinalysis.* This method involves the selection of an appropriately significant number as well as a scientifically drawn random sample of employees for screening. Screening is usually performed several times a year, each time on a different random sample. Basically, this means that all employees in a particular job category are eligible at any time for screening.

The testing cycle usually involves the initial screening of a urine sample, followed by a confirmatory test for samples suspected of containing drugs. These procedures are discussed in greater detail here:

- *Drug screening.* The methods used to screen urine samples are designed to be an accurate and reliable means to distinguish negative specimens from those that may contain drugs or drug metabolites. Drug-screening techniques should be precise so that operator technique cannot adversely affect performance. Examples of the major immunoassay technologies are:
  - *Abbott-Fluorescence Polarization Immunoassay (AFPI).* This system is an extremely sensitive, rapid, precise, and reliable screening technique that is also fully automated. The system functions on an inverse relationship between signal to drug concentration, which provides excellent sensitivity at low drug concentrations. The system also uses a reagent (chemical) bar-coding technology that virtually eliminates the possibility of operator error.
  - *Roche-Radioimmunoassay (RIA).* RIA technology is also an extremely sensitive and reliable screening system. It is even the U.S. Armed Forces' screening method of choice. Drawbacks to the system are that it requires expensive ancillary equipment for operation and that it uses radioactive reagents to detect the presence of drugs. This requires operators to wear special protective clothing and to be specially trained in handling discarded materials, all of which add to the cost of the testing procedure.
  - *Syva-Enzyme Multiplied Immunoassay Technique (EMIT).* The EMIT system functions on a direct relationship between signal to drug concentration; it is less sensitive than FPIA and RIA and less precise at low drug concentrations. A disadvantage of the EMIT

system is that there are significant variations in test results between technologies and a high rate of poor performance when challenged by blind testing. (For example, EMIT has a 40 percent false negative rate in that it will miss 40 percent of individuals who have smoked marijuana in the previous 48 hours.)

- *Confirmation tests*. As mentioned, when drug tests may affect an individual's personal rights, a positive drug screening must be followed by a secondary or confirmatory test. The second test must be based on different chemical principles with an equal or lower threshold value than the screening test and must specifically identify the drug present in the sample using a different portion of the original sample.

  The technology most commonly used for the confirmatory test is *gas-liquid chromatography* (GC) or *mass spectrometry* (MS). Of these two technologies, MS is considered the more reliable, but it is also more expensive to purchase and operate. More recently, Hewlett-Packard Company developed a detector called a *mass selective detector* (MSD), which is less expensive than a full mass spectrometer and provides the same high-quality data.

- *Chain of custody*. This is the method of documenting which urine sample belongs to which testee and who handled the sample from the time it was originally collected. Without strict procedures for establishing the chain of custody of the urine sample, even the most technologically advanced drug-testing method will be of no value. The issue of chain of custody involves several critical phases of the testing procedure. These are as follows:

- Collecting the sample
- Labeling the sample
- Limiting the number of individuals who handle the sample
- Ensuring that samples are stored properly
- Limiting access to information about test results to individuals with a legitimate need to know

Other important issues that should be considered in drug testing are:

- The passive inhalation of marijuana when an individual is present in a room where it is being smoked
- The ingestion of certain foods or substances that may result in false-positive drug readings (some claim that poppy seed bagels may test positive for opiates, for instance)
- The lack of standards directing drug-testing laboratories to operate under the same set of criteria
- The cause-and-effect relationship between the presence of drugs and one's behavior, which is usually an issue in "probable cause" testing
- The distinction between the different drug-testing arenas, such as hospitals, treatment centers, sports testing (discussed later in this chapter), the military, schools, probation and parole programs, and so on
- The adulteration of specimens, such as when urine substitution or dilution takes place

If it is true that a substantial group of drug users utilize drugs only on weekends, at parties, and for purposes of relaxation and diversion, then drug testing may alter drug-use patterns. For example, marijuana users will test positive for drug use for a far longer period of time than will cocaine users. A user who wants to get high on a Friday night is relatively safe from a positive drug test on Monday morning if he or she uses cocaine, but the same person can be almost certain of a positive test if he or she uses marijuana. The same relationship occurs with regard to amphetamine use. As a result, some theorize that for those drug users who are determined to get high, drug testing may lead many of them to switch to harder drugs, which last a shorter period of time in their systems.

As technology progresses, drug testing may someday be done by the analysis of human hair follicles. A 1987 study by Gideon Koren of the Hospital for Sick Children in Toronto compared urine and hair samples for evidence of drug abuse. Koren contended that once traces of drugs enter the hair, they are permanently registered there. Testing hair follicles, he asserted, would eliminate the problem of employees avoiding detection of drug use by abstaining from drug use just before being tested by employers.

In 1990, however, the American Medical Association (AMA) reported on Koren's findings and argued that although there is some credence to the testing of hair follicles for drugs, urine provides the most reliable data to date. According to the AMA, dyeing or bleaching hair, as well as exposure to other substances such as automobile exhaust fumes, can contaminate test results.

These issues and others pose important questions and considerations that must be addressed in this critical area of drug control. Because existing technology is generally considered reliable by professionals in the area, the "ironing out" of other ancillary issues may result in effective alternatives to traditional drug control methods.

AP Photo/Alan Mothner

Sunny Cloud poses with a Parent's Alert kit. Cloud invented her own home drug test kit after she caught her son smoking marijuana in her home.

Home Drug Testing

In November 1995 Psychemedics Incorporated of Cambridge, Massachusetts, began manufacturing a drug test for the home, known as PDT-90. Recent questions have been raised about home drug testing, a process designed to give parents a way to find out whether their child is using drugs. In one case, the parent cuts off a lock of the child's hair and the laboratory can tell whether drugs are present. Though the tests provide parents with answers, the more fundamental question remains whether it is appropriate for parents to check out their children surreptitiously. Opponents argue that such a system of home inspection creates resentment and ill will in families and may do more harm than good. Even the accuracy of hair testing is in question to an extent. Concerns include:

- Hair can pick up drugs from the environment.
- Coloring or bleaching can affect the amount of drugs that can be measured.
- The test may be biased against blacks and others with more scalp pigment.

Drug Testing in Schools

Concern about drugs has caused parents to demand more accountability on the part of schools to do something about the situation. As the practice of drug testing becomes more accepted and widely used, schools around the country are considering drug tests as a condition for playing sports. Some are even using part of their drug education funds to pay for the tests. It costs $30 a test to screen for alcohol and recreational drugs and more than $100 to test for steroids. Many school administrators have learned that drug testing for athletes is one way to help curb drug use.

The recent trend toward student drug testing sprang from a 1995 U.S. Supreme Court decision that cleared a major legal hurdle for schools. In a challenge to an Oregon school's random drug testing of athletes, the Court held that testing of public school athletes is constitutional. The Court essentially said that schools do not need to determine that students have a drug problem before forcing them to be tested. The Court narrowed its ruling to student athletes because sports is a voluntary activity and the use of alcohol and/or other drugs can pose a health threat to athletes and their teammates.

In most cases, a parent is notified immediately when a son or daughter tests positive. A second, unscheduled test is given to make sure no mistake was made. If results are positive a second time, the student must undergo counseling and face temporary or permanent suspension from the sport or activity. Although parents and students are still concerned about rights to privacy, support is nevertheless strong in the school districts where such programs are being implemented.

NEEDLE EXCHANGE PROGRAMS

Needle sharing is a major problem in inner cities in which heroin addiction prevails. The heroin addict typically injects himself or herself with the drug several times a day. Because sterile needles are not always available, the sharing of needles between one person and another sometimes occurs.

The problem of acquired immune deficiency syndrome (AIDS) dominates much of the medical profession's public health and policy concerns. Although the transmission of the disease is often accomplished through sexual activity, an estimated 20 percent of AIDS cases were reported to have been transmitted through intravenous drug users sharing needles. According to testimony before the U.S. House of Representatives in April 1989, one HIV-infected drug user can conceivably expose up to 100 other users over the course of a few months (ONDCP, 2002). (Other communicable diseases such as hepatitis are also transmitted in this fashion.) In an effort to curb the spread of the disease, both researchers and medical professionals have considered the controversial idea of exchanging clean needles for the dirty needles belonging to drug addicts.

Most needle exchange programs consist of three basic functions:

1. To dispense sterile needles to current IV (intravenous) users
2. To promote and accept returns of used needles to control how needles are discarded
3. To change the behavior of IV-drug users through health education and counseling

A debate continues to rage about needle exchange programs across the country. Needle exchange programs offer clean needles to drug users in exchange for dirty ones in an effort to cut down on the number of blood-borne diseases among intravenous drug users, but many feel that such programs encourage drug use, that the needles will not be used, and that the programs will only create more drug addicts and, accordingly, more AIDS carriers. The assertion that the needles will not be used is based on the view that needle sharing is a ritualistic practice, deeply embedded into the subculture of IV-drug users. Another argument against the exchange programs is that giving away needles is illegal. The question of legality may be a valid one, at least in certain jurisdictions, and is constantly being addressed at the state and local government levels.

Proponents of needle exchange programs argue that they help not only the drug users at risk but their sex partners and children as well. Opponents of needle exchange programs suggest that the programs may cost lives. At the political crux of the issue is this question: Should the federal government, which spends billions on the drug war, do anything that may encourage drug use? Supporters claim that the scientific case for such programs is overwhelming, since needle exchange programs have been shown to cut HIV infection rates without increasing drug use. Opponents claim that the studies showing this finding are flawed. However, scientific reviews sponsored by the federal Centers for Disease Control and Prevention, the Institute of Medicine, the

Critical Thinking Task

Assume you are on the New York City Council. Explain your "yea" or "nay" vote to continue the City Health Department's $230,000-per-year program to exchange addicts' used needles for sterile ones.

National Institutes of Health, and the General Accounting Office all have agreed with the usefulness of needle programs (Painter, 1997).

When considering the appropriateness of such a program, perhaps one should consider the success or failure of similar programs in England, the Netherlands, Sweden, and Australia, where needle-sharing programs have been operational since 1984. The results are extremely consistent. In Amsterdam, for example, researchers noted that 80 percent of needle exchange users in the program stopped sharing equipment since the program began, compared to 50 percent of nonexchangers.

FORFEITURE OF ATTORNEY'S FEES

Considering the enormous cash flow of many drug traffickers, it is logical to assume that much of the money earned through illicit drug transactions ends up in the bank accounts of lawyers who represent drug traffickers. Through the use of carefully sculpted laws such as the 1984 Federal Comprehensive Forfeiture Act (CFA), the instances of lawyers knowingly accepting "dirty" money or assets for legal fees have greatly decreased. The most conspicuous legal precedents addressing the issue were handed down by the Supreme Court in 1989 in *United States v. Monsanto* and *Caplin & Drysdale, Chartered v. United States*. These decisions basically held that the government's ability to enforce forfeiture extends to drug assets needed to pay attorney's fees.

In reviewing these cases, the *Monsanto* decision involved a defendant who was facing charges under the federal Continuing Criminal Enterprise (CCE) statute of creating a continuing criminal enterprise. The indictment asserted that the defendant had acquired an apartment, a home, and a sum of $35,000 in cash as a result of drug-trafficking activities. The government subsequently sought to freeze all of the defendant's assets until the trial was over. In response, the defendant claimed that those assets were necessary to retain a competent lawyer for his defense. His claim was rejected by the district court.

As the trial progressed, an appellate court reviewed the district court's ruling and found that the frozen assets should indeed be used to pay attorney's fees. The defendant, however, declined because of the advanced stage of the trial. He was ultimately convicted of the trafficking charges and was required to forfeit his assets. At a later stage in the appeals process, the Supreme Court agreed to hear the case involving forfeiture of attorney's fees. The Court ruled that the sale or transfer of potentially forfeitable assets is forbidden.

The issue of lawyers accepting drug assets in lieu of payment for services rendered raises several legal and ethical questions. Such legal questions include whether the defendant's Fifth or Sixth Amendment rights are violated through the use of such a tactic. Those opposed to the forfeiture practice point out that the Sixth Amendment provides the accused the right to counsel and the Fifth Amendment protects the right to due process under law. On both issues, however, the Supreme Court has upheld forfeiture sanctions against attorney's fees.

The ethical concerns of forfeiture have centered on three issues. First, in the two preceding cases, opponents to forfeiture argued that the CFA actually encouraged attorneys to be less than thorough in investigating a client's case, so that any fees they might have received would be protected from forfeiture. Additionally, some argue that when faced with losing legal fees under the CFA, an attorney may compromise his or her client's position during plea bargaining if a longer prison sentence were suggested in lieu of forfeiture of legal fees. In a third scenario, an attorney may be tempted to manipulate the justice system by representing a client on a contingency basis. Although the practice is considered unethical by the American Bar Association, the attorney could conceivably make an agreement with his or her client that only after the client's acquittal would the attorney be paid the designated fee. Thus, the unscrupulous attorney could avoid losing his or her fee under the CFA.

On the same day the government argued its case in *Monsanto*, the Supreme Court heard oral arguments in the *Caplin* case. In this case, illicit-drug importer Christopher Reckmeyer paid the law firm of Caplin and Drysdale $25,000 for preindictment legal services. Before the case could go to trial, Reckmeyer pleaded guilty to the charges, and virtually all his assets were declared forfeitable by the court, including fees paid to the law firm. After an extended legal process whereby the firm's lawyers attempted to secure a release of the fees already paid to them, the Supreme Court ultimately ruled that the forfeiture was lawful and that there are no statutory, ethical, or constitutional impediments to the forfeiture of attorney's fees under the Federal Comprehensive Forfeiture Act.

DRUG CONTROL AND SPORTS

Athletes have been forbidden from using artificial stimulants since the 1920s, and since the 1970s they have had to give urine samples to show they are not pumping up their muscles by injecting *anabolic steroids*—a class of synthetic drugs that promote tissue growth. Recently, however, athletes in a number of countries have been using a newly developed steroid known as *tetrahydrogestrinone* (THG), which was specifically designed to evade the sporting authorities' drug tests. In 2003, USA Track & Field (USATF) confirmed reports that four U.S. athletes had tested positive for the drug. Britain's fastest sprinter, Dwain Chambers, also admitted having tested positive for the drug, though he denied having taken it knowingly. In 2006, less than a week after the Tour de France, it was revealed that winner Floyd Landis had tested positive for THG after his stage-17 victory. In 2009, nearly 1 in 10 retired NFL players polled in a confidential survey said they had used now-banned anabolic steroids (Reinberg, 2009).

A watershed in the fight against doping in the United States occurred in June 2003 when an anonymous track and field coach sent the United States Anti-Doping Agency (USADA) a syringe containing a pale yellow liquid. Within a few weeks, the UCLA Olympic analytical laboratory team determined the structure of the compound as that of THG.

THG was not found specifically on the world antidoping agency list of prohibited substances and methods, but it fell within the category of "related substances." USADA contacted a variety of experts to verify the structure of THG because it was not clear whether THG or one of its components would be a detectable substance in urine. After considerable research, it was determined that THG had biological activities similar to other anabolic steroids and that it did indeed act like other potent steroids. In fact, studies stemming from laboratories at UCLA confirmed that THG had biological activity even more potent than that of testosterone. New protocols to test for the presence of the substance in body fluids has now been developed and has been made available to all accredited dope-testing laboratories throughout the world.

Why Athletes Use Drugs

Athletes face enormous pressure to excel in competition. They also know that winning can reap them more than a gold medal. A star athlete can earn a lot of money and fame, and athletes only have a short time to do their best work. Athletes know that training is the best path to victory, but they also get the message that some drugs and other practices can boost their efforts and give them a shortcut, even as they risk their health and their athletic careers.

For as long as there have been competitive sports, athletes have taken performance-enhancing substances, going back to the stimulating potions taken by ancient Greek sportsmen. In the nineteenth century, cyclists and other endurance athletes kept themselves going with caffeine, alcohol, and even strychnine and cocaine. In 1928, the precursor of the International Association of Athletics Federations (IAAF) became the first world sporting body to forbid stimulants. The ban was ineffective, though, because there was no way of testing for many of them. The invention of artificial hormones in the 1930s made the problem more severe.

In the 1960s, the world bodies for cycling and soccer became the first to introduce doping tests. However, there was no reliable test for steroids until the 1970s. Once a test was introduced, there was a big rise in the number of athletes being disqualified, culminating in the scandal of Ben Johnson, who broke the world 100-meter sprint record at the 1988 Olympics, only to be stripped of his gold medal afterward, when his urine sample showed the presence of steroids. Johnson insisted that he was far from alone in using banned substances, and he seems to have been right: In the 1990s, as improved doping tests made it harder to get away with such cheating, the results achieved by top-level athletes in some sports showed a notable decline.

To date it is unclear how long athletes have been taking THG or how widespread is its abuse. The THG doping threat raises the prospect of national

Figure 11.3

The U.S. Anti-Doping Agency is breaking ground in its attempt to sanction athletes for drug violations based on evidence other than a positive test. Though the process is unprecedented, the protocol will be the same as for a positive test. The process includes:

- Notification of a potential violation. The sending of notice letters is the first step toward determining whether sport anti-doping rules have been violated.

- An independent review board, consisting of experts with legal, technical, and medical knowledge of anti-doping matters, will consider the alleged violations and make a recommendation as to whether USADA should proceed with a formal charge.

- Under the USADA protocol, those who are notified of potential violations are innocent unless and until a formal charge has been brought and they accept the sanction, or a panel of arbitrators, after a full hearing, determines that a doping violation has occurred. The review panel's recommendation will be forwarded to the athlete, the sport's national governing body, the U.S. Olympic Committee, the international federation, and the World Anti-Doping Agency.

- Within 10 days after being notified of a sanction, the athlete must notify USADA in writing if he or she desires a hearing to contest the sanction.

- If an athlete accepts the sanction proposed by USADA, it then will be publicly announced.

- Or an athlete can choose arbitration. Athletes have two choices for the hearing, to be held in the United States:

  A. Selecting the American Arbitration Association (AAA). A single arbitrator will rule, unless either party wants a three-arbitrator panel. Arbitrators come from a pool of the North American Court of Arbitration for Sport (CAS) arbitrators. If an athlete chooses an AAA hearing, either party can appeal the decision to CAS.

  B. Or an athlete can choose to go straight to CAS for a single, final hearing. The CAS decision shall be final and binding on all parties and shall not be subject to further review or appeal.

How Doping Cases Proceed

heroes being stripped of their medals. In 2003, the USATF announced a "zero-tolerance" policy on doping that included plans to impose lifetime bans on athletes caught using illegal substances, rather than the former two-year ban.

The side effects of steroid abuse range from liver and kidney cancer to infertility, baldness, and even transmission of HIV (if the syringes used to inject the drug are shared). However, there seems no limit to the lengths that some athletes are driven to by their will to win. In the 1970s, some tried "blood boosting"—reinfusing themselves with their own blood to boost the level of oxygen, a practice banned by the International Olympic Committee in 1986. Some then turned to erythropoietin, a blood-enhancing drug. Though this was banned in 1990, a reliable test for the drug was not available until the 2000 Olympics. Now, though a test for THG has been developed, there are concerns that some athletes are taking human growth hormone.

Reports of athletes possessing, using, and distributing illicit drugs have become commonplace in newspapers, magazines, and on television. One popular illicit drug, cocaine, is used by many athletes for both recreation and performance enhancement. In addition, the nonmedical use of steroids is becoming more commonplace among athletes and nonathletes alike.

The high visibility of athletes, especially the successful ones, makes their drug problems more newsworthy than those of the average citizen. Most of the media accounts of drug abuse involving athletes report the use of illicit recreational drugs. Such activities have created a public outcry for control and have prompted athletic organizations to initiate antidrug programs. What is it that attracts athletes to drug abuse? Three different reasons can be identified to help explain their involvement with illicit drugs:

1. Drugs taken at the time of competition immediately enhance performance.
2. Drugs taken during training or well before competition enhance performance.
3. Athletes use recreational drugs for the same reasons that nonathletes do.

Drug Control in Amateur Sports

The two major governing bodies for amateur athletics in the United States are the United States Olympic Committee (USOC) and the National Collegiate Athletic Association (NCAA). Both organizations ban the use of certain substances by competitors:

- *USOC.* The USOC has developed a list of banned drugs. The list consists of five categories of drugs: psychomotor stimulants, sympathomimetic amines, narcotic analgesics, anabolic steroids, and miscellaneous central nervous system stimulants. Drugs in these categories are banned to

Figure 11.4

- The first recorded attempt to enhance performance occurred as early as the eighth century B.C.E., when ancient Greek olympians ate sheep's testicles; today we would recognize these as a source of testosterone. As early as the late nineteenth century, professional cyclists were using substances such as caffeine, cocaine, and ether-coated sugar cubes to improve performance, reduce pain, and delay fatigue.

- In the 1904 Olympics, Thomas Hicks (USA) won the marathon at St. Louis and collapsed. It took hours to revive him; he had taken brandy mixed with strychnine to help him win his gold medal. Nazi Germany's athletes were rumored to use the first rudimentary testosterone preparations in the 1936 Summer Olympics.

- The World Weightlifting Championships of 1954 was the event of the first unconfirmed testosterone injections by Soviet athletes, ending in the Soviets winning the gold medal in most weight classes and breaking several world records.

- In the early 1960s, Dr. John Ziegler (who was the U.S. Team Coach in the 1954 Soviet dominated World Weightlifting Championships) administered Dianabol tablets to his weightlifter and consequently Dianabol tablets and the United States dominated the 1962 World Championships.

- A famous case of illicit drug use in a competition was Canadian Ben Johnson's victory in the 100-meter event at the 1988 Summer Olympics. He subsequently failed the drug test when Stanozolol was found in his urine. He later admitted to using the steroid as well as Dianabol, Cypionate, Furazabol, and human growth hormone among other things. Carl Lewis was then promoted one place to take the Olympic gold title. Later it was revealed that he also had been using drugs.

- In the 1970s and 1980s, many athletes from Eastern-bloc nations were suspected of augmenting their ability with some kind of pharmacological help. After the fall of Communism in Eastern Europe and the reunification of Germany, documents surfaced proving that the East German sport establishment had conducted systematic doping of virtually all its world-class athletes.

- In 1998 the entire Festina team was excluded from the Tour de France following the discovery of a team car containing large amounts of various performance-enhancing drugs. The team director later admitted that some of the cyclists were routinely given banned substances. Six other teams pulled out in protest, including Dutch team TVM, which left the tour still being questioned by the police. The Festina scandal overshadowed cyclist Marco Pantani's tour win, but he himself later failed a test. More recently David Millar, the 2003 World-Time Trial Champion, admitted using erythropoietin (EPO), and was stripped of his title and suspended for two years. Still later, Roberto Heras was stripped of his victory in the 2005 Vuelta a España and suspended for two years after testing positive for EPO (erythropoietin).

- In July 2005, founders of California's Bay Area Laboratory Cooperative pleaded guilty to steroid distribution and money laundering. Those implicated or accused in the ensuing scandal include athletes Dwain Chambers, C.J. Hunter, Marion

Notable Drug Scandals in Sports

Figure 11.4—*continued*

Jones, and Tim Montgomery; baseball players Barry Bonds, Jason Giambi, and Gary Sheffield; and several members of the Oakland Raiders.

• At the 2006 Winter Olympics, cross-country skier Walter Mayer fled from the police when, acting on a tip, the Italian authorities conducted a surprise raid to search for evidence of doping.

• The 2006 book *Game of Shadows* alleges extensive use of several types of steroids and growth hormone by baseball superstar Barry Bonds. It also names several other athletes as drug cheats.

• In 2006, Spanish police arrested five people, including the sporting director of the Liberty Seguros cycling team, on charges of running a massive doping scheme involving most of the team and many other top cyclists. Several potential contenders in the 2006 Tour de France were forced to withdraw when they were linked to the scheme.

• Less than a week after the 2006 Tour de France, it was revealed that winner Floyd Landis had tested positive for an elevated testosterone/epitestosterone ratio after his stunning stage-17 victory. Currently, further testing is pending. On July 29, another U.S. champion—Olympic and world 100-meter champion Justin Gatlin failed a drug test.

• In January 2010, Mark McGwire ended more than a decade of speculation when he acknowledged that he had used steroids during much of his Major League playing career, including when he broke Major League Baseball's single-season home-run record. In 1998, McGwire and Sammy Sosa achieved national fame for their pursuit of Roger Maris's single-season home-run record. McGwire broke the record and hit 70 home runs that year. Barry Bonds (who allegedly took steroids as well) holds the current record after hitting 73 home runs during the 2001 season.

discourage use of them to improve an athlete's performance during competition. Drug testing is conducted by one of numerous methods for testing urine. The USOC tests athletes in events such as the Olympic and Pan American trials and games. Athletes are disqualified if they test positive for drugs or refuse to be tested. In the event that an athlete withdraws from a competition, no penalty is imposed.

• *NCAA*. During the 1986 NCAA convention in New Orleans, drug-testing legislation was passed. The list of banned drugs is similar to that of the USOC but includes substances banned for specific sports as well as diuretics and street drugs. The NCAA does not include narcotic analgesics, which are on the International Olympic Committee (IOC) list.

Drug testing is performed for 73 NCAA championships and football postseason bowl games. Drug testing during the regular season remains the responsibility of each school. If any player tests positive for any of the banned drugs, the NCAA can render the player ineligible for that particular postseason competition as well as for postseason play for a minimum of 90 days after the test date.

MEDICAL MARIJUANA

Medical marijuana refers to the use of cannabis as a form of medicine or herbal therapy approved by a physician. While the extent of the medicinal value of marijuana has been disputed it does have a number of documented beneficial effects that many researchers have applauded (Aggarwai, S. K. et. al., 2009). Among these are: the suppression of nausea and vomiting, stimulation of hunger in chemotherapy and AIDS patients, lowered eye pressure (for treating glaucoma), as well as general benefits of pain relief.

Synthetic marijuana is available as a prescription drug in some countries including the United States. There are numerous methods for administering the drug, including vaporizing or smoking dried buds, drinking/eating extracts and taking capsules. The comparable efficacy of these methods was the subject of an investigative study[5] conducted by the National Institutes of Health.

Marijuana as a recreational drug is illegal in most parts of the world. However, its use as a medicine is legal in a number of countries, including Canada, Austria, Germany, the Netherlands, Spain, Israel, Italy, Finland, and Portugal. In the United States, under federal law, marijuana is illegal for any type of use, while permission for medical marijuana varies among states. Distribution is usually accomplished within a system identified by local laws.

Medical marjuana remains a controversial issue worldwide. In a 2002 review of medical literature, medical cannabis was shown to have established effects in the treatment of nausea, vomiting, premenstrual syndrome, unintentional weight loss, insomnia, and lack of appetite. Medical marijuana has also been found to relieve certain symptoms of multiple sclerosis and spinal cord injuries (Grotenhermen, et. al. 2002).

In 2005, the United States Supreme Court ruled that the Commerce Clause of the U.S. Constitution allowed the government to ban the use of cannabis, including medical use. The United States Food and Drug Administration states "marijuana has a high potential for abuse, has no currently accepted medical use in treatment in the United States, and has a lack of accepted safety for use under medical supervision."

As of the preparation of this text, fourteen states have legalized medical marijuana. These include: Alaska, California, Colorado, Hawaii, Maine, Michigan, Montana, Nevada, New Jersey, New Mexico, Oregon, Rhode Island., Washington D.C. and Washington.

In 2008, California's medical marijuana industry took in about $2 billion a year and generated $100 million in state sales taxes. With an estimated 2,100 dispensaries, co-operatives, wellness clinics and taxi delivery services in the sector colloquially known as "cannabusiness" (Harvey, 2009).

At the federal level, cannabis per se has been made criminal by implementation of the Controlled Substances Act but in 2009, new federal guidelines were enacted. U.S. Attorney General Eric Holder announced that the federal government will not be a priority to use federal resources to prosecute patients with serious illnesses or their caregivers who are complying with state laws on medical marijuana, but drug traffickers who hide behind claims of compliance with state law will not be tolerated. Ironically, also in 2009, California Assembly Bill 390 was introduced. If passed, it would legalize the sale of marijuana to those twenty-one and older – a first for any U.S. state. As of the preparation of this text, the bill is still moving through California state governance.

In Seattle in 2007, a woman uses a vaporizer to get one of her daily doses of medical marijuana. Washington State's medical marijuana law is considered one of the weaker laws among states with medical marijuana protections.

Criticisms of Medical Marijuana

One of the biggest criticisms of marijuana as medicine is opposition to smoking as a method of consumption. The United States Food and Drug Administration (FDA) issued an advisory against smoked medical marijuana stating that, marijuana has a high potential for abuse, has no currently accepted medical use in treatment in the United States, and has a lack of accepted safety for use under medical supervision. Furthermore, there is currently evidence that smoked marijuana is harmful (Food and Drug Administration, 2006).

The Institute of Medicine, run by the United States National Academy of Sciences, conducted a comprehensive study in 1999 to assess the potential health benefits of cannabis and its constituent cannabinoids. The study concluded that smoking cannabis is not recommended for the treatment of any disease condition, but did conclude that nausea, appetite loss, pain and anxiety can all be mitigated by marijuana.

While the study expressed reservations about smoked marijuana due to the health risks associated with smoking, it concluded that until another mode of ingestion was perfected that could provide the same relief as smoked marijuana, there was no alternative. However, modern vaporizers and the ingestion of cannabis in a decarboxylated state have laid most of these concerns to rest (Joy, et. al., 1996). In addition, the study pointed out the inherent difficulty in marketing a non-patentable herb.

The fact is, pharmaceutical companies will not substantially profit unless there is a patent (see chapter 5). For those reasons experts argue that there is little future in smoked cannabis as a medically approved medication.

OTHER PUBLIC POLICY ISSUES

Reduce Aid to Source Countries

Advocates of reducing aid to foreign countries often argue that the only way to disrupt drug trafficking is to eliminate the source of supply. One possible means to use leverage against source countries is to cease trade practices and/or eliminate aid to them. The prevailing theory is that if drugs are made less available, their prices will rise, reducing the number of users. This theory may not be valid, however, because past increases in drug prices have proved to have little effect on the demand for drugs.

Opponents of this measure argue that it is not the supply but the demand that fuels the drug business and that cutting off one source will just force traffickers to find another. Additionally, many people feel that forcing source countries to eradicate crops and extradite their citizens would jeopardize already fragile economies and create political instability. Both of these possibilities would damage relations with the United States.

Increase Aid to Source Countries

Many observers feel that, instead, a concerted effort to revive economies and promote economic development in source countries is necessary to persuade these countries to stop trafficking drugs. Under this strategy, all countries affected by drug abuse would contribute some form of aid. The opposition to this proposal contends that such an action would, in effect, reward the drug traffickers and would encourage other countries to participate in the drug trade in order to qualify for aid.

Expand the Role of the Military

Some drug enforcement strategists debate the merits of economic strategies; still others have considered the use of force. The Reagan administration declared that drug trafficking posed a threat to national security. It has been suggested, therefore, that the U.S. military is better equipped to deal with such a threat than civilian law enforcement agencies. This theory is supported by arguments that the military has at its disposal advanced intelligence capabilities, training, equipment, and other resources to launch a successful, full-scale drug control initiative.

Some jurisdictions have implemented the National Guard to assist drug control officers in raids. The primary use of the National Guard is to augment staff in nonthreatening functions of certain operations. In addition to other tasks, these duties include transporting and booking prisoners as well as facilitating certain paperwork. Predictably, this school of thought has its critics, who hold that drug trafficking is not a military problem and that to empower the military with civilian police powers opposes the country's foundation of democracy, which is based in part on the separation of powers. Recent studies have also cast doubt on the military's ability to make an impact on drug consumption through interdiction.

Legalizing Drugs

Although the strategies discussed so far are aimed at reducing drug trafficking, another strategy is based on the assumption that drug abuse will never be eliminated. The strategy that accepts drug abuse calls for legalization of drugs and is aimed at reducing criminals' control over the drug trade.

The prospect of legalizing drugs has attracted considerable attention from the media, civil libertarians, some public officials, and some members of Congress. The arguments for and against the legalization of illicit drugs are many and should be carefully weighed with such considerations as public safety and personal freedoms. In addition, other considerations include the rights of the people as a free society versus the rights of innocent victims of the drug trade (see Chapter 12).

Increase Spending for Drug Education Programs

A final strategy focuses on the demand side of the drug cycle. One traditional school of thought holds that the government should continue to spend increasingly more on public education and treatment programs, although it is conceded that this strategy will take many years to be considered successful. In theory, once demand is under control, the supply will dry up. The response to this argument is that to stop drug trafficking, sources must be cut off at the supply side rather than the demand side.

SUMMARY

Controversy is nothing new in considering the fate of the drug abuse problem in the United States. Much of the controversy in drug control stems from the tactics adopted by law enforcement officials. On one hand, many traditional police tactics have proven less than effective, but on the other hand, the use of more unconventional enforcement techniques, such as needle exchange programs or the forfeiture of ill-gotten attorneys' fees, raises concerns for civil liberties and expanded police authority.

One controversial technique that has proved effective in identifying drug traffickers is the criminal profile. Although police tend to shy away from the word *profile*, the use of this tactic has resulted in many major seizures. The profiling procedure focuses on drug couriers in transit. The 1989 *Sokolow* decision gave legitimacy to this procedure, which enables agents to stop and question individuals who look or act like "typical" drug dealers. In this decision, the court recognized that certain traits are common to drug dealers and typically are not evidenced in the general population.

The reverse sting is another enforcement technique that has proved effective in identifying drug buyers (or users) rather than sellers. This technique requires the undercover officer to pose as a drug seller. The officer is authorized to sell a quantity of drugs to a prospective buyer, but the buyer is immediately arrested and the drugs are seized as evidence. People who criticize this technique claim that an atmosphere of entrapment prevails and that police are enticing people to commit crimes. The proper use of this technique, however, requires police to show a defendant's "criminal intent" and his or her predisposition to purchase the drugs.

The practice of surveillance is common. Because covert observation by the police has always generated a certain degree of skepticism by the public, the police must take great care in initiating certain surveillance operations. Officers must be careful that the activities for which the suspect is under investigation are authorized (for investigation) under federal guidelines. In addition, the concerns of both the government and civil libertarians must be observed throughout the operation.

Drug testing is not a new concern for drug control strategists, but the issue is far from being resolved. Most of the concern revolves around the questions of who should be tested, where, and under what sets of circumstances. Drug testing of federal transportation and law enforcement employees has been authorized, but what about drug testing in the general workplace? Some claim that the examination of a blood or urine sample violates one's Fourth and Fifth Amendment rights.

The subject of drug testing leads to the discussion of the problem of drugs and sports. This issue deals with several aspects, including nonaddictive and recreational drug use and the use of drugs such as steroids, which are designed to aid athletes in their particular sports. Regulatory agencies governing drug use in sports have created punitive provisions for those who use dangerous drugs. Such provisions may include fines, suspension, or expulsion from professional athletics and even criminal prosecution.

Do you recognize these terms?

- drug courier profiling
- entrapment
- gas-liquid chromatography
- mass spectrometry
- reverse sting
- zero tolerance

DISCUSSION QUESTIONS

1. Discuss some of the more valid concerns in the practice of "officially" abducting drug traffickers wanted in the United States.

2. List some possible options that the U.S. government could consider for the elimination of international drug trafficking.

3. What fears do civil libertarians have regarding the practice of drug courier profiling by police?

4. What is meant by the term *zero tolerance*, and why has the term become so controversial?

5. Discuss some of the legal and moral ramifications of the practice of seizing attorney fees.

6. Discuss why needle exchange programs are controversial throughout the world.

7. Discuss the different circumstances under which one may be tested for drugs in the workplace. What are the pros and cons of drug testing in such a manner?

8. Discuss the physiological effects of steroids on the human body.

CLASS PROJECT

1. Study the controversies surrounding drug control in your community. Discuss them in terms of both their strong and weak attributes.

Chapter 12

The Issue of Legalizing Drugs

This chapter will enable you to:

- Understand the basis for the drug legalization argument
- Understand the distinctions between decriminalization and legalization
- Appreciate public policy concerns with regard to the legalization issue
- Compare pros and cons of the drug legalization debate
- Learn why legalization has not worked in other countries
- Discover alternative solutions for the reduction of drug abuse

As an alternative to the growing problem of drug abuse in the United States, some politicians and social scientists have suggested that the laws governing drug control be repealed or at least modified ("decriminalized"). Glaring questions about the social responsibility of such a policy surface when a radical shift is considered. We have learned thus far that because attitudes about drugs are complicated and contradictory, resolution of the drug issue is enigmatic at best. For example, both cigarettes and alcohol are thought to be harmful, yet both are legal and readily available. On the other hand, cocaine and heroin are generally considered to be dangerous drugs, and both are controlled under federal and state laws. When we add in the factor of addiction, which is present in both controlled and legal drugs, the stage is set for combat between political conservatives and liberals.

Most people agree that the problem of drug abuse cannot be ignored. Crimes to which some addicts resort to finance their habits and in which suppliers of drugs regularly engage exact their price both financially and in terms of victims'

DOI: 10.1016/B978-1-4377-4450-7.00012-6
© 2011 Elsevier Inc. All rights reserved.

lives. Illegal drugs are the financial cornerstone for organized crime the world over. Drug abuse can draw users into a world of syringes, dirty needles, poisoned doses, disease, deceit, and drug dealers bent on selling increasingly more addictive and potent drugs. However, the manner in which government might undermine such effects has basically focused on tough law enforcement. We know that cigarettes are considered to be one of the most affordable causes of death in the world, second only to alcohol, which not only deprives drinkers of their health but causes many deaths along the highways as well. Yet, here the notion of dissuasion within the law is broadly accepted. To address the problem, some have suggested that drug *legalization*—or its lesser form, *decriminalization*—be considered. Concurrent with this proposition is the fear that changing the laws would increase drug consumption and addiction. An important question in the legalization issue is: How will legalization affect the crime rate and public health?

Opinions about the drug legalization/decriminalization issue span the spectrum. Some reformers argue that drug use is a personal moral decision and that it is not the responsibility of government to police social morality. Additionally, many people who want to legalize drugs claim that crime rates soar as high as they do because drugs are treated as a criminal problem rather than a medical problem. Opponents of legalization argue that although regulation of public morality may conflict with some personal freedoms, the government has a legitimate responsibility to ensure order and public safety in our society.

PUBLIC OPINION

Compared with the peak years of the late 1970s, in 2007 government statistics showed that drug use is down in the United States. In prior years, use of illicit drugs among adults was stable, and over the past decade the use of illegal drugs by workers declined by more than half. Teen drug use held steady for the past four years after rising sharply in the early 1990s. Teen use of some drugs, such as LSD, methamphetamine, and cocaine, is down somewhat, but use of some other drugs (e.g., ecstasy) has increased, according to the University of Michigan's annual *Monitoring the Future* survey.

Despite the overall decline, most Americans still regard illegal drugs as one of the nation's most serious problems. More than half of the public worries that a family member might become addicted, and 7 in 10 people say that the government is not doing enough to address the problem.

Getting Tougher with Dealers

Historically, federal and state governments have used two strategies to combat drug use: reducing the supply of illegal drugs and curbing the demand. When most people talk about the "war on drugs," they are thinking about efforts to reduce supply: more aggressive police investigations, tougher sentences for drug users and dealers, greater efforts to intercept drugs before they cross U.S. borders, and supporting antidrug efforts by drug-producing nations. The number of drug offenders in U.S. prisons has risen dramatically over the past two decades, and drug arrests have doubled since 1985.

Reducing demand has often meant drug education programs in schools, public service messages in the media, treatment programs, and drug testing. Despite civil liberties concerns, the courts have generally upheld drug-testing programs for employees and even students involved in extracurricular activities. In addition, over the years, the federal government has spent millions in antidrug advertising campaigns.

Critics of the "war on drugs," including an increasing number of law enforcement officials and even a few public officials (such as former New Mexico Governor Gary Johnson), say the campaign has not worked and have called for drug legalization. They argue that legalization, like the ending of the Prohibition on alcohol, would undercut drug gangs and allow the nation to focus on drug abuse as a medical problem. Those critics, however, are still a distinct minority.

Marijuana as Medicine?

One area in which advocates of legalization have made progress is in the medical use of marijuana. Although the federal government does maintain an extremely limited medical marijuana program, federal policy for decades has held marijuana to be a dangerous and addictive drug.

As noted in Chapter 11, in 1996 Californians approved a ballot proposition allowing physicians to prescribe marijuana for specific illnesses such as glaucoma, even though federal laws ban marijuana's sale and distribution. Several states followed suit, and similar ballot propositions have been passed and nullified or are pending in several other elections. In March 1999, a panel of experts convened by the federal Institute of Medicine found that marijuana does have legitimate medical uses for treating symptoms of cancer and AIDS. Although the panel found no evidence that marijuana leads to harder drugs like cocaine, the scientists did warn that marijuana smoke was even more toxic in the long term than tobacco smoke.

Polls vary, but nationwide at least two-thirds of the public supports the use of marijuana to ease severe pain. Although most people regard marijuana as a much less dangerous drug than cocaine or heroin, a solid majority opposes general legalization of marijuana. In a 2004 poll commissioned by the American Association of Retired Persons (AARP), 72 percent of respondents ages 45 and older thought marijuana should be legal for medicinal purposes if recommended by a doctor (ProCon.org, 2004).

Mixed Attitudes

Opinion polls show the public tends to favor a variety of approaches to the drug problem, mixing liberal and conservative attitudes. There is strong public support for doing everything possible to intercept drug supplies and punish dealers. At a time when the nation's prisons are filled with criminals serving sentences for drug-related crimes, most Americans want even stricter penalties for dealers. A substantial majority of Americans opposes the overall legalization of drugs.

Many people also think permissive messages from parents and the media are one of the main causes of the drug problem. They favor expanded antidrug efforts to discourage use. Expanded drug treatment is favored as well, although this tactic is not as widely supported as stepped-up enforcement.

The Basis for the Debate: Three Approaches

Based on surveys and opinion polls, three general approaches have been consistently identified over the years. Each point of view comes with arguments for and against, along with some potential costs and tradeoffs.

- One perspective emphasizes strict enforcement of the drug laws, intercepting drug supplies, and doing whatever is necessary to catch and punish drug dealers.
- A second perspective puts its emphasis on cutting demand by preventing drug use and doing everything possible to change tolerant attitudes toward it.
- A third perspective regards drug abuse primarily as a health problem and favors stepped-up treatment to help users rather than punish them. Advocates generally favor legalization of some drugs.

Approach #1: Stopping Drugs at the Source by Cutting Off the Supply

This approach takes a get-tough stance. Proponents hold that certain drugs are illegal for a reason—they are so dangerous that there is no safe way to have them in our society. We have to do everything possible to keep illegal drugs out of the country and off the streets. We need to cut off the supply of drugs by targeting traffickers and dealers, both wholesalers and street-corner drug dealers. Tougher enforcement and stricter sentencing of dealers and users helped to deal with the crack cocaine epidemic of the 1990s and kept overall drug use at stable levels. To win the war on drugs, we need to pursue this strategy aggressively, making every effort to identify, prosecute, and imprison drug dealers, thus cutting off the drug supply both at home and abroad.

Advocates for this approach suggest that the government take more aggressive measures to prevent drugs from crossing our borders while helping drug-producing nations with eradication efforts and other enforcement activities, including the destruction of clandestine labs and airfields. They argue that the United States should demand international cooperation in cutting off the drug supply while rewarding countries that crack down on drug growers. Rewards would be in the form of aid and support, and economic sanctions would be imposed on countries that refuse.

This approach holds that the United States should impose swift and certain punishment on drug dealers, including consistent mandatory minimum sentences, while expanding sanctions against convicted dealers. This would include confiscating automobiles and other personal property and taking away driver's licenses. Those who make the case for this approach typically argue that illegal drug use is morally wrong and terribly destructive and that there can be no compromises, no unenforced laws, and no distinctions between hard and soft drugs or between dealers and casual users. They further argue that drug dealers and users are also likely to commit other crimes, either to support their habits or protect their businesses. Consequently, they believe that cracking down on drug offenses will help cut crime in general.

Opponents argue that this approach is a losing battle and as long as drugs are illegal and very profitable, there will be dealers willing to sell them. They complain that the "war on drugs" comes at a huge cost in money and jail space and, thanks to rigid mandatory sentences, the country imprisons drug users who might be able to change if we gave them treatment. Furthermore, opponents contend that the get-tough policy has taken an unfair toll on poor, minority communities, where drugs are common and too many people have too few alternatives in life. This no-holds-barred approach to drug enforcement infringes on civil liberties.

The trade-off under this alternative is that it may be necessary to spend even more to imprison drug sellers, dealers, and users. Drug searches mean that the houses of innocent people may, on occasion, be searched by mistake, but proponents believe that is a small price to pay for a more effective war on drugs.

Approach #2: Reducing Demand by Holding Users Accountable

From this perspective, the drug problem has persisted because millions of drug users continue to buy them. Despite abundant evidence of their corrosive effect on users and the society as a whole, drug use is still widely tolerated and even glamorized in the media. Sports stars use steroids, and many people abuse even over-the-counter inhalants and prescription drugs. The war on drugs will be won only when millions of users are persuaded to stop and young people are persuaded not to start. We have to make zero tolerance for drugs a top national priority—starting at home, in the schools, and in the workplace.

This approach holds that society must do everything possible—in the schools, in the workplace, in homes, and in the media—to convey the message that drug use is dangerous, unacceptable, and not chic. In addition, drug users should be punished by fines, arrest, and forfeiture of driver's licenses. This would even apply to those who only occasionally use drugs. This is one of the strongest ways of sending an antidrug message.

Advocates for this approach argue that because it is impossible to stop the supply of illegal drugs, the only way to win the war against drugs is to reduce the appetite for them. They claim that because drug use is not always apparent, testing is the only way to ensure that people remain drug free, and it is an effective deterrent. Finally, another position is that drug users may be victims, but they do not hurt only themselves. Rather, the use of illegal drugs is linked to domestic violence, school failure, crime, AIDS, and workplace injuries. For everyone's sake, we need to force drug users to take responsibility for the consequences of their actions.

People who oppose this approach complain that although no one opposes antidrug educational programs, there is not much evidence that this approach actually reduces drug use. They suggest that addiction is a medical problem and that society should not punish people for getting sick. Besides, addicts need treatment to get clean—so how does it help to leave them unemployed and without health insurance?

A harder-line argument is that as long as illegal drugs are available, some people will be tempted to use them. The only way to win the war is to cut them off at the source by targeting growers and drug dealers, not drug users. Furthermore, alcohol and tobacco are both addictive substances that cause a great deal of social damage, yet both are legal. Millions more are addicted to drugs legally prescribed by their own doctors. So, why should we treat other drugs differently? Under this perspective, people must be ready to accept the notion that it may take a long time before expanded drug education efforts turn around the drug problem.

Approach #3: Redefining Drug Use as Addiction, Not Criminal Behavior

Those in support of this argument contend that the drug problem has persisted (and, in some respects, worsened) because we have gone about it the wrong way. The "war on drugs" is not working and, even if it was, the price is too high. The prohibition on drugs leads to black-market prices. It generates crime and violence as dealers fight over turf and sales, and drug users steal to buy illicit substances at inflated prices. The drug laws turn users—who need treatment—into criminals. We would be far better off if drug use were regarded as a health problem. We should legalize at least some drugs and reduce the harm they cause by regulating their sale and treating their victims.

To accomplish this goal, it is argued that society should treat drug abuse as a public health problem rather than a law enforcement issue and eliminate criminal penalties for personal drug use. The government should regulate drug sales and permit the use of some drugs (such as marijuana) under a doctor's care while expanding drug treatment programs, including those in prison. Furthermore, insurance companies should be required to cover substance abuse the same way they would any physical illness. The goal should be to provide treatment to anyone who needs it.

Those in favor of this approach argue that the harm done by drugs is predominantly caused by the fact that they are illegal. A more sensible policy would control their distribution and discourage their use. Prohibition of alcohol did not work in the 1920s and drug prohibition does not work now. Decriminalizing drug use would destroy the illicit drug trade. Advocates of this view also suggest that the war on drugs has done tremendous harm by sending thousands of drug users to prison instead of salvaging their lives and communities through treatment. Drug treatment should be widely available and stigma-free.

Those who oppose this approach argue that making it easier to get drugs would inevitably make them more widely available. For example, legal prescription drugs are tightly regulated but are still the second most common drugs of abuse. They are also concerned that too many people believe that making something legal also makes it moral. If one considers drug abuse to be morally wrong, blurring this fact by calling it a health problem will only compound the problem.

They further argue that treatment programs, though important, are not the whole answer to the illegal drug problem. This is because many treatment programs have low success rates (i.e., many people relapse). Additionally, opponents to this approach are concerned that organized gangs will not simply go away if we legalize drugs. Rather, they'll move into other forms of crime, just as the bootleggers did after Prohibition ended. The bottom line is that some people believe that a result of decriminalizing drug use is that more people may experiment with drugs. Legalizing drugs may lead to more drug abuse in inner cities, where addicts are more numerous and there are few treatment programs.

The Pros: Arguments for Legalization

Many people who advocate the legalization of drugs base their arguments on assertions of the historical practice of policing "victimless" crimes. The experience of Prohibition is particularly singled out. Reformers allege that the passage of the 1920 Volstead Act outlawing the production, possession, and use of alcohol created more problems than it resolved and that the end of Prohibition in 1933 saw bootlegging gangsters, along with their violence and corruption, fade away. This argument is now put forth to support legalization as a means of disbanding modern-day drug gangs in the same fashion.

Many scholars who support legalization assert that Prohibition was responsible for the transformation of organized crime from small, isolated vice peddlers serving urban political machines to major crime syndicates. This occurred as a result of the profits realized from Prohibition, the political and law enforcement contacts the gangsters made, the respectability that came from serving the drinking public, and the logistical and structural reorganization of organized crime that bootlegging required (see Chapter 13 for a more comprehensive look at Prohibition and public policy).

Proponents of drug legalization base their argument on a number of points. One such point is the traditionally liberal argument stating that a free society allows its people to do as they wish so long as they harm no one. The state, therefore, should be reluctant to use criminal law to constrict personal freedoms. In addition, drug reformers argue that drug laws fail to impact the availability of illicit drugs and may even make the situation worse. For example, a study of the national Marijuana Interdiction Program by Mark A. R. Kleiman of Harvard's Kennedy School of Government concluded that the interdiction campaign stimulated domestic production, increased the supply of marijuana in the United States, and raised the potency of marijuana available from 1 percent to 18 percent (Kleiman, 1992). A similar study of marijuana eradication campaigns in Kentucky also concluded that the result of the campaigns was increased supply, increased potency, introduction of new dangerous drugs to the market, and the creation of marijuana syndicates in place of the usually small, disorganized growers who had dominated the market before the eradication effort.

Skeptics question the specific correlations between the eradication program and the advances in the marijuana production trade. For example, since the late 1960s, trends toward the rising potency of marijuana and toward indoor hydroponic growing methods had been well documented prior to the implementation of the eradication program. Additionally, research has concluded that one fundamental reason that traditional organized crime (La Cosa Nostra) has been unable to dominate the domestic marijuana trade is because it represents an easy-entry market for entrepreneurs. According to a 1984 *DEA Special Intelligence Report on Domestic Marijuana Trafficking*, "efforts to organize certain dispersed [marijuana-trafficking] elements of society would prove futile and too costly." This illustrates how difficult and impractical (if not impossible) it would be for the government to attempt to control and tax the marijuana market after legalization.

Reformers also point to the connection between illegal drugs and crime, arguing that addicts are lured to other crimes such as prostitution, burglary, and robbery as ways to help finance their expensive habits. In addition, it is argued that the illegality of drugs forces consumers to enter a criminal underworld to purchase them, thereby having contact with criminal actors with whom they would not ordinarily interact, creating conditions for both victimization and subsequent criminality.

Proponents of drug legalization argue that those crimes traditionally associated with drug dealing would be greatly reduced if the context of drug control were changed from a law enforcement model to a *medical model*. The organized crime groups formed around the drug trade would find the illicit market constricted under a medical model and would leave the black market in drugs for other criminal opportunities. In addition, legalization proponents argue that law enforcement and political corruption associated with drug trafficking, abuse of due process and procedural rights sometimes associated with drug enforcement, and the problem of selective drug enforcement would also be mitigated under a medical model.

Let's now take a closer look at some of the most commonly advanced arguments for the legalization of drugs.

The Futility of Enforcement

As discussed, drug law enforcement has come under considerable critical scrutiny. Some researchers claim there has been no reduction in supply from enforcement efforts and point to an alarming fall in the retail price of drugs and an increase in their potency. Adding support to this claim are findings from a federally funded study of intensive street-level drug enforcement in Lynn, Massachusetts, which pointed to "temporary" and "transitory" successes. This finding is considered by some to indicate not much more than a marginal success.

In addition, it is argued that fully suppressing the demand for drugs would require the jailing of a large proportion of the nation's population. At least 70 million Americans have admitted to having used drugs. Federal studies estimate that despite constantly escalating numbers of drug arrests, we are still reaching less than 1 percent of users with law enforcement efforts.

The Restriction of the Drug Market

Reformers also argue that legalization of some drugs, particularly the so-called *recreational drugs*, would serve to restrict the drug market. Because most drug experts agree that marijuana, cocaine, and heroin are the preferred substances for most drug users, their legal availability might reduce demand for more dangerous illegal substances such as "ice" (Methamphetamine) and angel dust. This would reduce the economic incentive for the production and distribution of these more dangerous substances.

The Hypocrisy of Drug Laws

It is also argued that it is hypocritical to ban drugs when our society has already legalized two exceedingly dangerous drugs: tobacco and alcohol. The argument is that a much larger percentage of the population is threatened through health risks, automobile collisions, assaults, and associated family problems attributed to these drugs than it is by the drugs currently proscribed by law. One should recognize, however, that such a comparison is difficult to make, because legalized recreational drugs are not a reality, and no existing scientific or empirical data are available to support this assertion. The hypocrisy of drug laws is also apparent when we compare different state laws and offenses for drug offenses. For example, charges for possession of some drugs are based on the amount of the drug in the defendant's control. These charges not only vary from one state to another, but sentences for those convicted also differ greatly from one jurisdiction to another.

International Relations

Some drug reformers have also pointed to problems created by drug enforcement efforts—specifically, our strained relationships with some foreign countries. These reformers argue that foreign relations with countries such as Mexico, Peru, and Colombia are being hampered by the intensity of enforcement efforts and the political rhetoric attached to the drug war. More compellingly, some critics argue that foreign policy considerations have resulted in a double standard in drug enforcement in the United States. These critics point to the lack of intense criticism directed to countries such as the Bahamas (a major transshipment site for cocaine made safe by massive political corruption), Chile (where the DINA, Chile's secret police, has been actively engaged in cocaine trafficking for more than two decades), Thailand (a major heroin-refining center), and Taiwan (source of much of the financial backing and logistical support for the Southeast Asian heroin trade). Critics are also disturbed by the relations between U.S. intelligence agencies and drug traffickers; the CIA's role in Australia's drug money-laundering Nugan-Hand bank and in Caribbean drug money-laundering enterprises; and support for fundamentalist Moslem Afghan groups actively engaged in heroin trafficking.

Personal Freedoms

To some critics of present drug enforcement policies, the possibility of severe threats to personal freedoms posed by tougher drug laws creates concern. New and expanded search-and-seizure powers granted to law enforcement officers, random drug testing by employers, and the use of the military in domestic law enforcement raise major concerns about potential due process abuses, further erosion of constitutional protections, and the potential for serious systematic corruption.

Figure 12.1
Source: Adapted from Kurt Schmoke (May 5, 1994),"Side Effects," *Rolling Stone.*

In advocating a policy called *medicalization* for the city of Baltimore, Kurt Schmoke recommends setting up a private market like the ones we now have for alcohol and cigarettes. He takes a health-regulatory approach rather than a free-market approach.

According to Schmoke, medicalization entails giving the public health system the leading role in preventing and treating substance abuse. Under this plan, the government would set up a regulatory regime to draw addicts into the public health system. The government, not criminal traffickers, would control the price, distribution, purity, and access to addictive substances, just as it currently does with prescription drugs. Public health professionals would have the authority to provide addicts with what are currently illegal drugs, to maintain them as part of an overall treatment and detoxification program. Addicts would have access to counseling, health services, and AIDS-prevention information, with the goal that they break the cycle of addiction, crime, and incarceration. The rest of the public would, in turn, get relief from the fear that comes from having open-air drug markets, drug-related violence, and addiction in their communities.

According to Schmoke, changes in Baltimore's drug policy are not enough. He calls for a new national drug strategy that will reduce crime by taking the profit out of drug trafficking, make the criminal justice system more effective, and increase the availability of treatment. As a first step toward achieving those goals, he suggests the creation of a national commission to study how drugs—both legal and illegal—should be regulated. Hundreds of prominent Americans have already signed a resolution calling for the establishment of this kind of commission.

He notes that a similar commission was set up in 1929 by President Herbert Hoover to study the prohibition of alcohol. Hoover asked the commission to recommend ways in which Prohibition could be more strictly enforced. Instead, though, the commissioners concluded that alcohol prohibition was, in the words of American intellectual Walter Lippman, a "helpless failure." It is entirely possible that a similar objective study will come to the same conclusion about drug prohibition.

In Favor of Medicalization

The Crime Rate

As mentioned, reformers also claim that legalization would cut down on street crimes because addicts could acquire their drugs inexpensively rather than by committing burglary, robbery, and murder for drug money. Drug reformers also argue that legalization would reduce the drug turf wars that have driven urban homicide rates to record levels in recent years.

Public Health

Proponents of drug legalization argue that the drug laws themselves create many of the severe health problems normally associated with drug use. The spread of AIDS, closely associated with the sharing of needles by intravenous drug users, is one such concern. Reformers also point to the problem of pregnant drug addicts, who, out of fear of legal repercussions, may not seek prenatal care.

Finally, some have argued, at least in the case of heroin, that illegality of heroin means there is no control over the quality of the drug being purchased. Heroin and other drugs are commonly adulterated with dangerous substances by retail dealers, and users are unsure of the potency or quality of the drugs they have purchased. From a pharmacological point of view, unadulterated heroin causes little physical damage to the human body (this, of course, excludes such health threats as AIDS and brutal physical addiction). It is the uncontrolled nature of street heroin that causes poisoning and overdose.

Critical Thinking Task

Explain your own view of marijuana use. Defend or refute arguments in favor of decriminalizing the possession, consumption, and sale of marijuana.

Despite these arguments for the legalization of drugs, drug reformers have yet to come up with a comprehensive plan that delineates any practical program for legalization. Some reformers have complained they have not had equal access to federal research monies with which to formulate their approach. Those monies have been exclusively reserved for research on drug abuse pathologies and drug repression strategies.

Issues to Consider

In 1988, Democratic Congressman Charles Rangel, who represents the drug-infested Harlem district in New York City and who strongly opposes legalization, posed questions that drug policy reformers will have to answer in coming years:

1. Which drugs should be legalized—marijuana, or the harder drugs such as heroin and cocaine?
2. How would the legalized drugs be sold: by prescription or over the counter, by hospitals or pharmacies?
3. Would there be an age limit and, if so, how would it be enforced?
4. As addictions and dependencies developed, would any limit be placed on the amount of drugs that users could purchase?
5. Who would manufacture the drugs—private companies or the federal government?

6. Would the drugs be provided to the public at cost? If not, how much profit margin would be allowed?
7. Would they be taxed?
8. Who would assume the responsibility of allowing a drug user to take so much of a particular drug: the government or a physician?
9. Should recreational use of drugs be authorized or just drug use for treatment?

In response to these questions, some reformers have offered the argument that drugs could be sold in the same fashion as alcohol—that is, sold only to licensed dealers, who would be taxed and held under close government scrutiny. Regulations would include prohibiting the sale of drugs to anyone under 21 years of age. Another proposal is a lesser form of legalization, called *decriminalization*. This concept generally calls for the reduction of criminal penalties for drug use or possession while retaining a degree of social disapproval. Regardless of which approach is most popular, it seems increasingly clear, at least to some, that a serious fault does exist in the current public policy addressing drug control. The fault is that current policy has failed to cut drastically the supply of drugs through the use of police action alone.

Figure 12.2

- It is not the responsibility of government to regulate the private morality of its citizens.
- Legalization of drugs would provide new revenue to be used in drug education and rehabilitation efforts.
- Drug laws are unenforceable and result in selective and discriminatory enforcement practices.
- Drug laws are hypocritical.
- Drug laws create criminals out of otherwise law-abiding citizens.
- Drug laws strengthen and expand organized crime.
- Drug laws create an environment in which police officials are tempted to use unscrupulous enforcement tactics, and they increase the danger of corruption.

Arguments for Drug Reform

The Cons: Arguments Against Legalization

The prevailing opposition against drug legalization is voiced by many politicians, law enforcement officials, and concerned citizens. Opponents of legalization contend that the problems created by Prohibition were minuscule compared to today's situation. Specifically, children of the 1920s were not the victims of alcohol consumption, at least not in an addictive sense.

Additionally, according to opponents, users would possibly face a greater risk of debilitating dependencies from cocaine and narcotics if those drugs were legalized. Today, almost 80 years after the repeal of Prohibition, alcoholism is considered—more so now than ever—one of the United States' most lethal killers. The legalization of drugs would very likely provide drug lords, both foreign and domestic, the vehicle to success for which they have been waiting: the conversion of the black market to an open market.

A primary concern about the reform of drug laws is the erosion of public morals. Specifically, many feel that the simple act of legalizing drugs would send a message about society's lack of social responsibility and its unwilling-ness to deal with a major health and public safety issue, which would be tan-tamount to surrender to the drug dealers of the world. Opponents, therefore, predict that adoption of such a public policy would increase drug abuse and would multiply the ancillary problems of poor health, violence, and broken families.

Certainly, legalization could serve as a "quick fix." How responsible is it, some might argue, to take a crime against society and legalize it for the sole purpose of eliminating it as a criminal problem and as a threat to public safety? This is a complex question that has been raised with regard to the legalization of prostitution, gambling, abortion, and pornography, as well as drugs.

According to some treatment officials, the rate of addiction to alcohol is only 10 percent of those who use it. The addiction rates for crack cocaine and methamphetamine, however, would soar; these are statistics that reformers strategically avoid (ONDCP, 2006).

The Alcohol Argument

Opponents to drug reform acknowledge alcohol as a dangerous and addictive drug, but they believe that the fact that alcohol is so harmful to society is the very reason that other dangerous substances of abuse should not be added to the list of legal drugs. The toll of alcohol consumption is well documented in terms of broken homes, violence, ruined careers, accidents, and lost productivity on the job and in school. The question is whether legalized alcohol and other drugs would create a worse situation than has been realized by legalized alcohol alone.

The Crime Rate

Although proponents of reform argue that legalized drugs would cause a decrease in the crime rate, opponents claim just the opposite—that is, although some drug-related crimes would be reduced (for instance, smuggling), a black market would always exist. This idea is particularly significant, considering that many addicts would be unable to hold down jobs because of their addic-tions to even the cheapest of "government-issued" drugs.

Many people involved in drug enforcement have suggested that numerous drug-related felonies are committed by people who were involved in crime before they started taking drugs. The drugs, which are routinely available in criminal circles, make the criminals more violent and unpredictable. Certainly there are some kill-for-a-fix crimes, but how logical is it to assume that a cut-rate price for drugs at a government outlet will stop such behavior? It is a simple fact that under the influence of drugs, normal people do not behave normally, and abnormal people may function in chilling and horrible ways. This argument extends to children, who are among the most frequent victims of violent, drug-related crimes that have nothing to do with the cost of acquiring the drugs (Bennett, 1990).

New Revenues

In response to those who claim that legalizing drugs would save the public billions of dollars in taxes, opponents are convinced that the black market would actually be broadened because of the lack of taxes on illicit drugs. After all, cigarette bootlegging is still one of organized crime's varied enterprises because of high tax-rate differentials. Additionally, it can be argued that stepped-up enforcement in conjunction with powerful forfeiture laws providing for government seizure of drug money, property, and assets would substantially reduce the costs of drug enforcement. Furthermore, it is maintained that what the government might save in law enforcement costs would be spent many times over as a result of traffic deaths, lost productivity, and medical costs.

This photo, released by the Bureau of Alcohol, Tobacco, Firearms and Explosives, shows a vehicle that agents stopped on Interstate 95 in 2005, recovering 1,600 cartons of black market cigarettes from the vehicle. Opponents to drug legalization point out that black markets do not disappear just because a substance is legalized and regulated.

The Addicts

Another viewpoint opposing reform is the argument that money would still be required to purchase drugs even if drugs were legalized. Specifically, it is believed that many addicts would not hold regular jobs and therefore would continue to commit ancillary crimes such as robbery, prostitution, and theft in order to acquire money. Even though some studies have indicated that heroin addicts are able to lead fairly normal lives if their drug needs are met, there is no evidence that all addicts would choose to leave the drug-crime subculture. Additionally, the number of drug-related crimes committed by intoxicated drug users, including assault, spouse/child abuse, and drug-related traffic accidents, would no doubt rise.

Additionally, perhaps we should remember that when pornography was legalized de facto by the Supreme Court, it did not just go away, as some had anticipated. In fact, it gradually became more extreme because of public boredom with the product. For example, *Playboy* magazine was superseded by *Penthouse*, which was then outdone by *Hustler*. Then came the sadistic "snuff" films that depicted gang rapes, sadism, and, ultimately, murder.

Organized Crime

The legalization of drugs would likely have three profound effects with regard to the black market: (1) it would give drugs a social sanction, creating a broader use of drugs (as was the case with legalized gambling, which created more gamblers rather than reducing the influence of organized crime in the market); (2) it would make drugs available without risk of arrest and prosecution; and (3) if the legal price of drugs did not undercut the price on the illicit market, users would continue to purchase drugs from drug dealers on the street and organized crime would continue to reap its drug-related profits.

After all, as pointed out earlier, legal lotteries have not dismantled the illegal numbers racket. In addition, the end of Prohibition did not devastate organized crime—it merely led to diversification and new areas of criminal enterprise. Many supporters of legalization are willing to admit that drugs such as crack and PCP are simply too dangerous to allow the shelter of the law. Thus, as former drug czar William Bennett (1990) has suggested, criminals will provide what the government will not. "As long as drugs that people very much want remain illegal, a black market will exist," says legalization advocate David Boaz of the Liberation Cato Institute. Crack is a good example. In powdered form, cocaine was an expensive indulgence. Then, however, street chemists found that a better, far less expensive (and more dangerous) high could be achieved by mixing cocaine with baking soda and heating it. So, crack was born, and "cheap" cocaine invaded low-income communities with furious speed. It could be argued that if government drugstores do not stock crack, addicts will find it in the clandestine market or simply bake it themselves from their legally purchased cocaine.

Finally, there exists the issue of children and teenagers. Certainly, under the legalization model they would be barred from drug purchases, just as they are now prohibited from buying beer, wine, and liquor. Drug dealers, though, will no doubt continue to cater to these young customers with the time-honored come-on—a couple of free fixes to get them hooked. What good will antidrug education be if these children observe their older brothers and sisters, parents, and friends smoking, snorting, or shooting up with government permission? According to Bennett, legalization will give us the worst of both worlds: millions of new drug users and a thriving criminal black market (Bennett, 1990).

Personal Freedoms

Proponents of legalization contend that drug laws increasingly deprive people of their personal freedoms and that drug users should be permitted to consume drugs in their own homes if they desire. Although this argument entails a rather lofty debate over political philosophy, it should be pointed out that a counterargument can be made that whenever one person's personal freedoms are safeguarded, someone else's may be restricted. In a nation with more than 250 million people, carte blanche cannot be given to everyone who desires to live his or her own way without regard to rights and needs of others.

The Cost of Legalization

Although legalization proponents argue that taxes from legal drugs and reduced expenditures related to drug enforcement would result in reductions in government spending, that argument fails to provide for the exorbitant

Figure 12.3

- Legalization of drugs would allow organized crime groups to continue in the drug trade but on a legal basis, using established drug-distribution networks.
- The governing of morality through enforcing "victimless" crimes upholds the moral viability of our nation.
- Just because a law seems unenforceable is no reason to abolish it. For example, laws against murder or robbery have not eliminated such criminal acts; however, the states continue to make murder illegal.
- Legalizing drugs would create much regulation and licensing and would therefore create many new opportunities for official corruption.
- Just because the criminal justice system seems to be overburdened, laws should not be eliminated. The answer is to dedicate more resources to the system, thus making it a more effective one.

Arguments Against Legalization

social costs of such a program. For instance, a study prepared by The Lewin Group for the National Institute on Drug Abuse and the National Institute on Alcohol Abuse and Alcoholism estimated the total economic cost of alcohol and other drug abuse to be $245.7 billion. Of this cost, $97.7 billion was due to abuse of drugs other than alcohol. This estimate includes substance abuse treatment and prevention costs as well as other healthcare costs, costs associated with reduced job productivity or lost earnings, and other costs to society such as crime and social welfare. The study also determined that these costs are borne primarily by governments (46%), followed by those who abuse drugs and members of their households (44%) (NIDA, 2007).

Given that more than one-half of this enormous figure was attributed to work-related accidents and lost productivity, is it not logical to assume that legalized drugs, which probably would sell for a fraction of the price of illicit drugs and therefore be more widely used, might increase that cost figure by many times? Many experts in the field believe so.

Even those who oppose legalization recognize that drug enforcement places a critical financial burden on the nation's resources, but they argue that the price of not doing so would be too costly for society. After all, all civilized societies have seen fit to exert some form of control over mind-altering substances. Even the few experiments in legalization have shown that when drugs are more widely available, addiction increases. For example, in 1975, Italy liberalized its drug laws and now has one of the highest heroin-related death rates in Western Europe. As discussed later in this chapter, in Alaska, where marijuana was decriminalized in 1975, the relaxed atmosphere increased use of the drug, particularly among children. After 15 years, Alaskans successfully petitioned to "recriminalize" marijuana.

Let's now look at some examples of legalization around the world.

DRUGS IN AMSTERDAM: THE "DUTCH WAY"

Some countries, such as the Netherlands, have legalized drugs as a remedy for their drug problems. Although drugs are not totally legal in Amsterdam, they are, for the most part, tolerated. In fact, the law in the Netherlands allows marijuana to be bought, sold, and used openly by anyone over 18 years of age.

The country's policy on marijuana evolved from the Opium Law, passed in 1976, after a heroin epidemic in the Netherlands. The law allows coffee shops to sell amounts of marijuana to patrons over the age of 18 but does not allow for wholesale trade. The "open policy" was meant to distinguish between low-risk drugs such as marijuana and high-risk drugs such as cocaine and heroin. However, the open policy has resulted in Amsterdam becoming a center of the drug culture in Europe, spawning a whole new travel category dubbed "drug tourism" (Thomas, 1998).

There are more than 1,000 coffee shops around the country. Most of them also sell beer and other alcoholic drinks along with marijuana. At a small counter, customers can purchase marijuana in "joints" or loose in small plastic bags. Rather than listing food, the menu lists different grades of marijuana and hashish, with varying tastes and strengths. Coffee shop owners, like many Dutch officials, believe that allowing soft drugs to be used openly actually reduces the attraction by taking away the adventure (Thomas, 1998). Indeed, over the years Amsterdam, a city of 700,000, has earned the reputation of being a drug mecca in Western Europe. Only a few blocks from Amsterdam's business district, cocaine and heroin dealers operate without fear of being arrested, because the government has adopted a strategy by which these dealers are quarantined to the area of town designated as the *red-light district*, a location known for drug dealing and other "vice" activities. This selling is tolerated because Dutch police authorities feel that drug trafficking can be more closely monitored if it is confined to a small area, thereby providing controls not only over drug dealing but over all ancillary criminal behaviors. Throughout the rest of the city, marijuana and hashish are treated much like alcohol and tobacco are treated in the United States.

The Dutch policy separates marijuana and hashish from harder drugs. It is generally felt that if young people can purchase marijuana in coffee shops rather than from criminal drug dealers who also sell harder drugs, it is less likely the customer will be tempted by the seller to try other more potent and addictive substances.

In addition, the Dutch have adopted a policy they believe makes drug use "boring" and less glamorous. The ease with which cannabis products can be obtained removes the mystique often attached to acts of rebellion and non-conformity that many young people engage in as part of the maturing process. Marijuana reformers claim that available data indicate strikingly lower patterns of drug use in Amsterdam than in the United States. For example, in 1986, drug users under the age of 26 accounted for 28 percent of Holland's drug users, but by 1995, that number had fallen to just 4 percent (Thomas, 1998).

The Dutch government believes that young people will experiment with drugs no matter what laws the government tries to enforce. Because they also believe there is danger in using drugs, the government has adopted a policy called *harm reduction*. Rather than punish young people for experimenting, the government tries to supervise their drug use. For example, at a local all-night club where marijuana was being used, the Drug Advice Bureau set up a booth to test the drug ecstasy (MDMA), a popular but illegal stimulant, before people took it—with no threat of arrest. In this fashion, the government attempts to guard young people against drugs that are unusually strong or toxic, rather than enforce the law. The government claims this is why the number of young people addicted to hard drugs is so low.

Ancillary to the liberal law enforcement approach in Amsterdam is a concomitant medical model used to treat addiction and abuse. In Amsterdam, a widespread methadone maintenance program, targeting heroin addicts, makes use of mobile units that travel around the city bringing methadone treatment to addicts. The methadone program in Amsterdam is beset by many of the same problems as U.S. experiments with the heroin substitute. In particular, methadone, which is also an addicting drug, has failed to divert users from heroin, so that some addicts have adopted a style of use combining both heroin and methadone.

In 1988, the Amsterdam health department estimated that there were 7,000 addicts in the city, 20 percent of whom were foreigners. Additionally, police estimate that 60 percent of petty crimes are committed by members of the addict population in Amsterdam. It should also be noted, however, that drug-related homicides in Amsterdam are very rare events. Washington, D.C., has 15 times as many drug-related murders than does Amsterdam. On the other hand, it is likely that the Netherlands has considerably more control over street crime than does the United States.

Unlike many U.S. cities, Amsterdam has a large and well-funded police department. Amsterdam's police strength is about 3,500, of which 2,900 are uniformed officers assigned to street beats. An estimated 400 of these officers are assigned to the diminutive four-block area of the red-light district in order to contain the high rate of crime there.

Some Dutch police officials are concerned with the overall rise in the crime rate that has occurred since the tolerance policy toward drugs went into effect. This increase in crime cannot be blamed entirely on Dutch drug users. As with many countries that experience a flourishing drug abuse problem, blame is conveniently placed on other countries whose stringent drug control policies have succeeded in ridding the country of many drug abusers and related criminals. It makes sense to assume that someone who steals to support a drug habit in Germany would not pass up an opportunity to steal just because he or she is in Amsterdam, where there is greater availability and affordability of drugs. One side effect of the Amsterdam project is the emergence of droves of pornography shops and houses of prostitution in the drug district. Dutch officials are quick to admit that the crime rate has dramatically risen since the so-called Dutch way was adopted.

Those who lend support for the Amsterdam experiment, however, claim that the relationship between sexual trafficking and drugs is difficult to establish because of several perceived factors. For example, some of the prostitution and pornography enterprises in Amsterdam preceded the legalization of drugs in that country. In addition, such red-light districts exist in European cities where drug retailing is not tolerated, although history has shown that the sex and drug industries are very closely correlated. In the United States, one need only travel through Boston's Combat Zone, San Francisco's Tenderloin, or Philadelphia's Arch Street districts to find evidence of close links between the sex and drug industries.

THE BRITISH EXPERIMENT

Great Britain passed legal controls regarding dangerous substances at about the same time the United States passed similar laws; the first such measure was passed in 1916. The early drug control efforts in both countries were aimed at controlling drug addiction and abuse by outlawing cocaine and opium and their derivatives. Much confusion surrounded the application of drug control laws in both Britain and the United States.

A second piece of antidrug legislation, known as the Dangerous Drug Act, was passed by Parliament in 1920. Basically, the law prohibited possession of opiates or cocaine except with a lawful prescription. Paralleling problems with the Harrison Act in the United States, confusion over the specifics of the new British legislation led to difficulty in its interpretation and enforcement. In 1924, a committee of British physicians was formed to determine whether drug abuse should be approached as a criminal justice problem or a medical problem. The committee was inclined toward the latter and instituted the so-called *British system*, which prevailed well into the late 1960s.

The British system gave opiate addicts, most of whom were older persons, legal access to heroin and morphine. The goal of the program was to wean addicts from their addiction to heroin. This was done through medical supervision of addicts by physicians, who would prescribe just enough heroin for the addicts to stay "well" but not enough to get high. By the late 1950s, the number of heroin addicts began to grow. By the mid-1960s, England became a major market for smokable heroin, similar to the opium traditionally smoked by Chinese addicts. The availability of this type of heroin was thought to contribute to the increasing numbers of addicts. Compounding the problem was the diversion of heroin from legitimate sources (e.g., doctors' offices) to the streets.

Critical Thinking Task

Suppose that legalization of drugs is adopted as a public policy in the United States. Suggest guidelines to implement this policy.

The British system of drug maintenance by prescription is still in operation, although several factors have made it a less effective practice than it has been in the past. First, a sizeable increase in illegal heroin supplies was noted in the 1970s, offering a realistic alternative to visiting doctor's offices. This was accompanied by a general economic downturn, with high unemployment, declining wages, and racial tensions in most large British cities. Some students of the British system suggest that the real crisis came when British economic policies under the former Thatcher government resulted in declining buying power and an increase in the cost of alcohol, thereby making heroin a cheaper high than liquor.

No matter which of the many problems actually resulted in the increase in heroin use in Britain, the fact remains that the system is not as effective as it used to be. However, more recent legislation relaxed some of the restrictions imposed on heroin maintenance by the Thatcher government, making it once again a more viable option.

THE ALASKAN POT LEGALIZATION EXPERIENCE

Although now illegal, possession of marijuana for personal use was considered lawful in Alaska between 1975 and 1990. During that time, Alaska state law allowed people over 19 years of age to possess up to four ounces of marijuana in private without penalty, though it could not be sold or bartered. In addition to other public concerns, the Alaskan law conflicted with federal law prohibiting the drug.

The "legalized pot" experiment has since given researchers and policymakers a model to study. In this section we consider the history and repercussions of this controversial public policy. Alaska's 1975 legalization of marijuana was not a result of a public movement or one anchored by elected representatives of the people. Instead, it resulted from a decision by the Alaska Supreme Court. The landmark decision was in the case of *Ravin v. State* (1975), which was based on Article I, Section 22, of the Alaska Constitution, which states that "the right of the people to privacy is recognized and shall not be infringed." In deciding this case, the court held that the state had no authority to exert control over the activities of an individual unless their activities affected the public health and safety of others (or the public at large).

The *Ravin* decision was based on two basic premises: (1) that marijuana was a "harmless substance," and (2) that a 1972 state constitutional amendment guaranteeing Alaskans the right to privacy extended to marijuana use in one's home. Indeed, the court declared that the effects of marijuana were not serious enough to justify widespread concern "at least as compared with the far more dangerous effects of alcohol, barbiturates and amphetamines." The court further held that until conclusive evidence was available to show that marijuana is a dangerous drug, the state could not prohibit its possession and use in the home by adults. With regard to the use of marijuana by minors, the *Ravin* court also contended that "adolescents may not be equipped with the maturity to handle the experience prudently. . . ." Therefore, it still made it illegal for anyone under 19 years of age in Alaska to use or possess marijuana.

Despite the fact that marijuana possession by minors was outlawed, law enforcement officials in Alaska had a difficult time keeping it out of the hands of school-aged children. For example, in 1982, seven years after the *Ravin* decision, the National Institute on Drug Abuse disclosed that approximately 72 percent of high school students in Alaska had used marijuana at least once. The corresponding figure nationwide was 59 percent. Young people are aware of the hypocrisy of a government that restricts the use of a substance by one age group but authorizes its use by persons only two to three years older.

Figure 12.4

Irwin Ravin—a Homer, Alaska, lawyer—had deliberately set out to be stopped while driving and had purposely possessed a small amount of marijuana in his pocket. Later, in his defense, Ravin filed a motion to dismiss the criminal complaint in district court. During the court hearings, several experts testified and numerous books and written articles were introduced into evidence. The district court denied the motion to dismiss, so Ravin appealed to the superior court, which also denied the motion.

Finally, the Alaskan Supreme Court agreed to review the case. The court noted at the time that "most marijuana available in the United States contained THC content of less than one percent." After considering both long- and short-term effects of the drug on users, the court overturned the lower courts'decision and protected an adult's right to possess marijuana in his own home for personal use. In coming to this decision, the court placed more importance on an individual's right to privacy than on the state's responsibility to preserve public health and safety. The court, however, failed to define an "adult," how much marijuana could be "possessed," and what constituted a person's "own home."

A Synopsis of the Ravin Case

Yet another study of school-aged children was conducted in 1988 by Bernard Segal, professor of Health and Sciences at the University of Alaska. Segal reported that marijuana had "become well incorporated into the lifestyle of many adolescents" and, for them, could no longer be considered an experimental drug. The study revealed that overall use of marijuana rose between 1983 and 1988 and that its popularity was 16 percentage points above the national average.

Between 1975 and 1990, interest groups opposed to the legalization measure lobbied in the state legislature to outlaw the drug again. Large oil companies, for example, made substantial contributions in support of a recriminalization proposal. On the other hand, groups such as Alaskans for Privacy (a citizen group consisting of local professionals) and members of the National Organization for the Reform of Marijuana Laws (NORML) maintained their support for decriminalization.

In 1989, another citizens' group, frustrated by inaction in the legislature, began circulating petitions for a recriminalization measure. The result was the required 42,000 signatures that were obtained for the acclaimed "Proposition Two," which was then placed on the ballot. In examining the former state drug policy of Alaska, three distinct problems should be noted:

Problem #1. Because possession or distribution of marijuana was a violation of federal law in Alaska, any person using the drug in his or her own home was still in violation of the law. So, one could argue that the state of Alaska had basically sanctioned the use of a substance prohibited by federal law.

Problem #2. While federal agents, through interdiction efforts, were attempting to curb the flow of drugs into the country, a simultaneous signal was also sent to the traffickers in foreign source countries such as Colombia and Mexico. The dual message was that although the United States does not want foreign-made drugs brought into the country, at the same time certain jurisdictions in the United States condone drug use.

Problem #3. Although the state of Alaska permitted the personal use of marijuana in the home, it refused to allow the drug to be sold in the state. To support the marijuana appetite for drug users, a vast illicit pot-growing network was created to meet consumer demands. This network developed drug-manufacturing problems not just for Alaska but for neighboring states such as Washington and Oregon. In addition, when drug dealers were arrested in Alaska, the moral stigma was removed, since they were seen as merely trying to furnish a product that was already legalized by the state government. Additionally, the penalty for an individual over 18 years of age found in possession of marijuana in a public place was a civil fine of only $100. This modest amount scarcely poses a deterrent for others contemplating involvement in drug use.

In summation, after considerable public outcry over the rise of adolescent drug abuse in Alaska, a voter proposition was passed in November 1990 to "recriminalize" possession of any amount of marijuana.

A Proposed Solution

The issue of legalizing drugs should be debated, as should any other strategy for solving the nation's drug concerns. It would seem, however, that legalization is an option whose time has not yet come. To date, it appears that the best strategies for fighting the "drug war" are through education, prevention, rehabilitation, and innovative law enforcement strategies.

The appropriateness of some law enforcement tactics remains the topic of a vigorous debate, even among police executives. It is doubtful, however, that interdiction, eradication, and intensive street-level enforcement strategies alone will yield a "quick fix" to the drug problem. It should be remembered that the U.S. public's perceptions of its drug problem have emerged from more than a century of changing attitudes, morals, and standards of living. Because drug use is a complex social problem, we must expect the solutions to be equally complex.

In considering a solution to the problem, perhaps we should be aware of the successes that have been achieved in reducing tobacco consumption over the years. The positive image of the cigarette smoker has been greatly minimized over the past 10 years due to public campaigns deglamorizing tobacco. This began with a government antismoking campaign, which was later embraced by Hollywood and segments of the media. For example, in a report from the Surgeon General, the nation's nicotine addiction rate was at 40 percent in 1964;

today it stands at 30 percent, not a great difference but a significant one that public heath officials consider a notable victory. As part of a proposed solution, opponents of drug legalization are considering several possibilities as viable, although sometimes contradictory, alternatives:

- *Deglamorize drugs.* This may have been the single most important component of drug control in the 1990s. As mentioned earlier, the success of the deglamorization of tobacco became evident in the decrease in tobacco use and cigarette smoking over a 25-year period. In the deglamorizing process, massive drug education programs in the schools combined with antidrug advertising in the media would convince would-be drug users not to use illegal substances.

  All available evidence suggests that drug education is the most effective means of drug control. However, such a strategy would require either a massive infusion of new money into educational programs or a major diversion of present funds from other drug control efforts in order to be successful. Present drug education efforts are woefully underfunded.

- *Boycott drugs.* It could be argued that if people can successfully boycott grapes, fur and leather clothing, and the killing of baby seals, why not organize an embargo on illicit drugs? In addition to the deterrent effect of arrest and prosecution, education and prevention programs may be effective ways to encourage a national initiative to boycott the illicit drug trade and dry up demand.

- *Rehabilitate and counsel.* Considerable research points to great successes in drug rehabilitation and drug counseling. The problem is that these programs are simply not available where they are needed (particularly the inner city), nor are they available in sufficient numbers (most drug rehabilitation programs targeted at lower-income groups have long waiting lists). To make use of this strategy, new revenues would have to be created or present allocations would have to be diverted from other sources.

- *Target the drug user.* A fact of drug enforcement is that to quell the drug problem, either the drug supply or the demand (or both) has to be reduced. In focusing resources on interdiction of drugs (i.e., reducing the supply), international and political problems are encountered. These pose serious questions regarding the legality and appropriateness of international law enforcement. An alternative is to focus law enforcement resources on the drug user in the United States. This would send the message that even low levels of drug use are not tolerated.

- *Break down the trafficking infrastructure.* This solution is in precise contradiction to the idea of targeting the user. Experts in organized crime have long argued that criminal organizations cannot be controlled by either a "headhunting" strategy (arresting as many illicit entrepreneurs as possible) or by attacking consumers. They argue that the way to control organized drug trafficking is to make the business of drugs very difficult to conduct. Essential to successful criminal organizations are money-laundering mechanisms and corruption, because these make up the infrastructure of the drug organizations. It is argued that the United States facilitates organized crime of all types, and drug trafficking in particular, in that, unlike almost any other Western nation, little regulatory control is exercised over the activities of corporations, banks, holding companies, trusts, and the like. It is argued that stepped-up reporting requirements, stiff penalties, and the reallocation of law enforcement resources from users to the business-community allies of drug organizations would strangle the cartels in their own money. In addition, it is axiomatic in the organized crime literature that corruption is necessary for success. Targeting of law enforcement and political corruption would make the logistics of drug trafficking very difficult. This strategy would shift the aim of enforcement strategies from users and small-time dealers to their "upperworld" partners, who have much more to lose and are more easily deterred.

- *Broaden forfeiture sanctions.* The use of forfeiture sanctions against drug offenders has proved to be a valuable asset to law enforcement in the drug war. As an alternative to incarceration, perhaps imposing stricter forfeiture sanctions against dealers would deter some drug crimes and would supply law enforcement with additional financial resources. There is also an argument to be made for the expansion of forfeiture laws to include money-laundering activities by legitimate business allies of drug traffickers. An investment house faced with the seizure of its depositors' assets might be less likely to handle dirty money.

- *Impose harsh fines.* This is yet another alternative to incarceration of drug dealers and users. The use of strict and harsh fines might serve as a deterrent to criminal activity and would aid in financing drug education, rehabilitation, and law enforcement efforts.

SUMMARY

Debating such a controversial public issue such as drug decriminalization or legalization and adequately deliberating all the important considerations of the issue are not an easy task. Headway in arriving at a viable solution is frequently stifled by fragmented (mis)information promulgated by people who are merely trying to "muddy the waters" or promote their own personal interests. Drug dealers and consumers represent one such interest group, but so do some government bureaucracies that do not want to give up funding, private hospitals that profit from drug abuse and related problems, and politicians who seek votes through emotion and fear rather than reason.

Perhaps one can argue that the United States has slowly evolved into a passive society that is becoming both drug- and violence-tolerant. The drug problem for many citizens is merely something that is seen on television or read about in the local newspaper. Unfortunately, many people have an "ostrich-type" mindset that holds that just because they are not victims of drug abuse or because they do not personally know a victim, the drug problem is somebody else's concern.

Additionally, drug users frequently consider themselves victims of governmental and societal repression rather than victims of drug abuse. Accordingly, many people view a "victim" of drug abuse as one who suffers an overdose or experiences some negative physical manifestation created by the use of a particular substance. When this occurs, little consideration is given to the drug user's employer and coworkers who are affected by the user's inability to function on the job; the taxpayer who foots the bill for drug enforcement; and the costs of expensive and often lengthy drug trials, incarceration, and treatment programs for drug-dependent people. In addition, the unsuspecting victims of drug crimes often suffer from fatal accidents, assaults, robberies, or murders. In cases of drive-by shootings, the murderers are often intoxicated, under the influence of drugs, or consciously operating on behalf of drug-dealing groups.

Some people feel that the drug problem is one that needs a "quick fix" and therefore should be easily remedied either through legalization policies or, at the other extreme, through the introduction of repressive law enforcement measures. Our country's drug problems are the product of more than 100 years of social change and evolution, touch-and-go drug control policy, and a myriad of other factors, such as the media and the entertainment industry. Additionally, a passive reluctance seems to exist on the part of our present-day society to learn from past historical experience in dealing with drug abuse.

It is clear that solutions, whatever they are, will be time-consuming and will require equal participation on the part of law enforcement, schools, colleges and universities, researchers, and social treatment programs. In addition, an effective drug control policy must include unified participation from a general public that is willing, informed, and ready to make constructive choices about controlling drug use and related criminal activity.

Do you recognize these terms?

- British system
- decriminalization
- legalization
- medical model
- recreational drugs
- red-light district

DISCUSSION QUESTIONS

1. What are the arguments for the legalization of drugs, and how realistic are those arguments?

2. Discuss the possible consequences of drug legalization with regard to public health.

3. List the arguments for not legalizing drugs.

4.   If drugs are never legalized in the United States, what other measures could be considered to ensure public safety and health?

5.   What would be the possible effects of drug legalization on drug gangs and organized crime groups?

6.   How might legalizing drugs in the United States affect international relations or efforts to control black market drugs entering the country from foreign sources?

7.   How would legalizing drugs likely affect domestic production of black market drugs in the United States?

8.   Discuss the ways various jurisdictions (e.g., Amsterdam, Britain, Alaska) have handled legalization and the results of these approaches.

Class Projects

1.   In considering the question of legalization of drugs, what patterns of criminality or addiction do you feel would evolve if drugs were legalized?

2.   Survey classmates or friends to see what their position is on the legalization issue. Take note of the reasons they give to support their positions. Are these reasons realistic or rational?

Chapter 13

Understanding Drug Control Policy

This chapter will enable you to:

- Understand social and political philosophies of drug policy
- Learn which government and private agencies share responsibility for drug control
- Appreciate the contribution of private industry to drug control
- Compare and contrast federal drug control strategies
- Consider both supply- and demand-oriented drug policies
- Understand the utility of federal drug control legislation

Perhaps one of the greatest ironies in the search for a modern, workable drug control policy is that most people, despite their political preferences or social differences, desire basically the same thing: a safe society. As simplistic as that may sound, the truth is that most of us want to live in neighborhoods without fear of drive-by shootings and crack houses. We want our schools and places of employment to be drug-free, and we want to have the peace of mind of knowing that the lives of our loved ones are not ruined by drug abuse. So, what should be done? What approaches are best?

Over the decades, local and national drug control initiatives have resulted in the hiring and training of more law enforcement officers, a more expanded interdiction campaign, the development of more education programs, and the establishment of more treatment and prevention programs than ever before in history. Yet the drug problem persists.

419

DOI: 10.1016/B978-1-4377-4450-7.00013-8
© 2011 Elsevier Inc. All rights reserved.

To begin a discussion on drug control policy, considering one of the absurdities in modern drug control policy thinking might serve to illustrate the philosophy of today's failed drug policy. During the mid-1980s, it was surprising when the House of Representatives passed an amendment requiring the military to "seal the borders" against drugs within 45 days. Although the amendment was defeated by the Senate, the dysfunctional nature of our national drug control policy became glaringly apparent. After all, how could such a mandate be fulfilled with more than 88,000 miles of U.S. coastline, 7,500 miles of borders with Mexico and Canada, and 300 ports of entry?

Today, the "drug war" has resulted in more than two-thirds of the federal drug budget being diverted to law enforcement, interdiction, and foreign initiatives. This budgetary scenario was nearly the opposite when President Richard Nixon launched the war on drugs more than 30 years ago. Under Nixon's administration, two initiatives were pursued: enforcement through interdiction, and treatment through the then recently developed methadone maintenance program, which focused on treating hard-core heroin addicts. The Carter administration sought to downplay the drug problem and to scale back enforcement initiatives. Instead, a program of *eradication* was implemented, by which the herbicide paraquat was used to climinate marijuana fields in Mexico. Next, the Reagan administration took a hard stance against drug offenders by supporting the passage of several powerful drug control measures and initiating the Pentagon into the national drug control effort. The George H. W. Bush administration followed through by expanding Reagan's initiatives, spending more money on the drug effort than all previous presidents combined (Wilkinson, 1994).

Establishing a workable drug control policy is a complicated social undertaking. As we observed earlier, many countries, such as China and Babylonia, were early victims of drug use and also may have been among the first to recognize a fundamental correlation between drug use and crime. Lawmakers during those periods recognized that a large percentage of people were unable to make judgments about their own ability to make safe use of mind-altering and addicting substances and that therefore those substances posed a threat to public order and safety. Furthermore, early laws indicated the necessity for the government to attempt to control drug-related crime by making it unlawful to use, possess, or traffic in dangerous substances.

In the United States, the federal response to the nation's drug problem is dynamic, with both successes and failures. Many critics of current federal drug policy and proponents of drug legalization claim that laws designed to control drug use and related activity violate personal freedoms and the spirit of the Constitution and as a result are too repressive in nature (see Chapter 12). They maintain that the government has no business regulating and criminalizing public morals. However, if the history of global drug use offers any yardstick as to the dangers of drugs and related activity, as many feel it does, then the option of decriminalization or legalization is not a viable one. So, if we reject decriminalization/legalization, the remaining alternative is to outlaw dangerous drugs, prosecute offenders, and attempt through numerous public programs and policies to deter individual involvement with substances thought to be dangerous.

In addition to physical and psychological harm done by drug abuse, one of the most threatening components of the illicit drug problem is the parallel issue of organized crime. As discussed in Chapter 7, the term *organized crime* means many things to many people, but a significant number of groups that fit the definition of organized crime provide a mechanism for the manufacturing, trafficking, and managing of criminal drug operations. Ways to dismantle these groups must also be a part of today's drug policy approach.

The United States' drug control policy cycle shows that the government assumes a particular method of dealing with drug use and trafficking, and drug users and traffickers then take defensive measures to counter those policies. The government then assumes a different strategy, which causes the traffickers to again take defensive actions, and so the cycle goes. This reactive response has characterized the federal drug control strategy for decades—but especially since the 1960s. As we will see in the forthcoming discussion, federal controls in the last 80 years have generally focused on the supply of illicit drugs rather than attacking the public demand for them. In 1986, the President's Commission on Organized Crime (PCOC, 1986a) made the following remarks regarding supply and demand policies:

> Although the supply and demand of drugs have often been considered separate issues, by both the public and private sectors, they are in fact inseparable parts of a single problem. The success of supply efforts is related to commitments made to reduce the demand for drugs through drug abuse education, treatment, research, vigorous enforcement of drug laws, and effective sentencing. Drug supply and demand operate in an interrelated and dynamic manner. The strategies employed to limit each should be similarly connected.

Today, politicians continue to support measures designed to control drug use. These measures have been in response to growing public demands for increased use of drug testing in the workforce, stricter laws dealing with both drug users and dealers, and renewed attempts by government to curtail drug-related corruption. On one hand, it may seem that the national focus on drug control is so intense that faulty drug control initiatives go unchecked or are immune from critical examination. On the other hand, widespread community concern and a tendency for making the public more aware of domestic drug policy may provide an adequate check against misuse of governmental power.

SHARED RESPONSIBILITY

Over the years, drug control efforts have involved a fusion of agencies operating at virtually all levels of government. Essentially, these efforts call on the functions of local, state, and federal government. At the federal level, international relations are concerned with regard to the manufacture, smuggling, and sale of drugs in the United States. The primary responsibility for drug control,

Figure 13.1
Source: Bureau of Justice Statistics, 1992.

A wide variety of policies, strategies, and tactics have been used to control the illegal drug problem.

■ Policies

Prohibition is the ban on the distribution, possession, and use of specified substances made illegal by legislative or administrative order and the application of criminal penalties to violators.

Regulation is control over the distribution, possession, and use of specified substances. Regulations specify the circumstances under which substances can be legally distributed and used. Prescription medications and alcohol are the substances most commonly regulated in the U.S.

■ Strategies

Demand reduction strategies attempt to decrease individuals' tendency to use drugs. Efforts provide information and education to potential and casual users about the risks and adverse consequences of drug use, and treatment to drug users who have developed problems from using drugs.

Supply reduction focuses diplomatic, law enforcement, military, and other resources on eliminating or reducing the supply of drugs. Efforts focus on foreign countries, smuggling routes outside the country, border interdiction, and distribution within the U.S.

User accountability emphasizes that all users of illegal substances, regardless of the type of drug they use or the frequency of that use, are violating criminal laws and should be subject to penalties. It is closely associated with zero tolerance.

Zero tolerance holds that drug distributors, buyers, and users should be held fully accountable for their offenses under the law. This is an alternative to policies that focus only on some violators such as sellers of drugs or users of cocaine and heroin while ignoring other violators.

■ Tactics

Criminal justice activities include enforcement, prosecution, and sentencing activities to apprehend, convict, and punish drug offenders. Although thought of primarily as having supply reduction goals, criminal sanctions also have demand reduction effects by discouraging drug use.

Prevention activities are educational efforts to inform potential drug users about the health, legal, and other risks associated with drug use. Their goal is to limit the number of new drug users and dissuade casual users from continuing drug use as part of a demand reduction strategy.

Taxation requires those who produce, distribute, or possess drugs to pay a fee based on the volume or value of the drugs. Failure to pay subjects violators to penalties for this violation, not for the drug activities themselves.

Testing individuals for the presence of drugs is a tool in drug control that is used for safety and monitoring purposes and as an adjunct to therapeutic interventions. It is in widespread use for employees in certain jobs such as those in the transportation industry and criminal justice agencies. New arrestees and convicted offenders may be tested. Individuals in treatment are often tested to monitor their progress and provide them an incentive to remain drug free.

Treatment (therapeutic interventions) focus on individuals whose drug use has caused medical, psychological, economic, and social problems for them. The interventions may include medication, counseling, and other support services delivered in an inpatient setting or on an outpatient basis. These are demand reduction activities to eliminate or reduce individuals' drug use.

Policies, Stategies, and Tactics for Drug Control

however, rests with state and local agencies, since they are closest to the drug problem in our communities. For example, as discussed in the following chapter, education, prevention, and treatment programs exist almost exclusively at the local and state levels and are administered in our school districts and state and regional health organizations. Local schools provide drug abuse prevention information to children; treatment services are administered in residential and outpatient facilities in almost every community. The role of the federal government in these areas is essentially to provide funding and technical assistance through the Departments of Education and Health and Human Services.

DEVELOPMENT OF FEDERAL DRUG CONTROL EFFORTS

Although states have always had police authority, under the Constitution the federal government was originally granted power to raise taxes and handle international relations, not to police its citizens. As stated in Chapter 1, in the early 1900s, federal control over drug abuse and prescription practices was considered unconstitutional. Thus, federal drug control efforts were restricted to tactics within federal authority—in particular, the ability to tax the people and develop international treaties. During the late 1800s, state laws (specifically those aimed at cocaine and morphine) required that drugs be obtainable only by a doctor's prescription. These laws were generally ineffective because controlled drugs could be transported from other states that did not have such restrictions. At the turn of the Twentieth Century, the federal government became active in drug control efforts through the State Department's participation in international initiatives. The majority of these were in the form of international conferences such as the 1909 Shanghai Opium Convention, the 1911 International Conference on Opium (at The Hague), and the 1913 International Opium Convention. The result was the 1914 congressional approval of the Harrison Narcotics Act, which used the federal government's authority to raise taxes and regulate the manufacture and sale of certain drugs. The broad enforcement powers of the Harrison Narcotics Act were upheld in two crucial U.S. Supreme Court decisions: *United States v. Doremus* and *Webb, et al. v. United States*. For the following 50 years, the Harrison Narcotics Act remained the basis for federal narcotics regulation.

In 1970, the myriad regulations and amendments to the Harrison Narcotics Act were consolidated into a new piece of federal legislation that became known as the Controlled Substances Act (officially titled the Comprehensive Drug Abuse Prevention and Control Act). Under the new legislation, courts interpreted powers of commerce as the new basis for drug control, supplanting the need for government to portray the police function of drug control as a tax measure.

POLICY-RELATED FACTORS

Although the federal government has adopted its own drug control policy and enforcement initiatives, for the most part such efforts are a local option. This means that drug laws, policing policies, and prosecution philosophies are all driven by local governmental initiatives. For example, in the case of drug enforcement options, a drug dealer facing state criminal charges may be given the choice to cooperate with police, testify against other drug dealers, or risk going to jail. Local authorities have full authority to make such an offer, and they do so every day. Police can also choose any number of enforcement methods and techniques, including gang sweeps, undercover operations, wiretaps, and reverse stings.

Regardless of the enforcement options chosen, these tactics have a significant impact on the criminal justice system in the community, especially in the adjudicatory process, which includes the courts, prosecution, and public defense. For example, operations such as street sweeps result in a high number of people being arrested and ultimately being convicted and receiving prison sentences. On the other hand, so-called kingpin strategies, by which police target upper-level traffickers, often result in lengthy trials and related criminal proceedings that also place financial and logistical burdens on the justice system. Even the investigation phase of drug kingpins poses special concerns to police in that these investigations are costly and lengthy, and the only outcome may be the arrest of a handful of people. Although those arrested may be primary managers in crime organizations, members of the public are sometimes slow in realizing the importance of such investigations as opposed to street sweeps of low-level dealers whose arrests make attractive media headlines but in actuality are easily replaced by the kingpins whom they serve.

A factor complicating drug control policy is the problem of variances in drug use from one area to another. Crack cocaine seems to be the predominant problem in many major metropolitan cities, whereas in rural areas drugs such as methamphetamine and marijuana are more widely abused. In addition to the different drugs of abuse, consequences of the drug trade also differ from one area to another.

PRIVATE-SECTOR RESPONSES

Organizations and agencies not affiliated with government have also risen to combat the nation's drug abuse problem. Many companies have developed extensive drug prevention programs for their communities. As discussed in Chapter 14, the Drug Abuse Resistance Education (DARE) program frequently has corporate sponsorship. Furthermore, the media provide free airtime for public service drug abuse prevention announcements, and many companies require prospective employees to undergo drug testing. In recent years, private companies whose employees have developed drug problems offer employee assistance programs whereby referral services offer treatment options. In addition, many treatment facilities are privately owned, and benefits are usually covered by private insurance companies.

THE ROLE OF THE MILITARY

We learned how thousands of military veterans during the Civil War became hopelessly addicted to morphine. With the exception of that war, the military has had little experience with controlling drug abuse and trafficking. It was in 1967, during the Vietnam War, that a special Department of Defense (DOD) task force was established to study the extent of drug abuse by U.S. troops assigned to Vietnam and areas in Europe. In 1972, a key policy directive, born out of the "drug scare" of the 1960s, recommended preventive alcohol and other drug abuse education along with strict enforcement procedures and the establishment of treatment policies.

In 1980, a new DOD directive was established to replace the 1972 initiative. The new policy reflected a less tolerant attitude toward drug abuse and was a drastic departure from the military's previous treatment-oriented attitude. Nineteen-eighty was also important due to the investigation of a major incident—the crash of a jet airplane on the aircraft carrier *U.S.S. Nimitz* that killed 14 navy personnel and seriously injured 44 others. This incident uncovered widespread drug use on the ship, illustrating the extent of the military's drug problem and by 1981 resulting in the establishment of urine testing for drugs. The DOD's drug-testing policy is still firmly in place today.

DEVELOPMENT OF U.S. DRUG POLICY

U.S. drug control policy has evolved over time and has undergone a number of distinctive phases. As discussed in Chapter 1, the earliest drug control efforts focused on regulation (1906 Food and Drug Act), taxation (1914 Harrison Narcotics Act), and prohibition (1970 Controlled Substances Act). *Regulation* of drugs specifies the circumstances under which they can be lawfully distributed and used. Prescription medications and alcohol are the most commonly regulated drugs. *Taxation* requires those who legally produce, distribute, or possess drugs to pay a fee based on the quantity or value of the drugs. Criminal penalties result for failure to pay taxes rather than for specific drug violations themselves.

Next, international efforts attempted to establish cooperation between the United States and foreign countries sharing similar drug abuse problems. Afterward, policies moved toward prohibition efforts, with a focus on enforcement of criminal sanctions and, more recently, civil penalties. The essence of *prohibition* is the ban on manufacturing, distribution, and use of drugs that are designated as illegal under state and federal law. Violators face prosecution and an array of penalties, from the imposition of fines to imprisonment.

Today, criminal penalties for drug violations have become firmly embedded in drug control public policy. Although it is unlikely that there will be much support for the abandonment of criminal sanctions, a few scholars and legal practitioners have suggested that the *crime control* model of drug control be abandoned and that drug legalization be considered under a new *medical model* of drug control. Suggestions have ranged from totally removing criminal penalties to imposing a system of regulation similar to that used in the manufacture and distribution of cigarettes and alcohol. Instead of total legalization, some have even suggested a system of decriminalization whereby penalties for possession or distribution of certain drugs would be reduced. During the 1970s, several states attempted to do just that. Complicating the drug policy question is the fact that drug abuse trends change over time. For example, at the turn of the century, heroin and opium products were the main drugs of concern. Through the years, other drugs such as marijuana, barbiturates, LSD, PCP, and, more recently, crack cocaine rose in popularity.

Because of the complexity of today's drug problem, control initiatives are varied and widely utilized. Each policy incorporates its own tactics and strategies to further its successful implementation. For example, drug prohibition is the predominant control policy in today's local and national arena. Strategies for accomplishing drug prohibition include the reduction of both demand and supply, and each of these is supported by law enforcement and drug treatment programs.

Let's now consider some particulars of demand and supply, since these strategies are the cornerstone of our national drug control policy.

Demand Reduction

People who believe that the market for illicit drugs is the reason for the country's drug problem generally think that police should target drug users. In theory, once users are sufficiently afraid to purchase drugs for fear of being arrested, fewer customers mean higher prices for drugs. If prices can be raised high enough, the profit margin for dealers will be too low to make it worth their while. Another demand-reduction philosophy focuses on changing the behavior of drug users or potential users. This is to be accomplished by programs such as DARE, which are aimed at teaching children to resist peer pressure and informing people about the dangers of drug abuse. The power of such programs is supposed to be in their ability to thwart the onset of drug use by potential first-time users. Zero tolerance was discussed in Chapter 11 as a demand-reduction policy option. This policy holds drug users, sellers, and buyers fully accountable for their offenses under law. The philosophy behind zero tolerance is that violators of drug laws, even for the smallest amounts of drugs, should be held criminally responsible for their actions.

The Supply-Reduction Paradigm

The drug war is based on a supply-reduction strategy that seeks to (1) eradicate or control drugs at their source; (2) interdict or seize drugs as they enter the country; and (3) engage in intense domestic drug enforcement efforts primarily aimed at users and drug consumers. All three components of the supply-reduction paradigm are so seriously flawed and ineffective that they have made the problem of illicit drug sales and consumption much worse than a strategy of simply doing nothing.

The major problem with the supply-reduction paradigm is that it assumes a stable and static supply of illegal drugs. The fact is that such an assumption is wrong. The supply of drugs is infinitely elastic, and trying to seize enough illicit produce to impact the market is the rough equivalent of trying to empty the Mississippi River with a teaspoon. The river is always going to win. The fact is that "suppliers simply produce for the market what they would have produced anyway, plus enough extra to cover anticipated government seizures" (Rydell and Everingham, 1994:5).

The supply-reduction paradigm is doomed to failure by basic facts of geography and horticulture. Drugs such as heroin, cocaine, and marijuana can be grown and processed in a wide variety of locations, making crop eradication programs impossible to implement. Even if a particular locale is targeted and eradication programs are successfully carried out there, growers in other locations will merely make up for the deficit in supply. If heroin supplies in the Golden Crescent (Afghanistan, Iran, Pakistan) are targeted, opium growers in the Golden Triangle (Thailand, Myanmar, Laos), Mexico, or Colombia will simply grow more and supply the demand. These regions have had no problem supplying the demand for heroin for the last century, although the relative importance of each fluctuates with local growing conditions, enforcement efforts, and the vagaries of geopolitics.

The case of cocaine is even more instructive. In theory, cocaine should be the easiest of the illicit crops to subject to an eradication strategy. It grows only in South America and principally in Peru and Bolivia (with Colombia, Ecuador, and Brazil making small, but increasing, contributions to the supply). The world's entire cocaine supply is grown on 700 square miles of arable land. Even so, it would still be prohibitively costly to eradicate the crop. But the fact is that cocaine, even though it can be grown only in certain areas of South America, can be grown on 2,500,000 square miles of arable land (Nadelmann, 1989:945). Eradication as a control strategy is doomed to failure by Mother Nature herself.

Even assuming no expansion in coca leaf production, efforts to destroy the drug at its source have been miserable failures. For example, in 1998 the Colombian government seized a record amount of cocaine and related coca products—about 57 metric tons. In addition, it also destroyed 185 cocaine laboratories. The net effect was zero decrease in the processing or exporting of cocaine hydrochloride from Colombia and greater availability of cocaine within the United States (GAO, 1999:6, 12). In fact, the GAO reported that after a two-year program of extensive herbicide spraying of Andean coca fields (in Peru, Bolivia, and Colombia), net coca cultivation increased by 50 percent (GAO, 1999:2). Despite the expenditure of $625 million on narcotics control operations in Colombia between 1990 and 1998, cocaine availability in the United States increased, cocaine production increased, and Colombia surpassed Bolivia and Peru as the major source country for cocaine (GAO, 1999:3-6). According to the World Drug report, in 2009 Colombia remained the world's largest cultivator of coca bush, followed by Peru and then Bolivia (UNODC, 2010).

The cost of crop eradication is enormous, especially considering its failure to reduce drug supplies. To achieve a 1 percent diminution in cocaine consumption in the United States (assuming eradication programs were successful), the cost would be $783 million. To achieve the 1 percent reduction in cocaine consumption, the cost of a strategy emphasizing drug treatment programs would be $34 million (Rydell and Everingham, 1994). The lack of impact on the U.S. market is obvious. From 1982 to 1999, federal expenditures on the drug war increased from $1.65 billion to $17.7 billion. From 1982 to 1999, the percentage of high school seniors who said they could obtain their illegal drug of choice "fairly easily" or "very easily" increased from 82 to 89 percent (Johnston, O'Malley, and Bachman, 2000:3-6, 48).

One additional concern with regard to crop eradication programs is that in attempting to comply with U.S. demands for domestic control of drugs, source countries often engage in programs that are environmentally disastrous. Colombia is a case in point. To meet U.S. demands to control coca production, the Colombian government initiated a program of aerial spraying that drops herbicides on more than 100,000 acres of land each year. As a result, Colombian peasants who are dependent on the coca crop as their only source of income have moved into the Amazon rainforests. The movement of coca growers to rainforest has resulted in the clearing of at least 1.75 million acres of rainforest (Trade and Environment Database, 1997:4-8). This is important because Colombia's forests account for about 10 percent of the world's biodiversity. In fact, it is the second most biodiverse country in the world (Trade and Environment Database, 1997). Despite the obvious problems, the aerial coca fumigation program in Colombia has been a failure.

In addition to the aerial spraying program, the illegality of cocaine manufacture in Colombia is also a source of severe environmental damage. Cocaine manufacturers hide their laboratories deep in the Colombian forests. This obviously makes it impossible to dispose of hazardous wastes associated with the refining of cocaine. As a result, some 10 million liters of sulfuric acid, 16 million liters of ethyl ether, 8 million liters of acetone, and 40 to 770 million liters of kerosene are poured directly into the ground and into streams (Trade and Environment Database, 1997).

A word needs to said about domestic crop eradication programs as well. Efforts to eradicate the marijuana crop in the United States have not only failed but have made the marijuana industry stronger and more dangerous than ever (Potter, Gaines, and Holbrook, 1990). In Kentucky, where the state participates in a federally funded program to find and burn the marijuana crop, the net effect of the eradication program has been to spread marijuana cultivation throughout the state and to increase both the quantity and the quality of the marijuana being produced. In addition, the eradication program has taken what was essentially a "mom and pop" industry a few years ago and turned it into a highly organized criminal cartel that is not only dangerous but also enjoys a high degree of community support in the marijuana belt counties.

The second prong of the supply-reduction paradigm, interdiction, is no more successful. Interdiction assumes that with sufficient resources, drugs can be stopped from entering the United States by controlling the borders. Using the most optimistic claims of interdiction success, about 8 percent to 15 percent of the heroin and about 30 percent of the cocaine in international drug shipments is seized (UNODCCP, 1999:32, 40). The difficulty with interdiction strategies can be illustrated by taking a quick look at the cocaine market. The entire demand for cocaine in the United States, the largest market in the world, can be satisfied by 13 pickup truckloads of cocaine a year. Considering that the United States has 88,633 miles of shoreline, 7,500 miles of international borders with Canada and Mexico, and 300 ports of entry, finding 13 truck loads of anything is virtually impossible (Frankel, 1997:A1).

As these numbers indicate, interdiction has failed with regard to both heroin and cocaine. The only minor success that the interdiction campaign can claim is with marijuana, a bulky commodity that is difficult to transport. But the net effect of that success has been an even bigger problem. Marijuana smugglers and growers in other countries have simply moved to cocaine and heroin as substitutes for marijuana, resulting in even more of those drugs being imported to the United States, and in domestic marijuana production increasing dramatically in the past 10 years. A RAND Corporation evaluation study of interdiction determined that "even massively stepped-up drug interdiction efforts are not likely to greatly affect the availability of cocaine and heroin in the United States" (Reuter, Crawford, and Cave, 1988). Consider this simple fact: The criminal justice system cannot keep drugs out of maximum-security prisons, much less seal the nation's borders to drug trafficking.

One other point needs to be made with regard to interdiction and eradication as supply-control strategies. In addition to the false assumption that the world's supply of illicit drugs is stable, there is a similar assumption that drug traffickers do not adjust to the exigencies of new enforcement strategies—an assumption that is similarly incorrect. For example, U.S. enforcement efforts in Colombia in the 1980s and 1990s resulted in the creation of hundreds of small, decentralized drug-trafficking organizations that are virtually impossible to find, let alone control. And as mentioned in earlier in the text, these new traffickers have altered their product significantly by using a chemical process to produce "black cocaine," which evades detection by drug-sniffing dogs and chemical tests. The chemical process is simple and inexpensive, primarily requiring adding charcoal and a couple of chemicals to their cocaine shipments (GAO, 1999:4-5). Interdicting cocaine was a hit-and-miss operation before; now it is primarily a miss.

The final component of the supply-control paradigm is intensive street-level drug enforcement in the United States directed at consumers and users. These efforts have also shown little hope of success in the drug war. Intensive street-level law enforcement efforts are very expensive. Although they result in the arrests of thousands of low-level drug dealers and users, they have little impact on the other elements involved in illicit drug supply. Although some of these enforcement efforts have been able to claim "temporary and transitory success," they have not had any impact at all on the availability of illegal drugs (Chaiken, 1988). In fact, all illegal drug prices have fallen, purity has increased, the supply has increased, and use levels have increased in jurisdictions where intensive street-level enforcement has been tried. In addition, crimes ancillary to drug trafficking have increased in almost every case in which saturation enforcement strategies have been utilized.

Drug Use

The supply-reduction paradigm promises an enormous expenditure of resources, vast expansion of law enforcement authority, and large numbers of citizens being arrested and imprisoned. It is supposed to have a deterrent effect on drug use as well. Statistics, however, show that more Americans are using illegal drugs with greater regularity than ever before. Just a few statistics exemplify this trend:

- By 2008, more than 117 million Americans over the age of 12 (47% of the population) had used illicit drugs (SAMHSA, 2009).
- More than 102 million Americans (41% of the adult population) have used marijuana, and almost 26 million used marijuana in 2008 (SAMHSA, 2009).
- Almost 37 million Americans (almost 15% of the adult population) have used powder or crack cocaine, and a little more than 5 million of them used cocaine or cocaine derivatives in 2008 (SAMHSA, 2009).

Despite the arrests, the media campaigns, and the adoption of draconian penalties for drug-use violations, one of every eight adult citizens of the United States chose to violate the drug laws in 2001. But the numbers are even more compelling when we look at the youngest of drug users, the population group that will drive these numbers even higher in the future. Surveys of high school seniors show that more than half of them had used an illegal drug while in high school (Johnston, O'Malley, and Bachman, 2001:3-6). Despite the enormous law enforcement emphasis of the drug war, 89 percent of high school seniors reported that marijuana is "very easy" or "fairly easy" to obtain, and 49 percent of those high school seniors have actually used marijuana (Johnston, O'Malley, and Bachman, 2001:329). The United States, with its get-tough-on-drugs policy, has a higher rate of illegal drug use by young people than any European nation. In 1999, 41 percent of U.S. tenth graders had used marijuana, compared to 17 percent of similar students in Europe, where drug restrictions are much weaker (Johnston, O'Malley, and Bachman, 2001:363).

Researchers note that the legal threats accompanying drug use have little or no impact on use levels, describing the legal threat as "very weak" (Erickson and Cheung, 1992:258). Fagan and Spelman (1994:A34) have argued persuasively that market forces, not law enforcement efforts, have the most impact on patterns of drug use. They argue that legal institutions have almost no impact on the drug market. In fact, there is a credible argument to be made that the existence of drug laws and the intensive enforcement campaign accompanying them may stimulate drug use and may be responsible for the production of larger numbers of addicts than we might otherwise have had. Mishan, for example, suggests that the crucial factor in spreading addiction is the enormous profits in the drug trade made possible by the illegality of drugs (Mishan, 1990). As long as drugs are illegal, virtually every addict becomes a drug salesperson in order to raise sufficient funds to pay for his or her habit (Zion, 1993:A27). In addition to the profits that can be realized from the sale of illegal drugs, illegality also stimulates experimentation, particularly among adolescents, by raising the specter of the "forbidden fruit" that simply must be tasted in order to fully experience life (Ostrowski, 1989:1).

Despite the failure of intensive street-level drug enforcement, the law enforcement campaign to arrest as many drug users as possible and put them in prison continues unabated. As a result, the United States has the largest prison population in the world, with an incarceration rate of 756 per 100,000 adults (Walmsley, 2007:1). Not only are more drug offenders in prison, but they serve far longer sentences that most other offenders and have sentences almost as severe as the most violent offenders.

Figure 13.2
Source: Bureau of Justice Statistics, Federal Criminal Case Processing, 2002, With Trends 1982–2002; Washington, D.C.: U.S. Department of Justice, 12.

Offense	Median Sentence
Violent felonies	63.0 months
Drug felonies	57.0 months
Property felonies	15.0 months

Drug Case Processing with Trends

As a result of mandatory minimum sentencing requirements for drug users, the Federal Bureau of Prisons budget increased by a phenomenal 1,954 percent by the end of the 1990s (Bureau of Justice Statistics, 1997). By any measure, the drug war has not only failed to deter illegal drug use—it has done nothing to make drugs harder to find or obtain.

As we have learned with regard to reduction of illicit drug use, the drug war has been a dismal failure. The extent of that failure is easily gauged when drug use in the United States is compared to drug use in the Netherlands, where marijuana is available for legal sale and a harm-reduction policy has replaced a law enforcement emphasis as the keystone of efforts to control harder drug use.

Other Variables

Other factors that have an impact on supply and demand should also be considered. For example, intense police initiatives such as gang sweeps, undercover operations, and reverse stings also tend to (at least temporarily) disrupt supplies in local drug markets and make drug buyers themselves fearful of being arrested. In other cases, courts have imposed mandatory drug treatment of addicts, resulting in many of them reducing their drug usage and consequently reducing their frequency of drug purchases.

STRATEGIES IN NATIONAL DRUG CONTROL

Since the early 1970s, the U.S. government has devised a series of strategies designed to combat the nation's drug problem. Strategies are the means through which drug policy can be set in motion; they typically include an array of programs and tactics. During 1973, 1974, and 1975, Federal Strategy for Drug Abuse and Drug Traffic Prevention documents were published. Each was designed to identify problems and possible solutions to drug abuse trends in the nation. Similar publications were produced in 1976, 1979, and again in 1982, all focusing on similar drug-related issues. In 1984, the first federal effort referring to itself as a "national strategy" was published by the White House Drug Abuse Policy Office, followed in 1987 and 1988 by publications from the White House Conference for a Drug-Free America.

The 1973 strategies focused on the reduction of drug abuse and the identification of the drugs that cause the greatest harm to society. The focus shifted somewhat by 1976, when the federal strategy initiated the lead agency concept by making the Justice Department responsible for enforcement of federal drug laws. In 1988, the Office of National Drug Control Policy (ONDCP) was developed. As part of its charge, comprehensive plans are required to be published each year on federal drug control policy issues. Statistics are also offered regarding issues such as:

- Current overall drug use
- Cocaine use
- Adolescent drug use
- Drug availability
- Marijuana production
- Student attitudes toward drugs

In addition, each National Drug Control Strategy identifies national priorities in the areas of drug enforcement, prevention, treatment, international initiatives, and drug education.

Politics and the ONDCP

One of the perennial hindrances to a workable drug control policy is the political arena. This is apparent in virtually all political campaigns but can be best illustrated by the role and function of the Office of National Drug Control Policy (ONDCP). The ONDCP was created in 1988 at the behest of a Democratic Congress that forced reluctant Republican bureaucrats to make the concept a reality. As originally envisioned, the "drug czar" was to study the fragmented drug war effort and better organize, coordinate, and consolidate the "troops" (Witkin, 1993). In actuality, during its early phases the office had no real power and soon gained the reputation of being little more than a ministry of propaganda.

The first drug czar was former Education Secretary William Bennett, who brought respectability to the office by his zeal for media coverage and his willingness to take on difficult policy questions in many different public forums. Next, defeated Florida Governor Bob Martinez was appointed drug czar by President George H. W. Bush. Interestingly, none of Martinez's top 11 aides had ever worked for any of the nation's lead drug enforcement agencies; in addition, another 40 percent of the office's jobs went to political appointees, a figure that dwarfed the numbers in other federal departments (Witkin, 1993). Finally, with the election of President Bill Clinton, the staff of the ONDCP was cut from 146 people to 25, which forced many policy experts to question the sincerity of Clinton's drug policy intentions. Clinton's budget cuts also jeopardized many meaningful drug control programs, including the Counter-Drug Technology Assessment Center, which drug experts had touted as being an effective program. R. Gil Kerlikowske holds the "drug czar" position under the Obama administration as of the preparation of this text.

PROHIBITION THEN AND NOW

As discussed in Chapter 1, many social scientists have characterized Prohibition as a dismal failure to control human behavior. Although this premise is supported by many elements of the era, let us pose the question: Could any aspects of the experiment be termed a success? Surprisingly, the answer is yes. For decades many experts have suggested that alcohol abuse actually increased during the Prohibition years. In actuality, and contrary to popular myth, alcohol consumption was fairly well controlled during the Prohibition era; records reveal that levels of alcohol consumption declined significantly during the era and rose again sharply after its repeal (Goode, 1993). However, because alcohol consumption was a clandestine practice during Prohibition, no reliable data are available that can be scrutinized. In a thought-provoking discussion on the matter, Goode has suggested that rates of cirrhosis of the liver (which are closely related to alcoholism) be considered before, during, and subsequent to Prohibition to determine the extent of alcohol abstinence. He points out that the rate of death from cirrhosis of the liver remained between 12 and 17 per 100,000 people each year between 1900 and 1919, but it dropped to between seven and nine per 100,000 in the 1920s and early 1930s, a reduction of almost one-half (1993:170). After 1933 (the end of Prohibition), however, it began to escalate again.

So, why is it generally believed that excessive alcoholism during the period was common? One explanation could be the popular belief that speak-easies, jazz clubs, and the like existed around every street corner and that opportunistic gangsters such as Al Capone had bootleg beer and whiskey all but flowing in the streets. Movies, books, and other popular literature tend to foster the notion that everyone was drinking, partying, and living the high life. The truth about Prohibition, however, is that it was an unexciting period in which most Americans did not drink, and those who did drink alcohol drank considerably less than they did before or after the passing of the Eighteenth Amendment.

Despite the "successes" of Prohibition, several important lessons were also learned about the era and the notion of Prohibition as a public policy option. First, the illegal alcohol made available by criminal entrepreneurs during the era was considerably stronger than that was obtainable before the Prohibition period. Before Prohibition, low-alcohol beer made up almost one-half of the alcohol consumed, compared to the rise in availability of distilled spirits during the era. Second, much of the available alcohol was adulterated with toxins, which were used as substitutes for ethyl alcohol (Morgan, 1991). In fact, in one case, a medicinal tonic known as "Jake," a Jamaican ginger extract containing 75 percent alcohol, resulted in more than 50,000 people becoming permanently paralyzed. Finally, as we have learned, bootleg alcohol products provided organized crime groups the financial boost they needed to become more integrated into society. This resulted in their increased power on the street and in the ranks of politics. It has been said that Prohibition actually increased the number and types of people involved in the production and distribution of alcohol (Levine and Reinarman, 1992).

Comparative Lessons from Prohibition

So, what have we learned from all this? First, the Prohibition of the 1920s and 1930s did what it was intended to do—make people stop or reduce their alcohol intake. We have also learned that along with the medical successes of this policy, other unforeseen social problems resulted, which probably over-shadowed the original social concern of alcohol. Comparing Prohibition of alcohol during the 1920s to the prohibition of drugs is tricky, because many of today's social and political variables are considerably different. For example, the prohibition of alcohol gave rise to loose-knit gangs and transformed them into powerful crime organizations.

Today, however, these organizations are already in place—well funded, highly organized, and interlaced throughout both the criminal and legitimate business worlds. If drug legalization is being considered as a policy option, its intent must be carefully considered, especially if it is designed for doing away with these immense criminal empires. Would this be a realistic outcome today? Second, at the time of its imposition, Prohibition had the general support of the American people. Today's drug prohibition, according to national polls, also enjoys considerable support by the American people. Assuming that a democracy represents a government by and for the people, then if for no other reason, how socially responsible is it for our elected officials to pursue a public policy (e.g., legalization) that lacks public support? Next, we should consider how decriminalization or legalization has worked in other states. The discussion in Chapter 12 about Alaska's 15-year experiment with marijuana decriminalization shows how on the surface such policies appear to be a workable solution but in practice can create problems of their own.

A fourth point is that there is evidence that alcohol prohibition did work in reducing alcohol consumption. Accordingly, we see trends of reduced drug abuse in recent years under our current prohibition policy. We also see the positive effects of innovative drug laws such as RICO, CCE, and forfeiture statutes, which in many cases have resulted in the successful arrest, prosecution, and conviction of dangerous drug lords and organized crime figures.

Finally, though many experts have suggested the abolition of drug prohibition in place of a policy of regulation, we must remember that we have already been there. Our current policy of drug prohibition originated from a time when drugs were perfectly legal in this nation and readily available over the counter. Slowly, as the dangers of drug abuse were realized, taxation and regulation were imposed to "reduce and control" drug abuse without arbitrarily outlawing drugs. So, after 75 years of legally obtainable drugs (before 1878) and regulation (e.g., the 1906 Federal Food and Drug

Alcoholics still abound in today's United States. Erich Goode claims that alcohol consumption was fairly well controlled during Prohibition. He points to the decline in rates of death from cirrhosis of the liver that occurred during the era and the rise of those death rates after Prohibition's end in 1933.

Mark C. Ide

Act, the 1914 Harrison Narcotics Act, and the 1937 Marijuana Tax Act), the United States willfully adopted the current system of prohibition as its chosen public policy regarding drug control. Even inexpensive, highly regulated pharmaceutical drugs such as cocaine have not deterred Colombian criminals from producing large amounts of it on the black market at exorbitant prices.

This discussion illustrates how the solution to formulating a successful drug control policy is unclear. Contradictions in facts, opinions, and impressions of prohibition—both then and now—have only served to muddy the waters. Although it is difficult to recommend one policy option without condemning another, responsible social policy must consider not just what the people need but what they want as well.

Legal Tools in Drug Control

As discussed earlier, the use of innovative antidrug laws has proved to be one of the most powerful weapons against drug trafficking and a strong ally in the development of drug control policy. Although some of the most effective laws have been in place for some time, many new laws have been written to address the many unique aspects of the drug trade and the constantly changing structure of drug organizations. We now know that most drug prosecutions occur at the state and local levels; those laws are discussed in previous chapters of this book. However, due to the influence and mobility of organized crime groups in the drug trade, several significant federal laws have become widely used over the past two decades.

Our current system of justice is predicated on crimes that for the most part affect individual behavior and specific, unrelated incidents. For example, the burglar, the armed robber, the rapist, and the drug dealer are all persons whose behavior violates specific criminal codes. Organized crime represents group criminal behavior, which presents a more complicated way of viewing drug-related crime. In the past, prosecutors have been forced to approach organized crime with a narrow and shortsighted focus, convicting criminals either one at a time or in a single conspiracy. For example, over the past 60 years, federal prosecutors have attempted to prosecute the heads of the Genovese crime family, beginning with Charles "Lucky" Luciano, who was convicted of operating a prostitution ring in Manhattan. His successor, Frank Costello, was convicted of federal tax evasion. This was followed by the conviction of Vito Genovese, who was found guilty of running a drug conspiracy, and so on. For years federal prosecutors were able to incapacitate (temporarily) the heads of a crime organization for various crimes but were never able to sufficiently weaken the organization's power. When finally removed, the head of an organization was easily and quickly replaced, and the organization continued to flourish. As a result, in 1970 Congress passed legislation that incorporated antiracketeering elements that targeted the criminal organization instead of the individual. Such laws are today's primary weapon against organizations and the people who control them. This section looks at some of the most effective federal drug control tools.

The Racketeer-Influenced and Corrupt Organizations Act (RICO)

The 1970 Racketeer-Influenced and Corrupt Organizations (RICO) Act is an invaluable tool in the fight against organized crime in the drug trade. RICO's purpose is to broaden the prosecutor's power by allowing one prosecution of a multidefendant crime organization for all the criminal enterprises in which it is involved. In addition to imprisonment of members of the crime group, RICO allows for seizure of assets and proceeds from illegal enterprises. Successful application of the RICO statute in recent years has resulted in the conviction of top-level La Cosa Nostra members in Kansas City, St. Louis, Philadelphia, and Cleveland. Cases such as these help illustrate to the general public the magnitude of organized crime organizations and the extent of their operations.

Although RICO has been law since 1970, it was not widely used until the early 1980s. Before that time, prosecutors tended to apply the statute to criminals who were not members of large crime organizations or who were not management-level organized crime players. RICO is a statute that criminalizes a pattern of conduct characteristic of organized crime. Specifically outlined in the RICO statute are the criminal acts that constitute a *pattern of racketeering*, two of which must have occurred during the previous 10 years. Under RICO, racketeering is defined as "any act or threat involving murder, kidnapping, gambling, arson, robbery, bribery, extortion, or trafficking in narcotics or dangerous drugs."

The Continuing Criminal Enterprise (CCE) Statute

The federal Continuing Criminal Enterprise (CCE) Statute (Section 848 of Title 21, United States Code), enacted as part of the Comprehensive Drug Abuse Prevention and Control Act of 1970, is one of the strongest statutory weapons against drug trafficking. Like RICO, this statute gives prosecutors the means to reach the organizers, managers, and supervisors of major drug-trafficking organizations. Prosecution under this statute requires proof of five elements to sustain prosecution:

1. The defendant's conduct must constitute a felony violation of federal narcotics laws.
2. The conduct must take place as part of a continuing series of violations.
3. The defendant must undertake this activity in concert with at least five other individuals.
4. The defendant must act as the organizer, manager, or supervisor of this criminal enterprise.
5. The defendant must obtain income or resources from this enterprise.

CCE provides for some of the most severe criminal penalties for illicit drug trafficking. These include imprisonment for a minimum of 10 years with no possibility of parole. In addition, the court may impose a life sentence with no provision for parole and fines totaling $100,000. Moreover, under CCE, all profits and assets that have afforded the defendant a source of influence over the illegal enterprise are subject to forfeiture.

Conspiracy Laws

The use of conspiracy laws in drug enforcement has proven to be one of the most beneficial tactics of the last decade. Although conspiracy laws have existed for quite some time, their use is now common among federal, state, and local authorities alike. Although state law in this area may differ from one jurisdiction to another, the basic principles of conspiracy are the same. *Conspiracy* is defined as an agreement between two or more persons who have the specific intent either to commit a crime or to engage in dishonest, fraudulent, or immoral conduct injurious to public health or morals. In studying this definition, one can easily see the benefits of such a law in the area of drug control.

Drug trafficking is a criminal endeavor that usually requires more than one player: for example, a grower sells drugs to a manufacturer, who contracts with a smuggler for transportation. The smuggler then transports the drugs to a wholesale buyer, who in turn sells them to a retail distributor. The retail distributor then sells the drugs to numerous dealers and users on the street. Given the documentation investigators require, conspiracy charges can be brought against all such players in a drug operation. Because most conspiracy cases involve numerous defendants, a degree of confusion may result. Generally, three types of conspiracy cases are most commonly used in prosecutions of drug traffickers. These are the chain, the wheel, and the enterprise conspiracy:

- *The chain*. A *chain conspiracy* occurs when a criminal endeavor is dependent on the participation of each member of the criminal organization. Each member represents a link in the chain, and the success of the criminal goal requires all participants. If one link in the chain is broken (i.e., a member fails to accomplish his or her particular task), the criminal act will be incomplete. To successfully prosecute a chain conspiracy, each member must be shown to be aware of the operation's intended goal.
- *The wheel*. A *wheel conspiracy* comprises one member of a criminal organization who is the "hub," or organizer, of the criminal plan and members who make up the "spokes." Wheel conspiracies must show that all members who serve as spokes are aware of each other and agree with each other to achieve a common illegal goal. For this reason, the wheel conspiracy is a difficult one to prosecute, since it is difficult to show a common agreement between the spokes.

- *The enterprise.* As discussed under the RICO section, a person who has been shown to participate in two or more patterns of racketeering may be prosecuted. The definition of *enterprise conspiracy* makes it a separate crime to conspire to commit any of the substantive offenses under RICO. Basically, RICO defines the term as an agreement to enter into an enterprise by engaging in a pattern of racketeering. The enterprise conspiracy recognizes that in some criminal organizations, not all members have one common goal. Therefore, all that must be shown is a member's willingness to join a criminal organization (an "enterprise") by committing two or more acts of racketeering.

Forfeiture Sanctions in Drug Control

Forfeiture is the ancient legal practice of government seizure of property used in criminal acts. Such an enforcement strategy has proven to be one of the most effective legal tools in the fight against illegal drugs. The federal government's momentum was somewhat slow in the area of forfeiture until recent years. For example, as of 2006, the U.S. government obtained $192 million in forfeitures with the assistance of 23 foreign countries (ONDCP, 2007).

The 1984 Federal Comprehensive Forfeiture Act increased existing forfeiture powers under federal law. This was accomplished in part by lessening the degree of proof necessary for officials to seize property from the traditional "beyond a reasonable doubt" standard to "probable cause." The Act reads:

> [A]ny property of a person convicted of a drug felony is subject to forfeiture if the government establishes probable cause that the defendant acquired the property during the period of violation, or within a reasonably short period thereafter, and there was no likely source for the property other than the violation.

The Comprehensive Forfeiture Act, in addition to many state laws addressing forfeiture of assets, enables officers to seize automobiles, aircraft, vessels, bank accounts, and securities as well as real estate holdings and privately owned businesses. In addition, it enhances penalty provisions of the 1970 Controlled Substances Act to include a 20-year prison term and/or fines of up to $250,000. Basically, the act works in this fashion: If a drug dealer uses his or her automobile to drive to a location to sell a quantity of drugs, the car then becomes the conveyance the dealer used to facilitate the crime. Therefore, it is permitted to be seized under law. Along the same lines, if investigators can show that an automobile was purchased with drug money, it is also allowed to be seized under the law.

Critical Thinking Task

Create a scenario in which you are a prosecutor attempting to bring several organized crime racketeers to trial. Describe and illustrate the type of conspiracy involved and your methods of proving the racketeer's complicity.

Federal law also contains a sharing provision whereby an equitable transfer of the property can be facilitated. This provision basically divides property and distributes it among participating law enforcement agencies. After the seizure, a determination is made on the degree of involvement of each participating agency, and a proportionate distribution of the assets is then made between the agencies.

Drug Tax Laws

One innovative approach to drug enforcement is the implementation of drug tax laws. During the 1980s, such laws were enacted in 21 states, with provisions similar to the 80-year-old Harrison Narcotics Act. Most drug tax laws are covered under state tax codes, and failure to pay the required taxes on illicit drugs results in both civil and criminal penalties—in addition to any penalties the offender faces regarding the drug violation itself. State drug tax codes include stamp, sales, and excise taxes on specified criminal activities, which include the manufacture, sale, acquisition, and possession of drugs in the state—virtually all types of drug-related activities. Typically, the tax is $3.50 for each gram of marijuana and $200 for each gram of other illegal substances. In addition, there is a specified amount for drugs sold in a manufactured form of dosage units.

Drug taxes work as follows: When someone comes into possession of drugs, he or she is required to buy a state drug stamp—a procedure that is usually performed anonymously. Law enforcement officials are aware that in most cases drug traffickers will be hesitant to do so because they do not want to inform the police about being in possession of illicit drugs (this would warrant an investigation). If a person is found to be in illegal possession of dangerous drugs for which tax has not been paid, he or she is subject to a financial penalty and a prison sentence for tax evasion (not drug possession). Prosecution for possession of drugs is a separate criminal matter carrying additional penalties.

The primary reason for the drug tax is to give investigators a powerful tool for investigating large-scale drug traffickers, as opposed to small-time dealers. Such offenders can be found guilty of a civil violation of the state tax code, providing that the state can show they have not paid the tax. As a result, violators can be required to pay back taxes and fines that can be substantial. For example, a trafficker caught with one kilogram (2.2 pounds) of cocaine might be subject to taxes of $200,000 as well as a civil fine of $200,000. He or she might also be required to pay a criminal fine of up to $10,000 as well as serve a prison term. Revenues resulting from drug taxes are often used for drug enforcement efforts, treatment, and prevention programs such as DARE.

Grand Juries and Immunity

The use of the grand jury has proven effective in drug suppression efforts because of the broad range of power that it enjoys. The roots of the grand jury go back to the twelfth century, when it served as a safeguard against governmental abuse. The grand jury sought citizen approval for prosecutorial actions. Some of the more powerful rights granted the grand jury are represented by its authority to subpoena persons and documents, to punish, to grant immunity, to issue indictments, and to maintain secrecy of its proceedings.

The grand jury has been used successfully on both the federal and state levels, and in the case of the latter, the authority to call a grand jury may rest with the governor, the state attorney general, or the local prosecutor. As indicated, the grand jury's ability to grant immunity broadens the powers of this investigative body. This ability is particularly useful because many witnesses are criminals who have intimate knowledge of criminal operations.

Most criminals are aware that under the Fifth Amendment they cannot be compelled to give testimony against themselves. When a criminal "takes the Fifth," prosecutors may pursue one of several options:

1. The prosecutor can compel testimony by seeking a contempt citation if prosecutors can prove that the testimony would not incriminate the witness.

2. The prosecutor can release the witness and continue the proceedings without the benefit of the witness's testimony.

3. A plea bargaining agreement can be sought, whereby the witness's testimony would be given with the understanding that a lesser charge could be levied against the witness than if he or she did not give the testimony.

4. Total immunity from prosecution can be given by the prosecutor in exchange for the witness's testimony. In this case, once the witness is given total immunity, he or she can then be compelled to testify. Refusal under these circumstances can result in punishment of the witness.

Two kinds of immunity may be granted to witnesses in organized crime prosecutions:

1. *Transactional immunity.* A witness given *transactional immunity* for testimony about a specific criminal act is literally immune from ever being prosecuted for that particular crime in the future. Some witnesses in the past have attempted to blurt out additional crimes connected with the primary offense in an attempt to take an "immunity bath" and be free from all responsibility for those crimes. In fact, immunity is not attached when the witness purposely mentions additional crimes. It is extended to other crimes, however, when the prosecutor chooses to mention them during the examination of the witness in court.

2. *Derivative use immunity.* When *derivative use immunity* is granted to a witness, the witness is immune only from having his or her own

testimony later used against him or her. If evidence of an independent nature is uncovered, however, the witness may be prosecuted on the basis of that evidence.

Derivative use immunity has considerable advantages for the prosecutor over transactional immunity. When using transactional immunity, a witness may give broad-sweeping and vague testimony referring to specific criminal acts, thus bringing him or her under the "umbrella" of the immunity grant but being ambiguous enough so that specifics essential to prosecution are not provided (Kenney and Finckenaur, 1995). A grant of derivative use immunity will not bar prosecution.

The Witness Security Program

Before the inception of the Federal Witness Security Program, witnesses who testified on behalf of the government were sometimes brutally tortured or even murdered. Until 1970, the protection of government witnesses was left up to each individual law enforcement agency. Because of limited resources and inconsistent services, the need arose for a single unified federal program.

The Witness Security Program (WITSEC) was implemented in 1970; since then, more than 7,500 witnesses have entered the program and have been protected, relocated, and given new identities by the U.S. Marshals Service (U.S. Marshals Service, 2007). The WITSEC plan provides people with psychological counseling and training along with employment assistance and provides new identities for both witnesses and their families. The first of its kind in the United States, the program has served as a prototype for similar programs in other countries.

Critical Thinking Task

Evaluate the federal WITSEC program in terms of its success or failure to contribute to a reduction in drug-related crime in the United States. Do you believe that tax dollars are well spent in allowing drug criminals to evade prosecution and to begin new lives?

The WITSEC program has proved to be one of the most significant prosecution tools in cases involving large-scale organized crime figures. The program is one that basically offers witnesses lifelong protection if they testify against organized crime figures. The program is necessary because of criminal conspiracies, secretive and clandestine drug operations, and the general covert nature of organized crime. The WITSEC program is considered a successful program; more than 8 of every 10 defendants are convicted and receive substantial prison sentences.

SUMMARY

Modern drug control policy is earmarked by a number of policy strategies, each designed to address a specific aspect of the nation's drug problem. These strategies include demand reduction, supply reduction, eradication, education, and treatment. However, despite many notable successes, none of these policies has proven successful in reducing drug abuse to what could be termed an acceptable level. The implementation of control strategies involves a concerted effort by many organizations and agencies. Those in both the public and private sector share responsibility for fighting the drug abuse problem in our communities and schools. These include law enforcement agencies on the federal, state, and local levels as well as local schools, the military, and private businesses that offer support for prevention and treatment programs.

Today's drug control policy originated with a series of federal laws designed to regulate the manufacture, sale, and use of dangerous drugs. Drug control efforts in the United States, however, date back to the late 1800s, when opium and its extracts were first recognized as dangerous. Momentum on the federal level began in 1906 with the passing of the Pure Food and Drug Act, which required medications containing opium or coca derivatives to say so on their label. In 1914, the Harrison Narcotics Act further controlled opiates by restricting their dispensing to medical purposes and pursuant to a written authorization. Ambiguities in the law, however, prevented this act from being fairly enforced.

In 1937, marijuana was controlled under the Marijuana Tax Act in much the same way as opiates were under the Harrison Narcotics Act. Taxes were imposed for people who grew marijuana, in an effort to deter growers from involvement with this plant. Finally, in 1970, the Controlled Substances Act was passed as an effort to update all preexisting federal drug laws. This comprehensive act placed all supposedly dangerous drugs in one of five schedules. Each drug was categorized according to level of danger. The law also set forth new criminal and civil penalties for possession and distribution of drugs.

Nineteen-seventy also marked the enactment of several new and innovative drug control laws that are still being used today. One such law, the Racketeer-Influenced and Corrupt Organizations Act (RICO), enables law enforcement to prosecute leaders of large trafficking organizations and to seize assets associated with the organizations. A similar law, the Continuing Criminal Enterprise (CCE) Act, also affords authorities special powers in arrest and forfeiture of assets of drug kingpins. To provide further aid in the drug enforcement initiative, conspiracy and forfeiture legislation have greatly enhanced law enforcement officers' ability to arrest dealers and their associates. These laws also provide the legal basis to seize assets acquired by drug offenders.

Drug control, by virtue of its economic, political, and social implications, is extremely complicated. Not everyone agrees on the most effective and efficient manner in which to contain the nation's drug abuse problem, but the strategies and policies discussed in this chapter demonstrate the breadth and complexity of control efforts, regardless of how successful they are or have been.

Do you recognize these terms?

- chain conspiracy
- derivative use immunity
- enterprise conspiracy
- eradication
- pattern of racketeering
- prohibition
- regulation
- taxation
- transactional immunity
- wheel conspiracy
- WITSEC

DISCUSSION QUESTIONS

1. What major drug control legislation was passed during the Reagan administration?

2. The RICO statute requires that a pattern of racketeering be established. What are the predicate offenses that constitute a pattern of racketeering?

3. Discuss the elements of a conspiracy.

4. How do the forfeiture sanctions under federal law help in the national drug control effort?

5. Discuss why the grand jury is considered a valuable asset in the prosecution of drug offenders.

6. List and discuss the two types of immunity most commonly used in federal drug prosecutions.

7. Discuss how the federal witness security program (WITSEC) aids in the prosecution of high-level organized crime figures.

Chapter 14

Control Through Treatment and Prevention

This chapter will enable you to:

- Understand public opinion as it relates to drug treatment
- Understand the drug user
- Appreciate the plight of the drug addict
- Compare and contrast drug treatment programs
- Learn differences in treatment philosophies
- Discover what works in drug treatment and what does not

Although many drug enforcement and community efforts are designed to deter drug abuse, there will always be people who develop dependencies on addictive substances or who seek escape through the use of alcohol and other drugs. Drug addiction is a complex but treatable brain disease. It is characterized by compulsive drug craving, seeking, and use that persist even in the face of severe adverse consequences. For many people, drug addiction becomes chronic, with relapses possible even after long periods of abstinence. In fact, relapse of drug abuse occurs at rates similar to those for other well-characterized, chronic medical illnesses such as diabetes, hypertension, and asthma. As a chronic, recurring illness, addiction may require repeated treatments to increase the intervals between relapses and diminish their intensity until abstinence is achieved. Through treatment tailored to individual needs, people with drug addiction can recover and lead productive lives.

DOI: 10.1016/B978-1-4377-4450-7.00014-X
© 2011 Elsevier Inc. All rights reserved.

The ultimate goal of drug addiction treatment is to enable an individual to achieve lasting abstinence, but the immediate goals are to reduce drug abuse, improve the patient's ability to function, and minimize the medical and social complications of drug abuse and addiction. Like people with diabetes or heart disease, people in treatment for drug addiction will need to change their behavior to adopt a more healthful lifestyle.

In 2004, approximately 22.5 million Americans age 12 or older needed treatment for substance (alcohol or illicit drug) abuse and addiction. Of these, only 3.8 million people received it. Untreated substance abuse and addiction burden families and communities with significant costs, including those related to violence and property crimes, prison expenses, court and criminal costs, emergency room visits, healthcare utilization, child abuse and neglect, lost child support, foster care and welfare costs, reduced productivity, and unemployment.

In 2002, it was estimated that the costs to society of illicit drug abuse alone amounted to $181 billion. Combined with alcohol and tobacco costs, costs exceed $500 billion, including costs for health care, criminal justice, and lost productivity. Successful drug abuse treatment can help reduce this cost and related crime as well as the spread of HIV/AIDS, hepatitis, and other infectious diseases. It is estimated that for every dollar spent on addiction treatment programs, there is a $4 to $7 reduction in the cost of drug-related crimes. With some outpatient programs, total savings can exceed costs by a ratio of 12:1 (NIDA, 2007).

UNDERSTANDING THE DRUG USER

Drug-dependent people present a danger not only to themselves but to those around them. Users may lie to friends and family. They may take advantage of those who attempt to help them. They may steal from loved ones to support their habit and may be involved in a lifestyle that includes predatory criminal acts such as robbery, assault, and murder. This is why society's response to the drug problem involves not only the medical and healthcare industries but also the criminal justice system.

Today, society bears most of the burden for offering treatment to those who have fallen victim to drug abuse. Failure to provide a means for addicts to "get well" not only endangers the lives of the addicts but also threatens the well-being of those who become victims of drug crimes, communicable diseases such as AIDS, and other related problems. The belief that drug treatment is a supple, nurturing, and easy way out of drug dependency is quite far from the truth. Indeed, to the drug addict, the successful drug treatment program is one that imposes stringent physical and emotional demands and is therefore an unappealing experience.

It is also a misconception that all drug users develop a dependency and require drug treatment. Indeed, most people who use drugs do not become addicted the first time they use them. For example, the casual drug user (one who uses drugs no more than once a month) does not usually need drug treatment in order to stop using drugs. However, a social (which includes governmental) climate of intolerance of drug use is an important ingredient in building a drug-free community.

The heroin or cocaine user who uses the drug once a week is a different story. This person may be able to ward off dependency on his or her own but is more likely to require a treatment program than those users who fall into the once-a-month category. Still, there are others who are persuaded only by arrest and adjudication through the criminal justice system. Finally, there are those addicts who are physically and psychologically addicted to drugs and who genuinely require a formalized treatment program such as Narcotics Anonymous (NA).

Studies have been conducted over the past several decades in hopes of identifying biological or personality factors to connect drug use to potential drug users. To date, no empirical evidence exists to show what type of person is the most likely candidate for drug use or addiction, nor is there evidence as to which user can control drug use and which cannot. In reality, many drug users make poor assessments about their ability to tolerate the effects of drugs. In fact, they are often the last to realize that they are addicted.

The use-to-abuse cycle is one that slowly engulfs the drug user. For example, many addicts experience what could be termed a "honeymoon" of drug use early in their abuse cycle. Typically, this begins with the use of alcohol, cigarettes, and sometimes marijuana at a young age. The use-to-abuse cycle then expands over time to the use of harder, more effective drugs. The honeymoon stage may last several years and is usually a manageable period for the drug user. Once the potency of drugs and the instances of use increase, the honeymoon is over and the user is well on his or her way to physical dependency. Addressing the problem of treatment of drug abusers, former drug czar William Bennett stated in his 1989 National Drug Control Strategy:

> If our treatment system is to do the job required of it, the system must be expanded and improved. We need more treatment "slots," located where the needs are, in programs designed to meet those needs. We must improve the effectiveness and the efficiency of treatment programs by holding them accountable for their performance. We must find ways to get more drug dependent people into treatment programs, through voluntary and, when necessary, involuntary means. And we need much better information about who is seeking treatment, who is not, and why.

Adding to the list of drug abuse misconceptions is the premise that addicts will eventually come to their senses and seek treatment. Several reasons can be identified to explain why addicts avoid treatment. First, addicts have chosen to seek out the euphoric effects of drugs; they can logically be expected to prefer such effects to the demands of a formal treatment setting. Second, treatment by its very nature denies addicts a form of pleasure: drugs. Finally, because abuse usually involves ingesting illicit drugs, many addicts fear that confidentiality will not be maintained and that local police may learn their identities.

Many addicts who begin treatment programs eventually drop out and return to their drug-abusing lifestyle. Sometimes this is because addicts are lured back into drug abuse circles by associates. Additionally, they may hope to "stay clean" for a period of time so that their drug tolerance goes down; smaller and cheaper amounts of drugs will then produce better "highs." As mentioned, the drug addiction cycle is compounded by the common use of addictive drugs such as caffeine, alcohol, and nicotine. Regardless of the type of drug on which one becomes dependent, a treatment program must be identified. The immediate objectives of most treatment and rehabilitation programs can be generally characterized in three ways:

1. To control or eliminate drug abuse
2. To give the drug users alternatives to their (drug-using) lifestyle
3. To treat medical complications (both physical and psychological) associated with drug use

Problems of drug abuse and addiction also prevail, in part, because such activity is covert in nature. Accordingly, drug use usually comes to the attention of the family and the community only when it has developed into either a personal or a public problem. At this juncture, the drug-dependent person must pursue any of a number of treatment options, which we discuss in this chapter.

THE RISE IN ADDICTION

Chapter 2 discussed our nation's gradual acceptance of drug use over many decades, but the problem of addiction has not always been clearly understood. Historically, Americans have alternated between viewing addiction as a medical problem and as a social ill. Accordingly, the public's response to addiction has vacillated between treatment of offenders and aggressive police crackdowns. During the nineteenth century, medications such as opiates were essential for use by medical practitioners. By the late 1800s, thousands of middle-class women whose doctors had prescribed powdered morphine had become hopelessly addicted. Even then, physicians established asylums to treat those who had become addicted. By the early 1900s, however, synthetic, injectable forms of morphine had been developed, and public concern grew about so-called pleasure users of the drug.

In 1914, the Harrison Narcotics Act was passed as a measure to control the distribution of narcotics. This was followed by Prohibition in 1920, which was designed to curb alcohol consumption. During this period, the government also cracked down on drugs by closing the remaining municipal clinics that had provided low-cost morphine, heroin, and cocaine to registered addicts. As a result, virtually no treatment facilities remained in existence throughout the country. Soon the jails filled with addicts. To ease the overcrowding problem, Congress authorized the building of two massive prisons for narcotic addicts—one in Lexington, Kentucky, which opened in 1935, and the other in Fort Worth, Texas, which opened in 1938. Both institutions offered a mixture of penal and psychotherapeutic environments.

As the 1940s approached, heroin use was growing in major U.S. cities, followed by what was later called a heroin epidemic in the 1950s. In 1964, Vincent Dole, a physician, and Marie Nyswander, a psychiatrist, published an article about methadone in the *Journal of the American Medical Association*. They reported that addicts who took methadone orally experienced neither withdrawal symptoms nor euphoria from the drug. As a result, they were able to return to reasonably productive lives. Hence, the medical model of addiction was born. As a result, the Nixon-era war on crime helped finance the expansion of methadone maintenance clinics with the hope that addicts would no longer have to commit crimes to finance their drug habits.

Philosophies of addiction were reconsidered during the 1980s with the rise in cocaine use and the arrival of crack on the U.S. drug scene. Until then, cocaine was so expensive that it was affordable only by the rich and affluent. Almost overnight, crack was available in most major cities at a price almost anyone—especially adolescents—could afford: $5 to $10 per rock. Soon crack had replaced heroin as the inner-city drug of choice. This phenomenon forced drug treatment professionals to refocus their efforts from heroin and opiate addiction to cocaine dependency. Accordingly, special problems arose because cocaine use altered the brain's dopamine receptors, which govern the user's sense of pleasure, making users not want to stop. This factor alone presented new and special treatment concerns for clinicians in the 1980s and 1990s.

TREATMENT PROGRAMS

We have thus far learned that there exist many different types of drugs of abuse, drug users, and explanations for involvement in drug-abusing behavior. Just as there is no single typology of drug abuser, programs for drug treatment are diverse, since there is no single treatment for what we know as drug abuse. It might be tempting to think of drug abuse under a simple medical model of acute illness, but it is far more complex than that. Symptoms of this chronic disorder and those interventions employed to treat the symptoms range well beyond the physiological and psychological and may even include explanations that are social, legal, and economic. A treatment program that works well for one user may not work for another due to the dynamics of what motivates drug abuse in the first place.

Treatment programs incorporate psychological and pharmacological components but also rely on efforts to teach communication skills, interpersonal skills, and the ability to deal with one's involvement in criminal behavior. As noted in Chapter 6, many types of criminal activity are associated with the drug user. Included are drug crimes, such as dealing and possessing controlled drugs; property crimes, such as burglary and larceny; and acts of interpersonal violence. These actions depend on the type of drug being used and the extent of one's dependency. Experts believe a small number of drug users are responsible for the majority of drug-related crime. In general, treatment programs serve both alcohol- and drug-dependent clients, and most of the nation's 5,000 treatment programs take place in one of two settings: (1) nonresidential, where the client receives treatment at a specific location but lives elsewhere; (2) residential, where clients receive treatment and reside at the treatment facility. Typically, residential facilities include hospitals or halfway houses.

In addition to the two types of settings, treatment programs can be divided into one of five categories: (1) detoxification programs, usually inpatient, which have the short-range goal of ending a user's physical addiction to substances; (2) chemical dependency units, primarily private inpatient or residential three- to four-week programs; (3) outpatient clinics, offering counseling and support for those who want to stop using drugs while they continue to work in the community; (4) methadone maintenance programs, which treat addicts by coupling counseling with the administration of methadone, a prescription medicine that blocks the craving for heroin while eliminating the usual pain of withdrawal; and (5) residential therapeutic communities, where users may spend up to 18 months in a highly structured program.

Detoxification

When treatment alternatives are considered, the term *detoxification* (often abbreviated to *detox*) is frequently used. Detoxification is usually the first step of the treatment process and is designed to withdraw patients slowly from their dependence on a particular drug. Its aim is to stabilize heavy drug users until their bodies are relatively free of drugs. This process generally takes from 21 to 45 days and is best performed on an inpatient basis. Detox, in and of itself, is not considered a form of treatment. The distinction is that detoxification helps users get off drugs, whereas treatment helps them stay off. Therefore, experts generally agree that the detoxification process does little good unless it is followed up by a sound treatment program.

Subsequent to the detoxification process, the patient is no longer physically addicted to the drug and, theoretically, is able to abstain from future use of the drug. Research suggests there is no single method of detoxification that

Figure 14.1

> • *Outpatient programs.* Outpatient programs range from completely unstructured drop-in or teen rap centers located in storefronts to highly structured programs offering individual, group, and family therapy. Most outpatient programs provide basic individual counseling and require that patients be self-motivated. Generally, the programs are small in size and serve between 20 and 30 clients.
> • *Inpatient programs.* The inpatient programs for drug abusers are growing but are still relatively small in number. These programs provide more intensive service for patients who require a controlled setting. Unlike some other drug treatment centers, some inpatient programs have lock-up wards, which patients cannot leave. Services provided include diagnostic testing and evaluation, psychotherapy, group therapy, and counseling. The inpatient treatment program is generally the most expensive of the drug treatment plans and because of this is usually a shorter program in duration.
> • *The halfway house.* This option is offered as an alternative for those who need to be housed in a location away from their own homes but cannot afford an inpatient program. Clients attend school or work during the day and in the afternoon or evening return to the halfway house, where they eat and sleep. The halfway house is frequently used as a transition from a therapeutic community to the outside community or in conjunction with outpatient therapy.

Types of Treatment Programs

is considered effective in the treatment of all drug abusers. Detoxification procedures are, therefore, individualized to meet the needs of each patient.

A patient's susceptibility to this form of treatment depends on several variables. These include the type of drug to which the patient is addicted, the degree of tolerance that has developed, and how long the patient has been dependent on the particular drug. Let's now look at some typical detoxification scenarios:

- *Heroin detoxification.* The detoxification process for heroin addicts is often futile due to the high incidence of relapse among addicts. Opiate drug addicts tend to have a high relapse rate because they return to peer and social groups that are still involved in drug abuse. Methadone maintenance, discussed later in this chapter, is considered one of the more successful ways to accomplish the goal of detoxification.
- *Self-treatment,* or the "cold turkey" approach, is fairly common among heroin addicts and is usually attempted at the addict's home. In some cases, this approach is undertaken in therapeutic communities or with the support of friends. In almost all cases, this type of detoxification is not successful.
- *Alcohol and barbiturate detoxification.* Detoxification or withdrawal from either alcohol or barbiturates is considered extremely dangerous and should be performed only under medical supervision. In this situation, withdrawal may not occur until several days after the last dose. With

these two drugs, detoxification is usually accomplished by a physician administering increasingly smaller doses of the drug to the patient to ward off withdrawal symptoms.

- *Marijuana and other hallucinogens.* Because these two categories of drugs are not physically addicting and there are no withdrawal symptoms, detoxification can usually be accomplished with little or no hospitalization.

- *Cocaine and amphetamine detoxification.* Of the two, cocaine poses the greatest challenge in treatment, primarily due to the addict's craving for the drug. So far, there are no proven successful treatment strategies comparable to those that have been developed for heroin addiction. Depression is common in patients experiencing withdrawal from these drugs, and suicide attempts are prevalent. Treatment for cocaine and amphetamines is not usually life-threatening but can cause great discomfort for the patient.

Maintenance (Substitute Therapy)

Maintenance refers literally to maintaining a drug abuser on a particular type of drug for the purpose of helping him or her avoid the withdrawal syndrome. Opiate drug addiction, for example, is a common problem for many treatment programs because it is so widespread. Because a cross-tolerance and cross-dependence exist between all opiates, any of them can be used to eliminate withdrawal symptoms and to detoxify the addicted patient.

Methadone maintenance is the most common type of maintenance program. Methadone, a synthetic narcotic analgesic, was introduced during World War II because of a shortage of morphine. It is an odorless, white crystalline powder that shares many of the same effects as morphine, but the two are structurally dissimilar. Methadone is best known for its use in the controversial methadone maintenance program that was introduced in 1964.

The use of methadone in treatment of people addicted to opiates has always been a controversial practice. The drug does have one distinct advantage over heroin: Methadone is a longer-acting drug, requiring less frequent administering. Additionally, the effects of methadone differ from those of heroin. In particular, methadone has a longer duration of action, lasting up to 24 hours, thereby permitting the administration of the drug once a day as treatment for heroin addiction. Time-tested results of methadone maintenance reveal that addicts who went through the program had much less criminal involvement and were better able to function within their communities.

As mentioned, the effects of methadone closely resemble the effects of morphine and heroin but fail to provide the user the euphoric effects caused by those two drugs. Methadone is also an extremely physically addicting drug— a fact that has created much of the controversy surrounding its use. The program is structured so that the patient leaves a urine sample at the clinic, where the urine is tested for signs of morphine (heroin is excreted as morphine) and other drugs. Once patients have demonstrated that they are responsible and committed to rehabilitation, they are permitted to take a one-day supply of methadone. Later, the take-home dosage is increased to a three-day supply.

Detoxification is achieved through slowly reducing the amount of methadone mixture administered to the patient. Frequently, however, addicts find that their psychological dependence is more difficult to overcome than their physical dependence, and therefore many addicts remain in the program for most of their lives.

Narcotic Antagonists

The term *narcotic antagonists* refers to a category of drugs developed as a treatment for heroin addiction but that do not produce physical dependence. These drugs, as the name implies, block or reverse the effects of drugs in the narcotic category. Naloxone (Narcan), which has no morphine-like effects, was introduced in 1971 as a specific antidote for narcotic poisoning. Nalorphine (Nalline), introduced into clinical medicine in 1951 and now under Schedule III, is termed a narcotic agonist-antagonist. In a drug-free individual, nalorphine produces morphine-like effects, whereas in an individual under the influence of narcotics, it counteracts these effects. Another agonist-antagonist is pentazocine (Talwin). Introduced as an analgesic in 1967, it was determined to be an abusable drug and was placed under Schedule IV in 1979.

> ### Critical Thinking Task
>
> Assume that your community has committed local funds to building and maintaining a drug treatment center and you have been asked to serve on the center's board of directors. After studying various kinds of treatment centers, you decide which one would best fit the needs of the city. Defend your choice to the rest of the board.

Naltrexone

Naltrexone is a long-acting synthetic opiate antagonist with few side effects that is taken orally either daily or three times a week for a sustained period of time. For opiate addicts, treatment using naltrexone usually is conducted in outpatient settings, although initiation of the medication often begins after medical detoxification in a residential setting. To prevent precipitating an opiate abstinence syndrome, individuals must be medically detoxified and opiate-free for several days before naltrexone can be taken. When the substance is used this way, all the effects of self-administered opiates, including euphoria, are completely blocked. The theory behind this treatment is that the repeated lack of the desired opiate effects, as well as the perceived futility of using the opiate, will gradually over time result in breaking the habit of opiate addiction. Naltrexone itself has no subjective effects or potential for abuse and is not addicting. Patient noncompliance is a common problem. Therefore, a favorable treatment outcome requires that there also be a positive therapeutic relationship, effective counseling or therapy, and careful monitoring of medication compliance.

Many experienced clinicians have found naltrexone most useful for highly motivated, recently detoxified patients who desire total abstinence because of external circumstances, including impaired professionals, parolees, probationers, and prisoners in work-release status. Patients stabilized on naltrexone can function normally. They can hold jobs, avoid the crime and violence of the street culture, and reduce their exposure to HIV by stopping injection drug use and drug-related high-risk sexual behavior (ONDCP, 2006).

The Therapeutic Approach

As with most psychotherapeutic types of treatment, a lengthy commitment is generally required on the patient's part. The role of the psychoanalyst in drug treatment is to identify repressed feelings in the patient that were experienced early in life and may contribute to drug abuse. Once the feelings or thoughts are uncovered, they can be dealt with through traditional psychoanalytic methods. Studies have shown that the length of treatment ranges from a few weeks to several years and that the success rate for recovery is marginal at best.

Group Treatment

Group therapy in drug treatment has demonstrated one of the highest success rates of any type of drug treatment program. Group treatment programs use an approach that creates an environment of personal interaction between peers. In theory, group interaction is more successful than the one-on-one interaction between the psychoanalyst and the patient. This is because the analyst often lacks a basic understanding of the drug abuse process and other variables that contribute to addiction. The analyst, therefore, often acts as a facilitator for the group. The treatment group may be formed during different phases of addiction and treatment and may involve not just the patients but their families and friends as well.

Long–Term Residential Treatment

Long-term residential treatment provides care 24 hours per day, generally in a nonhospital setting. The best-known residential treatment model is the *therapeutic community* (TC), but residential treatment may also employ other models, such as cognitive-behavioral therapy. TCs are residential programs with planned lengths of stay of 6 to 12 months. TCs focus on the "resocialization" of the individual and use the program's entire "community," including other residents, staff, and the social context, as active components of treatment. Addiction is viewed in the context of an individual's social and psychological deficits, and treatment focuses on developing personal accountability and responsibility and socially productive lives. Treatment is highly structured and can at times be confrontational, with activities designed to help residents examine damaging beliefs, self-concepts, and patterns of behavior and to adopt new, more harmonious and constructive ways to interact with others. Many TCs are quite comprehensive and can include employment training and other support services on site.

Compared with patients in other forms of drug treatment, the typical TC resident has more severe problems, with more co-occurring mental health problems and more criminal involvement. Research shows that TCs can be modified to treat individuals with special needs, including adolescents, women, those with severe mental disorders, and individuals in the criminal justice system.

Short–Term Residential Programs

Short-term residential programs provide intensive but relatively brief residential treatment based on a modified 12-step approach. These programs were originally designed to treat alcohol problems, but during the cocaine epidemic of the mid-1980s, many began to treat illicit drug abuse and addiction as well. The original residential treatment model consisted of a three- to six-week hospital-based inpatient treatment phase followed by extended outpatient therapy and participation in a self-help group, such as Alcoholics Anonymous. Reduced healthcare coverage for substance abuse treatment has resulted in a diminished number of these programs, and the average length of stay under managed care review is much shorter than in early programs.

Outpatient Drug–Free Treatment

Outpatient drug-free treatment is yet another alternative that costs less than residential or inpatient treatment and often is more suitable for individuals who are employed or who have extensive social supports. Low-intensity programs may offer little more than drug education and admonition. Other outpatient models, such as intensive day treatment, can be comparable to residential programs in services and effectiveness, depending on the individual patient's characteristics and needs. In many outpatient programs, group counseling is emphasized. Some outpatient programs are designed to treat patients who have medical or mental health problems in addition to their drug disorder.

Narcotics Anonymous

Narcotics Anonymous (NA) is an organization devoted to helping addicts recover from drug addiction. It began in California in 1953. Since then, NA has spread to all parts of the United States (and some foreign countries) and supports a World Service Office that unifies its global efforts. The NA program was adapted from Alcoholics Anonymous (AA), from which NA borrowed its 12-step program for recovering addicts. The philosophy of NA basically says: If you want what we have to offer and are willing to make the effort to get it, then you are ready to take certain steps. The NA group operates in a relatively structured manner; that is, it has regular meetings at specified places and times. It is suggested that group members follow the Twelve Steps of Narcotics Anonymous. NA groups are registered with the World Service Office in Los Angeles.

The goal of the organization is to carry the wellness message to the addict as well as to provide group members a chance to express themselves and hear the experiences of others. NA offers two types of meetings: open (to the general public) and closed (for addicts only). The meetings vary in format from group to group; some are participation meetings, some are question-and-answer sessions, some are meetings for the discussion of special problems, and some are a combination of some or all of these formats.

Figure 14.2
Source: Reprinted by permission of NA World Services, Inc., from Narcotics Anonymous, Fifth Edition by NA World Services, Inc. All rights reserved. Twelve Steps and Twelve Traditions reprinted for adaptation by permission of AA World Services; see www.na.org.

1. We admitted that we were powerless over our addiction, that our lives had become unmanageable.
2. We came to believe that a Power greater than ourselves could restore us to sanity.
3. We made a decision to turn our will and our lives over to the care of God as we understood Him.
4. We made a searching and a fearless moral inventory of ourselves.
5. We admitted to God, to ourselves, and to another human being the exact nature of our wrongs.
6. We were entirely ready to have God remove all these defects of character.
7. We humbly asked Him to remove our shortcomings.
8. We made a list of all persons we had harmed, and became willing to make amends to them all.
9. We made direct amends to such people wherever possible, except when to do so would injure them or others.
10. We continued to take personal inventory and when we were wrong promptly admitted it.
11. We sought through prayer and meditation to improve our conscious contact with God as we understood Him, praying only for knowledge of His will for us and the power to carry that out.
12. Having had a spiritual awakening as a result of these steps, we tried to carry this message to addicts, and to practice these principles in all our affairs.

The Twelve Steps of Narcotics Anonymous

Does Drug Treatment Work?

Occasionally, newspaper articles about recovered addicts surface, giving the impression that another addicted life has been spared through successful treatment. However, one of the hard truths about drug treatment is that experts know very little about the effectiveness of such programs. The assumption that drug treatment works is based on reports from clinicians and recovered drug addicts. Most research is so poorly conducted that it is difficult to know whether treatment cures any more people than would have stopped using drugs on their own (Apsler, 1994). For example, studies have shown that between 45 percent and 70 percent of alcoholics are known to recover, but little empirical information is available for the rate of recovery for illegal drug users.

To assess the effectiveness of drug treatment programs, we should first consider the goals of treatment. Although total abstinence may seem to be a likely goal of treatment, experts have suggested that lifelong abstinence from alcohol or other drugs on the first try should not be the measure of success. Indeed, treatment goals are not restricted to simply reducing the consumption of drugs but also to reducing the demand for drugs, cutting down on related street crime, and improving the user's overall physical and mental health. Furthermore, clinicians have argued that the ultimate goal is to allow people to return to a normal, productive life—however that can be accomplished. Once again, this leads us back to the issue of gauging the "effectiveness" of treatment. However, as discussed earlier, a full recovery from drug dependency is not only unlikely but unrealistic. Complicating factors include the length of time that may be required for detoxification as well as the patient's inclination for relapse.

We do know that some treatment programs seem to have more positive outcomes than others. For example, the methadone maintenance program, which has been intensely studied since it originated in 1964, has the best documented success record. In the program, addicts are given a daily dose of methadone, which is designed to block the craving for heroin and other opiates. More than three decades of experience with methadone maintenance programs show that drug users tend to be less prone to drug consumption and criminal activity when maintained on the drug. Some controversy exists as to whether methadone simply substitutes one addicting drug for another (Apsler, 1994:52). Furthermore, drug addicts graduating from both therapeutic communities and no methadone programs seem to perform better than addicts who fail to complete these treatment programs. Length of stay seems to have a high correlation with better patient outcomes.

Most people who enter drug treatment do so reluctantly, often under pressure from family, friends, or the government. One of the most important observations regarding drug treatment is the positive effects of court-imposed treatment. From time to time, judges will impose treatment as a condition of probation. In addition, corrections institutions will sometimes offer treatment programs for inmates. Studies have shown, however, that legal pressure from

Figure 14.3

In 2003, Harris County, Texas, established a drug court program called Success Through Addiction Recovery (STAR). A voluntary program that bridges the gap between traditional criminal justice and therapeutic treatment, STAR works with up to 200 nonviolent drug offenders who are ready to lead clean, sober, productive lives. Since the first graduation in December 2004, individuals who completed the STAR program have a 1.25 percent recidivism rate, as compared to the national average of 16.4 percent for similar drug court programs.

A public unfamiliar with the program might assume that participation in the STAR drug court would be a "way out" of serving prison time. Nothing could be further from the truth. Not a pretrial diversion program, STAR provides a higher level of offender supervision than any program other than incarceration. In fact, some drug offenders prefer incarceration because completing the Harris County program is, in many ways, much tougher than merely sitting in a cell.

STAR requires participants to make difficult choices, to examine their path to addiction, and to take a hard look at themselves and the consequences of their actions. STAR clients actively participate in programs that will change the way they live and take responsibility for their choices—both good and bad. As Judge Brock Thomas often tells them: "From here on out you must realize that it's not your past that will define you, but the choices you make starting today which will define you most—for the rest of your life." A STAR graduate says it is a "fear of God and a fear of [STAR drug court] Judge Cosper" that keep her on the road to recovery. She said, "The STAR program gave me opportunities I never had before, and they promised that they would not let me fail."

A highly structured, three-phase treatment program, STAR involves 12-step programs or approved alternatives, group and individual treatment and counseling programs, frequent random drug testing, and regular interaction with the judges. Although designed to last at least 12 months, there is no "automatic" graduation from STAR. To graduate and successfully reenter society, participants must take certain positive steps to become drug and crime free, including demonstrating continued sobriety through drug testing and getting an education or obtaining gainful employment. Even after graduation from the program, STAR clients must participate in aftercare for a minimum of 12 months. Graduates must continue to report to a case manager who monitors their sobriety, and successful discharge is determined on a case-by-case basis. Considering the program's continued success, the folks at STAR must be doing something right.

A Closer Look: Tough Love in Texas

the criminal justice system tends to keep people in treatment longer. One such study is the Treatment Outcome Prospective Study (TOPS), a 1989 comprehensive study conducted at the Research Triangle Institute. The study showed that one of every two addicts seeking treatment did so because of an encounter with the criminal justice system and not just because of a personal desire to kick the habit. Ironically, another TOPS study concluded that those addicts required to undergo treatment by court order do as well as those who do so under their own volition. Such studies therefore support the role of the criminal justice system in drug treatment and control.

Figure 14-4
Source: Office of National Drug Control Policy: 2010 Drug Control Strategy (2010).

Josh's first encounter with meth at the age of 17 spiraled into a full-blown addiction. It cost him his job at a car dealership, his house, and the trust of his family. Soon after, Josh was arrested for meth possession. Through a drug court in Dunklin County, Missouri, Josh was provided the treatment, structure, and accountability he needed to turn his life around. His recovery is an ongoing process that continues today: Josh now works as a junior drug counselor and lives with his wife and kids.

Josh's story illustrates both the sheer destruction of methamphetamine and the promise of effective treatment for meth addiction. In Josh's case, a life of meth addiction and meth-related crime has been transformed into an example behind the statistics, bringing to life the national research finding that each dollar invested in recovery leads to $12 in societal savings as a citizen is returned to a productive life.

Josh's story was featured prominently in 2009 as part of a national anti-meth campaign. This national campaign, launched in 2007, takes the stories of real people at the heart of the methamphetamine issue—from law enforcement to drug court professionals and people in addiction recovery—and gives a face to the many facets of meth abuse. This testimonial approach allows a window into the real experiences behind the statistics of methamphetamine addiction, as a strategy to leverage media attention, raise public awareness, and create a dialogue around solutions. The anti-meth campaign began with a public service campaign centered on a photo series, Life After Meth, featuring real people across the country touched by meth addiction. The photo essays are available to local communities, government offices, and local nonprofit coalitions and groups to use their own efforts to fight meth.

Josh, now 32, was willing to share his experience in a open-letter advertisement published in 39 newspapers and news magazines in the states hit hardest by methamphetamine; the ads are now available as free public service announcements to local organizations to use in their own public outreach. The primary message of Josh's ad is from his own story: "People can—and do—recover from meth addiction."

Case in Point: How a Missouri Drug Court Turned a Meth User's Life Around

Drug Treatment in Lieu of Prison

It is in many ways ironic that the overwhelming proportion of funds allocated at local, state, and federal levels to combat the problem of drugs has been directed at law enforcement efforts, such as interdiction and intensive enforcement, which have shown little hope of positive results. Trying to solve what some perceive as a public health problem with punitive enforcement policies not only antagonizes the problem, it also ignores policies that show great promise of actually doing something about drug use and its ancillary problems. Law enforcement tactics spread a wide net that targets a majority of people who are engaged in behavior that is problematic for society, but it misses an enormous number of people whose behavior and health problems should be specifically addressed. It is important to note that more than 40 million U.S. citizens use illicit drugs, but only about 6 million of those drug users are classified as drug abusers or drug addicts (Association of the Bar of New York City, 1994).

Compounding this irony is the fact that those 6 million problem drug users are denied access to a policy initiative that would benefit them: drug treatment. Drug addiction and drug abuse are health problems that can be both treated and managed. The diversion of funds away from treatment programs to interdiction and enforcement assures the continuation of a stable population of individuals who are social problems, while arresting and incarcerating large numbers of people who pose little or no social threat.

No single type of drug treatment works for all drug abusers. As with cigarette smokers, users of other drugs often have to attempt several different approaches before finding one that works. Social factors, lifestyle factors, patterns of drug use, and available support networks in the family and community all combine to impact the effectiveness of drug treatment and on the appropriateness of treatment styles for individual users. Nonetheless, the fact remains that treatment works in reducing drug use and in ameliorating most of the troublesome ancillary behaviors associated with drug abuse. The only thing necessary for treatment to work is that it be available and that drug abusers be given sufficient opportunity to experiment until they find the modality that works best for them.

Many drug abusers are able to manage their problem through programs similar to those of AA. Narcotics Anonymous (NA) and other similar groups are voluntary self-help associations of drug abusers who follow a structured program that makes extensive use of member support as they progress through the several stages of recovery from drug abuse. Because these self-help groups protect their members' confidentiality and do not keep attendance roles at their meetings, it is impossible to measure their effectiveness statistically. There is, however, considerable anecdotal evidence for the effectiveness of this approach, and many other treatment programs have incorporated parts of the self-help regimen into their treatment plans.

Often when we think of drug abuse treatment programs, we think in terms of highly structured, long-term residential inpatient programs referred to as therapeutic communities. As a general rule, patients spend one to two years in these therapeutic communities, both living and working in the facility. Individual counseling and group therapy programs are used to help patients identify and deal with the causes and effects of their drug abuse and the other problems in their lives impacting on their drug abuse. Counselors and social workers work with the patients to help them rebuild their lives through education, vocational training, and work experience. The educational and training components are particularly important features of the treatment program because many drug abusers lack the necessary skills for attaining and holding on to decent jobs. As the therapy progresses, patients who are judged to be progressing and showing patterns of success are reintroduced to the outside world, first through jobs and then through halfway houses outside the residential community.

For drug abusers with available financial resources or private health insurance, a less demanding and restrictive alternative to therapeutic communities is available. Inpatient programs of much shorter duration are available for people of means. Probably the two best-known private inpatient treatment programs are at the Betty Ford Center in Palm Springs, California, and the Hazelden Foundation in Center City, Minnesota. In these programs, patients typically commit to four weeks of in-residence care involving intensive individual counseling, group therapy, and NA or AA meetings. Patients are then discharged to aftercare programs in which they receive continuing outpatient treatment.

The most commonly used outpatient treatment for narcotics (heroin and opiate) addiction in the United States is the methadone maintenance program. Methadone is a long-lasting synthetic opiate. When it is administered to heroin addicts, the addicts do not experience withdrawal symptoms and they lose the desire to use heroin. In addition, unlike heroin, methadone does not impair normal physical functioning or interfere with the ability to maintain a job and perform normal tasks such as driving. Initially, methadone patients receive daily doses. As the treatment progresses and the patient demonstrates that he or she is free of heroin and is maintaining steady employment, the dosage schedule becomes more flexible. Methadone maintenance programs also provide counseling, healthcare services, vocational rehabilitation, and educational services. Many methadone patients remain in the programs for many years at reduced doses, and some leave the treatment program entirely.

Finally, for some drug abusers who are unable to commit to residential treatment and who either do not want to be maintained on methadone or are abusing a drug other than an opiate, a wide variety of drug-free therapies are available. Some involve "talk therapies," but others involve treatments such as acupuncture, which is used to reduce the craving for drugs. An innovative program in this regard is found at Lincoln Hospital in New York City, which for the past 15 years has administered an acupuncture program designed to control withdrawal symptoms and reduce drug cravings. Like methadone treatments, acupuncture involves daily procedures in the beginning, gradually moving to less frequently scheduled treatments.

Critics of drug treatment programs argue that the failure rate is high and relapses are common, thereby ostensibly justifying a law enforcement approach to drug control. Herbert Kleber, former deputy director of the Office of National Drug Control Policy, now medical director of the National Center on Addiction and Substance Abuse and lecturer in psychiatry at Columbia University College of Physicians and Surgeons, identified the basic fallacy in this pessimistic outlook:

> Drug dependence has been viewed as a chronic relapsing illness with an unfavorable prognosis. However, there are thousands of formerly dependent individuals in the United States and elsewhere who have remained off both illicit drugs and excess use of licit drugs like alcohol for decades, functioning as productive citizens…. [T]here are already effective methods of treatment if the right approach [and] the right person can be brought together (Kleber, 1989).

As most people know, efforts to stop smoking cigarettes and to stop drinking alcohol often require several treatment efforts before they are effective. Similarly, few people are able to manage and overcome addictions to other drugs in an initial effort. Relapses are likely, primarily because several treatment regimes may have to be tried before finding the one that will best help a particular person in his or her particular social setting (Falco, 1992:108-109). On the other hand, there is one possible "bullet" that has not been fully tested because of the drug laws themselves. Ibogaine, a mild hallucinogen prohibited from use by federal law, has, in preliminary studies, shown a remarkable ability to break heroin addictions and addictions to other drugs after one administration. Drug prohibition probably has slowed down medicine in trying to assess the effectiveness of this therapy.

Beyond questions of resource allocation and possible relapse, one key statement about drug treatment can be made with certainty: Drug treatment works. Drug treatment not only can successfully break patterns of addiction and abuse, but much more important, drug treatment impacts positively on ancillary social problems linked to drug abuse. Virtually every evaluation study done in the past two decades has shown conclusively that the most commonly utilized modalities of drug treatment work. Whether the studies have evaluated methadone treatment programs, inpatient residential programs, or outpatient drug-free programs, they all produce evidence of dramatic and positive results (Hubbard et al., 1989).

As mentioned earlier, the Treatment Outcomes Prospective Study (TOPS), funded by the National Institute on Drug Abuse, is the most comprehensive evaluation study of the effectiveness of drug treatment done in the United States. TOPS found drug treatment programs to be extremely effective in reducing drug use (Hubbard et al., 1989). The researchers tracked 10,000 drug abusers for a five-year period following their admission to one of the 37 treatment programs being evaluated. Heroin and cocaine use declined markedly for patients in all three treatment modalities. After only one year in methadone maintenance programs, patients found that heroin use had declined by 70 percent. Heroin and cocaine use dropped by 75 percent for patients in outpatient drug-free programs and by 56 percent for patients in residential treatment. By the end of the five-year tracking period, less than 20 percent of the patients used any illegal drug except marijuana, and 40 percent to 50 percent of the patients abstained from all psychoactive drugs—legal or illegal—altogether.

Other evaluation studies have shown strikingly similar results. A NIDA-sponsored study looking at the risk of AIDS infection for intravenous drug users found that methadone maintenance reduced intravenous drug use by 71 percent (Ball et al., 1988). An earlier NIDA study, the Drug Abuse Report Program (DARP), followed the drug use patterns of 44,000 opiate addicts from 1969 through 1974. The DARP study found that most patients stopped using opiates daily upon the inception of treatment and had not resumed daily use after discharge. Seventy-six percent of the patients in methadone therapy, 74 percent of the patients in therapeutic communities, and 72 percent of the patients in outpatient programs did not resume the daily use of opiates (Hubbard ct al., 1989). Much more important, a follow-up study found that 74 percent of the patients were not using heroin on a regular basis 12 years after their treatment had ended (NASADAD, 1990:17).

What is remarkable about the evaluations of the three most common drug treatment modalities is that researchers have found them effective despite the many personal problems impacting clients, such as clients' long histories of deviant lifestyles, clients' long absences from medical care, and a lack of support for clients' efforts in their communities (Hubbard et al., 1989:163).

Although pessimistic appraisals of the efficacy of drug treatment programs in reducing drug use seem to be overstated, evaluations of the impact of drug treatment programs on problems ancillary to drug use offer even stronger evidence for a commitment to drug treatment rather than drug enforcement. For example, studies evaluating the impact of drug treatment on the transmission of HIV and other diseases carried in the blood show remarkable results. The rate of HIV infection for addicts living in New York City (46–47%) is twice that of addicts in methadone maintenance programs (23–27%). Even more notable is the fact that a study tracking the history of methadone patients with 10 or more years in treatment found that none of them tested positive for HIV (NIDA, 1988; Office of Technology Assessment, 1990).

Drug treatment also appears to reduce criminal involvement by drug abusers and drug addicts. The TOPS study showed that in the first six months following treatment, 97 percent of the residential therapeutic community clients and 70 percent of outpatient clients who had self-reported participation in predatory crimes during the previous year engaged in no criminal activity at all. Three to five years after treatment, the proportion of addicts involved in predatory crimes fell between 50 percent and 67 percent (Hubbard et al., 1989:128-129, 181). In looking at all treatment modalities, the DARP study found that arrest rates fell by 74 percent after treatment for all patients and clients (NASADAD, 1990:17-18).

In addition to reducing levels of criminal involvement and reducing high-risk health behaviors, drug treatment programs also show success in helping clients stabilize their lives. Only one-third of the 44,000 patients in the DARP study worked in the year prior to entering drug treatment. However, in the year following their discharge, 57 percent were holding jobs (NASADAD, 1990:17-18). More than two-thirds of the patients who had been involved in therapeutic communities were employed after ending treatment. The TOPS study found the same pattern. Three to five years after patients left treatment, the employment level of residential program patients had doubled and the outpatient program participants increased employment levels by more than one-half (Hubbard et al., 1989).

The other benefits of shifting priorities from law enforcement to drug treatment are equally important and less subtle. For example, addicts develop a wide range of health problems, including chronic illnesses such as hepatitis and tuberculosis as well as lifestyle maladies such as malnutrition and psychological difficulties (Tabbush, 1986). Addicts in drug treatment programs have access to regular medical care, nutritional counseling, and psychological services. The cost of supplying emergency and outpatient services to drug addicts is considerable. Drug treatment not only helps in diagnosing and treating existing conditions, it also places clients in programs in which health maintenance is easier. In addition, drug treatment programs reduce the spread of diseases from drug addicts to others, thereby lowering medical costs even more.

One research study calculated that when the costs of crimes committed, unemployment, and medical treatment for drug addicts are combined, they exceed the cost of supplying drug treatment by a factor of 10 to 25 times, depending on the treatment modality chosen. The most cost-effective of the modalities was treating addicts in long-term residential programs, which amounted to only 4 percent of the cost to society of not treating the addict (NASADAD, 1990:23-24). Drug treatment is clearly much more cost-effective than incarceration. In New York City, residential drug treatment costs about $17,000 a year per client and outpatient costs $2,000 to $4,000 a year per client. Putting that addict in a prison cell costs $40,000 a year, and the cost of building that cell is about $100,000 (Clines, 1993:B3). Recalling that the evaluation studies have also strongly suggested that drug treatment reduces the frequency of criminal behavior and recidivism, this is a savings that would accrue many times over for each addict treated.

The research clearly indicates that drug treatment works and works well. Not only is it less expensive than using a law enforcement strategy against drugs, it also does something prison cannot: It produces healthier, more productive individuals who engage in less criminality and make fewer demands on public coffers for social and medical services. Drug treatment also does what law enforcement has been unable to do—that is, it successfully reduces the overall demand for drugs.

SOCIAL REINTEGRATION

Social reintegration is the process whereby the benefits gained from treatment and rehabilitation are sustained and drug users adapt to a drug-free, productive existence within the community. This can happen in several ways: They can return to their families; they can complete or further their education; they can learn new skills; they can become employed on a full-time or part-time basis; they can continue participation in self-help groups; or they can develop friendships in nondrug-using environments.

Statistics show that most drug addicts lack a formal education. In many cases, they drop out of high school, and when they attempt to get jobs, they find themselves at a serious disadvantage. For those who do get jobs, frequently they are fired because of absenteeism due to drug abuse. Unemployment contributes to the drug-using cycle, and social reintegration then becomes difficult and sometimes impossible. We mentioned earlier that halfway houses were developed, in part, to help bridge the transition between drug abuse and reintegration back into the community. In these houses, residents have responsibility for their own lives, preparing food, cleaning their rooms, and managing their own money matters. Other members as well as therapeutic staff members offer the residents support and assistance in coping with the stress of learning to live independently.

The Talbert House in Cincinnati, Ohio, offers a variety of treatment services for offenders with substance abuse histories. This residential substance abuse program provides assessment, employment and chemical dependency services, and reintegration for drug-dependent men.

Relapse

Over a period of years, drug misuse may be somewhat cyclical, and many people grow out of their drug dependence over time. Studies have revealed that even during the course of abusing drugs, periods of abstinence occur. Thus, it is not uncommon for drug users to drop out of a program before its completion. Programs, therefore, must be prepared to readmit patients who have dropped out so that those patients have an opportunity to achieve control over their own drug use.

Research has shown that many drug users experience a temporary *relapse* (i.e., recurrence of drug misuse) at the end of treatment and rehabilitation. In many cases, however, after a period of a few weeks or months, these same users often achieve long-term stability and, eventually, abstinence. This finding strongly suggests that treatment opportunities offered by rehabilitation and social reintegration can be an important means of reducing the demand for drugs at early stages of abuse.

Problems with Drug Treatment

Factors that complicate the treatment process are attributed to both the psychological and the physiological characteristics of drug addiction. Addiction differs from diseases that are considered treatable through conventional medical methods. One major logistical problem to overcome is the lack of treatment capacity. Many publicly funded programs, particularly those in large cities, maintain long waiting lists. If addicts realize they may not get treatment for several months, their drive to seek help may greatly diminish.

Unfortunately, many treatment centers are not located in towns, cities, or neighborhoods where the need for treatment is greatest. For this reason, some programs have vacancies and others have waiting lists. Moreover, new drug treatment programs are difficult to begin, since funding is sometimes hard to secure and residents are frequently opposed to treatment centers being located in their neighborhoods.

Another problem in the drug treatment process is the soaring cost of health care. Drug treatment in the United States is a big business and accounts for millions of dollars in private, corporate, and insurance monies. For some employers, for example, costs of inpatient treatment may run as high as $1,000 a day for a 28-day treatment program.

Today, trends indicate that fewer patients are referred to inpatient care in lieu of the readily available, lower-cost outpatient programs. The dilemma becomes manifest when one tries to balance the cost of treatment with the quality of treatment—a frustrating and difficult task. Studies show that many people gravitate toward "brand-name" hospitals or rehabilitation services, regardless of their recovery rates.

When searching for a treatment solution, drug counselors tend to look for variables such as whether the hospital is approved by the Joint Commission on Accreditation of Hospitals, the availability of extended outpatient aftercare, the quality of the staff, and the institution's recovery rate.

As we have seen, many treatment programs exist for the drug-dependent person. The most effective programs insist on a sound code of conduct, individual responsibility, personal sacrifice, and sanctions for misbehavior. The evidence is mounting to support the contention that when these elements exist, the best results are attained.

The Cost of Drug Treatment

When considering the great need for drug treatment programs, one should first consider that the largest proportion of drug addicts are white males between the ages of 18 and 40. Many such individuals have the financial means or health insurance with which to pay for treatment. However, many do not. At private institutions, where these addicts most commonly seek treatment, it is not uncommon to have vacancy rates of up to 45 percent. Publicly supported facilities were financially strapped during the 1970s and 1980s and were unprepared for the great influx of addicts generated by the crack epidemic. Federal funding increased in the late 1980s and early 1990s to compensate for this rise.

If a single variable that most greatly impedes the improvement and expansion of treatment were identified, it would be the lack of trained, qualified personnel. In many cities, salaries are often too low to attract or retain people with proper training. Indeed, many starting salaries for drug treatment counselors begin at or below $14,000 per year, a figure that is unrealistically low for a professional position. Although improvements are slowly being made in this area, it will be some time before the competency and responsibility of treatment meets the needs of most communities.

DRUG PREVENTION

Although as a rule most drug abuse begins during one's teenage years, many young people start using drugs much sooner. For that reason, most prevention programs focus on younger people. The goal of prevention is to ensure that Americans, especially children, never begin the cycle of drug abuse, even through experimentation.

Unquestionably, drug prevention should begin in the home, with the parents of the potential drug user as the primary facilitators. After the home, school is probably the most effective place for the drug education process to take place. School is where children spend a majority of their time and where they are subjected to peer groups. Additionally, it is at school where first-time drug users frequently acquire their drugs.

Drug prevention through education is designed to reach people who are not yet personally affected by drug abuse, to inform people about the hazards of drugs, and to reduce curiosity about drugs. Prevention strategists have identified two ways to influence young people against taking drugs. The first is to make people not want to use them, and the second is to warn of severe penalties, to convince potential users that the consequences of drug abuse outweigh the advantages. One of the more disturbing trends revealed by surveys on drug abuse is the decline in the average age of first-time substance abusers. In numerous studies, substantial numbers of school-age children have reported initiating the use of alcohol, tobacco, and marijuana by the time they reach junior high school.

Schools are also primary sources of drug prevention programs and are well equipped for such undertakings. In addition to many community resources being housed within local schools, young people are required to spend much of their time there and are thus more accessible to prevention programs than are other people. As a rule, students in their final year of elementary school are targeted for prevention programs because the junior high school years are thought to be the time in which many students begin their drug experimentation. In addition to drug education classes, many schools have sponsored other types of prevention programs. For example, schools employ counseling and guidance for students in addition to sponsoring substance-free extracurricular activities and peer support groups. Each is thought to show promise in enhancing the quality and effectiveness of drug prevention.

Communities and neighborhoods also play a role in developing drug-related prevention programs. Many of these programs are sponsored by churches, civic organizations, or parent groups; their content, educational focus, and financial backing may differ greatly. An example of a community-based prevention program is SMART Moves, which is associated with the Boys and Girls Clubs of America. Trained staff involve youths in addressing problems of drug abuse, alcohol, and teen pregnancy. Other community-based prevention programs include a school-based program called the Midwestern Prevention Project, which interfaces with community groups and parents, and Fighting Back, which requires all participating communities to establish a task force of community representatives to join forces in drug prevention activities.

Various prevention efforts have also been implemented by law enforcement agencies to address the drug abuse problem. Conventional wisdom in recent years has held that the most effective initiatives should focus on building the self-esteem of young people, improving their decision-making skills, and enhancing their ability to resist peer pressure to use drugs.

Prevention Programs

An important part of drug prevention is the development of programs that prevent illicit drug use, keep drugs out of neighborhoods and schools, and provide a safe and secure environment for all people. Examples include these:

- *Boys and Girls Clubs of America.* Boys and Girls Clubs programs and services promote and enhance the development of boys and girls by instilling a sense of competence, usefulness, belonging, and influence. Their program areas include education, health, arts, careers, alcohol/drug and pregnancy prevention, gang prevention, leadership development, and athletics.
- *Centers for the Application of Prevention Technologies (CAPT).* The primary mission of the national CAPT system is to bring research to practice by assisting states and jurisdictions and community-based organizations in the application of the latest research-based knowledge to their substance abuse prevention programs, practices, and policies.
- *Center for Substance Abuse Prevention (CSAP) Model Programs.* The CSAP model programs offer a website that serves as a comprehensive resource on preventing substance abuse and creating sustained positive change in our nation's communities. The featured model programs have

been tested in communities and schools across the United States and proven to prevent or decrease substance abuse in youth.

- *Division of Workplace Programs.* The Division of Workplace Programs' drug-free workplace initiatives include a clear policy of no use; employee education about the dangers of illicit drug use and the workplace consequences of drug use; supervisor training about their responsibilities under the policy; access to employee assistance programs (EAPs) and treatment referral; and accurate and reliable drug testing, consistent with the policy.

- *Drug-Free Communities Support Program.* The Drug-Free Communities Program is designed to assist community-based coalitions' efforts to reduce alcohol, tobacco, illicit drug, and inhalant abuse by youths. The program enables the coalitions to strengthen their coordination and prevention efforts, encourage citizen participation in substance abuse reduction efforts, and disseminate information about effective programs.

Prevention Through Education

School- and community-based drug educational programs should be designed to educate children about drugs and the potential for drug abuse and provide children with alternatives to socialization experiences that might lead them to drug use. Both experience and logic convince us that education programs, if they are realistic and credible, should divert children from initial experimentation with drugs.

Education has been demonstrated to be an effective tool in preventing the initiation of tobacco use. Similar school- and community-based programs should be effective in preventing and reducing alcohol and other drug use among young people. Attention must be paid to what types of educational programs work and what types are less effective. There is a common public assumption that any form of "education" must be good. That assumption is incorrect; not all forms of drug education are equally effective (OSAP, 1991).

Evaluation research directed at drug education and prevention programs strongly suggests that long-term programs emphasizing the social influences leading to alcohol, tobacco, and other drug use are far more successful in diverting and reducing subsequent use than are other types of programs. These educational programs are typically conducted in concert with community prevention and home education programs. The short-term education programs, conducted outside overarching community programs, have proved ineffective in actually reducing drug use. Among the most successful drug education programs are the following:

- *Life Skills Training Program* is a 15-session program for junior high school students that emphasizes personal coping skills that will lead to better decision making and greater confidence in social settings. The program has been used for the past 10 years in 150 schools in New York and New Jersey. Evaluations of the program have demonstrated that rates of tobacco and marijuana consumption are one-half to three-quarters lower among program participants than among their peers.

- *Students Taught Awareness and Resistance* is a 13-session program for first-year high school students, coordinated with community, media, and family programs and emphasizing resistance skills and the social undesirability of drugs. The initial program is followed by a five-session refresher course the following school year. A five-year follow-up study to this program determined that it resulted in reductions of marijuana, tobacco, and alcohol use by between 20 percent and 40 percent and in cocaine use by 50 percent (Falco, 1991:41).

- *Project Healthy Choices* is a program directed toward sixth and seventh graders that integrates discussions about drugs and alcohol into the everyday curriculum of all students in all subjects. The program is being utilized in about 100 New York City schools.

- *Student Assistance Program* (SAP) has been implemented in high schools in more than 20 states. The program's primary focus is making available voluntary confidential counseling to students during the school day. A study of the program's effectiveness in the Westchester County, New York, school system found a significant reduction in alcohol and marijuana use. In addition, the study found that overall levels of drug use, drinking, and tobacco use were 30 percent lower among students at schools that had initiated the SAP program (Falco, 1991:56).

- *SMART Moves (Skills Mastery and Resistance Training)* is a program run by Boys and Girls Clubs in inner cities, particularly targeting children in high-crime neighborhoods. SMART Moves offers after-school prevention programs, along with recreational, educational, and vocational programs. The program teaches children to recognize the social pressures to use drugs and to develop the requisite verbal and social skills to resist those pressures. Evaluation studies have shown significant reductions in cocaine and crack use among participants as well as marked improvements in behavior at school (Falco, 1991:59-60, 63-64).

- *Seattle Social Development Project* is a comprehensive program that tries to strengthen the bond between children from high-crime neighborhoods and their families and schools. The program teaches parents various techniques for monitoring their children; it instructs teachers in how to maintain order and resolve conflicts in schools; and it teaches children how to resist peer pressure.

Finally, a number of cities are attempting to develop prevention programs geared toward the children of drug addicts. These programs attempt to teach parents communication and parenting skills and provide children with support and social skills.

These education programs are already available in communities throughout the country. Successful programs are those in which the school and the community have demonstrated a commitment to implementing comprehensive programs directed not just at children but also at parents and teachers. The most successful programs clearly demonstrate the need for education that goes beyond simple warnings about the dangers of drugs and alcohol. They also provide additional support structures that assist children in resisting the pressures of peer drug use.

Two additional prevention approaches are Drug Abuse Resistance Education (DARE), which originated in Los Angeles, and School Program to Educate and Control Drug Abuse (SPECDA), which began in New York City.

Project DARE

One of the main points of this chapter is that many different organizations and agencies, both private and public, are involved in drug prevention efforts. Project DARE (Drug Abuse Resistance Education) is one such example. It began as a joint project between the Los Angeles Police Department and the LA Unified School District. Its purpose is to equip fifth-, sixth-, and seventh-grade children with the skills and motivation to resist peer pressure to use drugs, alcohol, and tobacco. A particularly innovative aspect of the program is the use of full-time, uniformed police officers (selected and trained by DARE's supervisory staff) as instructors. The project uses a variety of educational techniques, including lectures, videotapes, and exercises, to teach students how to resist drugs. The community policing philosophy is also used in that attempts are made to develop positive attitudes toward police officers.

DARE programs send full-time, uniformed police officers to schools to teach grade-school children self-management techniques for resisting peer pressure.

The core curriculum consists of a 17-lesson program, each of which consists of a 45- to 60-minute lesson that teaches children various self-management skills and techniques for resisting peer pressure. The focus of the training rests on the premise that children who feel positive about themselves will be more successful in resisting peer pressure. Other lessons emphasize the physical, mental, and social consequences of drug abuse, and still others identify the different methods of coping with stress and having fun.

The scope of the 17-lesson DARE program core curriculum is as follows:

1. *Practices for personal safety.* Students are acquainted with the role of the police officer and methods to protect themselves from harm. The thrust of the lesson is to explain to the students the need for rules and laws designed to protect people from harm. The instructor and the students review a list of students' rights, which is contained in a notebook provided to each student. Finally, teachers instruct students in using the 911 emergency system to summon help.

2. *Drug use and misuse.* This segment explains the definition of drugs and the positive and negative effects of drugs on the body and mind. Each student then takes a true/false test that assesses understanding of the lesson. The teacher defines the word *consequences* and the class considers the consequences of various actions. The students then discuss the consequences of using and not using drugs.

3. *Consequences.* The class discusses both negative and positive consequences of using drugs during this lesson. The students fill out a worksheet that directs them to list positive and negative consequences of using marijuana and alcohol. The officer points out that those who try to persuade others to use drugs will emphasize positive consequences, leaving the many negative consequences unstated.

4. *Resisting pressure to use drugs.* A key component to this lesson introduces students to the different types of peer pressure to take drugs that they may face. It teaches them to say no to such offers by considering the negative consequences of drug use. DARE instructors introduce four different sources of influence on people's behavior: personal preferences, family expectations, peer expectations, and the mass media. After defining *peer pressure*, the DARE instructor explains different types of pressure that friends use to get others to use alcohol or drugs. These methods include threats and intimidation.

5. *Resistance techniques: Ways to say no.* This lesson reinforces the previous lesson by teaching students different ways to respond to peer pressure. Instructors write various techniques of resisting pressure on the chalkboard and discuss them with the class. These include giving a reason or excuse, changing the subject, walking away, and ignoring the person. The instructor also stresses that people can consciously avoid such confrontations by choosing to avoid associating with drug users. Because noting long-term consequences for not taking drugs is usually not as effective as citing short-term consequences, an emphasis is placed on explaining short-term consequences such as: "I don't like the taste."

6. *Building self-esteem.* In this lesson, DARE instructors explain that self-esteem is created out of positive and negative feelings and experiences. Students learn to identify their own positive qualities. They discover that drug use stems from poor self-esteem and that those with high self-esteem think for themselves and have accepted their limitations as human beings. In short, when people feel good about themselves, they can exert control over their behavior.

7. *Assertiveness: A response style.* Instructors teach assertiveness as a technique to refuse offers of drugs. The lesson begins with the DARE officer asking the class what occurrences happened during the previous week to heighten their self-esteem. They then emphasize that once people achieve self-esteem, they can more easily think for themselves without being pressured to do what they believe is wrong. The instructor defines the word *assertive* and stresses that people should learn how to assert their rights confidently without interfering with the rights of others. Role-playing occurs in which each student and his or her partner practice good posture, strong voice, eye contact, calm manner, and other elements of assertiveness.

8. *Managing stress without taking drugs.* This step helps students recognize stress in their lives and how to relieve it without taking drugs. The teacher presents the "fight or flight" response to danger along with the physiological changes that accompany that response. The instructor notes that modern-day stressors, such as taking a test, fail to provide the individual with a means to "flee" or "fight," and alternative ways of coping with stress must be learned. Students then work in groups and devise ways of dealing with two types of stressors (from a class list) in their lives. They then share their strategies with the rest of the class and discuss them. Methods include ways to relax and exercise, talk out problems with a family member or a friend, and so on.

9. *Media influences on drug use.* This lesson focuses on ways to resist media influences to use alcohol and drugs. The class discusses various advertising strategies to promote certain products, and the DARE instructor explains how to see through the strategies. For example, by showing a product being used by people who are enjoying themselves, the advertiser suggests that people who actually use the product will indeed have more fun. The students then work in groups to create an antialcohol or antidrug commercial while using the techniques employed by professional advertisers. Next, each group performs their own commercial before the class.

10. *Decision making and risk taking.* The objective of this lesson is to teach students to apply decision-making skills in evaluating the results of various kinds of risk-taking behavior, including drug use. First, the class generates a list of risk-taking behaviors, including the many everyday types of risks commonly encountered. Although many risks are worth taking (e.g., making new friends, trying out for a play, etc.), many are not and can result in harm (e.g., swallowing an unknown substance, riding with a drunk driver, etc.). Students learn that any assumption of risk involves a choice. The choices that we make are influenced by several factors, including family, friends, the mass media, and personal values. The key to intelligent decision making is to think through the likely outcomes of various alternative actions.

11. *Alternatives to drug abuse.* This lesson examines rewarding alternative activities that do not involve taking drugs. Students recount the reasons that people take drugs and what basic needs people have. They also learn that these needs can be met in healthier ways than taking drugs (such as playing games or exercising). The students then fill out a worksheet titled "What I Like to Do." They write down their favorite activities and explain to the class why these are better than taking drugs.

12. *Role modeling.* This phase involves older students who have resisted peer pressure to use drugs. The younger students ask the older students questions that they have previously prepared.

13. *Forming a support system.* Students discover that positive relationships with different people create a support system for the student. In this lesson, two fundamental questions are posed: Why do people need other people? What do other people do for us? The DARE instructor explains that everyone has needs that can be met only through positive

relationships with other people. The students then complete a worksheet titled "Choosing Friends," which requires them to indicate the qualities they look for in friends (e.g., people who are honest with me, people who won't get me into trouble, etc.). When they are finished, students share their responses and discuss barriers to friendship and how to overcome them.

14. *Ways to deal with pressure from gangs.* In this lesson, students learn how to deal with pressure put on them from gangs and how to evaluate choices available to them. The students begin with naming the social activities they most enjoy and with whom they like to share these activities. These relationships help satisfy needs for recognition, acceptance, and affection. It is also recognized that people join gangs to satisfy these same needs. Students see that gangs use strong-arm tactics to get what they want. The students then learn to cope with bullying and intimidation by first avoiding places where gangs hang out and by leaving money or other valuables at home. Other techniques include keeping busy with constructive activities that meet the needs for friendship and love.

15. *Project DARE summary.* This lesson is a summary of what the student should have learned through Project DARE. The class divides into competing teams, and the officer reads a series of questions about DARE, giving each team an opportunity to earn points for each correct answer. Scores are then computed, and a winner is announced. Each student then individually completes a true/false questionnaire titled "What Do You Know About Drugs?" The officer reviews the answers.

16. *Taking a stand.* As homework, students must complete a worksheet, "Taking a Stand," which asks them to articulate how they will (1) keep their body healthy, (2) control their feelings when angry or under stress, (3) decide whether to take a risk, (4) respond when a friend pressures them to use drugs or alcohol, and (5) respond when they see people on television using drugs or alcohol. This document represents the student's DARE pledge.

17. *DARE culmination.* The author of the winning DARE pledge reads his or her pledge in front of a school assembly. Each student who has completed the DARE curriculum receives a certificate of achievement signed by the chief of police and the superintendent of schools.

Concerns About DARE

The U.S. Department of Education concluded in 2003 that the DARE program is ineffective and now prohibits its funds from being used to support it. The U.S. Surgeon General's office, the National Academy of Sciences, and the Government Accounting Office also concluded that the program is sometimes counterproductive in some populations, with those who graduate from DARE later having higher rates of drug use. Studies by Dennis Rosenbaum and by the California Legislative Analyst's office found that DARE graduates were more likely than others to drink alcohol, smoke tobacco, and use illegal drugs (Rosenbaum, 1998).

Administrators of the DARE program have tried to suppress unfavorable research that found that DARE "simply didn't work." A federal judge ruled that DARE had sought to "suppress scientific research" critical of its program and had "attempted to silence researchers at the Research Triangle Institute," according to editors at the *American Journal of Public Health* and producers at *Dateline NBC*. Some reporters, like those at *Rolling Stone* magazine, who have written negative stories on DARE have claimed that they were the victims of harassment and intimidation as a result. Critics such as Students for Sensible Drug Policy, DRCNet, and Drugsense have exposed the DARE program for teaching misleading and inaccurate information about drugs and drug use.

Critics of DARE have the opinion that abstinence or "Just Say No" messages mislead students by treating recreational drug use as substance abuse or by labeling alcoholic beverages as gateway drugs. Supporters of DARE believe that educating students that alcoholic beverages and cigarettes are illegal substances is appropriate because underage drinking in the United States and cigarette purchasing are illegal for those of primary and secondary school age.

> ### Critical Thinking Task
>
> Assume you are a DARE officer working in a sixth-grade classroom. Create a role-playing skit by which children may learn methods of resisting peer pressure to experiment with illicit drugs. The characters and dialogue in your skit must be realistic yet suited for the age group.

SUMMARY

We have discussed many ways to deal with drug abuse in our society, and because of the social dangers of drug abuse, increasingly more attention is being given to this critical issue. In addition to education and law enforcement initiatives, treatment remains one of the most viable options. The immediate objectives of most treatment programs are to control or eliminate drug abuse, give the drug user alternatives for his or her lifestyle, and treat medical complications associated with drug use.

Treatment programs are varied in nature because of the personality type of the drug-dependent person as well as the specific drug of abuse for which the person is being treated. Options include detoxification, chemical dependency units, outpatient clinics, methadone maintenance programs, and residential therapeutic communities. After treatment, social reintegration is an important step in making the patient a productive member of the community. The halfway house is often used for this purpose; it permits members to assume some responsibilities in maintaining the operation of the house.

Drug prevention is another essential component to fighting drug abuse. The two ways most likely to achieve the drug prevention goal are to make potential first-time users not want to use drugs and to impose severe criminal penalties to deter first-time drug abuse. DARE and SPECDA prevention programs focus on children to teach them fundamental basics of individual thinking, decision making, and personal choices when faced with the prospect of using illicit drugs. Many experts believe that treatment and prevention programs offer the most hope for successfully dealing with the nation's drug problem.

Do you recognize these terms?

- chronic relapsing disorder
- DARE
- detoxification
- maintenance
- methadone treatment programs

- narcotic antagonists
- relapse
- SPECDA
- therapeutic communities

DISCUSSION QUESTIONS

1. List three characteristics of treatment and rehabilitation programs.

2. Compare and contrast the five categories of drug treatment.

3. Describe the detoxification process and its role in drug treatment.

4. Explain how the methadone maintenance program operates in treating opiate addicts.

5. Explain how the therapeutic community program treats drug addicts.

6. What are some problems with drug treatment in our communities?

7. List and discuss the two goals of drug prevention.

Appendix I
Drug Scheduling

This document is a general reference and not a comprehensive list. This list describes the basic or parent chemical and does not describe the salts, isomers, and salts of isomers, esters, ethers, and derivatives, which may also be controlled substances.

Schedule I			
Substance	**DEA Number**	**Non-Narcotic**	**Other Names**
1-(1-Phenylcyclohexyl)pyrrolidine	7458	N	PCPy, PHP, rolicyclidine
1-(2-Phenylethyl)-4-phenyl-4-acetoxypiperidine	9663		PEPAP, synthetic heroin
1-[1-(2-Thienyl)cyclohexyl]piperidine	7470	N	TCP, tenocyclidine
1-[1-(2-Thienyl)cyclohexyl]pyrrolidine	7473	N	TCPy
1-Methyl-4-phenyl-4-propionoxypiperidine	9661		MPPP, synthetic heroin
2,5-Dimethoxy-4-ethylamphetamine	7399	N	DOET
2,5-Dimethoxyamphetamine	7396	N	DMA, 2,5-DMA
3,4,5-Trimethoxyamphetamine	7390	N	TMA
3,4-Methylenedioxyamphetamine	7400	N	MDA, Love Drug
3,4-Methylenedioxy-methamphetamine	7405	N	MDMA, ecstasy, XTC
3,4-Methylenedioxy-N-ethylamphetamine	7404	N	N-ethyl MDA, MDE, MDEA
3-Methylfentanyl	9813		China White, fentanyl
3-Methylthiofentanyl	9833		Chine White, fentanyl
4-Bromo-2,5-dimethoxyamphetamine	7391	N	DOB, 4-bromo-DMA
4-Bromo-2,5-dimethoxyphenethylamine	7392	N	Nexus, 2-CB, has been sold as ecstasy, i.e., MDMA
4-Methoxyamphetamine	7411	N	PMA
4-Methyl-2,5-dimethoxyamphetamine	7395	N	DOM, STP

4-Methylaminorex (cis isomer)	1590	N	U4Euh, McN-422
5-Methoxy-3,4-methylenedioxyamphetamine	7401	N	MMDA
Acetorphine	9319		
Acetyl-alpha-methylfentanyl	9815		
Acetyldihydrocodeine	9051		Acetylcodone
Acetylmethadol	9601		Methadyl acetate
Allylprodine	9602		
Alphacetylmethadol except levo-alphacetylmethadol	9603		
Alpha-Ethyltryptamine	7249	N	ET, Trip
Alphameprodine	9604		
Alphamethadol	9605		
Alpha-Methylfentanyl	9814		China White, fentanyl
Alpha-Methylthiofentanyl	9832		China White, fentanyl
Aminorex	1585	N	Has been sold as methamphetamine
Benzethidine	9606		
Benzylmorphine	9052		
Betacetylmethadol	9607		
Beta-Hydroxy-3-methylfentanyl	9831		China White, fentanyl
Beta-Hydroxyfentanyl	9830		China White, fentanyl
Betameprodine	9608		
Betamethadol	9609		
Betaprodine	9611		
Bufotenine	7433	N	Mappine, N,N-dimethylserotonin
Cathinone	1235	N	Constituent of "Khat" plant
Clonitazene	9612		
Codeine methylbromide	9070		
Codeine-N-oxide	9053		
Cyprenorphine	9054		
Desomorphine	9055		
Dextromoramide	9613		Palfium, Jetrium, Narcolo
Diampromide	9615		

Diethylthiambutene	9616		
Diethyltryptamine	7434	N	DET
Difenoxin	9168		Lyspafen
Dihydromorphine	9145		
Dimenoxadol	9617		
Dimepheptanol	9618		
Dimethylthiambutene	9619		
Dimethyltryptamine	7435	N	DMT
Dioxaphetyl butyrate	9621		
Dipipanone	9622		Dipipan, phenylpiperone HCl, Diconal, Wellconal
Drotebanol	9335		Metebanyl, oxymethebanol
Ethylmethylthiambutene	9623		
Etonitazene	9624		
Etorphine (except HCl)	9056		
Etoxeridine	9625		
Fenethylline	1503	N	Captagon, amfetyline, ethytheophylline amphetamine
Furethidine	9626		
Gamma Hydroxybutyric Acid (GHB)	2010	N	GHB, gamma hydroxybutyrate, sodium oxybate
Heroin	9200		Diacetylmorphine, diamorphine
Hydromorphinol	9301		
Hydroxypethidine	9627		
Ibogaine	7260	N	Constituent of "Tabernanthe iboga" plant
Ketobemidone	9628		Cliradon
Levomoramide	9629		
Levophenacylmorphan	9631		
Lysergic acid diethylamide	7315	N	LSD, lysergide
Marijuana	7360	N	Cannabis, marijuana
Mecloqualone	2572	N	Nubarene
Mescaline	7381	N	Constituent of "Peyote" cacti
Methaqualone	2565	N	Quaalude, Parest, Somnafac, Opitimil, Mandrax

Methcathinone	1237	N	N-Methylcathinone, "cat"
Methyldesorphine	9302		
Methyldihydromorphine	9304		
Morpheridine	9632		
Morphine methylbromide	9305		
Morphine methylsulfonate	9306		
Morphine-N-oxide	9307		
Myrophine	9308		
N,N-Dimethylamphetamine	1480	N	
N-Ethyl-1-phenylcyclohexylamine	7455	N	PCE
N-Ethyl-3-piperidyl benzilate	7482	N	JB 323
N-Ethylamphetamine	1475	N	NEA
N-Hydroxy-3,4-methylenedioxyamphetamine	7402	N	N-hydroxy MDA
Nicocodeine	9309		
Nicomorphine	9312		Vilan
N-Methyl-3-piperidyl benzilate	7484	N	JB 336
Noracymethadol	9633		
Norlevorphanol	9634		
Normethadone	9635		Phenyldimazone
Normorphine	9313		
Norpipanone	9636		
Para-Fluorofentanyl	9812		China White, fentanyl
Parahexyl	7374	N	Synhexyl
Peyote	7415	N	Cactus which contains mescaline
Phenadoxone	9637		
Phenampromide	9638		
Phenomorphan	9647		
Phenoperidine	9641		Operidine, Lealgin
Pholcodine	9314		Copholco, Adaphol, Codisol, Lantuss, Pholcolin
Piritramide	9642		Piridolan
Proheptazine	9643		

Properidine	9644		
Propiram	9649		Algeril
Psilocybin	7437	N	Constituent of "Magic mushrooms"
Psilocyn	7438	N	Psilocin, constituent of "Magic mushrooms"
Racemoramide	9645		
Tetrahydrocannabinols	7370	N	THC, Delta-8 THC, Delta-9 THC, and others
Thebacon	9315		Acetylhydrocodone, Acedicon, Thebacetyl
Thiofentanyl	9835		Chine White, fentanyl
Tilidine	9750		Tilidate, Valoron, Kitadol, Lak, Tilsa
Trimeperidine	9646		Promedolum
Schedule II			
1-Phenylcyclohexylamine	7460	N	Precusor of PCP
1-Piperidinocyclohexanecarbonitrile	8603	N	PCC, precusor of PCP
Alfentanil	9737		Alfenta
Alphaprodine	9010		Nisentil
Amobarbital	2125	N	Amytal, Tuinal
Amphetamine	1100	N	Dexedrine, Biphetamine
Anileridine	9020		Leritine
Benzoylecgonine	9180		Cocaine metabolite
Bezitramide	9800		Burgodin
Carfentanil	9743		Wildnil
Coca leaves	9040		
Cocaine	9041		Methyl benzoylecgonine, Crack
Codeine	9050		Morphine methyl ester, methyl morphine
Dextropropoxyphene, bulk (non-dosage forms)	9273		Propoxyphene
Dihydrocodeine	9120		Didrate, Parzone
Diphenoxylate	9170		
Diprenorphine	9058		M50-50

Ecgonine	9180		Cocaine precursor, in Coca leaves
Ethylmorphine	9190		Dionin
Etorphine HCl	9059		M 99
Fentanyl	9801		Innovar, Sublimaze, Duragesic
Glutethimide	2550	N	Doriden, Dorimide
Hydrocodone	9193		Dihydrocodeinone
Hydromorphone	9150		Dilaudid, dihydromorphinone
Isomethadone	9226		Isoamidone
Levo-alphacetylmethadol	9648		LAAM, long-acting methadone, levomethadyl acetate
Levomethorphan	9210		
Levorphanol	9220		Levo-Dromoran
Meperidine	9230		Demerol, Mepergan, pethidine
Meperidine intermediate-A	9232		Meperidine precursor
Meperidine intermediate-B	9233		Meperidine precursor
Meperidine intermediate-C	9234		Meperidine precursor
Metazocine	9240		
Methadone	9250		Dolophine, Methadose, Amidone
Methadone intermediate	9254		Methadone precursor
Methamphetamine	1105	N	Desoxyn, D-desoxyephedrine, ICE, Crank, Speed
Methylphenidate	1724	N	Ritalin
Metopon	9260		
Moramide-intermediate	9802		
Morphine	9300		MS Contin, Roxanol, Duramorph, RMS, MSIR
Nabilone	7379	N	Cesamet
Opium extracts	9610		
Opium fluid extract	9620		
Opium poppy	9650		Papaver somniferum
Opium tincture	9630		Laudanum
Opium, granulated	9640		Granulated opium
Opium, powdered	9639		Powdered opium

Opium, raw	9600		Raw opium, gum opium
Oxycodone	9143		OxyContin, Percocet, Tylox, Roxicodone, Roxicet
Oxymorphone	9652		Numorphan
Pentobarbital	2270	N	Nembutal
Phenazocine	9715		Narphen, Prinadol
Phencyclidine	7471	N	PCP, Sernylan
Phenmetrazine	1631	N	Preludin
Phenylacetone	8501	N	P2P, phenyl-2-propanone, benzyl methyl ketone
Piminodine	9730		
Poppy Straw	9650		Opium poppy capsules, poppy heads
Poppy Straw Concentrate	9670		Concentrate of Poppy Straw, CPS
Racemethorphan	9732		
Racemorphan	9733		Dromoran
Remifentanil	9739		Ultiva
Secobarbital	2315	N	Seconal, Tuinal
Sufentanil	9740		Sufenta
Thebaine	9333		Precursor of many narcotics
Schedule III			
Amobarbital & noncontrolled	2126	N	Amobarbital/ephedrine capsules active ingred.
Amobarbital suppository dosage form	2126	N	
Anabolic steroids	4000	N	"Body Building" drugs
Aprobarbital	2100	N	Alurate
Barbituric acid derivative	2100	N	Barbiturates not specifically listed
Benzphetamine	1228	N	Didrex, Inapetyl
Boldenone	4000	N	Equipoise, Parenabol, Vebonol, dehydrotestosterone
Buprenorphine	9064		Buprenex, Temgesic
Butabarbital	2100	N	Butisol, Butibel
Butalbital	2100	N	Fiorinal, Butalbital with aspirin

Chlorhexadol	2510	N	Mechloral, Mecoral, Medodorm, Chloralodol
Chlorotestosterone (same as clostebol)	4000	N	If 4-chlorotestosterone then clostebol
Chlorphentermine	1645	N	Pre-Sate, Lucofen, Apsedon, Desopimon
Clortermine	1647	N	Voranil
Clostebol	4000	N	Alfa-Trofodermin, Clostene, 4-chlorotestosterone
Codeine & isoquinoline alkaloid 90 mg/du	9803		Codeine with papaverine or noscapine
Codeine combination product 90 mg/du	9804		Empirin, Fiorinal, Tylenol, ASA or APAP w/codeine
Dehydrochlormethyltestosterone	4000	N	Oral-Turinabol
Dihydrocodeine combination product 90 mg/du	9807		Synalgos-DC, Compal
Dihydrotestosterone (same as stanolone)	4000	N	See stanolone
Dronabinol in sesame oil in soft gelatin capsule	7369	N	Marinol, synthetic THC in sesame oil/soft gelatin
Drostanolone	4000	N	Drolban, Masterid, Permastril
Ethylestrenol	4000	N	Maxibolin, Orabolin, Durabolin-O, Duraboral
Ethylmorphine combination product 15 mg/du	9808		
Fluoxymesterone	4000	N	Anadroid-F, Halotestin, Ora-Testryl
Formebolone (incorrect spelling in law)	4000	N	Esiclene, Hubernol
Hydrocodone & isoquinoline alkaloid 15 mg/du	9805		Dihydrocodeinone + papaverine or noscapine
Hydrocodone combination product 15 mg/du	9806		Tussionex, Tussend, Lortab, Vicodin, Hycodan, Anexsia
Ketamine	7285	N	Ketaset, Ketalar, Special K, K
Lysergic acid	7300	N	LSD precursor
Lysergic acid amide	7310	N	LSD precursor
Mesterolone	4000	N	Proviron
Methandienone (see Methandrostenolone)	4000	N	

Methandranone	4000	N	?incorrect spelling of methandienone?
Methandriol	4000	N	Sinesex, Stenediol, Troformone
Methandrostenolone	4000	N	Dianabol, Metabolina, Nerobol, Perbolin
Methenolone	4000	N	Primobolan, Primobolan Depot, Primobolan S
Methyltestosterone	4000	N	Android, Oreton, Testred, Virilon
Methyprylon	2575	N	Noludar
Mibolerone	4000	N	Cheque
Morphine combination product/50 mg/100 ml or gm	9810		
Nalorphine	9400		Nalline
Nandrolone	4000	N	Deca-Durabolin, Durabolin, Durabolin-50
Norethandrolone	4000	N	Nilevar, Solevar
Opium combination product 25 mg/du	9809		Paregoric, other combination products
Oxandrolone	4000	N	Anavar, Lonavar, Provitar, Vasorome
Oxymesterone	4000	N	Anamidol, Balnimax, Oranabol, Oranabol 10
Oxymetholone	4000	N	Anadrol-50, Adroyd, Anapolon, Anasteron, Pardroyd
Pentobarbital & noncontrolled	2271	N	FP-3 active ingred.
Pentobarbital suppository dosage form	2271	N	WANS
Phendimetrazine	1615	N	Plegine, Prelu-2, Bontril, Melfiat, Statobex
Secobarbital & noncontrolled	2316	N	Various active ingred.
Secobarbital suppository dosage form	2316	N	Various
Stanolone	4000	N	Anabolex, Andractim, Pesomax, dihydrotestosterone
Stanozolol	4000	N	Winstrol, Winstrol-V
Stimulant compounds previously	1405	N	Mediatric excepted
Sulfondiethylmethane	2600	N	

Sulfonethylmethane	2605	N	
Sulfonmethane	2610	N	
Talbutal	2100	N	Lotusate
Testolactone	4000	N	Teslac
Testosterone	4000	N	Android-T, Androlan, Depotest, Delatestryl
Thiamylal	2100	N	Surital
Thiopental	2100	N	Pentothal
Tiletamine & Zolazepam Combination	7295	N	Telazol Product
Trenbolone	4000	N	Finaplix-S, Finajet, Parabolan
Vinbarbital	2100	N	Delvinal, vinbarbitone
Schedule IV			
Alprazolam	2882	N	Xanax
Barbital	2145	N	Veronal, Plexonal, barbitone
Bromazepam	2748	N	Lexotan, Lexatin, Lexotanil
Butorphanol	9720	N	Stadol, Stadol NS, Torbugesic, Torbutrol
Camazepam	2749	N	Albego, Limpidon, Paxor
Cathine	1230	N	Constituent of "Khat" plant
Chloral betaine	2460	N	Beta Chlor
Chloral hydrate	2465	N	Noctec
Chlordiazepoxide	2744	N	Librium, Libritabs, Limbitrol, SK-Lygen
Clobazam	2751	N	Urbadan, Urbanyl
Clonazepam	2737	N	Klonopin, Clonopin
Clorazepate	2768	N	Tranxene
Clotiazepam	2752	N	Trecalmo, Rize
Cloxazolam	2753	N	Enadel, Sepazon, Tolestan
Delorazepam	2754	N	
Dexfenfluramine	1670	N	Redux
Dextropropoxyphene dosage forms	9278		Darvon, propoxyphene, Darvocet, Dolene, Propacet
Diazepam	2765	N	Valium, Valrelease
Dichloralphenazone	2467	N	Midrin, dichloralantipyrine

Diethylpropion	1610	N	Tenuate, Tepanil
Difenoxin 1 mg/25 ug AtSO4/du	9167		Motofen
Estazolam	2756	N	ProSom, Domnamid, Eurodin, Nuctalon
Ethchlorvynol	2540	N	Placidyl
Ethinamate	2545	N	Valmid, Valamin
Ethyl loflazepate	2758	N	
Fencamfamin	1760	N	Reactivan
Fenfluramine	1670	N	Pondimin, Ponderal
Fenproporex	1575	N	Gacilin, Solvolip
Fludiazepam	2759	N	
Flunitrazepam	2763	N	Rohypnol, Narcozep, Darkene, Roipnol
Flurazepam	2767	N	Dalmane
Halazepam	2762	N	Paxipam
Haloxazolam	2771	N	
Ketazolam	2772	N	Anxon, Loftran, Solatran, Contamex
Loprazolam	2773	N	
Lorazepam	2885	N	Ativan
Lormetazepam	2774	N	Noctamid
Mazindol	1605	N	Sanorex, Mazanor
Mebutamate	2800	N	Capla
Medazepam	2836	N	Nobrium
Mefenorex	1580	N	Anorexic, Amexate, Doracil, Pondinil
Meprobamate	2820	N	Miltown, Equanil, Deprol, Equagesic, Meprospan
Methohexital	2264	N	Brevital
Methylphenobarbital (mephobarbital)	2250	N	Mebaral, mephobarbital
Midazolam	2884	N	Versed
Modafinil	1680	N	Provigil
Nimetazepam	2837	N	Erimin
Nitrazepam	2834	N	Mogadon
Nordiazepam	2838	N	Nordazepam, Demadar, Madar

Oxazepam	2835	N	Serax, Serenid-D
Oxazolam	2839	N	Serenal, Convertal
Paraldehyde	2585	N	Paral
Pemoline	1530	N	Cylert
Pentazocine	9709	N	Talwin, Talwin NX, Talacen, Talwin Compound
Petrichloral	2591	N	Pentaerythritol chloral, Periclor
Phenobarbital	2285	N	Luminal, Donnatal, Bellergal-S
Phentermine	1640	N	Ionamin, Fastin, Adipex-P, Obe-Nix, Zantryl
Pinazepam	2883	N	Domar
Pipradrol	1750	N	Detaril, Stimolag Fortis
Prazepam	2764	N	Centrax
Quazepam	2881	N	Doral, Dormalin
Sibutramine	1675	N	Meridia
SPA	1635	N	1-Dimethylamino-1,2-diphenylethane, Lefetamine
Temazepam	2925	N	Restoril
Tetrazepam	2886	N	
Triazolam	2887	N	Halcion
Zaleplon	2781	N	Sonata
Zolpidem	2783	N	Ambien, Stilnoct, Ivadal
Schedule V			
Codeine preparations 200 mg/100 ml or 100 gm			Cosanyl, Robitussin A-C, Cheracol, Cerose, Pediacof
Difenoxin preparations 0.5 mg/25 ml			Motofen ug AtSO4/du
Dihydrocodeine preparations 10 mg/100 ml or 100 gm			Cophene-S, various others
Diphenoxylate preparations 2.5 mg/25 ug AtSO4			Lomotil, Logen
Ethylmorphine preparations 100 mg/100 ml or 100 gm			
Opium preparations 100 mg/100 ml or gm			Parepectolin, Kapectolin PG, Kaolin Pectin P.G.
Pyrovalerone	1485	N	Centroton, Thymergix

Appendix II
Gangs Highlighted by the National
Drug Intelligence Center[1]

STREET GANGS

18ᵗʰ Street (National)

Formed in Los Angeles, 18ᵗʰ Street is a group of loosely associated sets or cliques, each led by an influential member. Membership is estimated at 30,000 to 50,000. In California approximately 80 percent of the gang's members are illegal aliens from Mexico and Central America. The gang is active in 44 cities in 20 states. Its main source of income is street-level distribution of cocaine and marijuana and, to a lesser extent, heroin and methamphetamine. Gang members also commit assault, auto theft, carjacking, drive-by shootings, extortion, homicide, identification fraud, and robbery.

Almighty Latin King and Queen Nation (National)

The Latin Kings street gang was formed in Chicago in the 1960s and consisted predominantly of Mexican and Puerto Rican males. Originally created with the philosophy of overcoming racial prejudice and creating an organization of "Kings," the Latin Kings evolved into a criminal enterprise operating throughout the United States under two umbrella factions: Motherland, also known as KMC (King Motherland Chicago), and Bloodline (New York). All members of the gang refer to themselves as Latin Kings, and currently, individuals of any nationality are allowed to become members. Latin Kings associating with the Motherland faction also identify themselves as Almighty Latin King Nation (ALKN) and make up more than 160 structured chapters operating in 158 cities in 31 states. The membership of Latin Kings following KMC is estimated to be 20,000 to 35,000.

---

[1] Source: *National Gang Threat Assessment, 2009.*

The Bloodline was founded by Luis Felipe in the New York State correctional system in 1986. Latin Kings associating with Bloodline also identify themselves as the Almighty Latin King and Queen Nation (ALKQN). Membership is estimated to be 2,200 to 7,500, divided among several dozen chapters operating in 15 cities in five states. Bloodline Latin Kings share a common culture and structure with KMC and respect them as the Motherland, but all chapters do not report to the Chicago leadership hierarchy. The gang's primary source of income is the street-level distribution of powder cocaine, crack cocaine, heroin, and marijuana. Latin Kings continue to portray themselves as a community organization while engaging in a wide variety of criminal activities, including assault, burglary, homicide, identity theft, and money laundering.

Asian Boyz (National)

Asian Boyz is one of the largest Asian street gangs operating in the United States. Formed in southern California in the early 1970s, the gang is estimated to have 1,300 to 2,000 members operating in at least 28 cities in 14 states. Members primarily are Vietnamese or Cambodian males. Members of Asian Boyz are involved in producing, transporting, and distributing methamphetamine as well as distributing MDMA and marijuana. In addition, gang members are involved in other criminal activities, including assault, burglary, drive-by shootings, and homicide.

Black P. Stone Nation (National)

Black P. Stone Nation, one of the largest and most violent associations of street gangs in the United States, consists of seven highly structured street gangs with a single leader and a common culture. It has an estimated 6,000 to 8,000 members, most of whom are African American males from the Chicago metropolitan area. The gang's main source of income is the street-level distribution of cocaine, heroin, marijuana and, to a lesser extent, methamphetamine. Members also are involved in many other types of criminal activity, including assault, auto theft, burglary, carjacking, drive-by shootings, extortion, homicide, and robbery.

Bloods (National)

Bloods is an association of structured and unstructured gangs that have adopted a single-gang culture. The original Bloods were formed in the early 1970s to provide protection from the Crips street gang in Los Angeles. Large, national-level Bloods gangs include Bounty Hunter Bloods and Crenshaw Mafia Gangsters. Bloods membership is estimated to be 7,000 to 30,000 nationwide; most members are African American males. Bloods gangs are active in 123 cities in 33 states. The main source of income for Bloods gangs is street-level distribution of cocaine and marijuana. Bloods members also are involved in transporting and distributing methamphetamine, heroin, and PCP (phencyclidine), but to a much lesser extent. The gangs also are involved in other criminal activity, including assault, auto theft, burglary, carjacking, drive-by shootings, extortion, homicide, identity fraud, and robbery.

Crips (National)

Crips is a collection of structured and unstructured gangs that have adopted a common gang culture. Crips membership is estimated at 30,000 to 35,000; most members are African American males from the Los Angeles metropolitan area. Large, national-level Crips gangs include 107 Hoover Crips, Insane Gangster Crips, and Rolling 60s Crips. Crips gangs operate in 221 cities in 41 states. The main source of income for Crips gangs is the street-level distribution of powder cocaine, crack cocaine, marijuana, and PCP. The gangs also are involved in other criminal activity such as assault, auto theft, burglary, and homicide.

Florencia 13 (Regional)

Florencia 13 (F 13 or FX 13) originated in Los Angeles in the early 1960s; gang membership is estimated at more than 3,000 members. The gang operates primarily in California and increasingly in Arkansas, Missouri, New Mexico, and Utah. Florencia 13 is subordinate to the Mexican Mafia (La Eme) prison gang and claims Sureños (Sur 13) affiliation. A primary source of income for gang members is the trafficking of cocaine and methamphetamine. Gang members smuggle multikilogram quantities of powder cocaine and methamphetamine obtained from supply sources in Mexico into the United States for distribution. Also, gang members produce large quantities of methamphetamine in southern California for local distribution. Florencia members are involved in other criminal activities, including assault, drive-by shootings, and homicide.

Fresno Bulldogs (Regional)

Fresno Bulldogs is a street gang that originated in Fresno, California, in the late 1960s. Bulldogs is the largest Hispanic gang operating in central California, with membership estimated at 5,000 to 6,000. Bulldogs is one of the few Hispanic gangs in California that claim neither Sureños (Southern) nor Norteños (Northern) affiliation. However, gang members associate with Nuestra Familia (NF) members, particularly when trafficking drugs. The street-level distribution of methamphetamine, marijuana, and heroin is a primary source of income for gang members. In addition, members are involved in other criminal activity, including assault, burglary, homicide, and robbery.

Gangster Disciples (National)

The Gangster Disciples street gang was formed in Chicago in the mid-1960s. It is structured like a corporation and is led by a chairman of the board. Gang membership is estimated at 25,000 to 50,000; most members are African American males from the Chicago metropolitan area. The gang is active in 110 cities in 31 states. Its main source of income is the street-level distribution of cocaine, crack cocaine, marijuana, and heroin. The gang also is involved in other criminal activity, including assault, auto theft, firearms violations, fraud, homicide, the operation of prostitution rings, and money laundering.

Latin Disciples (Regional)

Latin Disciples, also known as Maniac Latin Disciples and Young Latino Organization, originated in Chicago in the late 1960s. The gang is composed of at least 10 structured and unstructured factions with an estimated 1,500 to 2,000 members and associate members. Most members are Puerto Rican males. Maniac Latin Disciples is the largest Hispanic gang in the Folk Nation Alliance. The gang is most active in the Great Lakes and southwestern regions of the United States. The street-level distribution of powder cocaine, heroin, marijuana, and PCP is a primary source of income for the gang. Members also are involved in other criminal activity, including assault, auto theft, carjacking, drive-by shootings, home invasion, homicide, money laundering, and weapons trafficking.

Mara Salvatrucha (National)

Mara Salvatrucha, also known as MS 13, is one of the largest Hispanic street gangs in the United States. Traditionally, the gang consisted of loosely affiliated groups known as *cliques*; however, law enforcement officials have reported increased coordination of criminal activity among Mara Salvatrucha cliques in the Atlanta, Dallas, Los Angeles, Washington, D.C., and New York metropolitan areas. The gang is estimated to have 30,000 to 50,000 members and associate members worldwide, 8,000 to 10,000 of whom reside in the United States. Members smuggle illicit drugs, primarily powder cocaine and marijuana, into the United States and transport and distribute the drugs throughout the country. Some members also are involved in alien smuggling, assault, drive-by shootings, homicide, identity theft, prostitution operations, robbery, and weapons trafficking.

Sureños and Norteños (National)

As individual Hispanic street gang members enter prison systems, they put aside former rivalries with other Hispanic street gangs and unite under the names Sureños or Norteños. The original Mexican Mafia members, most of whom were from southern California, considered Mexicans from the rural, agricultural areas of northern California weak and viewed them with contempt. To distinguish themselves from the agricultural workers or farmers from northern California, members of Mexican Mafia began to refer to the Hispanic gang members who worked for them as Sureños (Southerners). Inmates from northern California became known as Norteños (Northerners) and are affiliated with Nuestra Familia. Because of its size and strength, Fresno Bulldogs is the only Hispanic gang in the California Department of Corrections (CDC) that does not fall under Sureños or Norteños but remains independent.

Sureños gang members' main sources of income are retail-level distribution of cocaine, heroin, marijuana, and methamphetamine within prison systems and in the community as well as extortion of drug distributors on the streets. Some members have direct links to Mexican DTOs and broker deals for Mexican Mafia as well as their own gang. Sureños gangs also are involved in other criminal activities such as assault, carjacking, home invasion, homicide, and robbery. Norteños gang members' main sources of income are the retail-level distribution of cocaine, heroin, marijuana, methamphetamine, and PCP within prison systems and in the community as well as extortion of drug distributors on the streets. Norteños gangs also are involved in other criminal activities such as assault, carjacking, home invasion, homicide, and robbery.

Tango Blast (Regional)

Tango Blast is one of largest prison/street criminal gangs operating in Texas. Tango Blast's criminal activities include drug trafficking, extortion, kidnapping, sexual assault, and murder. In the late 1990s, Hispanic men incarcerated in federal, state, and local prisons founded Tango Blast for personal protection against violence from traditional prison gangs such as the Aryan Brotherhood, Texas Syndicate, and Texas Mexican Mafia. Tango Blast originally had four city-based chapters: Houstone, Houston; ATX or La Capricha, Austin; D-Town, Dallas; and Foros or Foritos, Fort Worth.

These founding four chapters are collectively known as Puro Tango Blast or the Four Horsemen. From the original four chapters, former Texas inmates established new chapters in El Paso, San Antonio, Corpus Christi, and the Rio Grande Valley. In June 2008 the Houston Police Department (HPD) estimated that more than 14,000 Tango Blast members were incarcerated in Texas. Tango Blast is difficult to monitor. The gang does not conform to either traditional prison/street gang hierarchical organization or gang rules. Tango Blast is laterally organized, and leaders are elected sporadically to represent the gang in prisons and to lead street gang cells. The significance of Tango Blast is exemplified by corrections officials reporting that rival traditional prison gangs are now forming alliances to defend themselves against Tango Blast's growing power.

Tiny Rascal Gangsters (National)

Tiny Rascal Gangsters is one of the largest and most violent Asian street gang associations in the United States. It is composed of at least 60 structured and unstructured gangs, commonly referred to as *sets*, with an estimated 5,000 to 10,000 members and associates who have adopted a common gang culture. Most members are Asian American males. The sets are most active in the southwestern, Pacific, and New England regions of the United States. The street-level distribution of powder cocaine, marijuana, MDMA, and methamphetamine is a primary source of income for the sets. Members also are involved in other criminal activity, including assault, drive-by shootings, extortion, home invasion, homicide, robbery, and theft.

United Blood Nation (Regional)

Bloods is a universal term that is used to identify both West Coast Bloods and United Blood Nation (UBN). These groups are traditionally distinct entities, but both identify themselves by "Blood," often making it hard for law enforcement to distinguish between them. UBN started in 1993 in Rikers Island GMDC (George Mochen Detention Center) to form protection from the threat posed by Latin Kings and Ñetas, who dominated the prison. UBN is a loose confederation of street gangs, or sets, that once were predominantly African American. Membership is estimated to be between 7,000 and 15,000 along the U.S. eastern corridor. UBN derives its income from street-level distribution of cocaine, heroin, and marijuana; robbery; auto theft; and smuggling drugs to prison inmates. UBN members also engage in arson, carjacking, credit card fraud, extortion, homicide, identity theft, intimidation, prostitution operations, and weapons distribution.

Vice Lord Nation (National)

Vice Lord Nation, based in Chicago, is a collection of structured gangs located in 74 cities in 28 states, primarily in the Great Lakes region. Led by a national board, the various gangs have an estimated 30,000 to 35,000 members, most of whom are African American males. The main source of income is street-level distribution of cocaine, heroin, and marijuana. Members also engage in other criminal activity such as assault, burglary, homicide, identity theft, and money laundering.

Prison Gangs

Aryan Brotherhood

Aryan Brotherhood, also known as AB, was originally ruled by consensus but is now highly structured with two factions, one in the CDC and the other in the Federal Bureau of Prisons (BOP). The majority of members are Caucasian males, and the gang is active primarily in the southwestern and Pacific regions of the United States. Its main source of income is the distribution of cocaine, heroin, marijuana, and methamphetamine within prison systems and on the streets. Some AB members have business relationships with Mexican DTOs that smuggle illegal drugs into California for AB distribution. AB is notoriously violent and is often involved in murder for hire. Although the gang has been historically linked to the California-based Hispanic prison gang Mexican Mafia (La Eme), tension between AB and La Eme is increasingly evident, as seen in recent fights between Caucasians and Hispanics within CDC.

Barrio Azteca

Barrio Azteca is one of the most violent prison gangs in the United States. The gang is highly structured and has an estimated membership of 2,000. Most members are Mexican national or Mexican American males. Barrio Azteca is most active in the southwestern region, primarily in federal, state, and local corrections facilities in Texas and outside prison in southwestern Texas and southeastern New Mexico. The gang's main source of income is derived from smuggling heroin, powder cocaine, and marijuana from Mexico into the United States for distribution both inside and outside prisons. Gang members often transport illicit drugs across the U.S.-Mexico border for DTOs. Barrio Azteca members also are involved in alien smuggling, arson, assault, auto theft, burglary, extortion, intimidation, kidnapping, robbery, and weapons violations.

Black Guerrilla Family

Black Guerrilla Family (BGF), originally called Black Family or Black Vanguard, is a prison gang founded in the San Quentin State Prison, California, in 1966. The gang is highly organized along paramilitary lines, with a supreme leader and central committee. BGF has an established national charter, code of ethics, and oath of allegiance. BGF members operate primarily in California and Maryland. The gang has 100 to 300 members, most of whom are African American males. A primary source of income for gang members comes from cocaine and marijuana distribution. BGF members obtain such drugs primarily from Nuestra Familia/Norteños members or from local Mexican traffickers. BGF members are involved in other criminal activities, including auto theft, burglary, drive-by shootings, and homicide.

Hermanos de Pistoleros Latinos

Hermanos de Pistoleros Latinos (HPL) is a Hispanic prison gang formed in the Texas Department of Criminal Justice (TDCJ) in the late 1980s. It operates in most prisons and on the streets in many communities in Texas, particularly Laredo. HPL is also active in several cities in Mexico, and its largest contingent in that country is in Nuevo Laredo. The gang is structured and is estimated to have 1,000 members. Members maintain close ties to several Mexican DTOs and are involved in trafficking quantities of cocaine and marijuana from Mexico into the United States for distribution.

Mexikanemi

The Mexikanemi prison gang (also known as Texas Mexican Mafia or Emi) was formed in the early 1980s within the TDCJ. The gang is highly structured and is estimated to have 2,000 members, most of whom are Mexican nationals or Mexican American males living in Texas at the time of incarceration. Mexikanemi poses a significant drug-trafficking threat to communities in the southwestern United States, particularly in Texas. Gang members reportedly traffic multikilogram quantities of powder cocaine, heroin, and methamphetamine; multiton quantities of marijuana; and thousand-tablet quantities of MDMA from Mexico into the United States for distribution inside and outside prison. Gang members obtain drugs from associates or members of the Jaime Herrera-Herrera, Osiel Cárdenas-Guillén, and/or Vicente Carrillo-Fuentes Mexican DTOs. In addition, Mexikanemi members maintain a relationship with Los Zetas, a Mexican paramilitary/criminal organization employed by the Cárdenas-Guillén DTO as its personal security force.

Mexican Mafia

The Mexican Mafia prison gang, also known as La Eme (Spanish for the letter *M*), was formed in the late 1950s within the CDC. It is loosely structured and has strict rules that must be followed by the 200 members. Most members are Mexican American males who previously belonged to a southern California street gang. Mexican Mafia is primarily active in the southwestern and Pacific regions of the United States, but its power base is in California. The gang's main source of income is extorting drug distributors outside prison and distributing methamphetamine, cocaine, heroin, and marijuana within prison systems and on the streets. Some members have direct links to Mexican DTOs and broker deals for themselves and their associates. Mexican Mafia also is involved in other criminal activities, including controlling gambling and homosexual prostitution in prison.

Ñeta

Ñeta is a prison gang that began in Puerto Rico and spread to the United States. Ñeta is one of the largest and most violent prison gangs, with about 7,000 members in Puerto Rico and 5,000 in the United States. Ñeta chapters in Puerto Rico exist exclusively inside prisons; once members are released from prison they are no longer considered part of the gang. In the United States, Ñeta chapters exist inside and outside prisons in 36 cities in nine states, primarily in the Northeast. The gang's main source of income is retail distribution of powder and crack cocaine, heroin, marijuana and, to a lesser extent, LSD, MDMA, methamphetamine, and PCP. Ñeta members commit assault, auto theft, burglary, drive-by shootings, extortion, home invasion, money laundering, robbery, weapons and explosives trafficking, and witness intimidation.

Outlaw Motorcycle Gangs

Bandidos

Bandidos Motorcycle Club, an OMG with 2,000 to 2,500 members in the United States and 13 other countries, is a growing criminal threat to the nation. Law enforcement authorities estimate that Bandidos is one of the two largest OMGs in the United States, with approximately 900 members belonging to more than 88 chapters in 16 states. Bandidos is involved in transporting and distributing cocaine and marijuana and producing, transporting, and distributing methamphetamine. Bandidos is most active in the Pacific, southeastern, southwestern, and west central regions and is expanding in these regions by forming new chapters and allowing members of support clubs to form or join Bandidos chapters. The members of support clubs are known as "puppet" or "duck" club members. They do the dirty work of the mother club.

Hells Angels

Hells Angels Motorcycle Club (HAMC) is an OMG with 2,000 to 2,500 members belonging to more than 250 chapters in the United States and 26 foreign countries. HAMC poses a criminal threat on six continents. U.S. law enforcement authorities estimate that HAMC has more than 69 chapters in 22 states with 900 to 950 members. HAMC produces, transports, and distributes marijuana and methamphetamine and transports and distributes cocaine, hashish, heroin, LSD (lysergic acid diethylamide), MDMA, PCP, and diverted pharmaceuticals. HAMC is involved in other criminal activity, including assault, extortion, homicide, money laundering, and motorcycle theft.

Mongols

Mongols Motorcycle Club is an extremely violent OMG that poses a serious criminal threat to the Pacific and southwestern regions of the United States. Mongols members transport and distribute cocaine, marijuana, and methamphetamine and frequently commit violent crimes, including assault, intimidation, and murder, to defend Mongols territory and uphold its reputation. Mongols has 70 chapters nationwide, with most of the club's 800 to 850 members residing in California. Many members are former street gang members with a long history of using violence to settle grievances. Agents with the ATF have called Mongols Motorcycle Club the most violent and dangerous OMG in the nation. In the 1980s, the Mongols OMG seized control of southern California from HAMC, and today Mongols club is allied with Bandidos, Outlaws, Sons of Silence, and Pagan's OMGs against HAMC. The Mongols club also maintains ties to Hispanic street gangs in Los Angeles.

Outlaws

Outlaws Motorcycle Club has more than 1,700 members belonging to 176 chapters in the United States and 12 foreign countries. U.S. law enforcement authorities estimate that Outlaws has more than 94 chapters in 22 states with more than 700 members. Outlaws also identifies itself as the American Outlaws Association (AOA) and Outlaws Nation. Outlaws is the dominant OMG in the Great Lakes region. Gang members produce, transport, and distribute methamphetamine and transport and distribute cocaine, marijuana and, to a lesser extent, MDMA. Outlaws members engage in various criminal activities, including arson, assault, explosives operations, extortion, fraud, homicide, intimidation, kidnapping, money laundering, prostitution operations, robbery, theft, and weapons violations. It competes with HAMC for membership and territory.

Sons of Silence

Sons of Silence Motorcycle Club (SOSMC) is one of the largest OMGs in the United States, with 250 to 275 members among 30 chapters in 12 states. The club also has five chapters in Germany. SOSMC members have been implicated in numerous criminal activities, including murder, assault, drug trafficking, intimidation, extortion, prostitution operations, money laundering, weapons trafficking, and motorcycle and motorcycle parts theft.

References

Abadinsky, H. (1989). *Drug Abuse: An Introduction*. Chicago: Nelson-Hall.

Abadinsky, H. (1990). *Organized Crime* (3rd ed.). Chicago: Nelson-Hall.

Abadinsky, H. (2007). *Organized Crime* (8th ed.). Belmont, CA: Thomson/Wadsworth.

Abt Associates. (2001). *The Price of Illicit Drugs: 1981 Through the Second Quarter of 2000*. Washington, DC: United Nations Office for Drug Control and Crime Prevention.

Adams, E. (1994). "ABA Urges Additional Funding for Drug Treatment." *New York Law Journal*, (February 4), 1.

Adamson, S. (1985). *Through the Gateway of the Heart: Accounts of Experiences with MDMA and Other Emphogenic Substances*. San Francisco: Four Trees.

Adamson, S., & Metzner, R. (1988). "The Nature of the MDMA Experience and Its Role in Healing, Psychotherapy and Spiritual Practice." *ReVision*, 10, 59–72.

Adlaf, E. M., Smart, R. G., & Canale, M. D. (1991). *Drug Use Among Ontario Adults, 1977–1991*. Toronto: Ontario Addiction Research Foundation.

Adler, P. A. (1985). *Wheeling and Dealing: An Ethnography of an Upper-Level Drug-Dealing and Smuggling Community*. New York: Columbia University Press.

Aggarwal S.K., Carter G.T., Sullivan MD, ZumBrunnen C., Morrill R., Mayer JD (2009). "Medicinal use of cannabis in the United States: historical perspectives, current trends, and future directions." *J Opioid Manag 5* (3): 153–68. http://students.washington.edu/sunila/JOM_5-3-03.pdf. Lay summary – SF Weekly (15 September 2009).

Albanese, J. (1996). *Organized Crime in America* (3rd ed.). Anderson: Cincinnati.

Albini, J. L. (1971). *The American Mafia: Genesis of a Legend*. New York: Appleton-Century-Crofts.

Alexander, S. (1988). *The Pizza Connection: Lawyers, Money, Drugs and Mafia*. New York: Weidenfeld and Nicolson.

Allen, H., & Kaiser, R. (1987). "The Age of Aquarius Grows Up." *The Columbia Daily Tribune*, (November 26), 16.

American Heart Association. (2007). *Cigarette Smoking Statistics*. Found at www.americanheart.org/presenter.jhtml?identifier=4559.

Anderson, J. (1989). "Narcs Risk Their Lives Daily to Battle Drug Scourge." *The Columbia Daily Tribune*, (May 23), 6.

Anderson, J., & Van Atta, D. (1988). "The Medellin Cartel/M-19 Gang." *The Washington Post*, (August 28), 87.

Anderson, K. (1982). *The Pocket Guide to Coffees and Teas*. New York: Putnam.

Apsler, R. (1994). "Is Drug Abuse Treatment Effective?" *The American Enterprise*, (March/April), 48.

Arlachhi, P. (1986). *Mafia Business: The Mafia and the Spirit of Capitalism*. London: Verso.

Ashley, R. (1975). *Cocaine: Its History, Use and Effects*. New York: St. Martin's Press.

Associated Press. (2010). "La Familia Cartel Targeted, Police Arrest More Than 300 Across U.S." October 22, 2009. Retrieved January 1. Found at www.streetgangs.com/news/102209_lafamiliacartel.

Association of the Bar of the City of New York. (1994). "A Wiser Course: Ending Drug Prohibition." *The Record*, (49), 5.

Atkins, N. (1994). "The Cost of Living Clean." *Rolling Stone*, (May 5), 41.

AVERT. (2010). *United States: Statistics by Transmission Route and Gender.* www.avert.org/usa-transmission-gender.htm.

Backer, T. E. (1987). *Planning for Workplace Drug Abuse Programs.* Washington, DC: National Institute on Drug Abuse.

Bagley, B. M. (1988). "Colombia and the War on Drugs." *Foreign Affairs,* 67(1), 70–92.

Bakalar, J. B., & Grinspoon, L. (1988). *Drug Control in a Free Society.* Cambridge, MA: Cambridge University Press.

Ball, J. C., Lange, W. R., Meyers, C. P., & Friedman, S. R. (1988). "Reducing the Risk of AIDS through Methadone Treatment." *Journal of Health and Social Behavior,* 29, 214–226.

Barrett, R. E. (1987). "Curing the Drug-Law Addiction: The Harmful Side Effects of Legal Prohibition." In R. Hamowy (Ed.), *Dealing with Drugs: Consequences of Government Control* (pp. 73–102). Lexington, MA: D. C. Heath.

Beaty, J., & Hornik, R. (1989). "A Torrent of Dirty Dollars." *Time,* (December 18), 56.

Beck, A. J., & Harrison, P. M. (2001). *Prisoners in 2000.* Washington, DC: U.S. Department of Justice.

Beckett, K. (1994). "Setting the Public Agenda: 'Street Crime' and Drug Use in American Politics." *Social Problems,* 41(3), 425–447.

Bellizzi, J. (1989). "On the Legalization of Drugs." *International Drug Report,* (January), 6.

Bell, R. (1987). "Toward a Drug-Free America." *Challenge Newsletter,* National Drug Policy Board (March).

Bennett, W. (1990). "A Plea to Legalize Drugs Is a Siren Call to Surrender." *Reader's Digest,* (March).

Birdsong, C. (1986). "Why Athletes Use Drugs." *American Pharmacy,* (26)11.

Blok, A. (1974). *The Mafia of a Sicilian Village, 1860–1960.* New York: Harper and Row.

Bonnie, R. J. (1980). *Marijuana Use and Criminal Sanctions.* Charlottesville, VA: Michie.

Bonnie, R. J., & Whitebread, C. H. II. (1980). "The Forbidden Fruit and the Tree of Knowledge: An Inquiry into the Legal History of American Marijuana Prohibition." *Virginia Law Review,* 56(October), 971–1203.

Booth, C. (1996). "Caribbean Blizzard." *Time,* (February 26), 46.

Bower, B. (1988). "Intoxicating Habits." *Science News,* (August 6), 88–89.

Boyle, J. D., & Pham, T. (1988). "The Indochinese Community: A Police Perspective." *Law and Order,* (September), 69–72.

Bradley, B. (1988). "Drug Suspicions Follow Officials in High Places." *The Christian Science Monitor,* (February 26), 17.

Brantley, A. C., & DiRosa, A. (1994). *Gangs: A National Perspective.* Washington, DC: U.S. Department of Justice.

Braun, M. (2006). *Congressional Testimony on "Counternarcotics Strategies in Latin America."* Washington, DC: Drug Enforcement Administration.

Brecher, E. M., & the Editors of *Consumer Reports.* (1972). *Licit and Illicit Drugs.* Boston: Little, Brown.

Brooke, J. (1994). "Grim View from Brazil's Coffee Fields." *The New York Times,* (June 19), D1–D3.

Bureau of Alcohol, Tobacco, and Firearms. (1988). *Jamaican Organized Crime.* Washington, DC: U.S. Government Printing Office.

Bureau of Justice Assistance. (1987). *Report on Drug Control.* Washington, DC: U.S. Department of Justice.

Bureau of Justice Statistics. (1983). *Prisoners and Drugs.* Washington, DC: U.S. Department of Justice.

Bureau of Justice Statistics. (1986). *Drug Use and Crime: State Prison Inmate Survey.* Washington, DC: U.S. Department of Justice.

Bureau of Justice Statistics. (1987). *Drug Use Forecasting.* Washington, DC: U.S. Department of Justice.

Bureau of Justice Statistics. (1987). *Report on Drug Control.* Washington, DC: U.S. Department of Justice.

Bureau of Justice Statistics. (1989). *BJS Data Report*. Washington, DC: U.S. Department of Justice.

Bureau of Justice Statistics. (1991). *Sourcebook of Criminal Justice Statistics*. Washington, DC: U.S. Department of Justice.

Bureau of Justice Statistics. (1992). *Drugs, Crime and the Justice System*. Washington, DC: U.S. Department of Justice.

Bureau of Justice Statistics. (1996). *Correctional Populations in the United States, 1994*. Washington, DC: U.S. Department of Justice.

Bureau of Justice Statistics. (1997). *Sourcebook of Criminal Justice Statistics 1996*. Washington, DC: U.S. Department of Justice.

Bureau of Justice Statistics. (2005). *Substance Dependence, Abuse, and Treatment of Jail Inmates, 2002*. Washington, DC: U.S. Government Printing Office.

Bureau of Justice Statistics. (2006). *Drug Use and Dependence, State and Federal Prisoners, 2004*. Washington, DC: U.S. Government Printing Office.

Bureau of Justice Statistics. (2009). *Indicators of School Crime and Safety*. Washington, DC: U.S. Department of Justice, Found at http://bjs.ojp.usdoj.gov/content/pub/pdf/iscs09.pdf.

Burton, F. (2007). "Mexico: The Price of Peace in the Cartel Wars." *The Stratfor Global Intelligence*. Found at www.stratfor.com/mexico_price_peace_cartel_wars. May 2. Retrieved 8-16-09.

Califano, J. A. (1997). "Legalization of Narcotics: Myths and Reality." *USA Today Magazine*, (March), 46–50.

Canadian Friends of Burma. (1996). Found at www.web.net/~cfob/index.html.

Carver, J. (1986). *Drugs and Crime: Controlling Use and Reducing Risk Through Testing*. Washington, DC: National Institute of Justice, U.S. Government Printing Office.

CASA. *See* National Center on Addiction and Substance Abuse.

CDC. *See* Centers for Disease Control and Prevention.

Centers for Disease Control and Prevention. (1992a). "The HIV/AIDs Epidemic: The First Ten Years." *Morbidity and Morality Weekly Report*, *40*(8), Supplement.

Centers for Disease Control and Prevention. (1992b). *Surveillance Report*. (November).

Centers for Disease Control and Prevention. (1996). *HIV and AIDS Trends—Progress in Prevention*. Hyattsville, MD: National Center for Disease Statistics.

Centers for Disease Control and Prevention. (2002). *Drug-Associated HIV Transmission Continues in the United States*. Washington, DC: U.S. Department of Health and Human Services.

Centers for Disease Control and Prevention. (2006). *Web-based Injury Statistics Query and Reporting System (WISQARS)*. Found at www.cdc.gov/ncipc/wisqars.

Centers for Disease Control and Prevention. (2007). *Quick Stats: Binge Drinking*. Found at www.cdc.gov/quickstats/binge_drinking.htm.

CFOB. *See* Canadian Friends of Burma.

Chaiken, J. M., & Chaiken, M. R. (1990). Drugs and Predatory Crime. In M. Tonry & J. Q. Wilson (Eds.), *Drugs and Crime* (Vol. 13), *Crime and Justice* (pp. 203–239). Chicago: University of Chicago Press.

Chambliss, W. J. (1971). "Vice, Corruption, Bureaucracy, and Power." *Wisconsin Law Review*, (Spring), 4.

Chavez, E. J. (2001). *Congressional Testimony on "The Role of the U.S./Mexico Border in the Drug Trade."* Washington, DC: Drug Enforcement Administration.

Chin, K. (1996). *Chinatown Gangs: Extortion, Enterprise, and Ethnicity*. New York: Oxford University Press.

Clines, F. (1993). "Dealing with Drug Dealers: Rehabilitation, Not Jail." *The New York Times*, (January 20), B2.

Cloud, J. (2000). "The Lure of Ecstasy." *Time*, (June 5).

Cloward, R. A., & Ohlin, L. E. (1960). *Delinquency and Opportunity*. New York: Free Press.

CNN. (2009). "Former Mexican Drug Czar Arrested on Corruption Charges." CNN.com (January 26, 2009). Found at www.cnn.com/2009/WORLD/americas/01/26/mexico.drug.czar/index.html.

Cockburn, L. (1987). *Out of Control: The Story of the Reagan Administration Secret War in Nicaragua, The Illegal Arms Pipeline, and the Contra Drug Connection*. New York: Entrekin/Atlantic Monthly Press.

Coffin, P. (1996). *Cocaine and Pregnancy: The Truth about Crack Babies*. New York: The Lindesmith Center.

Cohen, P. (1989). *Cocaine Use in Amsterdam in Nondeviant Subcultures*. Amsterdam: Institut voor Sociale Geografie, Universiteit van Amsterdam.

Cohen, S. (1997). "Meth Madness." *The Columbia Daily Tribune*, (March 9), D1.

Congressional Research Service. (2007). *Mexican Drug Cartels*. October 16. Washington, DC: U.S. Government Printing Office.

Corcoran, D. (1989). "Legalizing Drugs: Failures Spur Debate." *The New York Times*, (November 27), A15.

Correctional Association of New York. (1992). *Injustice Will Be Done: Women Drug Couriers and the Rockefeller Drug Laws*. New York: Correctional Association of New York.

Cressey, D. (1969). *Theft of the Nation*. New York: Harper and Row.

Davis, R. (1995). "'Meth' Use in the '90s: A Growing Epidemic." *USA Today*, (September 7), 7A.

DAWN. *See* Drug Abuse Warning Network.

DEA. *See* Drug Enforcement Administration.

del Carmen, R. V., & Walker, J. T. (2006). *Briefs of Leading Cases in Law Enforcement*. (6th ed.). Anderson: Cincinnati.

Della Cava, M. R. (1995). "Drug Czar: It Is Time to Sound the Alarm." *USA Today*, (February 15), Al.

DeStefano, A. (1985). "Balkan Connection: Brazen as the Mafia, Ethnic Albanian Thugs Specialize in Mayhem; Active in the Heroin Trade, The Faction Is So Violent, Prosecutors Need Guards." *The Wall Street Journal*, (September 9), 1.

Diagnostic and Statistical Manual of Mental Disorders (4th ed.). Washington, DC: American Psychiatric Press.

Ditton, J., Farrow, K., Forsyth, A., Hammersly, R., Hunter, G., Lavelle, T., et al. (1991). "Scottish Cocaine Users: Wealthy Snorters or Delinquent Smokers?" *Drug and Alcohol Dependence*, *28*, 269–276.

Downing, J. (1986). "The Psychological Physiological Effects of MDMA on Normal Volunteers." *Journal of Psychoactive Drugs*, *18*, 335–339.

Drug Abuse Warning Network. (2005). *National Estimates of Drug-Related Emergency Department Visits*. Rockville, MD: U.S. Department of Health and Human Services.

Drug Enforcement Administration. (1984). *Domestic Marijuana Trafficking. Special Intelligence Report*. Washington, DC: U.S. Department of Justice.

Drug Enforcement Administration. (1985). *Drug Enforcement Administration Booklet* (Summer). Washington, DC: U.S. Department of Justice.

Drug Enforcement Administration. (1992). *Drugs, Crime, and the Criminal Justice System*. Washington, DC: U.S. Department of Justice.

Drug Enforcement Administration. (1996). *Drugs of Abuse*. Washington DC: U.S. Department of Justice.

Drug Enforcement Administration. (2005). *Drugs of Abuse*. Washington DC: U.S. Department of Justice.

Drug Enforcement Administration. (2007a). *About DEA*. Found at www.dea.gov/job/agent/about.html.

Drug Enforcement Administration. (2007b). "Two Tijuana Cartel Figures Plead Guilty." April 27. Found at www.justice.gov/dea/pubs/states/newsrel/sd042707.html Accessed January 4, 2010.

Drug Enforcement Administration. (2008). "Maps of Methamphetamine Lab Incidents." Found at www.justice.gov/dea/concern/map_lab_seizures.html.

Drug Enforcement Administration. (2009a). *175 Alleged Gulf Cartel Members Arrested in Massive International Law Enforcement Operation*. September 17. Found at www.justice.gov/dea/pubs/pressrel/pr091708.html. Accessed January 8, 2010.

Drug Enforcement Administration. (2009b). *DEA Announces Gulf Cartel/Los Zetas Most-Wanted List*. July 23. Found at www.justice.gov/dea/pubs/states/newsrel/2009/dallas072309.html. Accessed January 8, 2010.

Drug Enforcement Administration. (2009c). *DEA Targets Southern California Violent Mexican Cartels in "Operation Xcellerator."* February 25. Found at www.justice.gov/dea/pubs/states/newsrel/2009/la022509a.html Accessed January 11, 2010.

Drug Enforcement Administration. (2009d). "Hundreds of Alleged Sinaloa Cartel Members and Associates Arrested in Nationwide Takedown of Mexican Drug Traffickers." February 25, Found in www.justice.gov/dea/pubs/states/newsrel/2009/la022509.html. Accessed January 10, 2010.

Drug Enforcement Administration. (2009e). *La Familia Michoacana Fact Sheet*. October. Found at www.justice.gov/dea/pubs/pressrel/pr102209a1.pdf.

Drug Enforcement Administration. (n.d.). "Domestic Cannabis Eradication/Suppression Program." Found at www.justice.gov/dea/programs/marijuana.htm.

Drug Policy Alliance. (2007). *Drugs, Police & the Law: Police Corruption*. Found at www.drugpolicy.org/law/police/.

Drug Use Forecasting Program. (1996). *Drug Use Among Arrestees, 1995*. Washington, DC: National Institute of Justice.

Drug Use Forecasting Program. (2000). *Annual Report: Arrestee Drug Abuse Monitoring*. Washington, DC: National Institute of Justice.

DSM-IV. *See* Diagnostic and Statistical Manual of Mental Disorders.

DUF Program. *See* Drug Use Forecasting Program.

Duster, T. (1970). *The Legislation of Morality: Law, Drugs, and Moral Judgment*. New York: Free Press,

Eaton, T. (1995). "Heavy Trafficking: Methamphetamine Trade in Mexico Alarms U.S." *Dallas Morning News*, (September 5), 1A+.

Ellingwood, K. (2008). "Former Anti-drug Chief Is Arrested." *Los Angeles Times*. (November 22, 2008).

El Nasser, H. (1996). "More Schools Test Kids for Drugs." *USA Today*, (September 5), Al.

Embassy of the United States, Mexico. (2007). *"Major Mexican Drug Trafficker's Assets in U.S. Frozen."* Press Release, May 17, 2007. Found at http://mexico.usembassy.gov/eng/releases/ep070517Zambada.html.

Engelberg, S. (1988). "Nicaraguan Rebels Tell of Drug Deal." *The New York Times*, (April 8), L6.

Epstein, E. J. (1977). *Agency of Fear: Opiates and Political Power in America*. New York: Putnam's.

Erickson, P., & Cheung, Y. (1992). "Drug Crime and Legal Control: Lessons from the Canadian Experience." *Contemporary Drug Problems*, *19*, 247–260.

Erickson, P. G. (1993). "Prospects of Harm Reduction for Psychostimulants." In N. Heather, A. Wodak, A. Nadelmann, & P. O'Hare (Eds.), *Psychoactive Drugs and Harm Reduction* (pp. 184–210). London: Whurr.

Erickson, P. G., & Alexander, B. K. (1989). "Cocaine and Addictive Liability." *Social Pharmacology*, *3*, 249–270.

Eskridge, C. (1998). "The Mexican Cartels: A Challenge for the 21st Century." *Criminal Organizations*, *12*, 1, 2.

Fagan, J. (1989). "The Social Organization of Drug Use and Drug Dealing Among Urban Gangs." *Criminology*, *27*(4), 633–667.

Fagan, J., & Chin, K. (1989). "Initiation into Crack and Cocaine: A Tale of Two Epidemics." *Contemporary Drug Problems*, *16*(4), 527–533.

Fagan, J., & Chin, K. (1991). "Social Processes of Initiation into Crack." *Journal of Drug Issues*, *21*(2), 313–344.

Fagan, J., & Spelman, W. (1994). "Market Forces at Work." *The New York Times*, (February 11), A34.

Falco, M. (1992). *The Making of a Drug-Free America: Programs That Work*. New York: Times Books.

Fedarko, K. (1993). "Escobar's Dead End." *Time*, (December 13), 46.

Fedarko, K. (1995). "Bad Neighbors." *Time*, (May 29), 78.

Federal Bureau of Investigation, Adlaf, E. M., Murray, G. E., & Smart, R. G. (1987). *The Steel Drug: Cocaine in Perspective*. Lexington, MA: Lexington Books.

Federal Bureau of Investigation. (1995). *Uniform Crime Reports*. Washington, DC: U.S. Department of Justice.

Federal Bureau of Investigation. (n.d.). "Italian Organized Crime—Overview." Found at www.fbi .gov/hq/cid/orgcrime/lcnindex.htm#overview.

Federal Government Information Technology. (1985). *Electronic Surveillance and Civil Liberties*. Washington, DC: Office of Technology Assessment, Congress of the United States.

Fields, G. (1997b). "Drug Labs Leave Dangerous Residue." *USA Today*, (May 2), 3A.

Filippone, R. (1994). "The Medellin Cartel: Why We Can't Win the Drug War." *Journal of Studies in Conflict and Terrorism*, *17*, 323–344.

Fogarty, K. (1986). "Parents Who Use Drugs." *The Columbia Missourian*, (October 26), C1.

Fong, R. S., & Vogel, R. E. (1995). "A Comparative Analysis of Prison Gang Members, Security Threat Group Inmates, and General Population Prisoners in the Texas Department of Corrections." *The Journal of Gang Research*, *2*(2), 1–12.

Food and Drug Administration (2006). "Inter-Agency Advisory Regarding Claims That Smoked Marijuana Is a Medicine." News Release, April 20. Found in: http://www.fda.gov/ NewsEvents/Newsroom/PressAnnouncements/2006/ucm108643.htm

Frankel, B. (1993). "Ex-NYC Officer Tells Stark Tale of Cops Gone Bad." *USA Today*, (September 28), 3A.

Frankel, G. (1997). "Federal Agencies Duplicate Efforts, Wage Costly Turf Battles." *The Washington Post*, (June 8), A1.

Friend, T. (1996a). "Prescription Misuse Costs Nation Billions." *USA Today*, (August 7), 2B.

Friend, T. (1996b). "Colombia Now Source of Heroin." *USA Today*, (September 4), 1A.

Friend, T. (1997). "Report Shows that More Preteens are Trying Drugs." *USA Today*, (March 5), 1A.

Galeotti, M. (1998). "Turkish Organized Crime: Where State, Crime and Rebellion Conspire." *Transnational Organized Crime*, *4*(1), 25–41.

GAO. *See* U.S. General Accounting Office.

Gardiner, J. A. (1970). *The Politics of Corruption: Organized Crime in an American City*. New York: Russell Sage Foundation.

Gay, B. W., & Marquart, J. W. (1993). "Jamaican Posses: A New Form of Organized Crime." *Journal of Crime and Justice*, *26*(2), 139–170.

Gilbert, R. (1984). "Caffeine Labeling." *Journal of the American Medical Association*, *26*(August 10), 565.

Goldstein, H. (1975). *Police Corruption: A Perspective on its Nature and Control*. Washington, DC: Police Foundation.

Goldstein, P. (1985). "The Drugs/Violence Nexus: A Tripartite Conceptual Framework." *Journal of Drug Issues*, *15*(Fall), 493–506.

Goode, E. (1972). *Drugs in American Society*. New York: Knopf.

Goode, E. (1993a). *Drugs in American Society* (4th ed.). New York: McGraw-Hill.

Goode, E. (1993b). *Drugs, Society and Behavior*. Guilford, CT: Dushkin.

Grayson, G. W. (2009). "*La Familia: Another Deadly Mexican Syndicate*." Foreign Policy Research Institute. February. Archived from the original on 2009-09-15. Found at www.webcitation .org/5joR97DuX.

Greenfield, L., & Harper, S. (1991). *Women in Prison*. Washington, DC: U.S. Bureau of Justice Statistics.

Greenhouse, L. (1989). "High Court Backs Airport Detention Based on 'Profile." *The New York Times*, (April 4), A1.

Greenhouse, L. (2002). "Justices Rule Drug-Eviction Law Is Fair." *The New York Times*, (March 27), Found at www.nytimes.com/2002/03/27/us/justices-rule-drug-eviction-law-is-fair .html?pagewanted=1?pagewanted=1.

Greer, G., & Tolbert, R. (1986). "Subjective Reports of the Effects of MDMA in a Clinical Setting." *Journal of Psychoactive Drugs*, *18*, 319–327.

Grimes, C. (1990). "Details Given on Noriega's Surrender." *St. Louis Post-Dispatch*, (January 5), A14.

Grinspoon, L. (1987). "Cancer Patients Should Get Marijuana." *The New York Times*, (July 18), 23.

Grinspoon, L., & Bakalar, J. (1985). *Cocaine: A Drug and Its Social Evolution*. New York: Basic Books.

Grinspoon, L., & Bakalar, J. (1986). "Can Drugs Be Used to Enhance the Psychotherapeutic Process?" *American Journal of Psychotherapy*, *40*, 393–404.

Grinspoon, L., & Laszlo, J. (1988). "Should Cancer Patients Smoke Marijuana to Limit Nausea?" *Physicians Weekly*, (June).

Grob, C. (2000). "Deconstructing Ecstasy." *Addiction Research*, *8*(6), 549–588.

Grob, C., & Poland, R. (1997). MDMA. In Lowinson, J. P. Ruiz, R. Millman, & J. Langrod (Eds.), *Substance Abuse: A Comprehensive Textbook* (3rd ed., pp. 269–275). Baltimore: Williams and Wilkins.

Gropper, B. (1985). *Probing the Links Between Drugs and Crime*. Washington, DC: National Institute of Justice, U.S. Government Printing Office.

Grotenhermen, F. (2002). "Review of Therapeutic Effects." Cannabis and Cannabinoids: Pharmacology, Toxicology and Therapeutic Potential. New York City: Haworth Press. p. 124. ISBN 978-0-7890-1508-2. http://books.google.com/books?id=JvIyVk2IL_sC&pg=PA123.

Gugliotta, G., & Leen, J. (1989). *Kings of Cocaine*. New York: Simon and Schuster.

Guillen, E. M. (2000). *Congressional Testimony Before the House Subcommittee on Criminal Justice, Drug Policy, and Human Resources*. Washington, DC: Drug Enforcement Administration.

Guillen, E. M. (2000). *Statement by Edward M. Guillen, Chief of Financial Operations, Drug Enforcement Administration, before the House Subcommittee on Criminal Justice, Drug Policy, and Human Resources. Congressional Testimony* (June 23, 2000).

Gunst, L. (1995). *Born Fi' Dead: A Journey Through the Jamaican Posse Underworld*. New York: Holt.

Gusfield, J. R. (1963). *Symbolic Crusade: Status Politics and the American Temperance Movement*. Urbana: University of Illinois Press.

Haller, M. H. (1989). "Bootlegging: The Business and Politics of Violence" In T. R. Garr (Ed.), *Violence in America* (pp. 146–152). Newbury Park, CA: Sage.

Harvey, M. (2009). California dreaming of full marijuana legislation. The San Francisco Sunday Times, September 28, p. 1.

Hayslip, D. W., Jr. (1989). *Local-Level Drug Enforcement: New Strategies*. Washington, DC: National Institute of Justice.

Hellmich, N. (1997). "Diet Drug Risks Are a Balancing Act." *USA Today*, (July 10), 1A.

Helmer, J. (1975). *Drugs and Minority Oppression*. New York: Seabury Press.

Henningfield, J. E. (1989). *Insight Magazine*, (May 9), 53.

Heron, M. P., Hoyert, D. L., Murphy, S. L., Xu, J. Q., Kochanek, K. D., & Tejada-Vera, B. (2009). "*Deaths: Final Data for 2006. National Vital Statistics Reports*" (Vol. 57, No. 14). Hyattsville, MD: National Center for Health Statistics.

Hess, H. (1973). *Mafia and Mafioso: The Structure of Power*. Lexington, MA: D. C. Heath.

Huang, F., & Vaughn, M. (1992). "A Descriptive Analysis of Japanese Organized Crime: The Boryokudan from 1945 to 1988." *International Criminal Justice Review*, *2*, 19–57.

Hubbard, R., Marsden, M., Rachal, J., Harwood, H., Cavanaugh, E., & Ginzburg, H. (1989). *Drug Abuse Treatment: A National Survey of Effectiveness*. Washington, D.C.: National Institute on Drug Abuse.

Hunt, T. (1997). "U.S., Mexico Agree on Drug Policy." *Associated Press*, (May 7).

Hutchinson, A. (2002). *Congressional Testimony Before the Senate Judiciary Committee, Subcommittee on Technology, Terrorism, and Government Information*. Washington, DC: Drug Enforcement Administration.

Hyman, T. (1986). "The World of Smoking and Tobacco." *Journal of the American Medical Association*, (February 28).

Ianni, E. (1972). *A Family Business: Kinship and Social Control in Organized Crime*. New York: Russell Sage Foundation.

Ianni, E. (1974). *Black Mafia: Ethnic Succession in Organized Crime*. New York: Simon and Schuster.

Inciardi, J. A. (1986). *The War on Drugs: Heroin, Cocaine, Crime and Public Policy*. Palo Alto, CA: Mayfield.

Inciardi, J. A. (1992). *The War on Drugs II*. Mountain View, CA: Mayfield.

Innes, C. A. (1986). *Drug Use and Crime*. Washington, DC: Bureau of Justice Statistics.

International Association for the Study of Organized Crime. (1989). *Criminal Organizations*, *4*(2).

Isikoff, M. (1988). "'Zero Tolerance' Held in Low Regard." *The Washington Post*, (July 13), A18.

Jackall, R. (1997). *Wild Cowboys: Urban Marauders and the Forces of Order*. Cambridge, MA: Harvard University Press.

Jacobson v. United States, 503 U.S. 540 (1992).

Janice, J. (1999). "Jamaican Posses and Transnational Crimes." *Journal of Gang Research*, *6*, 41–47.

Jaschik, S. (1990). "Scholars Are Irked by Bennett Speech Criticizing Their Approaches to Nation's Drug Problems." *Chronicle of Higher Education*, (January 3), 1.

Johanson, C. E., & Fischman, M. W. (1989). "The Pharmacology of Cocaine Related to its Abuse." *Pharmacological Reviews*, *41*, 3–52.

Johnson, B. D., et al. (1985). *Taking Care of Business: The Economics of Crime by Heroin Abusers*. Lexington, MA: Lexington Books.

Johnson, K. (1998). "44 Law Officers Arrested in Sting, Cleveland-Area FBI Raids Hit Five Agencies." *USA Today*, (January 22), A3.

Johnson, K. (2010). "Violent Surge Doesn't Cross Border: Patrols Push Down Rate of Drug Killings." *USA Today, Mexican-Caribbean Edition*, (January 2–3), 3A.

Johnson, L. D. (1997). *Preliminary Results on Illicit Drug and Alcohol Use from Monitoring the Future 1997*. Ann Arbor: University of Michigan.

Johnson, T. (2009). "China Urges Burma to Bridle Ethnic Militia Uprising at Border." *The Washington Post*, August 29, 2009. Found at www.washingtonpost.com/wp-dyn/content/article/2009/08/28/AR2009082803764.html.

Johnston, L. D., O'Malley, P. M., & Bachman, J. G. (2000). *Results of Monitoring the Future Study*. Ann Arbor: University of Michigan.

Johnston, L. D., O'Malley, P. M., & Bachman, J. G. (2001). *Monitoring the Future: National Results on Adolescent Drug Use: Overview of Key Findings*. Washington, DC: U.S. Department of Health and Human Services.

Johnston, M. (1982). *Political Corruption and Public Policy in America*. Monterey, CA: Brooks/Cole.

Jones, H. B. (1985). *What the Practicing Physician Should Know About Marijuana. Narcotic Educational Foundation of America*. Washington, DC: U.S. Department of Justice/Drug Enforcement Administration.

Joseph, J. (1999). "Jamaican Posses and Transnational Crimes." *Journal of Gang Research*, *6*, 41–47.

Joy, J. E., S. J. Watson, Jr., & J. A. Benson, Jr., editors; Division of Neuroscience and Behavioral Health, Institute of Medicine (1999). Benson, John; Joy, Janet E.; Watson, Stanley J. ed. Marijuana and medicine: assessing the science base. Washington, D.C: National Academy Press.

Kakesako, G. K. (2004). "Pearl Ship Makes Huge Drug Bust." *Honolulu Star-Bulletin*, (September 28). Found at www.starbulletin.com/2004/09/28/news/story7.html.

Kalb, C. (2001). "Playing with Pain Killers." *Newsweek*, (April 9), 45–51.

Kantrowitz, B., & Gonzalez, D. L. (1990). "Still Shocking After a Year." *Newsweek*, (July 29), 48–49.

Kant, S. (1989). "Addicts Drawn to Life of Crime to Support Drug Habits." *The Kansas City Star*, (February 5), A14.

Kappeler, V., & Potter, G. (2000). *The Mythology of Crime and Criminal Justice* (4th ed.). Prospect Heights, IL: Waveland.

Karchmer, C. L. (1989). *Illegal Money Laundering: A Strategy and Resource Guide for Law Enforcement Agencies*. Washington, DC: Police Executive Research Forum.

Karchmer, C. L., & Ruch, D. (1992). *State and Local Money Laundering Control Strategies*. Washington, DC: National Institute of Justice.

Katel, P. (1998). "Elderly Caught in Drug Evictions." *USA Today*, (April 9), 3A.

Kazman, S. (1991). "The FDA's Deadly Approval Process." *Consumer's Research*, (April), 31–36.

Kelly, J. (2001). "U.S. Takes on War-Hardened Taliban it Helped Create." *USA Today*, (September 21–23), A1.

Kenney, D., & Finckenauer, J. (1995). *Organized Crime in America*. Belmont, CA: Wadsworth.

Ker v. Illinois. 119 U.S. 436 (1886).

Kleber, H. (1989). "Treatment of Drug Dependence: What Works." *International Review of Psychiatry, 1*, 81–100.

Kleiman, M. A. R. (1985). "Drug Enforcement and Organized Crime." In H. E. Alexander & G. Caiden (Eds.), *Politics and Economics of Organized Crime* (pp. 67–87). Lexington, MA: D. C. Heath.

Kleiman, M. A. R. (1992). *Against Excess: Drug Policy for Results*. New York: Basic Books.

Kleiman, M. A. R., & Smith, K. D. (1990). "State and Local Drug Enforcement: In Search of a Strategy." In M. Tonry & J. Q. Wilson (Eds.), *Drugs and Crime, Volume 13: Crime and Justice*. Chicago: The University of Chicago Press.

Klein, M. (1971). "Violence in American Juvenile Gangs." In D. Mulvihill & M. Tumin, with L. Curtis (Eds.), *Crimes of Violence* (Vol. 13). National Commission on the Causes and Prevention of Violence. Washington, DC: U.S. Government Printing Office.

Klein, M. (1991). "Youth Gangs." *Congressional Quarterly*, (October 11), 755.

Kline, H. (1995). *Colombia: Democracy Under Assault*. Boulder, CO: Westview.

Knapp, W. (1972). *Commission Report: New York Commission to Investigate Allegations of Police Corruption and the City's Anti-Corruption Procedures* (September 15).

Kramer, M. (1993). "Clinton's Drug Policy is a Bust." *Time*, (December 20), 35.

Kraska, P., & Kappeler, V. (1988). "Police On-Duty Drug Use: A Theoretical and Descriptive Examination." *American Journal of Police*, 7(1), 1–28.

Krogh, D. (1992). "Smoking: Why Is It So Hard to Quit?" *Priorities*, (Spring), 29–31.

Lamar, J. (1988). "Kids Who Sell Crack." *Time*, (May 13), 20.

Leinwood, D. (2001a). "Studies Show Ecstasy Can Damage Brain." *USA Today*, (July 20), 3A.

Leinwood, D. (2001b). "Panel Examines Ecstasy's Lows." *USA Today*, (July 31), 3A.

Lender, M. E., & Martin, J. K. (1987). *Drinking in America: A History*. New York: Free Press.

Letwin, M. (1994). "Sentencing Angela Thompson." *New York Law Journal*, (April 18), 2.

Levine, H. G., & Reinarman, C. (1992). "From Prohibition to Regulation: Lessons from Alcohol Policy for Drug Policy." *The Milbank Quarterly*, 69(3), 1–34.

Levine, J. (1997). "FDA Panel Recommends Approval of Thalidomide." CNN Interactive. Found at www.cnn.com/HEALTH/9709/05/nfm.thalidomide.vote/.

Levins, H. (1980). "The Kabul Connection." *Philadelphia* (August), pp. 114–120, 192–203.

Levinthal, C. F. (1996). *Drugs, Behavior and Modern Society*. Boston: Allyn & Bacon.

Levy, D. (1994). "46 Million Smoke: 70% Want to Quit." *USA Today*, (December 23), 1A.

Liester, M., Grob, C., Bravo, G., & Walsh, R. (1992). "Phenomenology and Sequelae of 3, 4-Methylene-dioxymethamphetamine Use." *Journal of Nervous and Mental Disease, 180*, 343–352.

Lintner, B. (1996). "Narcopolitics in Burma." *Current History, 95, 602*(December), 432–437.

Los Angeles County Sheriff's Department. (1991). *Gang Enforcement Manual*. Los Angeles: Los Angeles County Sheriff's Department.

Luntz Research. (1996). *National Survey on American Attitudes on Substance Abuse II, Teens and Their Parents*. New York: Center on Addiction and Substance Abuse.

Lyman, M. (1987). *Narcotics and Crime Control*. Springfield, IL: Charles C Thomas.

Lyman, M. (1989a). *Gangland: Drug Trafficking by Organized Criminals*. Springfield, IL: Charles C Thomas,

Lyman, M. (1989b). *Practical Drug Enforcement: Procedure and Administration*. New York: Elsevier.

Lyman, M., & Potter, G. (1995). *Organized Crime*. Englewood Cliffs, NJ: Prentice Hall.

Macko, S. (1997). "Today's Mexican Drug Cartels." *ERRI Daily Intelligence Report—ERRI Risk Assessment Services*, *3*, 338 (December 4).

Manning, A. (1997). "Patients' Pleas Yield Rash on Unneeded Prescriptions." *USA Today*, (September 28), D1.

Manning, P. K., & Redlinger, L. J. (2006). "Invitational Edges of Corruption: Some Consequences of Narcotic Law Enforcement." In P. E. Rock (Ed.), *Drugs and Politics* (p. 279). New Brunswick, NJ: Transaction.

Marriott, M. (1989). "Drug Needle Exchange Is Gaining But Still Under Fire." *The New York Times*, (June 7), B1.

Marshall, J. (1987). "Drugs and United States Foreign Policy." In R. Hamowy (Ed.), *Dealing with Drugs: Consequences of Government Control*. Lexington, MA: D. C. Heath.

Marx, G. (1988). *Undercover Police Surveillance in America*. Berkeley: University of California Press.

Massing, M. (1990). "U.S. on Full Drug-War Footing." *The Kansas City Star*, (January 28), G3.

Mastrofski, S., & Potter, G. (1987). "Controlling Organized Crime: A Critique of Law Enforcement Policy." *Criminal Justice Policy Review*, *2*(3), 269–301.

Mauer, M., Huling, T. (1995). *Young Black Americans and the Criminal Justice System: Five Years Later*. Washington, DC: The Sentencing Project.

McCoy, A. W. (1972). *The Politics of Heroin in Southeast Asia*. New York: Harper and Row.

McGarrell, E. F., & Flanagan, T. (1986). *Sourcebook of Criminal Justice Statistics*. Washington, DC: Bureau of Justice Statistics.

McGinnis, J. M., & Foege, W. H. (1993). "Actual Causes of Death in the United States." *Journal of the American Medical Association*, *170*(18), 2207–2212.

Merton, R. K. (1938). "Social Structure and Anomie." *American Sociological Review*, *3*, 672–682.

Merton, R. K. (1967). *On Theoretical Sociology: Five Essays Old and New*. New York: The Free Press.

Mieczkowski, T. (1986). "Geeking Up and Throwing Down: Heroin Street Life in Detroit." *Criminology*, *24*, (November), 645–666.

Milford, J. S. (1997). *Congressional Testimony on "Anti-Narcotics Cooperation with the Government of Mexico."* Washington, DC: Drug Enforcement Administration.

Miller, N. (1988). *Toward a Drug-Free America*. Washington, DC: The National Drug Policy Board, U.S. Government Printing Office.

Mills, J. (1986). *The Underground Empire*. New York: Dell.

Mintz, J., & Churchville, V. (1987). "Vice Officers Walk the Line Between Crime and the Law in Drug World Integrity Easily Eroded." *The Washington Post*, (February 11).

Mirkin, G., & Hoffman, M. (1978). "Drugs: Is the Prize Worth the Price?" In *The Sportsmedicine Book*. Canada: Little, Brown.

Mishan, E. (1990). "Narcotics: The Problem and the Solution." *Political Quarterly*, *61*, 441–458.

Mitchell, D. (2008). "Legitimizing Marijuana." The New York Times. May 31. Found in http://www.nytimes.com/2008/05/31/technology/31online.html. Retrieved August 10, 2010.

Moody, J. (1989). "Noble Battle, Terrible Toll." *Time*, (December 18), 33.

Moore, M. H. (1990). "Supply Reduction and Drug Law Enforcement." In M. Tonry & J. Q. Wilson (Eds.), *Drugs and Crime, Volume 13: Crime and Justice* (pp. 109–157). Chicago: The University of Chicago Press.

Moore, M. T. (1997). "Binge Drinking Stalks Campuses." *USA Today*, (September 23), 3A.

More, H. W. (1998). *Special Topics in Policing* (2nd ed.). Cincinnati: Anderson.

Morgan, J. P. (1991). "Prohibition is Perverse Policy: What Was True in 1933 Is True Now." In K. Melvin & E. Lazear (Eds.), *Searching for Alternatives: Drug Control Policy in the United States* (pp. 405–423). Stanford, CA: Hoover Institution Press.

Mugford, S., Cohen, P. (1989). *Drug Use, Social Relations and Commodity Consumption: A Study of Recreational Users in Sydney, Canberra and Melbourne*. Canberra, Australia: Research Into Drug Abuse Advisory Committee, National Campaign Against Drug Abusers.

Musto, D. (1973). *The American Disease: Origins of Narcotic Control.* New Haven: Yale University Press.

Musto, D. (1991). "Opium, Cocaine, and Marijuana in American History." *Scientific American,* (July), 40–47.

Nadelmann, E. A. (1988). "U.S. Drug Policy: A Bad Export." *Foreign Policy, 70*(Spring), 83–108.

Nadelmann, E. A. (1989). "Drug Prohibition in the United States: Cost, Consequences, and Alternatives." *Science, 245*(September 1), 939–947.

Narcotics Anonymous. (1987). *Narcotics Anonymous* (4th ed.). Van Nuys, CA: World Service Office.

NASADAD. *See* National Association of State Alcohol and Drug Abuse Directors.

Nash, J. M. (1997). "Addiction: Why Do People Get Hooked?" *Time,* (May 5), 69–76.

National Association of State Alcohol and Drug Abuse Directors. (1990). *Treatment Works: The Tragic Cost of Undervaluing Treatment in the "Drug War."* Washington, DC: NASADAD.

National Center on Addiction and Substance Abuse. (2001). *Shoveling Up: The Impact of Substance Abuse on State Budgets.* New York: Columbia University.

National Criminal Justice Association Newsletter. Washington, DC: National Criminal Justice (January).

National Drug Intelligence Center. (2007). *Domestic Cannabis Cultivation Assessment 2007.* Washington, DC: U.S. Department of Justice.

National Drug Intelligence Center. (2008a). *National Drug Threat Assessment 2009.* December. Washington, DC: U.S. Department of Justice.

National Drug Intelligence Center. (2008b). *National-Level Gang-Drug Trafficking Organization Connections.* April. Washington, DC: U.S. Department of Justice.

National Drug Intelligence Center. (2008c). *National Methamphetamine Threat Assessment 2009.* December. Washington, DC: U.S. Department of Justice.

National Drug Intelligence Center. (2009a). *National Gang Threat Assessment 2009.* January. Washington, DC: U.S. Department of Justice.

National Drug Intelligence Center. (2009b). *National Prescription Drug Threat Assessment 2009.* April. Washington, DC: U.S. Drug Enforcement Administration; U.S. Department of Justice.

National Drug Intelligence Center. (2010). *Domestic Cannabis Cultivation Assessment 2009.* Washington, DC: U.S. Department of Justice.

National Drug Intelligence Center. (2010). *National Drug Threat Assessment 2010.* February. Washington, DC: U.S. Department of Justice.

National Drug Policy Board. (1988). *Toward a Drug-Free America.* Washington, DC: U.S. Government Printing Office.

National Gang Intelligence Center. (2009). *National Gang Threat Assessment, 2009.* Found at www.justice.gov/ndic/pubs32/32146/gangs.htm

National Institute of Justice. (1987a). *Drug Testing, Crime File Study Guide.* Washington, DC: National Institute of Justice.

National Institute of Justice . (1987b). *Issues and Practices: AIDS and the Law Enforcement Officer: Concerns and Policy Responses.* Washington, DC: U.S. Department of Justice, Office of Communication and Research Utilization.

National Institute of Justice. (1987c). *Issues and Practices: Arresting the Demand for Drugs: Police and School Partnerships to Prevent Drug Abuse.* Washington, DC: U.S. Government Printing Office.

National Institute of Justice. (1987d). *Major Issues in Organized Crime: A Compendium of Papers Presented by Experts in the Field.* Washington, DC: U.S. Government Printing Office.

National Institute of Justice. (1988). *Attorney General Announces NIJ Drug Use Forecasting System.* Washington, DC: U.S. Department of Justice, U.S. Government Printing Office.

National Institute of Justice. (1989). *Drug Trafficking: A Report to the President of the United States* (August 3).

National Institute of Justice. (1992). *State and Local Money Laundering Strategies. Research in Brief.* Washington, DC: U.S. Department of Justice.

National Institute on Drug Abuse. (1982). "Drug Taking Among the Elderly." In *Treatment Research Report.* Washington, DC: U.S. Department of Health and Human Services.

National Institute on Drug Abuse. (1983). "Women and Drugs." In *Research Issues 31.* Washington, DC: U.S. Department of Health and Human Services.

National Institute on Drug Abuse. (1985a). *National Household Survey on Drug Abuse: Main Findings 1984.* Washington, DC: U.S. Government Printing Office.

National Institute on Drug Abuse. (1985b). "Effects of Drugs on Driving, Driver Simulator Tests of Secobarbital, Diazepam, Marijuana, and Alcohol." In *Clinical and Behavioral Pharmacology Research Report.* Washington, DC: U.S. Department of Health and Human Services.

National Institute on Drug Abuse. (1985c). *Treatment Services for Adolescent Substance Abusers.* Washington, DC: U.S. Department of Health and Human Services.

National Institute on Drug Abuse. (1986a). *National Trends in Drug Use and Related Factors Among American High School Students and Young Adults, 1975-1986.* Washington, DC: U.S. Department of Health and Human Services.

National Institute on Drug Abuse. (1986b). *Urine Testing for Drugs of Abuse.* Research 73, Monograph Series. Washington, DC: U.S. Department of Health and Human Services.

National Institute on Drug Abuse. (1988). *National Household Survey on Drug Abuse: Main Findings 1987.* Washington, DC: U.S. Government Printing Office.

National Institute on Drug Abuse. (1990). *Research on Drugs and the Workplace: NIDA Capsule 24.* Rockville, MD: U.S. Department of Health and Human Services.

National Institute on Drug Abuse. (1991). *National Household Survey on Drug Abuse: Main Findings 1990.* Washington, DC: U.S. Government Printing Office.

National Institute on Drug Abuse. (1992). *Annual Emergency Room Data, 1991.* Data from Drug Abuse Warning Network, Series I, Number 10-B.

National Institute on Drug Abuse. (1996a). *Cigarette Smoking.* Washington, DC: U.S. Government Printing Office.

National Institute on Drug Abuse. (1996b). *Cocaine Abuse.* Washington, DC: U.S. Government Printing Office.

National Institute on Drug Abuse. (1996c). *1992–93 National Pregnancy and Health Survey: Drug Use Among Women Delivering Live Births.* Rockville, MD: U.S. Department of Health and Human Services.

National Institute on Drug Abuse. (1996d). *National Household Survey on Drug Abuse.* Rockville, MD: U.S. Department of Health and Human Services.

National Institute on Drug Abuse. (1997). *National Household Survey on Drug Abuse: Preliminary Results for 1996.* Rockville, MD: U.S. Department of Health and Human Services.

National Institute on Drug Abuse. (2006). *National Household Survey on Drug Abuse.* Rockville, MD: U.S. Department of Health and Human Services.

National Institute on Drug Abuse. (2007). *NIDAInfo Facts: Treatment Approaches for Drug Addiction.* Found at www.nida.nih.gov/infofacts/TreatMeth.html.

National Institute on Drug Abuse. (2009). *Monitoring the Future: National Results for Adolescent Drug Use – Overview of Key Findings 2008.* National Institutes of Health. U.S. Department of Health and Human Services.

National League of Cities, National School Boards Association, Joe DiMaggio Children's Hospital, and Youth Crime Watch. (1999). *Ten Critical Threats to America's Children: Warning Signs for the Next Millennium.* Alexandria, VA: The National League of Cities.

National Narcotics Intelligence Consumers Committee. (1996). *The NNICC Report 1995: The Supply of Illicit Drugs to the United States.* Washington, DC: U.S. Government Printing Office.

National Survey on Drug Use and Health: National Findings. Rockville, MD: Office of Applied Studies, U.S. Department of Health and Human Service. Found at www.oas.samhsa.gov/nsduh/2k8nsduh/2k8Results.cfm#1.1; accessed March 15, 2010.

National Youth Violence Prevention Resource Center. (2007). *Youth Gangs*. Found at www.safeyouth.org/scripts/teens/gangs.asp.

Nelli, H. (1976). *The Business of Crime: Italian and Syndicate Crime in the United States*. New York: Oxford University Press.

NHSDA. *See* National Household Survey on Drug Abuse.

O'Brien, R., & Cohen, S. (1984). *The Encyclopedia of Drug Abuse*. New York: Facts on File.

Office of National Drug Control Policy. (1989a). *The National Drug Control Strategy, Executive Summary*. Washington, DC: U.S. Government Printing Office.

Office of National Drug Control Policy. (1989b). *Pulse Report*. Washington, DC: U.S. Government Printing Office.

Office of National Drug Control Policy. (1994). *The National Drug Control Strategy, Executive Summary*. Washington, DC: U.S. Government Printing Office.

Office of National Drug Control Policy. (1995). *What America's Users Spend on Illegal Drugs 1988–1993*. Washington, DC: U.S. Government Printing Office (Spring).

Office of National Drug Control Policy. (1998). *The National Drug Control Strategy, 1998: A Ten-Year Plan*. Washington, DC: U.S. Government Printing Office.

Office of National Drug Control Policy. (2001). *The National Drug Control Strategy, 2001 Annual Report*. Washington, DC: U.S. Government Printing Office.

Office of National Drug Control Policy. (2002). *The President's National Drug Control Policy, February 2002*. Washington, DC: Executive Office of the President of the United States.

Office of National Drug Control Policy. (2006). *The President's National Drug Control Policy, February 2006*. Washington, DC: Executive Office of the President of the United States.

Office of National Drug Control Policy. (2007). *The President's Drug Control Strategy, February 2007*. Washington, DC: Executive Office of the President of the United States.

Office of National Drug Control Policy. (2009). *The President's National Drug Control Policy: 2009 Annual Report*. Washington, DC: Executive Office of the President of the United States.

Office of National Drug Control Policy. (2010a). *National Drug Control Strategy 2010*. U.S. Department of Justice. Washington, DC: Executive Office of the President of the United States.

Office of National Drug Control Policy. (2010b). "*Source Countries and Drug Transit Zones: Colombia*." Found at www.whitehousedrugpolicy.gov/international/colombia.html. Accessed, 5-21-10.

Office of Substance Abuse Policy. (1991). "Promoting Health Development Through School-Based Prevention: New Approaches, in U.S. Department of Health and Human Services." *Preventing Adolescent Drug Use: From Theory to Practice*, OSAP Prevention Monograph-8, DHHS Pub. No. (ADM) 91–1725.

Office of Technology Assessment. (1985). *Electronic Surveillance*. Washington, DC: United States Congress, U.S. Government Printing Office.

Office of Technology Assessment. (1987). *The Border Patrol and Interdiction*. Washington, DC: United States Congress, U.S. Government Printing Office.

Office of Technology Assessment. (1990). *Protecting the Borders*. Washington, DC: United States Congress, U.S. Government Printing Office.

Office on Smoking and Health, Preventing Tobacco Use Among Young People. (1994). *A Report of the Surgeon General*. Rockville, MD: Centers for Disease Control and Prevention, U.S. Department of Heath and Human Services.

ONDCP. *See* Office of National Drug Control Policy.

Orcutt, J., & Turner, J. B. (1993). "Shocking Numbers and Graphic Accounts: Quantified Images of Drug Problems in the Print Media." *Social Problems, 40*(2), 190–206.

Organized Crime Drug Enforcement Task Force. (1988). *Annual Report*. Washington, DC: U.S. Department of Justice.

Organized Crime Drug Enforcement Task Force. (1990). *Annual Report*. Washington, DC: U.S. Department of Justice.

Organized Crime Drug Enforcement Task Force. (1991). *Annual Report*. Washington, DC: U.S. Department of Justice.

OSAP. *See* Office of Substance Abuse Policy.

Ostrowski, J. (1989). "Thinking About Drugs Legalization." In *Policy Analysis* (Vol. 121). Washington, DC: Cato Institute.

Painter, K. (1996). "Heavy Marijuana Use May Impair Learning." *USA Today*, (August 8), 2A.

Painter, K. (1997). "Needle Exchanges in the Eye of AIDS Debate." *USA Today*, (September 18), 1D.

Parker, L. (2001). "States Heavy on Drug Cleanup, Not Prevention." *USA Today*, (January 30), 10D.

PCOC. *See* President's Commission on Organized Crime.

Pellerano, R., & Jorge, E. (1997). "Money-Laundering Rules in the Dominican Republic." *Banking Law Journal*, *114*(2), 136–141.

Pennsylvania Crime Commission. (1974). *Commission Report*. Harrisburg, PA: The Commonwealth of Pennsylvania.

Pennsylvania Crime Commission. (1980). *A Decade of Organized Crime 1980 Report*. St. Davids, PA: The Commonwealth of Pennsylvania.

Perkins, K., & Placido, A. (2010). "Drug Trafficking Violence In Mexico: Implications for U.S." Statement Before the U.S. Senate Caucus on International Narcotics Control. *Eurasia Review*, (May 5, 2010). Found at www.eurasiareview.com/drug-trafficking-violence-in-mexico-implications-for-us.html.

Permanent Subcommittee on Investigations, Committee on Governmental Affairs. (1983). *Crime and Secrecy: The Use of Offshore Banks and Companies*. Washington, DC: U.S. Senate, 98th Congress, First Session.

Pincomb, R. A., & Judiscak, D. L. (1997). "The Threat of Jamaican Posses to the United States in the 1990s." In G. L. Mays (Ed.), *Gangs and Gang Behavior* (p. 396). Chicago: Nelson-Hall.

Pinkerton, J. (2005). "Freed Captives in Mexico Say Police Abducted Them." *Houston Chronicle*, June 29.

Post, M. (1990). "Colombian Crime and Cocaine Trafficking." *The Narc Officer*, (December), 11.

Potter, G., Gaines, L., & Holbrook, B. (1990). "Blowing Smoke: An Evaluation of Marijuana Eradication in Kentucky." *American Journal of Police, IX*(1), 97–116.

Potter, G., & Jenkins, P. (1985). *The City and the Syndicate: Organizing Crime in Philadelphia*. Lexington, MA: Ginn Press.

President's Commission on Organized Crime. (1984a). *Organized Crime and Cocaine Trafficking*. Washington, DC: U.S. Government Printing Office.

President's Commission on Organized Crime. (1984b). *The Cash Connection: Organized Crime, Financial Institutions and Money Laundering*. Washington, DC: U.S. Government Printing Office.

President's Commission on Organized Crime. (1985). *Organized Crime and Heroin Trafficking*. Washington, DC: U.S. Government Printing Office.

President's Commission on Organized Crime. (1986a). *America's Habit: Drug Abuse, Drug Trafficking and Organized Crime*. Washington, DC: U.S. Government Printing Office.

President's Commission on Organized Crime. (1986b). *The Edge: Organized Crime, Business and Labor Unions*. Washington, DC: U.S. Government Printing Office.

President's Commission on Organized Crime. (1986c). *The Edge: Organized Crime Today*. Washington, DC: U.S. Government Printing Office.

President's Commission on Organized Crime. (1986d). *The Impact: Organized Crime Today*. Washington, DC: U.S. Government Printing Office.

ProCon.org. (2010). "Medical Marijuana." Found at http://medicalmarijuana.procon.org/.

Pryor, D. (1994). "Prescription Drug Industry Must Be Reformed." *USA Today*, (March), 74–75.

R. Hamowy (Ed.), (1987). *Dealing with Drugs: Consequences of Government Control*. Lexington, MA: D.C. Heath.

Raich v. Gonzales. 545 U.S. 1 (2005).

Rake, A. (1995). "Drugged to the Eyeballs." *New African*, (June), 16–19.

Rangel, C. (1986). *The Crack Cocaine Crisis*. Committee on Narcotics Abuse and Control, 99th Congress, Joint Hearing.

Rashid, A. (1995). "Nothing to Declare: The Political Void in Afghanistan has Spawned a Vast Smugglers' Market That Is Crippling Pakistan's Economy and Threatens Those of Other Nations in the Region." *Far Eastern Economic Review, 158*, 58–60.

Raspberry, W. (1988). "Living and Dying Like Animals." *The Washington Post*, (November 2), A21.

Ravin v. State. 537 P.2d 494 (1975).

Reinarmann, C., & Levine, H. (1989). "Crack in Context: Politics and Media in the Making of a Drug Scare." *Contemporary Drug Problems, 16*, 535–578.

Reinberg, S. (2009). 1 in 10 Ex-NFL Players used Steroids Poll reports. U. S. News and Word Report. Health Day. February 20. Found at http://health.usnews.com/health-news/family-health/pain/articles/2009/02/20/1-in-10-ex-nfl-players–used–steroids-poll-reports.html

Renard, R. (1996). *The Burmese Connection: Illegal Drugs and the Making of the Golden Triangle*. Boulder, CO: L. Rienner.

Reuter, P. (1983). *Disorganized Crime: The Economics of the Visible Hand*. Cambridge, MA: MIT Press.

Reuter, P., Crawford, G., & Cace, J. (1988). *Sealing the Borders: The Effects of Increased Military Participation in Drug Interdiction, R-3594-USDP*. Santa Monica, CA: RAND.

Reuter, P., MacCoun, R., & Murphy, P. (1990). *Money from Crime: A Study of the Economics of Drug Dealing in Washington, DC*. Santa Monica, CA: RAND (June).

Richey, W. (2009). "U.S. Strikes at Mexican Cartel's Drug-and-Gun Trade." *The Christian Science Monitor*, October 22.

Riding, A. (1988). "Intimidated Colombian Courts Yield to Drug Barons." *The New York Times*, (January 11), A3.

Riedlinger, T., Riedlinger, J. (1994). "Psychedelic and Entactogenic Drugs in the Treatment of Depression." *Journal of Psychoactive Drugs, 26*, 41–55.

Rinehart, R., Kaplan, I., Whitaker, D. P., Shinn, R. S., Nelson, H. D., & Bunge, F. M. (1981). *Thailand: A Country Study*. Washington, DC: U.S. Government Printing Office.

Robbins, C. A. (1989). "Bloody Footprints on Peru's Shining Path." *U.S. News & World Report*, (September 18), 49.

Robinson, J. (1999). *The Merger: How Organized Crime Is Taking Over Canada and the World*. Toronto: McClelland and Stewart.

Rorabaugh, W. J. (1991). "Alcohol in America." *OAH Magazine of History*, (Fall), 17–19.

Rosenau, W. (1994). "Is the Shining Path the 'New Khmer Rouge'?" *Journal of Studies on Conflict and Terrorism, 17*, 305–322.

Roth, J. (1994). *Understanding and Preventing Violence*. National Institute of Justice, Research in Brief, (February).

Rovner, J. (1992). "Prescription Drug Prices." *Congressional Quarterly*, (July), 599.

Rydell, C. P., & Everingham, S. E. (1994). *Controlling Cocaine: Supply Versus Demand Programs*. Santa Monica, CA: RAND.

SAMHSA. *See* Substance Abuse and Mental Health Services Administration.

Schaffer, E. (1996). "Mexico's Internal State Conflict Over the War on Drugs." *Criminal Organizations, 10*, 14–16.

Schmetzer, U. (1991). "The Chinese Connection." *The Chicago Tribune*, (May 12), D1.

Schmitt, E. (2009). Many Sources feed Taliban's War Chest. New York Times, October 18. Found in: http://www.nytimes.com/2009/10/19/world/asia/19taliban.html?_r=1&hp=&adxnnl=1&adxnnlx=1281434453-R/H5H6liJIBpB/OuLEm2Iw. Located August 10, 2010.

Schroeder, W. R. (2001). "Money Laundering: A Global Threat and the International Community's Response." *FBI Law Enforcement Bulletin*, (May), 1–8.

Scott, P. D., & Marshall, J. (1991). *Cocaine Politics*. Berkeley, CA: University of California Press.

Select Committee on Narcotics Abuse and Control. (1986). *The Crack Crisis* (2nd ed.). Joint Hearing, 99th Congress (July).

Shannon, E. (1988). *Desperados: Latin Drug Lords, U.S. Lawmen, and the War America Can't Win*. New York: Viking Penguin.

Shannon, E. (1991). "New Kings of Coke." *Time*, (July 1), 29–36.

Shaw, C. R., & McKay, H. D. (1942). *Juvenile Delinquency in Urban Areas*. Chicago: University of Chicago Press.

Sheridan, M. (1996). "Mexico Fires 700 from Elite Police." *Los Angeles Times*, (August 17), A1.

Sherman, L. (1974). *Police Corruption: A Sociological Perspective*. Garden City, NY: Doubleday.

Sherman, L. (1982). "Learning Police Ethics." *Criminal Justice Ethics*, *1*(1), 10–19.

Shibata, Y. (1996). "Quaking Lenders: How Gangsters Complicate Japan's Banking Crisis." *Global Finance*, (10 January), 40–41.

Siegel, R. K. (1984). "Changing Patterns of Cocaine Use." In J. Grabowski (Ed.), *Cocaine: Pharmacology, Effect, and Treatment of Abuse* (pp. 92–110). Rockville, MD: U.S. Government Printing Office.

Smith, D. C., Jr. (1975). *The Mafia Mystique*. New York: Basic Books.

Smith, R., Holmes, M., & Kaufmann, P. (1999). *Nigerian Advance Fee Fraud*. Canberra, Australia: Australian Institute of Criminology.

Smith, R. N. (1986). "The Plague Among Us." *Newsweek*, (June 16), 15.

Smolowe, J. (1997). "Sorry Partner." *Time*, (June 30), 24–30.

Song, J., & Dombrink, J. (1994). "Asian Emerging Crime Groups: Examining the Definition of Organized Crime." *Criminal Justice Review*, *19*(2), 228–243.

Stein, B. (1988). "The Lure of Drugs: They Organize an Addict's Life." *Newsday*, (December 4), 6.

Steller, T. (1998). "Mexican Drug Runners May Have Used C-130 from Arizona." In *The Arizona Daily Star*. Archived at California State University Northridge (15 April). Found at www.csun.edu/CommunicationStudies/ben/news/cia/980415.steller.html. Retrieved 2007-09-26.

Stellwagen, L. D. (1985). *Use of Forfeiture Sanctions in Drug Cases*. Washington, DC: National Institute of Justice, U.S. Government Printing Office.

Sternberg, S. (1997). "Marijuana's Active Ingredient May Cause Addiction." *USA Today*, (June 17), 1C.

Sternberg, S. (1998). "Drug Reactions Kill 100,000 Patients a Year." *USA Today*, (April 15), 1A.

Stoddard, E. L. (1968). "The Informal Code of Police Deviancy: A Group Approach to Blue-Coat Crime." *Journal of Criminal Law, Criminology, and Police Science*, *12*, 37–39.

Substance Abuse and Mental Health Services Administration, Office of Applied Studies. (1997). *An Analysis of Worker Drug Use and Workplace Policies and Programs*. Analytic Series: A-2 Rockville, MD: U.S. Department of Health and Human Services.

Substance Abuse and Mental Health Services Administration. (1996). Preliminary Estimates from the 1995 Household Survey on Drug Abuse. In *The National Drug Control Strategy, 1997*. Washington, DC: U.S. Government Printing Office.

Substance Abuse and Mental Health Services Administration. (1997). *An Analysis of Worker Drug Use and Workplace Policies and Programs*. Rockville, MD: Office of Applied Studies, U.S. Department of Health and Human Services.

Substance Abuse and Mental Health Services Administration. (2002). *Results from the 2001 National Household Survey on Drug Abuse: Volume I. Summary of National Findings*. Rockville, MD: Office of Applied Studies, U.S. Department of Health and Human Services.

Substance Abuse and Mental Health Services Administration. (2006). *Results from the 2006 National Survey on Drug Use and Health: National Findings*. Rockville, MD: Office of Applied Studies, U.S. Department of Health and Human Services.

Substance Abuse and Mental Health Services Administration. (2009). *Results from the 2008*.

Sutherland, E. H. (1939). *Principles of Criminology* (3rd ed.). Philadelphia: J. B. Lippincott Company.

Szasz, T. (1974). *Ceremonial Justice: The Ritual Persecution of Drug Addicts and Pushers*. Garden City, NY: Doubleday.

Tabbush, V. (1986). *The Effectiveness and Efficiency of Publicly Funded Drug Abuse Treatment and Prevention Programs in California: A Benefit-Cost Analysis*. Los Angeles: Economic Analysis Corporation.

"Thai Democracy: Pass the Baht." (1996). *Far Eastern Economic Review*, *159*(28), 16–19.

Thayer, A. (1995). "Cambodia: Asia's New Narco State?" *Far Eastern Economic Review*, *158*(23), 24–27.

The Economist. (2005). "Instant Pleasure, Instant Ageing." *The Economist*, (June 16), 30–31.

Thomas, N. (1998). "Shopping Holland's Drug Policy." *ABCNews.com*.

Thrasher, E. M. (1927). *The Gang*. Chicago: University of Chicago Press.

Toborg, M. A., & Kirby, M. P. (1984). *Drug Use and Pretrial Crime in the District of Columbia. Research in Brief*. Washington, DC: National Institute of Justice.

Toufexis, A. (1994). "A Health Debate that Won't Die." *Time*, (April 18), 61.

Trade and Environment Database (TED). (1997). *TED Case Studies: Colombia Coca Trade*. Washington, DC: American University.

Trahan, J., Londondo, E., & Corchado, A. (2005). "Drug Wars' Long Shadow." *The Dallas Morning News*, (December 13). Retrieved 8-17-2009.

Trebach, A. (1982). *The Heroin Solution*. New Haven: Yale University Press.

Trebach, A. (1987). *The Great Drug War: Radical Proposals That Could Make America Safe Again*. New York: Macmillan.

U.S. Customs and Border Protection. (2006). *U.S. Customs and Border Protection Canine Enforcement Program*. Washington, DC: U.S. Department of Homeland Security. Found at www.cbp.gov/xp/cgov/newsroom/fact_sheets/k9_enforce/fact_sheet_canines.xml.

U.S. Department of Health and Human Services. (1988). "Mandatory Guidelines for Federal Workplace Testing Programs, Final Guidelines Notice." *Federal Register*, *53*, *69*(April 11).

U.S. Department of Health and Human Services. (1991). *Cocaine Trafficking. Special Intelligence Report*. Washington, DC: U.S. Department of Justice.

U.S. Department of Health and Human Services. (1993). *Special Report: Drug Trafficking*. Washington, DC: U.S. Department of Justice.

U.S. Department of Health and Human Services. (1999). *Blending Perspectives and Building Common Ground: A Report to Congress on Substance Abuse and Child Maltreatment*. Washington, DC: U.S. Government Printing Office.

U.S. Department of Justice. (1978). "The Investigation of Nicky Barnes." *Drug Enforcement Magazine*, (July), 11–14.

U.S. Department of Justice. (1983). "Investigation and Prosecution of Illegal Money Laundering: Narcotic and Dangerous Drug Section Monograph." In *A Guide to the Bank Secrecy Act*. Washington, DC: U.S. Government Printing Office.

U.S. Department of Justice. (1984). *Domestic Marijuana Trafficking Special Intelligence Report*. Washington, DC: Drug Enforcement Administration, U.S. Government Printing Office.

U.S. Department of Justice. (1986). *Black Tar Heroin. Special Report*. Washington, DC U.S. Department of Justice, Office of Intelligence.

U.S. Department of Justice. (1988a). *Drugs of Abuse*. Washington, DC: U.S. Department of Justice.

U.S. Department of Justice. (1988b). *Intelligence Trends Special Report: From the Source to the Street* (Vol. 1). Washington, DC: U.S. Department of Justice.

U.S. Department of Justice. (1989a). *Drug Trafficking: A Report to the President of the United States*. Washington, DC: Office of the Attorney General, U.S. Government Printing Office.

U.S. Department of Justice. (1989b). *Drugs and Jail Inmates*. Special Report. (August).

U.S. Department of Justice. (2008). *2007 National Money-Laundering Strategy*. U.S. Government Printing Office.

U.S. Department of State. (1997). *International Narcotics Control Strategy Report*. Washington, DC: Bureau for International Narcotics and Law Enforcement Affairs.

U.S. Department of State. (2000). *International Narcotics Control Strategy Report, 1999*. Washington, DC: Bureau for International Narcotics and Law Enforcement Affairs.

U.S. Department of State. (2006). *2006 International Narcotics Control Strategy Report*. Found at www.state.gov/p/inl/rls/nrcrpt/2006/index.htm

U.S. Department of State. (2010). *2006 International Narcotics Control Strategy Report* (Vol. 1). Drug and Chemical Control. Found at www.state.gov/p/inl/rls/nrcrpt/2010/vol1/index.htm

U.S. Department of the Treasury. (1987). *Anti-Drug Law Enforcement Efforts and Their Impact*. Washington, DC: U.S. Customs (August).

U.S. Department of the Treasury. (2008). "Treasury Designates Corporate Network Tied to the Amezcua Contreras Organization." October 3, 2008. www.ustreas.gov/press/releases/hp1171.htm.

U.S. General Accounting Office. (1999). *Drug Control: Narcotics Threat from Colombia Continues to Grow*. Washington, DC: U.S. Government Printing Office.

U.S. Marshals Service. (1988). *The Pentacle*. Washington, DC: U.S. Department of Justice.

U.S. Marshals Service. (2007). *Witness Security Program*. Found at www.usdoj.gov/marshals/witsec/index.html.

United Nations Office for Drug Control and Crime Prevention. (1999). *Global Illicit Drug Trends, 1999*. New York: UNODCCP.

United Nations Office for Drug Control and Crime Prevention. (2000). *Opening Statement to the Tenth United Nations Congress on the Prevention of Crime and the Treatment of Offenders*. Found at www.uncjin.org/Documents/10thcongress/10cStatements/arlacchi14.pdf.

United Nations Office on Drugs and Crime. (2003). *Global Illicit Drug Trends: Executive Summary*. New York: UNODC.

United Nations Office on Drugs and Crime. (2010). *World Drug Report 2009*. New York: United Nations Publications. Found at www.unodc.org/unodc/en/data-and-analysis/WDR-2009.html.

United Nations. (2000). *World Drug Report, 2000*. New York: United Nations.

United States Department of Health and Human Services. (1997). *Monitoring the Future Survey*. Washington, DC: United States Department of Health and Human Services.

United States v. Alvarez-Machain. 504 U.S. 655 (1992).

United States v. Caplin & Drysdale, Chartered. 491 U.S. 617 (1989).

United States v. Doremus. 249 U.S. 86 (1919).

United States v. Monsanto. 491 U.S. 600 (1989).

University of Amsterdam, Centre for Drug Research. (1999). *Licit and Illicit Drug Use in the Netherlands*. Amsterdam: University of Amsterdam.

University of Mississippi Potency Monitoring Project. (2002). *Quarterly Report #76* (Nov. 9, 2001–Feb. 8, 2002). Table 3 (p. 8). Oxford, MS: National Center for the Development of Natural Products, Research Institute of Pharmaceutical Sciences.

UNODC. *See* United Nations Office on Drugs and Crime.

UNODCCP. *See* United Nations Office for Drug Control and Crime Prevention.

Van Dyke, C., & Byck, R. (1982). "Cocaine." *Scientific American*, *236*(3), 108–119.

Voth, E. A. (1995). "This is a Dangerous Path." *USA Today*, (August 21), 10A.

Wagner, J. C. (1987). "Substance-Abuse Policies and Guidelines in Amateur and Professional Athletics." *American Journal of Hospital Pharmacy*, *44*(February), 719.

Walmsley, R. (2008). *World Prison Population List* (8th ed.). London: International Center for Prison Studies.

Watson, R., & Katel, P. (1993). "Death on the Spot: The End of a Drug King." *Newsweek*, (December 13), 18–21.

Webb, et al. v. United States. 249 U.S. 96 (1919).

Webster, B., & McCampbell, M. (1992). "International Money-Laundering: Research and Investigation Join Forces." *National Institute of Justice Bulletin*, (September), 1–7.

Weingart, S. N., Hartmann, F. X., & Osborne, D. (1994). *Case Studies of Community Anti-Drug Efforts*. Washington, DC: National Institute of Justice.

Weisheit, R. (1992). *Domestic Marijuana: A Neglected Industry*. Westport, CT: Greenwood Press.

Wells, M. (1998). "Converse Cans 'Young Guns' Shoes." *USA Today*, (April 15), 1B.

White House, The (1989). *National Drug Control Strategy*. Washington, DC: U.S. Government Printing (September).

White, P. T. (1989). Coca: An Ancient Indian Herb Turns Deadly. *National Geographic*, *175*(January), 1.

Wilkinson, E. (1994). "A Separate Peace." *Rolling Stone*, (May 5), 26–29.

Willing, R. (1997). "Football Led to Addiction, Suit Says." *USA Today*, (January 16), 3A.

Winick, C. (1965). *Epidemiology of Narcotics Use.* New York: McGraw-Hill.

Wisotsky, S. (1987). *Breaking the Impasse in the War on Drugs*. Westport, CT: Greenwood Press.

Witkin, G. (1993). "How Politics Ruined Drug-War Planning." *U.S. News & World Report*, (February 22), 29.

Witkin, G. (1995). "A New Drug Gallops Through the West: Mexicans Muscle in on Methamphetamine." *U.S. News & World Report*, (November 3), 50–51.

Yablonsky, L. (1966). *The Violent Gang*. Baltimore: Penguin Books.

Zhang, Z. (2003). *"Drug and Alcohol Use Among Arrestees, 2003."* Washington, DC: U.S. Department of Justice. Found at www.ncjrs.gov/nij/adam/ADAM2003.pdf.

Zinberg, N. E. (1984). *Drug, Set, and Setting: The Basis for Controlled Intoxicant Use*. New Haven, CT: Yale University Press.

Zion, S. (1993). "Battle Lines in the War on Drugs: Make Them Legal." *The New York Times*, (December 15), A27.

Zwerling, C., Ryan, J., & Endel, J. (1990). "The Efficacy of Pre-Employment Drug Screening for Marijuana and Cocaine in Predicting Employment Outcome." *Journal of the American Medical Association*, (November), 264.

Index

Note: Page numbers followed by 'b' indicate boxes, 'f' indicate figures and 't' indicate tables.